Contents

Preface to the Fifth Edition   xi

1 Marketing today   **1**
Definitions 4 • The concept in the firm 8 • Marketing throughout the
firm 9 • The emergence of marketing 10 • Supply and demand 15 • Who
are our customers? 17 • In search of excellence 18 •
The knowledge revolution 19 • Ethics, the environment and related
issues 19 • A global concept 20 • The marketing system 23 •
Specimen questions 27 • Case Study 1 28

2 Managing the marketing effort   **31**
Marketing management 31 • The marketing manager 32 • Marketing's role in the
organization 36 • Marketing and its environment 39 • Marketing policy 49 •
Marketing controls 53 • Conclusion 53 • Specimen questions 55 • Case Study 2 56

3 The marketing system   **58**
Introduction 58 • Market basics 58 • General environment 61 • The different
publics 72 • The marketing system 74 • Particpants and partners 77 •
Windows of opportunity 79 • Conclusion 79 • Specimen questions 80

4 The case of food marketing   **81**
Introduction 81 • External policy and regulatory pressures 82 •
Environmental pressures 83 • Regulatory and control systems 84 •
Investment and technology 85 • Structural and behavioural changes 86 •
Work patterns 86 • Trade structure 87 • Operations 88 • The future evolution
of the food marketing system 89 • Specimen questions 90

5 Offerings and organizations   **91**
Introduction 91 • The diversity of markets 92 • Raw materials 93 •
Agricultural markets 96 • Processed products 99 • Components 100 •
Finished goods 101 • Services 102 • Capital 103 • Plant 103 • Conclusion
104 • Case Study 3 106 • Specimen questions 105

6 Marketing research   **108**
Research today 108 • The 'science' of research 109 • Research in the firm 111
• Briefing for research 111 • The scope of research 112 • Secondary sources

114 • Primary studies (field research) 118 • Special areas of study 124 • Marketing information systems 125 • Decision analysis 126 • Conclusion 126 • Specimen questions 127 • Case Study 4 129

7 Buyers, consumers and influences   **132**
Social and economic variables 134 • Market segmentation 134 • Motivations 137 • Attitudes 138 • Images of reality 139 • Models of buyer behavious 139 • Diffusion and adoption of a new product 144 • Loyalty to store and brand 145 • Conclusion 145 • Specimen questions 146 • Case Study 5 147

8 Marketing analysis   **148**
Introduction 148 • Analyzing the market 149 • New information technologies 154 • Experience, shares and competition 155 • Conclusion 157 • Specimen questions 157 • Extended Case Study 6 158 • Extended Case Study 7 174

9 Marketing information systems and technologies   **181**
Introduction 181 • Change in the world 181 • Information technology and its impact 182 • Business links 184 • Internet hosts 187 • Computing and telecommunications 188 • Information technology and distribution 190 • The marketing information system 192 • Conclusion 196 • Specimen questions 198

10 Intermediary markets and marketing   **200**
Introduction 200 • Changes, development and competition 201 • Agents, distributors and wholesalers 202 • Retail marketing 204 • Franchising 209 • The future 209 • Conclusion 210 • Specimen questions 211 • Case Study 8 212

11 Industrial markets   **214**
Introduction 214 • Are industrial markets different? 214 • Derived demand 216 • Sellers and buyers 217 • Factors affecting the degree of risk from buyer's view 220 • The buying coalition 222 • Tackling industrial markets 223 • Segments and markets 225 • Industry 225 • Conclusion 226 • Specimen questions 227 • Case Study 9 228

12 The marketing of services   **230**
Introduction 5230 • Services: a definition 231 • The sources of growth 232 • The difference between service and product industries 232 • The range of service industries 234 • Managing the service offer 236 • Quality in services marketing 238 • Relationship marketing 238 • Innovation and productivity 240 • Conclusion 240 • Specimen questions 241 • Case Study 10 242

13 Export marketing and overseas trade   **243**
Introduction 243 • A historical perspective 243 • The marketing perspective 244 • Theory of comparative advantage 245 • Developments in trade 245 • The international marketing system 247 • Export-led growth 248 • Market selection and development 250 • Advertising and sale spromotion 251 • Selling overseas 252 • Intermediaries 252 • From export to international marketing 256 • Trade in 'invisibles' 258 • The multinationals 260 • New

Marketing
Principles and practice

Fifth Edition

TOM CANNON

CASSELL

Cassell
Wellington House
125 Strand, London WC2R 0BB

370 Lexington Avenue
New York, NY 10017-6550

First edition 1980
Second edition 1986
Third edition 1992
Fourth edition 1996
Fifth edition 1998

British Library Cataloguing-in-Publication Data
A catalogue record for this book is available from the British Library.

ISBN 0-304-70293-5 (hardback)
        0-304-70294-3 (paperback)

Designed and typeset by Kenneth Burnley in Irby, Wirral, Cheshire.
Printed and bound in Great Britain by J. W. Arrowsmith Ltd., Bristol.

issues and new challenges 261 • Conclusion 262 • Specimen questions 263 • Case Study 11 263

14 International marketing   **266**
Introduction 266 • From export to international marketing 267 • Moving overseas 267 • Building an international market 269 • The research base 272 • The operational structure 274 • Conclusion 275 • Specimen questions 276 • Extended Case Study 12 277

15 Managing the marketing mix   **291**
Introduction 291 • The mix elements 293 • Designing the optimum mix 295 • Mixes for levels 295 • Change over time 296 • The future 297 • Specimen questions 298

16 Product policy and innovation   **299**
Introduction 299 • The complexity of customer needs 300 • Selection of opportunities 302 • Brands and branding 303 • The changing environment and evolving needs 305 • What business am I in? 307 • The product life-cycle 307 • Invention, research and creativity 309 • Innovation 310 • Screening and testing 310 • Test marketing 313 • Success and failure 314 • The entrepreneur and the small firm 315 • Specimen questions 316 • Case Study 13 317

17 Test marketing   **319**
Introduction 319 • The controversy 319 • The scientific dimension 320 • The challenge of innovation 321 • Success, survival and failure 322 • Are test markets worth doing? 323 • Tests: exceptions and opportunities 323 • What can be tested in test markets? (Variables) 325 • Defining information needs, decisions and controls 325 • Setting up a test 326 • Are there alternatives? 327 • Where should I test? (The external variables) 328 • How long should the test last? 330 • The test 330 • Test area overlap 331 • How is performance judged? 331 • From test to launch 333 • Conclusion 334 • Specimen question 335

18 Price   **336**
Introduction 336 • The reality of pricing 336 • The just price 337 • The political dimension 338 • The price decision 339 • Non-core-price policies 343 • Setting prices 343 • Breakeven analysis 345 • Marginal pricing 345 • Conclusion 346 • Specimen questions 347 • Case Study 14 348

19 Channel management   **350**
Introduction 350 • The role of intermediaries 351 • Channel choices are long term 352 • Channel networks 352 • Channel design 352 • Push and pull 354 • Intermediary responsibilities 355 • Conflict and co-operation 355 • Conclusion 356 • Specimen questions 356 • Case Study 15 357

20 Physical distribution management and logistics   **358**
Introduction 358 • A historical perspective 358 • The physical distribution and logistics system 359 • Marketing, PDM and logistics 360 • The goals of

PDM and logistics 360 • The total-cost approach to distribution 362 • Conclusion 362 • Specimen questions 364 • Case Study 16 365

21 Advertising and sales promotion   **369**
Introduction 369 • The nature and scale of advertising 369 • Media advertising 369 • Setting the advertising budget 382 • Economics and ethics in advertising 391 • Public relations 393 • Conclusion 393 • Specimen questions 394 • Extended Case Study 17 395

22 Sales and sales force management   **408**
Introduction 408 • Selling 409 • The salesman's task 410 • Sales management 411 • Conclusion 417 • Specimen questions 418 • Case Study 18 419 • Case Study 19 420

23 Marketing communications   **421**
Introduction 421 • The communication process 421 • The means 425 • Symbolism 425 • The receiver 426 • Conclusion 427 • Specimen questions 429 • Project 430

24 Strategic marketing   **431**
Introduction 431 • Changing conditions 431 • The nature of strategic decisions 433 • Strategic analysis 433 • Tight-loose strategy 437 • Strategies and portfolios 437 • Strategic business units 440 • The mind of the strategist 441 • Specimen questions 441 • Case Study 20 442

25 Market planning   **447**
Introduction 447 • The plan 447 • Turning plans to reality 448 • Barriers to effective planning 449 • Marketing audit 450 • Forecasting 452 • Objectives 455 • Research 457 • Strategy 457 • Tactics 457 • Controls 458 • Contingencies 458 • Costs and timings 458 • Evaluation 458 • Different approaches to plans 458 • Implementing plans 459 • Barriers to effective implementation 459 • Conclusion 460 • Specimen questions 461 • Case Study 21 462

26 Marketing: the social, ethical and environmental dimensions   **465**
Introduction 465 • The wider agenda 465 • Ethics, values and standards 468 • Environmentalism 469 • Consumer action 471 • Consumerism 472 • Seller's response 474 • Marketing and non-profit-making organizations 474 • Conclusion 476 • Case Study 22 477

Appendix: Managing a marketing project   **481**
Defining the task 481 • Project search and initial development 482

Notes, references and further reading   485
Name index   513
Subject index   517

To Robin and Rowan

Preface to the Fifth Edition

Well, I survived. In the preface to the fourth edition I suggested that the pace of change in technology might even put the role of the author, the last piece of old technology left in the process, at risk. Happily, for me, information technology and word processing still depend on the writer's inputs. The theme of change does, however, persist. I am writing this Preface on my Gateway 2000 on a train to London. It is so small that it fits easily in my briefcase. Near me, a banker is using his portable telephone to fix a meeting in Paris tomorrow. It is a little reassuring that the train is late . . . some things are slower to change, even when Richard Branson is in charge!

Change is a continuing preoccupation among marketers. Some developments are gradual and progressive. Once a pattern is established, the trends can be discerned. Personal computers have become smaller and more powerful. The number of features in the software has rapidly increased. The same patterns can be seen in the achievements of many corporations. It is good to see that most of the firms identified in the Preface to the second edition have maintained their commitment to marketing. Despite challenges, ABB, Westinghouse, Hewlett-Packard, Shell, P & G, Exxon and Du Pont among multinationals have sustained their success through continuing commitment to marketing. In the UK the same phenomenon has been seen in companies like Marks and Spencer, and Guinness.

Some have faced major challenges, perhaps none more so than Guinness. Its survival and continuing prosperity are founded largely on the strength of its brands and its success in the market. These proved to be the best insurance against financial short-termism of the worst kind. In North America good marketing has proved to be a better investment than junk bonds. This is one of the factors which has provoked some financial analysts to look for ways to include brands and other marketing assets on the balance sheet.

The pattern of ailing giants regaining some of their former strength through embracing the marketing concept in depth persists. The car industry has been joined by firms in the chemical industry like ICI and Zeneca, metals and other industries in acknowledging the need to put the customer first. The nature and structure of some of the earlier examples has changed. The British financial system was not able to provide the resources to capitalize on the opportunities created at Jaguar, but Ford seem able to do this for the 'baby' Jaguar.

The role of marketing-orientated corporate leaders is consistently re-emphasized. They continue to display an ability to bring firms back from the brink or build their ventures by convincing their workforces that marketing starts on the shop floor. New challengers have achieved much of their growth through the same process of integrating marketing into the total corporate effort. All shared two characteristics:

1.   A commitment to marketing.

2.   Determination to sustain this despite difficult trading conditions.

The notion of the customer-driven company is central to attempts to improve the successful redirection of firms, especially through the long-term links that lie at the heart of relationship marketing.

In the conclusion to earlier editions, developing trends were explored. In the first edition there was the deepening recession in the industrially developed world and the impact of this on the developing world. The influence that this would have on the changing relationships between the North and South was discussed. It has become clear that the phenomena described have had a profound effect on marketing management's behaviour. The already discernible trend, for forward-sighted firms to reject the allure of 'easy' savings through cutting budgets and reap longer-term benefits, has occurred. Those firms which sustained or increased their marketing commitment overcame the worst effects of the recession. Many have sustained these levels of growth throughout the 1980s and 1990s.

In the second edition additional shifts and developments were flagged. The priority given to the strategic role of marketing has, if anything, increased. This is vividly seen in some of the newer fields of marketing endeavour. Public agencies and government and voluntary bodies recognize the vital contribution that marketing can make to achieving their goals. The rapid progress of the privatization programmes of the UK and other governments has underlined the significance of marketing.

In the third edition, internationalism and strategy were to the fore. Internationalism continues to grow in importance. In part this reflects the weight placed on international business by individual firms. Global competition is the primary driving force in the evolution of corporations like British Airways. Specific events affect these developments.

In the fourth edition, the moves towards the creation of the single European market in 1992 raised awareness of the challenges of trading in an increasingly cohesive trading block. Even the problems of the ERM and the Maastricht Treaty merely delayed progress which EMU could soon accelerate. Rapid increases in international trade and awareness of the benefits of open markets prepared the way for the wider political and economic changes.

It is becoming increasingly apparent that, quoting from the final chapter of the first edition, in a description of the success of Vickers during the Great Recession of the 1880s, those firms which coped best with the recession of the early 1980s, profited from the growth of the late 1980s and survived the early 1990s:

> innovated a way through it, exploiting rather than mislaying their
> technical strengths . . . [they have] turned about to face the ill winds, and,
> to beat through them [have] simply 'created a new business'.

Innovation, allied to a willingness to use new technologies to meet customers' needs, has proved (predictably) to be the best guarantee of success in changing economic circumstances. The advent of mass customerization is rewriting even this agenda.

The structural changes discussed in the earlier editions have continued. The move towards an increasingly service-orientated economy in Britain and Europe continues. This process was fuelled initially by the employment crisis of the early 1980s and later by the entrepreneurial revolution of the late 1980s and the information revolution of the 1990s. However, a far more important factor has been the rapid increase in the added value per employee from the increasing application of new technologies in manufacturing, retailing and services.

Today the scale and pace of technological progress continues to confound predictions. Innovations in information technology, communications, manufacturing processes and biotechnology have transformed key areas of industry and commerce. All are dedicated, in part, to increasing productivity and, from this increase, sustaining ever greater added value. Companies talk of doubling their total turnover with no increases in their workforce. These new technologies are extending their impact far beyond the traditionally 'automated' areas of primary industries and manufacturing. Automated warehousing, electronic point of sale, bar coding etc. are transforming retailing. Electronic funds transfer and cash dispensers have led to more changes in the face of banking over the last decade than occurred during the previous century. The change potential of the emerging technologies for electronic shopping and/or banking are even now not fully understood. The Internet is leading to even greater change.

The next generation, with its 'expert systems', biotechnologies etc. seems certain to see even more dramatic, discontinuous change.

The restructuring of the world economic order highlighted in the preface to the earlier editions has continued. New economic powers such as Korea and other 'Pacific Basin' nations seem certain to join Japan and Germany in their challenge to US dominance of the Western industrial world, despite the traumas of 1997 and 1998.

The growing confidence in European and other non-North American marketing ideas is shown in most aspects of marketing. Industrial marketing, especially the study of networking, innovation, services, small business and cultural aspects of marketing continue to be areas of special strength. Sectoral studies have grown in importance. New approaches and creative thinking continue to be the hallmark of the best marketing thinking.

The changing role of the state has emerged as a major feature of economic life. The Blair government continues British efforts to 'roll back' the direct involvement of government but sees effective marketing as a key element in government strategies as a 'third way' is sought for economic success. The radical changes in Central and Eastern Europe and China are especially dramatic illustrations of a global shift in attitudes towards state intervention through participation. The sale of major state-owned corporations has restructured relationships in this field. Despite these individual programmes of action, other developments are prompting counter-balancing pressure. The increasing size (now three times its original size), complexity and integration of the European Community is a notable illustration of this.

The overall approach of the text has remained constant. The heterogeneous nature of domestic and international markets and marketing is highlighted. Traditional forms and approaches are re-examined in this context. The diversity of different trading situations – industrial/consumer, producer/intermediary/service marketing as well as the non-profit organization – is examined, with the emphasis on integrating traditional ideas with specialist and sectoral needs.

It is in this context that more general global phenomena will be explored. These include consumerism, environmentalism and evolving attitudes to corporate responsibility, in addition to more industry-specific factors such as new technologies, fashions and trading conditions. All take forms which owe as much to the culture and tradition of their home market as to any wider movements.

The most significant changes in the content and structure reflect shifts in thinking, the growing importance of internationalism, especially in Europe and Asia, and the new emphasis of sectorialism. These have gathered pace over the last few years. The profound impact of the changes in Europe and the Pacific Rim is examined in depth. This is explored in terms of its impact both on markets and on marketing management. The additional discussion on strategic management reflects the growing significance of effective strategies in shaping the firm's future.

This book has been written to incorporate syllabus developments in the Chartered Institute of Marketing's Diploma in Marketing, especially since the award of Chartered status, NVQs, the CAM certificate and the continued evolution of business education under the auspices of the Ed Excel and QCA in England, and in Scotland through SQA. The growing importance of undergraduate education in marketing is reflected in the approach of the text. The changing shape of management education, especially the Management Charter Initiative, is incorporated. Together these demonstrate the extent to which marketing education has emerged as a powerful force in shaping the quality of marketing management.

Every effort has been made to trace the holders of copyright material and seek their permission to reproduce the tables and diagrams concerned. If any have inadvertently been overlooked, I hope that they will accept my apologies.

Any book as wide-ranging as this depends on the support and encouragement of many people. Numerous colleagues have played a part, especially Karen Smith. Particular thanks are due to colleagues at other institutions who have commented on the text. The many members of the Marketing Education Group who have advised and assisted me over the years were of great help. One of the most valuable experiences for any academic is the open and frank discussion of ideas with friends at other universities and colleges. My role as a visiting professor at Kingston, Bradford and Middlesex Universities, as an external examiner at City, Buckingham, Strathclyde, London Guildhall and Greenwich Universities and the University of the South Bank has given me access to a remarkable amount of expertise, experience and insight. A new dimension to my work was provided by my recent collaborations with Training and Enterprise Council (TECs) in England and Wales, Local Enterprise Companies in Scotland, and the Training and Enterprise Agency in Northern Ireland. Especially important were my experiences at Nanyang Technological University; Texas A&M; Kellogg Business School, Stanford; IMC (Budapest); Lahore University of Management Science; IMI Ahmedeba and Narsee Mungee, Bombay. My publishers continue to show patience above and beyond the call of duty. Their efforts – especially those of my editor, David Barker, and colleagues, notably in sales and marketing – continue to be enormously encouraging. Fran, my wife, has made the greatest individual contribution. Behind these there are many students and businessmen who have forced me to think, review and revise my ideas contained here. To all, my thanks are due. Although they have played their part, the final responsibility for the book in its final form must lie solely with the author – at least until the technology pushes even further into this area.

TOM CANNON

1

Marketing today

ECONOMIC TURBULENCE poses many challenges to marketing management. Changing growth rates, inflation, high interest rates, rapid technological change, recession and new aggressive rivals challenge firms to adapt and respond for survival and prosperity. Success means finding ways of achieving maximum effectiveness in the deployment of resources to meet client needs. Firms are obliged to scrutinize every area of expenditure to minimize waste and maximize returns. Management practice has been under the microscope to an extent unmatched in the past. Clear conclusions emerge from this re-examination. Perhaps the most clear and specific of these is the central role of marketing in determining the health of a firm and through this the entire economy.

In the mid-1990s, Michael Hammer and James Champy[1] reshaped thinking about the way businesses operate. They argued that customers and their expectations have changed:

> Sellers no longer have the upper hand; customers do. Customers now tell suppliers what they want, when they want it, and what they will pay. Customers – consumers and corporations alike – demand products and services designed for their unique and particular needs. There is no longer any such notion as 'the customer'; there is only this customer . . . customers expect and demand more, because they know they can get more . . . Customers don't need to deal with companies that don't understand and appreciate this . . . in the customer-buyer relationship.

Over a decade earlier, in their book *In Search of Excellence*, Peters and Waterman[2] pointed out that the 60 most successful US firms over the 25 years of their study shared a dedication to marketing as the key strategic discipline in their firm. All these firms were dedicated to that most important of marketing propositions, that the key to success lies in 'keeping close to the customer':

> IBM's marketing vice-president, Francis G. (Buck) Rodgers, says, 'It's a shame that, in so many companies, whenever you get good service it's an exception. Not so at the excellent companies. Everyone gets into the act. Many of the innovative companies got their best ideas from customers. That comes from listening intently and regularly.'

The subsequent fate of many of these firms illustrates the continuing importance of this notion. The drift into complacency, the failure to recognize the ongoing challenges imposed by changes in the market-place, meant that many of the firms in the original study lost ground and their performances deteriorated. The customer-driven company[3] is constantly on its mettle. The dawning age of mass customization[4] makes this sensitivity to client or customer needs even more important.

A decade after Peters and Waterman, Hamel and Prahalad[5] moved the agenda forward by pointing out:

> There are three kinds of companies. Companies that try to lead customers where they don't want to go (these are companies that find the idea of being customer led an insult); companies that listen to customers and then respond to their articulated needs (needs that are probably already being satisfied by more foresightful competitors); and companies that lead customers where they want to go, but don't know it yet.

Their triad reminds us of the old maxim that people can be divided into three groups:

- Those who make things happen.
- Those who watch things happen.
- Those who wonder what happened.

In the modern business environment the task of marketing is to make things happen by understanding customer needs and building customer-driven companies.[6]

Successful marketers rethink, review and redevelop their ideas constantly. The approaches to their market which had served IBM so well in mainframe computing in the 1950s, 1960s and 1970s posed major problems when the environment, the market and the technology changed in the 1980s and 1990s. Even the old maxim 'No one ever got sacked for buying IBM' came to plague the company. It was an asset when computers were surrounded by mystique and controlled from the data processing department. It is a liability when executives have a PC on their desk, read computer magazines and want to know whether the equipment is bought because it is the safest for the buyer or best for the company.

The value of the underlying lesson is not diminished by distance, company type or time. Saunders and Wong[7] found that successful British companies kept close to their customers through a mixture of regular and positive interaction. Client feedback was a crucial element in planning and policy formulation throughout their business. Cannon[7] returned to this theme in studies of growing companies. Successful internationalization by these firms was founded on a firm commitment to marketing. A decade on from the Peters and Waterman work, Porter[9] placed marketing at the centre of his analysis of competitive advantage:

> Firms that gain competitive advantage in an industry are often those that not only perceive a new market need or the potential of a new technology but move early and most aggressively to exploit it.

This view was reinforced by John Kay's analysis of the foundations of corporate success (Table 1.1).[10]

This notion of marketing as the power-house for industrial growth and the prime mechanism for sustaining growth and prosperity is not new. Sir Winston Churchill pointed out that: '[Advertizing] sets before man the goal of a better life, better clothing, better food for himself and his family. It spurs individual exertion and great production.'

It is a point of view increasingly adopted by firms of different types in many situations. A survey of small businesses[11] found that this was the area of greatest concern to owner-managers and the field in which they felt they needed most help in developing skills. The creation of the single European market is bringing to the fore those skills in market analysis, market development and marketing policy which lie at the centre of modern marketing. Anyone visiting the rapidly growing countries of the Pacific Basin such as Korea, Hong Kong and Singapore will find successful industrialists who see marketing as the foundation upon which their growth will be

Table 1.1 Added value statement: Glaxo 1990[12]

Relationships with	Financial flow	Value (m. Ecus)
Customers	Revenues	3,985
Labour	Wages and salaries	901
Investors	Capital costs	437
Suppliers	Materials	1,528
Added value		1,120

based.[13] The transformation of Eastern Europe was shaped by the determination of individuals to express their desires through the market.

This 'beneficial' view of marketing is not held universally. Vance Packard[14] claims that: 'The people of the United States are in a sense becoming a nation on a tiger. They must learn to consume more and more, or, they are warned, their magnificent economic machine may turn and devour them.'

This debate on the benefits and costs of marketing continues with vigour today. Some critics argue that marketing can lead to conspicuous, even unnecessary consumption while others argue that the commercial benefits are far less than claimed. Mant[15] suggests that many of the gains from marketing are less considerable than often suggested. This view has been echoed by articles in journals and magazines in Britain and North America.[16, 17]

Often these comments reflect exaggerated claims and expectations about marketing and a failure to distinguish the appearance from the reality of marketing. Lack of investment in R & D, poor product design, quality problems, alienated staff and weak support systems are not resolved by clever packaging and promotion. The reality of marketing is rooted in the research, production, human resources and financial policies of the enterprise. The strength of Japanese and German marketing lies in integrating these features into a powerful customer orientation. Doyle and co-workers highlighted this in their study[18] of British and Japanese marketing:

> The findings . . . confirm the Japanese astuteness in marketing. Strategies were clearly defined, decisive and aggressive. Not losing sight of new opportunities in the market, they time their opportunities in the market, they time their entry well. Their products had significant advantages and their marketing efforts were more efficiently targeted at well defined sectors of the market . . . The British were woefully weak and defensive, driven much less by market opportunities but more by survival needs.

It is, however, clear that many of the most successful firms are convinced that their commitment to marketing has been critical to their achievements.

The transformation of the service sector by firms like Mariott Hotels, and Florida Power and Light owes much to a recognition of the contribution that marketing can make[19] and the opportunities for genuine breakthroughs in customer service. The pressure for service excellence and exceeding customers' expectations is vividly illustrated by the Scottish company Kwik-Fit.

Much of the debate would appear to be based on very different understandings of the marketing concept. There is the view adopted by Drucker[20] that: 'Marketing is so basic that it cannot be considered a separate function . . . It is the view of business seen from the point of view of its final result, that is, from the customer's point of view.'

The reality of marketing is firmly rooted in the notion that the firm exists to meet customer needs. All the firm's efforts and the entire workforce is committed to translating these needs into profitable products and services. Some firms, however, confuse the appearance of marketing – large advertising budgets, big sales forces, prestige sponsorship and other symbols – with the reality. They would rather spend a fortune on an advertising campaign than try to understand customer needs.

Definitions

There are many alternative definitions of marketing. Frequently, the particular form reflects the preoccupations of individual authors. Most have certain basic features in common, especially the notion of looking at the firm from the point of view of the customer or striving to ensure mutual profitability from the marketing exchange. Other definitions place their emphasis on the essentially managerial nature of marketing. This can be seen in the definition put forward by the Chartered Institute of Marketing (UK):

> Marketing is the management process which identifies, anticipates and supplies customer requirements efficiently and profitably.

Or the American Marketing Association's definition that :

> Marketing is the integrated analysis, planning and control of product, price, promotion and distribution, to create exchanges and satisfy customer and organizational needs.

Recently, increasing numbers of writers have emphasized this process perspective on marketing, i.e. defining it in terms of the process of moving goods from concept to consumption in the most effective way (from both the customer's and the supplier's point of view). Runyon[23] captured this nicely with his description of it as:

> The performance of business activities that direct the flow of goods and services from producers to consumers.

Even this falls short of the all-encompassing approach, increasingly used to bring out the wider applicability of marketing. Kotler[24] provides one of the widest definitions:

> Marketing is a human activity directed at satisfying needs and wants through exchange processes.

This extends the approach to include many forms of non-commercial transaction, including education, community activities and most social and political processes. It is a perspective which has generated considerable controversy, not least because it challenges many traditional assumptions about roles and responsibilities in a variety of exchange-based situations. Crosier[25] draws these ideas together when he says:

> the single word 'marketing' is used in practice in three different contexts:
>
> *The marketing process* – enacted via the marketing channel connecting the producing company with its market.
>
> *The marketing concept* – the idea that marketing is a social exchange process involving willing consumers and producers.
>
> *The marketing orientation* – present to some degree in both consumers and producers; the phenomenon which makes the concept and the process possible.

All these definitions share certain basic characteristics which are the major elements of modern marketing:

1 *It is operational.* Managers must take action to achieve results. Benefits will not emerge from a passive attitude to the exchange.
2 *It is customer-orientated.* It makes the firm look outside itself, focusing on the needs or requirements of the customer. Its effectiveness lies in finding solutions to the challenges posed by these demands.
3 *It emphasizes mutuality of benefit.* The exchanges work and persist because it is in the best interests of both parties to continue. Through this, both prosper as needs are satisfied by goods and services which suppliers will continue to supply because they profit and which are bought because customers' benefits exceed costs.
4 *It is value driven.* The culture of the company, the values espoused by its leaders and communicated to all those involved in the firm, are based on a desire to build the business through meeting needs and responding to the market.

Baker[26] develops this theme when he argues that marketing has four key features:

1 Start with the customer.
2 A long-run perspective.
3 Full use of all the company's resources.
4 Innovation.

Grouroos[27] extends these notions to incorporate the powerful 'relationship' dimension to marketing with his argument that marketing exists in order:

> to identify and establish, maintain and enhance relationships with customers and other stakeholders, at a profit, so that the objectives of the partners involved are met; and that this is achieved by a mutual exchange and fulfilment of promises.

The long-term nature of most healthy marketing relationships is central to this approach. The satisfaction of both parties is dependent on the excess of return over investment. That encourages both to return and engage in further exchanges. For the firm it will mean a good return on the prices charged. For the individual or organizational customer it means greater satisfaction than could be achieved by refraining from the exchange. In simple diagrammatic terms it changes relationships from the supplier push described in Figure 1.1 to the mutual supportive in Figure 1.2. The supplier push approach emphasizes the directive role of the producer in determining the nature of the product and service then persuading the customer to purchase.

The interaction approach (Figure 1.2) highlights the importance of the customer as the originator of exchanges. It brings out the importance of an exchange of ideas. At the same time it suggests the scope for increased profits to the firm in supplying potential purchasers with items they need or want. Its real value lies in emphasizing the active role of the customer, who is not a passive participant led, directed or shaped by producers or suppliers.

The idea that production should be based on the goal of satisfying customer needs lies at the root of the 'marketing revolution' in management thinking. The impact of this has been world-wide. The roots of the revolutionary changes in eastern and central Europe in the early 1990s can be traced to earlier decisions by Communist Party Congresses which acknowledged the failure of the command economy and the urgent need to become more responsive to market needs. 'It is the specific responsibility of . . . [identified industries] to use their entire scientific

Figure 1.1   The supplier push view of transactions

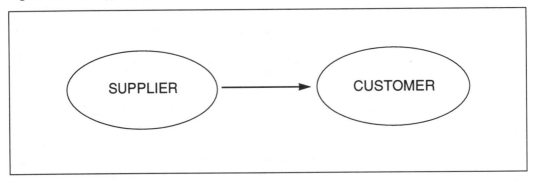

Figure 1.2   The interaction view of transactions

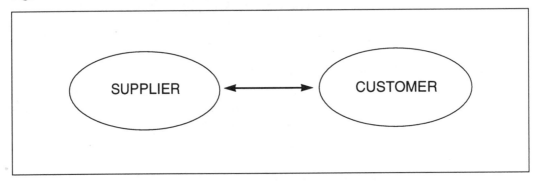

and technological potential to produce consumer goods which directly serve to satisfy the needs of the people.'[28]

Brown summarized the disparities created by the central direction of the economy in the Soviet Union: 'They could put people in space for a year, have the most advanced eye clinic in the world and yet were still unable to provide adequate food and accommodation to many of their citizens.'[29] The economic reforms initiated by former Soviet President Gorbachev made economic accountability central to policy. Acceptance of the notion that the market or the customer is the arbiter of success is crucial to changes in attitude and performance which are necessary to deliver customer benefits, economic growth and political stability in central and eastern Europe.

Similar statements emerged from leaders as diverse as Mrs Thatcher and Deng Xiaoping. The notion that it is both popular and effective to seek to give the customer what he or she wants is becoming generally recognized. It is a long way from the famous story of customer relations in eastern Europe:

> The traveller had lost his luggage on a flight to Sofia. Faced with no immediate prospect of its return he went to a giant department store. The process of purchasing goods involves choosing the item at the counter, paying at a separate till, returning with a ticket and obtaining the goods. Having completed this (laborious) process the traveller returned

to where there were stacked piles of shorts behind the counter. There were three stacks of white – one half sold – then three stacks of blue.

The assistant took his ticket, turned to the stack of white shorts and handed them over. The customer pointed out that he wanted blue shorts.

'When we have sold the white shorts . . . then we will sell the blue ones,' replied the assistant.

Production-dominated transactions can easily produce this response to customer needs. Organizations adopting this approach find it increasingly difficult to survive and thrive in today's competitive market-place.

Hammarkvist and others have taken this further by exploring the notion of markets as networks.[30] This approach views a market as a network of relationships. Different participants will adopt more or less active roles. Sometimes the producer will take the lead. In different circumstances, this might shift to middlemen of various kinds. Elsewhere, buyers will play a more active role. The successful working of the market will depend on all parties understanding the nature of the market-place, the efficiency of the exchanges and the ease with which new entrants can join the network and existing members can quit. A modern and efficient market is like an efficient network: it is organic and non-hierarchical.

Figure 1.3 The market network

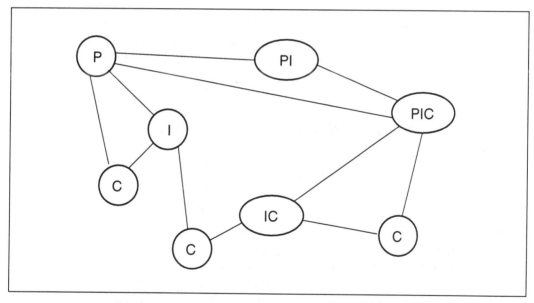

Figure 1.3 illustrates the typical network. Participants specialize as producers (P), intermediaries (I) and consumers (C) or adopt multiple roles as consumers as well as intermediaries or producers. Even a firm like IBM will buy in another company's products and re-badge them for resale as its own. Market leadership changes. Food retailing in Britain is not dominated by the packed food producers but by the large supermarket groups. However, this can change. In late 1990, Nissan cancelled the exclusive dealership agreement its UK distributor had held for 20 years. This intermediary had led the market development for Nissan for much of this period. Conflict can emerge. During the early 1990s, many leading publishers were in direct conflict with large book retailers over the maintenance of the Net

Book Agreement which regulated the prices charged for books. The collapse of the Net Book Agreement in 1996 led to a sharp growth in price competition in the book trade.

This view of markets contrasts with the traditional, mechanical and hierarchical ideal of marketing systems. In Figure 1.4 the market is presented as a hierarchy with the producer at the top. Intermediaries serve the needs of producers, and consumers respond to their offerings.

Figure 1.4   The market hierarchy

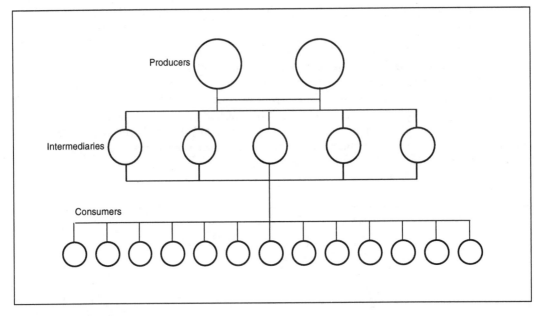

The concept in the firm

The concept that firms exist, first and foremost, to satisfy customers' needs has not been accommodated easily into the operations of many organizations. The notions that: 'Firms exist to make profits', 'Firms exist to create/protect jobs' or simply that 'Firms exist to survive' have been put forward as equally plausible purposes.

The real power of the marketing concept lies in three areas:

1   The reality of the market-place, i.e. the alternative purposes stated above can only be achieved, in the long term, if the customer is satisfied with the offering.
2   The recognition that firms will achieve their targets most effectively if they see that the closer they are to understanding the customer, the more likely they are to gain maximum profits, hence save/create jobs and survive.
3   The awareness that adding value to the customer offering provides the key to long-term and secure business development.

Marketing is not the philanthropic pursuit it is sometimes seen as in other areas of corporate activity. It is the formal recognition that the firm can adopt two routes to business development. It can produce something to fit its convenience and in a competitive environment face the massive risk and uphill struggle of pushing this on an unwilling public; or it can use its knowledge of buyer needs to design, develop or modify its offerings to meet those needs. Acceptance and returns will be earned in proportion to their understanding of these needs and ability to provide an offering to match them. The power of marketing lies in linking the firm's capabilities to the needs of the customers.

Marketing throughout the firm

Building effective marketing is the responsibility of everyone in a firm. The response of the market-place will determine its prosperity. This means that marketing is not an activity that can be confined solely to those specialists working in the marketing function: everyone is involved. The shop-floor workers can determine quality; the first-level supervisors are critical to output levels; the engineers design quality and reliability into the product; receptionists and administrative staff deal with customer queries.[31] All are part of the marketing team. It was a belief close to the heart of Sir John Egan when he was Chief Executive of Jaguar Cars. He brought the firm 'back from the brink' by espousing and communicating this belief. Jaguar have come back from being a fading British marque to an international success story. The firm is now the launch pad for Ford's worldwide effort to establish a premier, quality marque.

The notion of a total corporate commitment to marketing is extending beyond the private sector into public agencies. One of the most imaginative of these was the Stirling Futureworld programme launched by Stirling District Council in Scotland. This was promoted as strongly to the local authority's staff as to prospective visitors and investors. 'We recognized that if our own staff did not believe in it and work to make it a reality, we could not expect anyone else to support it' (Ian Wyles, Convener).

Figure 1.5 Different views of the same problem

As marketing requested it

As sales ordered it

As engineering designed it

As plant manufactured it

As field service installed it

What the customer wanted!

More recently, Birley's research[32] highlighted the importance of these internal attitudes. She indicated that the type of corporate culture[33, 34] which emphasized 'keeping close to customers', looking outside the firm for cues to business development and emphasizing quality, service and pride in the product, was the best predictor of marketing effectiveness.

The emergence of marketing

Many ancient civilizations based their prosperity on their skill as traders. This turned on their success in understanding the needs of their customers and finding ways of supplying them. Even the Vikings were more often traders than pirates.

Before the Industrial Revolution of the 1780s to 1830s, the lack of production skills and limited output restricted trade so much that the primary area of activity was in luxury goods.

The evolution of trade

The most basic form of trade, barter, has existed ever since man was capable of generating a surplus of some crop or other. In agricultural societies it provided the scope for exchanging specific surpluses for other desired commodities. The market or fayre evolved to facilitate these exchanges. In fact the process of making the exchange process more efficient has characterized the progress of civilization throughout the world.

Although the local market provided the venue for most barter trading, periods of stability saw the emergence of much wider networks of trade; primarily in luxuries but occasionally in far more basic items. The trade in corn between Egypt and Italy during the Roman Empire exemplifies this. Egypt was the breadbasket of the Empire during most of its later history. All the great empires provided an environment in which trade could prosper.[35]

The Middle Ages saw the formation of the Hanseatic League (Figure 1.6). The Hanseatic League was a grouping of cities in northern Germany in the middle of the thirteenth century as an association (Hansa) to advance their joint commercial interests. The most important cities were Lubeck, Riga, Hamburg, Danzig (Gdansk in Poland) and Bremen, but around 200 towns were members at different times. The League's strength reflected the weakness of central or national governments and their inability to implement laws, protect trade, or help navigation.

The League's period of greatest strength coincided with the weakness of the Holy Roman Empire and the younger nation states of Northern Europe. The League probably reached its zenith between 1350 and 1500 when it had 140 members with representatives in countries from England to Russia. In 1370, it defeated its greatest rival, Denmark, and won major concessions from the Danish Empire at the Treaty of Stralsund. The growing power of the nation states of northern Europe, notably England, France and the Netherlands, forced the League into decline as its rights and privileges faded and competition from London and Amsterdam increased. The last meeting of the League was in 1669 but former members such as Lubeck and Hamburg retained special rights and privileges in Germany until the nineteenth century.[36]

During these Middle Ages in Europe, traders, pedlars and hawkers provided not only goods but the only continuous form of communication available to most of the population.[37] The most famous of these traders, Marco Polo, provided insights into cultures in countries far beyond his native Italy, besides dealing in the luxuries demanded from these places for his

Figure 1.6 A map of the Hanseatic League

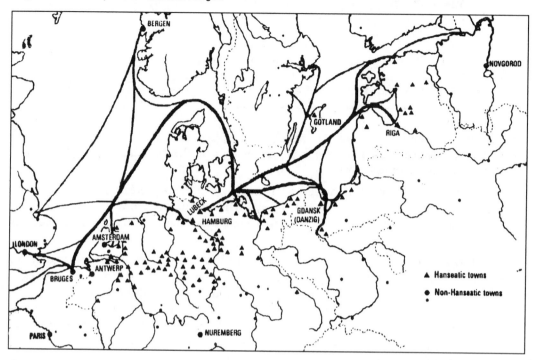

Venetian customers. Despite times during which this trade reached very large proportions, there were three major constraints, all directly associated with the exchange process itself:

1 The recurrent problem of obtaining acceptable currencies, hence the importance of imperial currencies and precious metals.
2 The limited production available in crafts-based industries.
3 The lack of a stable and secure environment.

The emergence of the great nations of Europe and their exploitation of the mineral and material resources of the New World, provided economic stability and raw materials. These changes were linked with problems with which we are very familiar today, including rapid inflation during the seventeenth century. Most importantly, the Industrial Revolution, first in Britain, and later in the United States, Germany, France and the other nations of Europe, solved the problems of secure, consistent and reliable production.

The impact of industrialization

Dramatic growth in industrial output was achieved in the early part of the nineteenth century (see Table 1.2). This capacity for growth continues to drive economies forward, especially those able to link enterprise and innovation.

The internal stability which occurred in the nation states provided an environment in which merchants could trade and reasonably expect to benefit from their efforts in the long term. In Britain it led initially to the era of mercantilism. Great trading companies such as the Muscovy, Levant, East India and Hudson Bay grew up. A number of today's major trading organizations can trace their descent from these, such as Jardines (Hong Kong) Ltd which has links with the

Table 1.2 Changes in industrial output 1785/1850

	1785	1850
Cotton	40 million yards	2,025 million yards
Coal	9 million tons	49 million tons
Iron	0.2 million tons	2.25 million tons

East India Company. These were not a purely British phenomenon. The struggle between the merchants of the Hanseatic League from Germany and the Merchant Adventurers from England has many parallels today.

It was the Industrial Revolution, however, which provided the real breakthroughs in volume, consistency of output, and price reductions.[38] The productive power of machines and industry made headway against the shortages which had held back trade and economic progress.

Despite this, for much of the history of the post-industrial world, demand for most goods and commodities has far exceeded supply. Under these circumstances, the primary interest of manufacturers was to increase their production efficiencies, normally striving to sell more at lower prices. This gives rise to what is generally described as the production orientation, i.e. the notion that customers will buy well-made products, produced in sufficient quantities to meet demand, with little or no marketing effort needed to achieve adequate sales.

The firm with this point of view focuses its attention on making a technically superior product, applying appropriate technologies to maximize output, and operating efficiently. It is assumed that the customer will respond favourably to these actions. A comment by Sir George Harriman of BMC (the British Motor Company, now Rover Cars) in 1959 epitomized this: 'We know what the customer wants: it's our job to make it at the right cost and then the public can be counted on to buy it.'

During periods of shortage and limited competition this *product orientation* can play a major role in corporate success. It provides the drive and commitment to achieve the increases in output necessary to sustain demand. However, a price has to be paid for success in this. Increases in output are linked to the emergence of competitors.

Many technical breakthroughs make it easier for competitors to enter markets. This leads to an excess of supply over (immediate) demand. A new perspective on business development is needed. The prime focus becomes the 'product push' or 'hard sell'. The overall corporate approach to the product remains virtually unchanged. Priority is still given to seeking increased efficiencies in manufacture or processing, generally with the aim of cutting prices. The firm still knows best; the problem now is to make sure the customer appreciates this.

This is the period in which a *sales orientation* dominates the firm. This is based on the notion that the volume needed to sustain the output generated by the new production efficiencies can only be achieved through heavyweight promotional efforts. Even now, it is the route taken by a firm that seeks to buy its way out of trouble. A decaying product, being overtaken by technology or consumer tastes, will often be heavily promoted to extend its life. The most vivid recent example of this was in the 'price war' launched by British Leyland (Rover) in the late 1970s to extend the life of its older models while waiting for the introduction of the new range of cars such as the Metro and the 600 and 800 series. Super Nintendo adopted the same approach –

cutting prices to 'buy' customers when struggling in the games console market. This response is not confined to manufacturers. Faced with loss of market share and Tesco's loyalty card, Sainsbury responded by cutting prices but with little effect. A similar phenomenon is seen when a new product which is falling short of its targets has large additional sums invested in its promotion in an attempt to make it 'lift off'. This pattern of behaviour can be seen in the numerous sales and discounting initiatives taken by manufacturers and retailers.

This approach occurs in industrial markets equally often. A particular form exists among the firms supplying a declining customer industry. Here a pattern can emerge where component and other suppliers fiercely compete on price to hold on to their share of a contracting 'cake'. Unfortunately this can lead to increasingly unprofitable business as the customers are frequently struggling to keep their costs down to stave off their own decline. The *declining market volume illusion* can mean that these suppliers meet the same fate as their customers despite the fact that their own technology or process retained considerable potential for expansion. Smaller firms supplying the shipbuilding industry tried to ignore the decline in the 1970s. They persisted in spending increasing amounts on advertizing, sales and promotion as the market disappeared in front of them. The same phenomenon occurred in the automotive products industry in the early 1980s. Ultimately such firms find that the cost of sustaining the uphill struggle against underlying market forces undermines the production process they are attempting to sustain. It drains scarce resources from R & D, quality control and process innovations, the cornerstones of the firm's future.

The strength of the *marketing approach* lies in the different view taken of the firm and its links with its customers and the wider market. Buyer needs become the starting point for the production process. The firm defines its offering, products, services and the means of getting these to their actual and prospective customers on this basis. This approach has a number of distinctive and unique strengths:

1 It recognizes that companies will only remain fit, healthy and competitive if they meet customer needs.
2 It highlights the real difference between the need and the means of satisfying it.

A series of studies have highlighted the commitment of Japanese firms to systematic, market-driven, research-based product development and improvement. Lorenz[39] found that Japanese companies gave far more attention to the future aspirations and desires of customers in their marketing research. This contrasted with the emphasis given by Western firms to existing products and services. Clark[40] highlighted the emphasis by Japanese companies on real improvements in performance at lower prices. Dace[41] summarized the results of his researches as indicating that 'Japanese marketing today represents not only a digest of the best marketing practices but an enhanced or improved approach to marketing.'

It is very easy for a firm, an industry or a community to convince itself that its products or services are indispensable. In reality, all are just ways of meeting needs. They can be replaced by alternative offerings which meet these needs better. Among the best examples were:

1 The railway industry's failure to respond to the transport revolution of the 1940s and 1950s.
2 The ineptitude shown by the producers of duplicators or copiers in responding to developments in word processing.
3 The dismal showing of virtually all the traditional consumer electronics firms in the personal or home computer market.

4 The failure of the film industry to move into television.

5 IBM's continued preoccupation with large, mainframe computers.

6 The inability of any of the established terrestrial TV companies to develop successful cable or satellite operations.

7 The inability of the Conservative Party to develop their policies and political campaigns, in response to the evolving political climate of the nation, which culminated in their defeat, by 'New' Labour, in the 1997 General Election.

In these and many other situations, established firms, even whole industries, with many apparent advantages have 'missed the boat' and seen their market disappear, contract or fail to grow while related or substitute products expand to meet customer needs.

This approach was the basis of one of the greatest marketing turn-arounds in modern business history. General Motors destroyed the overwhelming dominance of Ford. Its success highlights both the strength of the approach and the complex challenges it poses to management.

General Motors succeeded despite the apparently overwhelming strength of Ford in the US car market. In 1926 Ford sold 1,550,000 cars to General Motors' 750,000. The position was reversed within four years through two inter-related policies.[42]

1 *The understanding of needs.* General Motors' analysis of the US car market showed that it was made up of many different customer groups. These had some needs in common but more importantly had many diverse requirements in a car. The basic common need identified and successfully exploited by Ford was the need to get from A to B, 'basic transportation at a low dollar price'. This was surrounded by many other needs which would determine purchase once the basic need was met. A simple extension was to get from A to B in comfort, even if this meant paying more.

The success of General Motors did not lie merely in identifying this need or using a clever, related catchphrase in their advertizing. The key to its success lay in the delivery of an augmented product which satisfied this need. Its production staff capitalized on a breakthrough in steel technology which helped them to stamp out steel into a body shell. The result was a car with real protection from the elements and dramatic improvements in comfort: 'in less than two years the closed body made the already obsolescent design of the Model T non-competitive as an engineering design'. General Motors' efforts were complemented by promotional and distribution policies geared to realize fully the benefits of this total offering.

2 *The match of need with total product proposition.* The firm realized that the product – the car itself – met only certain of the customers' needs. The name and the image had to be right if the customer was to be happy to show it to his family, friends and colleagues. The price had to be presented in ways which made it possible for the purchaser to afford it. This involved different models, trade-ins, financial services etc. The customer needed the car to be available in the right place to view it, try it and, once bought, have it serviced. General Motors was among the first firms to draw together this marketing mix. This is the combination of product, promotion, price and place summarized by Alfred P. Sloan as 'instalment selling, the used-car trade in, the closed body and the annual model'. It delivered to the customer the right product, with the right reputation, at the right price, in the right place.

Figure 1.7 The four Ps satisfy the four Os

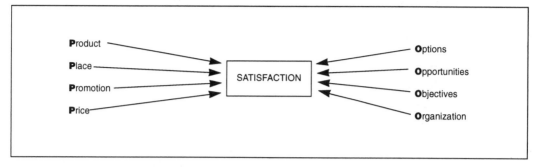

It is the fit of offering against needs which determines success. Thomas[43] brings out the importance of linking this notion to marketing planning if it is to be effective.

Marketing highlights the extent to which products and services are bought by different groups to satisfy different needs. Different items can be purchased to meet the same need. The need for esteem could be met through a prestigious car (Rolls Royce); type of credit card (American Express Platinum Card); accounts in a particular store (Harrods); holiday location (Aspen, Colorado).

Marketing demonstrates how immediate utility must be supplemented with information, image, price, physical distribution, availability, service and other facilities if customer satisfaction, repeat purchase and long-term market strength is to be achieved. For example, Fujitsu's computers matched IBM in their ability to process data, but lack of technical information, inability to match the quality image, shortage of outlets, lack of product availability, inadequate software and poor service support, especially in Europe. These gaps meant they failed to meet the total needs of customers and hence were uncompetitive. The acquisition of ICL (UK) is an attempt to add these market and service strengths to its technical and financial assets.

The emphasis on integrating these complex, dynamic and diverse forces takes the marketing concept beyond the traditional economic perspective of supply and demand. However, understanding the basics of supply and demand remains central to an appreciation of the underlying forces of the market-place.

Supply and demand

For the economist the interplay between demand and supply underlies the entire concept of the market. Demand is the quantity of a product that people will buy at any time for a given price. Supply is the quantity of a product that producers will provide at any one time for a given price. It is assumed that the demand curve is downward sloping: as prices go up, demand goes down. Similarly, it is assumed that the supply curve is upward sloping: as prices go up, supply goes up. From these two propositions the process by which prices and quantities are determined can be described graphically (Figure 1.8).

Equilibrium or balance is achieved when the amount which customers are willing to purchase at a given price matches the amount producers are willing to sell at the same price. When there is excessive demand, prices will be forced up until there are fewer customers at the new price. When there is excessive supply, prices will drop until producers leave the market or curtail supplies until a new equilibrium is reached.

Figure 1.8 How supply and demand determine price

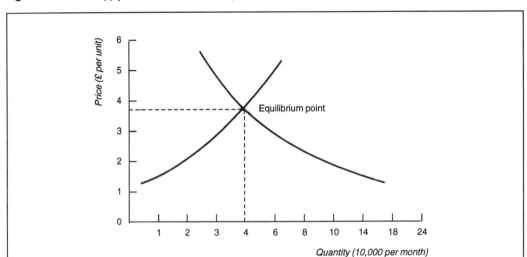

Like all theories, this is based on a series of assumptions:

1 *Perfect competition:* a standard commodity is provided by numerous sellers to numerous buyers.
2 *Perfect information:* all buyers and sellers have at their disposal all the information that they need to judge the offers of other parties.
3 *Ease of access and exit:* buyers and sellers can enter the market at little cost and withdraw equally easily.
4 *Economic man:* prospective buyers actively seek to maximize the utility of each purchase.

Although this may describe the conditions which prevailed at the great commodity auctions such as the Liverpool Cotton Exchange, it bears relatively little resemblance to the real situation facing managers in the modern industrial environment.

Massive capital investments, the skills and expertise of buyers and sellers, the mass consumer markets and the highly specialized requirements of certain buyers, have created a complex and highly differentiated market to contrast with the simple and undifferentiated market of perfect competition. It is in the interest of both customers and suppliers to identify clearly their requirements and, on occasion, to use their market power to achieve them. For example, Marks and Spencer sets high standards to its suppliers and uses its buying power to ensure that its requirements are met. Ford, Nissan[44] and Rover retain the power to withdraw their franchise from dealers who fail to maintain standards of service and business performance. At the same time the environment may be so complex that the time and effort involved in embarking on a full comparative evaluation of all alternatives would not be justified, even if the prospective buyer could fully evaluate the variables.

On a weekly shopping trip for a family, over forty different lines may be purchased. Ideally, 'economic man' considers the alternative outlets, say five supermarkets; the alternative producers, perhaps four for each line; the alternative brands, perhaps three from each producer; and the five or six variables on which they are judged. This would involve analysing over 14,000 pieces of information, a task well within the capacity of a PC, but hardly the average shopper. Instead, most people use their stock of experience, attitudes and loyalties, to simplify their buying (Figure 1.9).

Despite this, there are dangers in taking too complacent an attitude to the questions economists ask about the operating of the marketing system. Imperfections do exist, and it is in the interest of both producers and customers that the powerful analytical tools developed by economists are applied to this area. At the same time, the cross-fertilization of ideas which has proved to be so fruitful in the past should not be hampered by entrenched positions.

Who are our customers?

The preceding discussion made a number of assumptions about the firm's knowledge of its customers, their location, nature and likely purchase behaviour. Often this level of awareness does not exist or there are fundamental misconceptions about key facts. Companies frequently assume that:

1 All customers are the same.
2 They are equally important.
3 They seek similar satisfactions from the product/service.
4 That customers and consumers are the same.

Figure 1.9 Data for decision? An illustration of the customer's problem of coping with the range of variables for each product (here light-bulbs) and the number of items purchased on each shopping trip.

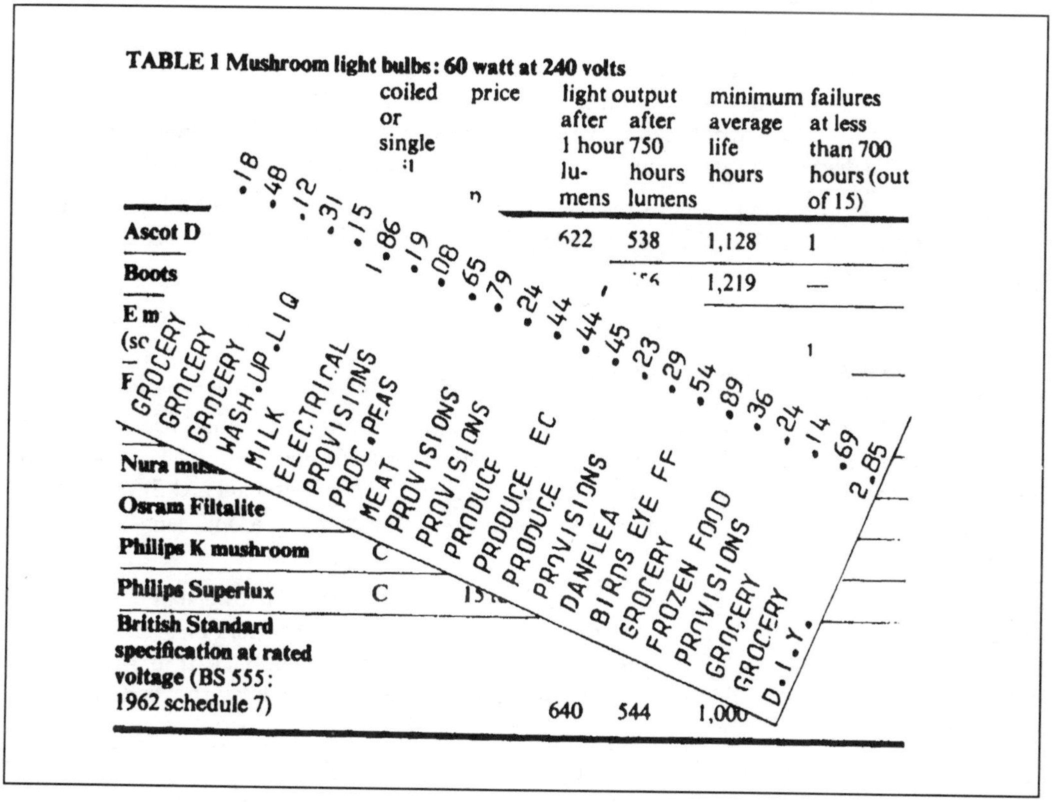

TABLE 1 Mushroom light bulbs: 60 watt at 240 volts

	coiled or single	price	light output after 1 hour lu-mens	after 750 hours lumens	minimum average life hours	failures at less than 700 hours (out of 15)
Ascot D			622	538	1,128	1
Boots					1,219	—
E m (sc						1
Nura mu						
Osram Filtalite						
Philips K mushroom	C					
Philips Superlux	C	1				
British Standard specification at rated voltage (BS 555: 1962 schedule 7)			640	544	1,000	

Often these assumptions are not true. The same product is bought by a very wide range of people with nothing more in common than this particular action. This is sometimes reflected in the very different levels of relative importance. The 80:20 rule is central to much modern marketing thinking. It highlights the differences in relative importance between customers. Frequently, 80 per cent of the firm's output is purchased by 20 per cent of customers. These provide the bedrock for the firm's prosperity. Failure to recognize this can mean that the 80 per cent of customers generating 20 per cent of demand can get vastly disproportionate attention. This is frequently to the disadvantage of key accounts. This phenomenon is called the *Pareto effect*.

Reid[45] brings out the problems firms have in implementing strategies even when they are established. Gray[46] points out that many firms are 'frustrated and disappointed'[47] with the ways their plans are implemented and the results they gain. This turns on the creation and executions of control systems which link the actions taken and the results observed with feedback systems which respond to success and failure.[48]

The same product can mean very different things to its many buyers. A car can be a means of getting from A to B, a status symbol, an employee perk and many other things to its buyers. Understanding this is vital if the design, its presentation, pricing and service support are to appeal to potential purchasers. Apparently minor slips can be fatal. A British firm launched its product into the market in Dubai with promotional material in Arabic, failing to realize that 90 per cent of the population originate from Pakistan, India, Iran or elsewhere. Simmons, the US bed manufacturer, made an even more basic error with its launch into the Japanese market. It failed to realize that most Japanese sleep on futons, and had no interest in Western-type beds. Even the eight salesmen the company recruited had never slept on a bed! Time has a profound effect, as the tour operators Thomson's found when it was obliged to drop its 'Thomson's Gaytours' range of packaged holidays.

Frequently, mistakes are made because the firm assumes that the individual making the purchase decision and the user are the same. The housewife may do most of the shopping but the tastes and wishes of the whole family will influence her. In industrial markets the buyer's ability to exercise discretion varies considerably between firms and across different items.

Few illusions are more dangerous to the marketing-orientated firm than the illusion that it 'knows' its customers, unless that 'knowledge' is backed by hard evidence, regularly and systematically updated.[49]

In search of excellence

In their book, Peters and Waterman[50] give numerous illustrations of the commitment of successful US firms to understanding their customers and keeping close to their changing attitudes and tastes. There was the case of the Hewlett-Packard development engineer: 'Damn! Here was an HP engineer behaving as enthusiastically as any salesman you'd ever want to see.'

The same phenomenon can be seen in the best European, Asian and Australasian companies. Charles Forte constantly sought for customer insights from his managers and staff. Derek Wanless of NatWest regularly examines ways of building client feedback into the bank's operations. Bob Ayling of British Airways places customer feedback at the centre of its operations.

The values they espouse can be illustrated by the following comments:

It used to be that marketing was a question of guessing consumers' desires and then responding to them, with words if not with facts. No longer. Today, words are not enough. Only the facts – better performance – will do. (Lindsay Owen-Jones, CEO, L'Oréal)[51]

Competition in our domestic market makes the consumer a king. (Akio Morita, Chair, Sony)[52]

These notions of partnership, delivery and response are central to the success of virtually all the most successful firms. It is an approach that pays off. A study of the innovation process by E. Von Hipple and J. Utterback found, in the words of Peters and Waterman:[53] 'Of eleven major innovations, *all* came from users. Of sixty-six major improvements, 85% came from users; and eighty-three minor improvements, 66% came from users.'

The knowledge revolution

It is no coincidence that the list of 60 'excellent' firms identified by Peters and Waterman was dominated by knowledge-based, high-technology companies. There is growing consciousness that the changes in economic and industrial systems currently taking place are part of a far wider process of change. This has been described as the 'knowledge revolution', and is a change which could prove to be as profound as the Industrial Revolution of the last century.

During this process the successful application of knowledge through products, services and the full range of offerings will determine the success, even survival, of companies in all sectors of industry and commerce. Although the most overt symbol of the application of knowledge will lie in the use of scientific and engineering knowledge to produce novel solutions to products and services, the key to success will lie elsewhere. The programme of research conducted at the Science Policy Research Unit (SPRU) has clearly demonstrated that the key to commercial success lies in combining engineering or technical innovation with understanding of the market-place and the customer. Piercy and Evans[54] take this a step further by suggesting that 'information processing' is the newest marketing mix element.

Ethics, the environment and related issues

The history of marketing has been characterized by extensive discussions of the ethical and moral issues raised by the actions of firms seeking to understand and respond to the needs of customers. The market power which emerges from success in both these areas has been seen as conferring a potential for exploitation, a challenge to others without the resources (or will) to achieve this, even a threat to certain forms of freedom. These are issues which the marketing person must understand and answer in a responsible way.

Traditionally much of the discussion has been focused on the role of advertizing; this is discussed at length in Chapter 23. More recently the actions of corporations operating in the less sophisticated developing countries have been challenged. The rise in consumerism is reviewed in Chapter 7. Today, three issues pose especially important challenges to marketing.[55] These are global environmental change, the needs of the newly emerging countries of central and eastern Europe, and corporate accountability. Debate on these issues has given rise to serious challenges to modern marketing thought and practice. Smith[56] highlights the need to review how marketing is taught, understood and implemented in the light of these challenges.

However, there is another side to the debate. Understanding leads far more often to positive action. This might be as clearly beneficial as the Volvo research into car safety. It can be very long term, such as the study of computer-assisted learning techniques for the physically and mentally disabled. It will frequently pose challenges to companies who fail to meet effectively the needs of their clients until obliged to by more responsive competitors. It is, however, the key to progress. On the wider issue of freedom, market power does exist but critics should never lose sight of the fact that: 'The international trade which led to the disappearance of the feudal and signorial regimes, by replacing serfdom by individual liberty, opened the way to freedom of thought.'[57]

This notion of responsibility is taking a number of forms today. In North America, 'Two per cent clubs' exist, with corporations pledging to give that proportion of their pre-tax profits to their community. In Britain 'Business in the Community' ('Scottish Business in the Community' in Scotland) is adopting a similar philosophy. Leading companies, including Pilkington Glass, United Biscuits, Shell, Marks and Spencer, IBM, Barclays Bank and the NatWest commit themselves to programmes of affirmative action to tackle the problems of communities across the UK.[58] Conscientious management is accepting the responsibilities that market power involves. Visionary entrepreneurs like Anita Roddick of Body Shop can redefine marketing practice while responding to the environment's needs.

A global concept

The underlying strength of the marketing approach to business is seen in the way in which it is adopted across much of the world. It is most clearly adopted and perhaps most fully accepted in the US. Over the last few decades practitioners and academics in Europe and the Far East have taken up this orientation with such enthusiasm and skill that the US position is now challenged. In the US market many of the most successful new products are from overseas as the battle for technological or innovative dominance shifts from US to foreign firms. These products illustrate the extent of overseas success in the 'home' of marketing. The 'decline' in US competitiveness during the late 1980s and early 1990s became a major political and economic issue, prompting organizations as diverse as the Business Round Table[59] and the US government to look closely at the underlying reasons. The impact of competition is vividly illustrated by the success of innovative products from overseas in the USA. During the decade 1983–1992, a high proportion of *Fortune* magazine's products of the year originated outside North America (see Table 1.3).

At the same time, other developments, often emerging from the special and different market, social, physical and cultural conditions of these societies, have taken place. The importance of international trade, the role of the state, the relative importance of industrial marketing, different values, mores and religions and the dramatic differences in technology, climate etc. all have to be incorporated into the overall perspective.

The basic dynamic of the marketing concept lies in its success in absorbing this diversity and adapting to these circumstances.

More recently the developing countries of the Pacific Basin, notably Taiwan, South Korea, Hong Kong and Singapore, have integrated this approach into their international and domestic environments. The forms of this process have varied from the decision of the

Table 1.3 The Fortune products of the year in the period 1983–1992

Year	US products	Non-US products
1983	Lotus 123, Procter & Gamble's Cookie, Bravo CAD/CAM, Cellular Mobile Phone, Kodak 1000 ASA film, Today Contraceptive Sponge, Apple LISA, IBM pc jr., Chrysler MiniVan	CD Player, Nuclear Magnetic Resonance Scanner
1984	B–1B Bomber, LA Beer, PC AT, Apple Macintosh, Nicorette,	Canon LBP–CX Laser Printer, Ibuprofen, Tonka Gobots, SWATCH watches, L'Oreal Hold Styling Mousse
1985	Coca Cola Classic, 'We Are The World' record, ETAK navigator, AIDS antibody test, Car Loan Bonds, Airfone, American Cynamid's Combat, NIKE AirJordon, IBM Sierra	Yugo, Minolta Maxxum
1986	Polaroid Spectrum, Plax Dental Rinse, Lithium Batteries, Bruce Springsteen 'Live' album, Lazer Tag, AZT, Pepsi Slice, Compaq Deskpro 386	Hyndai Excel
1987	Optima Card, Stainmaster Carpet Cleaner, Mevacor, Spare Chips, Equity Cds, Lifestyle Condoms, Interpak, People Meters	DAT Machines, Acura Legend Coupe, Disposable Cameras, Mini skirts, Casio SF–4000
1988	Genetic Mouse, ET on Video, Rogaine, No colour mascara, Ergon 2 Chair, Wilson 'Wide Body' profile tennis racket	Video Walkman, NEC Ultralight Laptop, Ricoh Mirai, Canon FaxPhone, Debt Swap, Erasable Optical Disc
1989	Batman – The Movie, Compaq Lte, Epogen, Gillette Sensor, Arco EC–1, HP Lasterjet IIP	Nintendo Game Boy, Sony CCD–TR5 Handycam, Mazda MX–5
1990	Windows 3.0, 386 Chip, Prozac Anti-Depressant, Ortho Diagnostic Systems, Healthy Choice Foods	PV–40 Palmcorder, Honda NSX
1991	Didge Viper, Smart Bombs, Neupogen, Low Fat Beef, Boyz in the Hood	Minolta Maxxum 7xi, Step Aerobics, Super Grip Ball
1992	The Nicotine Patch, Goodyear Aquatred Tire, Chrysler LH Series, AT&T Video Phone, Ben & Jerry's Cookie Dough Ice Cream, Apple Computer Powerbook, Eastman Kodak Photo CD	Sony Mini Disc, Philips DCC

Government of Singapore to standardize all school and college tuition on English 'because it is the language of international trade' to the successful adoption of marketing by leading Korean firms such as Hyundai, Samsung and the Lucky Group.

Those OPEC countries which are trying to broaden their industrial base are showing the same commitment to expanding their marketing skills. It is now argued with increasing vigour and commitment that those developing countries eagerly seeking growth will benefit considerably from the adoption of a clearer marketing perspective.

Agencies such as the World Bank, ILO and the International Trade Centre (Geneva) see this as central to their long-term strategies for economic development. The level of marketing skills in the West is seen by some as the most important 'non-tariff barrier' to trade facing developing countries. Increasingly, Third World leaders, those in central and eastern Europe and the socialist and social democratic parties are abandoning their traditional hostility to marketing. They are recognizing that this attitude frequently condemns their economy to low-price, low-added-value competition in products which does little to improve their long-term economic circumstances.[60]

> [Singapore's success] depends on a highly skilled and educated work force, which is willing to adapt to changing technology and changing markets. (Lee Kuan Yew)

It is the same trap out of which the countries of central and eastern Europe, ex-members of the Council for Mutual Economic Assistance (CMEA, more commonly called Comecon), are emerging. Marketing is playing an increasing role in domestic trade in these countries. The command economy was giving way long before Christmas 1989, when the Berlin Wall was destroyed. Goldman points out the positive effect that branding and promotion has in establishing and maintaining quality standards in production. In their overseas trade many of these emerging countries work hard to understand the needs of buyers despite being faced with the difficulties any country or industry with a traditional production orientation inevitably faces.

Introducing a marketing approach has produced some major successes, particularly in dealings with the Third World. Especially noteworthy has been the introduction of novel and sophisticated forms of the oldest method of trade, barter.

Compensation trading, as it is more generally known, has emerged as an invaluable mechanism to cope with the serious shortages of foreign exchange faced by many central and eastern European and Third World countries. There are indications from other countries, notably those with large raw material surpluses, that this form of trade will play an increasing part in world trade.

Barter in action

1 Pepsi-Cola agreed with the Soviet Union to build three major soft drink factories in the USSR. *Payment* came from sales of Russian vodka in the US, for which Pepsi-Cola was the sole agent.
2 Marlboro broke into the Soviet market by agreeing to *payment* from sales of Soviet tobacco in the US.
3 A consortium of European firms provided the technology for a major oil and gas pipeline from Russia to Western Europe. *Payment* came in the form of revenues from sales of the oil and gas in Western Europe.
4 Rank Xerox made major strides in Eastern Europe by accepting payment in a wide range of products.
5 Fiat takes products from Russian manufacturers in payment to add to its own production.
6 India exported food to Russia in return for oil.

The almost universal push towards growth and industrialization is creating increasing opportunities for the introduction and adoption of a marketing perspective.

W. W. Rostow[62] describes this process of economic development in terms of five stages: traditional society, transition, steady growth, drive to maturity and mass consumption. At each stage the demands placed on the marketing-orientated firm change as the elements in the marketing system interact and adapt.

Stages of economic growth

In the *traditional* society most economic activity is based around agriculture. There is little surplus, most of which is traded locally. The period of *transition* sees growing efficiency in agriculture as technology boosts agricultural productivity. There is a growing market for equipment, fertilizers and some consumer goods. Surpluses provide the resources for *steady growth*. This sees a growing emphasis on agricultural processing and infrastructure projects: schools, roads etc. (Figure 1.10)

Markets now exist for a wide range of capital equipment and development services. The growing urbanization of the population increases demands for entertainment and other

Figure 1.10 The stages of economic growth

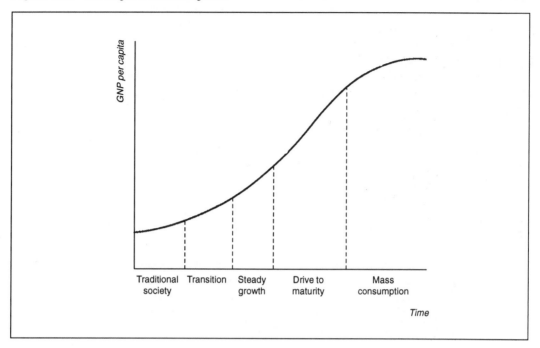

facilities. This provides the framework for the *drive to maturity*, during which there is a major shift to industrialization. An increasing proportion of the population works in industry and commerce as the country becomes increasingly self-sufficient and starts to seek export opportunities. The era of mass consumption sees an affluent and sophisticated population seeking a variety of means to meet the needs which their new affluence allows them to satisfy.

The marketing system

It is useful to think of the process of marketing as the links of a chain which stretches from the raw materials suppliers to the end user (Figure 1.11).

Figure 1.11 The food chain

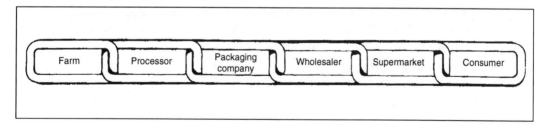

No firm simply sells goods to specific unchanging customers. It may believe that it does, like the suppliers to the shipbuilding industry mentioned earlier, but this is a dangerous, short-sighted fallacy. There may be intermediaries – probably suppliers. Few firms can avoid competitors. This network of relationships is continually interacting with the *cultural, technological, economic* and *political* forces surrounding it.

Figure 1.12 illustrates some of the numerous interacting forces which ultimately determine the future of a firm such as British Steel. It is tempting to think of British Steel's market in terms of its immediate customers but this gives only a partial picture. A steel producer can, for example, concentrate all its efforts on sales to middlemen, like steel stockholders, or sell through the manufacturers. A large firm like British Steel might need to help small customers to sell through their customers. British Steel might sell nothing to end-users but invest heavily in promoting distinct features of its products, e.g. ease of recycling to end-users.

The pattern of this trade is affected by influences which go beyond the buyer-seller relationship. British Steel might buy its iron ore from a country with a poor human rights record. A media exposure of this link can hurt sales throughout the market-place. Political action, for example, changes in competition law, might make it harder or easier to operate. The overall culture shapes trading relations. In the 1980s there was much interest in lightweight composite materials as alternatives to steel. These are, however, very difficult to recycle so that the 1990s saw a revitalized market for steel. The 1980s vividly illustrated the impact of these forces with:

1 The steel strike and the miners' strike affecting customer confidence and output.
2 Government policies on cash limits and borrowing influencing investment and development programmes.
3 Technological change stimulating new forms of competition.
4 The recession producing massive overcapacity.
5 Privatization.

Throughout the system companies are involved in a constant process of converting the goods found in nature or provided by suppliers into offerings designed to meet the needs of industrial purchasers, intermediaries or final consumers.

The central role of marketing is to give direction to this process. Co-ordination of the other functions within the firm is as important as managing the specific aspects of the marketing mix under their control.

 ## Key points

This chapter emphasizes how effective marketing management is built on:

1 Understanding the exchange process and the environment in which it operates.
2 Insight into the people and institutions involved in the marketing system.
3 Recognition that effective management of the forces involved provides the returns to sustain company and national prosperity.

However, introducing a marketing perspective is neither easy nor automatic. It calls for understanding, commitment, sustained effort and effective management of the total effort.

Figure 1.12 Interacting forces

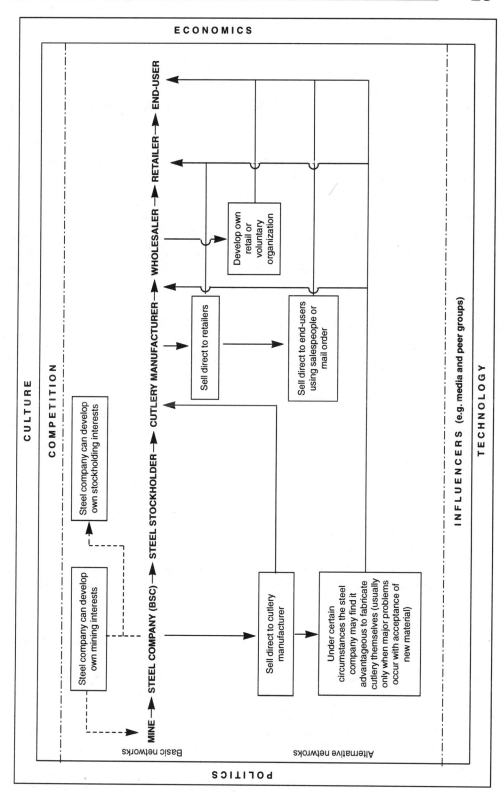

Glossary

Barter. Transactions which involve, in some form, the exchange of goods for goods, i.e. without the direct use of money. A number of forms exist today, notably:

1. Buy-Back: in development projects, where the supplier buys or gets some of the output from the project.

2. Switch trading: the supplier accepts the involvement of a third country outside the original two partners which accepts goods from the customer and provides either money or goods which are more acceptable to the supplier.

Barter trade is one of the most complex areas of international business today. Most firms are unwise to get involved without the involvement of outside specialists.

Consumer goods. Items provided primarily for purchase by, and the use of, individuals as opposed to organizations or groups. Sometimes subdivided into 'fast-moving consumer goods' (fmcg), i.e. the type of non-durable typically sold through supermarkets and similar outlets, and 'consumer durables', i.e. items designed to last a considerable time, e.g. televisions, cars.

Consumption. The pace at which a user consumes or uses up the items obtained. Economists sometimes use the phrase 'consumption function' to describe the means of measuring this.

Customer satisfaction. The degree to which the buyer finds the results of the transaction acceptable.

Developing countries. Those nations of the world with low levels of industrialization and generally poor standards of living seeking industrialization, urbanization, increases in productivity and technological progress. Frequently split into 'underdeveloped' with $300–$500 per capita annual income, 'less developed', with $500–$1,200, and 'newly industrialized', with over $1,200.

Industrial Revolution. The period during the late eighteenth and nineteenth centuries, when machines were first used on a wide scale to replace labour in the production process to dramatically increase output. Associated with the introduction first of steam engines then other means of driving equipment and vehicles (ships, trains etc.). The first industrial nation was Britain, followed by Germany, the United States and France.

Innovation. The technical, industrial and commercial steps which lead to the marketing of new manufactured products or services and the commercial use of new technical processes, products or services.

Law of demand. The law that the quantity of a good demanded by buyers tends to increase as the price of the good decreases and tends to decrease as the price increases, all other things being equal.

Marketing. The management process responsible for identifying, anticipating and satisfying customer requirements profitably (Institute of Marketing's definitions).

Marketing mix. The mixture of controllable marketing activities that are brought together to match the needs of a particular customer group. Normally seen in terms of combining the four utilities (benefits) of price (affordability), product (function), promotion (reputation and information) and place (availability).

Pacific Basin. The newly and rapidly industrializing countries of the Pacific region. A fully comprehensive list should include South Korea, Taiwan, Singapore, Hong Kong and probably Indonesia, Malaysia and the Philippines.

Raw materials. Sometimes called 'primary products', as they exist in their 'raw' or untreated state and are traded as such, e.g. coal, iron ore, oil, wheat, timber.

SPECIMEN QUESTIONS

1 Why is it that 'In so many companies, whenever you get good service it's the exception'? Illustrate your answer with personal examples of good and bad service and the reasons you think they occurred.

2 Describe the problems faced by IBM in entering the PC market. Why did their early success occur, and can you explain in marketing terms their subsequent decline?

3 Outline the economic argument for and against advertising.

4 Describe the stages which firms pass through as they evolve towards a marketing orientation. What are the distinct features of each stage?

5 Indicate the role that marketing can play in a public agency of your choice. Give examples of the way marketing might affect specific areas of policy and practice.

6 What are the dangers in Sir George Harriman's comment: 'We know what the customer wants'?

7 Use one of the examples of failure to adapt outlined on pages 13–14, e.g. railways, to explain:

   (a)   Why firms and even industries fail to adapt.

   (b)   The consequences of this failure.

   (c)   Ways firms might avoid this failure.

8 Indicate some of the threats and opportunities global environmental change creates for marketers.

9 For a product or service of your choosing draw up a marketing system which highlights the main forces which shape the market.

10 Define:

   (a)   Advertising.

   (b)   R & D.

   (c)   Marketing.

   (d)   Networks

   (e)   Barter.

   (f)   Industrialization.

   (g)   Mass customization.

   (h)   GATT.

   (i)   The stages of economic growth.

   (j)   The marketing mix.

CASE STUDY 1: BLACKTHORNE PUBLISHERS LTD

Introduction

In 1995 Blackthorne Publishers had established itself as one of Britain's leading educational publishers. Sir Alexander Blackthorne had founded the company in the late nineteenth century and had dominated the firm until his death in 1962. His deep commitment, particularly to the sciences, still influenced the policies and approaches of the firm. Although the Blackthorne family retain a substantial investment in the firm, the management structure has been thoroughly 'professionalized', with no direct family involvement in the company. Although the traditions of demanding academic excellence and publishing 'important' works are seen as important to the firm's management, pressures on the firm are mounting, particularly from cutbacks in educational expenditure, the introduction of the National Curriculum and new technologies.

Background

In the past, Blackthorne were actively involved in the school sciences market, university-level science texts, particularly biology and molecular science, and their university paperback series, which covers a wide range of subjects. Other subjects were included, as areas developed either through editorial interest or the acceptance of academically important texts. This has extended the firm's range into the social sciences, business and management and a number of arts subjects.

Although educational publishing is the firm's primary area of activity, the firm has a strong fiction imprint which has published a number of best-sellers over the past few years, and a paperback imprint handling a number of famous authors. For the sake of this analysis these will not be included in the case.

Organization and structure

The educational publishing activities are organized around a group of commissioning editors, as shown in Figure 1.13. As the name suggests, the primary task of a commissioning editor is to identify likely areas for developing books, commission authors, and manage the production of the text from manuscript to final production. All editors control a list of established texts, with responsibility to oversee their performance and authority to commission rewrites, order re-issues, add and delete texts from the series.

Although the commissioning editor has considerable authority over the development and production of material, the sales effort is handled through a sales manager with three full-time salesmen located in different parts of the country. Their activities are directed largely by the editorial board.

Figure 1.13 Blackthorne Publishers (Educational Division)

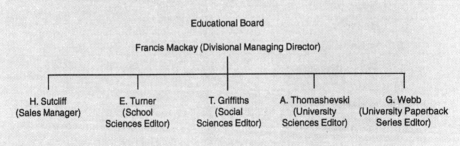

Educational Board

Francis Mackay (Divisional Managing Director)

| H. Sutcliff (Sales Manager) | E. Turner (School Sciences Editor) | T. Griffiths (Social Sciences Editor) | A. Thomashevski (University Sciences Editor) | G. Webb (University Paperback Series Editor) |

The work of the commissioning editor

All the commissioning editors have some degree of subject expertise, although, clearly, this cannot encompass all the areas they deal with. It is seen as very important that the editors can converse with some authority with experts in the fields they cover. Their picture of the environment is supplemented by a series of academic advisory committees. These operate both on an established formal basis (all major series, e.g. the 'Frontiers of Biology' series, have a standing academic committee chaired by a prominent academic) and on an *ad hoc* basis, any new developments being 'bounced off' such a group.

At the same time the editors see one of their primary tasks as establishing a broad network of contacts in educational circles to identify major developments and prospective authors.

The overwhelming majority of books published are commissioned by editors. Very few derive from unprompted manuscripts, although a large number of these are received.

Developments in the market

Although educational publishing has never been a particularly profitable area of business, the firm has historically managed to earn a good return for its efforts. However, the past five years have seen a significant decline in demand, largely because of the cutbacks in educational expenditure. This has had a particularly bad effect on the traditional educational publisher adopting a policy of: 'a very wide range of books published at relatively low prices (break-even not being achieved until years 2, 3 or 4). Marginal increases or reductions in sales have dramatic effects on profits. These lists reflect academic merit and importance.'

The effect has been felt at all levels: school expenditure *per capita* has actually declined in monetary terms; university libraries have been held back; and the 'book grant' element in a student grant has been held virtually static. The National Curriculum means that the market has changed dramatically. Instead of large numbers of books selling in small quantities, small numbers now sell in large quantities. The group's excellent profits for the last two years have been won largely through the success of the fiction imprint. The Education Division has contributed a declining share of the profits (Table 1.4).

To arrest this declining contribution is seen as a major task of the editorial group over the next three years.

> We cannot afford to bank on an annual best-seller to keep us in business. (Charles Forthrop, Group Managing Director)

Table 1.4 Selected financial statistics 1990–95 (£000)

Year	Net profit (Education)	Net profit of group	Group net worth	Group assets	Common Dividend paid
1995	514	746	7,776	13,203	365
1994	497	725	7,313	12,516	381
1993	485	614	6,648	11,846	301
1992	495	656	6,032	12,004	266
1991	605	748	5,677	11,187	266
1990	638	651	5,031	10,014	230

Developments proposed

In mid-1995 an editorial conference agreed that each member would review the means by which their individual areas could contribute towards the achievement of this broad task. These could include comments on overall developments likely to contribute towards the target. At the December, 1995 editorial conference the following proposals were put forward.

H. Sutcliff: 'The existing sales force is far too small to obtain any meaningful coverage of the market. At the moment they are chasing from school to school with little opportunity to sell properly and no opportunity to establish long-term relationships, particularly in the universities. The volume is in the schools, and that is where they must concentrate their efforts. Some increase in the sales force number is necessary, but I recognize that a significant increase is impossible at the moment. I would suggest that we recruit a number of part-time salesmen, perhaps retired school-teachers, and pay them a small retainer, with most of the income deriving from commission. This would enable us to establish a strong presence in the market.'

E. Turner: 'There are a number of exciting developments occurring in my area which can make a great contribution to the future of the school sciences division. A Swedish publisher has been in touch about giving us the rights to their 'Geography' series. This is directed towards the lower ability groups aged less than sixteen. My editorial advisers have pointed out that this group is very poorly served for reading material and the Swedish series looks relevant. I have been talking to the Qualifications and Curriculum Authority and they are looking for a schools' mathematics project. I think we stand an excellent chance of winning the commission to develop this.'

T. Griffiths: 'I really think that the selection of books and texts that is on my list at the moment is adequate; if anything, there are too many. I believe that we need to work much harder at publicizing and advertizing our material. We seem to be poor at getting our material reviewed in the major journals, and even when it is reviewed there is often a problem with stocks. Last year there was a full-page review of one of my books in *Campaign*, the advertizing magazine, but stocks had not been issued. Our publicity and promotion must be improved. We can steal some of the ideas and expertise of the fiction group.'

Ideas along these lines were reiterated by the other members of the editorial panel. At the end of the discussion, Francis Mackay concluded by saying:

> Although I have found everything that has been said here very interesting and relevant, I do not know whether we have really come to grips with the problem. I want to bounce these ideas off a few more people.

Tasks

1 Review the company's present position.

2 Highlight the problem areas as you see them.

3 Evaluate the suggestions put forward by the editorial team.

4 Put forward your ideas on the means of resolving their problems.

2

Managing the marketing effort

IN CHAPTER 1 the marketing approach to business was defined and placed into a broad context. It was noted, in defining marketing, that one of its essential features is that it is operational. Management means facing up to the need to make decisions in the real world of business operations. These decisions can never be made in a vacuum. Their effects frequently go far beyond the firm, and they may have interactions throughout the marketing system. The following are some examples of decisions and their possible effects.

1 A car manufacturer decides to reduce its distribution costs by cutting back drastically on the number of his direct dealerships. This provides the perfect opportunity for a foreign competitor to pick up a substantial dealer network by 'cherry picking' among the discarded dealers.
2 A small knitwear producer decides to promote direct sales of her goods by mail order. This might alienate all her existing retail customers.
3 A utility such as gas or electricity limits its service engineering apprenticeship intake, causing long-term problems of extended repair dates and alienated customers.
4 The trustees of an area of historical or natural interest neglect the provision of support facilities, e.g. catering, creating a situation which means that visitors come only once and stay briefly.
5 A bank manager tries to handle all her business accounts herself and neglects to pass on a small firm's request for specialist export advice to her international division, running the risk of providing inferior service to the client.
6 Rail operators replace several information centres to concentrate their facilities in a single unit, but lose large numbers of knowledgeable staff. Customer complaints about poor information soar, and the Rail Regulator intervenes.

There are few important decisions made in a company that do not have implications for the firm's marketing effort. The extent of this interaction is seldom fully recognized. At the same time the number of corporate personnel directly influencing the firm's marketing is frequently underestimated.

Marketing management

A casual glance at a newspaper almost any day will give the reader an idea of the range and depth of marketing management (Figure 2.1). Marketing directors, marketing executives, commercial strategy consultants, sales representatives, advertising managers, account executives, export sales managers, new product development managers, sales engineers, PR executives and many others are always sought. The demands placed on them, the skills needed, the resources at their disposal and their backgrounds are the primary interest of this chapter.

Marketing is not an activity that can be conveniently compartmentalized and handed over to the person with marketing in their job description. It is a total corporate commitment involving everyone. Appliance manufacturers may have a marketing department, but the service engineer probably has the most regular contact with customers. Banks may have a similar department, but the individual bank manager is in the front line of the selling effort. A university might have a public relations manager, but a lecturer's or professor's attitude to a journalist's questions is likely to be far more important in establishing the right climate of opinion. Video Arts Ltd, in an excellent series of short films, illustrated this clearly with the service engineer's comment, 'Who sold you this then?' (Figure 2.2).

Internal communication of this message of total company commitment is as important in effective marketing as any advertising or promotional expenditure.

The marketing manager

Job advertisements give some idea of the range of titles given to those involved in the marketing function. The precise names will vary among industries, firms and levels within companies. Despite this, there is a considerable degree of consistency in the functions and roles they perform.

The range of tasks and responsibilities undertaken by marketing executives has developed over the last decade. Traditionally, attention was concentrated on the presentation and sales of products as service. The growing importance of the marketing function has led corporate leaders to place far greater emphasis on its impact on overall company performance, notably: profits; leadership; strategy; integration of the firm; and long-term portfolio management. In the UK, business leaders like Sir Colin Marshall of BA came together to create the Marketing Council, which seeks to highlight the gains from effective marketing. Griffin's research[1] into the role given to marketing by senior executives found the priorities and responsibilities as follows:

- Profit responsibility.
- Profits a priority over volume.
- Long-term profits the goal.
- Cost control responsibility.
- Cost management a priority.
- Integrating company activities a priority.
- Sales management not a direct control area.
- Acts as a lead area at board level.
- Contribution to other areas a priority.
- Marketing a lead corporate function.
- Long-range planning and strategy a priority.

The most basic task of those with a management responsibility within the marketing operation is to control, allocate and use responsibly the funds and other resources at their disposal. The

Figure 2.1   Opportunities in marketing

* An able professional is required to join a young team to bring a fresh approach to international marketing of key equipment to professional users in a sophisticated and highly competitive world market.

* The role is to accelerate growth especially in Europe and North America, based on a new generation of products and a strong ...

We can provide you with the opportunity and encouragement to develop your potential and your ambition and ability allow.

Reporting directly to the Managing Director, the prime role will be to co-ordinate and develop all aspects of marketing strategy for specific products in order to achieve maximum growth and profitability. Management style allows for considerable autonomy and innovation. Candidates, male or female, will be highly motivated and of graduate calibre.

The variety of projects undertaken by our group is extremely large. You'll find great challenge in harnessing latest technology ... achieve optimum results.

For the posts of Operations Manager and Marketing Manager some years relevant experience in the oil industry is required together with, if possible, a relevant university degree. Applicants for the post of Financial Controller must be qualified accountants; an additional legal ... would be an advant...

If you believe you have the ... s and experience needed to reach the high standard we require, we are offering excellent salaries, supported by a full range of benefits.

Our Engineering Centre, which we believe to be one ...

He/she will be responsible to the Marketing Director for new product development and the design and implementation of marketing plans, including market information. He/she will also be responsible for the development and control of publicity policy.

Figure 2.2   'Who sold you this then?' Reproduced with the permission of Video Arts Ltd

product or brand manager of a consumer goods firm is likely to have a promotional budget amounting to many thousands, even millions, of pounds. The manager's task is to understand the objectives set for his or her product or service and deploy the budget in the way most likely to achieve this goal.

To this end the product or brand manager is likely to work with other marketing managers with different titles. Some may be juniors, such as assistant brand managers. Their role will be similar and supportive. However, the senior manager will have the additional responsibility to help the juniors develop their management skills, besides ensuring that they understand the objectives of the firm for the products and services under their control. This communication is central to all marketing relationships. The product manager needs to work through and with colleagues in sales, advertising, R & D, production, distribution, service etc. All are members of marketing management. Some are within the firm, e.g. sales, production. Others are outside the company, such as account executives with the company's advertising agency.

Piercy[2] describes the twin pressures being placed upon the marketing function. Growing awareness of the wider role of marketing throughout the firm is encouraging some writers and many firms to broaden the tasks given to marketing. It is intrinsic to all policies. At the same time its activities are becoming more compartmentalized. Piercy describes this as the 'disintegration' of the marketing department. This can take the form of giving specific functional areas considerable autonomy, hence 'diffusing' authority. In Britain this is seen most clearly in the freedom given to 'key-account staff' in their negotiations with major clients. This was formalized first in fast-moving consumer goods (fmcgs). The major retailers achieved such a dominant market position that manufacturers were obliged to set up highly specialized units to deal directly with them. Other facets of business have been viewed as so critical to corporate performance that their inclusion under the marketing function is questioned. Advocates of integrated physical distribution management are especially articulate in suggesting that distribution is a discrete function.

Awareness of the value of effective marketing has focused attention on the skills, attitudes and characteristics needed by marketers and the best ways to organize the marketing function. The

Table 2.1 Attributes sought in marketing management

Skills	Attitudes	Characteristics
Communication skills	Leadership	Creativity
Analytical	Entrepreneurial	Stamina
Logic	Initiative	Tenacity
Organizational skills	Tact	Innovativeness
Problem-solving skills	Implementation	Drive
Numeracy	Flexibility	Common sense
Persuasiveness	Attention to detail	Practicality
Planning	Practicality	Intelligence
Time management	Teamwork	Sense of humour
Salesmanship	Ambition	Individuality
Presentation	Confidence	Energy
Literacy	Empathy	Enthusiasm
Driving	Warmth	Friendliness
Management	Decisiveness	Good judgement
Product knowledge	Charisma	
Computer literacy	Adaptability	

most comprehensive recent examination of this was prompted by a mixture of the criticisms of skills of current managers and the desire to respond to initiatives like the Management Charter Initiative. This seeks to ensure that managers are competent to face the challenges of managing in a complex and changing environment. Middleton and Long[3] identified a wide range of skills, attitudes and characteristics as being those called for in marketing management (Table 2.1). There is considerable evidence that personality characteristics such as creativity, drive and innovativeness are at least as important as technical knowledge and functional skills.

Over the last decade, a major change in the way firms organize their marketing has occurred in Britain. Many companies have moved away from a structure based around a cluster of functions, e.g. sales, advertising and exports, often led by senior managers with similar status.[4] As recently as the early 1970s, the most senior executive with a clear marketing responsibility was the sales director. The majority of firms, especially those with turnovers exceeding £5m or more than 250 employees, now have marketing departments. In most cases, sales, customer service, trade promotion, advertising, exports and market research now fall under the direct responsibility of the marketing department. There does, however, remain a strong tendency for distribution to operate separately (Table 2.2). The senior marketing management hold a range of specialist functions but are expected to integrate the activities of others and work closely with their colleagues elsewhere.[5]

Table 2.2 The responsibilities of marketing

Marketing function	Part of marketing (%)	Not a separate function (%)	Not part of marketing (%)
Sales	59	4	37
Distribution	27	16	57
Customer service	45	15	40
Trade marketing	63	25	12
Advertising	81	10	9
Exporting	38	22	40
Marketing research	77	18	4

Source: Piercy.[6]

In most marketing relationships the key to successful management lies in effective communication, understanding and persuasion, not authority and power. The product manager will need to build up relationships with the sales force, and must understand the problems they face; the same responsibility lies with each member of the sales force. The lynch-pin of their relationships is the common purpose they share, in working to achieve the firm's marketing objectives through an agreed strategy.

The formulation of objectives and strategies is the central task of senior marketing management. They are responsible for identifying opportunities in the market-place, relating these to the capabilities of the firm and developing solutions and strategies designed to convert these opportunities to profitable business. In this work they need to work continually to relate these *externalities* (opportunities, threats) to the *internal capabilities* (strengths, weaknesses) of the company.[7] This can only be done effectively through teamwork which goes beyond the immediate confines of the marketing function.

Marketing is a *total* company activity. This applies with particular strength to the responsibility of top management. It is their task to relate the marketing operations, especially the strategies, to the other functions in the firm and to the corporate plan. Ballantyne[8] draws out the ways in which firms can build a virtuous circle, in which marketing is used as an internal management tool – to make all employees customer-orientated which then produces external benefits in customer service (see Figure 2.3).

Figure 2.3   The Virtuous Circle of Internal Marketing

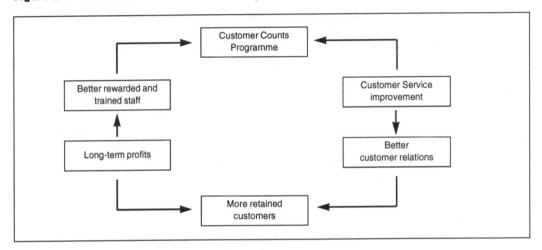

Success in marketing management lies in using the special techniques and skills developed in this area to understand the environment in which the firm must operate. This understanding needs to be wedded to the creation of plans and strategies which make the best use of company resources to earn profits and gain differential advantage. Understanding the function of marketing in the firm's operations lies at the centre of this. This highlights the conscious role that networking[9] plays in effective marketing management.

Marketing's role in the organization

In any organization, large or small, manufacturing or service, public or private, those formally responsible for marketing must work with their colleagues. Even in the small, entrepreneurial firm, where the marketing decision-maker may be also the owner, the external responsibilities for promotion, pricing, channel management and product management are matched with internal responsibilities.

A mini-case study: Grohman Engineering

A medium-sized firm which is, also, a world leader in supplies for the component industry has achieved its leadership by restating internal responsibilities. They employ no salespeople, but give their managers total responsibility for the projects they work on. They strive to make every project team act like a small company built around their customers' needs. Everyone adopts a holistic view of the project, with the customers fully integrated.

Promotional activities must be geared to adequate stocks, which in turn depend on the effectiveness of the forecasts. Production schedules are based on estimates of future demand.

Inaccuracies soon show up in production dislocations, high costs and inadequate supplies of raw materials or components. Buying decisions in industrial concerns are greatly influenced by marketing or sales force estimates of the design or product needs of customers.

An effectively co-ordinated management team can achieve results that are beyond the scope of ill co-ordinated teams. Under certain circumstances a production manager will be able to produce small quantities profitably when generally only very large runs are feasible. Transport departments can occasionally cope with special packings and promotional offers far outside the scope of their normal operations. The ultimate responsibility for creating a climate in which the type of flexibility or responsiveness occasionally demanded by the market can be achieved lies with top management. All those directly responsible for the marketing effort have a special role to play. Relatively simple exercises in communication and involvement can earn massive pay-offs. For example, the brand manager who gives production management good notice of actions likely to affect them, discusses the objects of special initiatives, e.g. requiring smaller quantities or new materials, and listens to their comments and advice is far more likely to earn real profits than those neglecting these activities. In many firms there is a hostile attitude to sales and marketing management, simply because of their failure to recognize the importance of effective internal communication and co-ordination. It appears to occur less frequently in smaller firms, where the tendency of top management to have a very intimate understanding of corporate capability is allied to easier and more frequent communication between areas.

A clear understanding of objectives and responsibilities is vital. Setting objectives and the entire planning process are discussed at length in Chapter 27. It must be recognized here that clear, actionable objectives geared to customer needs lie at the core of the operations of the marketing-orientated firm. In developing these, a clear view of total corporate capabilities must be wedded to a marketing audit.

The allocation of responsibilities within the marketing effort varies enormously between firms. Besides the differences at any particular point in time, the dynamic nature of the market-place has led to the emergence of new offices and areas of responsibility.

Product management emerged in firms like Procter and Gamble in the early part of the century. Its development and continuing popularity derive partly from the specific problems of the multi-product or multi-brand firm. In the inevitable debate about the allocation of corporate resources the product manager makes a major contribution by acting as the general manager responsible for the specific brand's sales and profitability. In this context he or she generally has responsibility for budgeting and planning, research and information systems, co-ordination, promotion and control:

> More than any other factor, it is his skill in working harmoniously with
> key people in the various disciplines that will heavily influence the success
> of the product and, of course, his own future with the company. (G. H.
> Evans)

In the 1950s and 1960s firms were faced with an environment of apparently limitless opportunity if only the company could respond quickly and creatively. The response of firms like Westinghouse was to institute the concept of venture management. Venture management is based on the creation of special groups to exploit opportunities, particularly of the new product type. The aim is to approximate the entrepreneur's willingness to become personally involved, committing large amounts of time and effort to achieve success. At a time of growth they could make progress where more conventional firms could not, particularly with marginal products.

In the adverse economic circumstances of the mid-1970s, success with this type of introduction became more difficult to achieve, while fully capitalizing on the potential returns from existing products grew in importance. Key-account management groups were set up by firms like Imperial Tobacco to handle their major customers. Their primary role is to earn the maximum returns over time from these key accounts.

Product management, venture management and key-account management are only three of the many developments in the organization of marketing that have emerged over the last half-century. At the same time, functional groupings under marketing or sales directors have retained their popularity. Here the key marketing decision-maker operates through his or her own department structure. This can be illustrated by the type of company organization chart familiar to most readers (Figure 2.4).

Figure 2.4   Marketing organizational chart

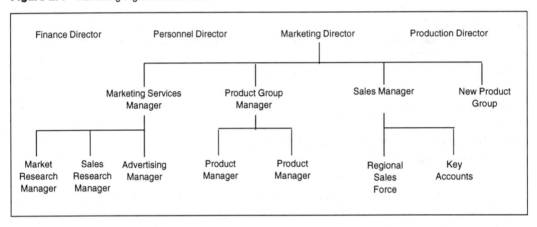

The optimum form of organization is largely dependent on the environmental forces affecting the firm. When the needs of buyers can be grouped together into separate customer groups, market-based management systems have considerable merit. Two points need to be made about the type of chart in Figure 2.4:

1   It is a highly simplified illustration of a complex system. The lines used for linkages are only a very small part of the network that will exist in a healthy firm. Communication, co-ordination and interaction will be operating horizontally as well as vertically. Equally important, the links will extend beyond the marketing department.
2   It reflects only the formal system. There will almost certainly be informal systems of great importance to the effective operation of the marketing function and the firm itself.

The optimum system will be the basis on which the firm will manage its exchanges with the market.

Marketing and its environment

Effective control of the exchange process goes far beyond the continual stimulation of demand. Kotler suggests that marketing management is faced with very different tasks depending on the existing demand state (Table 2.3). An understanding of the determinants of demand and the character of supply is vital to any manager attempting to carry out these tasks.

Table 2.3 The different tasks of marketing management

Demand state	Underlying buyer attitude	Marketing task	Formal name
Negative demand	Hostility	Disabuse demand	Conversional marketing
No demand	Indifference	Create demand	Stimulational marketing
Latent demand	Strong need but not gratified	Develop demand	Developmental marketing
Faltering demand	Declining interest	Revitalize demand	Remarketing
Irregular demand	Intermittent requirement	Synchronize demand	Syncromarketing
Full demand	Strong desire	Maintain demand	Maintenance marketing
Overfull demand	Excessive desire	Reduce demand	Demarketing
Unwholesome demand	Demand for undesirable product	Destroy demand	Countermarketing

Demand

The patterns of demand existing in any market are determined by a wide range of forces. The demand curve shown in Figure 1.8 (page 16) is made up of the demands of a number of individuals. Their specific social and economic circumstances, income or disposable funds, psychology, pressure from others (particularly in institutional or industrial buying), awareness and other factors influence the shape of the individual demand curve. For example, Mrs Brown may be forced to buy margarine as a low-priced substitute for butter because of her husband's low income. Mrs Jackson may buy margarine for cooking (Figure 2.5).

Figure 2.5 Different demand conditions

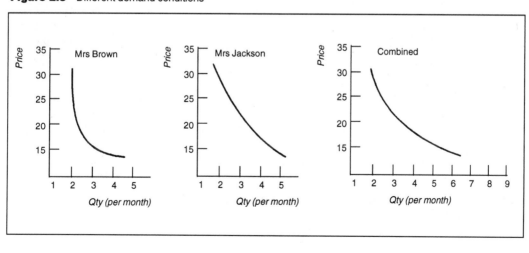

However, all these factors are subject to change. Mrs Brown's substitution of margarine for butter may be acceptable to her until her husband gets a new job with better wages, significantly increasing the family's disposable income. She switches to butter. However, his new position is far more sedentary than his previous post, and over time this leads to worries about his weight and desire for margarines higher in polyunsaturated fat.

Complex interrelationships exist between buyers, directly affecting a company's demand situation. This can even reverse the shape of the demand curve, for example when, during a period of increasing prices, people rush out to buy more. The expectation of continuing rising prices converts today's expenditure to investment in stocks. The effect of a combination of these phenomena was seen in the 'petrol panics' during the middle of 1979 in Britain and the US. Prices were going up and fears of shortages spread across both countries, resulting in long queues and worsened shortages.

Although demand is essentially a dynamic phenomenon a number of variables have a continuing impact.

Needs

To the marketeer, needs are the basis of the entire process of marketing. In its simplest form, need is any lack or deficit within the person or organization. Needs gain their special relevance to marketing when they are linked to the different phenomenon of drives:

> While need and drive are parallel, they are not the same.[10]

A drive is the internal pressure to satisfy a need. The interplay between needs and drives is determined by the motives of the individual or group:

> Motives initiate behaviour and direct it towards specific types of activity.[11]

The study of needs, drives and motives constitutes one of the main areas of study in both modern psychology and, more relevant to those involved in marketing, consumer behaviour and industrial buying. Needs are complex and varied. They range from physiological needs, such as hunger and thirst, through psychological needs, for example for love or esteem, to socially or culturally based needs, such as self-fulfilment and ambition. Although these are discussed at length in Chapter 6, it is useful to note here a few of the basic approaches, particularly the effects of the choices associated with selecting: which needs to satisfy and the alternative means of satisfying them.

Physiological needs. The most basic needs are physiological. People must eat, drink and breathe in order to survive. There is also a need to minimize, by prudence or escape, risks to the person's safety. These provide only a basic insight. The individual may have a wide choice of ways of satisfying his hunger need, or may take actions, such as driving dangerously, which appear inconsistent with the basic needs.

Psychological needs. Individual and social psychology provide insights into a range of different needs besides the process of motivation, drive and choice. The needs can include affection, ego boosts, membership of groups or communities, ambition, and relief from anxiety. At any point in time these needs are interacting, with some achieving a degree of dominance which can lead to action. The nature of this interplay and the specific motives, drives and choices of individuals and groups have been studied from a number of perspectives within modern psychology.

Motivational research explores the interplay between needs and motives. Special emphasis has been placed on different kinds of needs, and a great deal of research in conscious and subconscious motivation has been carried out.

Attitude research has emphasized the state of mind which the individual takes into any social situation, e.g. a shopping expedition, creating a predisposition toward certain types of response or choice.

Cognitive research examines the ways in which the individual perceives, evaluates and structures his or her environment. Even a simple newspaper advertisement can be understood, viewed and responded to in widely different ways by apparently similar individuals.

Personality research has focused its attention on the individuality and consistency of response shown by people in social situations. The underlying proposition is that an individual's response to a situation is determined by a combination of specific traits that are particular to him or her. With this as the starting point, considerable effort has been invested in examining whether particular, general personality types can be spotted. Their response to offerings could then be predicted with a high degree of confidence.

In the broad area of psychological study two notions have emerged as particularly interesting over the last 35 years: cognitive dissonance[12] and lifestyle analysis.

The theory of cognitive dissonance proposes that in his or her cognitive system the individual constantly strives for balance or consistency. When imbalance, inconsistency or dissonance emerges there will be a need to reduce it by avoiding the situation, restructuring perceptions, or gathering information to establish a new balance.

Lifestyle analysis has emerged from personality research. It is based on the proposition that study of the activities, interests, opinions and demographics of large numbers of respondents will highlight specific subgroups. These will respond to specific situations or offerings in broadly consistent ways. Lifestyle groups have been widely used in new product and promotional development.

Social and economic factors

It is important to recognize that people do not exist in isolation. They are members of a particular society, community and family. For part of their time they work, study or play. Typically, they do this in groups. This social and economic environment plays a major part in shaping needs as well as the specific pattern of motivations, values and drives which shape choice. Five aspects of the social and economic environment are especially important to the marketer: demography, location, income, socio-economic grouping and culture.

Demography is the study of populations. Its importance lies in the fact that all demand derives ultimately from people. Sheer numbers are only part of the picture. The structure of the population, i.e. the proportion in different age or sex groups, can have profound marketing implications. In Figure 2.6 the age profile of the UK is illustrated. Here we see relatively large numbers in the older age groups, especially among women. These have different needs from younger people. For example, they have probably passed their peak age for consuming products, especially consumer durables, but will have more opportunity for leisure. Their income-earning potential has probably peaked and most will have left the labour pool.

This population structure is in marked contrast with that seen in high population growth countries. In Figure 2.7 the population profile for India is shown. This population is heavily biased towards the young. The proportion aged over 60 years is less than 15 per cent of that in the UK. The needs of young families will dominate markets. Economic growth is likely to be increased by the entry of large numbers of new, economically active people.

Figure 2.6 The age profile for UK (1995)

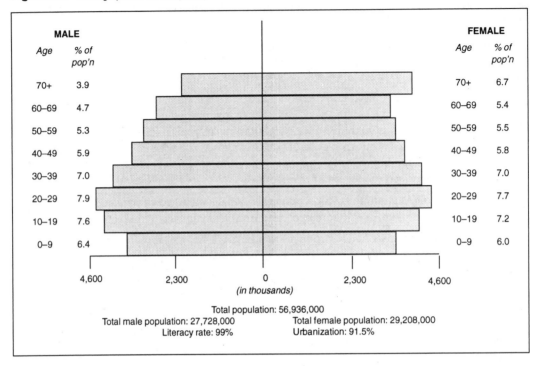

Figure 2.7 The age profile for India (1995)

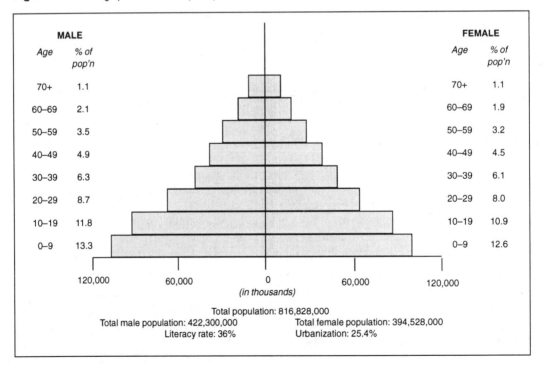

Figure 2.8 Regional profiles

Location of population is important in both domestic and overseas markets. Even in Britain, which is relatively small, the population is unevenly spread. Figure 2.8 indicates the economic regions of Britain. Population is concentrated in the South East, Midlands, North West and Strathclyde areas and is relatively low in the South West, East Anglia, parts of Wales and the Highlands of Scotland. Apparently simple local phenomena, such as hard or soft water, can have major long-term effects on sales of products like detergents. In larger countries like Germany, the US, Nigeria and Australia, climatic variations can have dramatic effects on a wide range of consumer requirements. In some of these countries these locational factors are strengthened by federal constitutions.

The US market is so large that it is common to see it subdivided into seven economic zones. In Table 2.4 these are grouped into regions which show similar industrial, climatic and communication systems.

The creation of the single European market has seen the emergence of similar regional clusters which cross national borders. They are likely to be shaped as much by location, communication and internal structure as national identity. It is already possible to talk about the 'golden triangle', the region bound by London, Paris and Hamburg. This contains many of the richest and most prosperous communities of Northern Europe. It is suggested that a new, South European 'triangle' is emerging bound by Lyon, Milan and Munich. The opening of Central Europe might see this stretch enlarging to include Vienna. Developments in transport and communication are reducing travel times and breaking down the barriers. By the end of 1996, the rail journey London–Paris, by Eurostar, took only half an hour longer than the London–Manchester trip (Table 2.5).

Income provides the individual, family or firm with its primary means of exchange. It is closely related to the notion of wealth, which also takes into account assets which may be disposable under particular circumstances. The overall pattern of national income provides considerable insight into the range and nature of opportunities in a community. This is especially true when income rises sufficiently for considerable discretion to be exercised in its disposal.

For this reason, the notions of disposable income and discretionary purchasing power are important. Disposable income is the amount available after taxes, mortgages and other fixed outgoings but not including food and other 'necessary' expenditure. Discretionary income is the amount left after these necessary expenses are deducted. The person can dispose of this as he or she wishes. Total income is often a poor predictor of the sums a person or group have

Table 2.4 The economic zones of the United States

North-East area:	Maine, Vermont, New Hampshire, Massachusetts, Rhode Island, New York, Connecticut, Pennsylvania, New Jersey, Delaware, Maryland
Great Lakes area:	Michigan, Wisconsin, Ohio, Indiana, Illinois
South-East area:	West Virginia, Virginia, Kentucky, North Carolina, Tennessee, Arkansas, Mississippi, Alabama, Georgia, South Carolina, Louisiana, Florida
Plains States area:	North Dakota, Minnesota, South Dakota, Nebraska, Iowa, Kansas, Missouri
South-West area:	Arizona, New Mexico, Texas, Oklahoma
Rocky Mountain area:	Montana, Idaho, Wyoming, Colorado, Utah
Far-West area:	Washington, Oregon, Nevada, California, Alaska
Pacific area:	Hawaii

Table 2.5 City centre to city centre rail journeys

Journey year 2000	*Present fastest*	*Projected*
Paris–Amsterdam	4h 13min	2h 48min
Brussels–Amsterdam	2h 41min	1h 28min
London–Paris	3h 0min	2h 30min
Frankfurt–Munich	3h 31min	3h 00min
Barcelona–Madrid	6h 13min	3h 00min
Rome–Milan	4h 05min	3h 05min

Source: The Economist.[13]

available to spend. A 35-year-old manager might have a monthly income of £3,000 but much of this will be taken up in mortgages, repayments on consumer durables, insurance etc. The costs associated with a young family will further reduce the money available. A 24-year-old earning only £1,000 per month but without these commitments can expect to have far more disposable or discretionary income.

Socio-economic structure is determined partly by the income levels of specific subgroups in the population. Basically it is the subdivision of the population into groups with broadly similar incomes, occupations, education levels and resources (Table 2.6).

Members of different groups are likely to give different priorities to certain needs, and the upper socio-economic groupings are likely to be able to satisfy certain needs more easily than others. Similarly, expectations, values, usage and attitudes are likely to vary between groups. Media research has highlighted the different media habits and approaches to communication of different groups. All these have direct implications for the approach to motivation within groups and the choice process.

Table 2.6 Socio-economic divisions in marketing in Britain

Registrar General	National Readership Survey	Occupation
I	A	Higher managerial, administrative or professional
II	B	Intermediate managerial, administrative or professional
III(n)	C1	Supervisory, clerical, junior managerial or professional
III(m)	C2	Skilled manual workers
IV	D	Semi-skilled and unskilled manual workers
V	E	State pensioners, widows, casual and lowest-grade earners

Culture is the basis of the entire social process, encompassing as it does knowledge, beliefs, art, morals, law and customs. It directly impinges on the values of every member of society. It influences both the needs themselves and the means of satisfying them. In Britain, despite the overall cohesiveness of our society, certain products, forms of entertainment and types of service that are acceptable in one part of the country have only a limited popularity in others. For example, working men's clubs used to play a major part in the social life in the North of England, while in the South they were almost non-existent. Participation in the National Lottery, by volume, is greatest in less affluent areas. This prompts the criticism that a tax on the poor is paying for the interests of the rich when grants go to, say, the Royal Opera House.

Institutional demand

In exploring the constituents of demand, attention so far has focused almost entirely on the consumer, with virtually no mention of industrial, commercial, intermediary, government or other demand. In fact the majority of companies are involved in servicing these markets, and the bulk of buying and selling is centred on this area.

One of the most critical features of demand in these markets is that it is primarily 'derived demand', i.e. it originates further down the marketing system. For example:

1   Industrial customers for specific raw materials or components will base the volume, timing, quality, type, and even price of their orders on their assumptions about their customers. Therefore the success of a product like stainless steel exhausts depends on the car manufacturer's judgements about their appeal to car buyers.

2   Commercial customers' demands for specific products or services is a function of their beliefs about how they will enhance their own offerings to their customers. For example, a bank installs outside cashpoint machines if it believes the extra customer service has commercial benefits.

3   Retailers base their purchasing policies on assumptions on throughput, 'stock turn rate' on goods. Therefore a new brand of chocolate is ordered if the combination of manufacturer 'push' and customer 'pull' means real pay-offs for the retailer.

4   A government department bases its requisitions on statutory obligations, specific regulations and the benefits of the goods to the public or section of the public. For example, a hospital invests in establishing self-contained cubicles for mental health patients rather than open wards if they are required to make provision for this type of patient, the funds are available, and it is judged that the patients will benefit.

Recent research highlights a powerful behavioural dimension to institutional demand. This brings out the degree to which many of the ideas mentioned earlier in exploring consumer demand can play a part in expanding our knowledge in this area.

All organizations have survival needs. These will range from the need for buildings and equipment, for power for lighting and heating, and for driving equipment, to the need for capital to establish and maintain the firm. As well as these basic needs, there may also be many less critical but often equally important needs, for example the need to present an image of social responsibility or to stay at the forefront of technology. These may play a part in contributing to overall corporate profitability but equally may reflect the values of company personnel.

Besides influencing the nature of the needs and the priority given to them, these behavioural factors directly affect the choice process. Source loyalty, innovativeness, and many similar phenomena have a major role in building up a picture of industrial demand. Location, prosperity, company resources, and technical background of personnel also play a part. Many large firms prefer to obtain supplies from firms in their immediate area. A firm with high profits or large resources is able to invest heavily in new equipment or provide better facilities for its workers. In some industries it can be difficult to get engineers to experiment with new materials or applications because of their traditional training.

Although these behavioural dimensions are more important than used to be thought, institutional purchasing is still characterized by a high degree of professionalism, information collection and analysis. The buyer is likely to conduct a more extensive search, employ more objective criteria, have greater technical expertise and back-up, and have far greater power than the individual consumer. Also, institutional demand is more directly affected by coalition purchasing, involving managers from a number of areas. For example, a marketing audit may highlight weaknesses in the firm's product array, so a need for research into the market emerges. The research indicates an opportunity for a low-cost economy brand, and a need for a new, cheaper packaging may occur, to keep costs down. The new packaging may be incompatible with existing machinery, requiring the purchase of new equipment. The buying process will involve top management anxious to resolve the company's weakness, brand management keen to ensure customer acceptability, production management, and personnel, besides the purchasing staff who will generally be responsible for information gathering and sometimes testing, as well as finally placing the order.

Supply

As long as people or institutions have needs, thus creating demands, there are opportunities to provide offerings to satisfy them. The means of satisfying needs are tangible products, perhaps to satisfy basic survival needs, and services, perhaps to meet more social needs.

These offerings can be directed either to the individual or to institutions; for example, Coca-Cola satisfies the thirst of an individual, and the ICI Agriculture Division provides animal foodstuffs to farmers. They can encompass services as well as tangible products; for example, Granada Television provides its audiences with programmes, and Securicor advises firms on how best to protect their property.

The suppliers of goods and services include private enterprise, non-profit-making organizations and the state. For example, farmers meet some of their needs, e.g. tractors, from private enterprise; other needs, e.g. insurance, are met by the National Farmers' Union, and yet other needs, e.g. advice and special grants, by government.

All these goods and services, and the different organizations and types of enterprise, are directly involved in the exchange process. In providing their offerings they are part of the marketing system. There are a number of ways of classifying these offerings.

The notion of a standard industrial classification is used throughout much of the world to classify economies into different industrial segments. All business activities are categorized into broad divisions, subdivided again, and then given a coding.

In international trade similar classification schemes exist in most countries. There is also the International Standard Industrial Classification (ISIC). Although there is not necessarily a relationship between the Standard Industrial Classification (SIC) and the International Standard Industrial Classification, most agencies working in this area are attempting to build in maximum consistency.

These classifications are based largely on the production process, technology or product features. It is equally important for marketing management to categorize offerings from the user's perspective.

Consumer offerings

Convenience goods are frequently-bought items requiring limited search and no delays in supply – the typical items in the supermarket or corner shop.

Shopping goods are generally purchased less often. Search and analysis are involved, particularly of price, product features, service and availability. Many consumer durables, e.g. washing machines and radios, fall into this category.

Speciality lines cater for the needs of special-interest goods. They include both subsets of more general areas, e.g. delicatessen lines, and autonomous groups, e.g. particular sports or hobbies.

Leisure services are those offerings geared to the non-domestic and non-work interests of people.

Domestic services are those services satisfying the home or work needs of individuals and families. Banks, building societies, certain local authority services and telephones are typical of these.

Although many organizations and companies are highly specialized, others cross a number of categories; for example, local authority parks and gardens are leisure services but the social services are generally domestic.

Industrial offerings

Industrial offerings are generally tied to the process of converting inputs into outputs which can be resold. They are thus related to three basic flows: information, goods and capital.

1   *Information.* Information services provide the basis for decision-making, resource allocation and communication. They include market research, advertising, and technical and consultancy services.

2   *Goods.* Raw materials are wholly unprocessed goods, e.g. grain and iron ore. Processed goods (fabricated materials) are items which have been converted from the raw material but are not usable unless combined with other items, e.g. plastic or aluminium mouldings and steel. Components are semi-finished goods which are brought together to make up the producer's offering, e.g. shock absorbers and cooker timers. Equipment includes items which are employed in the conversion processes but which are not transferred into the producer's goods, e.g. buildings, cement mixers and desks. Supplies are those items needed to sustain the production or commercial process but not directly incorporated in the product, e.g. gas and electricity.

3   *Capital.* Financial services are the services provided by those institutions which manage a firm's flow of funds out to its suppliers, through the organization and in from customers, e.g. banks, credit agencies and factors.

Although a thorough understanding of the firm's offering, whether product or service, is important to effective marketing management, long-term success in the market-place calls for a clear understanding that the buyer responds to a number of variables when making a purchase decision, and a recognition that it is the mix of these variables that determines the degree to which firms satisfy needs in the market.

The marketing mix

The variables are called the marketing mix (Figure 2.9). Individually they are the product or offering, price, physical distribution, intermediary or channel of distribution and promotion. This is simplified to the four P's: product, price, place and promotion. The combination of these constitutes the total product proposition. This provides the basic opportunity for satisfying customer needs.

Marketing calls for effective management of the individual mix elements and, perhaps even more important, their interaction. It is the right product, at the right time, in the right place, with the right price and presented in the right way that satisfies buyer needs, as the following example shows.

Dell Computers achieved rapid market penetration and became the fourth-largest computer manufacturer by using a simple formula for its marketing mix. At its heart is the virtual elimination of middlemen and the extensive use of direct mail plus heavy advertising in specialist press. Dell, also, keeps a very low inventory. Together, these policies allow Dell to supply high specification PCs at low cost.

Figure 2.9 Different mixes will meet different needs and appeal to different subgroups

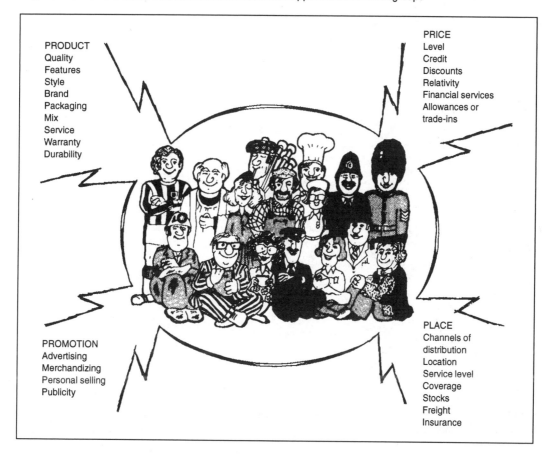

PRODUCT
Quality
Features
Style
Brand
Packaging
Mix
Service
Warranty
Durability

PRICE
Level
Credit
Discounts
Relativity
Financial services
Allowances or
trade-ins

PROMOTION
Advertising
Merchandizing
Personal selling
Publicity

PLACE
Channels of
distribution
Location
Service level
Coverage
Stocks
Freight
Insurance

Marketing policy

Marketing policy integrates the different aspects of the marketing mix. It involves:

1 Study of the likely future situations which the firm may face (scenario analysis).
2 Consideration of the different challenges which will be posed by these alternatives.
3 Careful examination of the company's ability to cope successfully with the challenges posed by changing conditions.
4 Review of the alternative strategies which the firm can adopt to make the best use of current or obtainable resources to achieve the best market position.
5 Taking the marketing management decisions, allocating resources and choosing the tactics which will convert these strategies to action in the market-place.
6 Setting up procedures which enable the firm to review progress and take action to adjust programmes of action in the light of changing circumstances and experience.

Figure 2.10 describes the formulation of marketing policy. It means looking into the future, considering how possible future situations (scenarios) will affect the firm. This examination is very long term in those areas in which 'lead times', i.e. the time it take the firm to adapt, are longest, such as technological change. This will then need to be related to the company's ability to adapt.

Figure 2.10 Policies, programmes and scenarios (adapted from R. E. Thomas, *Business Policy.*[14]

Scenario				Alternative technological economic and social futures	
Audit			Assess match of resources and requirements		
Scenario		Alternative markets and economic conditions			
Audit	Assess match of resources and requirements				
Mission	Define business mission				
Strategy	Strategy implementation	Strategic choice	Strategic analysis		
Programme	Schedule of activities (tactics) designed to implement strategy				
Budget/ Projection	Authorize and implement projects	Proposed projects			
Measure	Action now				
	1995	1996	1997	1998	1999

Pilkington Glass, for example, will invest tens of millions of pounds on a new float glass line. The line will take years to build and operate for over a decade. Their investment in the mid-1990s will only pay off if they have predicted accurately the likely market for their product at the end of the first decade of the next century.

The process of regular auditing of skills and capabilities is central to this and to the shorter-term 'scenario analysis' related to changing market and economic conditions. This is primarily designed to relate the firm's actions to short- to medium-term changes in trading conditions. These can include changes in demand, new competitors, and proposed novel courses of action, e.g. new product launches. Relating capabilities to costs is the key to this. The earlier the firm starts adjusting to changing circumstances, the more likely it is to adapt successfully.

At the core of the process of adjustment is an understanding of the 'business mission', i.e. the ability to answer the question 'What business are we in?' This is the most important question in marketing, as it requires that the firm looks beyond its current offering into the need it meets for its customers.

There are many examples of firms failing to appreciate the true nature of the business they are in. There was the failure of the railway companies to recognize that they were in the transport business (not railways), and of the motion picture companies to appreciate that they were in the entertainment business (not films).

A mini-case study: Parker Pens

A very clear illustration of the benefits of this vision lies in the realization by Parker Pens of the business this firm is in. Conventional analysis would see Parker as being in the 'pens' or perhaps the 'writing implements' business. This would lead to policies being adopted in product development, distribution, pricing and promotion based on this business definition, e.g.

1 People write all year so advertising should be constant over the various months.
2 Distribution should be concentrated in specialist outlets, e.g. stationers.

However, careful analysis of the market brought out evidence which challenged this conventional belief. It became clear that the vast majority of quality pens (the type that Parker produce) were not purchased by users. They were gifts! Parker was in the gift business. The implications of this affected virtually all aspects of marketing activity:

1 Products were designed to enhance their 'presentation as gifts' as much as their functionality.
2 Gift packs and packaging were critical to success.
3 Advertising schedules reflected gift-buying seasons, e.g. Christmas, more than use.
4 Distribution and production schedules were designed to reflect the same buyer and seasonal patterns.
5 Pricing became geared to competitive gifts, not other pens.

In arriving at this definition of its 'mission', Parker managed to combine a definition which was broad enough to provide new avenues for development while not being so wide as to be meaningless. The 'mission' described the nature of the firm. The 'marketing strategy' provides the firm with its sense of direction. Strategy involves the matching of the activities of an organization with the environment in which it operates.[15] It links the conclusions drawn from appreciation of the firm's current position in the environment with the future position the company seeks to occupy in the market-place. Marketing strategies should also contain within them clear indications of the immediate policies and programmes of action to be adopted by the company.

The marketing programmes adopted by the firm focus on the two areas previously introduced under the titles 'target markets' and 'marketing mixes'. Central to thinking in this area is the notion that the more activities are focused around the needs of particular groups, the more likely they are to be successful. The company should attempt to define and describe the customer groups it wishes to reach as clearly as possible. These become the 'target' for the specific market-orientated actions it is taking. These actions are built from the resources under the company's control in the areas of product, price, place and promotion. Specific combinations will have a different degree of appeal to alternative target groups or market segments. Establishing the specific mix is only the first stage. The actions which emerge will need to be integrated and scheduled into a programme of action designed to achieve the desired results over time and in the most cost-effective way.

Budgeting is an integral part of the process. Establishing realistic funding levels is necessary at this stage. Often firms draw up marketing strategies far beyond their capacity to fund them. This is particularly true in overseas trade. Research[16] has indicated that underfunding is one of the most serious problems faced by exporters, regardless of whether they are concentrating on a few markets or attempting to skim a large number of different countries.

Very few marketing activities can work effectively in isolation. Effective management has been described as 'Doing the right things, *not* doing things right'. Critical to this notion is the process of monitoring and measuring performance against the firm's corporate and marketing objectives.

Marketing success in the long term depends on learning from mistakes and continually striving for increased effectiveness and improved productivity. This can only be achieved if the company sets up systems to monitor and evaluate the returns from expenditures and actions.

Policy, strategy and structure

The earlier discussion of marketing's role in the firm indicates a number of the alternative approaches to organizing the marketing function in the firm. Two additional aspects of this need to be included in any consideration of this area:

1 The relationship between the organization of the marketing function and the rest of the firm.
2 The fit between the strategies adopted and the organizational arrangements (structure) to achieve them.

A number of distinctive organizational forms have been identified by researchers in Britain and the US:[17, 18]

1 *The entrepreneurial firm.* Controlled and managed by the owner-manager, who takes responsibility for most significant marketing decisions.
2 *The professionalized company.* The operations of the company are delegated to specific departments of functional areas managed and controlled by specialists, e.g. marketing, production, finance.
3 *The divisionalized firm.* A head office exists which determines overall policy but the divisions take most of the operational decisions. A firm such as Lucas with its specialist divisions illustrates this.
4 *The holding company.* The centre exercises very loose control over the operating companies. They have considerable freedom, operating at times like 'independent' firms.

The organization of the marketing operation, especially the responsibility for strategic decision-making, varies considerably between these different structures.

The best form of organizational arrangement is directly influenced by the environment faced by the company. Mintzberg[19] has put forward a matrix like that shown in Figure 2.11 to describe how the nature of the business mission (in terms of complexity) and the character of the environment can be related to suggest particular forms of organizational arrangement.

Figure 2.11 Organization and uncertainty. Adapted from G. Johnson and K. Scholes, *Exploring Corporate Strategy.* [20]

		Environment	
		Stable	**Dynamic**
Task	**Complex**	Banks and other highly centralized firms	Advanced electronics and other markets experiencing change
	Simple	Cars and other established single product consumer goods	Retailers and other firms where the market requires freedom of action

In the complex-stable situation strategies can be centrally set and monitored as the stability of the market enables the head office to use their greater resources while little is lost through central control. In the complex-dynamic case any attempt to impose too much central direction may stifle creativity, making it harder for the firm to adapt to changing circumstances. The simple-stable context gives considerable advantages to the firm that can mobilize its resources most efficiently against identified long-term goals. The simple-dynamic situation gives the maximum benefit to strategies built on people-based responses to customer requests.

More recently authors such as Kay[21] have emphasized the importance of understanding the organization's capability or 'architecture' first, then designing the strategy to achieve them. They suggest that this form of functionality in organizational design is the best defence against the inefficiencies which can emerge too easily in large and powerful corporations. The risk is that management may lose sight of the objectives and strategies while paying too much attention to company politics and personal position. A properly designed strategy should force the organization to shape itself around the best means of achieving goals if matched with effective controls.

Marketing controls

The excitement and challenge of deriving and implementing marketing strategies and programmes makes it very easy to lose sight of the equally important challenge of building systems of effective control into the firm's marketing procedures. Anyone familiar with Murphy's Laws – *If anything can go wrong, it will go wrong* and *Of the things that can't go wrong, some will* – will recognize the importance of building in controls to ensure:

1 That the firm making the mistakes is the first to be aware of them. Some of the cheapest lessons to be learnt in marketing are to be gained from the mistakes of competitors who fail to build in effective monitoring systems. However, this pattern works both ways.
2 That adjustments and adaptations are made to programmes before errors become fatal. Customers are surprisingly supportive of suppliers who realize their mistakes and try sincerely to correct them. The same client will have very little patience with the firm that is unaware of its failings.

Marketing controls exist to help management monitor and direct their actions in the field. They are intimately linked with supervision and surveillance. The controls set up by the firms should provide a basis for measuring performance against established and agreed criteria. The issue is discussed at length in Chapter 27; here it is important to recognize that the primary aim of marketing control is to ensure that actions taken and their consequences conform to the policies and strategies established by the firm.

Conclusion

In this chapter a number of issues were raised which are central to marketing practice today:

1 Marketing policy can only be effective if it is based on an understanding of the market, the firm's place within it and the likely consequence of actions.

2   Establishing 'what business we are in' is the cornerstone of the marketing approach.
3   The marketing strategy provides the firm with its sense of direction, besides providing the basis for the formulation of programmes of action and mechanisms of control.
4   Those involved in marketing management perform a wide range of tasks and hold a diverse array of job titles.
5   Marketing management is most effective when it operates in harmony with the rest of the firm's operational areas.

Throughout the rest of the text these issues will be central to discussion of the areas of management action.

Glossary

Account. (1) In sales, an invoice. (2) In advertising, a client of an advertising, or other agency. (3) Now being used far more widely to describe customers and customer groups. Key-account management is a term gaining increasing currency to describe selling arrangements made to deal with major customers.

Audit. The assessment of the assets and liabilities of the firm. SWOT analysis (Strengths, Weaknesses, Opportunities, Threats) is frequently used as the basis of the marketing audit.

Budget. Statement of income and expenditure over time, usually linked to a timetable of events and actions for which monies have been allocated.

Communication. This is the process of transmitting information from one human being to another whether directly and personally or indirectly and impersonally. Effective communication is a function of the reception of messages, not their transmission.

Control. This consists of directing and monitoring the actions taken by the firm and its members to ensure that the use of company resources contributes to the achievement of company goals.

Drive. An internal pressure to satisfy a need.

Mission. The statement of the nature of the firm in terms of the business it is in and the need(s) it meets.

Motives. The psychological state which affects the readiness of a person or organization to adopt a course of action or continue with an existing pattern.

Needs. Any lack or deficit within an individual or organization.

Objectives. The purposes and tasks set for the firm or a particular area of company activity, e.g. marketing.

Product/Brand manager. The executive with overall responsibility for a specific product or brand within a multi-product (or brand) firm. Typically he or she has specific responsibility for promotional expenditures with joint authority in other areas. The degree of profit responsibility varies between firms.

Programme. The schedule or sequence of events which draws together the specific actions or activities of the firm in a concerted way.

Scenario analysis. This is a strategic planning technique which involves the identification of a range of alternative future environments which the firm is likely to face. On the basis of these the company examines its ability to cope with the challenges which they will pose. The extent to which different strategies strengthen its position can then be related to these scenarios.

Strategy. The process of matching the company's resources to the wider environment to produce a statement (or statements) which summarize the overall route the firm will take to achieve its objectives.

Tactic. The specific action taken to move the firm in the direction of achieving its overall strategy.

Venture management. The approach to new product development which involves bringing together teams of specialists to develop an offering from concept to launch.

SPECIMEN QUESTIONS

1 For two marketing jobs which you find in a national newspaper indicate the mix of skills and knowledge which the successful candidate will need.

2 Why has the growing importance of the marketing function led corporate leaders to place greater emphasis on issues like profits, strategy and portfolio management?

3 'Marketing is a total company activity'. What are the implications of this statement for:
   (a) Marketing.
   (b) Production.
   (c) Finance.

4 Describe the positive gains from effective internal communication to marketing, and the costs of poor communication.

5 Explain the importance of the concept of need to marketing. Illustrate ways in which attention to customer needs changes the way a company of your choice might direct its efforts.

6 How might the different age profiles of the populations of the UK and India influence the kinds of products and services that might be successful? Produce proposals on ways in which a British holiday tours operator might redirect his services to meet the needs of the increasingly important older age groups.

7 How might a firm use the Registrar General's classification to plan their marketing?

8 Describe the ways in which institution demand differs from consumer demand.

9 Outline the steps in the formation of marketing policy for a new firm.

10 Define:
   (a) Cherry picking.
   (b) Brand management.
   (c) Product portfolio.
   (d) Key accounts.
   (e) The Marketing Council.
   (f) Fmcgs.
   (g) Venture management.
   (h) Syncro marketing.
   (i) Drives.
   (j) Cognitive dissonance.

CASE STUDY 2: CALEDONIA PLAIN CHOCOLATE

Introduction

In late 1997 the marketing audit conducted by Booker-Greer Limited's confectionery division highlighted a number of weaknesses in their marketing position. The two main weaknesses were:

1   Their strength in milk chocolate lines was matched by poor performance in plain chocolate. This situation was made more serious because of the growing importance of plain chocolate in the market.

2   In a number of parts of the UK their market share was significantly worse than in the country as a whole. Among these Scotland stood out as particularly important because of its high *per capita* chocolate consumption and the unusually high sales of plain chocolate in that area.

Competitive history

Both these factors could be explained in part by a series of decisions made in the past. In the early 1950s the company had been the first major confectionery manufacturer to spot the trend away from toffees and boiled sweets.

For over thirty years the firm had sustained its position as one of the three largest confectionery manufacturers through a small number of major milk chocolate count lines backed by heavy advertising and extensive distribution. These traditional favourites had been supplemented by a number of new product launches. During the late 1980s and early 1990s a very high rate of new brand introduction by themselves and their competitors had occurred. Overall, Booker-Greer had come out of this period worse off than before. Unlike their two competitors they had not established a major new large-volume count line on the market. (Although the two competitors had established only one new major product each, the long-term contribution of these was likely to be substantial.)

The current situation

Faced with the ever-escalating cost of introducing a new brand, the new product group embarked on a wide-ranging study of alternative strategies. In the light of the weaknesses in plain chocolate and in Scotland, it was recommended that the firm explore the scope for a brand geared to the specific needs of the Scottish market. It was hoped that this brand would take up some of the spare capacity then existing in the firm's manufacturing plant in Edinburgh. The large vote in favour of Scottish devolution, also, seemed to suggest that a distinct opportunity existed for a Scottish brand.

In the past the firm had always worked very closely with its existing advertising agencies on new product development projects. In this case it was decided that extra insight into the market in Scotland could be achieved through a local Scottish agency. Four Scottish agencies, two based in Glasgow and two in Edinburgh, were asked to compete for the business, as was the Edinburgh office of one of their London agencies.

Of the competing agencies Alexander Gooch and Co. stood out as most committed to a distinctly Scottish offering. There were briefed to develop and research a new brand for possible launch in late 1998 or early 1999. Clear volume targets were set, amounting to 25 per cent of plain chocolate count lines (10 per cent total count line sales) in Scotland. This would minimize the impact on current sales of Booker-Greer products while biting into their competitors' market.

A number of names, packs and related advertising themes emerged, notably 'Stuart', 'Saltire', 'Caledonia' and 'Stirling' brand chocolates. These were researched in conjunction with a brand name and proposition, 'Silhouette', that had performed reasonably well in national research studies among both adults and children.

The research indicated considerable interest in the concept of a Scottish brand. The Caledonia brand and campaign (emphasizing Scottish links, made in Scotland etc.) did consistently well, out-performing all other propositions, including Silhouette. Unfortunately, two major problems emerged:

1 Consumer preferences were for a milk chocolate Scottish brand.
2 The results, although promising, suggested a market of less than 18 per cent of the plain chocolate market (for the plain brand) and 9 per cent of total chocolate count sales (if a milk chocolate brand was launched).

These results created a major debate within the firm about further actions. The brand group and advertising agency favoured progressing with the launch, initially with the plain brand but with a view to introducing a milk brand later. Both pointed to the overall appeal of the basic concept and suggested that the results might easily be an understatement, given the newness of the proposition. They also pointed to strong nationalist feeling in Scotland, and the brand manager in charge saw increased pressure of greater economic, social and cultural autonomy as a possible platform for long-term strength.

The firm's research department recommended abandonment. In this they were supported by the corporate planning department, who pointed out the harsh reality that the offering had failed to meet its targets at a time when national sentiment was high. Also, any milk chocolate derivative would draw much of its sales from their current offering.

After considering these arguments the marketing director decided to abandon this initiative.

Tasks

1 Examine the thinking which led to this project.
2 Review its development.
3 Explore the final argument.
4 Evaluate the final decision.

3

The marketing system

Introduction

Understanding the environment and marketing system in which the firm and its competitors, suppliers and customers do business is central to effective marketing. Managers must fully appreciate:

The business environment: the conditions, primarily economic, political, cultural and technological, under which the marketing system(s) exists or is developed. (Adapted from the *Oxford English Dictionary*)

The marketing system: the set of significant institutions and flows that connect an organization to its markets.[1]

Market basics

The traditional, trading farmer is perhaps the simplest illustration of the system (Figure 3.1). Although perhaps the oldest marketing system, it persists throughout the world, adaptations have taken place even here, perhaps to capitalize on new opportunities or imposed

Figure 3.1   A simple marketing system

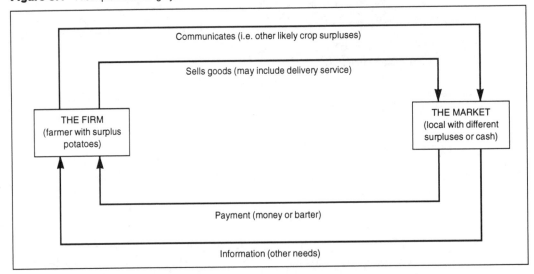

by law. The basic farm products market is unchanged, with goods moving from the farmer to the customer, roads have opened up a massive new travelling market, and cultural changes have encouraged motorists to buy direct from the farm.

Throughout the world, environmental factors have interacted with the marketing system to produce change and adaptation for both farmers and buyers. (The system's view sees the market as a series of inter-related processes made up of a number of parts (subsystems) operating in a more or less complex environment. The parts of the system demonstrate an ordered pattern of behaviour designed to achieve certain goals, either their own or the system's.) The results are markedly varied in different parts of the world. The political, cultural, economic and technological history and conditions of Britain have created many areas in which the systems differ dramatically from those in North America and the old Commonwealth (perhaps those nearest culturally) and in Europe (nearest physically). There are, however, some areas of similarity. For example, advertising/sales ratios in the UK have tended to be nearer US levels than European ones, and the Co-operative (retail and wholesale) movement is powerful throughout Europe, including Britain, but in Europe's semi-political form is virtually unknown in the US.

The environment

The environment is continually changing, partly from interactions with other systems (much of our thinking about marketing is derived from ideas and research originating in the US) and partly from internal factors (with the improving quality of British and European marketing has come a recognition of the real differences which exist and the confidence to recast some ideas and explore new areas). The ability to manage change effectively is one of the key determinants of corporate success.[2] Two of the most dramatic areas of change in Britain over the last hundred years have been the decline in primary production (agriculture and mining) and the growth in the service industries (Table 3.1). Over half the working population of the UK is already employed in service-related industries. It is a pattern which can be seen across the developed world. In the US, estimates now place the 'white collar' group as by far the largest sector of the population, with every indication that their relative significance is increasing rapidly with the introduction of new technologies.

Until recently, attention has been concentrated on the impact of marketing on commercial and consumer services such as banking, tourism and catering. The 'deregulation' of many areas of professional services, e.g. accountancy, law, opticians and architecture, has forced many professional groups to face up to the challenges of competition. The more sophisticated have

Table 3.1 Percentage distribution among industries of working population (UK)

	1861 (%)	1902 (%)	1921 (%)	1951 (%)	1971 (%)	1979* (%)	1989* (%)	1991* (%)	1995 (%)
Primary									
Agriculture and mining	23.2	14.8	14.4	8.9	4.4	4.1	3.7	3.6	3.6
Secondary									
Manufacture	38.6	37.9	36.2	39.0	34.9	31.3	29.5	27.9	26.4
Intermediate									
Transport, communication, utilities, construction	11.3	16.3	12.2	14.0	15.4	19.6	21.3	22.4	23.0
Tertiary									
Services, white collar	21.2	25.1	35.1	37.7	45.3	45.0	45.5	46.1	47.0
Other	5.6	5.9	2.2	0.4	–	–	–	–	–

Reproduced with permission, Gershung, J., *After Industrial Society*. London and Basingstoke: Macmillan, 1978.   * C.S.O.

become conscious of the potential impact of marketing on professional practice development. Mitchell[3] has explored the impact of this change in the professions as well as the differences in role that will emerge. In Britain many professional groups are seeking ways of building marketing into their client development strategies:

> It is not a question of whether professionals should adopt the marketing concept to assist in practice expansion, but whether they adopt it to survive and how well they undertake the tasks involved.[4]

Technology

New technologies are currently associated with major changes in patterns of employment and consumption to transform markets and commercial relationships. There has been a major shift in the balance of trade in technologies during the last twenty years. As recently as 1975 Western Europe had a trade surplus of $1.7 billion in high technology. By 1983 this was a deficit of $5 billion. This doubled by 1986. Every major European country saw its share of world exports of technology-based products reduced over the period 1978 to 1995 (See Tables 3.2, 3.3).

Table 3.2 Exports of high-technology products by selected countries (as a percentage of all exports)

Country	1972	1976	1978	1980	1982	1983	1990	1995*
Germany	26	22	22	20	17	15	15**	14.5
France	11	11	10	10	8	8	8	8
UK	14	12	12	13	11	10	9	9.5
Switzerland	4	4	4	4	3	3	4	3.5
Japan	13	18	19	18	20	25	28	28
US	32	34	34	35	40	37	36	36.5

Sources: Deutsche Bundesbank, 1984, Eurostat.   * Estimated. ** Includes former E. Germany.

Table 3.3 Percentage change in share of world exports in selected industries (1980 to 1987)

Country	Materials/metals	Semiconductors/computers	Telecommunications
Germany	−2.5	−1.4	−7.0
Italy	−0.4	−0.5	−0.8
UK	−0.4	−0.6	−2.2

The transformation is not restricted to these areas. Policy initiatives by government had a profound impact on commercial systems over a relatively short period of time. In Britain this can be seen in the extensive programme of privatization which has taken place over the last twenty years. This has led to drastic reductions in the state's involvement in telecommunications, oil production, gas production, airlines, shipbuilding, banking, gas distribution, railways, water services, postal services, electricity production and distribution as well as motor vehicle production.

Networks and relationships

Kotler[5] suggests that the company system and environment can be viewed in terms of three levels: the general environment, different publics, and the marketing system. These are in a state of constant interaction, not only within each level but across different levels.

Figure 3.3 illustrates how the general environmental forces – economic, political, cultural and technological – shape the marketing system and the commercial relationships within it. A free market economy, with competing political parties but sharing certain values and an advanced technology, will place very different demands on those involved in business from a closed, single-party, underdeveloped economy. The individual firm will have far more freedom of action but can expect far less protection from commercial difficulties. Management will be far more mobile, but so will competitors. The company will have access to high technology but will need to meet high research and development costs while being vulnerable to novel offerings.

The precise form and shape of the commercial relationships within these broad patterns will be determined by the publics which surround the 'core marketing system'. The financial community can affect many areas of action, ranging from investment programmes to international trade. In Britain it has been suggested that the banks do not provide as much support for R & D and innovation as banks in the US, Japan and Germany. At the same time foreign competitors look with envy on the skills in international trade and finance which the UK banks have acquired over the years. The approach of the media to industry has a direct effect on confidence and relationships. Many criticisms have been lodged against the UK media over the last few years:

> The media are determined to send up industry as making profits out of innocent, ill-informed members of the public. (Michael Shersby, M.P.)

The earlier comments on privatization illustrate the way in which direct intervention by government can shape commercial relationships. Perhaps even more important is the way in which government can use its legislative, administrative, purchasing and other powers to shape markets. In turn, government is affected by pressure groups. These can influence markets directly as the activities of groups such as the Consumers' Association, Friends of the Earth, and, after the Dunblane tragedy, the Snowdrop Campaign, show. A clear illustration of this was the pervasive influence over many years of the Lord's Day Observance Society. Even when the society was moribund, its policy was taken up by trade unions opposing (on very different grounds) proposals for repeal of the restrictions on Sunday trading in England.

In isolation or in concert these forces shape the pattern of the market. Looking at them in terms of one country can be deceptive. These systems interact within regions of the world, e.g. Europe and internationally. This was seen in the early 1980s when US legislation on restricting access to new technologies to the Soviet Union, then Russia, came into direct conflict with the policies of European and other countries.

In some markets other 'environmental' forces play a major part. Agricultural and food markets can be affected immediately and dramatically by climate or ecology.[6] These issues are elaborated in the discussion in Chapter 4 of the marketing of food case study.

General environment

Britain is a mixed economy in which both the state and private enterprise are directly involved in the marketing process. A series of political decisions, stretching back into the last century, have led to the state becoming directly involved in both the management of the systems and the operations of specific industries through direct intervention, regulation, inducement and direction, legislation and economic policies. The specific strategies of governments can vary considerably even over relatively short periods of time. The differences between, say, the Labour government of 1974 and Tony Blair's 'New Labour' government of 1997 illustrate this. The former was committed to direct intervention through such agencies as the National Enterprise Board. The latter endorsed the Conservatives' policy of privatization, designed to reduce public sector direct involvement, while exploring other ways to reshape

Figure 3.2   The water share offer

Public Application Form

This document contains a public application form and guide on how to complete it, a summary of the application and instalment arrangements and the terms and conditions of application. Please refer to the Prospectus and Mini Prospectus, copies of which are available at most clearing bank branches and post offices, for further information.

Anglian Water Plc
Northumbrian Water Group Plc
North West Water Group Plc
Severn Trent Plc
Southern Water Plc

South West Water Plc
Thames Water Plc
Welsh Water Plc
Wessex Water Plc
Yorkshire Water Plc

Offers for Sale

by

Schroders

on behalf of

The Secretary of State for the Environment

and

The Secretary of State for Wales

HM Government is now offering for sale 100 per cent of the Ordinary Share capital of each of the Water Holding Companies; 81.5 per cent is being offered in the UK and 18.5 per cent overseas.

The Offer Price of 240p per Share is payable in instalments of 100p now, 70p on 31st July 1990, and 70p on 30th July 1991.

The minimum investment is £240, of which £100 is payable now.

The information contained in this document is in summary form. It has been drawn from, and is to be read together with, the relevant Sections of the full Prospectus dated 22nd November 1989, which alone contains approved listing particulars relating to each Water Holding Company.

In applying for Shares in any Water Holding Company you will be treated as applying on the basis of the information in the relevant Sections of the full Prospectus and on the terms and conditions set out on pages 3 and 4 of this document, which together govern your rights and obligations. Expressions defined in the full Prospectus have the same meaning in this document.

Before deciding to apply for Shares you should consider carefully whether shares are a suitable investment for you. Their value can go down as well as up. If you need advice, you should consult a stockbroker, solicitor, accountant, bank manager or other professional adviser.

The Council of The Stock Exchange has authorised the issue of this document under section 154(1)(b) of the Financial Services Act 1986 without approving its contents. This document is not for distribution outside the UK, nor should it be treated as an offer to sell or solicitation of any offer to buy any securities outside the UK.

Figure 3.3 Interaction between the different levels in the marketing system

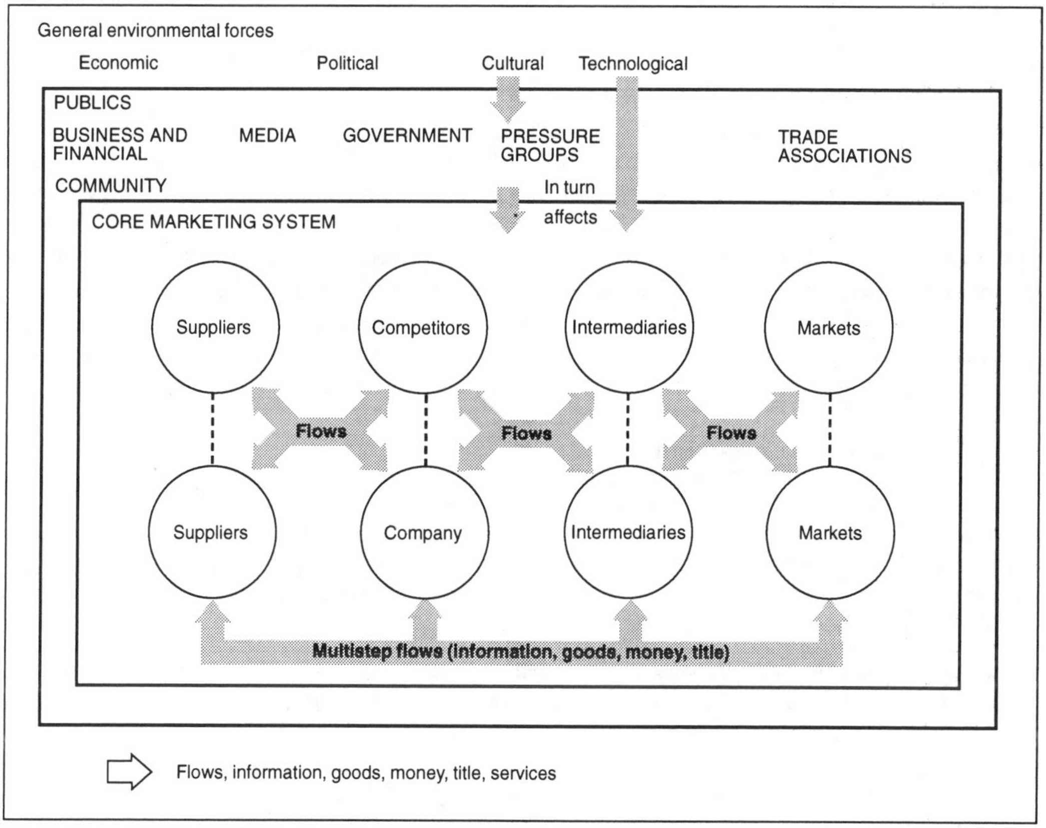

policy. Despite these differences in policy, both recognized the profound impact their programmes could have on markets and business relationships.

Pressure for 'deregulation' can be seen in many industries and a number of countries. Airlines, trucking, banks and professional services have been transformed. The reluctance of British firms to espouse marketing has been linked by King[7] with two aspects of recent industrial development: the emergence of 'producer bureaucracies' and the 'profit spiral'. Both reflect the changing competitiveness of UK industry. This has been linked with two contradictory explanations:

> The growth of competition and progressive removal of protectionism.[8]

> The increasing bureaucratization of trading relationships and the shifting patterns of regulatory interference.

The balance of evidence in those industries where deregulation has occurred suggests that the latter explanation is closer to the truth. This may reflect the failure of British companies to respond to the increasing 'globalization' of trade:

> Many observers have contrasted the long tradition of protected markets for British firms which has led historically to both buyers and sellers being resistant to change and competition.[9]

The evidence of the reluctance of sellers to adopt a marketing approach in certain key sectors has been demonstrated in a number of studies, notably machine tools,[10] textiles[11] and vehicles.[12] This theme recurs throughout the NEDO report on international competitiveness.[13] It is possible that the high import penetration of many UK markets indicates a less conservative approach among buyers.

The overall British strategy for economic development employs many of the approaches open to any similar governments. In North America different attitudes, decisions and traditions will produce variations in government policy with a broadly similar framework. In Europe a more directly interventionist approach has been adopted, especially in France and Sweden. In Japan the tradition of strong informal links between government and industry finds its expression in the dialogues held under the auspices of MITI (Ministry of International Trade and Industry). Elsewhere, detailed national plans are produced to assist and/or direct industry along certain lines. In Britain the review of the available alternatives and consideration of their strengths and weaknesses in this context have led to a particular pattern emerging.

Direct intervention

The last twenty years saw more substantial change in this area than at almost any time since the late 1940s. It is an area in which the marked contrast which existed between Britain and Europe on the one hand, and the US and Japan on the other, has been reduced. Recent changes reduced significantly the commercial transactions taking place in Britain today involving the state.

The process of intervention was so far advanced that even a government committed to reducing it faced severe limitations on its freedom of action, at least in the short to medium term. Some continuing involvement was acknowledged by the Thatcher and Major Conservative governments, at least until the free market institutions were in a position to take over a more active supporting role. This process of intervention has direct effects on the marketing system both at home and overseas. It is important to recognize that the UK was not atypical among European countries, most of which have adopted direct intervention under specific circumstances. The massive industrial enterprises in the UK are part of a worldwide pattern of government ownership of key industries, services and utilities.

Marketing in nationalized industries represents, in many ways, a very different competitive situation from that of the traditional free market. In some instances the firm has a monopoly of supply or service, e.g. gas, electricity, post, telecommunications and rail. This imposes special responsibilities, and may impose very real constraints on activities throughout the system. For example, even though a firm controls 80 to 90 per cent of customer sales, it may be restricted in the following ways:

1 *Supply policies.* It may be unable to apply maximum leverage to suppliers.
2 *Competitive strategy.* It may be unable to act with complete freedom against retail competition.
3 *Intermediary behaviour.* It may be unable to develop price and distribution polices to maximize profits, e.g. refuse to supply.
4 *End-customer service.* It may be unable to act with complete freedom on product usage or promotional strategy.

Pressure can come from Parliament; even when the utility resists it can be overruled. Consumer councils and other groups can by-pass management, by exerting political and media pressure.

Figure 3.4 The changing face of the public sector

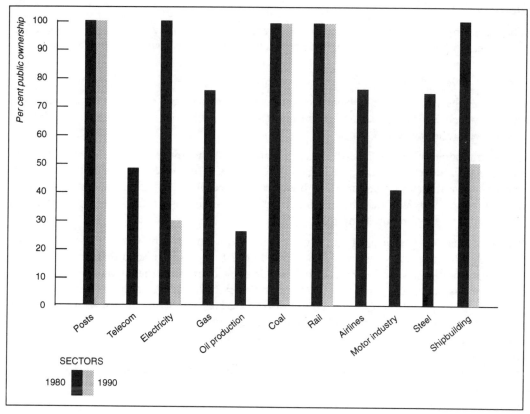

Despite these features, some nationalized industries demonstrated the scope for creative marketing over many years. In 1977 the *Financial Times* described the then publicly-owned Gas Corporation as one of the best marketing organizations in Britain. Nevertheless, creative freedom and flexibility have been key features of marketing in the newly privatized firms.

Regulation, inducement and direction

In most industrial economies in the Western world some degree of regulation, inducement and direction of marketing activity is accepted. In Britain this has ranged from the definition of technical standards (under the auspices of the British Standards Institute) to the direction of investment in certain parts of the country through regional aid.

Regulatory systems

These include technical standards, building regulations and requirements for health and safety at work. Regulatory systems can create new opportunities as well as impose rules, and there is now a service industry advising firms about the regulations.

Inducement

Inducements are often offered to persuade firms to implement government policies. Export policies are backed by an array of inducements from the British Overseas Trade Board, and innovation and investment are often grant aided.

Direction

The government sometimes attempts to direct firms into specific areas of activity, e.g. investment in North Sea oil and related activities, or even towards specific business stances.

Legislation

The last forty years have seen an ever-increasing pace of legislation affecting the ways in which the firm operates in the market-place. Much of this legislation is directed towards encouraging competition.

In the immediate post-war period the first major legislative move was the Monopolies and Restrictive Practices (Inquiry and Control) Act 1948. The overall aim of this Act was to establish a commission to enquire into business practices in industries in which one-third or more of an industry was held by one firm, cartel or less formal group, in order to establish whether this was in the public interest.

Partly because of a report of the Commission on restrictive practices in industry, the Restrictive Practices Act was passed in 1956. This set up a Registrar of Restrictive Trading Agreements and a Restrictive Practices Court. In the Court, judgement was made according to fixed provisions as to whether any restrictions were not against the public interest. In a series of important judgements the detailed framework of case law has been established. For example in 1962 the Court ruled that Net Book Agreements designed to enforce retail price maintenance were acceptable, as their removal would affect the viability of many bookshops and reduce the ability of publishers to publish small-volume texts. This decision was not reversed until the mid-1990s. In 1959 the Court ruled that price fixing and agreements on discounts by carpet manufacturers were not acceptable, as they were arbitrary and contrary to the public interest.

Government policies affect trade directly. In 1965 the relatively short-lived National Board for Prices and Incomes was set up with a brief to examine pricing policies referred to it by the government. The Board was abolished by the 1970 Conservative government. Within three years the Price Commission was established to scrutinize prices in private industry, and during the period of the 1975 Labour government the Price Commission played an increasing part in counter-inflation policies.

One of the first acts of the 1979 Conservative government was to introduce the Competition Act 1979. This abolished the Price Commission, transferring a number of its powers to the Office of Fair Trading and the Monopolies and Mergers Commission. These bodies were provided with additional 'competition reference' powers. As a result, Britain's competition laws are based on the Competition Act 1979, the Fair Trading Act 1973, the Restrictive Practices Act 1976, the Restrictive Practices Court Act 1976 and the Resale Prices Act 1977. These Acts generally operate under the auspices of the President of the Board of Trade.

Since its election in 1997, the Labour government has been renewing its approach. This is likely to be based on selective action in areas such as environmental protection while pursuing a strategy of minimum intervention elsewhere, except where competitiveness is affected or it falls under the new Companies' Act. The most significant change is the emphasis on international competitiveness as a defence against accusations of excess concentration at home.

Mini-case study: Virgin and British Airways

For several years, Richard Branson's Virgin Atlantic has been waging a campaign against the proposed link between British Airways and American Airlines. Branson argues that their partnership would create a near monopoly on some routes, especially across the Atlantic. This would, in his view, severely restrict competition. The British Airways response is that they need the tie-up with American Airlines to sustain their international competitiveness. Besides his media campaign, Branson is pursuing his case with UK, European and US regulators to attack anti-competitive practices and to ensure the proper operation of the market.

Although specific approaches by government have changed significantly over the last twenty years, all would probably subscribe to a general commitment to act by legislation if necessary, 'to attack anti-competitive practices and to ensure the proper operation of the market' (Mrs Sally Oppenheim, former Minister for Consumer Affairs).

Also, although there are very real differences in policies, there has been a broadly consistent direction of thinking about overall competition practice. The aim has been to reduce the direct role of government, substituting the 'market' or 'regulators' for government action.

A major plank of the previous government's programme was the reduction of statutory and voluntary restraints on trade. This process of 'deregulation' can be seen in areas as diverse as banking services, optical supplies and transport.

The Acts noted above reflect some of the major areas of policy and legislation, but government action has also been directed at a number of specific areas of marketing activity and particular industries. Pricing is directly affected by both the Resale Prices Act 1977 and the work of the Office of Fair Trading. Advertising for certain commodities (cigarettes, gambling, food, drugs etc.) and in some areas (e.g. affecting health and safety) is controlled by a number of statutory instruments, e.g. the Consumer Protection Act 1961 (as amended by the Consumer Protection Act 1971). Product and warranty are governed by such legislation as the Sale of Goods Act 1893 and the more recent Supply of Goods (Implied Terms) Act 1972, and the broad area of the Law of Contract. Other important legislation is the Trade Marks Act, the Copyright Act , the Trade Descriptions Act and the Patents Act. In the new privatized companies, their regulators, e.g. the Rail Regulator, play a key role in protecting the consumer's interest.

Europe

As a member of the European Union (EU – formerly the European Community), Britain falls under the auspices of its competition laws, which have always played an important part in the Union. They are encompassed by Articles 85 and 86 of the Treaty of Rome. Article 85 deals with agreements and practices which hinder the free play of competition, and Article 86 focuses on the abuse of a dominant market position. They apply only where trade between member states is affected. Responsibility for implementing these Articles lies with Directorate-General IV. All rulings by the Commission in this area fall into the scope of the European Court of Justice, to which firms can appeal if they are dissatisfied with the Commission's findings. Although there are areas of overlap between US and European practice, a fundamental difference exists in the approach to restraint on trade. Unlike the US, the EU is prepared to accept restraints which are economically useful and do not substantially reduce competition. The competition policies under the Single European Act will shape policy for much of the next few years. The Maastricht Treaty has had a major effect on trade within and between member countries.

These two areas of legislation, EU and UK, directly affect British firms at home and in Europe. Firms operating overseas must learn to cope with the specific legislation of the markets in which they operate. Most industrially developed Western economies have legislation and statutory bodies to protect customers and facilitate competition; a few are listed below:

1 *Belgium:* Consumer Council, General Economics Inspectorate, Commercial Economics Service.
2 *France:* Directorate General for Internal Consumers and Prices, Service de la Répression des Fraudes et du Contrôle de la Qualité, National Consumer Institute.
3 *Germany:* Although no specific ministry has responsibility, policies are co-ordinated by the Inter-Ministerial Committee on Consumer Matters.
4 *Japan:* Conference on Consumer Protection, Economic Welfare Bureau of the Economic Planning Agency.
5 *Sweden:* National Council for Consumer Goods Research and Consumer Information, Market Court, Consumer Ombudsman.
6 *United States:* Federal Trade Commission, Anti-Trust Division of the Attorney General's Office.

Even in the countries listed, many other government departments, ministries of finance or economics, are involved in what has become an almost worldwide movement by governments to legislate to achieve specific goals in competition policy and consumer protection. There is generally a close link between these and attempts to manage the overall economic progress of their countries.

Economic policies

Although the supply and demand issues which are the basis of any free market were discussed in Chapter 1, many other aspects of the economic environment help create the conditions under which firms operate.

Britain is one of the most economically developed countries in the world, accounting for about 5 per cent of the output of the 24 member states of the Organization for Economic Co-operation and Development. Although there has been a marked decline in the country's position relative to its major trading rivals, the British consumer has experienced significant real growth in living standards over the last decade, and much of British industry remains highly competitive and capable of winning business in highly sophisticated and technologically advanced markets, as Table 3.4 shows.

Table 3.4 Winners of the Queen's Awards for Exports

Firm	Technology	Markets
Anite Systems	Space software and systems	World-wide
Avalon Chemicals	Synthetic resins and adhesives	Scandinavia, North America
Biozyme Laboratories	Biochemicals	Western Europe, Japan, US
British Aerospace	Aerospace	World-wide
Crosfield Electronics	Electronics	World-wide
Davy International	Contracting	Japan, USSR
JCB	Materials handling	US, Europe
Medeva PLC	Pharmaceuticals (influenza vaccine)	World-wide

Marketing policies are directly affected by worldwide, regional and domestic economic forces. The scale of Britain's dependence on exports (over 20 per cent of the Gross National Product) means that movements in the world economy influence both foreign and domestic operations. The sharply changing world economy, caused by a mixture of energy shortages, inflation, protectionism and other factors, is forcing many firms to recognize the need to face up toturbulence in markets. Marketing resource shortage and intense competition are part of the business reality of the 1990s. These conditions highlight the importance of effective marketing:

1 Targeting will be critical; overall growth may be low but specific sectors will be far more resilient. During the slump in the UK furniture market in the mid-1970s the high-price, high-quality sector continued to grow while the low-price sector suffered.

2 Effective use of the marketing mix will be critical. According to a study of the economic recession of the early 1920s, 'the firms which increased their advertising also increased their sales'.

3 Continual monitoring of the changing character of customer attitudes and behaviour will be essential. There appears to be an increasing professionalism among consumers, who are seeking solutions to their new economic circumstances.

4 The balance of a firm's business will probably require a broader market base, increased added value and a rigorous approach to pricing, notably in industrial markets. 'In the post 1973 recession, the Third World was the most buoyant market.' Despite the turbulence shown by stock markets in 1997, the Pacific Rim, China and India are showing similar characteristics as the century closes.

Membership of the EU has subjected British firms to new economic pressures. The years between 1970 and 1997 saw a major shift in Britain's balance of trade as industry learnt to cope with new, sophisticated industrial markets. Figure 3.5 illustrates how Britain's overseas trade has been influenced by membership of the European Union and other developments over the last twenty years. As recently as the mid-1960s, the 'English-speaking' world of North America, the old and new Commonwealth plus the less developed countries accounted for over half of UK exports. They were twice as important as the EU. This situation has virtually

Figure 3.5 Distribution of UK exports by areas

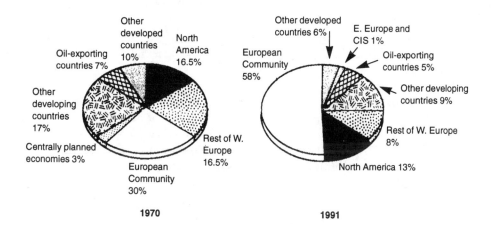

reversed. The EU is Britain's major partner. The impact of the EU goes far beyond the members. The signing of the Lomé treaty between the EU and 46 developing nations demonstrates how the economic and trading implications stretch outside the confines of the EU itself. As the EU becomes more fully integrated through the creation of the single European market and expands, this impact will grow. The move towards a single currency seems certain to accelerate these developments.

There is increasing recognition of the extent to which domestic marketing systems of most firms are influenced by external economic circumstances. However, it is the state of the domestic economy which generally has the most profound impact on the marketing system.

Incomes (real and monetary), prices, interest rates, credit, output and savings all have a direct influence on the fortunes of companies. Variations in the levels of inflation over the last decade were closely linked to shifts in interest rates.

These reductions in the rate of inflation are coinciding with significant improvements in the Gross Domestic Product after a decade of stagnation. The notion of the strong domestic economy as the basis for international competitiveness has influenced much government thinking. To encourage growth, some form of economic management, through either fiscal (tax) or monetary policies, has been tried by most British governments. Marketing people now pay close attention to actions in these areas, but their freedom to react is directly affected by their lead times. Fluctuations in the domestic economy often lead to high imports, as intermediaries respond to demand by buying from countries with larger industrial bases in order to satisfy consumer demand before local firms can respond. Stability or consistency are vital for long-term planning, particularly investment in technology.

Technology

Britain is familiar with the impact of technology on the market-place. The Industrial Revolution which started in Britain during the late eighteenth century affected all parts of the marketing system, from raw materials producers to manufacturers, intermediaries and final customers. There has been continuing change and development. In 1994 alone over 120,000 patents were applied for in the US.

Keeping pace with technological change is a challenge to which all firms have to respond. Large firms invest vast sums in basic and applied research. Smaller firms, although they may lack the absolute resources, have flexibility and commitment, which go a long way to compensate for resource limitations.

The large-scale investment of major firms, perhaps allied to government, university, college or other institutional research, plays a major role in advancing technology. The joint success in winning the Queen's Award for Technology of BDH Chemicals Ltd, the Royal Signals and Radar Establishment and the Department of Chemistry, University of Hull, for the development and large-scale commercial production of biphenyl liquid crystals, illustrates the potential in this area. The emergence of a significant group of new-technology-based firms, which are generally small, highly specialized, and with significant added value, in Britain and other advanced industrial countries, brings out the continuing role of smaller firms in this sphere of activity. The contribution is now seen as so important that many nations have devised special support schemes.

New technologies have an impact throughout the marketing system in shaping availability, cost and ultimate consumption of goods (Figure 3.6).

Figure 3.6 Technology and the system

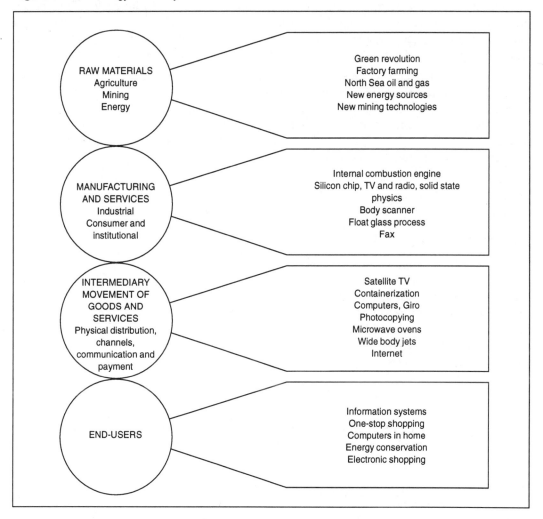

Marketing management's role in this area is to provide the spur to the company's innovation while supplying marketing insights into the broad patterns of technological change. Some new technologies affect marketers directly, notably the Internet, minicomputers and microcomputers for handling problems and analysis, besides satellite, videofilm and cable television.

Culture

The ways in which any society responds to the various pressures described above depend to a considerable extent on its history and culture. Britain, as the first industrial power, has made adaptations which are very different from those of other countries, both those which are industrially developed and those which are undeveloped. Language, religion, attitudes, social organization, education, the law, the arts and the very attitudes towards industry and materialism interact to create the special milieu in which the firm operates.

The existence of a single, shared language distinguishes the UK from many countries where tribal and 'national' subgroups sustain wide variations in dialect and language. This means that mass communication through large-circulation newspapers, magazines, television and radio is possible. The cohesiveness of British society has itself helped to create a broader-based national system of media, unlike countries such as the United States and Germany.

Changing attitudes and values continually create new opportunities. The emerging importance of a young, design-conscious, middle-income group in the 1960s provided the foundation of the success of Habitat stores. Growing geographic mobility, allied to the increasing desire of families to eat out but remain confident of consistent levels of quality, service and cleanliness, paved the way for the success of McDonald's hamburgers in the US, and subsequently throughout the world.

The cultural and ethnic subdivisions in society create their own marketing opportunities. In the US, African-Americans emerged as a powerful and important market sector, their impact ranging from product development to the models used in advertisements: 'If you want to reach the heart of a $20 billion-a-year market, you'll have to recognize that the negro is nobody's fair-haired boy' (*Ebony* magazine).

In Britain, ethnic heterogeneity has now been recognized as a factor in creating marketing opportunities and problems. For example: individual products may need to meet special religious needs, e.g. kosher foods; tastes may differ, e.g. Cadbury Typhoo's Poundo Yam, the Nigerian equivalent of instant mashed potato; intermediaries may be different, e.g. the importance of small, local, Asian-run shops; languages can be a barrier, e.g. over half of Pakistani women and around a third of Pakistani men struggle with English, according to one survey. The impact of these subgroups frequently extends beyond their confines into the broader population.

The different publics

Although the system operates within the general environment created by the forces described above, many are interpreted and gain immediacy from the impact of more specialized and cohesive publics.

The business and financial community

The community helps to create the trading and financial environment in which the firm operates. The confidence of manufacturers in very different sectors of the economy affects their willingness to recruit workers, give wage increases, invest and provide the overall stimulus to the market. The financial community provides the capital and credit to sustain this process. Its resources can be directed to both industrial and consumer credit. The confidence of manufacturers in the sustained demand for their products may lead them to seek funds for new machinery, which creates demand not only for the machinery supplier but also for all the component suppliers. Equally, the prevailing rates of interest and availability of credit will determine the firm's real returns from investment in capital and plant.

The media

The media can have a direct impact on business confidence besides influencing specific firms and markets. The mass national media can have a substantial effect on markets. For example, the link between the TV series 'Full Circle' with Michael Palin and the book of the same name helped keep the book in the best-seller lists for over twenty weeks.

In fashion markets, the impact of magazines such as *Vogue* and *Harpers,* allied to newspaper supplements, is considerable. It extends far beyond the £6 billion clothing and footwear market into general tastes and attitudes, from domestic furniture to shop, office and even factory canteen layout.

The trade and technical press play a critical part in disseminating news and information. The authoritative position they can adopt in specific circumstances, e.g. in reviewing new developments or in featuring a firm and its activities, can enhance both the firm and its offering.

An important manifestation of the emerging interest in consumerism has been the publication of special-interest magazines. In some instances they are purely commercial, such as *What Car?, What Buy?* or the short-lived *Value Today.* Many of these periodicals are linked to national consumer associations (Table 3.5)

Table 3.5 Some European consumer magazines and associations

Magazine	Association	Country
Which?	Consumers' Association	Great Britain
Consumentengids	Consumentenbond	Netherlands
Test	Verbraucher Rundschau	Germany

Pressure groups

Pressure groups have long been recognized as a vital part of the economic and social system. The emergence of the consumer movement and the organization of formalized pressure groups play a major part in the context in which the firm operates. These bodies examine specific industries, and over 350 industries were studied by *Which?* during the period 1975 to 1996. Their influence includes Parliamentary lobbying (the British Consumers' Association actively supported the passing of the Unfair Contract Terms Act 1977 and Consumer Safety Act 1978) and international co-operation through bodies such as the International Organization of Consumers' Unions and the Bureau Européen des Unions de Consommateurs.

The influence of groups with direct interests in particular consumer and industrial goods can be considerable. In some areas, such as photography, motoring, sport and travel, their role can be very important, for example that of the International Air Travellers' Association in the DC10 groundings of 1979.

In industrial markets groups of manufacturers and retailers can exercise great power over supplier industries, especially when acting to encourage improved standards. The work of trade associations illustrates very clearly the role that pressure groups of industrialists can play. For example, the British Plastics Federation argued for changes in the British Standards Institution, the technical specifications of the nationalized industries and clay pipe regulations. The work of environmental lobbyists like Greenpeace has helped to transform attitudes to environmental responsibility.

Trade associations

Throughout the world, trade associations play a major part in advancing the interests of their members, besides providing them with a range of support services. In some countries, notably Germany, trade associations play a consistently powerful role in policy formulation and implementation.

The barriers to effective environmental scanning

The interaction of these different forces, the rate and pace of the change and the various ways in which these can be interpreted creates significant barriers to effective environmental analysis. Figure 3.6 (see page 71) shows how Brownlie[14] uses Diffenbach's model[15] to structure and classify these barriers.

The marketing system

In examining the ways in which the firm operates within the marketing system, it is useful to think in terms of a conversion process. The company obtains an array of inputs which it converts into a selection of offerings for the market with a view to achieving some overall or specific goals (Figure 3.7).

Figure 3.7 The conversion process

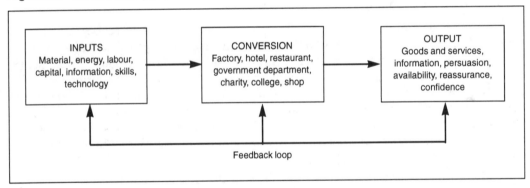

All members of the system are involved in some type of conversion as they seek to satisfy an array of needs and goals. The Rand Corporation proposes that system analysis is:

> Inquiry to aid a decision-maker choose a course of action by systematically investigating his proper objectives, comparing quantitatively where possible the costs, effectiveness and risks associated with the alternative policies or strategies for achieving them, and formulating additional alternatives if those examined are found wanting.[16]

Even the smallest organization may find that its inputs are extensive, complex, numerous and subject to change, while the conversion process and array of output demand effective management and control.

The primary producer

Primary producers, whether in extractive industries or agriculture, face the problems of bringing together equipment, labour and capital to ensure the effective exploitation of the minerals or land at their disposal (Figure 3.8).

Figure 3.8 The mine: a conversion process illustrated

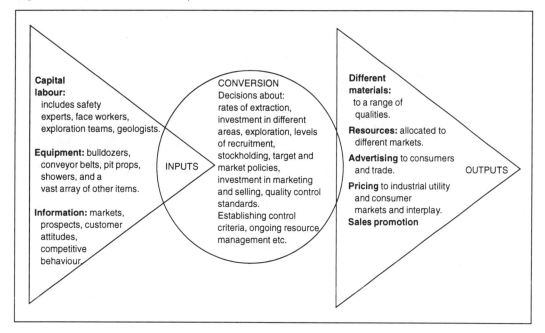

The manufacturer

The manufacturer of finished goods or components faces basically the same problems. These are complicated by the frequent need to introduce new products, which may mean extensive information-gathering, investment in large stocks of new materials and a large-scale logistics problem to ensure that all the elements come together at the optimum moment for introduction. The large number of product offerings by most firms adds a further dimension to the management of the system. A company's activities may extend into many distinct areas (Figure 3.9).

The systems approach

The systems approach tends to underplay this competitive element within a framework which emphasizes the process of integration and adaptation. An alternative 'action' approach, while accepting many of the systems assumptions, emphasizes the role of people, either individually or acting together, in shaping the market and environment to their own ends.

The power of the creative element in marketing, the achievements of managers, both entrepreneurs and working organizational managers, and the continuing dynamic of competition support this approach. In the overwhelming majority of successes in the market-

Figure 3.9 The multiple-market conversion process

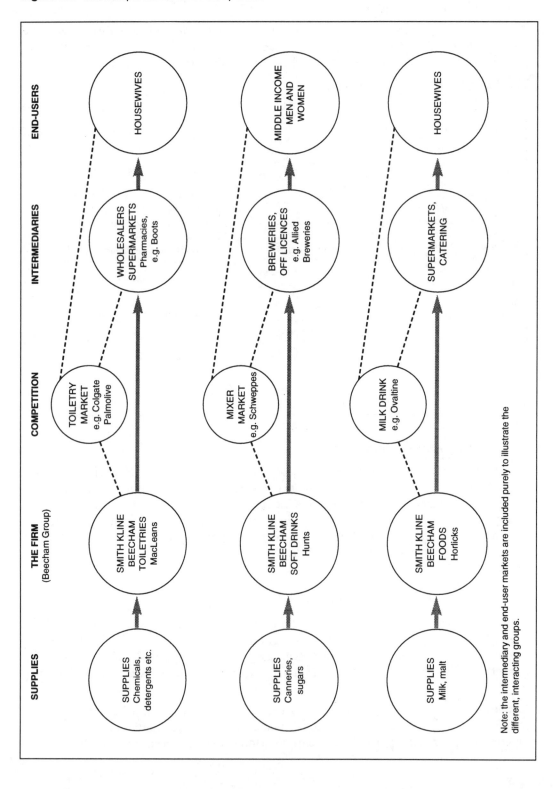

Note: the intermediary and end-user markets are included purely to illustrate the different, interacting groups.

place, individuals interpreting the interacting forces around them, willing to take risks and adopting a creative marketing approach have played a vital part.

Mapping

The data from the analysis of the marketing system can be used in the production of maps of the market. These help the firm to:

1 Clearly identify its competitive position.
2 Identify the relative strengths and weaknesses of rivals.
3 Highlight the major features of current offerings in the eyes of customers.
4 Spot gaps in the market.

Mapping provides a way of performing these useful analytical tasks in a graphic and easily understood way.

The first step in building a market map lies in identifying the major product/market features or dimensions. Illustrations of this could be as shown in Table 3.6.

Table 3.6 Examples of major product/market features

Market	Feature 1	Feature 2
Margarine	Price	Health
Bank	Convenience	Range of services
Breakfast cereal	Nourishment	Novelty
Shampoo	Medication	Cosmetic
Dentrifrice	Tooth care	Taste
Beer	Strength	Flavour
Yoghurts	Range	Diet/Health

These features can be used to construct scales along which specific offerings can be located.

The map in Figure 3.10 indicates how the brands in a market can be distributed. Specific gaps can be identified, e.g. the one that existed in the 'mild' end of the market prior to the launch of Timotei in 1983.

The same type of analysis can be used to explore the positioning of competitive companies, even retailers and advertising media[17]

Participants and partners

Analysis of the marketing system and effective use of techniques such as 'market mapping' calls upon firms to understand the character and role of all the other members of the markets in which they operate. Typically they will be only one of the participants in a complex and changing set of relationships (as in Figure 3.11). The marketing-orientated firm needs to know almost as much about its suppliers, immediate customers, competitors and end-users as it does about itself. Managers ought to be able to conduct a SWOT analysis (Strengths, Weaknesses, Opportunities and Threats) about each, individually, and in terms of their own company.

Figure 3.10 Mapping the shampoo market

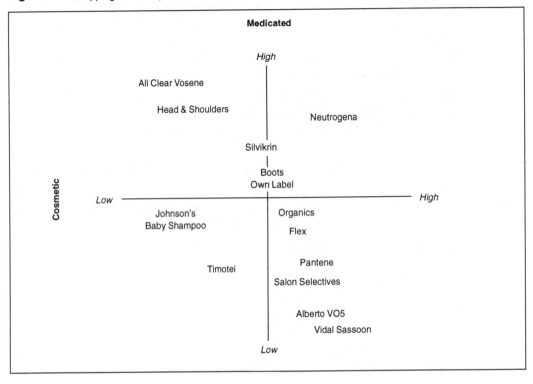

Figure 3.11 Manufacturers' share of the European car market (Source: *Fortune,* 12 November 1984)

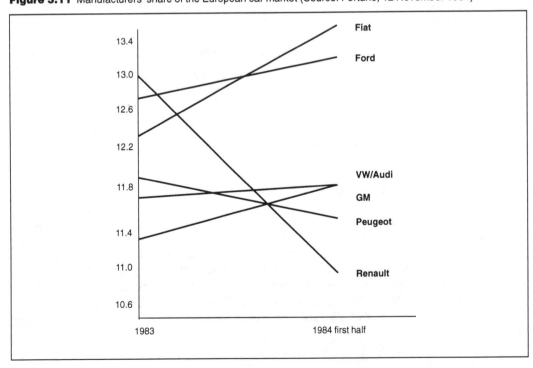

It is as important to comprehend the limitations and potential of suppliers as it is to understand customers. It is not unknown for a very efficient producer to be faced with decline because its immediate customer failed to compete effectively in its market. This situation has faced the British components industry over the last twenty years, as domestic vehicle and white goods producers have lost their market share to European and Japanese producers. Those firms which built up their trade in Europe before the crisis of the late 1970s and early 1980s found that their sales to the growth firms went some way to compensate for the decline of others. The growth of Japanese car production in the UK in the late 1980s and 1990s reversed this trend so that the UK is once again a net exporter of vehicles but without a single, major UK-owned manufacturer.

Windows of opportunity

Although the type of technique identified above can indicate opportunities, it is just as important to realize that most gaps in the market-place are temporary. Other firms can move to fill them. Changed conditions can eliminate the need for the particular offering. Customers can find an acceptable substitute. The 'windows of opportunity' that exist can close with surprising speed.[18]

This does not mean that firms should move without thoroughly researching the market and analysing the situation. It requires managers continually to seek for ways of matching care with decision.

Conclusion

A number of points which are central to understanding modern marketing relationships have emerged in this chapter. They have focused around four central points:

1 Marketing relationships involve sets of inter-relationships, many of which go far beyond the specific transaction or immediate customer.
2 These relationships are continually changing as they are influenced by, and in turn influence, their environment.
3 Techniques and approaches have been developed over the years to help managers understand and draw lessons from this network of relationships.
4 Effective management involves linking this appreciation to decisive action.

Glossary

Consumers' Association. Non-profit-making organization which provides a range of services associated with attempting to ensure effective representation of consumers to producers and government.

Demographics. The measurable, structural characteristics of a population, such as age, sex, income, family size, class, occupational distribution. Used a great deal to provide firms with profiles of the groups who may make up their market.

Deregulation. The process of reducing or eliminating the legislative interference in markets.

Environment. The context and set of forces which exist around the market and which shape it and determine its character.

Gross Domestic Product. The total value of all goods and services produced in an economy.

Inflation. Those increases in price which cumulatively produce a reduction in purchasing power or the real value of money.

M1. The measure of the money supply, defined as currency plus demand deposits.

M2. M1 plus savings and time deposits at the commercial banks.

Market. The arrangement individuals or groups have for trading with each other.

Services. Those offerings which involve no tangible or manufactured product but attempt to satisfy needs. The service industries include: banking, tourism, leisure, entertainment and communication, as well as numerous government activities.

System. The set of interconnected and interdependent relationships which as a whole is greater than the sum of its parts.

SPECIMEN QUESTIONS

1 How might the changing distribution of the working population among industries affect the type of marketing skills needed by industry?

2 What are the particular marketing techniques which will have special relevance to the successful development of professional service? Illustrate with reference to a specific profession.

3 Describe and illustrate the role of pressure groups in influencing the actions of firms within the marketing system.

4 Why have so many British firms failed to respond to the globalization of trade? How might a stronger marketing orientation help them reduce this failure?

5 Identify the main items of government legislation which affect the way in which a firm can promote their goods and services. Choose one of: food, pharmaceuticals or hotels to show the effect of industry-specific legislation.

6 Indicate the likely effects of the Maastricht Treaty on marketing in Europe.

7 How has the balance of British trade shifted since the UK entered the EU? What effect has this shift had on the way firms market their goods and services?

8 Identify the different ethnic foods currently on sale in a store of your choice. Suggest how their promotion might change to reach a larger market.

9 Describe the conversion process which makes up the marketing system. Spell out the role of the 'feedback process' in influencing decisions and policies.

10 Define:

(a) The business environment.

(b) Tertiary industries.

(c) The media.

(d) A mixed economy.

(e) Privatization.

(f) British Standards Institute.

(g) GDP.

(h) Trade press.

(i) Primary producers.

(j) Competitive mapping.

4

The case of food marketing

Introduction

A great deal of the recent literature on food distribution has emphasized the extent and rate of 'change in competitive processes'.[1] These changes affect every aspect of the distribution process. Developments in production affect not only yields but the location and nature of output. This can be seen in such contrasting areas as fish farming and grain production. The introduction of effective farming techniques for fish means that for some types, e.g. Atlantic salmon, farmed output greatly exceeds landings of wild salmon.[2] The introduction of intensive farming techniques in Britain means that drastic reductions in the amount of land given over to food production are likely over the next 30 years if over-production is to be avoided (Table 4.1).

The pattern of raw material production and technological development is stimulating changes which can be compared with the Industrial Revolution in terms of their impact on yields. India provides a graphic illustration of this. In the 1970s, few believed that India would be able to feed its growing population. Within a decade, one state in India was able to produce enough food for the entire population. India became a large net exporter of food.

The distribution systems for food across the world are experiencing comparable shifts in form and nature. This can be seen in physical distribution systems and channels of distribution. New technologies and the widespread use of more established systems shape the ways in which food products can be moved, which in turn influence their nature and customer appeal. Rawlings[3] illustrated the ways in which innovations in aseptic packaging were affecting the distribution and consumption of a wide range of liquid foods.

Table 4.1 Land for food production (millions of hectares)

	Used in 1985	Needed in 2015
Cereals	4.00	1.3–1.9
Grasslands	12.63	7.5–9.3
Other crops	0.68	0.6
Horticulture	0.21	0.2
Total	17.52	9.6–12.0

Source: Spedding, C., 'Diet and Agriculture', *Journal of the Royal Society of Arts*, May, 1988, pp. 388–392.

Alongside new technologies, other changes are occurring, most notably the increasingly international nature of food markets. In Britain, the Europeanization of food distribution can be seen in both the origin of food products and the trading polices of distributors and retailers.[4] There is evidence that patterns of food consumption are converging, at least among Western, more developed economies.[5] This trend is likely to be reinforced by the successful internationalization of major food companies. Examples of this range from the ubiquitous McDonald's to processors and manufacturers such as United Biscuits and, most recently, UK retailers such as Iceland, Marks & Spencer and J. Sainsbury. There is a progressive shift from a closed to an open system of food distribution in the UK.

The challenges posed by change can be seen vividly in the marketing and strategic dilemmas facing UK retailers and wholesalers. There are the conflicting pressures of the move towards conglomerates and the success of niche firms. The static nature of overall demand poses short-, medium- and long-term challenges to an industry which has been described 'as one of the most dynamic sectors within UK retailing'.[6] There is the immediate pressure to introduce more higher-margin ranges while maintaining total volume sales. The view that the market is rapidly approaching saturation is encouraging some firms to look for routes into diversification in the medium term. The success of the present generation of retailers will eventually depend on the extent to which they can institutionalize food retailing. This will confound those pundits who suggest that each generation of retailers is replaced by a new entrepreneurial revolution (see Chapter 28).

Ultimately, success depends on the ability of retailers and other members of the food marketing system to respond to the needs of consumers at a time of major behavioural and structural change. Concern with healthier eating is widespread in the economically developed world.[7] This reflects the increased choice; at the same time it links food consumption with a range of related market forces. These include the altering role of women within the family, reductions in product life-cycles, and modified cooking and eating habits. Comparable changes are occurring in the structure of the population. Perhaps the most dramatic is the shift to one-person family units. These have increased from 1 in 10 in 1951 to 1 in 3.5 in 1994. It is reasonable to expect that the proportion will increase to over 1 in 3 by the end of the 1990s. The transformation of the age structure of the population in Britain will influence both the nature and pattern of food consumption. This is not a local phenomenon: it is mirrored in North America and much of Europe.

External, policy and regulatory pressures

The current changes in the food marketing system are taking place against a policy background which is markedly different from that which has prevailed for most of the last half-century. The UK government has reorientated its approach to intervention. There is a new emphasis on improving the operations of the market instead of direct intervention. In the EU, completion of the single European market will produce a more consistent, less ambiguous and more open market for food.[8] Globally, absolute shortages are being replaced, at least temporarily, by imperfections in the food chain. Today,

> hope and despair [prevail] on the food front. Hope arises from our ability to produce more food from less land through a combination of technology, services and government policies. Despair looms large because of the growing dimensions of hunger in the midst of plenty.[9]

Each of these developments and many related shifts in policy and practice represent a growing recognition that centralist and producer-orientated programmes are giving way to distributed and market-based approaches.

Environmental pressures

The forces which underpin the patterns described above range from the highly individual to the global. In Britain and much of the developed world, prosperity has prompted increased demands for choice and freedom. The shift towards a healthier diet is affecting the stocking policies of major retailers, besides opening up new market opportunities in retailing and catering.

This is being reinforced by media and political pressures.[10] Slattery[11] suggests that 'many consumers face a new problem: that of deciding which "healthy" products are genuinely useful in a healthy diet'. Other writers are more sanguine: 'present policies artificially raise consumption of either potentially harmful products, such as sugar, whole fat milk and butter or less healthy products, such as white bread'.[12]

The market has responded at three levels. The most immediate has been the increased emphasis on the positive features of existing products, their repackaging or the introduction of new formulations backed by promotional claims.[13] Evidence from other markets would suggest that this might be an effective palliative or short-term measure. In the long term, however, the consumer will seek out products based on real product differentiation.[14] Trade structures are already emerging which will reinforce this response. It is estimated that there are now over 3,000 health or wholefood shops and a further 2,000 restaurants in the UK. Together, they could exceed the number of confectionery retailers by the end of the 1990s. Similar developments can be seen in Europe and North America. In Germany there are over 3,000 Naturkostladen (nature diet) outlets. In the US the shift towards healthier eating is affecting both the trading situation and the underlying product development process.

It is useful to counterpoint these alterations at the individual level with wider environmental concerns. Few human activities are more closely linked with the physical environment than food production and allocation. The shape of the landscape largely reflects priorities in these areas. It is unlikely that society will give producers the type of freedom of action that has been enjoyed in the past. In part, this reflects the successes achieved in boosting production, which in turn creates opportunities for greater restraint.

The FAO World Food Report in 1986[15] indicated that more food had been produced than ever before, leading to large surpluses in food grains, butter, milk powder and animal products. These surpluses have helped to keep prices down, enabling domestic consumers in Europe and North America to exercise more choice and spend less of their family budget on food. Retailers and wholesalers have been able to sustain their profits, even increasing margins in some areas in a static market. It is hard to see this pattern being sustained in the long term. Widespread concern exists in the West about the costs of intensive, chemical-driven farming. This concern is matched by worries in developing economies about the price being paid in those countries through falling prices and production imbalances.

The interdependencies in the food marketing system are becoming evident and their ramifications more extensive. This is prompting policy-makers to explore mechanisms which can increase control while improving the distribution and marketing system. The BSE crisis in the UK in the mid-1990s vividly illustrated these interdependencies.

Regulatory and control systems

There has been a steady and relatively consistent movement over the last decade in the mechanisms adopted by governments to achieve desired outcomes in terms of industrial and economic policy. It is common to see this described as a process of deregulation. It is probably better to describe this approach as a change in the nature of control and regulatory systems. In the European food distribution system it has three basic characteristics. First, there has been the move from intervention and regulation at the point of consumption to control at the point of production. Second, market mechanisms are being seen as an alternative to direct intervention. Third, selective targeting and differential support is being used to achieve policy objectives.

The move towards a single European market is the most wide-ranging and tangible expression of the commitment by policy-makers to market mechanisms to enhance competition and consumer choice. The highly concentrated nature of grocery retailing is often seen as a major constraint on the workings of the free market.

Table 4.2 Shares of grocery sales 1995–96

Category	Share of market (%)
Major multiples	59.8
Other multiples	15.4
Co-op	11.9
Independents	12.9
Total	100.0

Source: based on DTI data 1997.

It seems, however, that the slow growth of the market has encouraged retailers to adopt very distinctive and competitive marketing strategies. Brown's generic retailing strategy matrix[16] would suggest that the major food retailers could be described along the lines illustrated in Figure 4.1.

Perhaps more important, in the long term, to the government's 'Let the market decide' strategy is the increasing rate of new business formation, especially in specialist food processing, distribution and catering.

Figure 4.1 Generic retailing strategies: the major food retailers

		Price dimension	
		Price-led	*Image-led*
Assortment dimension	*Wide*	Tesco Co-op Gateway	Safeway J. Sainsbury
	Narrow	Kwik Save Asda Aldi	Marks & Spencer Waitrose

Investment and technology

The cost of entry into markets is an important element in the competitive process. Traditionally, the food distribution system has been characterized by relatively low entry costs. The classic 'wheel of retailing' model, shifting from small, low-cost units to large units with wide ranges, could reasonably describe the evolution of several of the leading UK grocery retailers. A number of recent changes in the food distribution system may change this.

The high levels of retail concentration are changing the nature of the retailer-producer relationship. The successful involvement of Marks & Spencer in new product development, allied to its positive purchasing strategies, has encouraged others to adopt some form of direct or indirect involvement in the production process. The separation between production and distribution which created gaps for entrepreneurs to exploit has been eroded.

Simultaneously, the locational and service opportunities which were exploited by earlier generations of entrepreneurs are shrinking, while existing traders are recognizing the importance of the 'service edge'. Ease of access to outlets is increasing. It is estimated that even in London, the most expensive and least developed area for superstores, there is one superstore to every 350,000 people. Outside London the ratio drops to one for every 150,000 in more developed areas. This type of saturation reduces the opportunities for new entrants adopting the classical strategies.

Scale can create its own problems. Purchase or operational economies can be eroded by managerial diseconomies. It would seem that the leading firms see investment in new information technologies as a vital element in the attempt to overcome these inefficiencies and maintain management control. Sawyers[17] found that new information technologies were introduced largely to improve management control rather than produce customer benefits. Dawson et al.[18] tended to reinforce this finding in highlighting the impact of new technologies on the structure of employment in retailing. The investment by firms such as J. Sainsbury and Tesco in new technologies would seem to provide the opportunity to increase the scale of their operations without paying an unacceptable price in terms of reduced management control. This has created an environment in which tighter space management will be possible through better information systems and the use of techniques such as direct product profitability.

This relatively stable environment encouraged major UK retailers to enhance facilities and improve margins. Their profits encouraged new entrants like Aldi and Kwik Save to enter the market and expand their operations on the classic 'Pile it high and sell it cheap' approach described in the retail literature.

Category killers – specialist retailers that sell a deep range of products at very low prices – have emerged as major players in a wide range of retail sectors. Typically these are giant outlets but with a relatively restricted range of products (Table 4.3).

The favourable financial environment of the 1980s and the strong share performance of the 1990s supported the investment strategies of the large retailers. The effects of this go beyond support for expenditure on new technology. The value of the larger acquisitions in the UK during the period 1986–87 exceeded £1,700 million. The food sector generally has found access to capital for acquisition and investment relatively favourable. In Britain the Nestlé/Rowntree take-over was merely an extreme example of a process which has seen firms like Northern Foods spend over £225 million on acquisitions over the decade. There is, however, nothing rivalling the KKR $25 billion leverage buy-out of Nabisco.[19]

Table 4.3   Hypermarkets and superstores in Western Europe, 1992

	Number of outlets		% Share of total retail sales
	Hypermarkets	Superstores	
France	914	765	29.4
UK	746	1,701	17.6
Netherlands	40	339	14.0
Germany	892	1,164	11.3
Norway	25	175	10.0
Switzerland	na	na	10.0
Spain	116	39	7.7
Denmark	15	–	6.0
Finland	57	–	5.8
Austria	77	152	5.0
Sweden	67	–	3.7
Belgium	70	30	3.0
Italy	118	na	1.8
Portugal	25	–	na

Source: Euromonitor

Structural and behavioural changes

The recent interest shown by the financial community in brands reflects a wider awareness of the value that can be placed on market power. This is a lesson which was learned very early in the evolution of the food industry in the developed world. The leading manufacturers and processors were among the first to recognize that an investment in identity and the creation of sense of product differentiation reassured customers while protecting the firm's position. This was an important feature of the processor's defence against commodity market pressures on prices and the power of the distributors. Until recently, the processors and manufacturers had no real rivals in terms of expertise within the sector.

A number of producer groups have achieved considerable success in building up trade and customer loyalty through effective marketing. This has been achieved with established products, e.g. the success of French apple producers. Innovations, notably the introduction of kiwi fruit, have benefited from the same improved understanding of marketing. Among the retailers the same learning process has occurred. The creation of a clear identity built around an understanding of customer needs shapes the location, size, store design, presentation and merchandizing decisions. The emergence of marketing as a central element in policy-making coincides with major structural changes in population and its food-buying habits. These reflect movements in work patterns, population structure and social attitudes.

Work patterns

Throughout Europe and North America the role of women in the workforce, and hence their domestic role, is changing. In the 1980s, the rapid increase in the numbers in employment in the UK was largely a function of the rapid increase in women entering employment. In North America the estimate[20] that 'more women in the workforce will mean more dual career families – as many as 75% of all families by the end of the decade vs. roughly 55% now' was met. In Europe, much of this expansion in the female labour force has been accounted for by relatively low-skill, low-wage, casual employment. It is unlikely that this will continue.

As workers and managers, women are increasingly important economic agents. They are likely to have a higher terminal education age than their older compatriots. Investment in education and training for higher-skill tasks will be worthwhile as their working life is relatively long. The dual-career family is emerging as the norm in the late 1990s. This will have a marked effect on shopping and domestic catering arrangements.

The nature of the adjustments which will be required in the supplier behaviour is hard to estimate. Some appear to be emerging already. The troubled, recent history of convenience store retailing is not likely to prevent the long-term growth and success of the sector. Seven-day/long-hour retailing seems inevitable. Increased levels of customer services, especially at the point of purchase, are already being demanded. Improved standards of food hygiene and production controls are certain to be expected by an increasingly affluent and discriminating buyer. There may be a change in the food shopping profile. One possibility is a switch away from 'bulk' buying of food towards 'top-up' shopping, especially among young marrieds and those with mature families.

This pattern may be reinforced by adjustments in the purchase behaviour of other members of the family unit. The drop in the birth rate is likely to have an immediate effect on sales of child- and youth-oriented food products. Volume consumption seems certain to drop significantly. The shift to healthier eating in the wider population may be even more marked among this group as increased purchase discretion and better health education have an effect. The catering industry may be the earliest beneficiaries as larger numbers with more disposable income enter the market. Niche retail outlets targeted on this group have grown in importance in North America. This is likely to be matched in Europe.

The analysis so far has concentrated on the traditional family unit. The food production, processing and distribution system will face a rapidly evolving client base. The most marked example of this is the increase in the number of single-unit households. It is estimated that one in three households consists of a single member. This may be an underestimate, as a combination of later marriages and ageing have a marked effect on household size. The move towards larger pack units and higher expenditures on each purchase occasion may be reversed. Changes in population structure are closely related to shifts in social attitudes. The preoccupation with youth which has been with us since the 1960s following the two baby booms of the mid-1940s and early 1960s may be replaced by a preoccupation with maturity or age. The greater prosperity of older age groups, which is associated with higher wages as well as better pension and assurance provision, will increase their purchase discretion. The existing trade structure will need to adapt to meet the new challenges.

Trade structure

The present food production and distribution system has evolved along relatively consistent lines over the last few decades. There has been a steady increase in the Europeanization of production.[21] Britain obtains over half its food from within the EU compared with a third in the late 1960s. This movement has been seen in all member states. The proportion of all food produced and consumed within the EU rose from one-third to just under two-thirds between 1958 and 1987. This trend has continued. Britain obtained over two-thirds of its food from within Europe in the first half of 1997.

This process is likely to extend beyond purchasing to a wider adoption of trans-European food processing practices. This trend is reinforced by the adoption of common regulations as outlined in the Single European Act. Non-European foods will gain entry to the market through distinctive trade regulations, e.g. New Zealand's historic link with Britain, or unique features.

Integration of production may be inseparable from consolidation of processing. Merger activity should increase as firms adopt a European approach to business development. The economies of scale will increase as standardization and consistency extend to new areas. Despite this, Nicholls notes[22] that 'most European food firms do not follow an EC-wide strategy'. Many non-European firms will see acquisition as the preferred route into the European market.

Increased concentration of the ownership of production within Europe will pose a new challenge to retailers and distributors. Firms with a track record of successful acquisition such as Argyll may find the smaller, less concentrated food retail sector in Europe more attractive than expansion in the UK. The freer movement of capital across Europe will reinforce this type of development. Other large food multiples may need to seek out alternative routes into European markets. The increasing overseas success of Marks & Spencer will reassure those firms with strong, high-quality images. Other forms of diversification may provide equally attractive opportunities. It is, however, worth noting that to date mainland European retailers like Aldi and Netto have had greater success in penetrating UK markets than vice versa.

Increased scale of operation has been identified earlier as one of the most distinctive features of the UK food distribution system. The shift towards smaller numbers of larger outlets has characterized the business development strategies of the majority of UK food retailers. In the 30 years to 1990 the number of food retail outlets was reduced by 60 per cent. There is some evidence that the increased buoyancy of specialist, niche retailing and convenience stores has slowed this rate of decline.

The redevelopment of inner city areas, allied to a growing interest in lifestyle shopping, has created a major opportunity for the development of niche-orientated food production and retailers. Specialist producers such as California Cake and Cookie, Derwent Valley Foods etc., have emerged to cater for these needs. The revitalization of inner city areas through projects such as the Waverly Market in Edinburgh and the Albert Dock in Liverpool create favourable environments for newly emerging and growing companies to establish a stable commercial base.

Franchising is increasingly important. There are presently over 8,000 franchised food and drink outlets in the UK. Their combined turnover exceeds £4 billion. Much of the early growth occurred through catering outlets such as McDonalds, Burger King and Spud-U-Like. So far none of the UK-based convenience store franchises has achieved a breakthrough in terms of customer awareness.

Operations

In the short to medium term, choice in the food sector is likely to be dominated by the type of concerns which have been to the fore over the last decade. Innovation and new product development activity is likely to increase as producers and retailers respond to changes in eating habits. Wheelock[23] vividly illustrated the reductions in consumption of established basics. He outlined the problems faced by producers and retailers in adapting to these needs. Producers cannot easily shift from production of potatoes to tomatoes or other growth products.

New product development is primarily in the hands of the producer/processor. This puts increasing demands on their resource base. The costs of innovation grow but the likely returns are declining. Few new food products reach the type of £7–10 million a year turnover needed to sustain marketing and development costs. Niche markets mean small volumes. This is unless ranging can be built in or the niche itself expanded, e.g. through internationalization. This is an international problem. In the US only eight new food products launched in the period 1982–87 achieved annual sales in excess of $100 million. The contraction in product life-cycles has increased over the subsequent years and is seen in food markets across the world.

Innovation is an important aspect of the business development of all members of the food production and distribution system. The success of Marks & Spencer in collaborative new product development and positive purchasing is an integral part of the growth of the firm's retail food operations. Other food retailers are likely to follow this route. This will involve greater integration of the retail chain as well as providing a framework for greater differentiation between outlets.

The future evolution of the food marketing system

The many and diverse pressures on the food production and distribution system would suggest that the changes being faced today go beyond mere incremental development. Modifications in patterns of consumer behaviour, shifts in the relationships between the key players, and wider movements in the economic environment are combining to produce a context in which discontinuous rather than continuous change will be the norm during the next few years. This transformation will affect the ways in which the existing forces interact. New forces will have a similar effect on the underlying dynamics of the food industry.

The internationalization of the production and distribution system has already been touched on. The European dimension has been emphasized. This is, however, only one aspect of the situation. Producers and distributors are building up their international networks. This is not one-way traffic. New entrants in the UK market from Europe, Asia and North America will provide severe competition for established firms. The success of Nissin in the US soups market indicates that no market is 'safe'.

The rapidly changing nature of food industry R & D is a crucial aspect of this. The costs are increasing and the technology is becoming more complex. Developments in biotechnology will enable growers to change key features of their crops. These developments are long term and involve high risks.

The nature of these changes will increase wider public concern about the workings of the food industry. Geoffrey Cannon[24] is not alone in calling for changes in trade practice. The BSE crisis added weight to his arguments. Major manufacturers are playing a crucial part. In the US, H. J. Heinz ordered its suppliers to cease using twelve named chemicals on crops grown for its use.[25] Goldie[26] took the debate a step further by arguing that the industry should develop strategies to deal with major problems.

The food industry has been remarkably successful in the past in satisfying customer demands for increased choice, lower prices and better quality. The environment and the nature of the client base will change profoundly over the next decade. The strategies adopted by suppliers will need to reflect this transformation if they are to prosper in the new market-place.[27]

SPECIMEN QUESTIONS

1   Describe with illustrations the food marketing chain; highlight the features which distinguish food markets from other consumer goods markets.

2   Visit your local high street or a major supermarket; indicate the extent to which the food products on the shelves confirm the 'increasingly international nature' of UK food retailing. Draw out the threats and opportunities this creates for a major food processor of your choice, e.g. United Biscuits or Unilever.

3   Indicate, with illustrations, the ways in which the single European market will change the sourcing, distribution and retailing of food products in Europe.

4   Outline the three basic characteristics of the recent changes in the European food distribution system. Indicate how these changes have affected the marketing of a food product of your choice.

5   Use data from a source such as *Mintel* or *Retail Business* to show how the grocery market in Britain has changed over the last twenty years. Indicate:

   (a)   What type of store has gained most from these changes.

   (b)   Which store group or type has lost most.

   (c)   Why you think these developments have occurred.

6   Use the type of generic marketing strategy model outlined in Chapter 4 to describe the overall approach used by three major retailers. Why do you think they are adopting these specific approaches? Indicate ways in which they might win competitive advantage by changing strategy.

7   Describe the 'Wheel of Retailing'; use it to outline the evolution of a major food retailer.

8   Why do you think 'most European food firms do not follow an EU-wide strategy'? What external forces are likely to stimulate firms to rethink this approach?

9   What does the BSE crisis tell us about the interaction of technology and marketing in modern food marketing? What can marketing do to help avoid future problems?

10   Define:

   (a)   Shelf life.

   (b)   Multiple retailer.

   (c)   Generic.

   (d)   Retail concentration.

   (e)   Category killers.

   (f)   Franchising.

   (g)   Convenience stores.

   (h)   Green marketing.

   (i)   '7 to 11' stores.

   (j)   Chilled foods.

5

Offerings and organizations

Introduction

The organizations or individuals existing within the marketing system, described in Chapter 3, introduce into this system their own history, technology, skills and other resources. These internal factors play a large part in determining the precise ways in which they respond, both as buyers and sellers, to environmental and system pressures. The whole, in sum, is greater than the sum of the individuals. Maximizing the value of this whole is the key to gaining and sustaining a long-term competitive edge.[1]

Recognition of an opportunity or threat emanating from outside the firm is likely to be followed up by a series of organizational and operational adjustments before market-orientated action can be taken. For example, the would-be restaurateur might take months to find a site, obtain planning permission, meet fire and hygiene regulations, and decorate and promote his premises before he can start serving customers. These time-lags affect the buyer as much as the seller, as the following examples show:

1 Lead times for certain types of plant or equipment can stretch into years if order, installation and running-in are included. This may effectively preclude some types of fast response to opportunities in the environment.
2 The British plastics industry has been precluded from capitalizing on some market opportunities because of shortages of skilled tool-makers.

The nature of the supplying industry and the purchasing groups directly affects the character of the buyer-seller relationship and the ways in which the firm operates. For simplicity, this chapter will concentrate on the single-industry, single-customer-type situation. In reality, however, many firms work within a number of situations or face special organizational or communication problems. Figure 5.1 illustrates how Kraft Jacobs Suchards fits into the giant Philip Morris organization. It operates in markets as diverse as the UK cheese market and the European confectionery trade. It needs marketing systems capable of tackling giant supermarkets while responding to the duty-free trade. Its internal systems will need to meet US, British and European expectations for operations, information and communication.

In some of these highly complex organizations, identifying the key personnel to approach when attempting to sell can be very difficult. For example,a small rubber company in south London eventually tracked down the key decision-maker, for its area, of the giant German company Kraftwerk Union at an exhibition in Brazil.

Occasionally the purchasing or consumption function is difficult to separate from the selling or supply role. End users may specify the use of certain components in the final item. For

Figure 5.1   Kraft Jacobs Suchard's role in the Philip Morris Organization

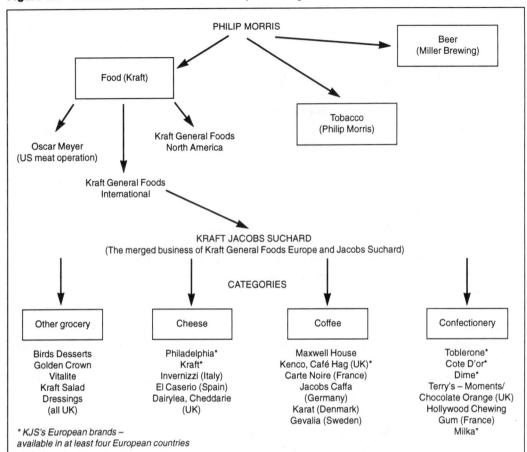

example, the Saudi Arabian Government may give the contract for fully equipping a new hospital to a German firm such as Labsco GmbH, but specify that all clean-air equipment is supplied by a UK firm such as Envair Ltd. In many government markets, policies of supporting local industry through directives such as 'Buy British'[2] or America First' may be adopted. Sales and marketing may insist that certain types or grades of material or components are used; for example, a Yorkshire footwear manufacturer gradually replaced synthetic materials with leather as sales staff noted the growing popularity of natural materials. Vertical integration may predispose the firm to use materials or products from a sister firm.

For example, when PVC-coated aluminium power cable was introduced into the UK market, the dominant cable manufacturer had little to gain in the short to medium term from introducing aluminium as it had an extensive interest in copper refining and no involvement in aluminium.

The diversity of markets

Despite the importance of these behavioural dimensions of the market, most managers find that much of their flexibility and the customers' responses are directly affected by established patterns of behaviour.[3] These are determined, at least in part, by their industrial situation as producers of raw materials, processed products, components, finished goods, services, capital or plant.

Analysis of the broad structure of how expenditure in Britain is allocated between different areas brings out the continuing significance and scale of government expenditure. Alone this accounts for almost a quarter of direct expenditure. It covers a vast assortment of items from military equipment through equipment for the National Health Service to supplies and services for all government agencies. Dealing with government calls for many skills and disciplines.[4] Some are common to all marketing areas. Others are highly specialized; for example, competitive tendering is more important in public sector activity than in most areas of commercial activity.

In international trade the same broad patterns exist. In some countries the state plays an even more central role. Considerable variations exist in the ways in which commercial dealings are handled between countries. The researches of the Industrial Marketing Group[5] indicate the degree to which organizational purchasing behaviour in different countries is influenced by:

1 The domestic environment.
2 The networks of relationships between suppliers and customers.
3 The nature of the offering.

The detailed discussion of this work will take place in Chapter 12; here the emphasis is on the interaction between the offering and the organization.

The conventional division between international and domestic markets has been challenged by those who have studied the 'global' marketing strategies of Japanese firms. Beal[6] indicates that in recent years: 'Although domestic demand has been sluggish, Japanese manufacturing industry has continued to grow and prosper.'

Porter[7] places this in the wider context by pointing out that 'a firm's home base defines, in part, its advantages and disadvantages in global industries'.

Raw materials

Raw materials, sometimes described as 'primary products', are so called because of their 'raw' or untreated state. The only processing they undergo will generally be for reasons of safety, economy, handling or avoiding deterioration. They are normally from extractive industries (mining, oil, gas and timber), agriculture and fisheries. In Britain these account for about 6 per cent of the GNP, employing about 3.7 per cent of the workforce. Figure 5.2 gives a breakdown of the 'industrial profile' of the UK and four other major industrial nations.

Although the dominant feature of this figure is the considerable similarity between these countries, some differences are worth noting. The sharp reduction in the proportion of the Japanese labour force employed in the 'primary sector' between 1962 and 1996 – from 12.9 per cent to 2.3 per cent – reflects the successful growth of Japan's manufacturing. The relative stability of this sector in Britain is partly a function of the earlier industrialization of Britain, the efficiency of the agricultural sector and new extractive industries, e.g. North Sea oil.

Britain's extractive industries and her richness of resources, from coal to North Sea oil, have long played a major part in the economic prosperity of the country, and the marketing of these extracted materials is conditioned by a number of specific features. One of these aspects, the finite nature of these materials, is central to current thinking about marketing in this area,

Figure 5.2 Industrial profile: GDP activity shares. (Sources: OECD, CSO.)

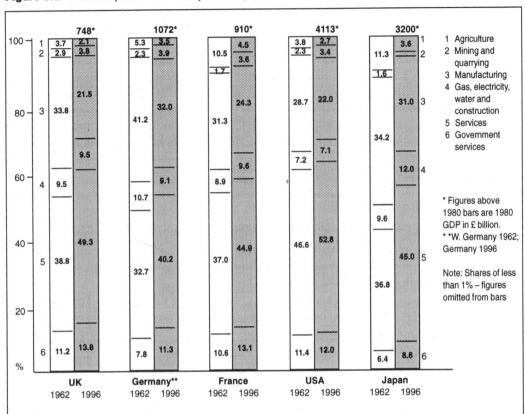

1 Agriculture
2 Mining and quarrying
3 Manufacturing
4 Gas, electricity, water and construction
5 Services
6 Government services

* Figures above 1980 bars are 1980 GDP in £ billion.
* *W. Germany 1962; Germany 1996

Note: Shares of less than 1% – figures omitted from bars

notably in fossil energy (although it has been argued that this 'finite' nature is exaggerated, particularly since large areas of the world's surface are as yet unexplored). This is clearly illustrated in the marketing problems of North Sea oil and gas. Although new discoveries are likely, the time span for depletion can be estimated at any given point in time. Achieving an effective balance between conservation and the effective exploitation of marketing opportunities is critical.

The scale of operations which is often necessary to open up a pit head or to explore for oil on the continental shelf has created a great deal of concentration in many of these extractive industries. British Coal, British Gas and the 'Seven Sisters' in oil illustrate this. (The Seven Sisters was the name given to the seven major oil companies: Exxon, Royal Dutch Shell, Texaco, Gulf, Mobil, Standard Oil of California and British Petroleum.) In some cases their control extends to the delivery of the product, sales and service.

In consumer markets this means that the primary area of competition is between the different energy sources: oil, gas, coal and electricity. There is generally a close link between sales and the basic material and appliance sales. Once an appliance has been purchased, conversion to an alternative energy source is expensive, and this is true for both industrial and consumer markets.

In the marketing of extractive industries the real price is a combination of material and installation costs. Distribution costs are often extremely high, leading to a tendency for industry to concentrate near the sources of raw materials. The cost and bulk factors have led some businessmen to doubt the scope for marketing in such product areas. In fact, the scope, particularly when recognized by creative marketing men, is considerable. For example, a quarry in northern England sends sand to Kuwait because top management recognized that its sand had technical characteristics lacking in Kuwaiti sand.

Raw material marketing, trading and usage are increasingly affected by political decisions. The types of fuel used in power stations, the rates of exploitation of forestry reserves and even the willingness to sell certain raw materials are influenced by government action. In much of the world, industry is being directed to move its materials further 'downstream', to add value or use in manufacturing in the home market rather than export. Third World countries have responded to fluctuating primary product prices by attempting to introduce local manufacture. For example, many European tanneries are suffering from shortages of untreated hides as Eastern European and Third World countries stop exporting and open their own tanneries, and acute shortages of certain types of timber have occurred as countries like Malaysia and Indonesia build up their furniture, giftware and other timber-consuming industries. Over time these considerations are likely to affect the operations of the London Metal Exchange and the other primary product exchanges. Although the conditions of rapid price fluctuations which occurred on the Rotterdam 'Spot' market for oil during the Gulf crisis of late 1990/early 1991 are unlikely to be paralleled in other primary markets,some hints of the challenges inherent in finite, even restricted supplies and substantial excess demand are given by this situation. The textile industry has long been a weather vane for these trends. The growth in textile sales to Britain by countries like India, Pakistan and China shows their increasing ability to cope in sophisticated markets (see Table 5.1).

The dramatic movements in prices in the extractive industries are matched by similar fluctuations in world agricultural and, to a lesser extent, fishery prices. In Europe, North

Table 5.1 Top twenty overseas suppliers of textiles to the UK

£ million	1989	1990	1991	1990/89 % change	1991/90 % change
Germany	587.0	582.0	504.3	−1	−13
Belgium	387.9	430.1	415.2	+11	−3
Italy	432.1	423.8	384.4	−2	−9
France	296.0	313.6	292.3	+6	−7
Netherlands	249.8	250.7	236.9	+0	−6
Eire	157.7	171.6	166.5	+9	−3
Portugal	177.1	171.9	154.8	−3	−10
India	104.2	136.1	153.0	+31	+12
USA	162.0	193.1	128.1	+19	−34
Pakistan	79.3	98.9	115.2	+25	+16
Japan	115.9	118.0	110.0	+2	−17
Switzerland	120.3	118.1	102.9	−2	−13
Turkey	98.5	87.9	75.9	−11	−14
Spain	50.1	73.4	73.2	+47	+0
China	57.9	60.1	72.6	+4	+21
Austria	78.7	85.6	66.9	+9	−22
Denmark	62.5	63.0	58.2	+1	−8
Hong Kong	70.0	57.4	50.4	−18	−12
Indonesia	26.0	45.0	47.4	+73	+5
Israel	36.9	38.1	42.6	+3	+12

Source: HM Customs and Excise
Quoted in Brown, M., 'Material World', Marketing Business, 20, May 1993.

Figure 5.3   The route to market for agricultural products

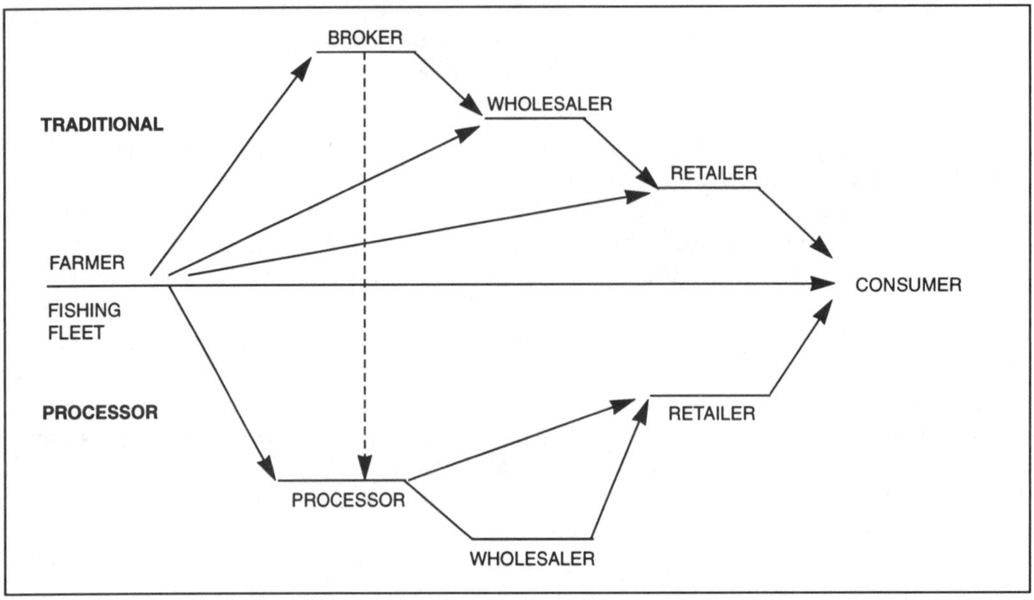

America and many other parts of the world, determined efforts have been made to introduce mechanisms to improve the basic stability of domestic (here including EU) farm prices. Policies like the Common Agricultural Policy (EU) and the Agriculture and Trade Redevelopment and Assistance Act 1954 (USA) illustrate specific programmes to influence agricultural production and prices.

Despite their ultimate success, the problems faced during the Uruguay Round of GATT negotiations vividly illustrate the importance and complexity of world negotiations on food prices. This round of negotiations was initiated by the US in 1986. In early December 1990, the failure to arrive at a final agreement on systems of support for agriculture was a primary cause of the near collapse of these talks. They were eventually suspended until early 1991. In part, this reflects concern in many parts of the world about systems of support for local output and their impact on exports. Since the mid-1980s the decline in the numbers of anti-dumping actions taken by states has been reversed. The power of key lobbies such as French farmers has delayed progress to a final settlement. It was not until 1994 that agreement was finally reached. The marketing of agricultural and fishery products follows two broad routes: traditional, untreated path to end use, and the food processor way to market (Figure 5.3). Although for many years the traditional path was dominant, the emergence of the giant processors during this century has revolutionized food marketing. Through canning and freezing they have offered assured long-term supplies, besides reassurances of quality. The farmers and fishing fleet operators have won long-term contracts to supply, resulting in freedom to plan and realize fully their potential.

Agricultural markets

The last few years have seen a rapid growth in interest in agricultural markets and marketing. A number of factors have helped to stimulate this:

1 The clear success of initiatives such as those taken by Danish bacon, Jaffa oranges and French apples.
2 The success of 'new' products like kiwi fruit and kumquats.
3 The demonstrated desire by consumers for quality reassurance and consistency.
4 The power of major retailers and their insistence on consistent quality.
5 Pressure and support from the UK government through programmes such as the 'Food for Britain' campaign.
6 The British beef crisis.
7 The wish by farmers to improve their returns.
8 Actions by the EU.
9 Research which has indicated the potential value and benefits from action in this area.[8, 9, 10]

It is useful to think of agricultural marketing in terms of the challenges posed to the farmer within the type of marketing system discussed earlier. All systems have unique features but in other ways show certain important similarities. Farmers wishing to develop their markets need first to understand the structure of their markets (conduct an audit).

The institutions in the market-place[11]

There are many private and public concerns and agencies active in agricultural markets, some long established, some relatively new. The three basic intermediary groups have existed in some form for many centuries, i.e. as long as farmers have wanted to move their output from the country to the city.

1 *The merchants.* These are the various retailers and wholesalers who buy from the farmer and supply to the consumer. They take many forms: the fruit and vegetable wholesaler based at one of the major markets in London or any big city (e.g. Vauxhall), the market trader operating in city centres such as Birmingham's 'Bull Ring', the major retailer such as Tesco, Sainsbury or Marks and Spencer.
2 *The agents.* These act on behalf of their client suppliers to seek out opportunities and trade in them. They are particularly important in two areas: horticultural products and international trade.
3 *The speculators.* Agricultural markets are characterized by serious problems of control of output. Periods of glut can be followed by severe shortage. The speculator attempts to profit from this variability of output level by attempting to predict patterns before the rest of the market. The extent to which his or her forecast is accurate determines the degree of success.[12]

The precise form and pattern of relationships varies considerably between countries and over time.

More recently two other organizations have grown in scale and importance.

1 *Processors, packers and manufacturers.* These take the raw product and convert it into a different form for onward sale. In scale, typically, they are much larger than farmers. They can exercise significant controls over the market. However, their capital investment often makes them vulnerable to supplier pressure. This has been very evident in the fishing industry over the last decade as fishing fleets have won major concessions from the processors in return for assurance of supply.
2 *Government agencies and facilitators.* These exist on a national and international scale. The UK government has a long tradition of involvement in the working of the

agricultural marketing system. It acts directly through legislation on standards and regulations, and indirectly through the various initiatives and agencies such as the Seafish Authority. The EU has had a major impact through the workings of the Common Agricultural Policy. Besides these bodies, many farming groups have organized themselves into co-operatives in attempts to achieve their marketing goals.

The role of the EU has increased with the implementation of the Single European Act and the creation of the internal market in foodstuffs; the original programme was harmonization and removal of internal barriers to trade. The legislative framework is in place which will establish common systems for labelling, control, composition, packaging and processing, besides establishing standards for nutrition levels, use of additives and food irradiation. A simple illustration of the impact of this programme is the Community directive which removed the use of 'Sell by' dates on perishable foodstuffs and replaced with 'Use by' dates. This came into effect in January 1991.[13] The Europe-wide ban on sales of British beef in 1997 is a dramatic illustration of the EU's power over agricultural markets.

It is within the structures described above that farmers and food producers design and develop their marketing strategies. The task is made more demanding by three unusual features of agricultural markets:

1   The importance of climate and related forces in determining the amount, range and quality of output.
2   The relatively small size of the producers (farmers) compared to their customers (the processors and middlemen).
3   The 'distance' between the supplier and the ultimate customer.

A number of approaches have been adopted by food producers to overcome these problems. Among the most significant are marketing co-operatives. These have been set up on both a national and local level. Some concentrate on particular commodities while others are more broadly based. There has been a rapid growth in interest recently in the role that new technologies, especially computers and telecommunications, can play in developing the market potential of farmers. Especially important has been their use in providing accurate market intelligence, particularly on prices and in increasing the scope for effective management control.[14]

The food chain

The food chain stretches from the farm to the shopping basket. In this section attention is focused on the steps from the food processor/broker/dealer to the retailer in Figure 5.3. Marketing has grown in importance in this sector until it is now estimated that marketing and distribution costs exceed production costs in this area.[15] This change has occurred at a time when there has been a marked increase in concentration among middlemen, notably wholesalers and retailers (Table 5.2).

Table 5.2 The number of auction markets in Great Britain

	1968	1974	1976	1978	1984	1987	1991	1994
England and Wales	453	369	354	332	254	227	214	210
Scotland	74	65	65	65	65	62	60	58

The reduction in the number of outlets gives greater power and responsibility to existing middlemen while restricting choices open to producers.

A similar pattern can be seen among grocery retailers, with equally rapid and substantial increases in the market shares for the multiples, e.g. Tesco, Sainsbury, Kwik Save (Table 5.3). This pattern poses major problems, especially for smaller producers. Major retailers require significant minimum order quantities as well as high standards in quality and consistency. It was reported recently that for fish products a major retailer required a minimum annual throughput per line of £600,000 for it to be stocked.

The scale of competition goes some way to explain the very high rate of new product introduction, the price rivalry, and advertising levels in this area.

Table 5.3 The growth of the grocery multiples

	1971 (%)	1976 (%)	1979 (%)	1982 (%)	1986 (%)	1991 (%)	1994 (%)
Multiples	44	48	53	65	70	73	74
Co-operatives	13	16	15	13	12	11	10
Independents	43	36	32	22	18	16	16

Based on Institute and Grocery Distribution and Nielsen data.

At the same time, new technologies had a major impact on food retailing. Electronic point of sale, laser scanning and bar coding are widespread at retail level. Companies such as Tesco and Sainsbury invested heavily in this area. These increased the pressures on smaller distributors while challenging the ability of major manufacturers to keep pace with developments.[16]

Processed products

The dividing line between processed goods and raw materials is sometimes very fine indeed. Generally, sufficient treatment has taken place to make them qualitatively different from their natural state. Processed goods include pig-iron, steel, concrete, cement, chemicals and solvents, resins, and processed rubber and plastics. Their form is frequently changed by the buyer before being assembled or inserted in the final end product.

A typical processed product is plastic moulding: extruded, injected, vacuum formed, sprayed or hand-layered. It ranges in scale from the small, injection-moulded, plastic pegs used in games like 'Mastermind' to the glass-reinforced plastic hulls of boats such as Royal Navy minesweepers. By far the greatest part of the output of the processing industries goes into industrial markets for inclusion (as in the case of the game), modification (for example when used in cars or domestic appliances) or assembly with other goods (as with a minesweeper). The scale of process industries is seldom fully appreciated: plastics processing alone employs over 130,000 workers in approximately 2,300 firms in the UK.

Marketing of processed products poses special problems, because in fact there is no product as such. The supplier generally works to the specifications of the customer, who will probably be incorporating the item into his own end product or component. The supplier will be providing machine capacity allied to his technical, engineering and design skills, perhaps allied to tool-making. The key purchasing decisions occur very infrequently, i.e. when laying down the tooling, designing the item or placing initial orders. Once a project is initiated repeat orders may be frequent, but are often a routine purchasing operation. This pattern of behaviour leads to an emphasis on three key areas: winning initial orders, sustaining quality standards and prompt delivery. A skilled technical representative, capable of interpreting buyer needs and adapting them to the material or technology, is invaluable. These requirements, as well as the limited scope for 'off-the-shelf' buying, reduce the middleman's contribution in many sectors.

Strong, direct, customer-producer relationships often lead to powerful supplier loyalties. The customer depends a great deal on his suppliers, since moving tools[17] can cause a great deal of disruption in supplies. At the same time, however, no customer can afford to have the entire production line disrupted because of poor delivery or low quality from a supplier whose item may be a very small part of a major line. For example, a mattress manufacturer cannot afford to have this bulky and expensive product held up because the polythene-bag supplier's deliveries are late; and the production lines of a cooker manufacturer can be quickly reduced to chaos if the silicon rubber seals on the doors are substandard or late. This explains the speed with which Total Quality Management was adopted by companies across the world. Japanese producers adopted the ideas of authorities like the late Bill Demming to transform their industries and image.

In some industries intermediaries play a large role. In steel, stockholders play a major part in distribution, generally to smaller customers or where analysis of the 'cost of possession' has indicated the scope for economies by larger buyers. (The 'cost of possession' differentiates between the monetary cost of buying direct, probably in bulk from producers, and the real costs of larger stock-holding and labour for handling and warehousing. See Chapter 19 for fuller discussion.)

Components

In the components area there is the additional need to develop lines of the producer's products for direct insertion in the buyer's product. Girling Brakes, Lucas Electrics, NSF Cooker Timers and Perkins Engines all offer lines of proprietary products to industrial customers but generally provide scope for adaptation or modification to special customer needs. In certain circumstances items are made to specification but probably only if the volume justifies it.

The cost per unit of components tends to be higher than that of processed goods, emphasizing the importance of price. However, in many fields reputation and appropriate technology play an equal role. In a rapidly advancing field such as electronics, decisions about technology are critical. Firms like Perkins Engines have demonstrated the role that effective marketing can play in ensuring long-term profitable business.

Normally, demand for an item is inelastic, but it may be met from a number of sources. This creates an environment in which distributors play a major role for both suppliers and customers. There are some elements of vertical integration in this area, with distributors becoming involved in limited assembly work. The complexity of the resulting distribution systems can be quite considerable, as illustrated in the case of hydraulic hose and couplings in Figure 5.4.

Figure 5.4 A distribution system for industrial products

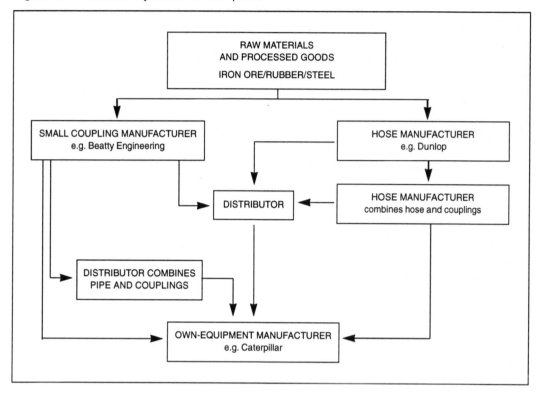

Finished goods

Finished goods are sold to all the different customer groups. Although they may require energy to drive them, operators to work them or machines to employ them, no other additions are normally required for their use or consumption. The majority of consumer marketing behaviour is directed towards finished goods, from fish fingers to motor-cars.

In industrial markets finished goods are made up primarily of equipment and supplies. Equipment ranges from large capital items destined to be part of fixed plant and fundamental to the manufacturing process, to everyday items such as small tools. The purchasing decision in equipment will normally be occasioned by one of four situations: replacement of old equipment; expansion of capacity; change of production process; or production of a new product.[18] Suppliers in some areas may be able, through their own innovation policies, to create a fifth situation in which capital investment will take place: the opportunity for differential advantage from adopting new technologies as well as the limitations.[19] In most situations customer investment is non-routine and involves substantial investment and, from the buyer's perspective, a certain element of risk. In today's inflation- and energy-conscious markets, the life-span of equipment and primary energy sources are increasingly important.

Supplies can generally be divided into two broad groupings: accessory equipment and operating supplies. Accessories include office equipment, tills, sales force cars, promotional materials, photocopiers and computers (although the increasing extent to which computers are aligned with production may make this classification more and more inappropriate). Operating supplies are the convenience goods of the industrial field. They include such diverse items as pens, stationery, cleaning equipment and books. In many of these areas the relatively small unit investment and the repeat-order character of much of the buying have led to the emergence of middleman groups such as Rymans, Office 1 and others.

In certain parts of the commercial environment supplies constitute, after labour, the largest single area of direct expenditure. Handling other types of finished goods provides intermediaries with their primary source of revenue.

The massive government markets concentrate much of their expenditure on finished goods. Their requirements include machinery and machine tools for colleges and government training centres and defence, and medical and educational equipment.

Services

Throughout the developed world the service sector of the economy is growing, and in many countries it is the most rapidly growing sector. Service workers can be broadly divided into two groups: those employed in other key areas, e.g. doctors employed by British Coal or the marketing staff of large manufacturers; and those directly involved in the service industries.

The main service industries are transport, post and telecommunications, communication, entertainment, holidays, hotels and tourism, government, intermediaries, maintenance and repair, domestic help and laundry, design, research and consultancy, medical, educational, legal and other professions and finance.

Some important features of the marketing of services are as follows.[20]

1 There is a broad division between profit and non-profit operations, with government, education and health dominating the latter.
2 Most offerings are of an intangible nature.
3 There is a tendency for the lack of a physical product to reduce the need for distributors and most forms of middlemen.
4 There have emerged agency systems in some markets, mainly those with very diffuse franchises, e.g. holiday, travel, tourism, some types of transport, some aspects of entertainment, communication, insurance and credit.
5 In the commercial sphere low barriers to entry often occur, leading to considerable emphasis on skill differentiation, reputation, availability and a high degree of responsiveness to the market.
6 In many areas of government services the conventional pattern of demand stimulation is replaced by demand control, even reduction.

Services are used by all the customer groups. Consumers use travel agents and the postal service, watch television, go to the cinema and theatre, have their cars repaired, raise funds and come into contact with the law, education and medicine. The organizations which provide these services attempt in various ways to manage the exchange with the prospective user, the travel agent promoting holidays and the university recruiting students.

Industry provides much of the demand for the service sector, often requiring special talents or skills. For example, the travel agent may develop a special business travel service, and the telecommunication needs of the business world have led to the emergence of firms like America Online and products like the fax. Some services are highly specialized, e.g.

management or marketing consultant, consultant engineer, fashion designer, market research bureau and advertising agent.

Commercial markets are closely linked to the service sector. The retail groups demand specialized logistics and location analysts, and the management service companies, such as computer bureaux, may need freelance systems analysts.

The state's need for services is perhaps the most extensive. The Central Office of Information is by far the largest advertiser, at one time employing over 27 advertising agencies. State requirements include architects, engineering research and consultancy, specialist advisers on areas of policy, and decision-makers. As well as these specialists, they make use of almost all the other service organizations.

The scale of Britain's invisible trade illustrates the importance of this area overseas. Foreign governments make extensive use of UK services.

Capital

Capital is the life-blood of the market-place. It is the mechanism for exchange, and as such it provides a vital service to consumers, industrialists, commerce and government. The marketing of capital or money is dealt with in the general section on services. However, in Britain it is only over the last two decades or so that finance has been recognized as a commodity like any other.[21]

Although the rate of growth has slackened, the general awareness of the need for a more positive approach to marketing this most intangible of commodities has grown. To a considerable extent the newer forms of credit and finance, e.g. credit cards, charge cards, and financial services have led the way, followed by personal financial services through the major banks.

Perhaps the slowest area to change has been the area of corporate finance. The growth of competition in this area, partly from overseas and partly from new institutions, is already having a noticeable effect on policies and practices.

Plant

Plant, sometimes called capital projects, constitute some of the largest individual market opportunities. They range from the construction of houses and industrial and commercial properties to the giant projects to construct power-stations, harbour installations and sometimes, in developing nations, whole townships. Their very scale can be daunting to even the largest international construction groups.

Although individuals may commission private projects, most of the activity is industrial, commercial and governmental. The scale of some projects is so great that tendering is increasingly conducted through consortia (Consortium: 'a partnership of corporations, firms or partnerships, generally for a specific project or time period'[22]).

The traditional pattern of winning business in these areas is through successful tendering: the government or a firm announces a project, provides specifications and calls for tenders. Inevitably this system places considerable emphasis on the price element in the project. Despite this, other aspects of marketing can play a major part in building up a pattern of successful tendering. Preparing the ground is vital. Many firms find that close links with governments and other bodies prior to formulation of the project through advice and technical guidance may help sway judgement towards factors more favourable to them. The notion of systems selling is particularly important in deveoping nations. Firms which provide a more complete service (design, development, management and assembly of associated parts) meet the needs of countries with very limited resources in skilled management.

The scale of some projects and the central importance of finance led many governments to sponsor or establish support schemes such as the UK Export Credit Guarantee Department's Specific Guarantee and the US government's EXIM Bank. The merchant banks are very active in contracts of over £1 million. They help to build up the loans necessary for the project, establishing competitive interest rates and agreeing the premium. In some instances groups of banks, perhaps in association with international agencies such as the World Bank, provide special 'lines of credit' for a country, a development plan or a specific project.

For the firms entering this type of activity, notably turnkey projects ('the construction, under contract, of a project up to the point of operation, at which time it is turned over to the owner') the potential returns are enormous. The costs and risks are commensurate, notably in areas of political and economic turmoil, demanding the highest levels of marketing and financial and strategic management commitment. In many cases the monetary price will be less important than the form of payment, the availability of funding and follow-up service and support.

Conclusion

In these very different product, process or service areas, the intrinsic character of the industry and the firm plays a major role in determining the possible and appropriate marketing responses. The effective marketing person will need to build upon these internal capabilities to design offerings to meet the real needs of the customers, whether they are less developed countries seeking coastal shipping but lacking the foreign exchange and needing new lines of credit, or students looking for low-price travel during the summer holidays.

In this chapter it was noted:

1 How the fundamental nature of the industry in which the firm operates – raw material, agricultural etc. – does much to shape the possible and appropriate form of marketing.

2 That changes in many of these areas are posing increasing challenges to traditional ways of developing business.

3 That there are various ways in which marketing techniques can be used to modify, design or change offerings to increase their appeal to existing and new customers.

4 How effectiveness in many of these areas calls for skill in integrating marketing actions with technical and financial skills and resources.

Many of the areas presented here as separate and discrete for the sake of discussion also need to be reviewed in terms of their inter-relationships, if a proper appreciation of their character is to be achieved.

SPECIMEN QUESTIONS

1 Describe, with illustrations, some of the ways in which the nature of a supplier, industry or firm can affect the character of the buyer-seller relationship.

2 Outline the factors which can influence the nature of organizational buying behaviour. Show how these might be different between a public agency and a small privately owned firm.

3 Why do customers need protection in a competitive market?

4 What are the differences between an 'asset led' approach to marketing and a 'market led' approach?

5 Industrial marketing is sometimes defined as being wholly dependent on developing and managing the buyer-seller relationship.

    (a)   What does this mean?

    (b)   Why is it different from consumer markets?

    (c)   Give a specific illustration of this approach in action.

6 Draw a diagram which describes the various routes to market followed by:

    (a)   Fresh, farmed fish.

    (b)   Frozen peas.

Identify specific firms and give illustrations of the approaches these employ to generate push and pull in the market.

7 Why have French apples been such a success in UK food markets? Outline the marketing policies and practices which have produced this success. Are there lessons which British producers can learn from this success? If so, outline them – if not, why?

8 Indicate, with illustrations, the ways in which component or engineering companies like Perkins Engines can use marketing to increase their penetration of market and reinforce customer loyalty.

9 Examine in-depth and describe the marketing policies adopted by a bank or other financial institution. Indicate ways in which their approach differs from that of a producer of fast-moving consumer goods.

10 Define

    (a)   Lead times.

    (b)   Vertical integration.

    (c)   Raw materials.

    (d)   Competitive tendering.

    (e)   Category management.

    (f)   Facilitators.

    (g)   Merchants.

    (h)   EPoS.

    (i)   Supplies.

    (j)   Integrated marketing.

CASE STUDY 3: WESTWARD PLASTICS

In 1996 Charles Price, the managing director, could look back on three years of sustained growth by Westward Plastics. The firm was a general plastics processor, with injection moulding dominant but some foam-extrusion capability, and was part of the giant Marchmont Group.

The firm had been acquired in the late 1960s with two basic objectives in view: entering into a new area of business; and meeting some of the group's own plastics processing needs. Despite the latter goal, the group is committed to the notion that all units are independent profit centres. This means that Westward have no special advantages in inter-group trading. In 1993, 1994, 1995 and 1996 sales within the group never accounted for more than 15 per cent of the turnover.

Business profit

When the company was acquired by Marchmont it was located in High Wycombe, near London. Much of the firm's business was drawn from the local furniture industry.

The proximity of London had given access to a much wider industrial base. Their customer list encompassed both the manufacturing industry (a number of lorry manufacturers, with ERF particularly important) and telecommunications (both the Post Office and key suppliers such as GEC). Just before the take-over important new accounts had been opened with South East and North Thames Gas (components for equipment used by service engineers in North Sea gas conversion).

In 1971 it was decided by the group to shift the firm's factory from High Wycombe to a new plant in the North West of England, to capitalize on various regional development grants. Just before the move the composition of the company's output was: furniture, 35 per cent; goods vehicles, 20 per cent; telecommunications, 15 per cent; gas regions, 10 per cent; and others, 10 per cent. On 1 January 1971, forecast income for the year was £750,000.

The new location

The immediate fears that the move would seriously weaken the company's business base, especially in furniture and gas, rapidly proved to be unfounded. In fact the furniture industry was in the process of becoming more evenly distributed across the UK.

Growth during the 1970s and 1980s

In the early 1970s business boomed: the furniture industry prospered; the gas conversion programme accelerated; and the telecommunications industry expanded. In September 1973 record monthly sales of £100,000 were recorded. This had been achieved almost entirely from the same industry profile as the firm had held before moving north.

The technical expertise and wide contacts of Ian Graham, the sales director, had played a major part in holding on to these accounts. Despite the distances involved, he kept close and regular contact with these accounts. Ian was viewed as an important part of their 'problem-solving capacity'. Despite various highs and lows, growth continued in the 1980s. In September 1983 monthly sales averaged £300,000. They steadily grew until 1985 when they peaked at £425,000.

Economic recession in the late 1980s

A number of Westward's key customers were hit very hard by the economic recession of the late 1980s. Furniture companies were particularly seriously affected. Its largest single customer, Johnson's Furniture, cut back orders from £82,000 per month in September 1988 to under £28,000 per month a year later. The ending of the post-privatization investment programme by British Gas posed further problems. At its lowest point the firm's turnover was less than £200,000 per month.

The workforce was pruned severely as part of a general economy programme. At the same time a number of avenues for new business were sought. Three major paths were followed: new own products, new industries, and new processes.

The first new product introduced was a Do-It-Yourself brick mould. The product was designed to enable DIY enthusiasts to manufacture their own garden-wall bricks. They launched the product at Interbuild (the building industry's main exhibition), and considerable initial interest was shown. A major Midland DIY group stocked the product during the first year. Unfortunately, consumer 'pull' was very limited. The launch of a more expensive competitive brand backed by a heavyweight advertising campaign led Westward to abandon active promotion of the mould in the trade.

This coincided with the skateboard boom at the end of 1987. Westward introduced a medium-priced skateboard in September 1987, and sales rapidly built up through the major sports and leisure groups. In November 1987 £80,000 worth of boards were dispatched. Attempts were made to open up accounts abroad since it was felt that the earlier skateboard boom of the 1970s had shown that only the strongest, best-resourced firms would survive.

The current situation

In late 1996, the profile of business is: furniture, 25 per cent; toys, 20 per cent; goods vehicles, 13 per cent; telecommunications, 10 per cent; gas regions, 7 per cent; electrical, 7 per cent; group, 5 per cent; and foam, 10 per cent. The projected turnover for the year is £7.5 million.

Charles Price is determined to sustain this success. The overall target for the forthcoming year is to achieve sales in the region of £10 million. He feels that it is important to adopt a positive attitude to this, believing that the company cannot afford to rest on its success.

A number of areas of development appear to present themselves: explore new products again; seek new markets, e.g. export; and build up local strength, since very little business comes from the North West.

Task

To realize fully these and to identify new avenues in which to capitalize on their strengths. Charles Price feels that a stronger marketing orientation is needed. Explore what this will mean for Westward Plastics.

6

Marketing research

The growing importance of marketing has been paralleled by the emergence of marketing research as a major area of business activity. In 1977, it was estimated by Simmons[1] that £55 million was spent on commissioned research. By 1979, Crimp[2] placed the size at £80–85 million or 7–8p for every £100 spent by customers. Moire recent indications are that the turnover of the industry in 1996 was over £500 million.[3] Internal changes in the Marketing Research Sector are being dramatically affected by the Information Revolution, which is transforming industrial and consumer practice. The most public feature of this revolution is the increased access to information produced by the Internet. Where possible in this chapter, Internet addresses are included.

Research today

The Market Research Society[4] is the professional institute of market research practitioners in Britain. It has over 3,500 members and 401 MRS listed suppliers. Three useful definitions of market research are:

> Market research is the means used by those who provide goods and services to keep themselves in touch with the needs and wants of those who buy and use those goods and services.

> The systematic collection and objective recording, classification, analysis and presentation of data concerning the behaviour, needs, attitudes, opinions, motivations etc., of individuals and organizations (commercial enterprises, public bodies etc.) within the context of their economic, social, political and everyday activities.
>
> (International Chamber of Commerce[5]
> European Society for Opinion and Marketing Research[6])

> The systematic and objective search for analysis of information relevant to the identification of any problem in the field of marketing.[7]

These definitions go beyond the confines of market research, with its emphasis on the measurement and analysis of markets, 'to solve a particular company's marketing problem'[8] in an attempt to encompass the broad field of marketing.

Four factors were instrumental in encouraging the development of both market and marketing research:

1 The size of firms has grown with the resulting distance between marketing decision-makers and consumers, buyers and users.
2 The scale of the market has increased notably as costs and risks grow with the shift from local to national, even international, markets.
3 The commitment of marketing men and women to look outside the firm, particularly at buyer needs, for clues to the company's future.
4 Greater awareness of the forces affecting both need creation and the choice process has highlighted the extent to which many and complex non-price factors influence behaviour.

These four factors interact to place a massive premium on information for effective marketing decision-making.

> To manage a business well is to manage its future: and to manage the future is to manage information.[9]

Traditionally, information management was a personal and subjective process. Top management had close, day-to-day links with their customers, and a continual process of review and updating was possible. The personal links were often strong, response was swift, and the number of customers small enough to be managed. In many of these situations an overall pattern of stability existed, posing no challenges to assumptions about market behaviour. Today, markets have been transformed in scale, distance, range and technology. Together, they are transforming information gathering.[10]

The four factors listed above gradually undermined these traditional patterns of behaviour. Bigger operations and greater risks required new approaches to information gathering and use. At the same time the accelerating rate of change in markets and research in other areas created a need for a deeper understanding of the more fundamental features of the market-place. In seeking insights into these issues marketing followed the example of the other social sciences and looked to the model of empiricism, objective and systematic study, set by the natural sciences.

The 'science' of research

The question whether marketing research is a 'scientific' pursuit raises issues which are central to the study of human behaviour. The founders of the three major disciplines from which much marketing thought has evolved, sociology, psychology and economics, saw the 'scientific' status of the enquiry as a matter of considerable importance:

> Our principle . . . demands that the sociologist puts himself in the same state of mind as the physicist, chemist or physiologist when he probes into a still unexplored region of the scientific domain.
>
> Emile Durkheim[11]

> The goal of psychological study is the ascertaining of such data and laws that, given the stimulus, psychology can predict what the response will be; or on the other hand, given the response, it can specify the nature of the effective stimulus.
>
> John B. Watson[12]

> The . . . period, from 1820–1830, was notable in England for the lively scientific activity which took place in the field of political economy.
>
> Karl Marx[13]

These writers saw the achievements of the natural scientists as evidence of the enormous power of the approach to investigation employed by workers in these fields. Adoption of a scientific approach was therefore seen as the best route to matching their achievements. However, this attitude is strongly challenged by others. Some question the relevance of this approach to the complex and changing world of human behaviour, while others doubt the scope for working within the basic disciplines of scientific methodology. The two major elements of these disciplines are a firm commitment to empiricism, i.e. the importance of observation and experimentation, and the search for objectivity by researchers. Beyond these there is no general consensus on the specific nature of a science.[14] The key points are: the relative status of scientific knowledge versus other forms, e.g. common sense; the roles of theories, laws, hypotheses and models; and the relationship of the hypothesis, the law, the model and the theory.

In modern marketing research we can see examples of the two broad approaches to the accumulation of knowledge and the explanation of behaviour which exist in the social sciences.

1 Inductivism: the observation of the world with a view to identifying regularities which are, once tested by repeated empirical studies, then raised to the status of universal laws.
2 Deductivism (encompassed by the hypothetico-deductive theory of explanation): 'explanations require the adducing of general laws, with the status of empirical hypotheses about the natural order, from which, in conjunction with statements of initial conditions, we can deductively infer statements about empirical consequences',[15] which are then subject to attempts at falsification.

In the overall approach to statistical inference in some modern research there are clear links with the inductivist approach.

Ehrenberg[16] indicates that several hundred cases examined support the relationship (but provides no clues as to how the relationship fits existing knowledge).

The approach of Zaltman et al.[17] is much closer to the deductivist approach, with its nine steps:

1 Assessment of relevant existing knowledge.
2 Concept formulation and specification of hypotheses.
3 Acquisition of meaningful data.
4 Organizing and analysing data in relevant ways.
5 Evaluating and learning from results.
6 Dissemination of research information.
7 Providing explanations.
8 Making predictions.
9 Engaging in necessary control activities.

But with a vital tenth step: integration into existing stock of knowledge.

Both routes are part of powerful strands of scientific knowledge, the former encompassing Bacon, Copernicus and J. S. Mill, the latter Newton, Laplace and, more recently, Popper.

As Hesketh[18] states, 'marketing research is as close to science as we get in this field', when properly conducted with rigour, objectivity and a clear empirical base. Although the emphasis is on the 'scientific' method, there are different ideas of precisely what that means, and it is important that the notion that creativity and insight have no role is avoided. The history of science abounds with individuals whose methodological discipline was a launching pad for their genius, not a straitjacket.

Research in the firm

Despite the importance of information to effective marketing, there is a tendency in many firms narrowly to define the role of the market or marketing research department as simply to gather data, and this is a role which has been welcomed by some researchers whose dedication to their methodologies outweighs their desire to make a real contribution to corporate effectiveness.

Many involved in both marketing and research recognize that this approach diminishes the contribution that research can make to improving the quality of planning and decision-making, as well as more conventional information-gathering to answer more or less urgent questions. In playing this larger part in the firm's activities the fundamental disciplines retain their importance but become part of a larger system of information and knowledge.

For many firms the first step towards this means giving a manager specific responsibility for marketing research or establishing a marketing research department.

Market research deals with data for specific studies or to a particular brief, and usually involves specific aspects of customer or buyer behaviour. Most of this work involves a combination of secondary (employing existing sources) and primary (original studies usually involving direct market contact) data. Sales research is generally associated with the analysis of patterns of customer behaviour as manifested in purchase patterns or through syndicated research. It attempts to forecast sales or quantitative response to specific company actions. Invariably there is considerable overlap between these two areas of the firm's research activity.

As research departments have grown or been started by firms, management of their relationships with outside agencies has become a large part of their work. Very few manufacturers, financial institutions or service companies can fully employ a substantial, national field force of researchers. The market research agency (including the large research departments of advertising agencies who work to outside clients' briefs) can do this, as well as providing the variety to keep staff motivated, giving clients access to different levels of expertise, skill, and objectivity.

Although some agencies with field forces will simply recruit respondents from a firm's own staff to interview, most clients avail themselves of a wider array of agency services. Most marketing research departments are active in reviewing prospective agencies, assisting marketing management in the formulation of briefs, briefing agencies, helping with the analysis of information, participating in the dissemination of acquired knowledge, and setting quality standards and managing costs. To perform these tasks effectively, while contributing to the general activity of the department, requires staff of very high calibre. Research managers in particular must be able to deal with the techniques involved, at the same time contributing their and their department's special skills to corporate policy and decision-making. Research managers, to realize the inherent potential of the area, require direct access of decision-makers to play their full role in business development.

Briefing for research

In order for these tasks to be undertaken efficiently the relevance and quality of the information collected must be carefully scrutinized. Nowhere is the saying 'rubbish in, rubbish out' more true than in the process of briefing for a research study.

Deciding on the topic to be examined is central to all scientific investigation. Unfortunately, it is often glossed over in some broad description of an area of interest with few clear clues to specific issues or likely courses of action.

In a succinct and practical paper on the subject, Ehrenberg[19] proposes seven basic rules for effective briefing for a marketing problem. The research brief should:

1 Mean the same thing to all concerned. This may call for detailed discussion of the problem and the goals of the marketing staff. It is better to invest time before the study than lament failure afterwards. Often the research firm's proposal for the study following its briefing highlights these misunderstandings.

2 Not ask for irrelevant information. All research involves some pay-offs between cost and time. Irrelevances cost time and money and can easily detract from the time spent on the substantial issues, as well as clouding the findings.

3 Define the population(s) to be sampled. This focuses attention on the specific contribution that the particular sample is seen as making to the project's findings.

4 State the variables to be measured. Most activity likely to be researched is multi-dimensional, involving many variables. A rigorous approach here will force managers to review their existing knowledge carefully as well as making them think through the problem fully.

5 Give some indication of the required accuracy of the results. Almost all research is geared to planned or likely action by the firm, so a clear view of the likely course of action and the criteria for judging results will be of importance in designing a good brief.

6 Give an order of priority for the required accuracy of the various specified breakdown analyses.

7 Ensure that the research brief does not prejudge the selection of research techniques and procedures.

The scope of research

The scope of research which can be encompassed by this type of brief is enormous. A number of typologies have been put forward, of which the most generally accepted is that of Crisp, which is as follows.[20]

1 *Research on markets:*
    (a)   analysing market potentials for existing products and estimating demand for new products;
    (b)   sales forecasting;
    (c)   characteristics of product markets;
    (d)   analysing sales potentials;
    (e)   studying trends in markets.

2 *Research on products:*
    (a)   customer acceptance of proposed new products;
    (b)   comparative studies of competitive products;
    (c)   determining new uses of present products;
    (d)   market testing proposed products;
    (e)   studying customer dissatisfaction with products;
    (f)   product-line research;
    (g)   packaging and design studies.

3 *Research on promotion:*
   (a)   evaluating advertising effectiveness;
   (b)   analysing advertising and selling practices;
   (c)   selecting advertising media;
   (d)   motivational studies;
   (e)   establishing sales territories;
   (f)   evaluating present and proposed sales methods;
   (g)   studying competitive pricing;
   (h)   analysing salesmen's effectiveness;
   (i)   establishing sales quotas.

4 *Research on distribution:*
   (a)   location and design of distribution centres;
   (b)   handling and packing merchandise;
   (c)   cost analysis of transportation methods;
   (d)   dealer supply and storage requirements.

5 *Research on pricing:*
   (a)   demand elasticities:
   (b)   perceived prices;
   (c)   cost analysis;
   (d)   margin analysis.

Even this list, however, fails to encompass such important areas as international and export studies, economic and business forecasting, lifestyle research and corporate responsibility research.

Research, like most other areas of marketing, responds quickly to developments and new ideas. Until fairly recently motivational research was seen as being very important, but now interest has shifted to lifestyle and psychographics or qualitative research. Overall there is a constant process of accretion, with the basic skills and techniques constantly supplemented by new ideas. There are considerable variations across Europe in the client base of research firms (see Table 6.1).

Table 6.1 Sources of market research revenues

	Manufacturing %	Services %	Advertising agencies %	(Semi) government %	Wholesale/ retail %	Research organizations %	Other %
Belgium	35	20	10	10	10	15	0
Denmark	20	10	15	15	10	20	10
France	50	19	4	11	6	4	6*
Germany	61	9	5	13	4	4	4
Greece	64	7	9	4	2	7	7
Ireland	40	35	5	8	5	5	2
Italy	61	9	5	7	3	3	12
Luxembourg	3	20	10	30	10	27	0
Netherlands	40	23	3	15	10	9	0*
Portugal	48	5	19	6	4	13	5*
Spain	51	8	11	9	7	6	8*
UK	50	16	4	4	3	n/a	23
EC average	52	14	5	9	5	4	10

*Estimate based on average of comparable countries.
Sources: Trade associations and estimates: other countries data not available.
Quoted in Miles, L, 'Leader of the Pack', *Marketing Business,* January 1993.

Agencies undertake a range of work for different clients. Although non-consumer goods companies are the majority of clients, consumer market research, especially for fast-moving consumer goods, forms a large part of the work undertaken, especially in terms of total expenditure.

Secondary sources

The search through secondary sources ('data neither collected directly by the user nor specifically for the user, often under conditions that are not well known to the user'[21]) should be the first step in any marketing research project. It is sometimes called desk research, although this may encompass a slightly broader operation, involving the collection of information from internal staff, salesmen and even outside individuals.

The firm itself is a vast store of marketing intelligence, ranging from the insights of top management to the detailed, day-to-day information held by delivery or sales staff. The major sources of quantitative material are:

1 Production: output, inventory, costs, utilization etc.
2 Distribution: goods in transit, stock levels and locations; stock turn rates and absolute throughput.
3 Purchasing: costs, rate of change of costs, materials, sources.
4 Sales: distribution and location of accounts, value and volume of trade, major developments.
5 Marketing services: expenditure, forecasts of turnover or likely developments.
6 Finance: costs, depreciation, overheads etc.
7 Personnel: staff and wage costs, trends, shortages and efficiency levels.

Much of this information can be matched with industry statistics collected and distributed by trade associations, industry research associations and, in specific contexts, chambers of commerce and development agencies.

The Information Revolution of the middle of the twentieth century emerged as large numbers of organizations became involved in the gathering of data. This has created a rich field of potential insight for the marketing person. Although the development of data processing systems has greatly facilitated the handling of this material, coping with the sheer scale of the information does pose many problems.[22]

The Information Revolution of the 1980s added a new dimension to this with electronic transmission of information through CompuServe, Janet and other systems.

Government and international agencies

In Britain researchers are fortunate in having access to invaluable directories of both UK and international marketing information, through organizations like Dun and Bradstreet.[23] The task of keeping this material up to date is generally beyond the scope of any individual or commercial concern, although magazines such as *British Business* play a vital role here. Fortunately the Central Statistical Office (CSO)[24] of the UK has adopted a very positive marketing-orientated approach.

Figure 6.1 The range of work that agencies do for different clients.
Source: Goodyear, J. R., 'The Structure of the British Market Research Industry', *Journal of the Market Research Society*, 31, No. 4, 1989, p. 429

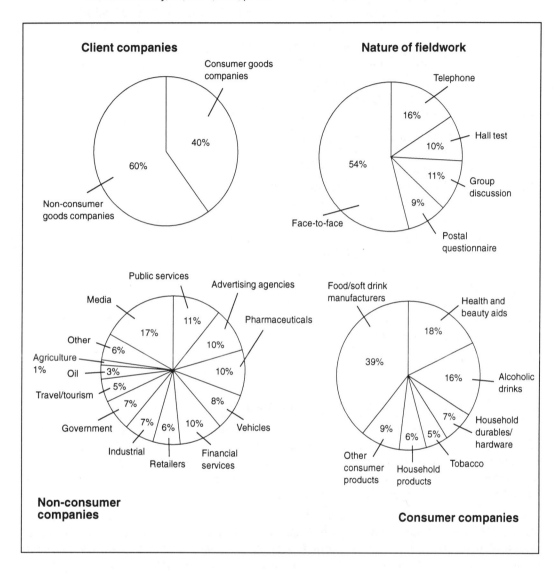

Many other countries have a similar interest in providing a statistical picture of their country and its economy. International and export marketing researchers should be familiar with the data provided in their target market, for example, *Statistical Abstract of the US*, US Department of Commerce.[25]

International bodies such as the United Nations,[26] EU[27] and OECD[28] are making a growing contribution. It is impossible to list more than a few organizations and publications here, but important sources are:

1 United Nations:[29]
   (a) Directory of International Statistics
   (b) Demographic Yearbook
   (c) Yearbook of Industrial Statistics (formerly Growth of the World Industry)
   (d) Statistical Yearbook
   (e) Yearbook of National Accounts Statistics
   (f) Monthly Bulletin of Statistics

2 International Monetary Fund:[30]
   (a) Balance of Payments Yearbook
   (b) Direction of Trade (annual).

3 Statistical Office of the European Communities:[31]
   (a) General Statistical Bulletin
   (b) Agricultural Trade in Europe (various reports)
   (c) Bulletin of the European Communities
   (d) Economic Survey of Europe

4 Organisation for Economic Co-operation and Development:[32]
   (a) Economic Surveys of Member Countries
   (b) Economic Outlook (biannual)
   (c) Consumer Price Indices (monthly)
   (d) Financial Statistics
   (e) Food Consumption Statistics
   (f) International Tourism and Tourist Policies in OECD Member Countries
   (g) Main Economic Indicators.

Much of this information is now available electronically, e.g. on CD ROM or over the Internet.

Commercial and semi-official sources

General data. The main sources of general data are: the Statistical Information Service at Warwick University Library;[33] Extel Statistical Services; the British Middle Market Directory (Dun and Bradstreet[34]); the Guide to Key British Enterprises (Dun and Bradstreet[35]); and Companies House.[36] Most banks also offer their clients some form of economic or commercial information service.

Specific data. Data specific to particular areas of business activity or industry can be obtained from: trade associations, identifiable through the Directory of British Associations (CBD Research[37]) (most offer a very limited service to non-members); industry research associations, generally restricted to members; the Advertising Association;[38] the Incorporated Society of British Advertisers;[39] the Institute of Practitioners in Advertising;[40] the Confederation of British Industry;[41] the Market Research Society;[42] the Chartered Institute of Marketing.[43] Some advertising and research agencies also issue special bulletins or reports on particular issues and general topics.

A number of organizations publish excellent subscription-based industry or marketing studies: *Retail Business; Mintel;*[44] *IPC Consumer Marketing Manual;* and *IPC Industrial Marketing Manual.*

Occasionally, studies of specific markets are published by research companies, e.g. *British Toys and Games Industry,* Jordan Dataquest Limited, London.

Research for overseas markets. Research for overseas markets is carried out by broadly the same set of organizations. In most countries this is complemented by the work of the national export promotion bureau. A number of commercial UK and international research agencies are active in this field of published information: Economist Intelligence Unit,[45] Marketing in Europe, *Multinational Business* and *International Tourism Quarterly;* Frost and Sullivan Ltd,[46] special industry studies, e.g. *Food Service: USA;* Predicasts Inc., *Plastic Trends,* etc.

Libraries

Every student and researcher should become familiar with the rich store of information available throughout the UK in libraries: local, central, college and university, industry and trade associations. Even relatively small local libraries are likely to have various relevant publications and the central libraries of the major cities such as Birmingham, Manchester, Bristol, Liverpool, Newcastle, Glasgow and Cardiff have specialist staff and a large stock of material. (Birmingham Public Library and a number of others publish short guides to their business information collection.)

Colleges and universities frequently have major data sources and subscribe to such periodicals as *Retail Business.* Many universities have enormous stocks of economic information, although some have much to learn from the colleges about making it available to industry.

Industry research associations, trade associations, chambers of commerce and specialized bodies such as the Advertising Association,[47] the Institute of Management[48] and the Chartered Institute of Marketing[49] frequently hold material relevant to their members or specialization.

Particularly important libraries are: The City Business Library;[50] the Statistics and Market Intelligence Library; the University of Warwick Library,[51] Birmingham Central Library;[52] the British Library of Political and Economic Science[53] and the libraries at London[54] and Manchester Business Schools.[55]

Electronic media

Electronic transmission of information is transforming both the range of available information sources and the ways of handling information. Two basic forms exist. Teletext is transmitted through the broadcast media of the BBC[56] (Ceefax) and the IBA (Oracle). Although Teletext is useful, more commercial material is organized through Viewdata, which provides access to a vast store of data through the telephone network. The real breakthroughs come through interactive (two-way) systems such as Janet, CompuServe and other on-line databases.

It is impossible to arrive at accurate figures about the use of the Internet. In 1996, Hoffman[57] estimated that 37 million Americans had access to the Internet, with roughly 18 million people using the Internet. The best estimate is that US usage accounts for roughly half the world usage. The resources available on the Internet are virtually limitless.[58] Despite this, potential use of the web for marketing is uneven. The problems have led firms like Werbal Advertising[59] to publish guidelines and checklists.

Primary studies (Field research)

Field research provides access to primary information, normally through direct contact with consuming, buying, intermediary or influencing groups. As indicated above, the specific design of field research should be based on a thorough review of secondary sources of information and a carefully designed and agreed brief. Research is generally divisible into qualitative and quantitive studies for one of a number of client groups, e.g. consumer, industrial, intermediary, commercial or governmental.

Although quantitative studies commissioned by consumer-goods producers and the government tend to dominate research activity, there has recently been a growth in qualititative research and research commissioned by industrial and commercial firms, notably banking and tourism.

Sampling

Once a project is initiated the first decisions normally involve the sample of respondents to be studied. 'A sample is a subgroup selected from the market, chosen usually to provide insights into a larger population with a view to drawing general conclusions about the population.'[60]

In research, samples are generally used instead of censuses (surveys of the total group), primarily on the grounds of cost and speed. In some limited industrial studies, however, the prospective purchasing population is small enough to justify a census.

The skill in sampling determines to a considerable extent the degree to which accurate statements about the total population can confidently be made. Two important factors are the sample size and selection of the sample.

The size is usually computed on the basis of acceptable levels of accuracy. The extensive literature in the field highlights the importance of this decision, which is occasionally influenced by cost factors. All too often decisions or findings are based on samples with little statistical credibility, especially when sub-samples of the main group are discussed; e.g. rejection by 1 per cent of the population in socio-economic groups A and B living in the Merseyside area and aged over 35 might mean rejection by only one hundred people.

P. G. Moore[61] identifies four basic approaches to selecting samples:

1   Random sampling: every member of the population has an equal and constant chance of being selected.
2   Systematic sampling: a set numerical routine is used to select the sample, e.g. every twentieth passer-by or house.
3   Stratified sampling: this attempts to bring out the differences which may exist in particular strata or groups in the population. Quotas are often used by the researcher to achieve this; i.e. the interviewer is given a quota of respondents in a group.
4   Cluster sampling: the respondents are selected on the basis of their grouping or clustering around a particular area or location. They may then be randomly selected within this area.

Although these approaches were developed primarily for use in quantitative studies, they can provide a framework for selecting respondents in a qualitative study. It must, however, be recognized that a qualitative study is not a substitute for quantitative investigation.

Piloting

Far too often the pilot study is omitted. However it plays a vital part in both interview approach development and questionnaire design. It should be carefully planned and the objectives clearly understood. The goal of the pilot is to assist in the development of full-scale investigations, and this should be borne in mind when briefing the interviewers and designing the format of the questionnaire. The pilot study should not be confused with 'dip-stick' research (designed to obtain a quick and limited insight into the market) carried out by managers who start looking for conclusions about the substance of the investigation rather than the research design.

Researchers in the UK have available to them the Market Research Society's *Handbook for Interviewers*.[62] This provides a practical guide to the problems and issues associated with the personal interview. Interviewing, however, is only one of a number of methods of establishing a direct link between the firm and the respondent in order to gather data, as Table 6.2 shows.

Table 6.2 Research methods other than personal interview and experimentation

Method	Some uses	Some advantages	Some disadvantages
Telephone	When simultaneous interviews are needed; when individual calls are very far apart.	Cost, speed.	Lack of rapport, interviews must be fairly short, cannot use showcards or pictures, low incidence of telephone ownership.
Mail	When respondents are difficult to contact.	Cost, no interviewer 'interference'.	Unrepresentative sample, lack of control of questionnaire completion.
Self-completion	When interview should be carried out but interviewer cannot be present.	Cost, accuracy of reporting close to action reported.	As with mail survey (e.g. misunderstanding bias; only short questionnaire possible).
Psycho-galvanometer	When respondent unlikely to be aware of own responses.	Prestige and similar answers need not be considered.	Unreal surroundings, little data about 'why', cost of large samples.
Tachistoscope etc.	To test detailed physical behaviour, particularly of eye reaction.	Ability to measure action in a detail not available by other methods.	Unreal surroundings, little data about 'why', cost of large samples.
Count	When requirement implies total numbers of people involved in certain actions.	Cost, speed, large samples.	Little data about 'why', no analysis possible by profile of individual.
Observation	When the concern is more with how people act than why.	Direct observation of what people do rather than what they say they do.	Cost, sample structure.
Participant observation	When only information at a very detailed level is of value.	Depth of response.	Very high cost and very long time taken, problems of representative sample.
Syndicated Research	Where regular insights into behaviour patterns needed	Low cost and regular insight.	Limited control.
Mystery Shopping	The direct purchase link gives researchers 'purchase' experience.	Immediate picture of way customer treated.	High cost. Blurs line between research and behaviour.
Focus Group	Gains understanding of group behaviour.	Highlights group nature of such action.	High cost and subject to interviewer bias.

It is in situations involving direct personal contact with the respondent that the role of the interviewer is of real importance. Personal interviewing calls for a range of professional skills normally requiring careful selection, training and close monitoring of the staff involved. In most consumer research the interviewing is conducted by part-time staff. This places a special responsibility on the firm to ensure that the field force of researchers is well managed; the briefing for the project carefully conducted; the piloting involves the field force; continual effort is invested in minimizing 'interviewer bias', and close control and monitoring of the work of the field force is carried out. (Interviewer bias is the introduction of bias into the research situation behaviour, comment, appearance or other features of the interviewer.)

In industrial markets there is a far higher likelihood of the interview being conducted by the research company's own full-time staff. They can bring a high level of training, skill and knowledge into situations which may require the ability to probe and analyse in the course of the interviews. Despite this, the basic control and management disciplines retain their role. In industrial situations careful management is necessary to maintain a level of consistency and comparability between interviews.

Questionnaires

The questionnaire is central to proper management of the interaction between researcher and interviewees. The basic rules of good questionnaire design are easy to state – keep it short, keep it simple and make sure that it is understood – but very difficult to put into practice. This is because the purpose is usually to elicit meaningful answers, from what is often a large and disparate group of respondents, to questions which may have little immediate relevance to those interviewed.

Planning the questionnaire is very important. The briefing, the initial discussion and the pilot all provide clues to the key issues under investigation, the forms of response required and likely reactions to particular formats, and these should be built into the overall structure of the questionnaire. The effect of the sequence of questions has been widely discussed and the following pattern found useful:

1. Open with a few factual, easy-response questions.
2. Lead into a small number of factual multiple-choice questions.
3. Follow with questions designed to gauge whether the interviewee has thought about or knows about the topic(s) under review.
4. Move into a series of structured and semi-structured questions designed to cover very specific issues.
5. Introduce a selection of open-ended or wide-open questions so that the respondent can fully express him- or herself.
6. Close with 'filter' questions, i.e. questions designed to locate the respondent according to the sampling frame.

In the questionnaire, some double-check questions to check for consistency of response and control questions to compare answers with information from other sources are invaluable.

Although this framework works in most situations it is not a universal model. The brief, the topic, the sample and the pilot determine the appropriate structure for each situation.

Questionnaires are part of a broader research study, so it is their overall contribution that is important. Computer-based data-handling techniques are normally used to handle aggregate data, so coding frames and the pattern of information should be borne in mind when designing the questionnaire.

The rules mentioned earlier – simple, short and easily understood – are doubly relevant to specific questions within the overall goal of gathering the required information. Respondents often fail to understand the interviewer's questions fully. Common causes of these failures are: ambiguity; the use of unfamiliar words; difficult and abstract concepts; overloading the respondent with too many instructions; vague concepts; and trying to ask two questions in one. Questionnaire and question design in industrial market research pose special problems for the researcher. The project may probe highly specialized areas where:

1 Technical terminology in the questions is unavoidable, posing real problems for the interviewer.
2 There may be only a small number of possible respondents in a particular sphere.
3 Major problems and reservations about confidentiality can occur.

Careful control of the response rates is essential to all forms of questionnaire-based research. Although it is virtually impossible to avoid some level of non-response, particularly in mail or telephone studies, sustained follow-up to minimize it and a close watch on its possible effects are necessary.

Completion of the fieldwork is not the end of a research effort. The project was set up to make a contribution to policy formulation and decision-making and to assist in resolving certain issues. The presentation of the findings and their dissemination are therefore two critical final steps.

Presentation usually involves a written and a verbal report. The Market Research Society's[63] minimum acceptable content of a written report involves overall purpose and specific objectives, details of the principals and researchers, a description of the population covered, sample and sampling frame, methodology, details of research staff, timings, the question-naire, findings, the data base and locations of interviews.

The report must face up to the problems posed by the client. The researcher has the responsibility to ensure that technical terminology which may be necessary for effective communication between specialist researchers does not become a barrier to understanding for the non-expert general marketing staff.

So far, discussion has concentrated on questionnaire-based studies. However, other approaches to market intelligence-gathering, experimentation and observation also have an important role to play.

Experimentation

Experimentation is the cornerstone of investigation in the natural sciences, and as such it has always been of special interest to the behavioural scientists. Its use, however, in the social sciences is restricted by the difficulties of setting up experimental situations and the dangers of the experimental situation itself affecting the research behaviour. Despite these difficulties the need to study, under certain circumstances, in a closely monitored situation, specific behaviour and responses has led many researchers to sustain their commitment to experimental marketing.

'A subject that covers the entire range of situations involved when a company first decides to introduce changes into a small part of its market so as to gain information before becoming committed to innovation on a wider scale.' In using this definition we go beyond the traditional area in which experimentation is used – test marketing of new products – into a much broader sphere of testing changes in controlled market situations.

As an area of investigation it has the scope for providing management with the opportunity to explore the impact of their ideas and developments in the real world. Attention is focused not on respondents' intentions or stated attitudes, but on their actual behaviour. The potential power of the approach is matched by the need for considerable skill in setting up the experiments and rigour in their application. Without doubt it is the most demanding area of marketing research.

To overcome some of the problems associated with real-world experiments, many companies have explored the scope for simulation. Simulation involves:

> The process of modelling things, problems or concepts.
>
> Definitions Committee of AMA

> Techniques for manipulating a model of some real-world process for the purpose of finding numerical solutions that are useful in the real process that is being modelled.[64]

Although there is considerable interest in this approach, particularly in the US, its contribution in the UK is largely confined to new product development, physical distribution and brand choice. There is continuing interest in its use in other areas and the scope for its simplification in order to overcome the recurrent problem of complexity in simulation research techniques, especially as the speed of PCs increases and the cost of processing power drops.

Observation

Observation is an approach that is extensively used in the social sciences and plays a major role in a number of important studies of behaviour, notably in the workplace and the small community.[65] The basic idea is that by watching the behaviour of specific respondents in controlled situations researchers can gain insights into their reactions. Its most popular uses are:

1 *Direct observation:* examining how people behave in specific situations. Although until recently direct observation was largely confined to retail studies, a number of industrial researchers are now exploring its use, notably for views of how machinery is used and opportunity spotting.
2 *Recording devices:* in this controversial area a number of electromechanical devices have been developed for monitoring respondents' reactions. Two commonly used devices are the eye camera, for recording eye movements (generally in advertising testing) and the psychogalvanometer, for measuring perspiration as a gauge of involuntary physical response, usually to advertisements.

The real value of observational studies lies in their ability to describe routines and patterns of behaviour. The nature of the approach calls for the researcher to infer causality if that is sought by the study.

Qualitative research[66]

As well as the data provided by quantitative studies of the market size and composition, there exists a mass of material required for a deeper understanding of the customer. Perception, motivations and attitudes cannot readily be discovered at an acceptable cost in large-scale quantitative studies. Qualitative research focuses on the less easily measured facets of perceptions, thoughts, motivations and attitudes in new, unfamiliar or changing markets. It deals in concepts rather than numbers.

There are three basic methods of inquiry:

1 *Non-directive group discussion:* this brings together members of the target group to explore and discuss specified themes. The 'group' situation can lead to a heightened willingness to contribute besides highlighting the special features of group-influenced behaviour.

2 *Non-directive individual interview:* this provides the opportunity to examine in depth the respondent's behaviour, attitudes, opinions and needs. It is particularly relevant in industrial market research where in-depth analysis of confidential material is sought.

3 *Projective techniques:* these involve different forms of stimuli – story-boards, sentence completion, Rorschach ink blot tests – to prompt the respondent to talk in an unstructured manner about specific topics. By letting the respondent range freely over a subject it is hoped that some unconscious or hitherto unmentioned views will emerge.

Qualitative studies play a significant role in current research, but place tremendous demands on the skills of the researcher and those involved in briefing and reporting.[67]

Syndicated research

Syndicated research is performed for a combination of firms involved in a sphere of activity which provides the research firm with scope to conduct large-scale and regular studies of a selection of consistent topics. In Britain it takes four basic forms: trade audits, consumer panels, omnibus surveys and TV ratings.

The general pattern of development involves the identification of a broad sphere of activity, e.g. consumer purchasing or fast-moving non-durables. The research firm conducts regular studies of a sample, providing a number of clients with the information gathered.

Trade audits

Trade audits are conducted among panels of wholesalers and retailers. The research firm sends 'auditors' into the selected outlets on a regular basis to count stock and record deliveries, this providing a measure of throughput. From their raw data a number of basic tabulations can be produced, notably consumer sales, stocks, price and brand distribution. A firm may find that, although its sent-out sales (from the factory) are high, retail stocks are growing rapidly. This may require immediate corrective action. Another company might note a weakness in a specific type of outlet, e.g. retail off-licences, and specific tactics can be considered to overcome this problem.

A number of highly specialized services have emerged, notably specialized area studies, e.g. Nielsen Drug Index, Nielsen Food Index etc., special analysis of particular topics, and test market studies. The leading retail audit company in Britain is A. C. Nielsen and Co.[68]

Consumer panels

Consumer panels provide a continuous survey of a consistent and large sample of consumers. A complete picture of their purchasing pattern is built up over time, and this provides an incomparable base for statistical and econometric analysis of patterns of behaviour.

Two types of panel exist: home audit (an auditor visits the home to check purchases, stocks and used cartons, wrappers etc.) and diary panel (the respondent completes, on a daily, weekly or other regular basis, a diary of his or her purchasing). Panels are either long term or set up on a short-term basis to study specific patterns or situations. A later development was the establishment of specialist panels in certain markets.

The availability of continuous time-series data provides the framework for the use of sophisticated forecasting and diagnostic techniques in research. One of the earliest uses of consumer-panel data was in Brown's classic studies of loyalty and repeat purchasing.[69] This broad approach is employed by several specialist companies.

Omnibus surveys

As implied by their name, omnibus surveys represent attempts by firms to minimize the costs of surveys by participating in a single large study made up of a large number of small questionnaires.

Normally, responsibility for designing the firm's questions lies within the client company. They will invariably be required to meet certain conditions imposed by the research company concerning number, location and support materials. As the majority of omnibus surveys are operated on a continuous basis the firm will be able to build up a picture of performance over time, as well as making savings.

TV ratings

TV ratings are probably the most famous forms of syndicated research. They are sponsored by television companies to build up a picture of patterns of viewing behaviour. A number of different approaches are used, notably:

1 *Meter recording of sets:* a meter is attached to the set to monitor the precise times of watching and the channels (and hence the programmes) viewed. (As the meter is automatic there is no guarantee that the viewer is actually in front of the set.)
2 *Interviewing:* this is conducted soon after the evening's viewing. A mixture of aided (prompted) and unaided (non-prompted) recall approaches are used.

Mystery shopping

This is the fastest growing aspect of marketing research. Researchers visit outlets as 'customers' to test services, products and delivery. Results of their purchasing are integrated into reviews of the ways outlets respond to true purchase situations.

Special areas of study

So far the particular problems associated with areas such as industrial market research were noted as the discussion progressed. A few comments are necessary about the major non-consumer goods fields: industrial market research; services, notably finance, research; and non-profit organizations. All require special skills and disciplines for effective marketing research.

Industrial marketing research

Industrial marketing research usually calls for grounding in the specific industries being studied. When managers who have used industrial marketing research are interviewed they frequently complain that researchers have not thoroughly conducted preliminary investigations. It is often difficult to identify the responsible decision-makers in the areas being studied, since formal job titles may have only limited relevance to the work done. In many instances no one individual is responsible; a purchasing coalition (formal or informal) may exist. Respondents are likely to be more conscious of the real cost of their time, so this calls for a disciplined approach to questionnaire length.

Services

The major banks, unit trusts and insurance companies conduct research regularly. They often work in areas that are personal and often highly confidential, e.g. salaries, tax, investments. Respondent reservations are made greater by the use of false questionnaires by some firms. Research here therefore requires considerable tact to overcome these problems.

Non-profit organizations

Probably the largest sponsors of research in Britain are government and the local authorities. Studies of social problems, leisure and the elderly are increasingly important parts of the research environment. Much of this research is focused on the poor, the aged and the disabled, groups which have in the past posed considerable recruitment and communication problems for researchers.

There is increasing interest among non-government, non-profit-making bodies, from pressure groups to colleges. This has been marked by an almost anti-professional stance by those conducting the research, and has usually been associated with unsystematic and subjective accumulations of dubious information. Although it is possible to self-conduct limited types of research, the disciplined approach still retains its importance.

Marketing information systems

The collection, communication and dissemination of data in all areas is seen by more and more marketing people and researchers as part of the continuing process of building up a corporate marketing information system.

The notion of constructing marketing information systems is fundamental to the entire approach of this chapter. Marketing intelligence is the life-blood of the firm. It is not sufficient that it exists; managers must be in a position to use it to formulate policies, make decisions and resolve problems. As such the marketing information system is best described as:

> A structured, interacting complex of persons, machines and procedures designed to generate an orderly flow of pertinent information, collected from both intra- and extra-firm sources, for use as bases for decision-making in specified responsibility areas of marketing management.[70]

All the salient features of good MIS design are encapsulated in this definition:

1 'A structured, interacting complex of persons, machines and procedures': it is carefully planned and constructed to achieve the maximum pay-offs for the organization, within specified goals.
2 'An orderly flow of pertinent information': this emphasizes the need for the patterns of communication to be thought through to ensure that those needing the information get it at the right time and in the required form, but at the same time ensuring that other managers are not swamped by irrelevant material.

3 'From intra- and extra-firm sources': the total network of contacts with the environment and sources of relevant data are effectively tapped and built into the system.

4 'Bases for decision-making': these flows of material are directed to the areas of need, where new information can help managers to more effectively resolve problems or minimize the risks involved in their decisions.

Constructing a marketing information system calls for a careful study of both the information needs of the company and its managers and the methods of acquiring the material required.

As early as 1972 Briscoe[71] identified the problems faced by the British Steel Corporation in matching the various sources of marketing intelligence with the information needs of management. Later, Jobber and Rainbow[72] found that almost 50 per cent of the large firms responding to a questionnaire on the topic had established, or were in the process of establishing, a marketing information system. By the mid-1990s most consumer and a large majority of industrial marketing companies had well-established marketing information systems. The advent of the microprocessor is creating many new opportunities and demands for system design and use. Now, Marketing Research gains much of its value from its incorporation in corporate marketing information systems.

Decision analysis

One of the primary roles of market and marketing research is to gather information to assist managers to resolve uncertainties, generally with a view to more effective or lower-risk decision-making. Information cannot make these decisions or eliminate the risks. As information cannot eliminate the risk, but merely reduces it, some might ask why money should be spent on collecting it. It is the issue which is faced by modern theories of decision, notably the Bayesian approach to decision-making under conditions of uncertainty.

Although there is not the scope for a full review of this complex and controversial topic here, the major aspects are:

1 It is possible to identify for any decision a series of likely outcomes.
2 These outcomes can be identified and the returns for the firm in each situation detailed.
3 A subjective probability can be assigned to each outcome.
4 By multiplying each outcome by the appropriate probability and summing, the products and expected return can be established.
5 Where a manager has imperfect information upon which to base his probabilities, he can elect to gather more information if the value of the additional information is greater than the cost of obtaining it.

Bayesian statistics provide a framework for handling this computational problem.

Conclusion

Marketing research is one of the most dynamic and rapidly developing areas of study and effort in modern marketing. In Britain large numbers of skilled managers and researchers are actively involved in improving and developing research techniques and working on approaches to the effective managerial use of market information. It is a context in which both the power of discipline and the potential of creativity must come together to produce more effective company marketing. The breakthrough made possible by electronic systems will produce dramatic changes over the next few years.

SPECIMEN QUESTIONS

1   What distinguishes market research and marketing research?

2   Is marketing research a science?

3   It is sometimes suggested that the most common problems in questionnaire design are linked with the effort to ask too few questions in order to keep the interview as short as possible.

   (a)   Is this fair?

   (b)   What would be the negative and positive consequences of longer questionnaires?

4   Draw up a questionnaire to help a West End impresario:

   (a)   Gauge the audience reaction to his show.

   (b)   Establish ways in which the pricing and promotional policies might be improved.

   (c)   Decide how long to keep the show running.

5   'Dish Sales Disappoint' was the newspaper comment about the sales of satellite dishes in the UK. Outline a programme of research to identify the reasons for low sales among one of the following groups: couples with young families; socio-economic groups AB; single households; sports fans.

6   Outline the ways in which an Italian manufacturer of bicycles can use 'secondary sources' of information to establish the nature and extent of the opportunities for his products in the UK. How can the use of secondary sources of information help with design of a market research investigation?

7   What research problems are likely to face a company trying to undertake a study of the opportunities for their products in one of the following markets:

   (a)   The Czech Republic.

   (b)   China.

   (c)   Kenya.

   (d)   Pakistan.

8   It is common for the following disclaimer to be used when opinion poll results are presented in the media. 'These results are based on a sample survey of about 1,000 people and the figures are liable to sampling error of plus or minus 3%'
How adequate is this disclaimer in the context of total survey error?

9   Define:

   (a)   Market research.

   (b)   Interviewer bias.

   (c)   Qualitative research.

   (d)   Self-completion questionnaires.

   (e)   Deductivism.

   (f)   Primary sources of information.

   (g)   E-Mail.

   (h)   Sampling.

   (i)   Pilot studies.

   (j)   Observation studies.

10 The following data are results from a survey conducted among farmers on behalf of a manufacturer of agricultural machinery. During the interview, respondents were asked to rate the importance of a number of attributes, including four items relating to maintenance, in respect of:

(a) Tractors.

(b) Combine harvesters.

(c) Balers.

Other questions in the interview covered: size of farm, in hectares; crops grown; number of workers; age of farmer; number and make(s) owned of each of the three types of machine.

You have been asked by the Marketing Department (Tractor Division) to prepare a note on farmers' views on tractor maintenance. These data come from a preliminary analysis, a count of responses with the sample broken down by size of farm (200+ha; under 200ha).

Write a brief summary of these results, including any table(s) and/or chart(s) needed to illustrate your comments, and discuss the further analyses you would require in order to pursue any hypotheses arising.

		Total sample (300)	200+ ha farms (100)	20–199 ha farms (200)
(a)	*Availability of spare parts*			
	very important	73	27	46
	fairly important	174	54	120
	not important	45	17	28
	don't know	8	2	6
(b)	*Cost of spare parts*			
	very important	119	41	78
	fairly important	153	49	104
	not important	26	10	16
	don't know	2	0	2
(c)	*Access to factory-trained mechanics*			
	very important	85	3	82
	fairly important	62	18	44
	not important	152	78	74
	don't know	1	1	0
(d)	*Good instruction manual*			
	very important	7	5	2
	fairly important	110	56	54
	not important	176	36	140
	don't know	7	3	4

CASE STUDY 4:
PRICE AWARENESS IN THE TOILET SOAP MARKET

Background

The toilet soap market is a large, fairly stable market. Toilet soap is a household staple with a high purchase frequency. There are many brands but only a few major manufacturers: Procter and Gamble, Unilever Cussons and Colgate Palmolive. Demand is concentrated among the top five brands. There is a high brand advertising, industry advertising/sales (A/S) ratio, and earlier work indicates a relatively high degree of brand loyalty. However, price cutting is endemic and appears to be growing.

Objectives of the research

Putting ourselves in the position of a leading manufacturer we hope to discover:

1 Consumer price awareness: how knowledgeable consumers are about the price of a block of soap, particularly the brand they bought last and the brand they buy regularly (if different). As there is some variation in sizes, e.g. standard and bath, interest is focused on the size they purchased and the size they regularly purchase.

2 The relationship between awareness and the outlet from which the product is purchased. Thus we need to know:
   (a) where the product was bought;
   (b) whether that outlet stocks an own-label brand;
   (c) whether consumers consider purchasing the own-label brand;
   (d) where they do (or do not) buy it;
   (e) what the effect of the outlet is on the consumers' price perception.

3 The assumptions made about the consumer's knowledge of the price of other brands. Thus we need to know:
   (a) how aware customers are of the price of brands other than those recently or regularly purchased;
   (b) whether they actively compare prices in stores;
   (c) whether they compare the recommended prices, the size of the price cut or the final price;
   (d) whether there is any concept of a fair price for soap;
   (e) whether the research can support Gabor's contention that definable price brackets exist in a market.

Target population

Women aged between 25 and 55, with particular emphasis on married women with two or more children under 15.

Annual size/value of the market

The figures for production of toilet soap seem to offer very little indication of the probable trends in the retail market: variations between 107.2 and 70.9 thousand tonnes in 1962 and 1972 respectively (Table 6.3) seem to suggest a seriously declining volume in total in a period when, with rising standards of living, greater attention to hygiene and a growing population, one would expect that volume would be rising slowly.

The value of the retail market was estimated at £140–£170 million (1993).

Table 6.3 Production of toilet soap (000 tonnes)

1982	1983	1984	1987	1990	1992	1994
107.2	91.3	99.6	96.7	93.4	82.8	98.2

Table 6.4 Sales by UK manufacturers

	1992	1993
Home market/wholesale, retail, '000 tonnes	65	72
Home market/other	n.a.	5
Export	29	38

Principal advertisers and brands

(those spending £100 000 or more in 1993 or 1994)

Table 6.5 Press and TV advertising (£000)

Advertizer	Brand	1993 TV	Press	Total	(%)	1994 TV	Press	Total	(%)
Procter and Gamble	Camay	794	30	824	(27)	798	3	801	(23)
Cussons	Imperial Leather	488	–	488	(16)	648	31	679	(19)
Procter and Gamble	Fairy	410	–	410	(13)	386	8	394	(11)
Lever Bros	Lifebuoy	180	20	200	(7)	400	2	402	(11)
	Lux	414	11	326	(11)	425	2	427	(12)
Colgate	Palmolive	322	–	406	(13)	504	2	506	(14)
Gibbs	Pears	334	67	401	(13)	278	14	292	(8)
Total for group	'Soaps Toilet'	2942	128	3055	(100)	2660	305	3501	

Channels of distribution

The main channels of distribution are grocers (predominantly), variety stores, chemists and departmental stores. Supermarkets and self-service grocers may account for half of the purchases.

Indications of brand shares

The pattern presented suggests that the overall (or subgroup) leadership could be continually changing within the top brands.

Camay, Lifebuoy and Fairy are rather further behind Lux and Palmolive. Private-label brands were estimated to account for 16 per cent (including Boots).

Table 6.6 Brand choice

Lux	16%
Palmolive	16%
Cusson's Imperial Leather	15%
Fairy	15%
Camay	14%
Lifebuoy	14%
Boots	11%
Knights Castile	6%
Wrights' Coal Tar	5%

Other points of interest

Virtually all housewives buy toilet soap. Ten per cent were classified as 'heavy users' by TGI. On the other hand IPC recorded an 86 per cent usage level among women, for 'use on the face'. Non-users were biased towards younger women and towards London and the South East.

Below-the-line activity (price-offs etc.) is used very extensively in this market. Fairy is very heavily supported 'below the line': price-offs, coupons, sampling etc.

Heavy users occur disproportionately in the 35–44 age group, in the C2D class and among families with children aged 10–15 (TGI 1974). In this latter group 22 per cent of housewives were classified as 'heavy users'.

Decisions required

As the major manufacturers are engaged in considerable price competition, particularly through the major supermarket groups, we need to know the following:

1 Is this an efficient means of competing and can we consider discontinuing it?
2 Should we give greater prominence to price in our advertising?
3 Are brand-loyal customers impervious to price cutting, i.e. do they even bother checking?
4 How important are the brand-loyal customers and should we concentrate on giving them rewards, e.g. improved imagery?
5 Is our policy of giving bonuses and discounts to the supermarket groups paying off or are we merely lining ourselves up for price comparisons in store?
6 Does the concept of a fair price exist, and if so, what promotional or product development opportunities does it stimulate?
7 Can we identify any new brand or new product opportunities through pricing?

7

Buyers, consumers and influences

In Chapter 2 some of the factors that make up demand for a firm's product were introduced. It was noted that the market's requirements were usually the results of the needs of a number of different customers. In industrial, commercial and government markets this is not necessarily the case; Marks and Spencer take all the output of some suppliers, and firms in the medicare and defence fields may sell all their output to the government. Each customer purchases the product for his or her own reasons, some shared with others, some individual. At the heart of the marketing concept is the proposition that the firm's ability to understand and meet the needs of sufficient numbers of buyers is the essential precondition for long-term success.

In this chapter the implications in consumer markets of this notion will be explored in depth. Consumer markets are those concerned with the private end-users of a product, service or other form of offering. Our knowledge of the forces shaping consumer and buyer behaviour is built on the foundations laid in the more general behavioural sciences. Although this was once a highly dependent relationship, advances in this area in marketing, notably the increasing amount of empirical study, have altered the balance over the last decade.

Despite the considerable amount of investigation carried out, no current theory or approach fully satisfies the needs of the marketer or researcher. The forces affecting behaviour are complex and wide-ranging. They have been viewed from a number of different perspectives: economic, psychological, physiological and sociological. In an attempt to understand the buying process more fully, models of the buyer's or consumer's approach to purchasing have been constructed. A model is an attempt to represent visually or verbally the most important element in a real-world situation as a basis for achieving greater understanding or conducting experiments to test the part or the whole.

The extent of the factors which influence the buyer are illustrated in Figure 7.1. These affect the consumer not only directly but through their interaction. For example, Mr Khan's desire for a sports car may be affected by his economic circumstances and his wife's fears for his safety.

Kotler[1] suggests that a useful way of considering this process is to think of purchasing in terms of four broad characteristics:

1 *Objects:* the classifications of goods and services.
2 *Objectives:* the factors affecting the customer's search for satisfaction and choice.
3 *Organizations:* the groups involved in achieving this satisfaction.
4 *Operations:* the actions needed to carry out this process.

These four O's can be matched against four P's of the marketing mix (see Figure 1.7).

Figure 7.1 Influences on the buyer

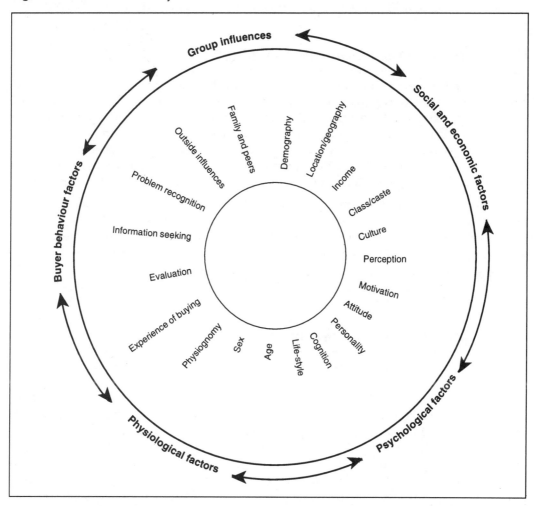

Buying can be seen in terms of a simple 'black box' system (Figure 7.2). The idea of the 'black box' is used to show the fact that what goes on inside is not fully understood.

Figure 7.2 The 'black box' system

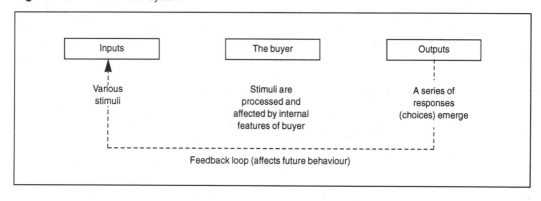

In order to understand the factors that influence the consumer we must return to some of the concepts introduced in Chapter 2.

Social and economic variables

The socio-economic forces of demography, location, income and class establish many of the preconditions for particular types of needs, drives and actions. These pressures are not constant. They change over time for both the total society and the specific individual or family. Some major socio-economic changes occurring now in Britain are: the increasing economic power of women, from 30 per cent of the labour force in 1951 to about 50 per cent now; a progressively older population profile; the increasing terminal education age of population; the shift from manufacturing industry to services; and the growth in leisure time.

These create problems for some firms and types of organizations while opening new opportunities for others. For example, the traditional male-only pubs and clubs are being forced more and more to admit women, and organizations such as the tour operators Saga are catering for the increasingly important subgroups.

In exploring these patterns and trends the danger of thinking in terms of single, mass homogeneous markets has been recognized.

Market segmentation

Market segmentation, as an approach, emerged from the recognition of the danger of thinking all customers are the same. Segmentation is based on the proposition that, if a holiday package is designed for a market consisting of three age groups (14 to 25, 26 to 45 and over 46) and three different types of participant (single, married with children, and married with grown-up children), and each group is willing to spend different amounts (up to £700, £1,000 and £2,000), then two different methods are available. A single general holiday – a low price, two weeks' full board holiday in an English holiday resort – could be offered. All the potential holidaymakers would be able to afford this, but younger holidaymakers may want more freedom, family units may need 'evening supervision' for the children, and older groups may require a greater educational or cultural interest. Therefore the approach of 'any holiday so long as it's full board in Blackpool' will succeed only until competitors satisfying the basic 'affordability' requirement also start meeting other needs.

Market segmentation is 'the subdividing of a market into distinct and increasingly homogeneous subgroups of customers, where any group can conceivably be selected as a target market to be met with a distinct marketing mix'.[2] There are two important features of this definition: the segments are more homogeneous than the market from which they are chosen; and they can be reached through a marketing mix which is specific to them. The basic aims are: to meet the needs of subgroups, protect the firm's offering from competition on price, and improve customer loyalty and company returns (Figure 7.3).

The routes taken to reach different segments are as varied as the different perspectives towards understanding consumer behaviour and the forces prompting purchase action.

Segmentation by location

Segmentation by location is probably the oldest and most established method. Here, firms target their offerings on specific local communities or groups. The retail trade has traditionally adopted this approach, since the shop serves its own community, and the range of goods offered reflects their needs rather than national or regional patterns of brand share or market power. There may be stottie cakes in the bakers' shops on Tyneside, black puddings in the butchers' shops in Lancashire, enormous arrays of exotic fish in the Birmingham Bull Ring fish market, and kosher food in north-west London. The local shop probably often meets convenience needs, and this fact is reflected in their pricing policies. Until very recently the growth in personal mobility had created a very high failure rate in small local shops, but now niche marketing by small retailers, new emphasis on less mobile groups and the success of the Lottery has slowed this trend. Location is very important in certain industrial markets.

Figure 7.3 Subdividing the market

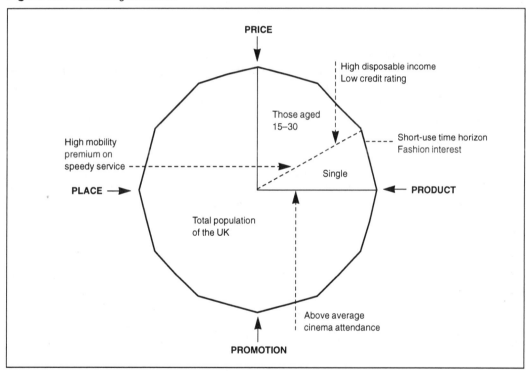

Socio-economic factors

Socio-economic factors are used as a basis for segmentation. Shared economic position and broadly similar incomes, levels of literacy and viewing habits, as well as some shared values, give many firms clues to the appropriate product offering, pricing, promotional and distribution mixes.

This is an approach to the market which is particularly important to the media, especially newspapers. Segmentation by class helps them to design their own special mix to appeal to specific groups. Equally important, newspapers and magazines can use the make-up of their readership as part of the offering to prospective advertisers.

Research into segmentation highlights weaknesses in these approaches, emphasizing external, non-product-related criteria. It is implied that 'differences in reasons for buying, in brand choice influences, in frequency of use or in susceptibility will be reflected in differences in age, sex, income and geographical location. But this is usually not true.'[3]

Out of this emerged a number of specific new approaches to segmentation and a new perspective on the entire process. Benefit segmentation attempts to get to the roots of the causes of action in particular markets. The customers' opinions and attitudes to specific brands and products are explored in depth and from this a number of segments with shared product requirements are identified. Recent developments in the toothpaste market illustrate this approach clearly. Consumption is dominated by families with children, but they share with other groups a specific requirement or benefit: protection from tooth decay. This theme is developed in product promotion: classless groups are used to communicate the message, and pricing and distribution are geared to maximize availability.

Lifestyle

A development of this approach, but drawing on research from elsewhere, is segmentation by lifestyle. 'Lifestyles are the patterns in which people live and spend their money.'[4] These patterns are determined by three behavioural components: activities, interests and opinions (AIO). Activities are observable behaviour, interest is the attention given and its importance, and opinions are the responses to various stimuli, especially questions.

Lifestyle analysis, by examining the patterns which emerge when these issues are explored in a population, seeks to identify groups which behave in a broadly consistent manner, have shared interests, share certain values and opinions, and are probably consistent demographically. A manual worker in a factory who actively plays soccer, is home-centred, adopts conservative, traditional standards for judging products, and has two sons and a daughter is likely to respond to product, promotional and other mix stimuli in a manner broadly similar to others with this lifestyle.

Lifestyle analysis is seen as particularly useful in helping the firm to reconsider its markets. Traditional structures such as 'our target audience is ABC males in NE England' can be re-examined, and even retitled 'traditionalist executives'. This may provide clues to new customers who share all the needs satisfied by the product but who are located elsewhere or are not approached for other reasons. Equally important, this perspective can provide creative clues for advertising and new product development. For example, a soccer-playing worker may respond very positively to promotion of clothes for himself and his children using soccer stars, while a traditionalist executive may provide a market for an array of new products designed to meet the needs which underlie his values.

Although these groupings can be identified it should never be assumed that the members of the groups will respond in exactly the same way to the stimuli they receive. Many internal, psychological forces intervene.

Motivations

When an individual or group embarks upon the act of purchase, even the so-called impulse buy, the buyer is driven by motives. These may be personal and idiosyncratic, but still exist for the person. These in turn are probably only part of a complex range of forces determining and motivating actions. Some aspects of the notions described earlier – the economic or social roots of behaviour – are relevant here. Much of the study of motives has developed from the work of psychoanalysts and psychologists.

Psychoanalytic views

These views of motivation are founded on the ideas put forward by Freud that people's needs operate at various levels of consciousness. The most important of these needs are subconscious and not readily observable. Although many psychoanalysts have rejected Freud's ideas on the specific drives, most concur with the emphasis he places on the subconscious.

The study of subconscious motivation has been rich in theories of the best way to stimulate required responses among buyers. In the US the success of a number of products has been ascribed to the extent to which they effectively capitalize on these subconscious drives.[5] In Britain most market research agencies have used or use research techniques to probe into the subconscious.

There have been a number of fruitful outcomes of this area of investigation. Unfortunately, a recurrent problem in the study of subconscious motivation has been the lack of any objective or replicable evidence. In fact, the researcher appears to affect the results appreciably.

The behavioural approach

This approach to motivation contrasts diametrically with the interpretative study of the subconscious favoured by Freud. Emphasis is placed on the observable and measurable aspects of behaviour. The individual is seen as responding to various stimuli, so a drive originating from some inner need (e.g. thirst) leads to specific responses to particular cures or stimuli.

The pattern of responses is conditioned by the effects which follow a specific response. Thus a severe headache, when associated with taking an aspirin and the response of pain relief, reinforces the belief that aspirins relieve pain. A pattern of aversion will emerge if the response is discomfort, e.g. a particular food gives stomach-ache. In this framework we see the foundations of one of the most important aspects of consumer behaviour – the notion of learning. This approach has been closely associated with the work of J. A. Howard[6] and will be discussed later in this chapter.

In the study of motivation in marketing, the work of A. H. Maslow[7] occupies a particularly important place. Maslow suggests that we are motivated by individual motivating factors which interact in terms of recognizable hierarchy (Figure 7.4).

Although this approach provides some useful clues about generating ideas and organizing the manager's thinking about his or her offerings, its predictive and diagnostic value in specific situations is very limited. At the same time Chisnall[8] has placed emphasis on the need to recognize that wants do not exist in isolation.

Figure 7.4 The hierarchy of needs

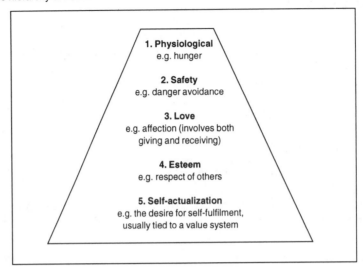

Attitudes

Any individual considering a purchase or entering a buying situation takes into it certain attitudes:

> An attitude is a mental and neural state of readiness to respond, which is organized through experience and exerts a directive and/or dynamic influence on behaviour.[9]

We all have attitudes of one kind or other. When we watch TV in the evening, our attitudes to the advertisements, and hence to the products they promote, are influenced. Unfortunately, beyond the knowledge that attitudes exist, very little else is actually known about them. This is particularly true of the critical relationship between attitude and behaviour. The traditional assumption in advertising has been that change in attitudes would be followed by change in behaviour:

> to result in a sale an advertisement must bring about a positive change in the attitude of the reader or viewer.
>
> Grey Advertising Inc., 1968

It is a viewpoint which contains a certain logical appeal. 'I like the image of Guinness portrayed by advertisements.' Result: favourable attitudes to Guinness. 'I value the ideas inherent in Ford's advertising.' Result: favourable attitudes to Ford. 'I recognize the merits displayed in Sony's advertising.' Result: favourable attitudes to Sony. Therefore I should drink Guinness, drive a Ford and install a Sony hi-fi. The crux of the attitude dilemma is that I don't. This does not mean that my favourable attitudes turn me against the brands: it merely means that the relationship is far more complex than traditionally has been assumed.

Bird et al.,[10] in a series of important empirical studies, examined this problem and the closely related view that people's attitudes are influenced by their use of particular goods and services. They found that spontaneous awareness, intention-to-buy and favourable attitudes were all closely related to past or current usage patterns. At the very least this suggests that attitude-action relationships are two-way rather than unidirectional, as was supposed in the past.

This lack of empirical corroboration for the relationship between attitude and behaviour provided the starting-point for Martin Fishbein's study of attitudes.[11] He rejected the more complex definitions of attitudes, preferring instead 'a relatively simple unidimensional concept connected with the amount of affect or feeling for a particular object'.[12]

These attitudes are in turn determined by certain beliefs. From attitudes are derived not specific actions but merely intentions. The link between intention to buy and actually buying therefore becomes the key point for further research (Figure 7.5).

Even in this newer formulation it appears that the predictive power is fairly limited. Engel *et al.*[13] suggest that this is because 'we still have not taken into account the full range of situational influences'.

Figure 7.5 The relationship between attitude and behaviour

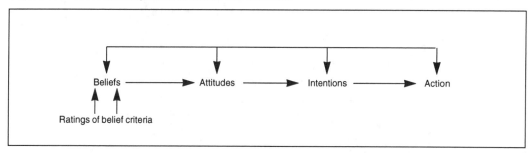

Images of reality

In this examination of the consumer it has become clear that marketing people face a continuing conflict between two goals. On the one hand they need a greater understanding of the buyer in order to design suitable offerings, and on the other hand this understanding must be matched with profitable action. It is always a problem in research that the search for averages and consistencies to guide behaviour is tempered by the fact that these may merely cloud judgement (Figure 7.6).

Segmentation studies illustrate one solution to the problem. They recognize that 'The world is made up of minority markets.'[14]

The firm can explore its own information to arrive at target segments. Outside sources such as BMRB's Target Group Index (an annual study of 25,000 self-completed questionnaires) can also be employed. Ultimately, however, segmentation gives only limited insight into the behavioural processes. More recently, there has been a growing interest in the modelling of behaviour to obtain some further insight into the processes of consumer behaviour.

Models of buyer behaviour

J. A. Howard[15] argues for the contribution that models of behaviour can make to our understanding of the processes involved. In his book he introduces the notion that behaviour could be thought of in terms of a learning process. He suggests that when people are purchasing an item they rely heavily on experience. If the item has been bought before and was satisfactory, the chances that it will be bought again (repeat buying) are increased (higher probability), as Figure 7.7 demonstrates.

Figure 7.6 The dangers of averages blurring real differences

Figure 7.7 The learning curve. Adapted from Howard, J. A., *Marketing Management*. Homewood, Ill.: R. D. Irwin, 1963.

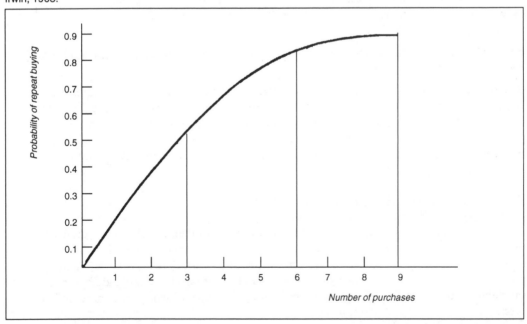

The curve can be divided into three distinct phases. Initially a buyer's experience is very limited, so she (or he) cannot draw on it to help her choose brands or products. Therefore she goes to various sources of information for help. At this stage she is involved in extensive problem-solving (Figure 7.8). This involves the most conscious and rigorous active evaluation of alternatives. Theoretically, it is closest to the idea of economic man. In a market such as the hi-fi market, individuals may be buying their first stereo system. They therefore ask friends for information and read a popular hi-fi magazine. They visit shops such as Dixons to listen to different makes. They may already have some biases or preconceptions such as 'big speakers give the best response'. They may even defer decisions because events led them to spend money elsewhere. All these factors affect the marketing of both the retailers and the manufacturers.

A major change occurs as buyers' experiences build up. They rely increasingly on their own knowledge and experience of purchasing. Information may be sought, but usually only when some outside event, for example a new product or a bad purchase experience, triggers it. What they are now doing is termed 'limited problem-solving' (Figure 7.9), when only a few alternatives are considered. Under certain circumstances, especially when buying low-cost, frequently-bought items, buying becomes totally routine. This is known as automatic response behaviour (Figure 7.10).

Like all valuable contributions to marketing knowledge, this approach provides the starting-point to investigation, not a conclusive statement.

It has prompted research into the following areas to provide guidance for the marketing person:

1 The influence of the outside variables which directly or indirectly influence purchasing: the housewife's decisions are affected by family pressures; individuals may be buying for themselves, but are conscious of the effect of the purchase on friends or colleagues.
2 The ways in which which people process the information they receive from a battery of sources: a statement on a consumer affairs programme might conflict with information from advertisements.
3 The process of motivation itself.
4 Under certain circumstances the search will be active and rigorous: what prompts this, how can the firm capitalize on it, and what type of information is sought?

Ultimately, firms seek methods of measuring these forces and weighting actions by them (usually at a cost) against returns.

Almost inevitably, as information and knowledge have increased, the complete model has become more complex and the relationship more tortuous.[16] Partly to overcome this problem, as well as to provide a model to give a clearer insight into such areas as information processing, Kotler, and Engel, Blackwell and Kollat, introduced models based on stages in the buying process (Figure 7.11). These stages provide a useful vehicle for analysing buyers and their behaviour, particularly exploring the objectives of marketing mix strategies. Among the more fruitful areas of current research is the work which locates buyers in their purchase situation.[17]

Figure 7.8 Extensive problem-solving. Adapted from Howard, J. A., *Marketing Management*. Homewood, Ill.: R. D. Irwin, 1963.

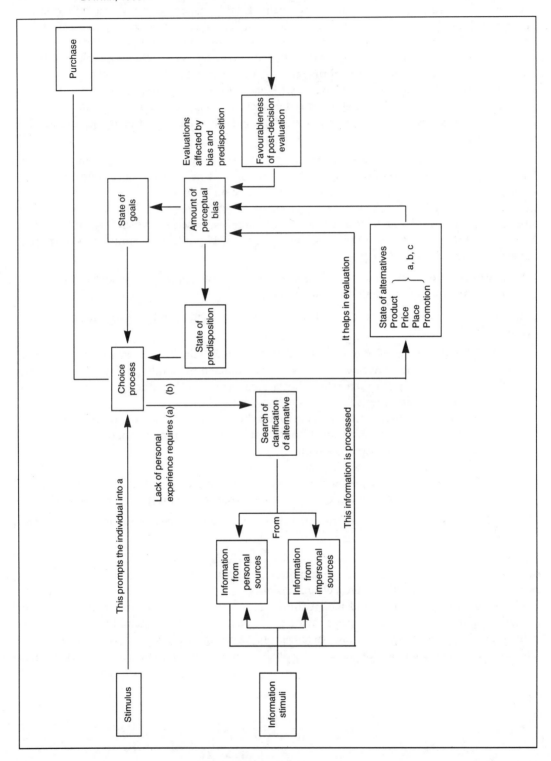

Figure 7.9 Limited problem-solving. Reproduced with permission. Howard, J. A., *Marketing Management*. Homewood, Ill.: R. D. Irwin, 1963.

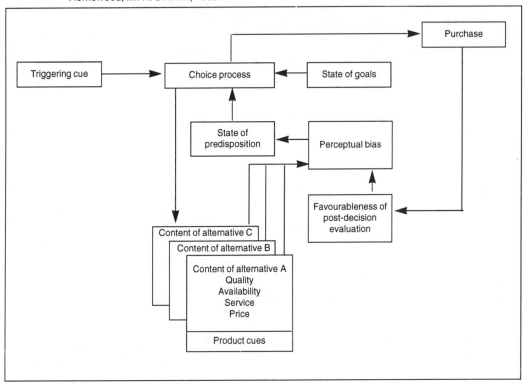

Figure 7.10 Automatic response behaviour. Reproduced with permission. Howard, J. A., *Marketing Management*. Homewood, Ill.: R. D. Irwin, 1963.

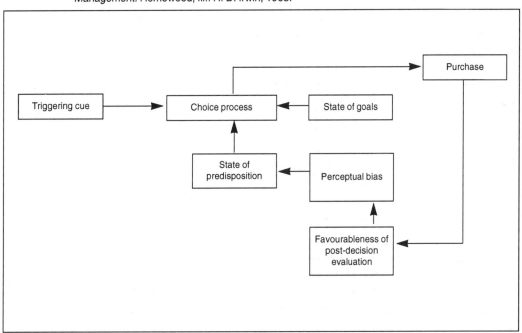

Figure 7.11   Different visions of the stages in the buying process. [a]Kotler, P., *Marketing Management*. Englewood Cliffs: Prentice-Hall, 1997. [b]Engel, J. F., Blackwell, R. D. and Minard, P. W., *Consumer Behaviour*, 8th edition. Hinsdale, Ill.: Dryden Press, 1995.

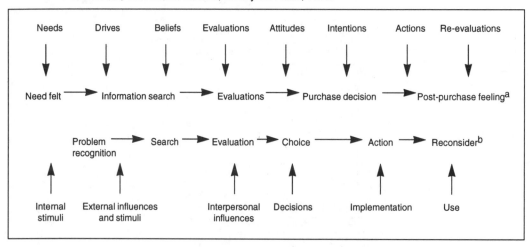

Diffusion and adoption of a new product

An understanding of the processes described above is critical to the study of innovation and new product development. In his research Rogers[18] suggested that a pattern similar to that described above occurred in the adoption of new products: need exists (conscious or unconscious) → awareness (as potential means of satisfying this need emerges) → interest (thus created leads to information search) → evaluation (of information, tempered by beliefs) → trials (probably preceded by 'intention to buy') → adoption (or rejection) occurs.

Although this is what occurs on an individual basis, the producer's main interest is in aggregate behaviour. The entire target population is unlikely to respond immediately, even if awareness were instant (Figure 7.12).

Figure 7.12   Relative time of adoption of innovation. Adapted from Rogers, E. M., *The Diffusion of Innovations*. New York: Macmillan, 1962.

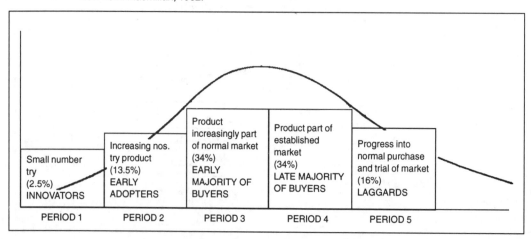

Rogers' model seems to make sense, but although he introduces a breakdown of the population he studied in terms of unconsciousness, early adoption etc., there is little support for this as a universal formulation. Equally important, there is no evidence to suggest that the groups are consistent across product fields. For example, the well-educated, self-confident farmer may innovate in terms of new machinery or hybrid crops, but be a laggard in terms of music. His innovativeness may be related far more to his peer group than to the product category; e.g. in fashion goods an innovative farmer may be a member of the late majority of the total population. This more holistic view of the diffusion of innovations is developed further by Lancaster and Taylor.[19] They highlight the strategic and competitive dimension to adoption.

Current research into product and corporate re-engineering, mass customization and process models of innovation suggests that a new pattern for the management of change and innovation is emerging.

Loyalty to store and brand

The study of customer loyalty demonstrates the importance of research into behaviour. Brand loyalty is the tendency of some customers to purchase a brand consistently. In a fast-moving consumer market it was seen as manifesting itself in such patterns as those shown in Table 7.1.

Table 7.1 Buying profile of detergent

Weeks	1	2	3	4	5	6	7	8	9	10
Mrs Osborne	A	A	A	O	A	A	O	B	A	A
Mrs Turner	B	A	B	B	B	A	A	O	O	B
Mrs Griffiths	A	B	D	D	D	D	O	O	B	A
Mr Marrion	–	–	A	–	–	–	A	–	–	A

(A = Ariel, B = Bold, D = Daz, O = Others.)

Some customers, it was believed, show undivided loyalty; others have either unstable or no loyalty. The phenomenon was seen as so important that Cunningham[20] commented:

> Brand loyalty is a substantial asset . . . in promotional planning. They (firms) should consider brand loyalty carefully.

However, some authors, notably Ehrenberg, question the value of aspects of the basic concept, preferring instead the notion of patterns of repeat purchasing. It appears that the levels of loyalty are virtually a constant for all brands, suggesting that loyalty-building advertising policies have not changed the levels of loyalty. In Table 7.1 Mr Marrion, the most 'loyal' customer, was a light user, a pattern consistent with research in the field.[21]

Conclusion

Over the last twenty years the study of consumer behaviour has emerged as one of the central themes of modern marketing, but in a short chapter such as this only a few of the central themes could be explored. Many important contributions have been excluded largely on the grounds of space.

Consumer behaviour is a fruitful area for marketing research. Concepts such as segmentation, learning and motivation play an important part in policy-making. In the future the marketing manager will need to be as familiar with these as he is with the notions of media selection, sales force territorial allocation, etc.

One issue that should be borne in mind is that the construction of models and theories is of extremely limited value if a large-scale and firmly empirical stance is not adopted to their evaluation and modification.

SPECIMEN QUESTIONS

1   What are the four 'O's and how do they relate to the four 'P's? Illustrate your answer in terms of a specific company operating in a consumer or industrial goods market.

2   Discuss the usefulness for marketing management of an understanding of:

   (a)   Opinion leadership.

   (b)   Group decision-making.

   (c)   Peer group behaviour.

3   The Fishbein extended model argues that certain behaviour is more strongly influenced by attitudes or subjective norms. How useful is this model to marketing policy-makers? Illustrate your answer in terms of a firm or market of your choice.

4   Describe through a model or flow chart the decision process that might be followed by the Dean of a business school choosing the type of PCs to use in a new computer lab. The lab is primarily for the use of first degree students but might, on occasion, be used by MBA students and executives on short courses.

   (a)   Indicate the factors the Dean will need to take into account and the influences that might come into play.

   (b)   How might a producer of PCs use this type of model to design an effective approach to the business school market?

5   What are the major practical benefits that can be gained by firms from a thorough understanding of the industrial buying process?

6   Do you believe that the purchasing function is the primary influence on organizational buying decisions? Justify your answer in terms of at least two types of organization and three purchase situations, e.g. capital goods, supplies.

7   How useful are expectancy value models, e.g. Fishbein, in understanding high and low involvement decision? Describe the way in which this type of approach might be used to examine a low involvement and a high involvement purchase decision of your choice.

8   Outline, with illustration, the benefits and limitations of benefit segmentation.

9   Use Rogers' model for the diffusion of innovations to describe the development of the market for a new marketing text book. Outline ways in which a publisher might use this model to increase the rate of penetration, sales and adoptions of the book.

10 Define:

   (a)   Consumer markets.

   (b)   Personality.

   (c)   'Black box' models.

   (d)   Psychographics.

   (e)   The buying coalition.

   (f)   Perception.

   (g)   Extended search behaviour.

   (h)   Market segmentation.

   (i)   Motivational analysis.

   (j)   Self-actualization.

CASE STUDY 5:
THE BUYING PROCESS IN THE TOILET SOAP MARKET

Using the information obtained from the research project in Chapter 6, highlight salient aspects of the buying process for key subgroups in the toilet soap market.

8

Marketing analysis

Introduction

In 1997, Apple Computers announced that the great enemy, Microsoft, was making a $150 million development in the company as part of a rescue package. This ended a bitter dispute between the two firms. The two cornerstones of Apple's strategy – narrow defence of its technology and defence of its independence – had crumbled. This type of problem was not confined to the turbulent 1990s.

In December 1984, a series of announcements by Philips of Eindhoven suggested that one of the longest-running battles 'against the market' of the 1980s was coming to an end. The struggle by Philips to introduce Laser Vision as an alternative to tape cassette-based video recorders for consumer markets in Britain and North America appeared to be almost over. The cost of this attempt to 'buck the market' was millions of guilders, pounds and dollars.

The same month saw Dysan Corporation (the US floppy disk manufacturer) give up its attempts to introduce a new standard 3¼-inch disk; British American Tobacco sell off its loss-making International Stores Group; and Hewlett-Packard announce further reorganizations of its consumer products division in an attempt to achieve its targets for personal computer sales. What makes sophisticated companies with technically excellent products misjudge the temper of the market and lose vast sums of money? This is a question which observers have posed ever since Ford launched the Edsel, Du Pont launched Corfam, Imperial Tobacco launched NSM (New Smoking Material), IBM the PCjr and its 'portables' that soon became known as 'luggables' (if you were fit), Kodak launched its 'instant' camera, BSkyB introduced its Squariel, Philips 'laserdisk' and Sony its 'minidisk'..

The problems are as likely to afflict new, growing companies as established, stable firms. Sock Shop's misguided attempts to repeat its UK success in North America almost destroyed the firm. The evidence suggests that the clearest explanation for these and the myriad earlier, simultaneous and future similar problems lies in the inadequate attention that firms give to the analysis of their markets.[1]

The weakness is not confined to the management of new products, companies and services. WD & HO Wills saw the sales of Woodbine cigarettes collapse when novel packaging was introduced to modernize the image of the brand. Unfortunately for the firm, existing customers preferred the old image and new customers did not want to smoke Woodbines in any guise. The decision by British Leyland (Rover) to cut back on its dealer network gave foreign manufacturers their opportunity to build their distribution system. Tesco almost left it too late to replace its large numbers of small (relatively inefficient) stores with smaller numbers of larger outlets. The clearing banks, notably Midland, have found that acquisition of US subsidiaries can cost far more than the purchase price. IBM and Xerox played their parts in creating Microsoft and Apple, IBM by giving Microsoft control over operating systems for PCs, and Xerox by giving Apple the mouse. Firms constantly fail to invest time and effort into systematic analysis of the market that its importance demands.

Interest in planning and strategy highlights the critical role of marketing analysis as the foundation stone for future policies.[2]

Analyzing the market

Effectiveness in this area is built on the implementation of a series of relatively simple steps in a rigorous and systematic way.[3] The approaches that can be used vary in complexity but virtually all are founded on:

1 Asking basic questions, especially the who, what, where, when, hows and whys of the markets the firm is in or seeks to enter.
2 Challenging assumptions, especially those which fit neatly into the way the firm wishes the market to be operated.
3 Never taking anything for granted.

On these fundamentals, most techniques for marketing analysis can be built.[4] The procedure can be seen in terms of two parallel processes shown in Table 8.1.

Table 8.1 Techniques for marketing analysis

Steps in the process	Exploring the issues
Define the market.	Measure its scale, character and key features.
Diagnose the purchasing process.	Describe the needs, goals and benefits sought by customers in their terms.
Define the target groups and segments.	Explore the levels of satisfaction, potential, saturation and structure of the market.
Describe the groups and segments.	Detail the salient features objectively with maximum accuracy.
Analyse competitive positions.	Conduct brand and market share analysis and distribution studies, as well as likely competitor action.

This process of market analysis should go alongside the regular internal audits of Potentials And Needs, Investments and Capabilities (PANIC).

Defining the market

A definition of the market is built around an up-to-date picture of the parameters of the market: its size, composition, consumption patterns and internal structure. This needs to be done regularly, as changes can occur rapidly with little apparent warning. The basic data can be built from consumption and usage statistics. Current and previous buyers are measured using either company statistics or data gathered by public or private agencies. Wider issues can be brought into this analysis, such as the impact of unemployment on demand. It is normally necessary to extend this analysis to look at trends in development as well as the immediately current position.

Mini-case study: Krona

The success of Krona margarine was based on wedding this type of analysis to a distinctive offering. Van den Berghs, the producers, highlighted a number of key features in the market.

1 It is huge (worth over £1,300 million at 1993 retail prices).
2 It is generally static.
3 It has experienced major shifts in demand over previous years, a major shift to butter post-war followed by a trend to margarine as quality improved and customers became interested in diet and health-related products.
4 Increasing price sensitivity.
5 A history among customers of seeking a 'butter substitute'.

The product was targeted on a key sector of the market – a group who were both significant in buying potential and likely to be responsive to the particular characteristics of this product:

> Housewives currently spreading salted butter, who are being forced to
> trade down because of the increasing price of butter, but who do not wish
> to sacrifice the taste and texture of butter.

A media campaign and budget was established to achieve awareness, trial and repeat purchase among this group. Following its launch in October 1978, it achieved 'brand leadership' with a market share of 18 per cent of the margarine market by August 1979, with 43 per cent trial and 80 per cent prompted awareness.

The ability to define the market as tightly and accurately as possible is the measure of marketing staff who are on top of their jobs. Many companies maintain a 'Marketing Fact Book' for each product and brand area in which they have an interest. In industrial markets the difficulty of defining markets causes problems in categories such as components or processed products. This places greater pressure on marketing executives to produce specific measures for their areas of activity.[5]

Environmental scanning

Environmental scanning has emerged as a powerful set of techniques and tools to inform the enterprise about the world in which it operates. This scan includes analysis of the environment, forecasting, industry and competitor analysis besides more narrowly defined market research. Environmental scanning is not solely concerned about the external context in which the firm operates, it includes the ways in which the firm processes inputs and its sensitivity to the material. An environmental scanning system incorporates the ways the enterprise learns from these insights.[6]

Browlie[7] identifies twelve environmental trends for the 1990s that organizations will need to monitor and for which they should establish response mechanisms:

1 Continued slowdown of international growth.
2 Splintered markets.
3 Irreversible inflation.
4 Uneven distribution of world resources.
5 Increasing exports from newly industrializing countries.
6 Globalization of markets.
7 Shortening product development cycles.
8 Shortening product life cycles.

9 Increasing capital intensity.
10 The emergence of the multilocal company.
11 Declining fixed to variable cost ratios.
12 Technological maturity and the growth of new, science-based industries.

Even if some of the trends are overtaken by events, they address many of the key issues facing firms. The integration of information and insights from their environmental scans allows firms to increase policy-makers' awareness of environmental changes.

Diagnosing the purchasing process

In Chapter 7 considerable attention was paid to issues of buyer and consumer behaviour. Understanding this process is vital to any manager seeking to develop an effective marketing strategy. The examination of buyer characteristics such as demographics, location, lifestyle (in consumer markets) and professionalism, training, discretion and reporting systems (in industrial, commercial and government markets) is only part of the picture. It is important to build up models of the buying process to explore the benefits sought, the stages in decision-making through which the buyer passes in order to understand the information sought, and the best means of influencing actions.

Parkinson's research[8] on the adoption of new manufacturing systems indicated the different role played by customers in two situations. Industrial buyers in West Germany expected to play a more proactive role in the development of products for their use than their British counterparts. They invested considerable time and effort in supporting the development process and expected to be sold total 'systems' rather than individual items. There is an important 'political' dimension to this.

In consumer and commercial markets, the same pattern of diversity in purchase behaviour can be seen. This highlights the importance of understanding the buyer's approach to the decision, ability and willingness to buy as well as the influences that bear upon decisions in this area.

Defining the target groups and segments

The greater the firm's awareness of a market, the more management becomes conscious of the different groups which make it up. This process of breaking up large heterogeneous groups into a more homogeneous target audience is central to the marketing process. The notion of differentiation has grown in importance within marketing.

It is based on the proposition that the firm's competitive position is strengthened and its appeal to customers is greatest if it is based on a combination of meeting generic needs and supplying special benefits to customers or groups of buyers. This usually calls for greater specificity in offering (avoiding the attempt to be all things to all people). Often it can lead to reduced marketing costs and increased productivity in expenditure. Effectiveness in this area turns on:

1 The ability to define the market.
2 The skill to provide offerings which the customer group sees as providing sufficient added benefit to buy.

Analysis of segments should be linked with some appreciation of the market potential provided by these groupings. The potential will vary considerably over time and between sectors, and can be influenced to some degree by the actions of firms and their competitors.

The growth of the 'pot snacks' market in the UK illustrated this in the late 1970s. The sector grew from nothing to over £80 million (RSP 1994) within fifteen years. A number of successful new products were launched during the early part of the period. However, the market soon began to show clear signs of saturation as rates of trial of new brands declined, advertising expenditures rose and retail discounting increased.

The purchase patterns on which this type of analysis is based can alter considerably over time as economic and other circumstances change. The early stages of recession frequently see the phenomenon of 'deferred purchase', as certain customer groups put off their buying of certain items until they feel more economically secure. The furniture market has been especially prone to this as householders reschedule purchasing of major items. The pattern is not uniform across all categories. The mid and late 1980s saw a much more dramatic drop in purchases at the lower price end of the market than among premium price lines.

The same overall pattern was seen in recent years. The late 1980s illustrated the importance of expectations of consumers' willingness to invest in certain types of products and services. As long as they expected house prices and wages to increase, they were willing to accept high interest rates and take on large commitments. There was a long lag between interest rates being increased and a significant cut in consumer spending. The early 1990s saw this reverse as 'negative equity', i.e. their mortgage was greater than the value of their house, which made people reluctant to increase their indebtedness when savings increased.

Describing the target groups

The earlier discussion of the nature of marketing placed considerable emphasis on its action, its *operational* role. This is critical to successful targeting and segmentation. Once the different groups within a market have been defined, the optimal means of reaching them should be detailed. A sector that cannot be accessed cannot be a meaningful target market. In this context the notion of 'access' refers to the firm's ability to reach a sector in a way which delivers the benefits sought by the customer.

Paliwoda's analysis[9] of the French packaging industry indicated the scope for segmentation. Out of it specific strategies for reaching these groups can be described.

> The French carton market is highly fragmented, served by some 550 small and medium-sized companies. Whilst it must be acknowledged that the economic crises of the 1970s led to many companies going out of business there is still substantial over-capacity in the carton industry and competition is intense. With margins being low over the last decade many companies have been unwilling to invest and there is thus great inequality in the technological sophistication levels of the companies. It is to be noted that whilst printing methods may remain fairly stable, there is much innovation in machinery, and as machines modernize there are greater demands on the mechanical properties of the cartons, to obtain higher performance and greater productivity.

> The French carton industry may be divided into three broad sectors; 50 per cent of carton producing companies serve the food industries, 40 per cent serve the pharmaceutical industry and only 10 per cent serve diverse industries of which the perfumes and cosmetics industry is one.

Within these groups, three subgroups can be identified: 'commodity producers' (large volume/low margins), 'systems producers' offering integrated ranges of multi-packs, and 'high quality packaging suppliers'. A technique such as gridding (see Figure 8.1) can be used to define specific segments for which suppliers of machinery, supplies and services can develop

Figure 8.1 Gridding the French packaging market

	TYPE OF OUTPUT		
	Commodity	System	High added value
M A R K E T Food			
Pharmceuticals			
Other			

Figure 8.2 Electronic mail evaluation chart

	E-mail features	Microsoft Mail	Lotus® CC Mail
1	Automated Directory Synchronization with built-in fault tolerance	☑	☐
2	Capacity to synchronize across backbone of a foreign system	☑	☐
3	Common gateway and server administration program	☑	☐
4	Batch User Creation Facility	☑	☑
5	Graphical Move User Facility	☑	☐
6	Computer-based training for new users	☑	☐
1	Circular route detection of mail messages	☑	☐
2	Hop count tracking to detect routing errors across complex networks	☑	☐
3	Multitasking MTA (message transfer agent)	☑	☑
4	Wide Area Network (WAN) support	☑	☑
1	Backbone capacity through other mail systems	☑	☐
2	Encapsulation to ensure message integrity	☑	☐
3	Automated notification of gateway status	☑	☐
4	Integrated X.400 MTA and gateway	☑	☐
5	Fax directly from any Windows-based application	☑	☐
1	Client for Windows	☑	☑
2	Client for MS-DOS	☑	☑
3	Client for Macintosh	☑	☑
4	Client for OS/2	☑	☑
5	Client for UNIX®	☐	☑
6	Remote client for MS-DOS	☑	☑
7	Remote client for Windows	☑	☐
8	Server for MS-DOS	☑	☑
9	Server for Macintosh	☑	☐
10	Multiplatform client software included in the server box	☑	☑

unique and distinctive marketing mixes. Companies can target their product, such as Microsoft Mail on a specific subgroup by comparing its ability to meet their needs in comparison with a rival's (see Figure 8.2) by using knocking copy.

A paper company might target its product on system producers supplying the pharmaceutical industry. It would be in a position to specify very clearly the range and qualities of product acceptable (product). It could tailor its advertising and exhibition policy to reach this group with messages that would appeal to them (promotion). At the same time the pricing policies could reflect its detailed knowledge of acceptable levels and price structures (price). The ability to identify them and analyse their demand patterns would make distribution and servicing more effective (place).

Analysing competitive positions

The identification of a market and the presentation of distinctive offerings to the target group are only the first stages of effectively developing a market. Having taken the ball and run with it, the firm must hold on to it. This involves competitor analysis. Frequently firms develop approaches to their markets which assume that they and their customers exist in a vacuum. This gives the competition the chance to develop approaches which learn from their mistakes and exploit weaknesses. The most obvious form of this is in the area of new product development, where certain firms deliberately adopt the policy of 'poisoned apple marketing'. This involves never being the first into a market. The competition takes the first bite and takes the biggest risk. There are clear risks to this approach, especially where lead times are long or the innovator recognizes the risks and does all in its power to avoid them.

A regular feature of this marketing analysis should be the review of the competition. This should range very widely to include external threats to the firm as well as immediate rivals.

New information technologies

New developments in information technology are having a wide-ranging influence on marketing. They make data available more quickly, in larger volumes and in relatively easily manipulated forms. This is changing the nature of business fundamentally. Piercy[10] argues that the impact is so great that the most basic marketing concept will need to be revised: 'Information processing should be regarded as the fifth 'p' in the marketing mix.'

The availability of the new technologies should not be confused with their use. Many managers remain reluctant to employ the technology that is available today. They often lack the skill to use it effectively.[11] Others believe that experience and intuition are substitutes for new technology-based data.[12] Lyons and Thakur[13] have highlighted the challenges that the combination of these traditional attitudes and the potential of the new technologies will pose to marketing education. The widespread use of electronic spreadsheets such as Excel and Lotus 123 gives managers the scope to ask the type of 'What if' questions that were impossible to handle manually. Databases give immediate access to high quality information. Specialist packages provide a host of new insights.

The impact of information technology varies considerably between markets. The information technology industries themselves use information technology in a host of different ways to analyse their markets. Cunningham and Culligan, for example, found that in producers of value-added data services 'data is analysed using complex statistical packages'.[14] Use of information technology to assist marketing analysis is expanding in industrial markets. In some sectors, early reservations[15] were replaced by increased recognition of the marketing and competitive advantages that are available. This has prompted banks, notably TSB and the Bank of Scotland, to identify information technology as the central feature in their search for a competitive edge. Mitchell and Sparks[16] found that by the late 1980s UK banks were already extensive users of information technology in their marketing intelligence systems (Table 8.2).

Table 8.2 Use of technology in marketing informations systems in the late 1980s

Form	Clydesdale	Royal	Lloyds	TSB	NatWest
Marketing Intelligence	IBRO Prestel	IBRO FRS	IBRO	IBRO Online Info EDP	IBRO FRS EDP
Modelling	ACORN	ACORN	ACORN	ACORN PINPOINT	ACORN PINPOINT FINPIN
Productivity Marketing research	All banks use accounts		CACI	CACI	

Source: adapted from Mitchell and Sparks,[17] p. 53.

The introduction of some forms of new technologies can face considerable customer resistance. McKay and Fletcher found that customers were reluctant to use teleshopping as an alternative to traditional forms.[18] More recent innovations, especially cable television initiatives, seem to be changing this. Despite some resistance and the increasing cost, firms are using information technology in a number of ways to support their marketing analysis. Those identified by Arnold and Penn[19] are summarized in Table 8.3. In some circumstances customers seem to prefer technology-based solutions to human interactions. Cashpoint machines, for example, are now ubiquitous. Frances Cairncross argues that the IT and communications revolution is already transforming markets and relationships.[20]

Table 8.3 The uses of information systems to support marketing analysis

Application
Customer analysis
Profit analysis
Sales force control
Competitor analysis
Cost control
Data retrieval
Sales forecasting
Planning and decision support systems

Source: Arnold and Penn,[21] p. 20

Experience, shares and competition

Examination of competition and competitiveness in business is intimately associated with issues of returns to relative effort, productivity and profits. These topics provide the focus for a programme of research conducted in the US to examine the 'Profit Impact of Marketing Strategies'. This work is more usually referred to in terms of its initials,

PIMS.[22] More specifically the study sought to establish the marketing factors which had the greatest impact on return on investment (profits).[23] The initial study was based on 50 companies with 600 business units. This has been expanded to over 240 firms with 1,800 business units. A number of specific conclusions were drawn from the research, especially the close relationship between market share and profitability (Table 8.4).

Table 8.4 The relationship between market share and profit

Market share	Profitability (return on investment)
Under 7%	9.6%
7–14%	12.0%
14–22%	13.5%
22–36%	17.9%
+36%	30.2%

Source: Buzzell and Gale[24]

These results appeared to demonstrate a strong and clear link between increased market shares and increased profits. The concept was taken further with the notion that this increased performance was a function of an experience or learning curve, i.e. the more the firm learnt about its market the better it would perform in terms of both sales and profits. This has been spelt out more fully as:[25]

1 A high market share requires high output.
2 Production costs go down as output increases.
3 Reducing production costs plus stable prices equals higher unit margins.
4 Higher unit margins equals greater ROI.

Assuming that this relationship holds true, the optimal strategy for most firms is to seek out policies to increase market shares.

However, the research indicated a number of significant additional factors and limitations on these findings, notably:

1 The strong relationship between product quality and ROI.
2 The poor return on heavy marketing expenditure where product quality is low.

More recent research highlights flaws in the PIMS work, especially in terms of the weakness of the claims for causal links between the variables and the strength of the relationships for very high share business.

Hammermesh *et al.*[26] tackled the converse of this problem; the strategies open to firms either operating in 'low market share' businesses, i.e. where the market was highly fragmented, or low-share brands. They highlighted the importance of:

1 Segmentation and targeting of specialist sectors.
2 Seeking improved returns through the more efficient use of R & D.
3 Exploiting relative smallness through short lines of communication, decisiveness and creativity.

In sum, they appear to be reverting to the traditional marketing strategy: 'If you have problems competing with your rival in his market, on his terms, redefine the market and fight on the ground of your choosing.'

Conclusion

This chapter highlighted:

1 The role of marketing analysis as the foundation stone on which marketing policy is built.
2 The need to bring together objectivity, systematic study and appropriate techniques in marketing analysis.
3 The links between profitability and market share.

However, this process is dependent on the existence of an effective marketing information system and reliable marketing research.

Glossary

Benefit. The perceived advantage or satisfaction sought by a customer or potential buyer.

Differentiation. The process of establishing a distinction between one offering and another.

Lifestyle. Usually employed in terms of 'lifestyle analysis', the programme of research designed to explore the differences in behaviour which emerge from the different ways of living and different attitudes of groups who behave in similar ways.

Market share. The percentage of a market or sector held by a specific brand or company.

Return on investment (ROI). The amount earned in proportion to the capital invested.

Segmentation. The subdivision of a larger, more diverse market into smaller, more homogeneous parts.

SPECIMEN QUESTIONS

1 Discuss the proposition that much recent marketing theory seems more designed to produce 'paralysis through analysis' than effective and practical marketing.

2 Twenty years ago the notion that British supermarkets would be selling water was ridiculed. Now, bottled water is a significant and growing product line in supermarkets. What has happened to produce this change? What can marketing staff looking for new opportunities learn from this success?

3 Identify three recent marketing failures:

   (a) Analyse the causes of their failure.

   (b) Indicate any common flaws in their marketing that might explain these failures.

   (c) Identify for one of these failures a change to their marketing that might have prevented failure.

4 Choose a product or service you purchase regularly, analyse the aspect of the communication, advertising, product, distribution or pricing policies that most strongly influence your choice.

5   How far is it true that a 'firm's competitive position is strengthened and its appeal to customers is greatest if it is based on a combination of meeting customers' needs and supplying special benefits'?

6   Which is more important to the effective marketing executive – logical analysis or creativity?

7   What are the key components of a marketing audit? Undertake a systematic audition of the strengths, weaknesses, opportunities and threats facing an organization of your choice.

8   Is Piercy's claim that 'information processing' is 'The Fifth P in the marketing mix' true? Justify your answer in terms of its implications for marketing analysis.

9   Define:

   (a)   Target marketing.

   (b)   Demographics.

   (c)   Market potential.

   (d)   Customer expectations.

   (e)   Added value.

   (f)   Market gridding.

   (g)   Market mapping.

   (h)   Knocking copy.

   (i)   ROI.

   (j)   Strategy.

EXTENDED CASE STUDY 6: DETTOL

Introduction

In this case history we have set out to demonstrate in two distinct ways that Dettol's advertising works and is effective.

Firstly we show that, by virtue of a change in creative strategy that was implemented at the beginning of 1978, consumer attitudes to Dettol have been modified in the directions intended. The research also shows that the use and purchase of Dettol have increased in this period.

Secondly, an econometric analysis of factors affecting Dettol's sales during the period 1974–78 is used to demonstrate that the sales response to the advertising expenditures put behind Dettol generated profitable increases in sales.

Other factors influencing Dettol's sales are also identified and it is clear that two 'non-marketing' variables – seasonal factors and consumers' purchasing power (disposable income) – have a major effect.

We conclude, however, that it is the long-term effects of Dettol advertising that lead consumers to purchase Dettol when these factors are favourable.

In consequence the dramatic decline in Dettol sales that occurred in 1975–77 was converted into an equally dramatic improvement in 1978 and maintained in 1979 (Table 8.5).

Many brands enjoyed increased sales as a result of rising consumer prosperity in 1978, but not to the extent of these figures, which underline the importance of maintaining a brand franchise by sustained and effective advertising support.

Table 8.5 Dettol ex-factory sales index

1973	100%
1974	100%
1975	85%
1976	87%
1977	83%
1978	100%
1979	100%

Background
Dettol has been marketed in the United Kingdom since 1933.

It is promoted as both an antiseptic and a disinfectant and is used in a wide variety of ways ranging from personal antisepsis of cuts and grazes, through to disinfection of surfaces in the kitchen and bathroom and, in some instances, as a more general disinfectant down lavatory bowls, waste pipes and drains. It is sold in three sizes, 100ml, 250ml and 500ml.

Dettol is not only a mature brand but an extremely well-established one. There is universal awareness of it by housewives: 70 per cent of housewives claim to use it nowadays – a figure which has not changed over the past eight years – and it has virtually 100 per cent distribution in chemists and grocers.

Although there are many alternative antiseptics and disinfectants on the market including many low-priced retailer own brands, there is only one other product that is promoted as a direct alternative to Dettol in its range of uses: Savlon Liquid. For many years Savlon had been available only through chemists' shops, but since the beginning of 1979 it has been heavily advertised and its distribution widened into grocery outlets.

Advertising support for Dettol has been provided consistently over the last twenty years and is considered to have been a major factor in the brand's development to the position it now occupies (as described above). The case history described in the following pages, however, relates to the period 1974–79 and describes, in particular, the changes to the advertising campaign that were implemented in 1978.

The 1977 scenario
Sales of Dettol had reached a peak in 1973–74. However, a combination of factors – rapid inflation and declining consumer purchasing power, reduced advertising investment, some production problems – had led to a sharp decline in sales in 1975, 1976 and 1977 (see Table 8.5).

Additionally, a situation had been developing which was of concern to the future promotion of Dettol. A significant personal use of Dettol was in bathing, which involved claims which could not be proved or disproved. Therefore, the ITCA would not permit the claims for this area of usage to be advertised.

So the problem that Reckitt and Colman (the manufacturers) and the agency faced in 1977 can be concisely expressed as: 'How can we restore sales volumes to the 1973–74 levels when a major usage area of Dettol is no longer open to direct advertising, and inflationary pressures are affecting sales volumes?'

Development of the 1978 strategy

Where is increased volume going to be obtained?
Research had shown that amongst Dettol users its use as an antiseptic was virtually universal; fewer housewives used it in its disinfectant role. Further research using diary panel techniques showed that there were certain household cleaning functions where Dettol was more widely used than others, e.g. in wiping lavatory seats, cleaning up after pets, but even in these instances Dettol's share of products was relatively low.

We nevertheless argued that, to increase Dettol volume sales to any marked extent:

1   We could not expect to obtain additional users – household penetration was extremely high (70 per cent).
2   Increased volume was more likely to occur from the advertising of disinfectant uses of the product.

But this conclusion presented its own problems.

1   The earlier success of Dettol had been built on the personal/antiseptic uses of the product: heavy promotion of disinfectant uses could well destroy the extremely favourable attitudes housewives had with regard to its personal benefits.
2   Dettol's price was considered to be a problem in the market-place (dictated by the high cost of ingredients). If Dettol is looked upon primarily as a disinfectant then the price differential with its main alternatives becomes particularly large – in some instances two or three times the price of own-label disinfectants.

How should we approach the problem of price?
An econometric analysis (described in full later) had shown that consumers appeared to be relatively insensitive to changes in Dettol's price, but sales were found to be affected by the decline in disposable income. This apparent anomaly can be explained by the fact that the housewife's need for Dettol has a lower priority than essential items such as food. In other words, for Dettol to be included in a housewife's grocery purchases, she must have sufficient money left after buying the essential items; and relatively small variations in the price of Dettol do not therefore affect her decision to buy. As a result the decision was taken to allow the price to rise generally in line with inflation and to confine any price-cutting to short term, tactical retail promotions.

A new creative strategy based on disinfectant usage
In developing a creative strategy for Dettol based on disinfectant usage it was essential to be aware of consumer perceptions of Dettol and to provide advertising consonant with them. Research had shown that advertising centred on the scientific basis for Dettol's performance in killing bacteria was ineffective in changing consumer attitudes and behaviour. The high regard which consumers have for Dettol is based on confidence and trust derived from its history, its name, its smell and clouding in water. As one interviewee commented: 'You can't see germs being killed. I have to use Dettol to be sure.'

New advertising for Dettol had to reflect such attitudes.

1978 advertising

At the beginning of 1978 Dettol introduced new TV and press advertising which took account of the thinking outlined in the previous section.

1   *TV:* Two TV commercials, entitled 'Beginning' and 'Discovery'. These two commercials addressed themselves to the need for environmental protection in the home in the context of a new-born baby and a toddler, Dettol providing protection and confidence. In parallel a TV commercial for Dettol Cream – an antiseptic cream – was also transmitted, assisting in the reinforcement of Dettol's traditional first aid usage.

2   *Press:* Full-colour page advertisements were produced in both 1978 and 1979 pinpointing specific disinfectant usage areas for Dettol. The subjects chosen were ones in which Dettol already had relatively high usage, although still low in absolute terms: the lavatory seat, kitchen waste bins, cleaning where pets have been, e.g. the kitchen floor.

3   *Media:* In each of 1978 and 1979, TV advertising amounted to approximately 20 weeks at an average of 50 to 60 TVR per week in all ITV regions. The press advertisements appeared in women's weekly and monthly magazines providing 70 per cent cover and 7.0 OTS.

To summarize the advertising changes:

1   *Content.* A switch from advertising which had been primarily concerned with the antiseptic use of Dettol to its environmental/disinfectant role.

2   *Weight.* Although the budget was maintained in cash terms in 1978, owing to media cost inflation the effective weight of advertising was reduced by about 20 per cent compared to 1977.

Results and evaluation

1   Volume sales of Dettol increased substantially in 1978, and this achievement was maintained in 1979.

2   Consumer research clearly indicates the improvements in consumer attitudes to Dettol that occurred during the period of the 1978–79 advertising campaign as well as changes in consumer usage of Dettol.

3   An econometric analysis of the factors affecting Dettol sales volume conducted over the period 1974–78 shows the profitability of the advertising investment throughout that period and suggests also that the long-term investment in advertising is a major factor in determining consumer purchasing of Dettol.

It should be noted that the periods covered by the econometric analysis and the consumer research are not exactly coincident. The reason for this is simply that the two pieces of research were not planned as a co-ordinated programme.

Consumer research

Two disinfectant and antiseptic usage and attitude studies have been carried out amongst consumers: the first in January 1978, the second in January 1980. These two surveys reflect the extent to which the advertising for Dettol has been successful, both in increasing its usage and changing perceptions of the brand.

The broad objectives of these studies were to monitor trends in the usage and image of disinfectants and antiseptics in terms of the following:

1 Brand awareness.
2 Brand penetration.
3 User profiles.
4 Usage patterns for the major brands.
5 The image of the major brands.
6 Detailed purchasing habits.
7 Usage and purchase patterns of antiseptic creams.
8 Advertising recall.

The research method
For each of the studies, 1,200 housewives were interviewed at 120 sampling points throughout Great Britain by Public Attitude Surveys Ltd. They were located by means of Random Location Sampling. In each case the sample was restricted to housewives aged 15 to 64.

A non-interlocking, two-way quota was set on working status (working full time/others) and whether they had children.

Weighting factors were applied to ensure that the sample was representative of the population.

The findings
In the two-year period since the beginning of the new Dettol strategy, research indicates that Dettol has:

1 Retained its leading position in terms of the penetration measurements.
2 Achieved increases in terms of the frequency with which it is bought and used.
3 Achieved increases in the applications for which it is used, reflecting the success of the advertising strategy of the past two years.
4 Achieved positive shifts in its image as a disinfectant.
5 Retained its positive image as an antiseptic.

There has been a substantial and significant increase in the frequency with which Dettol is used (Table 8.6). Just over one quarter (an increase of 7 percentage points) of users now use Dettol every day: 53 per cent of housewives use it on average every two to four days.

Table 8.6 The frequency of using Dettol

Base: all current users	January 1978 835 %	January 1980 849 %	Change 1980 vs. 1978
Every day	19	26	+7*
Every 2–3 days	28	27	−1
Every 4–6 days	12	11	−1
Once a week	19	18	−1
Once every 2–3 weeks	6	6	—
Once a month	7	5	−2
Less often	8	7	−1

*Statistically significant at 99.9 per cent confidence level.

There has been a substantial and significant increase, of 10 percentage points, in the number of housewives buying Dettol once a month or more often (Table 8.7). These findings are consistent with the increase in ex-factory dispatches during 1978 and 1979 and the improvement in consumer sales audited by Nielsen.

Table 8.7 The frequency of buying Dettol

Base: all current users	January 1978 835 %	January 1980 849 %	Change 1980 vs 1978
Once a month or more often	39	49	+10[a]
Once every 6 weeks	22	18	−4
2–3 times a year	29	26	−3
Once a year	7	5	−2
Less often	3	2	−1

[a]Statistically significant at 99.9 per cent confidence level. .

In terms of usage, Table 8.8 shows increases in the areas of Dettol usage which clearly reflect the positive effects of the advertising strategy over the past two years. This table also shows that increased household usage has not resulted in a decline in personal usage – in fact, upward movements have been noted in some areas of personal use.

Table 8.8 The usage occasions for Dettol

Base: all current users	January 1978 835 %	January 1980 849 %	Change 1990 vs. 1978
Selected household uses			
Cleaning lavatory seat	51	56	+5[a]
Lavatory bowl	43	46	+3
Bath and handbasin	32	36	+4
Kitchen rubbish bins	29	34	+5[a]
Kitchen sink and waste pipe	28	32	+4
Kitchen floor	23	32	+9[c]
After pets	23	25	+2
Kitchen surfaces	16	23	+7[c]
Outside dustbin	13	14	+1
Selected personal uses			
Cuts and grazes	64	71	+7[b]
Bath	55	55	—
Bites and stings	38	45	+7[b]

Statistically significant at:
[a] 95 per cent confidence level.
[b] 99 per cent confidence level.
[c] 99.9 per cent confidence level.

The image of Dettol: method
The image questions were structured so that respondents could make a free association with attitude couplets by brand. Thus, the respondents were introduced, by a preamble, to mention whatever brands on the list were appropriate to the stimulus (attitude couplets). The respondents were free to mention as many or as few

brands as they wished. In each study half the sample were given a list of antiseptic brands to associate with the attitude couplets while the other half of the sample were given a list of disinfectant brands.

Table 8.9 shows the number of positive mentions achieved by Dettol over several selected dimensions. Aside from illustrating the positive overall image of Dettol, it also shows upward shifts in perceptions of the brand's image in those areas for which it has been advertised.

Table 8.9 The image of Dettol as a disinfectant

Base: all respondents rating the disinfectant products	January 1978 583 %	January 1980 592 %	Change 1980 vs. 1978
A product you can really trust	91	94	+3[a]
Particularly effective against infection	90	90	—
Strong enough for my needs	83	82	−1
Goes a long way	73	73	—
Particularly suitable for cleaning the lavatory	52	56	+4
Particularly suitable for sinks and drains	47	50	+3
Particularly suitable for kitchen surfaces	37	41	+4

[a] Statistically significant at 95 per cent confidence level.

Table 8.10 shows the number of positive mentions achieved by Dettol when the product is rated amongst a list of other antiseptics, and illustrates the overall stability of the brand in this area.

Table 8.10 The image of Dettol as an antispetic

Base: all respondents rating the antiseptic products	January 1978 614 %	January 1980 602 %	Change 1980 vs. 1978
A product you can really trust	92	92	—
Particularly effective against infection	88	86	−2
Strong enough for my needs	82	82	—
Particularly suitable for adding to bath water	78	77	−1
Goes a long way	66	66	—

Economic analysis of the factors affecting Dettol sales
Outline of method of analysis. Common sense dictates that variations in the weight or content of the advertising are not the only factors which will influence a brand's sales. Even with the benefit of a carefully controlled area test specifically designed to measure the effects of advertising, it is usually necessary to check and allow for the influence of other marketing factors which may have caused a differential sales effect between areas. In the case of Dettol, no controlled experiment was carried out and thus the evaluation of the sales effects of Dettol's advertising requires that any other influences on sales are isolated.

In essence, the method involves setting up a simple hypothetical model of the market which describes the likely relationship between the brand's sales and the marketing factors which are believed to influence sales. For example, a very simple model might be of the form:

$$\text{Brand Sales} = K_1 \text{ Advertising} - K_2 \text{ Price} + \text{Constant}$$

This means that for each unit increase in advertising weight the brand's sales increase by K_1 units; and for each unit price increase sales will decrease by K_2 units. The technique of multilinear regression analysis is then used to find the values of the constants in the model (the K's) which provide the best fit to the historical sales data.

There are, of course, many different formulations of the model that are hypothetically possible, which then raises the question as to which is the right one. To answer this, the chosen model must satisfy three basic criteria:

1 The model must agree with common sense. In other words, the variables influencing sales must satisfy our intuitive understanding of the market.
2 The model must be capable of accounting for a large proportion of the historic sales variation. Unless this is so, one cannot tell whether the marketing variables in the model really do significantly affect sales.
3 The model must be able to predict sales once the new values of the various marketing variables are known. This last condition is an acid test of whether the model really does explain the behaviour of the market.

The mechanics of the analysis involve the use of real-time computer facilities. With this aid it is possible to evaluate many different models rapidly and at low cost, and thereby find a model which meets the three conditions described above. The following sections describe the evaluation of Dettol's sales performance. Details of the statistical analysis are shown in the appendix at the end of this chapter.

The construction of the model. Dettol occupies a unique position in that it is used both as a disinfectant and an antiseptic; consequently the definition of its competitors, and hence its market share, is somewhat arbitrary. In the event, we found that the most satisfactory explanation of the brand's sales performance was achieved by modelling Dettol's actual volume sales rather than its share of a defined market.

The model was constructed from Nielsen bimonthly consumer sales audit data covering the period 1974–77, and the 1978 data were then used to test the model's predictive capability. (In the initial stages national data were used, which provided 30 observations, and the analysis was subsequently expanded by including the data for five individual regions, giving a total of 150 observations.)

Four factors were found to have a statistically significant influence on Dettol sales:

1 Real personal disposable income.
2 Dettol's price (adjusted by the retail price index).
3 An underlying seasonal variation (this is common to all disinfectants and antiseptics, sales being higher in the warmer summer months).
4 Accumulated advertising weight (described in detail in the next section).

Figure 8.3 (p. 168) shows how each of these factors has varied over time. When combined they account for 90 per cent of all the variations in Dettol's national sales. This is demonstrated in Figure 8.4 (p. 169), which shows the bimonthly sales of Dettol as recorded by Nielsen from 1974 to 1977, together with the fit to these data provided by the model which has the four factors above as its components. In statistical terms the correlation between sales and the component factors is highly satisfactory; the chance that the result is merely a random coincidence is substantially less than one in a thousand.

The significance of the relationship between sales and each individual factor is demonstrated by the cross-plots shown in Figures 8.5 to 8.8 (pp. 169–71). For example, Figure 8.5 shows the correlation between the variation in accumulated advertising weight (expressed as an effective advertising weight in TVRs) and Dettol sales after removing the effect of the other three factors (price, disposable income and seasonal variation).

An important feature of the analysis is the substantial effect that the 'non-marketing' variables have on sales. Together, the underlying seasonal variations and the influence of disposable income account for more than half the total variation in Dettol's sales. This underlines the need to take account of such effects before examining the influence of factors which are within the control of the advertiser, i.e. price and advertising.

The predictive capability of the model was tested by comparing the model's sales forecasts (based on the known values of the four variables during 1978) with the actual sales achieved in that period. This is shown in Figure 8.9 (p. 171). The model estimates closely follow the actual sales achieved, which is a very satisfactory result, particularly in view of the fact that the reversal of the previously declining sales trend has been correctly predicted.

The effects of advertising. The weight of advertising was expressed in terms of television rating points. Press expenditure, which formed only a small proportion of the total, was included in the television figures assuming it to be equally cost efficient. Using the larger sample of 150 observations available from the regional Nielsen data, it was possible to investigate the duration of the advertising effect, i.e. previous advertising influencing sales in the current period. The analysis (which is described in the appendix) provided strong evidence that the advertising effect decayed over time at a rate of about 10 to 15 per cent per month, i.e. half the full sales effect is achieved within about four months. This is an important result since it means that it is the accumulated weight of advertising which influences sales and not simply the advertising in the current period.

The economic implications. One of the most important features of this type of statistical analysis is that it is possible to quantify the effects on sales of changing the price and the weight of advertising. Because Nielsen reports at bimonthly intervals, and hence the number of observations is limited, only the average effect over a number of years can be calculated with any degree of reliability. The results in Table 8.11 are presented in the form of elasticities, i.e. the percentage change in sales that results from a 1 per cent change in each of the four variables.

Table 8.11 Elasticities calculated from economic model, 1974–78

	Best estimate	95% confidence range
Advertising elasticity	0.19	0.11–0.26
Price elasticity	−0.44	−0.64–0.23
Disposable income elasticity	2.26	1.66–2.86
Temperature (pr°C)	1.85	1.49–2.21

The price and advertising effects are clearly of most interest to the advertiser, since they have a direct bearing on decisions regarding the marketing strategy. The most useful way of interpreting these results is to compare the estimated elasticities with the 'breakeven' values (Table 8.12).

Table 8.12 Elasticities calculated from economic model, 1974–78

	Best estimate	Breakeven
Advertising elasticity	0.19	0.16
Price elasticity	−0.44	−0.20

For example, the breakeven price elasticity of −2.0 means that a 1 per cent increase in price would generate an increased profit for the brand provided that sales volume did not fall by more than 2 per cent. The estimate of the actual price elasticity is substantially less than this breakeven figure; had price been increased by 1 per cent the best estimate is that sales volume would have declined by 0.44 per cent. Thus, there is strong evidence that the brand has been underpriced.

By contrast, the estimate of Dettol's advertising elasticity, 0.19, is higher than the breakeven figure of 0.16 (this is the percentage increase in sales required to recover the costs of a 1 per cent increase in advertising expenditure).

The implications of this are:

1 The advertising expenditure over the period 1974–78 has generated profitable increases in sales for the brand. Even allowing that a degree of uncertainty is associated with every statistical estimate, there is only a 1 in 5 chance that the advertising was not profitable (i.e. the advertising elasticity was actually less than breakeven).
2 Given that our best estimate of the advertising elasticity is correct, the level of expenditure should have been higher to maximize the profit returned. By definition, at the optimum expenditure level the breakeven and actual elasticities will be equal. However, it is not possible to say what the optimum level should have been; to do so requires that the precise shape of the advertising/sales relationship is known.

The consumer research described above showed that the 1978 advertising campaign had generated significant improvements in consumers' attitudes, accompanied by increases in claimed usage. This certainly suggests an increased advertising effectiveness in 1978. Unfortunately, it is not possible to confirm this finding via the econometric analysis, for two reasons:

1 First, as previously stated, there are only a limited number of sales observations for any one year, which means that an estimate of the advertising elasticity based on one year's data will be very unreliable. In fact, a statistically significant result would only have been obtained had the advertising doubled in effectiveness.
2 Secondly, 1978 was a period when consumers' disposable income rose rapidly. In this situation it becomes very difficult to separate the contributions that advertising and disposable income made to the improvement in sales. (A very small change in the weight of importance given to disposable income would allow a substantial improvement in the effectiveness of the 1978 advertising.)

However, the assessment of the average advertising effectiveness over the period 1974–78 almost certainly understates the contribution that advertising made to the substantial improvement in sales during 1978. The rapid increase in consumers' spending power was a necessary precursor, but it is not axiomatic that this increased prosperity should have been directed to purchases of Dettol. Consumers must have a reason for purchasing the brand which involves a belief in its value, and this in large

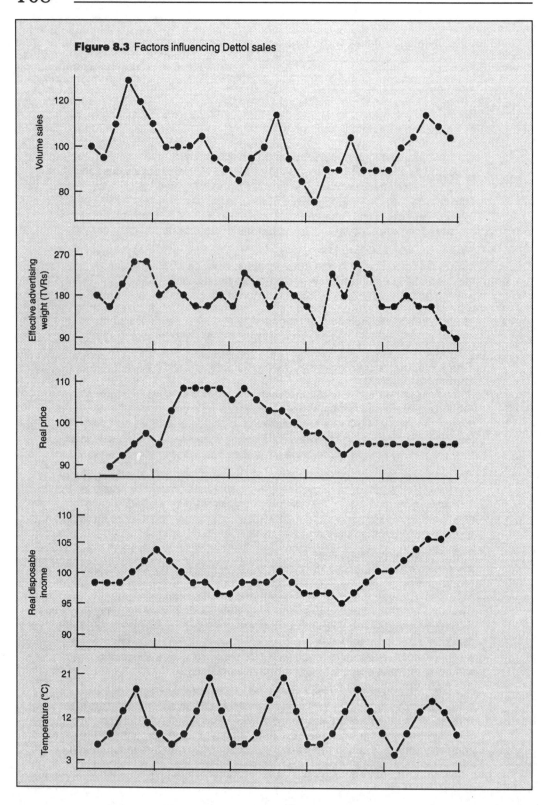

Figure 8.3 Factors influencing Dettol sales

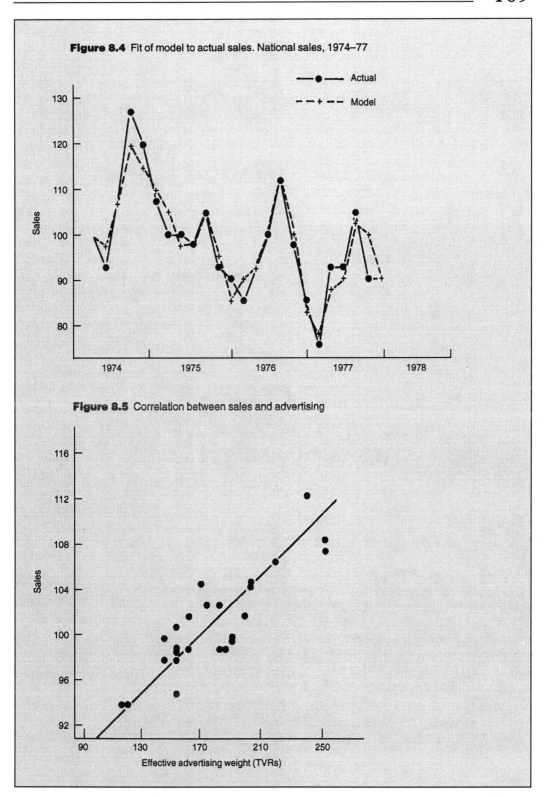

Figure 8.4 Fit of model to actual sales. National sales, 1974–77

Figure 8.5 Correlation between sales and advertising

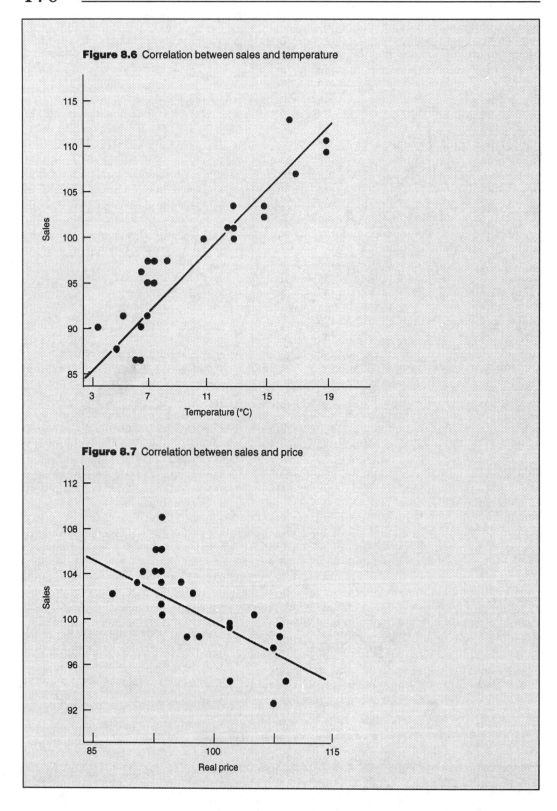

Figure 8.6 Correlation between sales and temperature

Figure 8.7 Correlation between sales and price

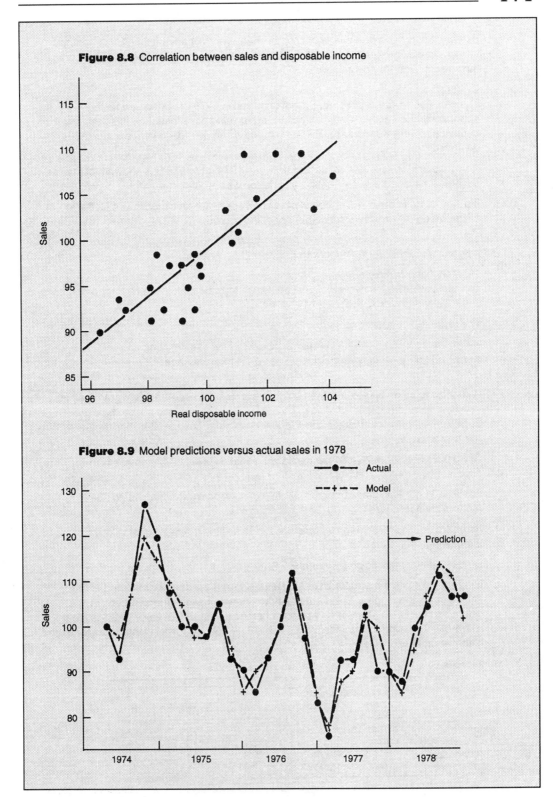

Figure 8.8 Correlation between sales and disposable income

Figure 8.9 Model predictions versus actual sales in 1978

part must depend on the image built up by many years of advertising. Such benefits cannot be readily quantified, but they nevertheless provide additional justification to the value of Dettol's advertising.

Conclusion

The change in advertising strategy that occurred in 1978 provided us with the opportunity of demonstrating that Dettol's advertising does influence attitudes and behaviour. There were shifts in consumer usage and attitudes along each of the desired dimensions.

The econometric analysis conducted between 1974 and 1978 has shown that the advertising expenditure on Dettol in this period was profitable.

Further, in 1978, the combination of past and current advertising allowed Dettol to capitalize on the growth in consumer spending power.

Appendix: Technical Appendix to Econometric Analysis

1. Model based on national sales data

The results shown below were achieved using stepwise multilinear regression on 24 observations, covering the period 1974–77.

The regression equation is:

> Sales Volume = 1.7 x Temperature +2.2 x Disposable Income
> +0.183 x Accumulated Advertising – 0.241 x Real Price
> –131

With the exception of temperature (which is expressed in degrees centigrade) all other vehicles were computed as indices about their mean values and hence the coefficients represent the elasticities for each variable. The key statistics for the regression equation are as follows:

R^2 = 0.909: This shows that 91 per cent of the variation in sales volume has been explained and thus it is unlikely that another factor of major importance has been ignored.

F ratio = 35.85: This means that the chance of such an explanation being due to random chance is less than one in a thousand.

Standard error as % of mean volume = 4.13: This is the measure of the likely forecasting error.

Durbin-Watson statistic on residuals = 1.8.

It is important that the error term (residual variation) is randomly distributed. If this is not the case, then the variables are not independent of each other, and errors in estimation are likely. There is no evidence here of colinearity (a value of 2.0 is ideal, with 1.5 to 2.5 being acceptable limits). Table 8.13 below shows key statistics for each of the variables in the regression equation.

Table 8.13

	Mean[a]	95% confidence limits upper	lower	T statistics[b]	Partial P[c]
Temperature	1.7	2.15	1.24	7.89	62.2
Disposable income	2.2	1.11	4.25	4.25	18.1
Advertising	0.18	0.07	3.47	3.47	12.1
Real price	–0.24	–0.52	–1.82	–1.82	3.3

[a] The mean is the most likely estimate of the coefficient for each variable, and the 95 per cent confidence limits indicate that there is a 5 per cent chance of the coefficients lying outside the range shown.

[b] The T statistic is a measure of the extent to which the coefficient is significantly different from zero (i.e. the variable has no effect on the regression equation). A value greater than 2.0 is significant at the 95 per cent confidence level.

[c] This is a test of whether the variable in question explains a significant amount of the sales variation. A value of 4.0 would be significant at the 95 per cent confidence level.

2. Model based on regional data

The regional model was based on 150 observations using Nielsen data from the five largest areas (London, Midlands, Lancashire, Yorkshire, Wales and West). Each variable was expressed as its index about the regional mean.

The existence of long-term advertising effects was established by first testing for an immediate advertising effect and then by introducing lagged advertising variables, examining whether the fit of the model (R^2) improved significantly (an R^2 lower than that for the national model is to be expected, since the regional Nielsen shop sample is smaller). With only immediate advertising considered, the R^2 was 0.50 and the F ratio for immediate advertising 19.1; by including advertising variables successively lagged up to six periods ago, the R^2 improved to 0.58.

A plot of the lagged advertising coefficients is shown in Figure 8.10. Compared with the coefficient for immediate advertising, those for the lagged variables diminish the longer the lag. The rate of advertising decay implied by this is of the order of 25 per cent per bimonthly period.

This information was used to construct a transformed advertising variable, representing the accumulated advertising effect, assuming a decay rate of 25 per cent per bi-month:

Accumulated Advertising Weight = $a_0 + 0.75 a_1 + (0.75)^2 a_2 + \ldots$
where a_0 = current advertising
where a_1 = advertising lagged by 1 periods

Using this variable the R^2 achieved was 0.65, with the F ratio for advertising increasing to 57.5.

The full results were as follows:

Sales volume = 1.85 x Temperature + 2.26 Disposable Income
+0.188 x Accumulated Advertising −0.44 x Real Price
R^2 = 0.653 F Ratio = 44.7

Standard error as % of mean volume = 8.3

Durbin-Watson statistic on residual = 2.1

Table 8.13

	95% confidence limits upper	lower	T statistic	Partial F
Temperature	2.21	1.49	10.04	100.82
Disposable income	2.86	1.66	7.4	54.9
Advertising	0.264	0.111	4.86	23.6
Real price	−0.23	−0.64	−4.15	17.25

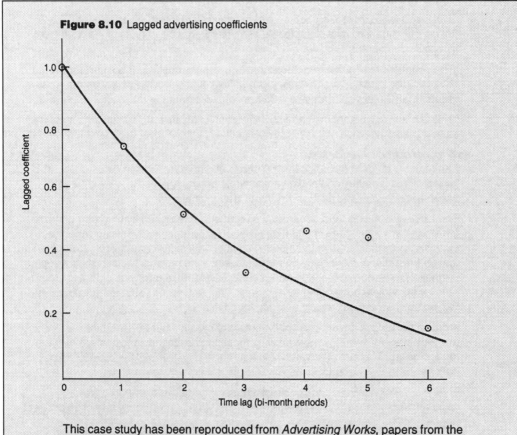

Figure 8.10 Lagged advertising coefficients

Y-axis: Lagged coefficient

X-axis: Time lag (bi-month periods)

This case study has been reproduced from *Advertising Works,* papers from the Institute of Practitioners in Advertising's 'Advertising Effectiveness Awards, 1980', edited by Simon Broadbent and published by Holt, Rinehart and Winston, 1981.

EXTENDED CASE STUDY 7: THE MARKETING OF CLOTHES

Introduction

The clothing industry and its markets illustrate many facets of marketing analysis development, and information systems management, during a period of rapid change. It is a highly diverse industry. Firms vary in size and nature from giant conglomerates such as Coats Viyella with its various specialist subsidiaries like Jaeger, to small local retailers. Some companies are specialist, international firms like Benetton. Others, such as Dewhursts, are major suppliers to large, national retailers like Marks and Spencer. There are dramatic changes in the markets and marketing of clothes. Some of these transformations will reflect the increasing competition which is already being seen as firms learn to use marketing techniques in increasingly innovative and sophisticated ways. At the same time, new material, new technologies and new ideas are entering the market-place. These create opportunities for market leaders while posing specific challenges to all producers and middlemen. The effect of these developments have been powerfully influenced by the changes in market structure and competition prompted by the creation of the single European market.

The context

A clear commitment to a market-led approach is a necessary prerequisite to long-term success in any market but it has to be linked to deliverables which meet market needs. The larger, more fully integrated European market of the 1990s has created major opportunities for firms who understand strategic positioning and build up their own niches. Success turns on the ability of firms to develop policies which meet the needs of all members of the marketing system while building in a competitive edge. Traditionally, the clothing industry has been shaped by a mixture of design push and retailer pull. The challenge lies in blending these and other aspects of marketing into an integrated approach to marketing. Success depends on management skills, and co-ordinating design activities with other tasks in the firm, particularly marketing, manufacturing and finance.[27]

Market changes

Changes in taste and attitude emerge at all levels in the market. New technologies have created new opportunities. Competitors have emerged from both new and emerging firms and foreign industries. At the same time the retail and wholesale trade was transformed through the same processes which can be seen in producer and end-user markets. All these factors converge to create the opportunities and threats which a clothing firm faces in today's environment.

Technological, economic, cultural and political forces affect the clothing industry directly as well as through such important interpreters as the media, banks, educators etc. Today's clothing firm has to learn to play its part in shaping this environment to maximize its opportunities and minimize its risks. Marketing managers need to be able to:

1 Explore the meaning of the marketing concept.
2 Examine ways in which the idea can be converted to action.
3 Highlight the ways in which the environmental changes of the next decade will place an even greater premium on an ability to understand the reality of marketing rather than its appearance.
4 Seek ways to add value down the marketing chain by exploiting Porter's[28] three generic strategies: price, focus and differentiation.

Porter's three generic strategies emphasize the need to gain competitive advantage. Price strategies are built around the attempt to develop and design products which enable the firm to reduce costs and compete through price. Focus strategies highlight the ways to win competitive advantage by identification of a specialist niche and effective integration of operations to maximum effect. Differentiation strategies emphasize the scope for gaining advantage by emphasizing the distinctive nature of the offering within its segment. Suppliers to Marks and Spencer are under steady pressure to keep prices down while maintaining quality. Hong Kong clothing manufacturers are past masters at winning business through price competition. Benetton built up its global market position through effective implementation of a niche strategy. Monsoon deliberately differentiates its offering.

It is clear that many of the most successful firms of the last decade have learned this lesson. Peters and Waterman[29] point out that 'keeping close to the customer' was the cornerstone of success for the leading US firms:

> These companies learned from the people they serve. They provide unparalleled quality, service and reliability – things that work and last. They succeed in differentiating – à la Frito Lay (potato chips), Maytag (washers), or Tupperware – the most commodity-like product.

McBurnie and Clutterbuck[30] found the same when they looked at Britain's most successful firms:

> Successful companies create their own values, appropriate to their own markets and circumstances, and it is the ability to do so in a purposeful and effective manner that sets them apart from those who never quite seem to achieve that essential rapport with their market.

In many ways, the clothing industry in Britain faces a marketing paradox. The leaders of British industry, on the whole, have heard and understood. Despite this there is still a real sense in which the approach has not been internalized. The quote: 'The problem in Britain isn't selling – it's buying' strikes too many chords for us to feel comfortable. It is far too easy to find the types of attitude listed below:[31]

1   UK manufacturers have neither the low prices of the Far East nor the design skills of the continental Europeans.
2   UK manufacturers are slow to react to changes in the market.
3   UK manufacturers produce very few innovative ideas.
4   Some manufacturers are very poor at meeting delivery dates (50 per cent) of respondents.
5   Labelling and packaging could be improved considerably.
6   Willingness to respond to requirements at a detailed level is low.
7   UK manufacturers are slow to produce samples of made-up garments for buyers to evaluate.
8   Quality controls are variable between companies.
9   Branded goods are weak.

The message has reached the market but change inevitably takes time. Unfortunately, time is not the resource in greatest supply. Just three of the environmental factors mentioned above illustrate the time pressure: technology, economics and politics.

New information technologies are eradicating the time lags that were once a barrier to entry to fast-changing fashion markets. The full specifications for a range can be with a manufacturer in Hong Kong as quickly as a firm in Huddersfield. Firms such as Federal Express have slashed the time taken to get samples to customers. The creation of the single European market means that firms across Europe are seeking to use any edge they have to break into UK markets. These changes affect home and international markets.

Domestic
At all stages in the buying chain there are changes in attitude emerging. The modern retailer epitomizes this with the following type of perspective:

1   Far more precise views of needs.
2   Unwillingness to accept products and services which fall short of specification.
3   Greater professionalism in the buying function.
4   Greater willingness to undertake extensive search.
5   Specialization with a willingness to employ and capitalize on technology, design, merchandizing, promotion, advanced concepts in presentation and packaging.
6   Wider sourcing.
7   Investment in R & D.

Table 8.14 shows how the expectations of buyers are increasing and putting further demands on suppliers.

Other members of the marketing chain show these patterns to a greater or lesser degree but the overall trend to a more self-aware, confident and skilled buyer is universal.

International

It is far too easy to imagine that the creation of the single European market is a limited and highly specific event. It is far more than that. It is the logical conclusion to the last ten years of profound structural and competitive change in markets. It is a process which events like the Maastricht Treaty have reinforced. The most obvious feature is the drastic reduction in barriers to intra-European trade. This is associated with two distinct and apparently contradictory developments. The first is greater homogeneity in certain areas. This has already been seen in labelling but now affects very many more areas. The truly European manufacturer or retailer may be inevitable. At the same time changes in market structure allied to innovations in communications are providing major opportunities for niche markets, growth through innovation and creativity in many forms. Operationally, firms need to adapt to the far more integrated marketing strategies of their European rivals. Links with customers must be earlier and more extensive. The types of shift which the research mentioned earlier has highlighted will continue.

Table 8.14

	Yes	No	DK
Expecting shorter lead times	14	1	0
Planning order further ahead	5	10	0
More conscious of design	13	1	1
Less concerned about price	2	13	0
More concerned about price	12	3	0
Tighter delivery specs.	11	4	0
Expecting more innovation	12	2	1
More innovative	6	8	1

Source: Dawson *et al.*[33]

Other changes in the trade environment include:

1   Expectations of more frequent product changes.
2   Holding wider ranges.
3   More frequent but smaller orders.
4   Increased vertical integration.
5   Transfer of quality ownership.
6   Increased integration and sophistication of buying.

Market structure

Retailing

The retail sector is one of the most dynamic in the British economy. Sales rose by 21 per cent by volume over the period 1989–95 and a further 17 per cent to 1997. Generally, expenditure in non-food areas is growing faster than in food areas. This is despite the fact that the relative prices of goods such as clothing have increased less rapidly than those of food. This increases the trend towards consumers spending an increasing proportion of their income in these areas. It is confidently anticipated that UK expenditure on clothing will increase by about 6 per cent per annum over the next five years.

This pattern of overall development masks significant changes in the overall structure of the retail clothes sector. The sector is increasingly concentrated. There is a tendency for the large multiple and the single outlet to lose share to the very large multiple. This squeeze occurred much earlier in other sectors and can be expected to level out when the medium-sized sector reaches 3–4 per cent sector share.

The most vivid illustration of this pattern of growth is the decline of the smaller regional group in favour of specialist, niche-orientated groups, e.g. Next, Sock Shop. Despite their recent difficulties the potential for this type of niche retailer is now well established. This may evolve into more use of multiple-format stores as gaps for growth through specialization or acquisition decline. The market segmentation which was the norm until recently seems likely to be integrated with multiple delivery systems. This can already be seen in the renewed interest in mail-order. The notion of lifestyle markets is likely to be reflected in a rapid growth of lifestyle shopping. In other parts of the world this has taken many forms, e.g. mall shopping in the US. Britain is not likely to be immune from developments which reflect increased leisure time and greater disposable income.

Wholesaling

The wholesale trade accounts for roughly 3.5 per cent of trade in clothing, furs, textiles and footwear. It is hard to arrive at any precise figure for the clothing proportion of this. The entire sector is, however, worth about £6,250 million. Overall, there has been a decline in the share of goods passing through the sector. Despite this, there was an increase of 12 per cent in the number of businesses undertaking retailing and wholesaling activity over the last fifteen years.

The pattern which can be seen in other sectors, i.e. overall decline with the emergence of specialists, seems to be occurring in this sector. The large numbers of smaller regional wholesalers seem especially vulnerable. At the same time, one can expect the growth of specialist wholesaler/manufacturers with selected client groups or branded lines.

Internationalization

The burgeoning success of UK clothing retailers overseas seems likely to stimulate others to follow their lead. The increasing concentration of the retail clothing sector will further stimulate this process. This will open up new markets to existing suppliers while creating new routes into the home market for foreign producers.

The increased concentration in the established retail clothing sector is creating major opportunities for the emergence of new forms of competition. The early success of the Sock Shop and Tie Rack demonstrated the opportunities which will encourage entrepreneurs to identify openings in areas such as franchising, mail order, speciality shopping and integrated operations. Their failure showed the volatility of the market.

Technology

New technologies affect all aspects of the firm's marketing effort. Product development is shaped by the new materials that are likely to emerge from research into new synthetics as well as novel production processes linked with established materials. Super-lightweight material is likely to compete with wool which can be cut by machine. More immediately, CAD and CAM either separately or together will allow firms to turn concepts into finished garments at speeds undreamed of a decade ago. This is likely to produce twin pressures on manufacturers.

Some will be able to compete for new materials and processes. They will accept the high investment in R & D and seek technology-driven routes into the market. Almost inevitably this will involve some degree of backwards integration with strong links with supplier industries. Other producers will cater to relatively volatile niche markets. The returns will be high but the risks considerable. The traditional mid-size/mid-range producer will be fortunate to escape this pressure from both ends.

Some protection may be afforded through especially close customer links, exploiting the access potential of new information technologies. These technologies with their high availability, high customer specificity, speed of adaptation and potential for networking provide the scope for full supplier-customer interaction. The information processing revolution will allow firms to realize fully the benefits of incorporating marketing intelligence into marketing action.

Associated changes in telecommunications technologies will radically change the range, type and price of promotional opportunities. Faxes are now commonly used for 'instant' direct mail. This illustrates the changes which are becoming possible as the cost of information processing and telecommunications drops. Direct mail operations are likely to expand and become increasingly selective and specific. They may be challenged in the very near future by electronic mail systems linked through computerized systems which allow transactions to be completed using the Internet. In the USA, clothing groups like Eddie Bauer (HYPERLINK http://www.ebauer.com) have pioneered the use of the Internet. More traditional, direct mail retailers like Land's End (HYPERLINK http://www.landsend.com) and Innovations (HYPERLINK http://www.innovations.co.uk) are using the Internet to reach their customers while expanding their market reach. The diversity of these new media allied to changes in existing media, e.g. digital television, are likely to force prices down and increase the variety and range of services offered.

Over the last twenty years, changes in distribution systems and technologies have probably had more immediate and direct effects on clothing markets than any other factor. There is every indication that this pattern will continue. The single European market, with the direct challenge it poses to logistics and related systems, has acted as a major spur to this. More obvious but equally dramatic developments such as the Channel Tunnel have had more immediate effects on the technologies of distribution.

The future
Success in the markets in the remainder of the 1990s calls for the skilful combination of established marketing disciplines and novel developments reflecting the needs of the period. Firms must learn to accept not only that marketing matters but also that it matters to all aspects of the firm's operations. It is too easy to lose hard-won orders on the cutting room floor. Some of the disciplines are easy to state but hard to implement. Commitment to effective implementation must come from the top, not just in terms of broad statements of principle but also in attention to the detail of marketing. It is easy to pay lip-service to understanding the firm's position in the market but hard to undertake rigorous marketing audits. The creation of a marketing strategy does not end when there is general acceptance in the boardroom but when everyone knows their role in executing it.

At an operational level, clothing firms will need to understand the changes in market structure that have occurred. In the retail sector it means developing an understanding of the structure and roles of the buying team. More generally it means appreciating the strategic value of network-based relationships.

Networking will mean that clothing firms will need to match integrated marketing with positive sourcing. In the increasingly extensive but more integrated distribution systems of the late 1990s, chain-based strategies are crucial. These require firms to understand fully the chain so that they can sell through it. In turn this will require a high order of professionalism in the sales and promotional effort. This will require a combination of better control systems and increasing professional freedom. In many situations this will involve smaller firms in systems selling in collaboration with others' suppliers if they are to win orders, especially overseas.

These challenges will create opportunities for the marketing-orientated firm. Growth opportunities will proliferate but only for the firm that fully appreciates the true marketing opportunities of the late 1990s.

Project

The clothing industry moves rapidly through fashions and style changes. Choose one retailer and examine the way the marketing policies for the store and the products on offer interact. Try to identify any developing trends in promotion, display and advertising.

Specimen task

Complete a detailed analysis of a market of your choice. This analysis should incorporate:

1   A clear and specific definition of the market. This should indicate any substitute products and the market's distinguishing features.
2   An overview of the current size, structure and nature of the market.
3   An examination of any recent changes in the market plus some attempt to identify likely trends or developments, in particular describe how a firm of your choice could use the Internet.
4   Wherever possible an international comparison should be undertaken. Where possible the emphasis should be given to European market comparisons.
5   The market structure must be described in some detail especially in terms of the chain or network of relations from the point of production (or extraction) to the point of consumption.
6   Technology is having an increasing impact on markets. The analysis ought to highlight the role of technology and how the market is influenced by different kinds of technology.
7   It is advisable to describe the advertising, promotional and merchandizing policies adopted by the different players. Where possible indicate any underlying differences in strategy.
8   Complete a SWOT analysis for the key producers or retailers.
9   Put yourself in the position of one of these 'players' and indicate any changes in marketing strategies or tactics that might significantly improve their position in the market.
10 What does the future hold for the market, and what type of information systems are needed?

Students who complete this type of project have a unique opportunity to get their work published in the next edition of *Marketing*. If their work is nominated by the member of staff who placed *Marketing* on their reading list, they will enter a selection process which might lead to one of the nominated projects – if they are judged by the author to be good enough – getting included, possibly in an edited form, in the next edition of *Marketing*. Anyone getting their work included in this way will also get a prize of £100 (or marketing books chosen by the author of *Marketing* to the value of £150). Nominated work, clearly ascribed and identified, should be sent to the publishers by 1 August of the year after publication and in subsequent years until the new edition.

9

Marketing information systems and technologies

Introduction

Although the gathering and analysis of data continues to be a central preoccupation of those involved in marketing, attention over the last few years has swung increasingly towards the issue of organization and application of information. Three factors have contributed to this trend:

1 The scale of the 'information revolution'.[1]
2 Technological progress in handling data.
3 Recognition that effective strategic and operational management requires good quality, usable and manageable data.

These issues provide the central focus for this chapter.

It is difficult to arrive at a totally satisfactory definition of 'information technology', as it is largely 'a new label for a collection of old ingredients, technologies which up to now have enjoyed disparate natures and histories'.[2]

Any definition will need to encompass both the diversity of the area and the debate on the range of activities which can be incorporated into the field. This may be best achieved through an approach which recognizes its eclectic and dynamic nature.[3]

Information technology is the generic term used to describe those technologies concerned with the collection, storage, transmission and reception of information. It incorporates both the 'hardware' needed to handle these activities and the 'software' required to organize and process the data.

Changing the world

There is little doubt of the interest of government and industry in this area. Information technology has provided the driving force for the growth of key firms, industry sectors and countries. Companies such as Sun, Hewlett-Packard and Microsoft grew and prospered at a time when the more common pattern was retrenchment and decline. Firms which effectively applied the new information technologies, investing to stay ahead rather than saving to survive, have prospered.[4]

The lead established by the US in information technology was a major factor in its economic growth during the mid-1980s. The gap that emerged between North America and Japan on the one hand, and Europe on the other, helped to explain the latter's relatively poor economic performance. This prompted British and European governments, often in collaboration with the European Commission, to embark on a range of initiatives to support the development and application of new information technologies. They range from the Alvey programme, designed to support research through assistance with applications projects such as CAD/CAM, to the Europe-wide programmes like ESPRIT (the European Strategic Programme for Research and Development in Information Technology).[6, 6]

Table 9.1 Information technology initiatives sponsored by the EEC

Euronet DIANE	Direct Information Access Network for Europe
INSIS	Community Inter-Institutional Information System
CADDIA	Co-operation in Automation of Data and Documentation for Exports, Imports and Agriculture
ESPRIT	European Strategic Programme for Research and Development in Information Technology
RACE	Research in Advanced Communications for Europe

Source: Budd.[7]

US decline during the early 1990s was attributed, in part, to a failure to build on its early lead. President Clinton's advocacy of the 'electronic highway' of IT and fibre optics is an attempt to restore this advantage.

The spread of the Internet, allied to sharply increased access to information, has seen the USA's competitive edge restored in many new areas. The Internet has the potential to transform the nature of trading relations by transferring real power to users and customers. The transfer of ideas, concepts and technologies on the Internet exploits the interactive power of new communication and information technologies. Typical of new sources is the online dictionary of computing.[8]

Marketing is at the centre of these developments in both the introduction of the technology through existing and novel products and services and the use of information technology to assist its own operations. The pace and scale of change has absorbed the attention of increasing numbers of researchers who see this as an area of vital significance to the marketing operations of industry and commerce.[9]

Information technology and its impact

The early emphasis in research into IT concentrated on developments in 'hardware'. The balance has shifted in two important ways. First, the distinction between hardware and software has diminished. At the same time, more attention is paid to the human and organizational aspects of IT, its use and application. IT is changing many industrial, commercial and public agencies, from engineering design through retailing to library services. The challenges posed will go far beyond the technical and procedural difficulties of adopting or using the technologies themselves. In the recent past when innovations or new products became available they affected throughput or efficiency but not the nature of the work itself. IT is different.

> Thus, information technology, even when it is applied to automatically
> reproduce a finite activity, is not mute. It not only imposes information
> (in the form of programmed instructions) but also produces information.
> It both accomplishes tasks and translates them into information. The
> action of a machine is entirely invested in its object, the product.

> Information technology, on the other hand, introduces an additional dimension of reflexivity: it makes its contribution to the product, but it also reflects back on its activities and on the system of activities to which it is related. Information technology not only produces action but also produces a voice that symbolically renders events, objects, and processes so that they become visible, knowable, and shareable in a new way.[10]

The change will be as profound as the previous 'industrial revolution'. This will see changes on two levels:

1 In the nature of the goods and services sought by customers.
2 In the ways companies organize themselves to produce, supply and distribute these goods.

In this chapter both these areas will be examined.

The new technologies provide a range of technological and commercial opportunities for firms, based on the accelerated transmission and recovery of data and the scope for rapid organization and close specification of material. This is occurring at a time when the real cost of the new technologies is declining almost as rapidly as the technological performance is increasing. In a speech in the early 1980s Dr D. Dekker of Philips pointed out that the amount of information that could be stored on a 'chip' had doubled virtually ever year for the past decade. At the same time the price had approximately halved. He forecast that this rate of increase would continue. In fact, it has amplified. The introduction of the 286, 386 and 486, then the Pentium series chips augmented processing speed at an increasing rate.

More graphically it was pointed out that:

> If the internal combustion engine had developed at the same pace, it would cost about 25p, generate enough energy to drive the QE2 and fit inside a match box.[11]

The existence of this potential will not guarantee a relevant response by current providers of equivalent services. In other areas the opposite has generally held true.

1 The railways were providers of transport services but did not respond to the transport revolutions of the twentieth century.
2 The department stores provided mass retailing but failed to move into supermarket trading.
3 The manufacturers of mechanical calculators completely missed out in the move to electronic calculators.
4 Producers of television sets in North America and Europe almost wholly failed to establish themselves in the video cassette recorder market.

There is now sufficient evidence available to suggest that established providers find it very difficult to respond to 'discontinuous' changes prompted by technologies which call for major modifications of behaviour. This is the case in information technology.

Five features of the new technology will create new options for provision and call for new patterns of behaviour:

1 *High availability.* Access points can be large in number and highly diverse. Britain has one of the highest levels of per capita computer ownership in the world. It is estimated that a town such as Luton now has more computing capacity than existed in the world 15 years ago.

2 *High customer specificity.* Services and products can be designed to very close tolerances, jointly by customers and suppliers. This degree of tailoring has only been possible in relatively high-price products in the past. The 'Cabbage Patch' dolls of 1983 and 1984, and the Nintendo 'Game Boy' portable video games of the early 1990s illustrate this technology.

3 *Recurrent adaptation.* The rate of change is now so fast that the notion of a fixed product or service may disappear.

4 *Interaction.* The facility now exists for users and suppliers to set up a communications network capable of virtually instantaneous interaction and response. Systems like CompuServe already reach large numbers of users.

5 *Relationship marketing.* This uses better information technologies to understand, and manage, the whole relationship between all the parties.

Few areas illustrate the potential impact of the new information technologies more clearly than CAD/CAM (Computer Aided Design/Computer Aided Manufacturing): this allows those working on projects to design, draft and analyse their offerings using computer graphics on a screen. It eliminates enormous areas of routine and 'chores', while giving the designer the opportunity to analyse, review alternatives and experiment which would have been impossible in the recent past. The newer systems enable the firms to take the newly designed offerings and use the computer to conduct a range of simulated tests on the product.

The application of CAD/CAM makes traditional procedures more efficient and provides avenues for innovation and new development. The use by car manufacturers illustrates both sides of this process. A traditional task such as designing the boot of a car to ensure maximum capacity used to require models and mock-ups. This was expensive. Building a full-size wooden model of the boot could take days and cost thousands of pounds. Now it can be done in moments with optimization techniques displaying the alternatives open to the producer. The even more expensive and time-consuming task of producing and testing new body designs has seen the same process of change. The more demanding, expensive and complex the area, the greater the potential for change.

Business links

The Department of Trade and Industry established a national network of Business Links to provide business counselling for firms through personal business advisers (PBAs). These PBAs were provided with on-line access, through laptop computers to a national database. This allowed them to benchmark the firms against performance in their business sector while providing up-to-date information.

The same technology provided the opportunity for Just-in-Time manufacture which dramatically cut costs and improved links between producers and customers. Total Quality, Exceptional Service Guarantees and Time Based Competition are part of a process of re-engineering[12] which is transforming industry by exploiting information technologies.

Desk-top publishing transfers the same scope for speed, flexibility and creativity into the production of published material. The user can achieve a quality of production and a range of materials comparable with the highest capabilities of traditional publishers. The software developments have occurred alongside innovations in printing and transmission of information. Full page make-up is transforming newspapers, as journalists can input directly, while pages can be reset quickly and at low cost. News on the Internet through companies like CNN[13] is transforming the access and use of information.

Parallel developments in telecommunication have seen the fax and the mobile phone become the standard tools of the marketing executive.

The evolution of 'expert systems' is taking this process of applying the technology even further. These systems are based on attempts to build models of how the mind works. Typically, they are built from two parts. The first, i.e. 'the knowledge base', provides the loosely structured collection of rules which summarize the state of 'expertise' in a field. The second provides the 'logic' for the system which allows the 'knowledge base' to manipulate and combine data. It is an attempt to mimic the way an expert in a field handles a question or issue. The strengths of expert systems are likely to lie in the type of structured selection tasks often handled today by libraries. So far the promise of expert systems exceeds their performance.

It is clear that change at this rate, with the diverse array of alternative avenues, cannot be handled with traditional tools. It requires a re-examination of the roles as well as tasks of companies and managers. Priority was given to either widening services or reaching more potential users: these are akin to the production and distribution tasks of manufacturers or service companies. Faced with the current environment, a new perspective is required. This emphasizes the needs to be met rather than the means used to satisfy them. Emphasis will be placed on needs, such as leisure or information, rather than specific and potentially outdated means of meeting them.

In marketing, four variables are seen as critical to this process of tailoring services to target groups: the product or service; its availability; awareness or attitudes; and cost. Specific customer groups seek particular combinations of these variables. The new information technologies enhance the scope for novel combinations while increasing the competitive pressures on providers. The four features of the new technologies mentioned earlier each illustrate this, while having differential scope to influence the above variables.

The high availability of home and personal computers allied to the increasing penetration of television-based information services dramatically reduces the cost of information search while raising questions about the viability of established cataloguing and referencing procedures. Already, almost ten million homes in Britain have access to on-line data through Ceefax or Teletext while services like Intertext, the Internet, and Intranets, are growing rapidly. In France, government policies designed to stimulate domestic information technology-based industries allied to incentive pricing are stimulating demand for Teletel.

Systems are transforming the current cumbersome access procedures while expanding the capacity for downloading material for reference and analysis.

A number of important initiatives have already been taken. The links between Aslib in Britain and services such as DIALOG, ESA-IRS and Orbit give some indication of the networking potential. Parallel developments across Europe and in North America incorporating novel and existing technologies to provide access to national and international data systems are illustrating the potential of both computer-based and telecommunications systems. Preliminary research results suggest that the process of adoption of these new technologies is broadly following the Rogers model of the line-process of adoption as indicated in Figure 9.1.

In the US, innovative systems are being developed which seek to capitalize on distinct market opportunities. In Germany, the progress with Bildschirmtext was greatly stimulated through links with the banking sector. The Canadian Telidon system developed through public and

Figure 9.1 From E. Rogers, *Diffusions of Information*, New York: Free Press.

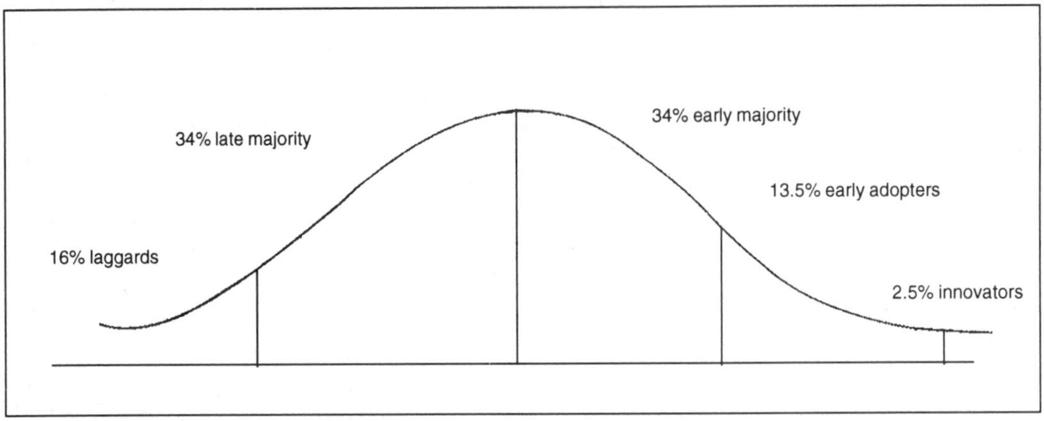

private sector co-operation to meet sectoral needs. In the near future, increased scope for interaction will expand demand for these systems.

In the different sectors of the market – consumer, industrial, commercial, and services (public and private) – this type of pattern can be seen. However, it is clear that a high degree of variation exists. This is affected by a number of factors. Techno-commercial factors, especially the need for real-line access, have assisted the rapid diffusion of this type of technology in sectors such as travel agencies. Techno-cultural factors are causing resistance to adoption among certain groups, e.g. older, less well-educated males.

Despite these factors, the pace of change is remarkable. The diffusion curves for a number of media can be compared:

1 *Newspapers:* Expansion of the market to virtually all households took almost 80 years (from the 1850s to the 1930s).
2 *Films:* The same pattern of access took place over less than 40 years (from the early 1900s to the late 1930s).
3 *Radio:* The expansion of the network took just 25 years (from the mid-1920s to the early 1950s).
4 *Television:* The penetration of TV took place in about 12 years (from the late 1940s to the early 1960s).
5 *Electronic calculators:* The widespread adoption of these took less than ten years (from the early 1970s to the late 1970s).
6 *Home and personal computers:* It took less than five years for over 20 per cent of all households to have a personal computer.
7 *The Internet* took around three years to reach almost a quarter of all US households after the creation of effective, user friendly search engines.

The rate and scale of future changes will challenge many of our preconceived ideas.

It is a mistake to assume that there are no potentially negative consequences other than those indicated above. Perhaps the most fundamental change may occur in organizational relationships and structures. Traditionally these were hierarchical and localized; that is, the overall structure of the commercial firm or public body was based on a relatively simple internally structured hierarchy, often with localized centres of knowledge and power.

This pattern may be challenged in both the short and long term. In the short term, the pace of change is likely to pose serious operational problems of adaptation and absorption to hierarchically or bureaucratically structured entities. Innovation is generally achieved more easily and effectively through open organic structures. These permit information flows, rather than structure, to be directed. A parallel pattern can be seen with task versus purpose-orientated structures. The latter finds the management of change easier than the former. Absorbing, responding to the innovations indicated above, requires profound short-term organizational adaptation.

Internet hosts

Hosts are the computer server, filled with various types of information and linked together creating the World Wide Web (www). Most are freely accessible. Surfing this information highway, one can access millions of documents, photos, books, and movies as well as e-mail friends and associates anywhere, any time. The number of Internet 'hosts' has grown dramatically during the 1990s (see Figure 9.2).

Figure 9.2 From R. McKenna, *Real Time*, Cambridge, Mass.: Harvard Business School Press, 1997.

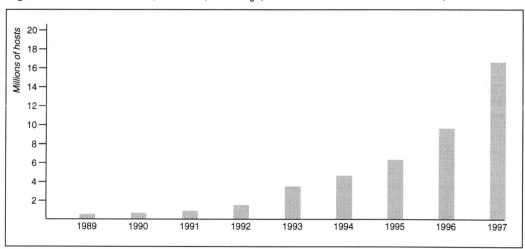

The direction taken with this general phenomenon will be influenced by the nature of the technologies themselves. Researchers are only now becoming fully aware of the appropriate organizational structures within a wider society. The introduction of the factory system, widespread mechanization and industrialization were major factors in the emergence of the type of bureaucratic, hierarchical structure dominant throughout modern industrial society. This pattern of organization extended far beyond the factory or commercial firm to a point where it is sometimes perceived as a 'natural' way of organization.

However, modern information technologies are built around a different model. Networks, rather than flows or hierarchy, predominate. Multiple access points, vertical as well as horizontal communication, unit-separation, gate-keeping are replacing the single access, hierarchical structure implicit in older systems. Organizational forms will inevitably change as 'loops' replace 'lines', and 'open' rather than 'closed' systems become the norm.

Figure 9.3 Diffusion curves for a number of media

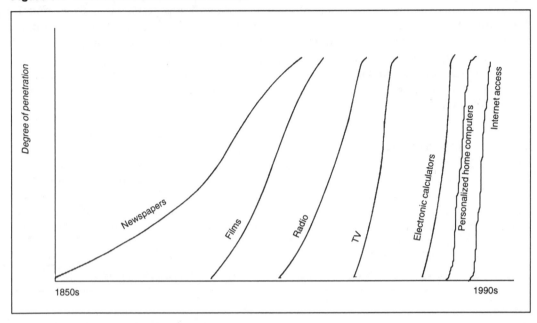

The organizational changes and the diffusion process mentioned earlier will have a social cost, at least in the short term. It seems, however, that although the direct effects on manufacturing employment have been less dramatic than earlier anticipated, a number of issues need to be borne in mind.

1 Firms introducing new information technologies so far (the innovators) were the more prosperous, more successful enterprises. Their growth compensated for potential job losses.
2 The increase in turnover associated with new information technologies was accompanied by increased added value per job, not new jobs.
3 The greatest impact has been on older, less well-educated males, i.e. a sector which is particularly difficult to reach through retraining and other schemes.

The work of L. Sawyers[14] in the retail sector arrived at broadly similar findings, but noted that among female workers there is evidence of:

1 Resistance to developing the skills to use the new technologies at a level far greater than their male counterparts.
2 De-skilling, as first and second levels of supervisory management are cut back in numbers as central control becomes easier.

These broader organizational and social consequences will need to be overcome if the potentials inherent in the technologies are to be realized.

Computing and telecommunications

The emergence of Viewdata systems was one of the early symbols of the telecommunications and computer-based systems. The link enabled computer systems to provide a wide range of data to a diverse array of users albeit in a static and non-interactive way.

The computer remains the most potent symbol of the information revolution of the second half of this century. It has been the basis on which major corporations have been built, attitudes challenged and new skills developed and demanded.

Table 9.2 The major computer companies, 1985, 1989 and 1993

1985		1989		1993	
Name	Country of origin	Name	Country of origin	Name	Country of origin
IBM	US	IBM	US	IBM	US
Philips	Netherlands	Digital	US	Apple	US
NEC	Japan	NEC	Japan	NEC	Japan
Honeywell	US	Hewlett-Packard	US	Compaq	US
Sperry	US	AT&T	US	Toshiba	Japan
Hewlett-Packard	US	Apple	US	DEC	US
Control Data	US	ICL/Fujitsu	Japan	Sun	US
Burroughs	US	Sun	US	ICL/Fujitsu	Japan
Digital	US	Olivetti	Italy	Tandy/Grid/Viclo	US
Wang	US	Siemens	Germany	Sieko/Epson	Japan

The position of the leading firms has changed rapidly over the 1980s as some responded to new challenges and others have failed to maintain their position. Philips, Honeywell, Sperry, Control Data, Burroughs, Wang and ICL all lost ground over the last decade. Others, notably the Japanese IT companies, Apple and Sun made progress. The virtual elimination of European producers from the top ten raises wider issues of competitiveness. The stages of the development of this area were as follows:

1 *The introduction of mainframe computers into industry, commerce and government.* Mainframe computers were generally expensive and required specialist staff to operate them efficiently. The primary role of the computer in these early years was in the performance of traditional computational or calculation 'number crunching'. Markets for these items were specialized, generally based on the notion of 'expert to expert' sales and service. The customer expected a high degree of customizing of project, software and service. Many organizations structured their internal operations around their 'data processing' department. Typically such departments were responsible for all policy and development.

2 *The launch of the minicomputer (1960s).* Generally minicomputers met the same broad array of needs but they were smaller, cheaper and generally more tolerant of their operating environment. The rapid growth of the producers of 'minis' was based on the combination of low price and robustness. This meant that they could be used for applications and in areas closed to the traditional mainframe and the data processing specialists. They rapidly penetrated novel areas such as science laboratories as users with specialist needs explored potential uses. Marketing and sales relationships were generally based on the applications-orientated non-computing expert in dialogue with the supplier firm. Buyers still expected a great deal of client service but tempered this with a recognition of their responsibility for 'applications packages'. Despite these developments the computer remained a highly specialized 'expert'-orientated tool until the early 1980s.

3 *The introduction of the microcomputer (1980s).* The dramatic reduction in entry costs mentioned earlier meant that access to the technology was opened to a vast array of non-specialist users. The limitations were primarily in user awareness and software. This era saw the computer change from a highly specialized tool to a universal aid in every area from work to entertainment. This in turn has broken up the market.

4 *The specialization of the market.* Diversity of machines, software and users dominates today's markets. Equipment varies from the super-computer to the Sony Playstation. Users might move from one piece of equipment to another, depending on need. Lines between types are becoming blurred as processing speeds increase and the lines between types disappear.

5 *The development of the Internet and intranets.* The Internet was originally established as a public network linked to US defence interests. It was gradually taken over by academic and specialist interests. Only recently have the commercial opportunities been recognized and exploited through speciality stores like the on-line bookstore Amazon[15] and general stores like Wal-Mart[16] in the USA.

Amazon, the online bookstore, highlights the Web's potential. It has no premises, originally operating out of the front room of its founder. It has access to over 2.3 million titles, and ships books around the world. It provides background and information that is impossible to deliver by conventional means. This background support includes expert reviews and even author comments.

It is very difficult to predict the direction that computational technology will take over the next decade. It is clear that the range of applications will continue to increase as customer confidence and the range of technology increases. Developments like the launch of Windows 98 highlight both the changing nature of the market and the power of Microsoft, although this power has been questioned by the US government At the same time it seems likely that research into 'expert systems' will bear some fruit. Perhaps the most important likely development for marketing people will emerge from the developing links between computers and communications systems (more precisely, telecommunications). The last few years saw a host of emerging technologies emerge in a fragmented form. The mobile phone, the laptop computer, cable television, the fax and electronic mail systems seem certain to come together into flexible, quick and easy-to-use communication and information systems.

Information technology and distribution

Retailers, wholesalers and distributors use computers and their associated technologies to perform the types of function described above. However, the newer, lower-price, easier-to-use systems provided an opportunity during the late 1980s to introduce a range of innovations especially suited to the trading practices and traditions of the retail and distributive sector. These include EPOS (electronic point of sale systems) and EFTS (electronic funds transfer systems). In particular they provide:

1 Opportunities for decentralization.
2 Scope for storage, assembly and analysis of the vast number of transactions whose volume defeated earlier attempts to gather and use it effectively.
3 Increased opportunities for effective management control in key areas such as stock control, inventory management and order/payment processing.
4 The potential to link transactions into 'electronic' funds transfer.

Besides these general opportunities there is increasing interest in the integration of retailing with the new technologies in a more active way. Many experiments have been tried: several have failed. Tesco's 'armchair shopping', i.e. where the items for sale are listed on the TV screen, made little headway in the face of customer resistance. Similar experiments, including Birmingham 'Club 403' and the home banking initiative of the Bank of Scotland, had varied success. They do, however, indicate the avenues which are likely to open over the next few years. The success of QVC on cable television and the growth of Internet shopping is shifting this pattern with varying responses in terms of consumer satisfaction, e.g. the Fortune Report.[17]

However, it is at the 'point of sale' that most immediate changes have taken place. The introduction of electronic point of sale systems (EPOS) and associated bar coding systems gives firms the opportunity to:

1 Check and monitor prices.
2 Store and retrieve accurate up-to-the minute information.
3 Print detailed till receipts.
4 Measure performance.
5 Improve cash control (even eliminate cash if electronic funds transfer is introduced).
6 Price goods more accurately and easily.

These improvements in the management functions have direct impacts on the marketing policies of the retailer and distributors and their relationships with manufacturers. Traditional problems such as 'out of stock' difficulties should be drastically reduced, while the ability of the trader to monitor the performance of products will pose major challenges to the producers.

Traders and suppliers use the new technology in merchandizing and promotion to improve layouts, quickly introduce special promotions, especially those based on price, and provide accurate information and promotional material for customers, perhaps using interactive video and computer graphics. A bar code, such as that in Figure 9.4, contains coded information which can be read by a laser scanner or light pen linked with a computer.

Figure 9.4 Illustration of a bar code

The marketing information system

The increased access to data provided by the new information technologies imposes extra responsibilities on management to use it effectively. This requires the construction of carefully planned and well-organized marketing information systems:

> The MIS is the organized arrangement of people, machines and procedures set up to ensure that all relevant and usable information required by marketing management reaches them at a time and in a form to help them with effective decision-making.

This definition highlights the important features of a marketing information system.

Management control

Central to marketing information systems is the notion that they are set up and organized to ensure the most effective use of marketing intelligence. This normally calls for planning, research, experimentation and introduction to ensure that the objectives of the MIS are achieved. Establishing these 'goals' for the system is the first step. These aims should be as clearly defined and as fully understood as possible. Specific responsibility for managing and monitoring the system is allocated to ensure continuing system efficiency as needs change and the range and variety of data develop. The system will only work if it is operated effectively.

This calls for the integration of people, machines and procedures. People are frequently the primary sources of information as well as responsible for its efficient allocation and distribution. Machines are the tools of the system. It is a common fallacy that equipment can solve the problems in this area. It is generally more accurate to say that machines can only make good solutions work better (or bad solutions worse). Procedures for review, access and allocation are vital to system maintenance.

User friendliness

Despite these organizational and control considerations, marketing information systems exist for only one reason: to assist with effective decision-making. It is critical that those responsible for decisions, the users, provide the basis on which the system is designed. This means involving line marketing management at an early stage in specifying their requirements. Frequently this does not mean additional information:

> Some Management Information Systems (MIS), as well as much of the literature on MIS, are based on a significant misconception. The assumption is made that the computer systems will benefit the management of the enterprise by providing more historical or projected data, of greater accuracy, in a more timely fashion, directly to the line manager for use in managing . . . (but) very few line managers want more data than they now get whether historical or projected; most managers are inundated with data.[18]

The design of effective marketing information systems calls for the integration of the sources with needs. Figure 9.5 illustrates the twin processes which come together in an effective information system.

Figure 9.5 The marketing information system development process. Reproduced with permission.

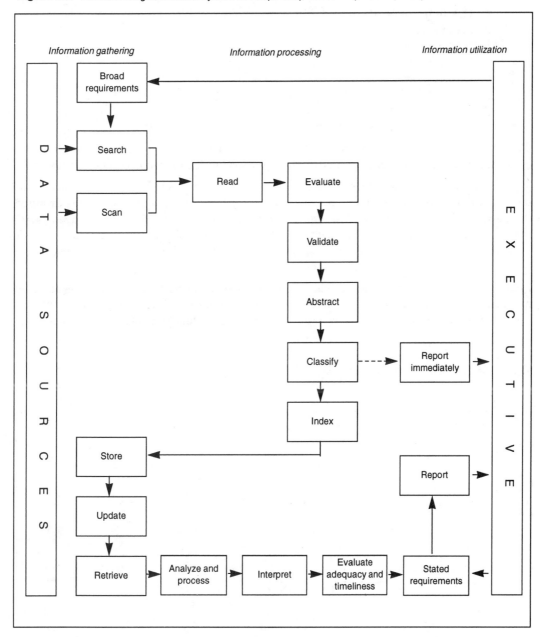

Watkins[19] identifies the three essential features of a marketing information system as:

1 Sources of information.
2 Mechanisms for handling and manipulating data.
3 Decisions requiring information.

In Britain, Fletcher[20] identified eight common uses for information systems:

1 Customer analysis.
2 Profit analysis.
3 Sales force control.
4 Competitor analysis.
5 Cost savings.
6 Improved data retrieval.
7 Sales forecasting.
8 Planning and decision-making.

These are listed in order of frequency. Some companies have used IT for much more extensive consultation and research projects like the Philips consultation on products and attitudes.[21]

The rapid reduction in the price of information has made it relatively cheap and easy to distribute microcomputers widely in firms. The real price of computing power has dropped dramatically. The data in Figure 9.6 suggests that the cost of information processing capacity measured in MIPS (Millions of Instructions Per Second) has also tumbled over this period. Parallel improvements in software, especially in 'user friendliness', have increased the willingness of managers to use these data.

Piercy[22] highlighted the degree to which conventional institutional barriers are eroded by modern information technologies. The integration of data from 'scanning', cable TV and Viewdata sources, besides more conventional means of gathering data, provides opportunities

Figure 9.6 The reducing cost of information

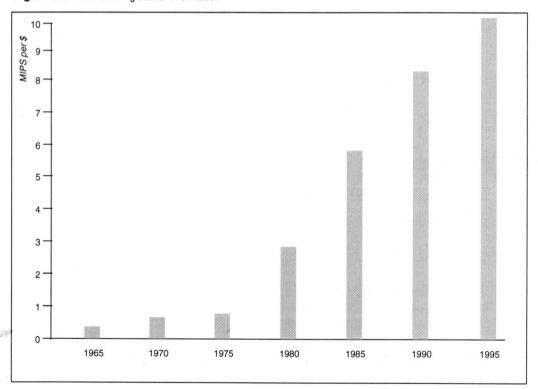

for manufacturers and retailers to co-operate to improve customer services. At the same time, new avenues for competition will emerge as firms realize that whoever controls the information system controls the market. Piercy's Product-Market Macro-Marketing Information System illustrates how the data sources of suppliers and intermediaries can dovetail through the 'central market data base' (Figure 9.7). Although Information Processing has exploded since 1983, the structure at the heart of Piercy's system still holds true.

Figure 9.7 The product-market macro-marketing information system. *Source:* Piercy, N., 'Information Processing – the Newest Mix Element', Marketing Education Group Conference, 1983.

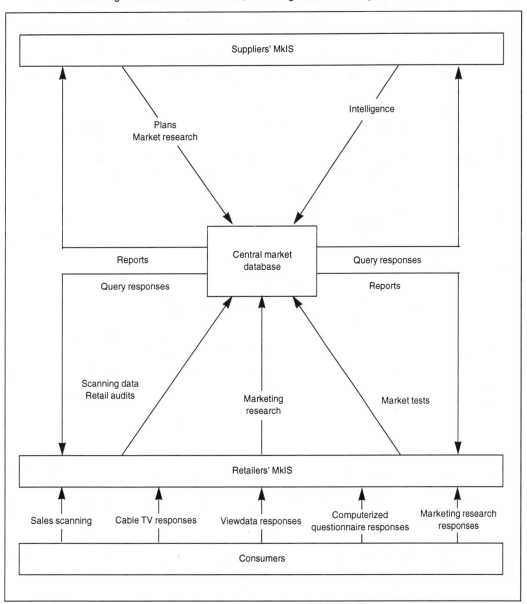

Conclusion

Information technologies and marketing information systems are increasingly important features of modern marketing. They affect a rapidly expanding number of transactions and exchanges between buyers and suppliers. Credit cards, electronic funds transfer,[23] stock management, product design and development, and logistics are integrated and shaped by information technologies and their effective use. Major developments such as Just-in-Time production, TQM and Time Based Competition are made possible by these new technologies.[24] This is prompting marketing educators to place marketing information systems and technologies at the core of the education, training and development process.[25] This in turn will produce new generations of marketers capable of exploiting fully the potential of these new systems.

In an area as complex and dynamic as this it is difficult to be confident that the aspects identified as central today will remain so. However, the following points should be borne in mind:

1   Information technology is transforming a wide range of commercial relationships.
2   It is influencing both the nature of the goods on the market and the ways firms organize themselves.
3   Historically, those firms already established in markets have faced very real difficulties in coping with the type of discontinuous change taking place today.
4   The retail and wholesale distribution along with the office and business services sectors are at the centre of many of the innovations in the application of IT in customer transactions.
5   The access to data places special demands on those involved in information systems design and implementation.

Glossary on information technology[26]

Alphanumeric key pad. A small calculator-type keyboard containing both numbers and letters, used to give instructions to the computer in a viewdata system.

Bar codes. A series of black lines of varying widths, each width representing a number from 0 to 9. Used in combination they form a digital code which can be identified by a laser scanner or light pen linked to a computer.

Computer terminal. A device that provides input/output facilities to a computer, often from a remote location.

Electronic cash register: ECR. A device which serves as a cash register but because of its electronic components can be enhanced to perform calculation and price look-up functions.

Electronic funds transfer system: EFTS. A system which communicates information about payments electronically instead of on paper and, as with cheque payment, minimizes the physical handling of cash.

Electronic point-of-sale systems: EPOS. A general name for systems which record sales data at the point of payment on to a cassette tape or computer file.

Electronic pricing. Price information that is held in computer files and is communicated automatically to the cash register upon the manual or automatic entry of a product code.

Encodation. The process of incorporating a code, usually into the magnetic strip on a credit or charge card.

Fibre optics (or optical fibres). An optical system that uses one or more glass Perspex fibres as a light guide. The fibre optics system now used for telecommunication purposes use electronic signals from a transmitter to modulate a laser beam, which is then transmitted through the fibres. Many more signals can be carried through a bunch of fibres than through a conventional copper cable of the same diameter.

Laser scanner. A fixed, flat-bed device which uses a laser beam to measure the width of the black lines of a bar code when products incorporating such a code are passed over it. Since each different width has a unique numerical identify the scanner is able, when linked to a computer, to convert the series of lines into a digital code for product identification purposes.

Light pen or wand. A similar concept to the laser scanner except that the beam emanates from a hand-held device resembling a pen or wand which is moved across the bar code by hand.

Machine readable code. Any form of coding which can be identified by an electronic device, e.g. bar code.

Modem. A device which fits between computing equipment and British Telecom equipment to convert data into a form which allows it to be transmitted over telephone lines.

Off-line. A term which identifies those items of equipment that are part of a computer system, but are not controlled by a central computer. Information that is to be communicated to the computer is stored on magnetic tape, cassette, or disk, which is then dispatched by post or messenger service.

On-line. A part of a computer system is on-line if it is directly under the control of a central processor.

Optical character recognition: OCR. A form of coding in which standard typewriter characters and numbers can be read by an optical device connected to a computer, as well as the human eye.

Packet switching. A technique in which data is transmitted across a data network in discrete, addressed blocks (called packets). Terminals on a packet network may send and receive packets to and from a number of other terminals simultaneously.

Portable data capture unit: PDCU. A device like a calculator which acts as a small, portable computer. Typically it can be used by a salesman, or stock checker, to record information for subsequent entry into a computer.

Price look-up: PLU. A facility for obtaining price information that is held on the computer and using it to record a sale through the cash register, usually by means of entering a product code.

Protocols. A formal procedure for the exchange of data between computers or computer terminals.

Visual display unit: VDU. A computer terminal comprising a video display and keyboard which allows data to be entered, displayed, dispatched or received from a computer.

Wanding. The process of moving a light or magnetic 'pen' or 'wand' across a machine readable code in order to record the coded information into a computer.

SPECIMEN QUESTIONS

1 It has been asserted that computers will eventually take over all manufacturing, selling and customer care activities and functions within the company. How far is this true and to what extent are the traditional functions of marketing being overtaken by computers?

2 Identify two markets that might be significantly changed by the 'electronic highways' being advocated in North America and the UK. Identify the strategies that firms in the affected markets might use to maximize their potential gains from these changes.

3 Zuboff argues that information technology will change the very nature of business activity in areas like marketing. What are these changes and what is meant by changing the nature of business?

4 What is meant by 'mass customization'? Identify a market in which firms are trying to introduce 'mass customization' and describe the ways in which business and relations with customers are being affected.

5 It is suggested that new information will have four broad effects on patterns of market behaviour; describe with examples:

   (a)   These four effects.

   (b)   A market that was affected at an early stage by these changes.

   (c)   A market that might be immune from these changes.

6 Describe the impact of 'full page make-up' on national newspapers. What effect is this change likely to have on newspaper advertising?

7 It is often argued that the 'life-cycles' of products are rapidly contracting in the face of new technologies and innovations in marketing development. How true is this claim? Support your argument with detailed analysis of a market or markets.

8 Why have European producers of computers virtually disappeared from the international lists of the top ten computer companies? Can anything be done to reverse this trend? Illustrate your answer with references to specific firms.

9 Design a marketing information system for an organization of your choice. In this design indicate:

   (a)   The direction of the different flows.

   (b)   Any filters that might be built in.

   (c)   The key decision points.

   (d)   The marketing advantages that will be gained from a well-designed system.

10 Define:

   (a)   Information technology.

   (b)   Electronic retailing.

   (c)   ESPRIT.

   (d)   JIT management.

   (e)   CAD.

   (f)   Total Quality.

(g)   Expert systems.

(h)   User friendliness.

(i)   The Intranet.

(j)   MIPs.

10

Intermediary markets and marketing

Introduction

David Morrel, then Assistant Managing Director of Tesco Stores, once gave a talk at a conference in London. Two inter-related themes dominated his lecture:

1 The lack of proper consultation of the retailer by the manufacturer. 'All that manufacturers in this country are concerned about is "What can we get in to the store?" not, "What does the supermarket operator want?"'

2 From the trader's perspective, retail marketing and selling (in this case super-markets) are very different from manufacturer marketing. 'The principles of supermarket selling are quite simple: pile it high and sell it cheap; the best selling line in the best selling position; if you have any money to spend at all, spend it on discounts, spend it on incentive.'

Later, the Annual Conference of the Advertising Association returned to these issues when the main topic at the Conference was: 'Is the growing power of the retail chains against the public interest?' The recurrent theme was that the power of the retail groups was so great that competition, innovativeness and profitability among manufacturers were being seriously eroded. Geoff Darby of Smith Kline Beecham summarized these views later with the comment:

> So much buying power is today concentrated into the hands of so few
> retailers that these retailers are able to exert considerable influence upon
> the marketing activities of the manufacturer.

In the years which followed, the discussion of retail or trade power has been a recurrent feature in marketing. Although the views have mellowed, the discussion has spilled into other areas of intermediary behaviour:

1 The BETRO Report on Britain's exports suggested that UK exporters were overdependent on agents.

2 British Leyland (now the Rover Group) criticized many of its dealers for failing to increase their throughput.

3 Appliance manufacturers have demanded better service and repair facilities.

These discussions clearly demonstrate the importance of intermediary relationships and the part they play in the marketing system. Despite this, there remains a tendency to view intermediary marketing as largely a service to manufacturers. The success of many intermediaries has been based on the recognition that building up their business and its prosperity is dependent on understanding the needs of their customer. This goes far beyond customers' needs to have specific products stocked, and encompasses location, price stock levels, range of goods, hours of opening and many other elements that make up customers' relationships with their stores. The returns to the retailer who recognizes the value of marketing are enormous. Marks and Spencer have been so successful at this, that Piercy recently described it as 'perhaps the most spectacular success in retailing anywhere in the world'.[1] This view was confirmed in 1997 when Fortune magazine[2] ranked Marks and Spencer as one of the most admired retailers in the world.

Changes, developments and competition

An intermediary or middle man is any firm or individual who provides a service between manufacturers and end-users in a channel of distribution (Figure 10.1). Continual pressures to improve channel services and reduce costs, along with relatively low costs of entry, result in intermediary patterns being in an almost constant state of change and development. For example, the Iceland Group grew from a market stall to a turnover of over £1 billion in 20 years. Although the cost of entry can be low and the potential enormous, substantial risks face the intermediary. In fact, the largest group of bankruptcy cases each year is normally drawn from the retail trade.

Figure 10.1 Trading patterns

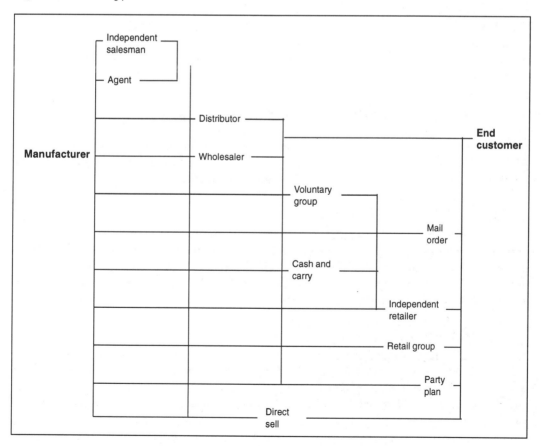

This pattern of change and development is so significant that the concept of the 'wheel of retailing' has been coined to describe how new retailers can enter markets, generally as low-status, low-profit-margin, low-price operators. As they move upmarket, through improved customer service, better design and display etc., opportunities are created for new types of retailer. An illustration of this can be seen today in the way firms like Amazon[3] are using the Internet to keep their costs low while delivering high standards of customer service.

AutoWeb Interactive is a low-cost, high-feature US car trader operating on the Internet. AutoWeb helps buyers to find their desired car and identify available deals. The facilities extend beyond new to used cars. The service incorporates trade-in support and access to sources of finance. From a private operation trading out of the founder's home, AutoWeb is now one of the largest car traders on the Internet in the USA.

Firms like Tesco were originally small outlets, providing a minimum array of services, often trading in lower-cost urban areas. Their recent growth is characterized by an expansion of services, from bottle banks to restaurants. The scale of their operations has increased. They have moved from smaller, high street locations to giant suburban sites. Prices have gradually increased. Convenience and the ability to do 'One stop shopping' has replaced the 'Pile it high and sell it cheap' maxim mentioned earlier. The gap left in the market is filled by new entrants. Kwik Save, Aldi and others grow by exploiting the traditional price/convenience opportunity. The scope that exists to grow by cutting costs while enhancing service and perceived benefits is vividly illustrated by the success and growth of Daewoo Cars. They have, in effect, taken over the middle man's role.

The 'wheel of retailing' is a useful rule of thumb that can partly explain some of the major changes in retailing over time (Figure 10.2). However, it fails to explain either the persistence of certain types of outlet (e.g. fruit and vegetable markets continue to prosper) or some relatively high-price entries (e.g. vending machines and craft shops).

Agents, distributors and wholesalers

Agents, distributors and wholesalers are the middle men's middle men. Their primary role for the customer is to provide access to a broad range of supplies so that the customer does not have to deal with each individual manufacturer.

Independent salespeople

Independent salespeople are sometimes called factory representatives, although they are not employed by any one firm. They act partly as salespeople and partly as intermediary managers. In the Western industrial economies their role has generally been taken over by the selling agent, but in the Third World countries they provide local retailers with access to goods or opportunities to become dealers or distributors.

Agents

The major role of agents is the management of relations between customers and manufacturers. They do not become principals in the purchasing transaction but usually operate for a fee or commission. The agent's skill lies in selecting his or her client list carefully and then effectively selling their goods to appropriate wholesalers, distributors, and even end-users.

Figure 10.2 The changing and overlapping pattern of trade

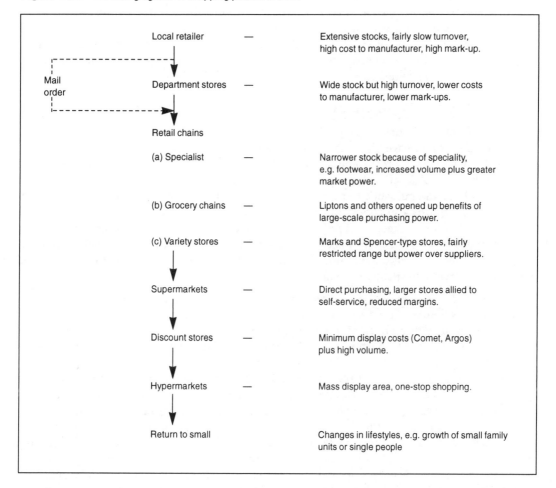

Local retailer	—	Extensive stocks, fairly slow turnover, high cost to manufacturer, high mark-up.
Mail order		
Department stores	—	Wide stock but high turnover, lower costs to manufacturer, lower mark-ups.
Retail chains		
(a) Specialist	—	Narrower stock because of speciality, e.g. footwear, increased volume plus greater market power.
(b) Grocery chains	—	Liptons and others opened up benefits of large-scale purchasing power.
(c) Variety stores	—	Marks and Spencer-type stores, fairly restricted range but power over suppliers.
Supermarkets	—	Direct purchasing, larger stores allied to self-service, reduced margins.
Discount stores	—	Minimum display costs (Comet, Argos) plus high volume.
Hypermarkets	—	Mass display area, one-stop shopping.
Return to small	—	Changes in lifestyles, e.g. growth of small family units or single people

Although the pure selling function is important, the more sophisticated recognize that they are at the centre of a two-way communication process. Their customers will often have a number of different needs, and the agent's task will be to transfer information about these needs to his or her current clients as well as to seek new suppliers.

Distributors and wholesalers

Distributors and wholesalers share a willingness to hold stock, thus providing access to the physical product (rather than order processing by agents). Traditionally the distributor is linked to a single supplier for each line carried, while the wholesaler will often carry a number of competing lines.

The direct link between distributor and supplier usually means that far more extensive support facilities are provided, often in return for regional or industry exclusiveness. The provision of back-up services, as well as more extensive stockholding, is critical to effective distributor marketing. In the past, wholesalers played a dominant role in the distribution of many goods, and their scale of operation permitted them to exercise considerable power over their retail customers. In the first half of this century, however, this position of leadership was eroded by the giant manufacturers who stimulated customer 'pull', in part through media advertising and promotion. Since the 1950s their position has been further eroded by the growth of the major retailers, whose market power enabled them to by-pass the wholesaler to deal direct with the manufacturers. More recently, cash and carry wholesalers have built up a strong position as suppliers to smaller, local retailers. It will be interesting to see whether 'discount club or warehouses' can reverse this trend.

Self-service wholesaler

Wholesalers have exploited a number of inherent strengths to stage a limited comeback. A number have made use of their tradition of strong retailer links (primarily with the small independent stores) to build up voluntary groups such as VG, Mace and Spar. The sales forces of wholesalers (especially those in voluntary groups) have become skilled in providing advice and guidance to customers which goes far beyond the traditional sales task. The voluntary groups also conduct joint advertising. Credit, delivery and high service levels are critical to their success. The restricted financial resources and limited staffing characteristics of most retailers make the 'service' cost well worth paying. This pattern of support has been helped by the move by many manufacturers to restrict their selling and distribution services to smaller accounts.

For example, in the cigarette market these patterns created a gap that Philip Morris successfully exploited. This firm's launch into the UK was targeted on the wholesaler. It capitalized on the cutting back of direct supplies by some of the UK majors to small outlets with their inevitable move to wholesalers. At the time the UK majors were slow to react to this increased wholesaler significance. The most important growth area in wholesaling has been in cash and carry operations. The idea behind these is simple: retailers, hoteliers and caterers are given the opportunity to 'supermarket shop'. Acting almost as giant supermarkets, with suitable trade discounts, they keep their overheads down while providing traders with access to goods. They are normally located in out-of-town areas, and their low overheads keep costs and prices down. A recurrent problem for cash and carry outlets is the 'rogue' buyer, i.e. the individual who uses the outlet for personal shopping. Retailers are hostile to any cash and carry which permits this to develop to proportions threatening their own livelihood. The skill with which the major full-service wholesalers, such as Palmer and Harvey, the cash and carry firms and the voluntary chains have employed the marketing approach, often in the face of adverse trading conditions, demonstrates its relevance, in its fullest sense, in this sector.

Retail marketing

The direct nature of the relationship between the retailer and customer has always given a sense of immediacy to the satisfaction of buyer needs in this area. The great retail entrepreneurs – Thomas Lipton, Lord Sainsbury, Marcus Sieff, Isaac Wolfson, Terence Conran and many others – have succeeded by adapting their complex offerings to customer needs. Over the past twenty years this traditionally intuitive approach has been matched by a determination to fully exploit the marketing concept.

Retail advertising leapt from £80 million in 1975 to almost £2 billion in 1996. This is a sixteen-fold increase, against an overall national seven-fold increase. Although main media advertising plays an important part in the promotion of the retail trade, the stores themselves still dominate their image. The character of the store – Next, Marks and Spencer, Boots,

Tesco, Sainsbury, Habitat, John Lewis and almost every retail outlet – is created to a considerable extent by the design, layout, appearance and staffing of the store itself. The pattern of increasing retail concentration mentioned earlier has created a situation in which the store groups must invest in these areas to ensure their continued growth and prosperity.

 ## Major types of retail outlet

The following are the main retail outlets:

1 *Independent retailer:* corner grocer, independent chemist, small group of retailers (probably not more than fifteen outlets).
2 *Retail chains:* typified by the large supermarket chain but including some speciality stores, e.g. W. H. Smith or Boots.
3 *Department stores:* large general-goods stores offering an enormous array of goods.
4 *Co-operative societies:* usually 'owned' in some way by consumers. Traditionally, profits are returned to them by dividends or stamps.
5 *Voluntary trading groups:* alliances of independent traders who act together to realize economies.
6 *Door-to-door delivery:* specialist carriers, usually delivering a limited selection of goods to customers.
7 *Cash and carry discount shops:* retailers offering a minimum of service and presentation at low prices, e.g. Comet.
8 *Electronic retailers:* includes cable companies like QVC, and Internet traders like Amazon.

The post-war period has seen an increasing concentration in virtually all sectors, with the independent retailers, co-operative stores and department stores steadily losing ground to the retail groups and chains.

Successful marketing among retailers is based on the effective management of product array, location, pricing and promotional policies.

 ## Product

The product mix offered provides the customer with clues to the type of offering and fashion changes. Adaptability in this area is a major problem: strengths can become liabilities as tastes and fashions change. An illustration of this is provided by the problems which faced the Burton Group in the 1970s and 1980s. The established strength of the group in providing reasonably priced, made-to-measure suits, with substantial vertical integration (from sheep to shop), caused major problems when tastes moved to ready-to-wear, high fashion clothing. The response of the group was to develop a wide range of high-volume speciality stores. They exploited the group's merchandizing strengths. Sales grew and Burton became one of the success stories of the 1980s. The depressed markets of the late 1980s saw sales slump. The architect of the earlier successes, Sir Ralph Halpern, was forced to resign as the company looked for new policies to renew its successes. In the early 1990s, the debts of the group grew as it paid the price for policies initiated in the 1980s.

Stock is not there merely to attract customers. Stock turn-around is a major factor in determining retail profitability. It therefore requires a thorough appraisal of all lines in terms of their contribution to income and the part they play in moving other items and lines. The idea of the 'loss leader' in supermarket shopping illustrates this interdependence of lines. Specific products are sold at very low prices, perhaps even at a loss, with the aim of drawing in customers who will purchase enough other items to pay off the firm's investment. As a concept, it has become linked in supermarkets and hypermarkets to the notion of one stop-shopping, where customers are encouraged to do all their shopping in one outlet. This saves time but also gives significant boosts to the average shopper's expenditure. 'Own-label', sometimes called 'private-label', brands play an important part in retailing:

> Own-label products are defined as consumer products produced by, or on behalf of, distributors and sold under the distributor's own name or trade-mark through the distributor's own outlet.[4]

For a time during the late 1960s and early 1970s the growth of own-label brands in supermarkets was seen as a threat to the viability of many manufacturers' brands:

> The manufacturer finds that his brand is under fire from the private label products which usurp what he has come to regard as his own shelf space in the store and consequently part of his sales.[5]

For a time the strength of own-labels such as St Michael and Sainsbury's, allied to the appearance of own-label products in most major retail groups and the voluntary associations, seemed to confirm this. However, over the past few years the share of own-label brands has stabilized, and even shown indications of decline, although individual own-label brands have grown. The policies of particular stores vary (see Table 10.1).

Table 10.1 Private-label share of grocery sales

Twelve weeks ending	Aug. 1975	Aug. 1976	Aug. 1977	Aug. 1978	Aug. 1983	Aug. 1985	Aug. 1987	Aug. 1993
Tesco %	24	24	23	23	24	24	25	25
Sainsbury %	67	65	62	57	63	62	64	65

Source: AGB/TCA

Private-label is now recognized as a tactic which can play a part in building a product mix and reinforcing imagery, but only one aspect of this. The key factors in introducing own-label are: improved gross or net margin; low prices; own-label brands which are good value becoming associated with the store and assisting in building loyalty; and supply problems with established brands.

Location

Perhaps the most important decision facing a retailer or distributor is the location of the outlet. In many senses the primary offering to the consumer is location, or availability. In the past such decisions have been simplified by the desire to establish outlets in or near shopping centres or on the high street. More recently, however, some major stores have established an ability to attract custom. A Marks and Spencer shop nearby might ensure sufficient interest in the location to justify the high rents involved in being near Marks and Spencer.

One of the earliest attempts to provide a more systematic approach to retail location analysis was the work of Reilly[6] on the gravitational pull of specific positions on trade from adjoining areas. This model has been developed further to incorporate such issues as the relation between distance and size, the topography of the area, ease of access (public transport, road networks and parking) and communication (catchment areas of local radio, television and newspapers) (Figure 10.3). Absolute distance from an outlet is less important than, say, motorway access. Retailer B in Figure 10.3 can draw significant numbers of customers from Store C's catchment because of easier access. Checklists are commonly used to gauge the potential of specific locations in terms of such criteria. An example of a location checklist is: rent; rates; frontage (to main street); area of shop; local expenditure on items held; competition in area; distance from firm's other outlets; local population (catchment area defined); composition of population; physical characteristics of outlet; availability of labour; character of area; adjoining outlets.

The success of retail parks, notably Metrocentre in Gateshead, has highlighted the value of the total retail experience and the scope for linking retail outlets.

Figure 10.3 The drawing power of different outlets A, B and C, weighted by ease of travel. From Cannon, T., *Distribution Research*. London: Intertext, 1973

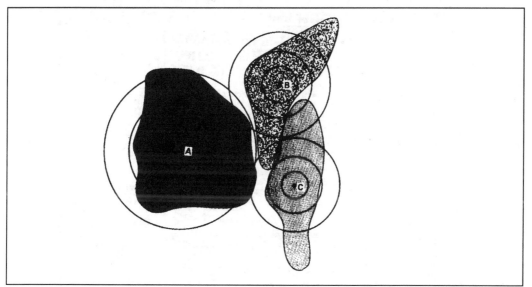

Prices

A glance at the type of advertising used by retailers or in store promotion shows the importance given to price in retail promotion (Figure 10.4). Most retail pricing is a mixture of mark-up prices, specific promotion and targeting on specific markets. The overall level of prices and prominence given to price in promotion (both in and out of store) are generally conditioned by the store's target market and desired image. For example, price may be an aspect of the appeal of Sainsbury's but it generally receives relatively little prominence.

The major exception to this in retailing is the sale. Sales are used by retailers for a variety of reasons: clearing stock, ironing out seasonalities, renewing interest in the store, and publicity. They have the special characteristic that even a store which targets itself on upper-income groups, such as Harrods, can run a sale with no risk to its overall image.

Until now the discussion of retailing has focused on semi- and non-durable goods. Traders in durables (cars, household appliances etc.) face many of the same stocking, pricing and location problems, but their marketing also needs to take into account the high value (per unit) of their items and the service and warranty requirements of their customers.

Figure 10.4 Consumer advertising by retail group highlights the importance of price. Reproduced with the permission of Morgan.

Stock turnover is critical when the item could be worth anything between £1,000 and £40,000. This places particular importance on the role of the salesperson in the transaction. Generally the durables salesperson will be expected to do far more than simply collect an order. He or she may need to arrange credit, handle technical questions, negotiate trade-ins and handle immediate post-sale problems. The scale of this involvement and the need for manufacturers to be confident that these transactions were being conducted effectively contributed to the growth of producer franchising.

Franchising

Until very recently franchising in Britain was associated with manufacturer-led operations. Two forms dominated:

1 *Agencies:* in areas such as cosmetics, it is frequently the policy of manufacturers to give individual pharmacists or other outlets sole rights to retail a product in return for some agreements about display and support service, e.g. a trained beautician on the staff.
2 *Dealerships:* in the case of many consumer durables, such as cars, dealers are given exclusive rights to an area. Traditionally they were not allowed to handle competitive lines. They may also be required to meet a number of predetermined conditions and be subject to inspection.

The operations of dealer-owned petrol stations and tied houses in brewing meet the broad definition of a franchise: 'a contractual agreement allowing a customer to use a supplier's name and receive assistance in location, merchandising, or other matters in return for the purchase for resale of the supplier's product or a separately specified franchise fee'. The strength and value of these 'contracts' was closely scrutinized in the *Monopolies Commission Report on Brewing,* and pressure from the EU to reduce uncompetitive practices. This prompted the government to force the large brewers to sell many of their 'tied' houses.

Recently, there has been a surge of interest in franchising[7] as new firms, building on the American experience, use franchise arrangements as a spur to growth. In the US it is estimated that franchise operations account for just over 30 per cent of all retail sales and 10 per cent of the gross national product. The appeal of franchising is threefold:

1 To the customer it offers a reassurance of quality and service based on previous awareness or experience of the franchise.
2 To the prospective franchiser it offers fast growth with minimum strain on capital.
3 To the prospective franchisee it offers the chance to become an entrepreneur while having the reassurance of a tried and tested product or service, backed by promotion and support services.

Although there has been criticism, there is little doubt that many existing franchises are operating very effectively and that scope for growth, in both the concept and the range of industries encompassed, exists.

The future

If franchising provides one insight into the future, a number of other aspects are likely to play at least as significant a role. Marketing under conditions of recession and turbulence presents the intermediary with specific problems.

The major retailers have responded to the prospect of difficult trading conditions by:

1 *Developing the service offering*: the wage inflation and interest rates hit hard an industry which is both low-wage and labour-intensive. Consequently, retailers have been looking for ways to reduce their labour bill while expanding services. Policies have included staff reductions, less overtime, increased use of technology and greater use of part-time staff.

2 *Reducing stock levels:* most retailers claim to carry fewer brands and fewer variations within product lines so as to reduce the capital tied up and improve cash flow. Just-in-Time delivery systems are used extensively.

3 *Closing smaller outlets.*

4 *Pushing own labels:* there has been a swing back to own labels in some retail chains in the 1990s, but Tesco's success against Sainsbury raises new questions about this approach.

5 *Offering more price-off deals:* recession means that price offers are the only guaranteed way of moving stocks.

6 *Operating differential price polices:* as price has become more and more important to the consumer, store loyalty has weakened.

Almost universally, major retailers de-stocked during the recessionbut they have been reluctant to restock to the same extent since the recession.

The fact that there is a general de-stocking in the retail trade does not mean that there is any less interest in new products. If anything, the reverse is true. There is one phrase that seems to be universally used to describe new products: they are 'the life-blood of the business'; they are welcome any time. The larger retailers, particularly in the food field, no longer think so much of the terms that they can get from manufacturers, but rather of the total 'deal' or 'package' that they can negotiate. There is no doubt about the importance that retailers attach to 'price' as the key factor in determining consumer purchasing patterns: all put it at the top of the list and say that its importance is increasing.

Although one of the main developments over the last decade was large-scale, out-of-town retail units, other developments might prove to be equally important. Niche retailing seemed to go from boom to bust with the fortunes of Next, Sock Shop and Tie Rack. It is likely that others will learn from their mistakes and develop new niche retailing. The arrival of Next highlights its ability to survive. Speciality sectors will become areas of major interest, especially if the very different speciality retailers, e.g. Body Shop, continue to prosper. Environmental concerns may have an effect on the move towards out-of-town shopping. Increasing petrol prices and the prospect of shortages may lead to a revival of the local store, especially if price gaps disappear. This, however, is unlikely to be a mere copy of the traditional outlet. It is more likely to be modelled on the successful US 7-Eleven Stores. Changes in legislation will influence this. The restrictions on trading hours are disappearing and Sunday opening is becoming commonplace.

Conclusion

The history of innovation and dynamism that has characterized intermediary marketing suggests that radical new development, perhaps based on new technologies or techniques or the entrepreneurial flair of an individual, will emerge. These changes seem certain to incorporate elements of the innovative thinking of service management,[8,9] the exploitation of new technologies, and the traditional routes[10] into retail dominance. Tele-shopping has not yet made the impact expected. We can, however, guarantee that some novel development is in the wings which will reshape our shopping behaviour.

SPECIMEN QUESTIONS

1 'The growing power and concentration among retailers is against the public interest'. Discuss this proposition and weigh the different arguments for and against this proposal.

2 Marks and Spencer has been described as 'perhaps the most spectacular success in retailing anywhere in the world'. Why do you think this kind of praise might be justified? What contribution, if any, has effective marketing played in this success?

3 Describe the stages of 'the wheel of retailing'; use this analysis to describe the evolution of a retailer of your choice.

4 Critically assess the prospects of 'from home shopping' over the next three, five and ten years. What market factors are likely to increase the prospects of failure or success during these periods?

5 You are the Marketing Director of a local soccer club; you know that you could be earning more from your souvenir shop:

   (a) Indicate the steps you might undertake to get a proper picture of its potential.

   (b) Identify the three marketing factors that will most influence your short-term success.

   In the course of your analysis, you are approached by the Marketing Director of Manchester United (or Rangers if you identify with Manchester United), offering you the chance to include a Manchester United franchise in your outlet. How would you reply? Justify your response in marketing terms.

6 Compare the approach to own label adopted by C&A and Marks and Spencer. What are the implications of the different approaches to the way each firm develops its market position?

7 Outline the broad principles of gravitational modelling in retailing. Spell out some of the factors that a DIY superstore might build into its model to avoid too much overlap with rival superstores.

8 Define:

   (a) Party plan.

   (b) Voluntary group.

   (c) Cash and carry wholeselling.

   (d) Hypermarket.

   (e) Own label.

   (f) Franchising.

   (g) Stock-turn rate.

   (h) Factory outlet.

   (i) Loss leader.

   (j) Mystery shopping.

CASE STUDY 8:
PANDORA (ARTS AND CRAFTS) CONSIDERS A NEW OUTLET

History

Pandora is a group of three retail craft shops based in south-west England. It was started in 1982 by John Jackson and Graham Lonsdale, two graduates of Bristol Polytechnic's BSc in Management Studies (now University of the West of England).

Their first shop was in Bristol. Eighteen months later a store was opened in Bath and two years after this an outlet in Cardiff was added. Since then, the shops' turnover and range of items carried have grown steadily. John and Graham have been reluctant to consider further shops while consolidating their existing business. This has not prevented their moving premises twice in the last three years as superior sites in Bristol and Bath became available.

Their original concept in starting Pandora was to provide an outlet for the increasing numbers of individual craftspeople, both those already working and those just starting up, in the South West and South Wales. Although individual local craftspeople, potters, jewellers, brass-workers etc. continue to provide a large part of their range the business has expanded in a number of other directions. Links have been built up with a number of cottage industries, primarily knitwear. Graham in particular has played a substantial role in encouraging a few of their better 'designer/craftspeople' to expand in this direction, recruiting knitting or dressmaking outworkers.

A recurrent problem of obtaining good-quality stock has encouraged this development. This problem led to a more widespread search for stock, and they now have goods coming from all parts of the UK. This has led to links being established with craft guilds in the Midlands, the Lake District, Northumbria and Scotland, as well as with local groups. A few years ago the stock problem was so serious that quite large quantities of goods were being imported from Europe and North Africa. This led to some adverse comment from some craftspeople and arguments between John and Graham, as Graham was very worried about losing their high-quality craft position in the market. However, the problems have eased as their supplies of UK crafts have increased. Imported items are now less than 15 per cent of turnover (by volume) and are concentrated in the low-price end of their range.

Over the last year they have had a number of approaches from Central European countries, notably Poland and Hungary, asking them to stock their traditional crafts. Prices are very good but quality is not reliable.

The current situation

The financial period 1995–96 was the best year Pandora has ever had. Profits were good while the range and quality of the items carried were probably better then ever before. Pandora held a number of exhibitions for well-known artist-craftspeople, which gained excellent publicity both locally, with major features in the *Bristol Evening News* and on BBC South-West, and nationally, in a number of craft magazines.

In the light of these developments, John is keen to open a new outlet. Although an equal partner, he has a full-time job as a lecturer in computer science at Portsmouth Polytechnic, and would like the shop to be in this area. Graham, however, who works full-time in the business, is uncertain about this. Both agree to a more wide-ranging review of their options, and this results in the following choices:

1   Continual consolidation with a progressive improvement in range: Graham greatly prefers this as it would probably free him to develop his own craft interest as a carpenter/toymaker.

2   Open a new outlet in the same general South West region, in Cheltenham, Exeter or Plymouth.

3   Use their links with the craft community to develop a wholesale side to their business, perhaps even involving them in exports or imports, e.g. from Central Europe.

4   Hold back on developments until the economic situation improves.

5   Open the outlet in Portsmouth suggested by John, but bearing in mind that he will still work only part-time in the business.

This is perhaps the most critical problem facing them in 1998.

Task

Advise on a policy.

11

Industrial markets

Introduction

In 1965 Aubrey Wilson introduced a collection of readings on the subject of marketing industrial goods with the comment:

> Industrial marketing is so broad a subject, so vital for individual firms and for the economy, that it is truly remarkable why so few books specifically on this subject have appeared in the UK.

That book itself is now out of print and, apart from a relatively small number of exceptional contributions, the area is still badly neglected, relative to consumer-goods marketing. This does not reflect any relative insignificance of the sector: there are more firms and more areas of activity encompassed by industrial marketing than by consumer marketing. Britain's exports are dominated by industrial goods: an estimated 60 per cent of manufactured exports.

One of the fundamental objectives of this text is to seek to give a better balance in coverage. As a deliberate policy, discussion of the implications for industrial marketers of many of the points made are included in the specific sections. In this chapter some of these points will be brought together and the special character of industrial markets reviewed.

Federal Express has grown into one of the world's most successful delivery companies, by combining astute targeting of customers with use of advanced technologies and the use of technology. In order to encourage high levels of customer service, staff can win the Golden Falcon Award. This occurs when a customer comments positively about a specific aspect of customer service provided by an employee. This type of individual reward is underpinned by a series of service guarantees on delivery speed and quality.

Are industrial markets different?

Two definitions help show the area in which industrial markets may have their own special character:

> Industrial marketing: All those activities concerned with purchases, sales and service in industrial markets and between organizational buyer and seller.[1]

> Industrial buyers are those buying goods and services for some tangibly productive and commercially significant purpose.[2]

The character of industrial marketing lies partly in the goods and services offered, partly in the goals of buying and partly in the buyers themselves.

The goods themselves are not necessarily unique. A manufacturing firm buys paper, tea, tools, food, banking services, telephone and postal services, cars, travel, adhesives, pens, pencils and many other items that end-users buy. The DIY enthusiast might even be buying bricks, sanding equipment or gravel, items which are traditionally associated with builders, manufacturers and other industrial markets. However, in the purchasing of many items, such as heavy lifting gear, many components, manufacturing and processing equipment, advertising and promotional services, no ambiguity exists. These 'industrial' goods and services are identifiable, but the borderline, if we use products to differentiate, is hazy.

The purpose for which items are purchased provides a clearer area of difference. The industrial firm buys goods and services for a 'tangibly productive and commercially significant purpose'. The company wants to earn some form of tangible return from its purchase. Paper for correspondence is part of the communication process, and assists internal efficiencies or external relations. At least in theory, a balance between pay-offs and expenditures can be specified. Tea might be bought for the works canteen, itself an element in the effective management and operation of the organization.

Xerox built much of its early market power through its control of a unique technology and technical support. In the 1980s, its market position in the UK was eroded through innovative rivals and cut-price competitors. It restored its market lead by putting 'customer satisfaction' at the top of its corporate priorities, then using novel advertising to reassert its technical leaders and its ability to meet needs.

This should not be taken to mean that behavioural factors do not affect choice or even the decision to purchase specific items. In a now famous experiment, Levitt[3] demonstrated how a minor design change enhancing the appearance of a piece of industrial equipment significantly improved its sales. More recently, a northern plastics moulder used models to promote his chair mouldings at an exhibition, with startling improvements in orders taken. This does not mean that this type of tactic *will* improve performance, merely that it *can*, even in a relatively undifferentiated area such as chair mouldings.

Although in consumer markets there are cases in which goods or services are purchased with a view to returns (e.g. housing repairs and specific items such as installing central heating may be viewed as improving the selling price, or individuals may get their cars serviced and buy touch-up paint to improve the car's price), in the normal course of events the purchaser probably owns the items concerned for reasons other than their resale value.

The part played by the industrial buyer or purchasing officer is an important area of differentiation. Done[4] estimates that around sixty per cent of the production costs of a car are accounted for by bought-in components. For a firm like Ford (UK), this could add up to over £2 billion per year. They enter the purchasing process for commercial reasons, and it is their job to ensure that efficiencies exist and that optimum policies are adopted by the firm in all areas of organization purchasing. Organizational purchasing is the process by which organizations define their needs for goods and services, identify and compare the suppliers and supplies available to them, negotiate with sources of supply or in some other way arrive at agreed terms of trading, make contracts and place orders, and finally receive the goods and services and pay for them. The buyer may be a senior executive of a large corporation, versed in value analysis, material management and other developments, or the chief executive of a small firm.

Although the housewife, car buyer, photo-freak or house buyer may be able to invest considerable expertise in specific areas, the continuing need to weight consequences and alternatives is far more real for industrial buyers. Their position may be enhanced by greater market power, closer relationships and technical expertise.

Although industrial markets and consumer markets often merge, there are substantial qualitative differences with which the industrial marketer must learn to cope.

Derived demand

Holding together the points of difference mentioned above is a central, common element: the demand state of industrial customers derives from the demand by others for their offerings.

For the consumer-goods producer in Figure 11.1, their demand for the various items bought is a function of the state of markets. They might open up a new export market generating a further 10 per cent demand. This will increase raw material needs and perhaps equipment and labour requirements, but probably not plant. Loss of a market such as (b) will probably reverse these trends. Over time, equipment ordering and labour needs will be affected, particularly if other losses occur. It will be only when the business has ceased to be viable that the plant needs change.

This derived demand goes some way towards explaining the lags that occur in demand for industrial goods. Increased demand will show itself first to the consumer-goods producers, then in the demand for raw materials, and later in the equipment, labour and plant markets. Similarly, these markets tend to be slower to respond to downturns. External factors can directly affect these patterns: the heralded economic downturn of the early 1990s saw firms deferring plant, equipment and labour recruitment decisions in anticipation of a future decline in demand, before their own order books were affected. When the up-turn occurred, firms ran their stocks down before re-ordering from suppliers.

Figure 11.1 Derived demand

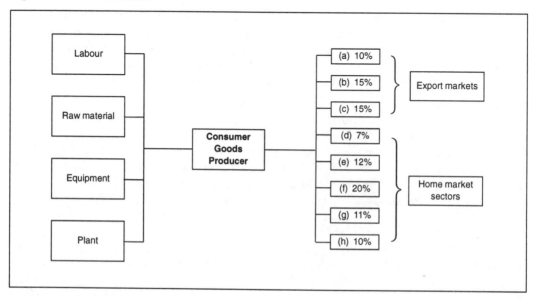

The derived nature of demand places an onus on industrial-goods suppliers to think their systems through. Customer 'pull' can be a more important determinant of demand than any sales effort.

> To effectively break these (resistances to new products) down, the manufacturer must accept the prime responsibility for approaching all levels of the system.[5]

> The rapid growth in the market for silicon rubber heat seals in cookers derived in part from fears among consumers of asbestos seals. (Managing Director of silicon rubber producing firm)

An awareness of the customer markets and an understanding of the forces affecting them plays a major part in ensuring the firm's long-term prosperity.

Figure 11.2 The main categories of industrial or organizational purchases

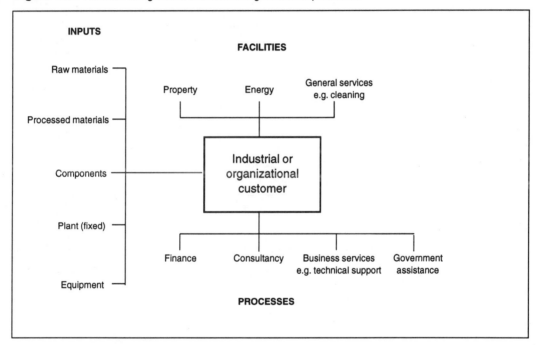

Sellers and buyers

It is a mistake to see the industrial buyer as a passive participant in this push–pull process. It is as much his or her job to buy as it is the seller's to sell, and to that extent they are in partnership. Clearly this does not mean that the buyer is under an obligation to buy from a specific supplier. It does mean that understanding marketing is an increasing feature of the purchasing officer's job.

Traditionally, industrial or organizational marketing was viewed in terms of two 'funnels' that interacted through the sales and purchasing operations of the supplier or customer respectively. The supplier funnelled its engineering and financial etc., services through their sales staff (see Figure 11.3) while the purchasing department performed the reverse process.

This is sometimes called separated marketing. Increasingly, firms have extended these networks far deeper into both enterprises. They use integrated marketing to build more powerful relationships with sales and purchasing staff performing more of a brokerage role (Figure 11.4) and managing contract compliance.

Figure 11.3 Separated marketing

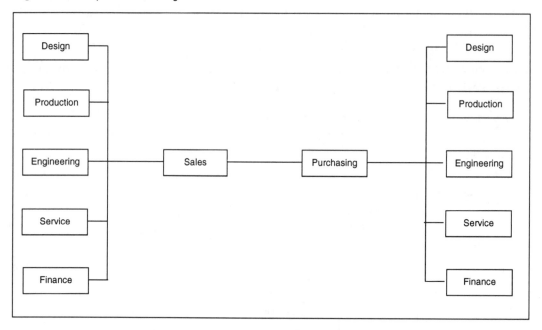

Figure 11.4 Integrated marketing

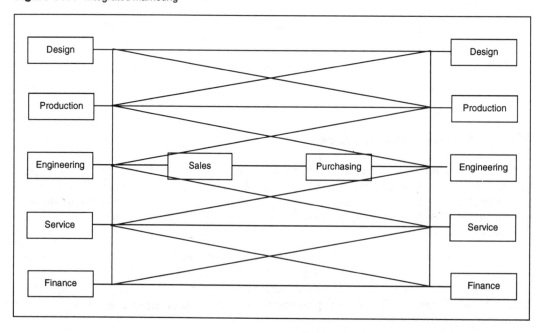

In many industrial buying situations the industrial, technological and negotiating skills, as well as the overall professionalism of the buyer, are important factors in the selling/purchasing context. Often the buyer operates in a fairly narrow and technical area, e.g. they might be responsible for all packaging requirements of a large consumer-goods manufacturer. Their knowledge places a considerable 'product knowledge' requirement on the seller.

This professionalism means that industrial buyers are capable of seeing criteria other than price on which to judge a firm's offerings. At the same time, the behavioural forces mentioned earlier influence decisions. In studies of how industry buys[6] it was found that: a significant proportion of buyers would not switch suppliers for price cuts of up to 10 per cent; and assured delivery was normally more important than quick delivery. More research is needed into the relationship between these attitudes and buyer actions. Nevertheless, current evidence suggests that professional buyers recognize the relevance of product development, service levels and communications as much as price in their purchase choices (Table 11.1).

Table 11.1 Industrial buyers and their expectations

	Yes %	No %	DK %
Expecting shorter lead times	90	10	0
Planning order further ahead	25	75	0
More conscious of *design*	85	5	10
Less concerned about price	10	90	0
More concerned about price	85	15	0
Tighter delivery specs.	90	10	0
Expecting *more innovation*	90	5	5
More innovative	65	25	10

The emerging recognition of this broader purchasing role has led to significant advances in the 'art and science of source management' over the last decade. Procurement, supplies and source management are key areas of management decision. In a wide range of industrial goods purchasing staff are adopting a more active role in:

1 *Resource planning:* evaluation of likely resource situations is becoming a part of corporate planning. This in turn places extra responsibilities on purchasing staff to recognize the impact of political, economic and other environmental forces.
2 *Purchasing research:* some companies are attempting to make routine the search process itself. Technical staff may be given responsibility for seeking ways of improving purchase performance, even to explore current manufacturing procedures.
3 *Value analysis:* the firms adopting this perspective call upon their buyers to review the whole purchase act, not just the price but also specification, stocks and delivery times, in order to bring out the real savings that are possible.
4 *Materials analysis:* this focuses on two aspects of supplies: the total costs of key items and the real returns from being involved in these expenditures. Materials-analysis teams involve staff who have a range of functions, enabling them to get to the root of total produce make-up and hence procurement policies.

Purchasing staff are being directed more and more toward a constant scanning of the horizon. There is some evidence that besides placing pressures on the salesman's product knowledge, demands on the supplier's communication, and calls on suppliers to consider carefully their service and delivery levels, these developments are posing questions for supplier technology.

The product life-cycle is likely to shorten if the purchaser actively searches for newer, superior or simply cheaper ways of more effectively meeting procurement goals. Research into user-initiated innovation vividly illustrates this role.[7]

Hitherto in this discussion a critical aspect of the buyers' situation has been played down: this aspect is risk. All their purchasing involves some degree of risk. For example, a new supplier may not deliver, thus disrupting product schedules; a new material may not run properly, costing large sums in machine time and waste; or an established supplier's service may deteriorate. The risks involved directly affect all the buyers' evaluation processes, and their response to salesmen is affected by this.

Risk avoidance, allied to certain minimum 'satisfying'[8] policies, may lead to a considerable degree of conservatism in purchase policies. Swedish researchers[9] found that procurement staff were reluctant to buy from smaller overseas firms: when trial orders were placed, they kept in very close, almost daily contact, for reassurance. Breakdowns or problems in communication, e.g. home staff not passing on messages or being unable to speak any foreign languages, created tensions even when not accompanied by a failure to perform well. This Swedish research has much in common with Levitt's findings[10] on the interplay between communication and industrial setting, discussed later. Important recent European research with contributions by Cunningham and Ford[11] has highlighted the interactive and continuous nature of the purchasing process.

It is tempting to assume that price is the sole criterion for industrial buying. It is now clear than in many situations the importance given to price is balanced by a range of other factors

Table 11.2   The non-price factors identified as helping to determine organizational purchasing decisions

Service
Availability
Reliability
Ease of use
Technical support
Quality

Factors affecting the degree of risk from buyer's view

The following factors have the greatest effect on the degree of risk:[12, 13]

- size of expenditure;
- degree of novelty;
- extent to which product is essential;
- source of purchase decision;
- self-confidence of buyer (general);
- self-confidence of buyer (in this specific situation);
- experience;
- purchasing history;
- professionalism;
- size and financial position of firm;
- company purchasing structure,
- lead time etc.

All these factors do not come into play every time a purchase is made. There are a number of different buying situations faced by the buyer, which in turn pose problems for the prospective or actual supplier. These can be broadly compared with the problem-solving situations noted in consumer behaviour.

The most complex purchase situation is probably the first-time purchase, involving new products, new material, new services, new suppliers or even a new buyer. In this situation there is likely to be an extensive search. This provides the supplier with a major opportunity, as the customer is looking for solutions to a recognized problem. An important difference between consumer and industrial 'extensive search' is that the technical knowledge and buying power of the industrial customer provides the scope for far more substantial dialogue. In many instances the customer specifies his requirements in considerable detail through drawings or a specification sheet. The most extreme case of this is when individual projects are put out to tender, allowing a number of firms to bid for particular work.

A recurrent problem of firms supplying industrial customers is deciding which, of the many requests to quote that they receive, they should follow through completely. A medium-sized engineering firm may receive as many as 30 invitations in a single week, both from home and from overseas, so quoting fully for each would take up a considerable amount of time and resources. There is no simple answer to this problem. It involves having a clear strategy indicating the types of business desired and continuing research into the market-place to more effectively estimate which business can be won.

A great deal of industrial business involves modified rebuys. Here, changes may have been introduced internally, perhaps in the product sold by the firm, in required technical specifications, or in purchasing policies or personnel. The degree of source loyalty generally determines the extent and commitment to the search (comparable with 'limited problem-solving').

Under normal circumstances the modified rebuy involves approaching a restricted number of prospective suppliers. It will be more extensive when a technical or material change is being introduced, i.e. when existing suppliers cannot adapt, as in the case of asbestos cooker seals mentioned earlier.

For the supplier the most intractable situation is the straight rebuy. The customer is likely to have established suppliers and no immediate, internal reasons to look for alternative sources. These situations can encompass items like stationery, raw materials and mouldings. In the case of moulds or components the situation may be more complex because ownership of tools is often shared. An injection moulder may have part ownership of the tool, and to move to another supplier could mean £40,000 to £100,000 for a new tool, or a proportion of this to buy the old tool from the current supplier. The likelihood of reduced services while the account is being changed compounds the problems.

These situations apply to service requirements as well as to physical goods. Advertising agency services are an industrial supply. An agency looking for business must consider: accounts where they have been asked to 'pitch' because the business is being moved; situations where the current agency will be making a presentation of its own, to try to hold on to the account; those occasions on which it is believed that the client is dissatisfied with the performance of the existing agency; trying for some desired accounts where there is no current movement. This introduces another aspect of industrial buying. The purchasing officer is very unlikely to be involved in recruiting, selecting, or managing advertising agencies. In most firms this is firmly rooted in top management or marketing.

In many industrial selling situations, identifying exactly who controls, specifies and even places the order is a major part of the selling task.[14]

The buying coalition

In many industrial buying situations other members of the firm's management and staff are directly involved in deciding whether to buy, specifying the product, considering alternative offerings and supplier choice. The location of those members of the firm and their influence can vary enormously (Table 11.3)

Table 11.3 Those involved in buying

Group	Areas
Top management (board level)	Plant, capital equipment, key services, e.g. banking.
Product management	Raw materials, printing and packaging, main energy sources.
Engineering	Equipment, tools.
Marketing	Raw materials and components, advertising, promotional services.

In some firms and in certain areas purchasing may not be directly involved at all: a secretary ordering an airline ticket for a director is buying, but this may not involve purchasing. In the majority of firms and in most situations the purchasing staff will be involved but as part of a buying coalition. This is a group, organized formally or otherwise, of staff or management involved in industrial procurement policy through specification, advice, information, transference or discretionary authority.

Hill and Hillier recommend comparing the firm's buying operation with the structure of an atom (Figure 11.5). Next to the core (1) lie those directly involved in the decision (2). The company may be introducing a new product, so purchasing staff, production, research and development and marketing will be directly involved. Other members of the firm (3) may be requested to provide specific or general information, e.g. distribution management on problems of packing or transport, market research on market testing. Outside the firm are various other individuals or organizations (4) who may exert influence, e.g. the advertising agency might point out that delivering the advertising promise calls for product improvements, or the Motor Industry Research Unit might point out that specifications fall short of UK or overseas standards.

Most industrial marketing is directed at the buying centre (those directly involved), so identifying them is the first stage in the selling effort. Their relative positions and relationships are critical. For example: marketing may have the final say in display materials but consider it totally inappropriate for companies selling display materials to approach them, other than through the purchasing department; media salesmen may approach brand management with 'special deals', but the firm may take a very firm line that all bookings are made directly with the retained agency; in some firms minor modifications in product make-up, and even supplies, may be vetoed by sales and marketing, if it is felt that they will significantly affect sales.

Figure 11.5 The buying operation. Reproduced with permission. Hill, R. W. and Hillier, T. J., *Organizational Buyer Behaviour.* London and Basingstoke: Macmillan, 1977.

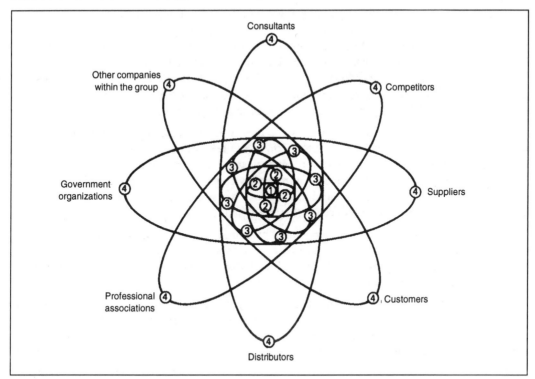

A number of studies of how industry buys have been conducted which clearly show the importance of understanding these interrelationships. Just-in-Time (JIT) manufacture emerged as a new approach to ensuring a perfect fit between quantities ordered and produced. Costs are cut, waste eliminated and quality is enhanced by rethinking the entire production process.[15]

Tackling industrial markets

The difference in the structure of the buying process and the types of buyer pose a challenge to the firm operating in industrial markets. In the past the supermarket philosophy 'Pile it high and sell it cheap' was echoed all too often. In an environment in which the range of skills invested in the purchasing process is considerable, the best approach is one which recognizes the many variables influencing choice. This is especially important given the renewed emphasis on supplier development.

Price is important. Comparing prices is part of the buyers' job, and where no difference in the offerings of the suppliers exists it is their duty to purchase the cheapest. Competing on price and seeking ways to keep prices down is part of the marketing effort in industrial markets. It also exists in consumer markets, but the consumer may lack the time or skill to judge offerings, so some simple rule of thumb may be developed. Cost and price cutting should not mean merely biting into profitability. Standards can be checked. Some customers who are particularly sensitive to price may accept product adaptations (cheaper materials, shorter life-span) to keep prices low. Others may accept shorter credit, longer lead times or reduced warranty.

Many firms embarking on this type of exercise soon find that the single homogeneous price-conscious customer group is actually a far more complex group accepting rather than preferring certain standards. Minor adaptations to meet their particular needs can become a hedge against cut-throat price competition. Warranty and service policies can be particularly effective here. Machinery breakdowns or production lines out of action can quickly offset small price savings. Warranties have the important side-effect of reducing buyer risk. The commitment to ISO9000 by many firms has transformed quality standards.

It is not enough to introduce improved standards in these areas: communicating them to existing and prospective customers is vital. Considerable evidence now exists to illustrate how important a well-thought-out promotion strategy can be to the industrial-goods producer. Buyers are constantly seeking information that they can use or store, and media advertising can do much to enhance awareness and the image of firms. Small companies often suffer from buyer reluctance to trade simply because they are small and unknown.

Brochures are probably the main non-personal promotional medium for the majority of firms. One merely needs to go into the sales office of a small engineering firm to see stacks of expensive brochures stored in cupboards or piled on selves to realize the importance of planning the use of material.

The media balance in industrial markets shows great differences. It is, however, in the contribution of the salesperson, technical representative or sales engineer that the difference in the promotion mix is most clearly demonstrated. The salesperson is the main intermediary between the firm and its customers. His knowledge, skill and authority must at least match those of his customer. In smaller and medium-sized firms, top management often recognizes this by becoming directly involved in the selling exercise. This is unfortunately an area in which Britain lags behind its major industrial rivals – in the qualifications and rewards of industrial sales staff as well as in active support for them. Expenditure on the sales force is estimated to account for 60 to 70 per cent of total promotional expenditure.

Systems selling has emerged as vital to the marketing effort in capital-goods markets. It is based on the proposition that the real cost to customers includes their management and organization of the project they are developing. Suppliers, by taking over the functions of project control, purchasing related items, planning, and even construction, offer significant savings to the buyer. As sellers are likely to have more experience of this type of exercise than buyers, they have scope for further economies. The expertise of the systems selling team becomes a major asset to the producer. They can seldom replace individual representatives, but can become a major feature in their selling armoury.

Selling agents play a major part in the marketing of industrial goods, particularly in overseas markets. The carefully recruited, selected and managed agent can play an important role in the firm's success. It is an unfortunate feature of the approach of some firms that, instead of seeing agents primarily in terms of the special contribution they can make, they view them in terms of the money saved through not employing salesmen. A well-managed agent need not save money but should provide expertise, knowledge and access to markets.

Large capital-goods projects introduce into the marketing effort a need to appreciate the workings of the financial and credit systems. The probability that any industrial order involves issues related to cash flow means that finance and credit are integral parts of industrial marketing. Negotiating the length of credit and chasing up late payments may be part of the industrial marketing person's job. Judging the credit risk in dealing with specific customers is a recurrent problem, and credit policies are a major feature of the industrial marketing mix. Recent interest in rental and leasing policies reflects the priority given to this area.

Segments and markets

The concept of subdividing markets into more homogeneous segments is one of the more successful transfers of a consumer marketing idea to industrial markets. The basic notion of geographical segmentation has guided industrial operations, at least unconsciously, for many years. A good illustration is the concentration of certain supply industries around the main fabricator industries. (The word 'fabricator' describes a company making some item from some other firm's goods. It is often used to describe producers of final customer lines.)

Shipbuilding in the North East and Scotland attracted large numbers of companies serving their needs, providing everything from welding equipment to steel. Motor-car production in the East Midlands and the South East helped create and sustain major supplier industries, many of whom are not independent of the motor trade.

Standard Industrial Classifications provide guidelines for segmentation for some firms. The company targets its efforts on, for example, the foundry industry or small boatbuilders. Government statistics can then provide information about numbers of firms, their average turnover and other aspects of their operations. As in the case of consumer markets it is now recognized that these externally measured (organizational) demographics are, at best, a very crude mechanism of targeting.

Approaches focusing more closely on behaviour and need are emerging from the study of industrial buying. Some of these are based on actual operations. For example: firms in industries such as plastics moulding, rubber processing etc. have a recurrent hopper-feeding need, and producers might concentrate on firms with this type of requirement; companies operating in overseas markets may require special types of financial services, so finance houses may introduce special types of credit factoring.

Other approaches, focused on new buying, are employed in specific firms. Sheth[16] raises the potential contribution of lifestyle as a determinant of buyer behaviour. As interest in this area grows, the type of approach and the skill with which it is applied are likely to improve considerably.

Industry

So far in this chapter the complex nature of the industrial market-place has been played down to provide a fairly consistent basis for discussion. There is a considerable amount of variation in the types of industrial customer and industrial firm. Often there is some ambiguity in the approach to the topic of industrial marketing in this area: is the marketing *to* or *by* industrial firms? The answer is both. Many of the firms operating in the industrial market-place face special problems caused as much by the character of their offering as by the customers they deal with.

Process producers

Process producers, typically, work entirely to customer specifications. To talk of their product is wrong, as their real offering is capacity, technology and service. The salesperson's technical abilities are often the most important feature, but generally they need to be backed by flexible and fast-moving production units. As a result many process industries are characterized by large numbers of small firms built around sales-orientated, engineering entrepreneurs.

Capital goods

Capital goods industries are a total contrast to process industries. Since the scale of projects is enormous, some of the world's largest firms have been daunted by the risks involved. Governments have become major participants in this area, by providing insurance and coverage against certain types of risk.

This area of business encompasses large construction projects, technological development, projects such as supplying a new engine for an aircraft project, shipping, aircraft and some specialized areas of engineering or exploration. In these projects even the smallest details can involve large sums of money, even determining the profitability of the entire venture. The sales and marketing staff involved will need a breadth of vision capable of ranging over different types of payment systems, levels of liability and the form it takes, and perhaps relations with other members of a consortium. Stamina is necessary, since such contracts may take months, or even years, to finalize. Throughout that period an error of judgement can endanger the long period of time invested. With costs involved, targeting on specific projects or areas of activity can be essential, and accumulated expertise can save considerable time and reduce costs dramatically.

Even in areas where there are traditions of operating all projects on a one-off basis, marketing principles can play a major part. The success of SD14 by Austin and Pickersgill exemplified this. Shipbuilding has a long history of tailor-making every vessel to the owner's specification. Sunderland Shipbuilders reversed this by producing a standard vessel based on careful market appraisal. This resulted in one of the most noticeable post-World War 2 success stories in British shipbuilding.

Engineering firms, highly technical companies and basic-material producers

These and many other types of firm face particular problems in trying to open up industrial markets. Marketing staff involved in these areas are recognizing the scope for adapting the marketing concept to match their particular circumstances.

Conclusion

There remains a continuing need to invest time and effort in the study of industrial markets. Some of the researchers mentioned earlier, centres such as Aston, organizations like the Chartered Institute of Marketing, specialized bodies, and journals such as *Marketing*, *Industrial Marketing* and *Industrial Advertising and Marketing* are making a real contribution to progress.

SPECIMEN QUESTIONS

1 Describe and analyze the ways in which industrial markets differ from consumer markets.

2 Outline the role played by purchasing officers or other buyers. Indicate the differences and similarities between their role and that of consumers in the purchase of:

    (a)   Stationery.

    (b)   Cars.

    (c)   Property.

3 'The concept of the purchasing centre is of little practical value in industrial markets.' How true is this comment? Illustrate your answer in terms of a specific purchasing situation or market.

4 Why do you think that research suggests that many industrial buyers are reluctant to buy from small firms even when prices and quality are better? Can you recommend marketing policies that might assist small firms to counteract this trend?

5 Using the data on the changing expectations of industrial buyers, indicate the ways in which suppliers might adapt to these changes.

6 For an organization of your choice, identify all those who will influence the choice of a new item of capital equipment. Indicate the stage of the decision process when their influence is greatest and suggest ways in which a supplier's knowledge of this choice process and structure can help it win business.

7 Your college is attempting to build up its range of short marketing courses for local firms. Prepare a brochure to promote this programme and identify the key individuals within firms to whom they should be sent.

8 Why is it that both buyers and suppliers in industrial markets seem to prefer long-term relationships?

9 Indicate the ways in which effective advertising can make the work of sales staff more productive. In the light of these arguments give reasons why many industrial firms are reluctant to invest in advertising.

10 Define:

    (a)   Derived demand.

    (b)   Modified rebuy.

    (c)   The buying coalition.

    (d)   TQM.

    (e)   Systems selling.

    (f)   ISO 9000.

    (g)   Batch production.

    (h)   Flexible manufacturing.

    (i)   Product liability.

    (j)   R & D.

CASE STUDY 9: HALFORDS DROP FORGINGS

Halfords Drop Forgings Limited is a small company, located in old-fashioned premises on the outskirts of Birmingham. It has been producing high-quality forgings for the last 60 years, and although it has been recently taken over by a larger general engineering group, it continues to operate fairly independently. The firm takes all the business it can and boasts in its literature that: 'We can supply any type of forging, and of any quality, from 10–10,000 units.'

It operates a wide range of hammers and all die-making is done on the premises, and a small technical and design service is available to all customers.

The Managing Director, Brian Day, has been with the firm 25 years, working his way up from the shop floor. His management team is organized as follows:

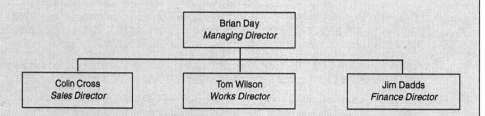

Halfords obtains business in three ways – it has a small proportional budget of £15,000 for trade advertisements, and this generates some new enquiries. These leads are followed up by the Sales Manager. Existing customers tend to recommend Halfords to other customers, who in turn contact Halfords direct. The firm also manages seven field agents, who obtain sales leads on a commission basis. These agents report to Colin Cross, who complains: 'I don't have enough time to manage or motivate them effectively.'

Most of Halfords' business, some 60 per cent, comes from the automobile industry. Their major customers are the Rover Group, Automotive Products, David Brown and Rolls-Royce, and Colin spends most of his time with these key accounts.

Halfords has dabbled in export markets and has supplied one order to Murphy Engineering in Dublin. Because of transport and clearance problems, there have been no follow-up orders. They have also received *ad hoc* orders via the Crown Agents and a London-based export house: these bodies arranged collection and delivery of the forgings. A recently appointed German agent has generated some enquiries, but these have not been converted into orders – price is the major barrier.

Brian Day is disturbed by the decline in the automobile industry and his firm's over-dependence on this sector. At the same time, by operating as a jobbing shop, he is unable to schedule in production effectively – the firm has recently reverted to a four-day week. The problems in the market are compounded by the increasing level of Far East and Eastern European importers who are able to undercut UK manufacturers by up to 50 per cent on certain forgings. At the monthly sales meeting, the following discussions take place.

Brian Day:	'The holding group have expressed doubts about our recent sales performance and are recommending that, in line with other group companies, a Marketing Manager is appointed, to generate a more positive, marketing-orientated way forwards, both in the UK and overseas.'
Colin Cross:	'I could certainly use somebody to get those commission agents moving. But on a brighter note, the Sterling launch at Rover has gone very well, which must mean more repeat business for us.'
Tom Wilson:	'That ball joint we developed for towing trailers – a new Marketing Manager could help promote that as a finished product and that could help my production scheduling problems.'
Brian Day:	'A new appointment could certainly help generate new business, but something needs to be done. There have been eight company closures in the forging business in the last six months and the price war is getting worse.'

Brian has to report back to the Group Managing Director before the next board meeting on the best means to get the firm into a growth position. At the end of the sales meeting he feels they cannot continue along their present lines.

Task

Advise Brian on the best ways to generate growth; highlight in particular ways in which he can use 'integrated' marketing to support these policies.

12

The marketing of services

Introduction

The growth of the service sector in industry is perhaps one of the most striking features of modern society. US writers have dubbed the last decade of the twentieth century the 'post-industrial' or 'service' society.

> The United States is now pioneering a new stage of economic development. During the period following World War 2, this country became the world's first 'service economy'.[1]

The shift from agriculture to manufacturing is now being followed by a move from production (including agriculture, mining and fishing) to services. Britain and Western Europe are following the US pattern, with an increasing proportion of the working population involved in service (Table 12.1).

Table 12.1 Percentage employed in services

	1960 (%)	1970 (%)	1975 (%)	1980 (%)	1989 (%)	1993 (%)	1996 (%)
United Kingdom	47.6	52	56.4	59.3	66	70	72
Total for EC (Eur. 9)	39.5	45.6	49.7	54.7	57	64	61

EC figures for 1989 are for enlarged Community of nine countries; for 1996, they are for twelve countries.
Reproduced with the permission of the Office for Official Publications of the European Communities.

The growth of the service sector has had two distinct 'knock-on' effects on all aspects and contexts for marketing. First, it has highlighted the importance of 'core' marketing capabilities such as: understanding the customer, working to achieve genuine two-way communication, ensuring good access by buyers to suppliers and intermediaries. Second, it shows how the line between the service sector and manufacturing or retailing has diminished. A good service gains immensely from the effective use of technology while an excellent product can be destroyed by bad service.[2, 3]

> The growth of marketing in the services sector in developed economies has been accompanied a changing environment with respect to consumer awareness and requirements, advancing technology and competitiveness.[4]

In this environment, three issues have grown sharply in importance in both research and practice in service marketing. These are: quality in services, relationships and the use of technology.

Services: a definition

It is not easy to define exactly what is meant by the service sector. One of the main points of the marketing concept is that a firm's offering goes far beyond the physical product offering into a broader array of need satisfactions. This means that firms must recognize that everyone in business sells some element of service. The standard definition of services:

> Those separately identifiable, essentially intangible activities which provide want-satisfaction, and which are not necessarily tied to the sale of a product or another service. To produce a service may or may not require the use of tangible goods. However, when such use is required there is no transfer of the title (permanent ownership) to these tangible goods.[5]

can usefully incorporate the notion that:

> The service is the object of marketing, i.e. the company is selling the service as the core of its market offering.[6]

Even using this definition, organizations, individuals and offerings vary enormously in scale and type of offering. They can range from BT, where the service problem is to match capacity to wide fluctuations in demand, to management consultancies where all staff are freelance.

The service sector does not present a uniform or homogenous sector. Service firms can vary from giant international banks like Hong Kong and Shanghai Bank to individual business counsellors working for a small number of local clients. Lowell[7] suggests that it is useful to classify services by sellers, buyers or the nature of the service offered (Figure 12.1).

Figure 12.1 Some ways of classifying services[7]

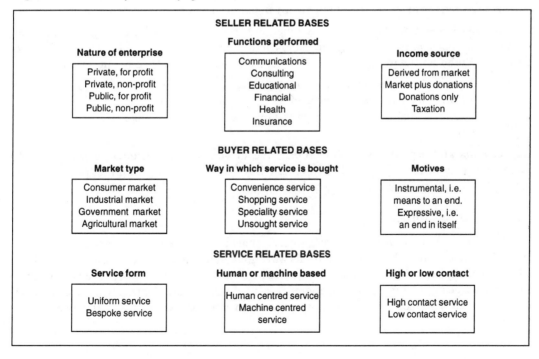

SELLER RELATED BASES

Functions performed

Nature of enterprise	Functions performed	Income source
Private, for profit Private, non-profit Public, for profit Public, non-profit	Communications Consulting Educational Financial Health Insurance	Derived from market Market plus donations Donations only Taxation

BUYER RELATED BASES

Market type	Way in which service is bought	Motives
Consumer market Industrial market Government market Agricultural market	Convenience service Shopping service Speciality service Unsought service	Instrumental, i.e. means to an end. Expressive, i.e. an end in itself

SERVICE RELATED BASES

Service form	Human or machine based	High or low contact
Uniform service Bespoke service	Human centred service Machine centred service	High contact service Low contact service

The sources of growth

A number of factors have contributed to the growth in the service sector. In consumer markets increased discretionary income and additional leisure time have stimulated the demand for education, grooming, travel and entertainment. In industrial and business markets, the growing complexity of the environment, along with specialization and fierce competition, has created new service markets. Government has faced demands from articulate and powerful groups for action in specific areas. At the same time, broad economic and social movements have forced government action. For example, the importance of geographical mobility among the workforce and the growth of the nuclear family in modern industrial society have transferred many roles, e.g. caring for the ill, away from the person on to the state. There is every evidence that these forces will continue in the future.

The difference between service and product industries

There are five basic differences between a service industry and a product industry. Services are usually *heterogeneous, intangible, inseparable, perishable* and *not owned by the buyer*. It is the combination of these five factors which creates the particular context in which the service company develops its marketing policies.

Heterogeneity

Services are usually designed around the specific requirements of the individual customer. For example, an insurance company will quote for each person a policy based on their specific industry, goods, prospects, even location, albeit using a fixed formula. There is an element of this in some product marketing, notably in industrial markets, but here there is usually a fair degree of standardization, e.g. by machine capacity or specific industry types.

A move towards standardization is now emerging in some service industries. An essential feature of franchising is the attempt to establish and comply with certain norms, which the customer can be confident of obtaining. For example, part of the 'Holiday Inn' offering is:

> Everything in our hotels must measure up to our 'no surprise' standards.
> From things you will notice, like every mattress in every room . . .
> specified 'manufacturer's top of the line' . . . to things . . . like cleaning
> your carpet every day.

Expectations and aspirations play a crucial role in consumers' attitudes to services. US researchers found, for example, that travellers liked hotels to have swimming pools, games rooms, work-out equipment and secretarial services, but seldom used them!

Intangibility

You cannot touch, taste, smell or take apart to examine the working of a service. A lawyer's services cannot be evaluated in this way; nor can a hotel, club, consultant, or barber. The opinions or attitudes of others can of course be obtained, but the 'trial' element is lacking. Even when free or low-price trials are offered, e.g. by car hire firms, the trial will not be exactly the same as the actual offering; for example, the car may be different or the staff may change.

These are intangibles which may be involved in any purchase. The BMW may be dirty or earn a poor reputation for performance, but the physical offering is what is important. This introduces the 'no bench-mark' aspect of service markets. When purchasing a new television set or hi-fi, the service in the shop can be terrible and the staff unpleasant, but the product itself can compensate for this. The same does not apply with a service: the facilities of a restaurant, the attitudes of the staff and the quality of cooking determine to a far greater extent the customer's rating of the offering.

The popularity of 'affinity' cards in the UK is, in part, explained by the intangible benefits provided by the association with 'other' causes.[8]

Inseparability

Production of the service and consumption occur at the same time. This concept is particularly important in the realm of personal services. It limits the scope to which dealers, distributors or agents can be effectively used, and places considerable emphasis on the skill and attitudes of those involved in selling. For example, in Britain, very few bank managers would see themselves as salespeople, but to a considerable extent that is their job. They are selling credit, financial services or advice to customers. Like all salespeople, they select their buyers (for creditworthiness) when selling; the bank manager's service and consumption of the offering occur at the same time (although of course the credit may be over a much longer period). This is an area in which progress has been made by service companies trying to combine a degree of standardization with opening up new markets. Insurance brokers, travel agents and some franchise operations achieve this very effectively.

Perishableness

Services cannot be stocked or held over: hotel rooms left vacant one night do not add to the following night's capacity. This creates massive problems when demand fluctuates, as in the case of some utilities, e.g. British Telecom. To cope with peak demand, massive capacity, much of it idle during the rest of the day or night, is needed (Figure 12.2). A variety of policies have to be developed to cope with this inability to store for more than a very short time, e.g. differential prices, promotion of evening use. It has even been proposed that private telephones or home extensions could be distributed free (although it has been suggested that unless some form of time lock (stopping peak hour use) could be installed, these would merely serve to amplify the trends).

Lack of ownership

In a service industry, access to or use of a facility does not mean that the customer obtains ownership of it. The hotel room, car, telephone or computer service is only hired for a period, and ultimately possession reverts to the firm offering the service. For example: 'This card remains the property of the issuing Bank.' – Access; 'This card is the property of American Express Company.' – American Express; 'This card remains the property of Barclays Bank Limited.' – Barclaycard. Payment is for the use of, access to, or hire of items. This does create some overlap with product markets, notably when an item is purchased but a warranty is attached.

Figure 12.2 Fluctuation in demand for telephone services

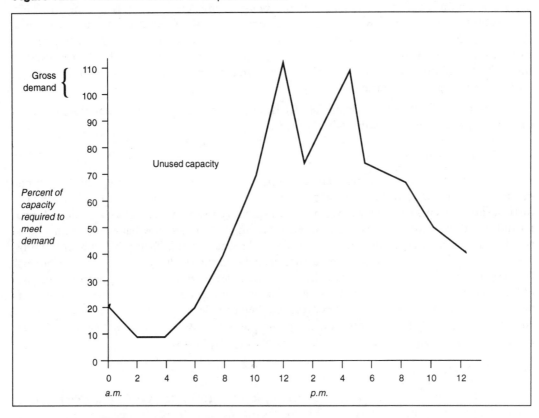

The range of service industries

Service industries are extremely wide-ranging. They encompass some of the largest commercial concerns, e.g. Barclays Bank, Marks and Spencer, Czarnikow Group (commodity brokers), and Inchcape and Co. The largest organization of all, government, is also a service concern. The following is a selection of just a few of the service industries:

• accountancy	• credit agencies	• information collection
• advertising	• dentists	• insurance
• airlines	• decorators	• law
• architects	• designers	• leisure
• banks	• doctors	• market research
• barbers	• dry cleaners	• office services
• brokers	• education	• personnel counselling
• cafes	• entertainment	• post
• car hire	• factors	• recreation
• circuses	• franchising	• recruitment
• cinemas	• freight forwarding	• repairs
• clubs	• hospitals	• research laboratories
• computer services	• hotels	• restaurants
• consultants	• hairdressing	• sport

- surveying
- symphony orchestras
- telecommunications
- theatre
- transport
- travel
- universities and colleges
- valuations
- window cleaning

In reviewing these areas some broad generalizations are necessary. Some service industries are closer to the product model than others. Some authors[9] have suggested that the differentiation itself is of limited value. However, the combined effect of the areas of difference and, perhaps more important, the comments of practising managers, suggest that in a number of key areas of marketing the circumstances demand policy adaptations. Although there is some truth in the suggestion that this argument 'seems to result from a "production" as opposed to a "market" orientation', it is equally true that the problems appear so severe, the differences so significant, that the adaptation should be two-way, with marketing people themselves steering clear of a product perspective on their own offering.

Government services

The state is the largest provider of services in the UK and in most societies today. These services range from information, advice and counselling to health care, credit and education. Most are provided on a non-profit-making basis, but there are a few which act or have acted on a more commercial basis, such as parts of the Department of Trade and Industry.

In many government services there is a growing recognition that they need to establish some form of effective control over their demand. This can encompass such actions as:

1 Overcoming objections to certain kinds of government actions, even persuading people to participate, e.g. in vaccination programmes: conversional marketing.
2 Creating demand among indifferent groups of the population for certain government priorities, e.g. persuading firms to employ more export salesmen: stimulational marketing.

When government activity was confined to the fundamentals of law, order and defence, the need to think seriously about the market was fairly limited, since legal enforcement and acceptance of specific social values dominated relationships. The extent of government involvement and the range of areas into which policy now intrudes have made the state very much an active participant in the market. The traditional roles of *regulator* and *customer* have been joined by *participant*. This is not, in fact, a totally new development, but is only now being recognized.

Choice is now a very real factor in many areas of government action. The industrialist can reject calls to export, invest or recruit. The mother can refuse to have her children vaccinated against certain diseases. The trade unionist can reject pay restraint. The family can refuse to insulate their home.

In attempting to understand the nature of choice in government markets, the notion of 'distress purchasing' is important. The traveller seeking a hotel bed for the night acts with considerable freedom and choice; the new admission to hospital can seldom exercise this choice. Distress purchasing occurs when personal 'distress' limits the effectiveness of the marketing exchange.

The traditional government approach is broadly similar to sales orientation: heavyweight advertising backed by ministerial speeches. To a certain extent this is inevitable so long as ideological commitments by political parties broadly determine policies. There are, however, many areas in which these general perspectives do not intrude directly, and where a marketing perspective could play a very positive role, for example in export promotion, relocation of industry, health care and provision of educational services. In doing this some new and different approaches to marketing may have to be adopted. As the overwhelming majority of government departments are involved in services, the ideas built up in this area are perhaps the most relevant.

Managing the service offer

People are at the centre of any business. They provide the direction and much of the motivation behind its development and success. In service industries the 'people dimension' gains added power from the lack of a tangible product offering:

> In product-orientated business, the physical reality of the product provides a simple but powerful base on which to build a business description.[10]

> In goods marketing there is a tangible core around which the offering can be developed.[11]

In service industries people are this central core. Consumers define the organization in terms of the ways in which the personnel behave or respond to them. For example: the uninterested or hostile waiter defines the restaurant; the lax lawyer determines the client's view of the law firm; and the unhelpful official determines attitudes to the government department. The impact of this is made even greater by the ability of the service organization's personnel to determine the character of the service and the form of the offering. For example, the consulting engineer is responsible for translating the customer's needs, using his (or her) own knowledge and expertise, into a clear project proposal. He may have more people to back him up, but he is the designer.

Even in a franchise operation the goals of standardization and uniformity are interpreted and judged by the franchisee's and franchiser's personnel. Some mechanization has taken place (automatic car washes, automatic bank services, launderettes), but to date its impact has been very limited and restricted to highly routine and low-skill areas.

The impact of the people element is taken even further by customer access and expectations. In industrial markets access to operatives is extremely limited: the industrial customer may meet the tool- and jig-maker but that will probably be all. No customer expects to meet the packers in a sweet factory, let alone expect them to have any responsibility for the total product offering. In service markets, however, access is far greater. The overwhelming majority of staff have some form of direct customer contact. The clerks in an insurance company, the operators in the telephone company and the porter at a business school all meet customers and help form their impression of the institution. Equally important, the buyer has high expectations of these staff.

Staff management is a major part of the design of the service organization's offering. The bank manager who threatened to 'bounce' Richard Branson's cheques during the launch period for Virgin Atlantic paid a high price in lost business and public ridicule.

In service markets the 'official' sales force tends to be more important than it is in industrial markets. Although the definition of a salesman is far broader, his role is significantly more substantial.

The extent of their knowledge and skill should reflect the importance of differentiation of skill, expertise and approach in most service industries. Among advertising agencies, Mark Craze of TMD Carat, Martin Boase of BMP and many other senior executives provide the basis of the skill/style differentiation which clients seek. Maintaining these standards throughout the organization is particularly difficult in the larger organizations such as the government, banks and insurance companies. A ministerial commitment to exports can be frustrated by civil servants building barriers between themselves, the services provided and firms.

The complex nature of this differentiation creates special problems in pricing policies. The price itself is often as intangible as the product. For example, it can be very difficult to work out exactly what is paid for bank services. Is the price the access to your deposits, the bank charges, special interest payments for loans, or some abstract combination of all three? Traditional cost-plus pricing poses problems when the primary costs are personnel. The low-cost entry in some service industries and problems of customer evaluation often keep prices very low. High levels of differentiation supported by individual negotiations occur, especially in situations where personal service is involved. In general, price information is difficult to obtain in these situations.

In some professions, regulatory agencies have been set up which exercise control over entry and sometimes fees. The bodies often adopt policies towards advertising and promotion, prohibiting it in some cases, regulating it in others.

Advertising has long played a substantial and central part in development of some services. Some of the finest creative advertising has been conducted for services, e.g. Toulouse-Lautrec for the theatre. A number of specific opportunities for promotion do emerge in the service sector. Sports and entertainment are frequently featured on specialized television programmes and often have their own sections in newspapers. Conferences, seminars, symposia and journals may provide the opportunity to disseminate information about the individual or firm, as well as the formal topic.

Promotion has a particularly important role in these services where indirect representation through agents (travel) or distributors (franchising) is not possible, and where the client may need to initiate the search or approach, i.e. through briefing or invitations to tender for business.

Grönroos[12] suggests that the concept of accessibility provides a major clue to both the difference between service and product marketing and the direction service and product marketing should take:

> Resources influencing accessibility are, for example, human resources, machines, offices, building and other physical things as well as extra services.

His basic proposition is that service marketing should be centred round the notion of maximizing access to the service industry for the target market(s). Barriers to access and factors interfering with access to the essential offering (or understanding this offering) should be overcome.

Quality in services marketing

Each of the distinctive features of the service offering – heterogeneity, intangibility, inseparability and perishableness – combine to increase the importance of quality while making the maintenance of high levels of service hard. In part this reflects the wide variations in customers' expectations but the amount of noise (extraneous forces) and the number of intervening variables are probably more important. The people sitting at the next table in a restaurant chain can 'ruin' the experience almost regardless of the quality of the food. Berry[13] claimed that customers' expectations should be explored along five dimensions:

- *Assurance:* suppliers' perceived trustworthiness and the confidence inspired in customers.
- *Empathy:* rapport between customer and supplier.
- *Reliability:* consistent delivery to a high standard.
- *Responsiveness:* willingness to adapt to needs.
- *Tangibles:* physical appearance of environment in which service is provided or service itself.

Disney place a high priority on customer service. The staff at their theme parks are called 'cast members'. They are expected to use all their efforts to ensure guests 'enjoy' the Disney experience. Immense efforts are invested in recruitment, selection and training to ensure that staff understand and deliver their role.

Ballyntyne's framework for service quality development[14] places people development alongside creating the right atmosphere, effective processes for managing the service offering, and proper task defining (see Figure 12.3).

Relationship marketing

Relationship marketing has emerged recently to express a shift in marketing thinking away from the emphasis on a particular transaction or series of transactions between a supplier and a customer (or set of customers and suppliers). It emphasizes the wider pattern of activities, interactions and communications inside or outside those participating in the exchange. Relationship marketing emphasizes not only the internal culture of the supplier, e.g. commitment to exceeding customers' expectations, but the links with others who can enhance and sustain customer satisfaction, e.g. intermediaries or service providers.

Central to relationship marketing is the notion that suppliers, intermediaries and customers create a partnership which blurs the lines between the organizations and dedicates itself to meeting long-term and short-term needs. The commitment to this link extends beyond those at the direct interface between supplier and consumer. Internal marketing plays a crucial part in sensitizing the supplier to customer needs – creating, in effect, the customer-driven company.

British Airways used its Customer First programme to shift thinking within the company from dealing with passengers to establishing long-term relationships. Once top management determined on this course of action, a programme of training, development workshops and communication was established to ensure that everyone – not just those dealing directly with customers – understood the importance of long-term customer relationships and appreciated the role they could play in establishing and maintaining this partnership.

Gunnesson[15] claims that the distinguishing feature of relationship marketing is that collaboration in a market economy needs to be treated with the same attention and respect as competition.

Figure 12.3 The diagnostic levels in service system design and redesign. (Ballyntyne, D., Christopher, M., and Payne A. 'Improving the Quality of Services Marketing: Service (Re)design is the Critical Link', *Journal of Marketing Management,* Vol. 11, January–April 1995.)

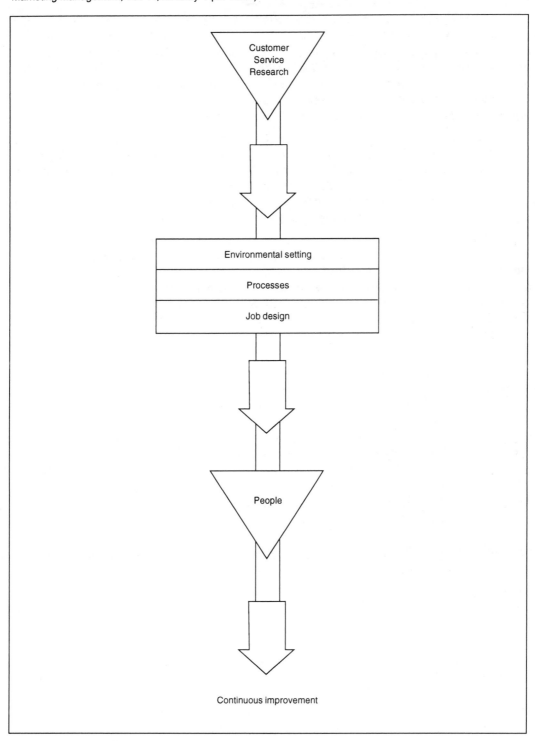

Innovation and productivity

The people-based nature of service industries has tended to mean that contrasting patterns of innovative activities have emerged. In highly skilled sectors innovation has frequently been individualistic. Sometimes this has been comfortably encompassed in existing organizations, e.g. the long and successful history of some research laboratories, but probably more often the low cost of entry and the close client contact have led to new enterprises being established. This problem of 'ownership' of new concepts may discourage some service organizations from formal innovation policies.

The larger people- or machine-based services have generally adopted a more formal policy towards innovation.[16] The high labour content in services such as banking, travel, leisure and recreation has created considerable interest in productivity improvements through automation or standardization. Low labour productivity is a recurrent problem in the service industries and is one reason why the percentage of the population involved has risen so dramatically. The productivity of manufacturing has improved while that of services has stabilized.

This has prompted deep concern in the service sector and growing attention to issues like standardization, competitive benchmarking and other techniques that have traditionally been more closely linked with manufacturing. Such benchmarking goes on more and more frequently today. Telephone companies benchmark against their regional competitors, but many also compare themselves to Southern Bell. Xerox Parts distribution people benchmark themselves not only against competitors, but against L. L. Bean, the leisure-wear manufacturers.[17]

Conclusion

Productivity and people are the keys to the future of service industries. Computers and information provide a significant contribution to productivity in some industries, but past performance suggests that other, probably more labour-intensive services, will emerge to satisfy new needs as the demand for skills and knowledge to cope with the new environment or leisure requirements increases. Technology is seldom, if ever, enough to meet client needs in service industries.

Attitudes to service industries will play a part in their development in the UK. For a significant proportion of the male UK workforce there appears to be prejudice against service industries, reflected in reluctance to seek employment there, negative attitudes when working, and the low priorities given to the service sector. Many government support schemes in development areas specifically exclude service industries, despite their high employment potential.

SPECIMEN QUESTIONS

1 Outline some of the reasons why the service sector has grown so rapidly over the last twenty years in Britain.

2 Use two industries of your choice to indicate the main differences between service and product markets – employ the advertising used by a firm in each of these sectors to illustrate these differences.

3 Analyze the current advertising of BT and Orange and indicate which, in your opinion, most clearly relates to the distinct nature of the service sector. Changing the service delivery approach is especially difficult for those firms for whom personal service is the key element in the client's purchase, e.g. legal services. What are the most important factors service firms must take into account when trying to change this delivery system?

4 'Unconditional service guarantees achieve significant breakthroughs in market penetration but at unacceptable costs.' Use the experience of Domino Pizza or another named company to analyze this proposition.

5 Most service companies struggle to create real and sustainable levels of differentiation. Use examples of different service businesses to show the ways in which companies have succeeded and failed to create this kind of differentiation.

6 Techniques like standardization and competitive benchmarking that have traditionally been associated with product markets are now becoming commonplace in service markets. What are the gains and losses to service firms using these approaches?

7 Outline the key steps in establishing an effective and sustainable, marketing-based, service strategy.

8 Tom Peters suggests that service firms, in particular, should 'under-promise and over-achieve'. What does this mean and why is it especially relevant to the marketing of services?

9 What are the main factors which a service firm must take into account to ensure high levels of quality assurance and customer satisfaction?

10 Define:

    (a)   Inseparability.

    (b)   Heterogeneity.

    (c)   Distress purchasing.

    (d)   Benchmarking.

    (e)   'Aggressive listening'.

    (f)   Accessibility.

    (g)   Perishableness.

    (h)   A profession.

    (i)   Public relations.

    (j)   Added value.

CASE STUDY 10:
MARKETING DEVELOPMENT AND EXPORT SERVICES

In 1995, Marketing Development and Export Services (MDES) completed a major development programme designed to draw up a framework for a specialist export course to meet the needs of small firms. A complete package of teaching aids, course notes and case studies had been drawn up following four years of extensive research. Pilot courses had been conducted with a number of key industries.

These pilot programmes had been very successful. The sponsoring bodies of these (primarily Training and Enterprise Councils and ITOs, but one or two trade associations had been involved) were very keen to greatly expand their involvement with these courses, and with MDES in general. Within a few months it became clear that conducting these courses for existing clients would take up all the firm's resources in this area for the foreseeable future.

Rapid expansion of facilities was not seen as possible by the firm's top management. The demands placed on tutors by the courses were so great that they could be involved in only a very small number each year. At the same time, severe problems had been experienced in recruiting staff with the thorough knowledge of export and small firms required to conduct the courses effectively.

Faced with the dilemma of meeting the needs of current clients or expanding, as planned, into new industries, it was decided to expand as intended. This meant that the desire of some current clients for courses in the near future was frustrated.

Top management felt that this extra exposure and the opportunity to establish extra networks of relationships were worth the risk of alienating existing clients. At the same time, it was decided to explore the scope for reducing the scale of tutorial involvement, perhaps through greater TEC and training adviser involvement or working with other consultants or agencies.

Despite this decision there were still worries about the wisdom of this step and the choices that had led to this position. The company therefore set itself the task of examining the situation for clues to the ways in which a marketing perspective could assist them in the future. The first topic examined was the decision to follow the expansion route described above.

13

Export marketing and overseas trade

Introduction

The international market-place provides one of the most challenging environments for the marketing person. The scale is enormous: during 1994 world trade in manufactures exceeded £700 billion, world trade invisibles, although much harder to calculate, was probably over £300 billion, and the population of the world was over five billion.

Britain is, and has been for a very long time, one of the world's great trading nations. In fact, the share of Britain's Gross National Product that is exported exceeds that of many of its leading industrial rivals (Table 13.1). The picture of Britain's export performance is very mixed, with some very bright spots and some areas in urgent need of improvement. Exporting is, perhaps more than any other, the area in which a marketing perspective can earn the greatest returns.

Table 13.1 Percentage of national product exported

Country	%
UK	24
France	21
Germany	21
USA	10
Japan	9.3

Source: OECD[1]

A historical perspective

Britain's long overseas trading history covers only a part of the time during which trade between independent communities has been important. It is possible that the earliest developed forms of commerce existed between autonomous groups, and it is this independence which characterizes international trade. Although today the international market-place is dominated by the nation state, in the past, groups from tribes, cities, regions and empires followed patterns of trade which in their broad principles would be familiar to today's international or export marketing person.

Four factors have determined the extent of trade: political stability, urbanization, some medium of exchange (acceptable currencies) and most recently, industrialization. The rise of the nation state from the thirteenth century provided a high degree of domestic political stability. The growth of the cities over the last 700 years was dramatic. Although specific currencies have declined during this period there has been greater convertibility of currencies. No single factor was more important to the dramatic growth in world trade than the Industrial Revolution. Besides the surge in volume of trade, a continuing pattern of change and counter-change typifies this period.

Despite its importance and the complex problems it poses, international export marketing is neglected in many books. Throughout Western Europe, and for Britain in particular, the application of a marketing perspective to all areas of export and international marketing is vital.

Although traditionally there has been a tendency to confuse the terms 'export marketing' and 'international marketing', there are very real differences between them. Export marketing is the marketing of goods, produced in one or more countries, in other countries. International marketing, on the other hand, gives weight to the development of business in a number of countries or regions, with a framework capable of incorporating the establishment of local manufacturing, distribution and marketing systems.

For most small firms the majority of their overseas trading is directed towards exports. Larger firms take a more international or global perspective with manufacturing and distribution located in overseas markets. Some of Britain's largest firms now view the world as a single market and devise policies and services to respond to diverse needs. There is an urgent need to strengthen this pattern of behaviour and firmly establish the marketing dimension of exports, as well as international marketing.

Table 13.2 The top UK exporters of 1996, and the proportion of turnover exported

Exports	Turnover (£billion)	(£billion)	%
British Aerospace	5,248	6,167	85.1
BP	4,483	22,872	19.6
Rover Group	4,005	6,491	61.7
Shell UK	3,357	7,067	47.5
IBM UK	3,069	5,115	60.0
British Steel	2,722	4,976	54.7
Ford Motor Co.	2,611	7,114	36.7
Rolls-Royce	2,512	4,294	58.5
Motorola	2,208	2,798	78.9
Zeneca	2,076	2,445	84.9

Source: Financial Times Exporter, October 1997.
All figures refer to accounting year ended 1996.

The marketing perspective

At its most fundamental this involves viewing the world from a new perspective. The traditional, physical geography viewpoint has only a limited value. More important to the marketing person is the economic geography of the world. Population, national income, educational standards and levels of economic development provide better clues to opportunity for the marketing person than do land masses. Also important are variables such as culture, language, attitudes towards change, wealth or achievement and social systems, as well as the very different ways of conducting business around the world.

Theory of comparative advantage

Adam Smith (1776) pointed out that in the case of two countries like Britain and France, each has its own special characteristics and endowments enabling it to produce certain goods. If each could provide one product better than the other, absolute advantages would exist, and the profits from trade would be very clear. The warmer climate and special soil conditions of France may be more productive of grapes for wine, while cooler weather and different soils of Scotland are more suitable for grains for producing whisky. When each country specializes, the sum of production will be greater than if each attempts to produce both.

Problems emerge, however, when one country is more efficient than the other in producing every product. The question of whether there is still any point in trading then arises. The answer from the theory of comparative advantage is yes. So long as there are differences in the relative efficiencies of producing goods in each country there is a value in trade. The more productive country would still benefit from specialization in those goods it is best at producing while importing from the less productive country those goods it is comparatively worse at producing. Thus, in Japan it may take ten person-days to produce a car and one person-day to produce a television set, while in Britain it may take fifteen person-days to produce the same car and two person-days to produce the television set, yet it still pays both of them to trade, as the total output will be greater than if they both try to produce both items.

Although economists such as Samuelson can state that 'The theory of comparative advantage is a closely reasoned doctrine which, when properly stated, is unassailable', many forces act against the implementation of policies based upon it. High tariffs, protectionism, local preference and the fear of competition are facts of life for the exporter, although attempts continue to be made, to reduce these pressures, especially through international agreements like GATT, the General Agreement on Tariffs and Trade.

Developments in trade

Since the end of World War 2 a number of major developments in international trading have taken place, generally with a view to facilitating trade and building up prosperity.

GATT is probably the most important attempt at international co-operation to reduce tariffs. The IMF (International Monetary Fund) was established to iron out the fluctuations in the international monetary system created by foreign trading. Credits are provided for countries with short-term trading deficits while longer-term assistance is given to countries with more intractable problems. The World Bank provides a more general banking role, supplying loans to people or countries unable to get private funding for apparently economically sound projects. All these and other institutions operate to widen the scope for successful international trade and prosperity.

On a narrower base, but equally important, the last twenty years have seen a movement towards powerful regional or common-interest groupings. The formation, development and success of the European Union (EU) has revived interest in customs unions and other associations geared to stimulate world trade within a number of linked countries. The broad policy of the EU has been to eliminate tariffs between member countries while setting up common tariffs against non-members. The Union is now only one, albeit probably the most powerful, of a number of similar groupings throughout the world. The creation of a single internal market after 1992 has further spurred interest in regional economic co-operation while the creation of the single European currency seems set to transform European trade. 1993, for example, saw the formation of NAFTA, the North American Free Trade Area, a customs union even larger than the EU based on Canada, Mexico and the USA. Even the collapse in Europe of the internally more cohesive but economically less developed association of socialist states, the Council for Mutual Economic Assistance (CMEA, more commonly know as Comecon) has not reduced this interest. The pattern of establishing unions of states in particular regions is paralleled by specific-interest groups such as OPEC (the Organisation of Petroleum Exporting Countries).

The major economic groupings and customs unions are: European Union (EU), North American Free Trade Area (NAFTA), Caribbean Community and Common Market (CARICOM), Latin American Free Trade Area (LAFTA), Central American Free Trade Area (CACM), East African Community (EAC), West Indies Associated States (WIAS), Caribbean Free Trade Area (CARIFTA), Central African Customs and Economic Union (UDEAC), West African States Customs Union (UDEAO) and Association of South East Asia Nations (ASEAN). Although all these organizations inevitably focus their attentions on their member states, most have established trade agreements or some associations with non-member countries or other associations. Countries which have trade agreements, are seeking entry to or are associated with the EU are: Turkey, all the Central and Eastern European countries, Israel, Cyprus, Malta, certain African, Caribbean and Pacific states, Argentina, Uruguay, Brazil, Mexico, Bangladesh, India, Pakistan and Sri Lanka.

The majority of these developments are designed to reduce the barriers to trade either globally, as in the case of GATT, or in a specific region, as in the case of the EU.

Although there has been progress in reducing the tariff barriers to markets, less success has been achieved in limiting the non-tariff barriers to entry. Non-tariff barriers to entry are all obstacles placed in front of prospective importers which are not incorporated in formal tariffs. They range from specific trade practices designed to limit competition to differential levels of skill and willingness to adapt. Japan in particular is often accused of conscious attempts to baffle would-be importers by 'Japanese methods of negotiating and the complexities of Japanese law and language', as well as by specific actions designed to limit imports in certain areas. The difficulties of penetrating the export market are nowhere more clearly seen than in attempts to understand the Japanese distribution system, in which products may go through the same trading company several times before they reach the market. The industrialized nations of the West are frequently accused of having similar policies designed to keep out of their markets goods produced in the Third World.

Even within groupings such as the EU it is recognized that reductions in tariffs have only limited impact in the face of national preferences, trading advantages by local companies and specific regulations. The 'Buy British' policies often adopted by government departments, local authorities and firms are real barriers to foreign firms, but they are matched by both formal rules and informal policies in most countries of the EU. 'Italians always prefer their own goods', 'The French are fiercely patriotic', and 'The Germans never buy foreign goods when they can buy German' are all frequent comments of UK businessmen. It has been claimed that as fast as tariffs are removed non-tariff barriers are erected, thus holding back progress towards the 'single home market' goal of the member states. These are problems to which the export or international marketers must find solutions by superior marketing in all spheres.

The international marketing system

The need to understand the marketing system in order to effectively develop business is nowhere more important than in export and international marketing. The picture built up of a country or market is complicated by the differences and interrelationships which occur with foreign business, and by the recurrent problem, particularly in exporting, of viewing the market as an outsider. These can lead to grave errors and misunderstandings. It is important to recognize that, although a market may be foreign to the exporter, it is the user's home market. Too many firms believe that inferior service is acceptable because the market is so far away, because of logistics problems, or because of the costs involved, ignoring the fact that no buyer willingly accepts these propositions. Firms may find certain markets too difficult to manage effectively, but this poses questions about both their market selection and total product proposition.

Economic, political, cultural and technological factors determine both the international environment in which the firm operates and the specific circumstances of target markets.

Economic factors

The three major economic factors are the trading relations within and between countries, the economic structure and policies of specific nations, and the level of economic development.

In the first part of this chapter trade relations have been extensively reviewed. It is important to recognize that many countries have very different economic structures and policies from those of the UK. Many countries in the world now operate within some form of economic or national plan. Even Britain had an industrial strategy identifying key areas of economic development until the election of the Conservative government in 1979.

This is a pattern which was far more developed in the countries of Eastern Europe and the Third World. Here, the National Plan would set targets for output along the lines below, but with little attention to demand.

> A total amount of 2.6 million tonnes of plastics materials was manufactured during the last five years. In the next five this figure will have to be brought to almost four million tonnes.[2]

The level of economic development is extremely important for highlighting the kinds of opportunity overseas. Models such as that put forward by W. W. Rostow, suggesting five stages of economic growth (traditional agricultural society, transition from agriculture to industry, steady growth to a strong industrial base, drive to mature employment of modern technology, and high mass consumption), are helpful in organizing our understanding of markets and grouping similar markets together to assist in identifying and meeting common needs.

Political factors

The nation state is the central feature of modern export and international marketing. Its domestic freedoms, national system and structure and links with other countries are critical to any picture of the available opportunities.

The federal nature of many countries, such as the US, Germany and Nigeria, can have a direct impact on factors as varied as local taxation and regulations on warehousing. The centralization typical of the remaining communist countries is in total contrast to this. Here all buying for an entire national industry is likely to be conducted through a single, state-controlled foreign trade enterprise. In international marketing in particular, a willingness to adapt to different political systems is critical to success.

Culture

This pervades all aspects of foreign trade, from the character of the needs and the forms of gratification which are acceptable, to the response to particular forms of communication.[3] No one faces these problems more directly then the export salesman. He must be able to respond positively to the culture shocks which are always possible in new situations. Their impact can range from the simple and procedural:

> An American customer receiving a letter bearing a subscription 'dictated by Mr Exporter, and signed in his absence by A. Smith, Secretary' experiences a rising wave of personal insult, occasioned by what is, to him, a plain condescension[4]

to the profound rethinking of overall value and attitudes. For example, there is in many parts of the industrial world:

> An increasing disenchantment with the artificial and man-made aspect of the modern world.[5]

Technology

This provides the thrust behind the market economy. Under its pressure the past 200 years have seen a profound transformation which has reached almost all parts of the world. Technology, through direct sales, transfer of capabilities or adaptation, creates many opportunities in international trade. It has been proposed by Louis T. Well Jnr that there exists an international product life-cycle, which is based on the proposition that innovations will generally occur close to the more sophisticated markets, those most capable of employing new developments. From there, four distinct stages can be identified with potential policy responses. (In Figure 13.1 the US is used to illustrate this proposition.) Although this suffers from the weakness of all life-cycle models, oversimplification of very complex phenomena, it does give some insight into key aspects of the spread of technology.

In exploring responses by the innovator or adapter the importance of market-orientated research and development cannot be overstated, and it gains considerably in importance when the issue of export-led growth is raised.

Export-led growth

Most national governments are committed to creating and maintaining domestic employment opportunities through manufacture at home and sales overseas. A healthy balance of payments created by this is generally seen as an indication of economic success. Besides this, it is generally argued that striving for domestic growth is far less risky when based on exports than home sales because there is less impact on inflation.

Many countries have built much of their prosperity on overseas sales. For example: British exports of wool and later textiles were major contributors to growth in the last century; since the war both Germany and Japan have used earnings from exports to lead home growth; and France has, over the last decade, successfully used export earnings to boost national growth. Although it is now becoming clear that domestic economic strength is as important as export earnings, these still have a major part to play in national prosperity.

Figure 13.1 The international product life-cycle

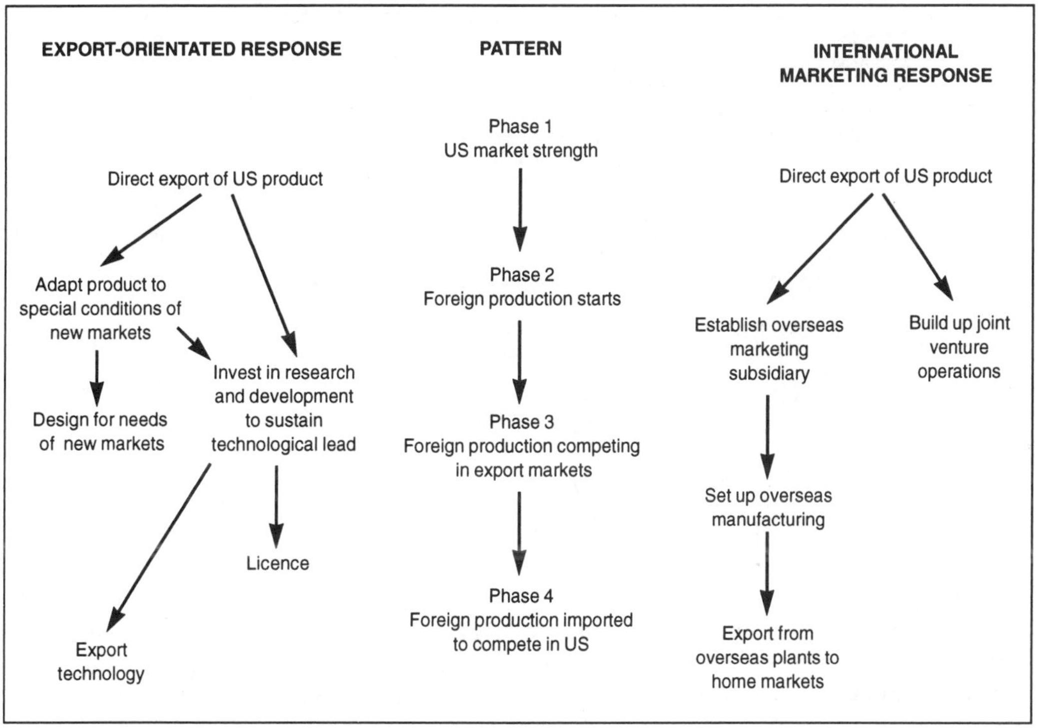

Most countries offer an extensive array of incentives to exporters. In Britain the main government help is directed through the British Overseas Trade Board, operating through the Department of Trade and Industry and overseas through the Foreign Office (Table 13.3).

British exporters are fortunate in having access to assistance from many sources, including government departments, banks, trade associations, chambers of commerce, industry research associations, specialized bodies (e.g. British Standards Institution), colleges and universities. It is a pattern of support paralleled in many other countries, but seldom equalled. One area of help, direct financial support for sales, is specifically forbidden by EU rules.

Despite this help, the problems faced by the exporter and the international marketer are enormous. Unfortunately, many firms invest relatively little time and effort in overseas market analysis and selection:

> British companies appeared to sell to more markets, i.e. 40 per cent of the
> British companies interviewed sold to more than 100 markets compared
> to 32 per cent in France and only 20 per cent in Germany.[6]

Table 13.3 Resources for export promotion

Expenditure net of receipts from users of services (£ million)	1991/92	1992/93
Overseas trade fairs	12.6	14.9
Overseas store promotions	0.8	0.7
Outwards missions	1.1	1.3
Overseas seminars	0.3	0.4
Inward missions	0.7	0.6
Export Marketing Research Scheme	1.2	1.2
Market Entry Guaranteed Scheme (closed to new applications – figures for receipts)	(0.8)	(0.3)
Overseas Projects Fund	3.3	3.1
Marketing and publicity	2.1	2.6
Simpler Trade Procedures Board (SITPRO)	0.8	0.9
Technical Help to Exporters (THE)	0.2	0.3
Other schemes of assistance to industry (excluding expenditure on Expo '92)	0.6	1.2
Area Advisory Groups and other non-official trade organizations	3.6	3.5
Export Market Information Centre publications	0.4	0.4
Other	0.3	0.4
Production of export publications	0.7	0.3
Net total direct expenditure	27.9	31.5
Staff costs and overheads (£ million)		
DTI HQ Divisions	44.8	48.6
DTI Regional Offices	5.3	5.0
Export sections of Territorial Departments	1.0	1.1
Foreign and Commonwealth Office commercial staff overseas	76.2	76.7
Total (including net total direct expenditure)	155.2	162.9

DTI HQ overheads include some estimated and notional costs.
Source: British Overseas Trade Board, Annual Report 1994. Reproduced with the permission of the Controller of HMSO.

Policies similar to the undifferentiated mass-market approach of the product-sales-orientated firm seem to characterize many firms. Consequences such as greater vulnerability to fluctuating exchange rates because of simplified price competition tend to follow.

Market selection and development

Concentration on key markets or opportunities provides firms with the chance to build a fuller picture of market conditions, understand the details of customers' specific requirements, design and develop offerings adapted to meet buyers' needs, establish and sustain a long-term marketing presence, and minimize costs while maximizing the returns from individual markets. When key markets are examined it is essential to avoid the trap of equating a market with a country. A firm's target may just as easily be a segment within an overseas country or a segment crossing national boundaries as a specific country:

> Silentnight (Kenya) Ltd . . . Has supplied the bed, furniture and furnishings for most of the tourist hotels developed in the area.[7]

> In its export range Van Heusen attempts to cater for the junior executive group . . . in all its export markets.[8]

In approaching and concentrating on target markets the progressive improvement in international statistical information is increasing the scope for constructive desk research and employing quantitative techniques to group or cluster markets. Organizations such as the EU, UN World Bank and the Organisation for Economic Co-operation and Development (OECD) regularly publish data to complement national statistical information. Commercial organizations such as the Economist Intelligence Unit also gather data on a systematic basis both for publication and for specific clients.

There has been a progressive worldwide improvement in the facilities for good-quality market research, and many UK companies conduct research in foreign markets. ESOMAR (European Society for Opinion and Market Research) has played a major part in the improvement of international standards. The ESOMAR Handbook and the American Association's *Green Book* list potential agencies and give an insight into the scope for obtaining good-quality research, at least in the industrially developed world.

Despite these developments there does appear to be some reluctance to conduct detailed studies. Many firms have got themselves into a vicious circle: large numbers of markets and lack of differentiation because of a reluctance to conduct detailed investigations caused, at least in part, by the costs of studying such large numbers of markets. Carefully planned investigations based on rigorously thought-out briefs, which take into consideration the differences in practice and approach which may occur overseas, can play a major part in identifying key market opportunities and the best means of developing them.

Advertising and sales promotion

The need for in-depth understanding of a market is nowhere more important than in designing advertising and sales policies. In some instances it has proved to be possible to transfer advertising campaigns overseas, either to specific markets or to many countries. The Esso tiger, the Marlboro cowboy and the Coca-Cola bottle are recognized throughout the world. However, even here it has been found that such similar campaigns can mean very different things in different markets. The overwhelming majority of consumer-goods firms adapt or totally revise their message to fit into the culture, values and language of their target markets.

Language alone can make a dramatic difference to meaning. In some countries a direct translation of 'Come Alive with Pepsi' is 'Come out of the Grave with Pepsi'. In the UK, if a product went 'like a bomb' it would be a great success, but in the US it would be a total failure. Spanish and Portuguese as spoken in South America are very different from the languages of Spain and Portugal. An English manufacturer of KD kitchen furniture would have faced disaster if the buyer for a Canadian store has not noticed that the proofs of its instructions were in European, not Canadian, French.

Many industrial firms believe that they are immune to these problems, but translators of technical copy must be thoroughly conversant with the appropriate and current usage in the target market. The amount and form of technical information required vary enormously. In Eastern Europe, for example, far more detailed material is required than in Britain. The role of visuals in advertisements and brochures is also very important, since the relevance and impact can vary considerably. For example, pictures of female operatives may totally alienate buyers in some countries, specific colours may arouse very different sentiments, and in developing countries endorsements and acknowledgements by previous clients can be a very important form of reassurance. In the development of promotional and advertising material, local staff or agents can provide valuable insights.

Exhibitions and trade fairs probably play a more important role in export and international marketing than in domestic business. They bring buyer, intermediary and seller together, minimizing for all the costs and time involved in the international search for supplies and custom. In scale they range from the giant international exhibitions and fairs such as Leipzig, Hanover and Poznann ,to the highly specialized Telecom, London Boat Show and Semaine de Cuire, and national or local exhibitions, e.g. Scandinavian Furniture Fair, Royal Melbourne Show.

Selling overseas

In the vanguard of much of this marketing effort is the salesman, whose continuing importance in modern marketing is discussed more fully in Chapter 22. In export markets new and different problems are often faced, and the salesman must learn to operate in alien, sometimes hostile, environments. The distance from head office makes communication difficult, and often the issues raised by prospective customers are new or unpredictable.

Some firms, particularly medium-sized or large ones, overcome some of these problems by employing only locals wherever they go. This effectively solves the language and culture problems, and also gives access to contacts and leads. However, many firms find it hard to understand their foreign employees, and there can be problems about remuneration, especially in markets where wage rates are much higher than in Britain. Also, in relatively small markets there may be no scope for advancement, creating the risk of demotivation.

Maintaining the representatives' level of technical knowledge is vital in industrial markets, and partly for this reason industrial firms tend to use UK-based technical staff to a greater extent than do consumer-goods firms. Their technical knowledge enables them to reassure clients, and they can also fully appreciate the needs of both supplier and customer.

Recent research has highlighted the importance of giving the overseas representative a great deal of discretion, since failure to do this can adversely influence customers. The same research highlighted the importance of a very high degree of technical competence in sales staff operating in conditions which may stretch their knowledge to its limit.

The export salesperson is the main point of contact in many cases. Often he (or she) handles far greater volumes of business than his home-based colleague,[9] and therefore is likely to remain crucial to most firm's success in the foreseeable future. However, because of the problems involved in operating an export or international sales force, many firms give intermediaries a far greater role than salespeople in foreign markets.

Intermediaries

It has been estimated that agents and distributors acting on behalf of overseas manufacturers or service companies handle about half the world's overseas trade, and these are only two of the many different types of intermediary available to the firm attempting to develop a foreign market. The term 'intermediary' is used to describe all those persons and organizations providing the service of representation between sellers and buyers.

Although intermediaries frequently represent the producer, a number of organizations act on behalf of the prospective purchaser, searching out suppliers using their specialist knowledge and expertise.

There are also firms like Macy's (New York), 'the world's largest department store', who have offices in London to search out prospective suppliers. The great Japanese trading houses such as Mitsui have offices in London performing basically the same role in the Japanese market.

However, the problems of the majority of firms lie in finding the right type of intermediary, choosing the best individual or firm and establishing a system of management, motivation and control geared to win initial business, sustain customer loyalty and provide a basis for a profitable long-term presence in the market. There are many different ways open to the firm looking for overseas representation (Figure 13.2).

The initial decision faced by the firm is the best form of overseas representation: direct or through intermediaries. Policies adopted at this point are critical to the firm's future in a market. The position may be made more complex by the laws of the country in question. For example, in Sweden employee protection legislation is extremely rigorous, making the dismissal of Swedish sales staff extremely difficult, and in France, agency law classifies buyers as the customers of the agent, not of his or her client, the producer. In virtually no country is the termination of an agency agreement easy and without costs or risks.

Figure 13.2 Export representation, home- and overseas-based. Adapted from D. Tookey, *Export Marketing Decisions*. Harmondsworth: Penguin Books, 1975.

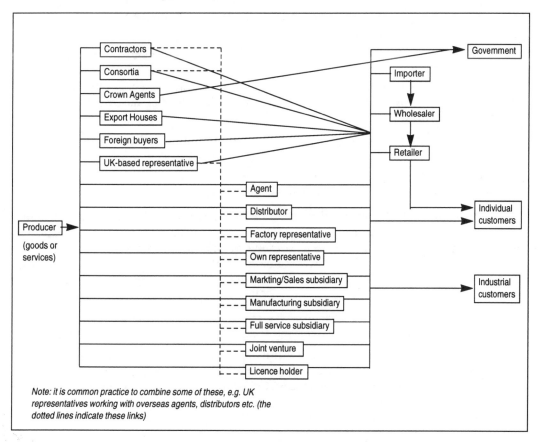

An agent is a firm or individual acting on behalf of another, generally in the sales process but occasionally in a technical or advisory capacity. Agents and distributors are the main forms of representation of UK firms overseas, and agents are of three basic types: those acting with the exporter as principal; those acting with the buyer as principal; and those specializing in certain tasks, e.g. technical support. Remuneration systems vary considerably between industries and countries, but can be broadly divided into fee- and commission-based, with some involving a combination of both.

Distributors can generally be distinguished from agents by their willingness to invest in stock (they are the principals) and their ability to hold stock. They are often much larger organizations with more extensive facilities and resources.

Both agents and distributors offer manufacturers a permanent presence on the market capable of making repeated customer contact, gathering information and clinching business. The fact that they are generally local firms (although there are some important international agencies providing worldwide cover) means that they understand and can adapt to local conditions. Equally important, they give the prospective customer a degree of reassurance. (The meaning of 'local' here must be fully understood. In some countries major social and political divisions may pose problems, e.g. a Greek Cypriot agent could gain very little access to Turkish Cypriot business.)

Despite these strengths some firms find that direct representation offers more advantage:

> All our experiences (with agents), Britain excepted, were disappointing.

> Their products need selling techniques that are much too sophisticated
> for the average agent.[10]

It provides a degree of control that is impossible to achieve through intermediaries. In technical areas many agents and distributors have neither the resources nor the desire to follow through opportunities in the way the producer can. In some instances small firms have found it impossible to find good agents, but through careful market selection have built up business in markets close at hand:

> The 400 miles I drive to visit my customers in Benelux from Leeds is less
> than the distance to my customers in Glasgow, Aberdeen and Exeter.
> (Managing Director of small giftware firm)

Direct representation is wholly dependent on the personnel involved.

Some forms of access to foreign markets can be achieved through the home market. Sub-contracting for overseas contracts won by other firms is a major source of indirect exports, particularly for smaller firms. The very scale of some projects dwarfs the resources of even the largest firms. Consortia (groups of firms coming together to tackle projects beyond the resources of an individual firm) are becoming increasingly common, particularly for government projects in less developed countries (Table 13.4).

British firms trying to build up their overseas business at a low cost but capitalizing on established market links are fortunate in having access to the expertise of export houses.

> An export house is any company or firm not being a manufacturer whose
> main activity is the handling or financing of British export trade and/or
> international trade not connected with the UK. (British Export Houses
> Association, 1978)

Table 13.4 Projects and consortia

Location	Type of project	Amount	Contractor and nationality
Iran	Petrochemical complex at Bandar Shahpur	$2.3 billion	Iran–Japan Petrochemical Co., joint venture composed of Mitsui Group (Japanese) the Iranian government.
Egypt	Sponge iron plant	$212 million	Arab Asian Development Partners, joint venture formed by: Development Consultants International Ltd (Indian) Bancom International (Filipino) Arab Export Trade Co. (Egyptian).
Jordan	Fertilizer complex	$180 million	Joint venture including: Agrico Chemical Co. (US) The Jordanian government International Finance Corp. (The World Bank) Jordan Phosphate Mines Co. (Jordanian).
Iran	Hospital	$235 million	United Kingdom Hospitals Group (co-ordinated by Orion Bank and Allied Medical Group Ltd, British).
Saudi Arabia	Desalination and thermal power generation facility	$167 million	Sasakura Engineering (Japanese) C. Itoh & Co. (Japanese) Brown, Boveri & Cie (German subsidiary) Saline Water Conversion Corp. (Saudi Arabian).
Iran	Expansion of port of Bandar Abbas	$1 billion	Italian consortium of state-controlled companies, including: Condotte d'Acqua Co. Costruzioni Motalliche Finsider Italdeii Dragomar, Ing. Mangelli & Cia.
Saudi Arabia	Direct reduction	$200–$300 million	Marcona Mining (US) Gilmore Steel Corp. (US) Nippon Steel Corp. (Japanese) Nippon Kokan K.K. (Japanese).

Adapted from *Harvard Business Review*

In scale and expertise export houses vary enormously. Companies like Booker offer expertise equal to any of the larger British exporters, while other houses are highly specialized; for example, Jardines (Hong Kong) can trace its history back to the East India Company.

Choice of the type of intermediary is only the first step in a continuing process. The firm must match the exporter's needs and be able to work effectively to develop his business. Unfortunately, many firms lack method in their choice. Some choose to approach firms in a specific country, on the dangerous premise that 'We haven't got anyone there, so we've nothing to lose'. The marketing-orientated firm, however, draws up a clear brief describing the type of intermediary required, a detailed job description and a plan of their respective roles in building up a market.

Once an agent, distributor or other representative has been chosen, the task of sustaining their motivation and working together for long-term success begins. It will involve regular contact and repeat visits by the exporter to the market-place, but it provides the opportunity for fully realizing the company's potential.

From export to international marketing

As foreign business grows many firms are faced with pressure to establish a more substantial overseas presence. It is a problem that has faced many of today's giant corporations:

> In the first part of this century, when today's giants were embarking on international expansion, the term international marketing was practically synonymous with exports . . . [Now] their quest for even larger markets has led them to invest in foreign production facilities. (Business International Corporation)[11]

This pressure can come from many sources: governments reluctant to see a continuing drain on their foreign exchange, local competition, a desire to spread the firm's risks, special opportunities or incentives, cost or marketing benefits.

Many of the problems discussed earlier – adaptation to overseas conditions, designing policies – are as important in international marketing as in exports. The advantages which can be gained from establishing a major presence overseas are matched by new problems.

Many of the advantages centre on two recurrent and thorny issues of overseas trade: pricing and product development. This development from home to overseas is complex, and full of challenges and potential setbacks – far from the simple process sometimes implied.

Pricing overseas

In launching a new product overseas a firm has open to it many pricing options (these are discussed in Chapter 18). Often firms use home-market prices plus cost for freight and insurance, but this fails to take into account the different market conditions the firm is likely to face in opening up new markets. Also, many hidden costs emerge which may directly affect the company's real returns (Figure 13.3).

Figure 13.3 Costs over time deriving from export business

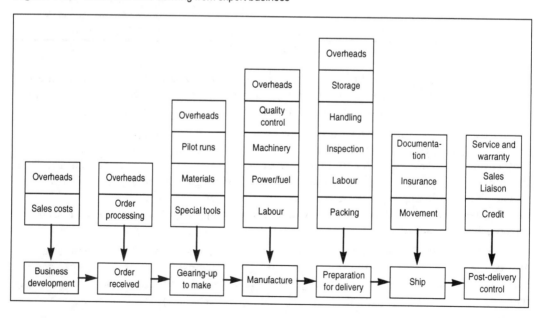

In determining prices and agreeing terms, parties in international trade operate under the terms agreed in Incoterms 1953 (revised 1967 and 1974). These set out rules to prevent misunderstanding and dispute over the precise meaning of an agreed price.

The company setting up a manufacturing plant in the target market can avoid many of these trading problems, and may also benefit from lower production costs or distribution savings. It is generally in a position to price much more competitively. For the overwhelming majority of firms, overseas production involves establishing a limited number of plants (generally small in proportion to the number of markets), the location of which should be carefully considered by marketing staff to fully exploit their marketing potential as well as any production or financial benefits, e.g. development grants from governments.

Distribution

For many firms one of the main advantages in establishing manufacturing plants overseas is reduced distribution costs. Research by organizations such as the National Economic Development Office highlighted the effect of service and other aspects of distribution on overseas trade. Poor delivery and service are seen as 'the British disease' by foreign buyers, and although a great deal of progress has been made in this area it remains a recurrent criticism by customers.

Manufacturing from a point much closer to the market can improve service levels and lower distribution costs. However, control of production and other operations can be a major problem, especially in plants at a considerable physical distance or operating in very different societies. Two fundamentally different approaches to those problem have been adopted in international marketing: centrist and devolved policies. Centrist operations are organized around and tightly directed by head office, while with a devolved policy the local operations have considerable authority. Most companies locate themselves somewhere between complete head office control and total operating freedom.

Products

One of the areas in which issues of central or local control come most clearly to the fore is in product development and management. The Wells international product life-cycle discussed earlier suggested that offerings emerged from the home market out into new markets. The pattern emerging today is a continuous flow of ideas and products from many parts of the world. Although Britain and the US are the only net exporters of licences, a study of new product directories will show inventions and innovations from all corners of the world:

> Gas alarm instrument using fixed electric current by a Japanese firm.
>
> Licence is offered by US company for a patented process for disinfecting liquids by irradiation.
>
> A blocking mix against enzymatic action . . . developed in Scandinavia.[9]

Overseas subsidiaries are increasingly geared to adapt existing products to their own special market conditions as well as producing their own innovations. These patterns of research and development require careful monitoring by the parent firm to maximize returns while minimizing waste and duplication.

Up to this point discussion has been focused broadly on British exports of manufactured goods. The rest of our trade falls broadly into the area of 'invisible exports', an area of recurrent balance of payment surplus.

Trade in 'invisibles'

The trade in 'invisibles' is so called because it deals in intangibles, in contrast to the physical tangible nature of visible trade.

> The invisible account is concerned with the payment and receipts derived from the provision of services. It includes payments and receipts derived from shipping, air freight, tourism and insurance: income earned and paid on overseas investment and foreign-owned home investment; current government expenditure abroad on the maintenance of forces, the provision of grant aid to underdeveloped countries (and contributions to bodies such as the EU).[13]

Four broad areas are of interest to the marketing person: finance (including insurance); shipping, freight and related services; consultancy and advisory services; and tourism. These are becoming increasingly important areas of opportunity for marketing-orientated executives. Their long-term strength and sustained growth are leading some authorities to suggest that Britain's economic future is more closely linked with these service sectors than with manufacturing.

Although it will be many years, if at all, before the service sector can provide either the foreign exchange earnings or the job opportunities to make this type of forecast come to pass, its growing importance appears to be certain.

Finance

The City of London is one of the world's leading centres for banking and insurance. Marketing financial services throughout the world is a major source of the UK's export earnings. Income is generated from returns on investment, loans, advisory and counselling services and the highly publicized but relatively small area of currency management.

> The government (Uruguay) in 1975 received capital from various sources including an allocation of SCR 46.6 million from the IMF's special oil deficit facility plus a loan for an initial amount of $110 million from a consortium of banks in London.[14]

The strength of the British banking system is matched by the power and authority of the insurance community. Lloyd's coverage is sought throughout the world. Some brokerages earn the overwhelming majority of their income from export transactions in this complex and highly specialized field.

No discussion of international or export marketing is complete without a mention of the specialized trading companies, although these are not, strictly speaking, in the finance area. Merchants such as European Grain and Shipping, Frank Fehr and Co. and Star Diamond Co. play a vital part in international trade, especially in primary products and raw materials.

Shipping, freight and related services

Britain's long history as a trading nation has built up a wealth of knowledge and expertise in the international movement of goods and associated services which is unsurpassed; the shipping lines and the air and road freight organizations have accumulated expertise which is in demand throughout the world. Some companies, such as Overseas Containers Ltd, established extensive networks of support services throughout the world to facilitate the movement of clients' goods. The operations of the transport firms are complemented by freight forwarders and other specialized organizations. It is an area in which radical change has occurred during the post-war era as the shipping firms have competed vigorously for a share of the movement of goods in world trade. A good illustration of the pace of development is the 'container revolution' which, from beginnings as recent as the mid-1950s, has changed the entire face of surface transport (Figure 13.4).

Figure 13.4   Types of liner vessels. From Thomas Meadows and Co., *Understanding the Freight Business,* 1979.

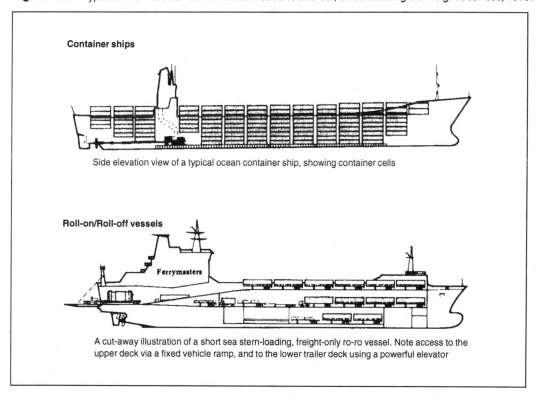

Container ships

Side elevation view of a typical ocean container ship, showing container cells

Roll-on/Roll-off vessels

A cut-away illustration of a short sea stern-loading, freight-only ro-ro vessel. Note access to the upper deck via a fixed vehicle ramp, and to the lower trailer deck using a powerful elevator

Consultancy and advisory services

Knowledge is rapidly becoming recognized as one of the most valuable international commodities. There has been a surge in demand for advice, technological skill and design, consultancy and other knowledge-based services over the last decade, particularly from the rapidly developing economies of the Middle East, Africa, the Far East and South America. The main demand in the initial period has been for technical assistance in areas such as construction and agriculture. Architects, designers and building, civil, mechanical, mining and electrical engineers have been at the forefront in opening new markets. More recently, the scope for business development in this area has been recognized by consultants and advisers in many fields.

As the industrial base of these emerging countries grows there is a growing demand for management and marketing expertise. Business schools, polytechnics and colleges of further education, as well as the more commercial concerns, are finding opportunities based on the need in many overseas countries for expertise in these critical areas.

Tourism

Today tourism is one of Britain's most important and vigorous industries. It provides employment to hundreds of thousands across the country, from museum keepers on Hadrian's Wall to waiters in London restaurants. It is, however, an area in which 'the marketing concept is yet to (fully) permeate'.[15] Although progress has been considerable since that comment was made, tourism remains an area of real opportunity for the creative marketer, from the large national concern catering to mass markets to the small local firm meeting the needs of special interest groups.

The requirements of customers go far beyond the 'tangible' aspects of the product. Also important are the attraction of the destination, the facilities (accommodation, catering, entertainment and recreation), the means of getting to and from the destination, the availability of goods and services, and the entire cluster of presentation, promotion, advice, finance, general atmosphere and, increasingly important, local attitudes to visitors.

A recurrent problem of tourism marketing is the impact of the 'total experience' on the holidaymaker or visitor and the number of uncontrollable factors which can influence their satisfaction. Weather, general impressions of the environment and interaction with residents can be as important as the stated purpose of the visit. Promotions geared to encourage overseas visitors can be nullified by hostility to them once they are here.

In tourism marketing there must be a recognition of the very different marketing opportunities which can arise from the varied holiday needs of customers from different parts of the world. The 'negative' cultural, environmental and economic impact of tourism is emerging as an issue of growing concern to policy-makers.

The multinationals

It is impossible to review international and export marketing without some discussion of the multinationals. Multinationals are firms which have direct investment in a number of countries, generally deriving 20–50 per cent or more net group profits from markets other than their original or home country. Management makes policy decisions based on the relative merits of alternatives anywhere in the world, and this feature places them, in part, outside the scope of international or export marketing. They generally try to minimize, if not eliminate, the foreign or alien nature of their offerings. Wherever they operate, their aim is to become a local firm. Lever Bros (US) might be part of Unilever, but generally its actions are those of a US firm in the American market. The Ford Corporation is a giant US concern, but Ford UK is almost as British as Rover (Ford UK contributed exports of over £1 billion to UK trade in 1993). The recent improvement in UK car exports is in large part due to 'foreign' manufacturers like Nissan in Sunderland.

Multinational corporations are now among the major forces in the world economy. Although it is impossible to obtain accurate figures, it is estimated that the 300 largest account for over 20 per cent of world trade, a proportion which is steadily growing. Their size, power and apparent independence from national governments have raised many fears among politicians, economists and others. Although these fears persist, large-scale unemployment has led many governments to mute their criticism while wooing them for investment and jobs.

Despite their apparent power, the multinationals face enormous management and marketing problems. At the centre of these lies the problem of control, discussed earlier. For the multinational firm this issue looms large. Marketing planning has become a powerful element in ensuring optimum returns and minimum duplication and in establishing control. In some firms the process of centralization has gone so far that totally standardized marketing plans are used throughout the corporation, from the group itself to the smallest operating unit. Other firms have placed considerable faith in building up shared ideas and values among corporate staff throughout recruitment, training and development.

The problem of standardization has also emerged in product, distribution, pricing and promotional policies. Five basic strategies have been identified in marketing and communication:[16] same product, same message world-wide; same product, different communication; different product, same communication; dual adaptation (product and communication adapted to local needs but little questioning of basic proposition); and autonomy of foreign operations.

In the past the discussion of multinational corporations focused on the activities of US firms, e.g. IBM and Coca-Cola, but recently British firms like BAT, Beechams and ICI, and even more recently European and Japanese companies like Philips, Nestlé, Toyota and Hitachi have become very powerful. The multinational company is increasingly becoming a worldwide phenomenon, and the Third World multinationals are demonstrating very rapid growth .

New issues and new challenges

The international marketing environment is likely to be characterized by operational and intellectual challenges. Buckley[17] highlighted these when he identified six of the themes most likely to change the nature of international business theory during the 1990s.

1   The simultaneous increase in both competition and collaboration.
2   Political change driven by political integration and deregulation.
3   Technological change.
4   Social change and reform driven by growing customer expectations.
5   Restructuring of international trade links.
6   Shifting relations between developed and underdeveloped world.
7   The growth of electronic, boundaryless retailing.

Conclusion

The export and international market-place is a complex and changing environment. It is made up of five basic types of firm:

1 Non-exporters: firms which, although they may have exported in the past or perhaps will export in the future, do not now.
2 Passive exporters: probably the largest group (in terms of numbers). Willing to service foreign business but do little to win it.
3 Active exporters: from a production base in one country these firms search out overseas business.
4 International marketing firms: production is spread over a small number of overseas plants.
5 Multinational corporations: giant firms operating throughout the world with an overlap between domestic and foreign business. Individual units of these corporations can fall into any of the above categories.

Although some firms progress from the first type through to being a multinational, the overwhelming majority operate for long periods in a specific category. Progress usually occurs because of a combination of the determination of specific executive, effective marketing backed by mobilization of all company resources and favourable demand conditions.

There are some constraints on the firm in international trade. One of the major disincentives to the newcomer is the complexity of documentation and payment systems, although bodies such as SITPRO (Simplification of International Trading Procedures Board) are attempting to solve some of these problems. However, while there are nations looking to protect their interests the problem will never entirely disappear. Care in these areas is vital in international trade.

Operating effectively in the international market-place is essentially to the economic well-being of the UK. Success in the single European market is increasingly important to the survival and prosperity of firms across Britain. Over the past 500 years British businessmen have demonstrated their ability to compete successfully, and success in the future will depend on their ability to effectively adopt a marketing stance in the overseas trade.

SPECIMEN QUESTIONS

1 Explain the Theory of Comparative Advantage. Give some reasons why such a sophisticated theory is hard to implement in mature markets.

2 Outline the ways in which marketing might help a manufacturer of craft goods in a developing economy win export sales in Britain or another rich, mature economy.

3 'We all pay lip-service to the notion of adapting our approaches to the different cultural environment of export markets but seldom make any significant changes.' Why do you think it is so hard for firms to make the type of changes needed to adapt to other cultures?

4 Outline the main features of the international product life-cycle. Using illustrations wherever possible indicate the strengths and weaknesses of this model of international trade development.

5 Define:

(a) GATT.

(b) IMF.

(c) Non-tariff barriers.

(d) Commission agents.

(e) Confirming-houses.

(f) Joint ventures.

(g) FOB.

(h) CIS.

(i) Invisible exports.

(j) Ro-Ro ships.

CASE STUDY 11: KIRKBY CARPETS

The company

Kirkby Carpets has been established as a carpet manufacturer in Kirkby, near Liverpool, since 1947. John Smith, the present Managing Director, is the son of the founder and, although it has been a public company since 1964, the family influence remains strong. The bulk of its production is medium to high quality Axminsters, with wool being the primary material, reinforced by nylon. A wide range of designs is produced:150 designs in 70 colours with ten alternative qualities. It was this range and variety of product which convinced the firm that real export opportunities existed. All its production is concentrated at its Kirkby site, which is well placed for Liverpool and its docks. The workforce of 180 is drawn largely from the surrounding towns. The current turnover of £3.5 million is divided into 70 per cent home market and 30 per cent exports. Its existing costing system does not permit the firm to separate the different markets to identify any differential experiences.

Export organization

The firm operates primarily through appointed agents working on a percentage basis. Its agents vary considerably in size, from large firms with well-established sales organizations to small firms depending to a considerable degree on Kirkby Carpets' products. The company prefers agents to have a range of complementary products. This flexible policy has enabled the firm to build up a very extensive network of national agents throughout the world.

Traditionally the old Commonwealth has been its largest market, with Canada and Australia as the leading markets (good sea links from Liverpool have assisted this process). The recent past has seen some decline in sales to both countries, with import restrictions making it difficult to build up trade. However, the growth of demand in Europe, the US and the OPEC countries has more than compensated for the decline in the traditional markets. In Europe prior to EC (now EU) membership a healthy trade had developed with EFTA countries, of which Switzerland and Sweden provided the biggest sales volume. The links with these countries have continued since Britain joined the EC, and in 1980 it made a serious attempt to tackle EC markets. Agents were recruited in all member countries, France and Germany being given priority:

> The Germans were already importing similar quality products at much higher prices from Belgium and Holland, so we felt that we had a real chance of success.

The French are not large users of carpets but the comments in the press about the likely growth in national income during the 1970s stimulated this move. The Netherlands, Italy and Spain were also seen as potentially lucrative markets.

Even more recently a serious attempt has been made to establish a sales organization in the Middle East. The oil price rises and comments about the oil-rich Arab states have promoted an initiative in that area. Two basic approaches have been taken: working through contractors in the UK, particularly those involved in major building projects, and building up a network of agents. A number of relatively small orders have been won, and the firm is currently tendering for a major order in a planned hotel complex. David Smith, the sales director, is planning to go to Saudi Arabia on a trade mission with the Liverpool Chamber of Commerce.

The most recent decisions have been to give considerable priority to developing the US and Japanese markets. David Smith, who is the Managing Director's younger brother, sees this search for new markets as clear evidence that 'it is from exports that we will be looking for growth'. He is very much the motivating force behind this search for market opportunities. His wife is Italian, and he believes this gives him a more international perspective than most of his rivals in the carpet industry.

The current sales set-up is based on David Smith as sales director, and export sales managers organized on a regional basis (Figure 13.5).

David Smith takes personal responsibility for the contracts side of the business and developing markets (Table 13.6). Co-ordination of their activities takes place through sales group meetings, the sales group reporting directly to the board.

Task

John Smith has called for a review of current export activities and for proposals to improve sales and profitability. Put forward recommendations to increase the share of export sales over the next three years from 30 per cent to 40 per cent, with no overall decline in UK sales. He is especially anxious to develop a 'post-2000' strategy for the firm.

Figure 13.5 Kirkby Carpets: sales division

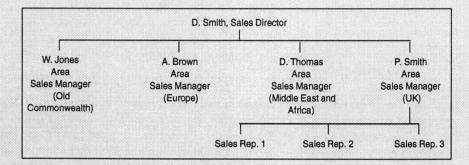

Table 13.6 Markets as a percentage share of Kirkby Carpets' business

Country	1976	1980	1988	1992	1997
UK	80	74	70	70	65
Australia	7	6	5	4	5
Canada	5	3	2	2	1
New Zealand	2	2	2	2	2
Sweden	1	1	2	2	1
Switzerland	–	1	3	1	1
Germany	–	1	2	3	6
South Africa	2	1	–	1	–
Irish Republic	2	–	–	1	1
US	–	2	2	4	3
Netherlands	–	–	–	1	3
Iran	–	2	–	1	–
Saudi Arabia	–	1	3	2	2
Nigeria	1	1	1	1	1
Other Commonwealth countries	–	1	3	1	1
Other European countries	–	1	3	2	3
Other OPEC countries	–	2	1	1	4
Others	–	1	1	1	1
Total	100	100	100	100	100

14

International marketing

Introduction

A cursory examination of almost any high street, shopping centre or mall in Western Europe, North America, Japan and most developing countries highlights the importance of international marketing. Products from many countries, shipped and distributed by international carriers, abound. These compete for space on shelves owned by retailers for whom the global market-place is a reality which is reinforced by their increasingly international ownership. Buyers seek out supplies and services whose origins are an increasingly secondary consideration. They are helped in this by greater personal and organizational experience of buying abroad and dramatic increases in the quality and amount of information available.

These developments lead some authors[1] to emphasize the similarities between domestic and international marketing. Others note that marketers who have gained their experience in a domestic market often find the transition to the international scene fraught with difficulties.[2] An understanding of this debate and its origins is central to any attempt to appreciate the nature of international marketing today and the demands it makes on managers, policy-makers, researchers and teachers.

Today's discussion of international trade and markets is greatly influenced by major changes which have occurred in the nature, shape and scale of activity. There has been a shift away from exports towards international or global marketing.[3] Interregional and international patterns have changed as countries and firms have challenged the 'established order'. The creation of the single European market produces pressures for similar groupings in America, Asia and Africa like NAFTA and ASEAN. This has occurred at a time when the volume of international trade has doubled every decade since the end of World War 2.

International trade takes many forms. Traditionally, exporting (discussed in Chapter 13) was dominant. In its basic form, this involves the movement of goods produced in one country to another separate nation state. Its existence reflects both the need of different societies to exchange their products and the opportunism of individuals and firms.

This need to exchange provides the foundation upon which economists' theories of international trade have been built. In essence they have asked the fundamental question – why enter international trade at all? Their answer is built upon the notion of specialization in those areas in which the nation has an absolute or the greatest comparative advantage. Simply stated by Ricardo[4] it means that specialization will maximize total output. This, in turn, ought to be based on each nation concentrating on those areas where it is relatively most efficient. His theory was later revised by Heckscher and Olin[5] to emphasize the importance of factors of production such as land, labour and capital.

In practice, this knowledge has demonstrated the value of international trade without being able to solve the problems resulting from the wish of individuals, firms and countries to achieve a differential advantage while protecting themselves from the rigours of the open market. The prevailing patterns of trade tend to reflect the opportunism and skill with which firms and managers develop their export or international markets. This notion that traditional theories are inadequate to explain differential, competitive advantage provides the basis for Porter's[6] approach to competitive advantage. His explanation is based upon the notion that competitive advantage among nations is built around powerful, internationally competitive firms. These shape the competitiveness of nations through the skills with which their managers exploit new technologies and use the resources available to them in order to win shares in global markets. The notion of competitiveness is developed further by Buckley et al.[7] They highlight the value of viewing competitiveness from different perspectives. They categorize it in terms of:

1 Competitive performance.
2 Competitive potential.
3 Management process.

Each plays its part in determining the international competitiveness of firms. They affect all forms of international trade, from exports to licensing. Performance is best measured in terms of profitability while potential is shaped by investment in R & D and the firm's skills in converting technologies to successful products. Success is underpinned by the effective deployment of management skills inside and outside the firm.[8]

From export to international marketing

In export marketing, attention is concentrated on the approaches which firms adopt to build up foreign sales of goods produced in the 'home market'.[9] In developing this side of their business, firms need to develop their policies on a number of levels. There are strategic questions of coverage of markets and direction of marketing efforts as well as tactical questions about specific means, e.g. agents or distributors, used to appeal to customer groups and win business.[10] But the emphasis lies in ensuring the maximum gains for a single or small number of 'home' producer markets. This is largely an 'ethnocentric' view of trade.[11] This means the needs of the home market are paramount.

This approach reduces the flexibility of the producer. Opportunities to establish stronger links with intermediaries or customers, even to develop new products collaboratively, call for marketing strategies based on a stronger, international perspective. The greatest benefits are linked with a more clearly defined international marketing strategy which may involve market concentration but could mean product specialization,[12] niche marketing[13] or some other coherent and effectively implemented, international marketing strategy. The nature of this strategy and the likely returns from it will depend largely on the capability of the firm, the environment faced, notably the stage of development of the market, and the competitive posture adopted.[14]

Moving overseas

The decision to move overseas either to win business or obtain supplies is often described in terms of the 'evolution' of a firm's operations. Perhaps the most popular of such models is the Wells International Product Life Cycle (1968). This model describes the process of the firm moving overseas in terms of a series of stages broadly as described in Figure 13.1 (see page 249) and summarized as follows:

- Phase 1: The firm innovates in the home market.
- Phase 2: The strength of the offering attracts overseas interest.
- Phase 3: Passive exporting takes place.
- Phase 4: Overseas demand prompts the firm to export actively.
- Phase 5: Creation of a strong foreign market leads to local production.

The model provides a useful heuristic with many implications for those trying to build up overseas business. It suggests that innovation is technology/demand driven. During phase 1 the most technically advanced markets will provide the best environment for new products and services to survive and thrive. The evidence that exists tends to support this but with certain notable exceptions.[15] These tend to occur in areas of particular strength for a particular nation or among countries of comparable economic development. More importantly it suggests that during phase 2 firms should be approached spontaneously by the more advanced companies in less advanced economies. This creates an opportunity to build up exports, initially by supplying the most technologically advanced customers in markets at a similar or a slightly lower level of development.

This poses the first dilemma for the international marketer – how to manage entry into the market so that short-term returns are earned while recognizing the likelihood of increased competition in the long term, notably during phases 4 and 5. Figure 13.2 (see page 253) illustrates the wide range of alternative entry strategies open to the new entrant to foreign markets.

In exporting, during the intermediate phases, it is common for firms to take the largely 'passive' or 'supply only' approach described in phase 3. This means doing virtually nothing to adapt the company's offering to export needs. Responsibility for finding the supplier lies with the customer. In the UK boatbuilding industry it is common to find enterprises with significant 'export' business which is won solely through the London Boat Show.

Three factors are associated with 'success' using this strategy. Most commonly, it is linked with patterns of international buying. In markets ranging from boats to finance, buyers expect to seek out offerings by searching out overseas suppliers. The stronger this pattern, as in the luxury yacht industry, the more often it provides a viable alternative. In some industries, new technologies have greatly contributed to this. The finance sector has been transformed to the extent that buying and selling can occur almost instantaneously, with the participants located across the world. In some instances, the market position of the supplier prompts customers to seek it out. Certain types of luxury goods, technologically advanced products or unique services are associated with this phenomenon. More often, this passive approach is employed by firms who see export business as a marginal activity not meriting any investment. The maintenance of a 'passive' stance leaves the firm vulnerable to local competition or rivals adopting an 'active' approach to export market development during phase 4.

Some firms respond to this by servicing the overseas market from a domestic base. This can be made easier by the existence of Confirming Houses or Export Trading Houses in the home market. Many companies build and maintain their exports by employing home-based sales, marketing and promotional staff. The notion of the complete trade 'package' has grown in importance with the scale and complexity of international capital goods transactions. Firms seeking to win this type of business match their product offering with financial, human resource and even counter-trade agreements. It is common for there to be significant participation by governments, international agencies and third countries.

Despite the importance of these and other home-based options, the active exporter normally seeks some form of overseas representation. There are three basic options open for firms pursuing this route: some form of agency arrangement (without stock-holding), a dealership or distributorship (involving stock-holding) or a wholly or partly owned subsidiary or joint venture. The specific option selected tends to reflect the nature of the firm's commitment or local legal circumstances.

The early discussion about concentration or spreading approaches under-stated the options open to firms in servicing markets. The importance of UK-based trading houses allied to the apparent preference for intermediary-based marketing arrangements makes market-spreading policies far more viable. Firms can use a network of agents or distributors to 'skim' a large number of markets with low costs and good returns. Their learning process involves learning to manage this form of distribution. This can earn the firm the same benefits as concentration. The most vivid illustration of the success of this strategy today can be seen in the achievements of the Sogu Shosha or General Trading Houses of Japan. Exporters who rely on this route are, however, very vulnerable to erosion of their market position by more active or local competitors. These are likely to emerge during phase 5. All other things being equal, they will have the advantages of being local, facing lower costs and exploiting local preferences.

Those firms which substitute agency arrangements for comprehensive and carefully thought out international marketing strategies are especially vulnerable to this threat. The NEDO report[16] on machine tool exports highlighted the importance of well-designed, customer-orientated approaches. Ultimately, the firm which is seeking to establish a secure international position must adopt a more clearly defined international marketing strategy.[17]

Building an international market

The Wells[18] Life Cycle Model presents the maturity phase of the international market for a product in terms of greater competition and reducing options. In practice, companies have three broad strategic options open to them: withdrawal, innovation or full internationalization. Withdrawal can be whole or partial. The former involves some recognition of the difficulties of competing when the advantages of local firms seem insurmountable. Partial withdrawal may mean the originator of the product transferring licences, even product capacity, to indigenous suppliers. Innovation-based responses seek to build on the technological or commercial lead of the home market. New products or services are fed into the overseas market as demand emerges. The problems of this approach are highlighted by the criticisms of the life-cycle models which have emerged. Innovation-driven strategies place major demands on the capacity of the enterprise to sustain its success in this area.

Implementing an effective programme of internationalization puts pressure on all aspects of the firm's marketing effort. This is valid for firms operating at both ends of the spectrum between 'standardized' offerings and those adapted to meet local needs.[19]

Standardization

There is increased interest in deliberate or conscious policies of standardizing products or services in international markets.[20] Two factors combine to produce this outcome. First, are efforts to reduce R & D production, human resource and marketing costs. Second, there is the view that some markets are becoming increasingly 'global'.[21] Both are seen in

Table 14.1 Regional analysis of US MNE product line composition

	North America	Central America	South America	Western Europe	Africa	Asia	Oceania	Other
% US product	60	74	58	57	62	61	45	75
% Non-US product	16	21	20	20	21	32	30	14
% Local goods	25	5	21	22	6	16	25	11
No subsidiaries	11	21	28	88	14	44	13	9

Source: Hill and Kwon[22]

industries as diverse as automobiles and fast food. Hill and Kwon[23] illustrate the extent to which US multinationals standardize their product offerings (Table 14.1).

In the car industry the massive tooling and other costs associated with new models led producers to give a high priority to efforts to build cars which meet the needs of a global market. The success of McDonald's hamburgers demonstrates the scope for an apparently simple product proposition to build a global franchise. These illustrations show how standardization can occur in either a single element in the marketing mix, the product, promotion, price, service and distribution, or across all elements in the total offering. They should not be exaggerated. Often, there are subtle yet significant adaptations to products or services that 'seem' global. Amazon, the electronic bookstore, uses the Internet to sell books in a wholly standardized way. Buyers can choose from a stock of over 2.5 million books. The same prices are offered to all customers with only postage costs varying.

Successful standardization programmes in consumer product markets are usually built around commonly held aspirations, e.g. a particular lifestyle, or generalizable needs. The success of the small number of lifestyle brands and products has lured some commentators into the view that standardization and uniformity are the same or that global products are the norm. In truth there are far more examples of failed attempts to transfer an unchanged product into international markets than successes. These failures have included products ranging from 'Shake 'n' Vac' to Hershey Bars.

Adaptation

In industrial markets, uniformity in production systems makes *de facto* standardization the norm among markets at similar levels of development. The needs of white goods manufacturers for certain types of plastic components is the same for all those producing similar ranges. Even here, local requirements affect the acceptability of certain products. In the domestic ovens market, the use of asbestos for seals was banned very early in certain countries. This forced suppliers to use alternatives which might not be needed in their home market. Government markets are especially vulnerable to pressures which undermine sales of standardized products.

Local cultural, legislative, technical, climatic and economic forces generally combine to make each market relatively distinct. This is likely to mean that most active international marketers will undertake some form of adaptation of their offering to maximize local sales. This is observed in each element of the marketing mix. The product features of a car are adapted to cope with the extremes of weather seen in the tropics. Distribution in countries like Nigeria, Bangladesh and Brazil is often easier by the extensive river system than by road. Counter-trade is essential in some countries to overcome shortages of foreign exchange. This, in turn, allows suppliers to charge more than the 'cash' price. Certain images are taboo in advertising in some countries.

Price

Changes in prices are almost inevitable. Those firms which adopt a cost-plus approach to pricing will typically 'add in' the costs of reaching an export market. This is true even among those exporters using the same 'ex-works' price. Companies adopting a market-orientated approach generally find that local conditions, taxes etc. require some form of modification. It is far too early to see the likely effects of international developments such as EU currency harmonization. The pressure for this, however, comes from the wish to overcome the 'market imperfections' which allow firms to vary prices. Some price changes reflect the needs of the local distribution system. Others reflect variations in the type of support available from government.[24]

Distribution

Methods of supplying markets evolve over long periods of time to meet many local needs. This means that the international marketer must learn to cope with wide variations in distribution systems. Standardization is likely to occur only in those markets in which the firm can 'impose' its own system or where a specific international trade intermediary emerges. The most obvious example of the former today is the success of the US-style franchise operations. The recurrence of import agents or similar distributor systems across the world is based in part on their ability to eliminate the problems of adapting to local distribution needs and minimizing the cost of entry.

Advertising

Some of the best-publicized examples of standardization in international markets are found in advertising and promotion polices. Coca-Cola, Bic, Esso and Marlboro are among brands which have been sold around the world under the same advertising message. Their apparent success prompted Saatchi and Saatchi to argue that global brands promoted with standard messages offer major growth opportunities for ambitious firms. It does seem that certain preconditions are needed for this approach to work. It is useful to build the advertising around a universal 'image' such as the Marlboro cowboy, a clear and simple proposition, e.g. Bic's 'throw-away', or a distinctive symbol analogous to the Coke bottle or Kodak logo. Douglas and Craig[25] highlight the advantages in terms of transfer of knowledge and expertise, uniformity of image and the easier control and co-ordination which this approach offers the international firm.[26]

These operational advantages have not persuaded the majority of firms to standardize their promotional policies. These advertisers find that structural and market forces require a locally specific approach. In some cases the law precludes the same approach being employed. Images which would be accepted in the West might be banned in Islamic countries. Approaches which are effective in one country might be counter-productive elsewhere. Certain types of advertising might be banned – such as television advertising of cigarettes in Britain. Some media might not be available. The costs of standardization might not be worth paying if it means missing opportunities or reducing overall advertising effectiveness.

The high costs that are generally associated with change or modification make firms reluctant to revise their product mix for each market. In consumer industries such as automotive products and white goods, this prompted firms to seek increased standardization, especially within ranges. Adaptations tend to reflect specific market developments, e.g. pressure for lead-free petrol in the US. Companies concentrate on the less tangible aspects of the product mix, notably service and warrantee policies or 'add-in' features. The shift to mass customization among key producers will change the basis on which the debate about standardization will be agreed.

Standardization is increasingly the norm among those firms striving to meet the needs of government and industrial markets. This has been spurred by the convergence of these markets as access to technology increases and the sourcing policies of enterprises become more international. A firm in Malaysia supplying components to a European firm must have access to the same type of industrial equipment. Some of the clearest illustrations of this are seen in the internal markets of the large multinationals. Components are purchased from across the world on the basis of quality, price and service standards, with country of origin a minor consideration. Simultaneously, products manufactured in many parts of the world from within the firm's range will be supplied to each market. In Britain, IBM's range might include personal computers produced in Scotland, peripherals made in three or four European countries and major items from the US.

Even here the freedom of action of firms can be affected by tariff barriers, quotas or other restraints on trade. These derive from the policies of the originating or purchasing country. The US government's restriction of sales of 'strategic' materials is a good illustration of the former, while 'Buy local' policies are common, especially in large contracts involving direct government subsidies or guarantees. In major contracts, there are pressures which encourage firms to include agreements to incorporate a significant proportion of local manufacture.

The research base

The variety of options open to firms, allied to the diversity of situations facing them, places enormous demands on their marketing research and intelligence systems. Three aspects of this are especially important in export and international marketing:

1 Sources
2 Values
3 Integration.

Sources

There are several levels at which the information needed by the international trader is available. At the most aggregated level, there is material gathered by agencies such as the World Bank, the ILO, OECD and the UN as well as their specialist bodies and agencies. Unfortunately this is often far too aggregated to be of much use to specific firms. Besides this, the data collection process generally depends on national bodies. This means that the quality can be very suspect and data may be out of date. The more specialist the agency, the less serious these problems are likely to be.

The interplay of these factors is especially noticeable at the next level – data available from regional bodies such as the European Union. Most parts of the world are now covered by some forms of regional economic or customs union. In some cases, the combination of high standards in data gathering and specialization in economic policies means that the quality and relevance of data is very good. The material provided by the European Commission, 'EuroStat' falls into this category. Elsewhere, lack of resources, especially trained manpower, mitigates against this.

The information gathered by national governments shows the same variation in quality but with some crucial distinctions. The material gathered tends to revolve around internal economic management questions, or its external trade, for example Customs and Excise data. In most countries, the national economic plan or assessment is an integral part of that country's economic programme. A company seeking to build up its trade is likely to find this a crucial document, as it normally highlights national economic priorities, key areas of development, especially those requiring foreign investment, and spheres of activity for which foreign exchange is available.

Relatively few firms have the skills, resources or need to use the type of highly aggregated data outlined above.[27] Those gathering information on a systematic basis often depend on the services of market research agencies. The major agencies will often operate internationally or be linked with associated firms overseas. The improved standards in research expertise around the world are reflected in the reaction of professional bodies committed to maintaining standards in many countries. The exporter or international marketer can call on a growing pool of good, indigenous researchers in target markets. At the same time the reservoir of published research is steadily increasing, while the Internet is transforming access to data.

Value

It would be a grave mistake to assume that increases in the quantity of material and comparability of standards mean that uniformity exists. Language, culture, politics and environment can change the meaning of responses. In some countries, a 'Yes' answer is as likely to mean 'I don't want to offend' as 'I like the product'. Taboos may exist which preclude discussion of certain issues.[28] The difficulties encompass research into industrial and government markets. Managers may provide output data which reflect their planned targets rather than true production. Government officials might be reluctant to say anything which conflicts with official positions.

Integration

International marketing decisions at virtually every level – choice of export market or strategic allocation of marketing and production resources – require some form of marketing intelligence. The greater the interdependence of these decisions, the more important is the underlying marketing information system. In practice this means that the international marketing information system operates at a number of levels.

The most basic is normally the individual market. This is typically defined in terms of a country or product. This requires its own integrated information loop. Data are gathered and fed directly to those requiring them for local use. In a well-designed information system, the specification of information needs lies with the users. At the next operational level, subsystem needs are integrated. Here, it is likely that resources to achieve agreed tasks are allocated and control systems implemented. Information is needed to manage short- and medium-term plans. Much of this is provided through the individual market. These feedback loops need to be integrated to ensure maximum consistency. Simultaneously, some checking mechanisms are needed.

Managing standards and comparing intelligence is a crucial task for those responsible for the subsystem. They provide the primary material for international strategic planning at a corporate level. For this, the key data needs must be specified in terms of 'deliverables'. Some firms have moved towards standardized reporting and planning systems. This enables them to cross-check material against comparable areas of norms. Corporations without this type of system face major problems of integration. They can become overdependent on head office-based 'interpreters' of non-standard material or local operators. This type of loss control poses major problems for firms, especially those striving to manage internationalization within a wider portfolio of developments.

The operational structure

The conventional classification of firms operating internationally is based on the division between exporters, international marketers and global or multinational enterprise. *Exporting* emphasizes the successful marketing of goods produced in one or more countries in other overseas markets. *International marketing* highlights the wider development of business in a number of countries or regions within a framework incorporating the establishment of local manufacturing, distribution and marketing systems. *Global* approaches tend to avoid the very notion of a distinction between home and foreign trade. The separate operating units in the multinational enterprise act like local firms. The shift from exporter to international marketer, then multinational, reflects the response of the originator to market pressures of the type touched on by Wells.[29]

In the past, the pressures to move production overseas were predominantly cost and resource-driven – cheaper raw materials and labour. More recently, access to markets and technologies are equally important, especially in plant location or inward investment decisions.[30] The immediate consequence of the move from exporter to international marketer is generally a far more active involvement in the market. Many exporters leave *de facto* control of their market in the hands of their agents or distributors. This typically reflects a relatively low investment in building up the customer base. The price of market entry paid by the international or global marketer is normally too high to allow such a transfer of ownership.

Figure 14.1 Diversification and internationalization alternatives

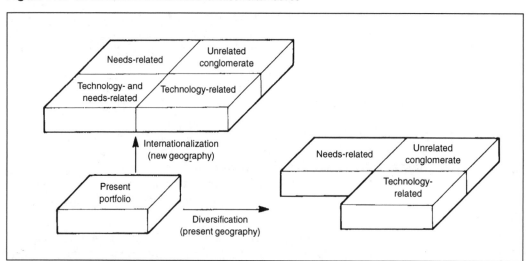

The discontinuous nature of internationalization is poorly reflected in the 'progress' models presented by writers who describe 'stages of internationalization'.[31] Withdrawal from overseas markets is not unusual, especially when the cost of exit is low. In some cases this reflects the limited nature of the initial investment. The firm which merely supplies items for a domestic range to overseas clients may cease supplies if home demand grows. This partly explains the recurrent findings that supply constitutes the major constraint on UK exports.[32] It is possible to identify 'transitional' firms who regularly enter and withdraw from export markets on the basis of their domestic demand or the price of access.

This reflects the overall posture to international trade adopted with the enterprise. Heenan and Perlemutter[33] suggest that there are four basic predispositions that a multinational firm can adopt:

1 *Ethnocentrism.* All strategic decisions reflect the home-market needs and interest of the parent enterprise.
2 *Polycentrism.* Decisions are tailored to satisfy the requirements of all countries in which the firm operates.
3 *Regiocentrism.* The needs of different regions are balanced against home-market requirements to shape posture.
4 *Geocentrism.* The global position of the enterprise takes precedence.

The posture that the enterprise adopts will shape both overall strategy and the way this is implemented. It seems that local and international pressures are forcing all but the smallest firms to move away from ethnocentric approaches.

The growth of regional trading blocks, notably the EU, prompts many firms to set up subsidiaries, acquire companies or use other approaches to build up their market position.[34] Nicoliades[35] points out that foreign direct investment, the amount invested by companies in countries other than their own, has increased faster than world trade.

This reflects three pressures. The improved flows of information and knowledge make it easier to establish and control overseas operations. There is increased resistance in markets to exporters who do not invest in market development. This is best illustrated in the tariff and non-tariff barriers to entry. The convergence of management and operational skills makes managers from different operations across the world able to share common values and assumptions, e.g. about the crucial importance of marketing. Wong et al.[36] highlight the emphasis given by Japanese companies in the UK to product differentiation, segmentation and marketing planning. This is underpinned by their confidence in their marketing skills despite the questions raised elsewhere about their global competitiveness.[37] This awareness of the power of international marketing has simulated recognition of the range of market entry strategies open to firms. Joint ventures and foreign licensing are strategic options which may prove to be as important as exports and overseas manufacture.

Conclusion

Over the last decade, international markets were shaped by the conflicting demands for greater integration and increased protection. The former was seen in developments as diverse as the European Community's moves towards a single market, increased integration of financial and banking systems, and the strides made to agree standards in information technology. These contrast with the demands for increased protectionism in vital markets such as the US, and Third World complaints about exploitative investment. The latter taps cheap labour or raw materials without truly investing in economic development.

Alongside these macro-economic developments, many micro-economic factors shape the way that specific communities, firms and managers respond to the opportunities of international trade. The dominance of manufacturers is being challenged by trade-based export channels. The clearest illustration of this lies in the success of the General Trading Houses of Japan. More recently, retailers such as Marks and Spencer, Sears and Benetton have initiated distinctive approaches to their internationalization. The pool of managerial expertise is expanding rapidly. Underpinning these diverse developments is the growing recognition of the importance of the global market and the risk of overdependence on vulnerable domestic markets.

SPECIMEN QUESTIONS

1 Buckley has suggested that international markets are seeing simultaneous increases in both competition and collaboration.

   (a)　What does he mean by this?

   (b)　Why does he believe that this will occur?

   (c)　What are the marketing implications of this notion?

2 Progress models of international trade development are often used to describe the way firms move from non-exporting to genuine international trade. What is the value of this type of approach and what are the flaws in progress models?

3 Porter argues in *The Competitive Advantage of Nations* that the international competitiveness of countries is built around the strength of internationally successful companies. To what extent does this explain the relative decline of Britain's share of world markets and the success of either Germany or Japan?

4 The shift from being a small profitable 'passive exporter' to a large, successful 'active exporter' poses a host of problems for the growing company.

   (a)　What are these problems?

   (b)　What steps can firms take to minimize the costs and risks of this change?

   (c)　What marketing case can be made to justify this move?

5 When General Motors were looking for new markets for their NOVA car range they found that NOVA meant 'No go' in Spanish. What are the implications of this kind of finding for name and advertising research and development for international firms?

6 A buyer for whom you have previously carried out plant construction asks you to quote a fixed US dollar price for a capital project worth £20 million. Roughly half your costs are in sterling, the rest in US dollars. This is a closed competitive tender, i.e. not open to many offers but restricted to you and one other. Your chances of winning are about 50:50. Outline and discuss the way you would manage the currency risk.

7 Explain the concept of ownership specific advantage in the theory of foreign direct investment and the multinational enterprise. Indicate the implications of this notion for a large European or US multinational seeking to establish a plant in India, Japan or Australia.

8 What factors will a multinational personal computer manufacturer need to take into account in choosing between sites in: Eire, the Central Belt of Scotland, North West England, Spain and Southern Germany for a new manufacturing plant? Indicate any ways in which the balance or mix of these factors has changed over the last twenty or thirty years.

9 Wong has highlighted the emphasis on product differentiation, segmentation and market planning in the successful development of international markets by Japanese companies. What is meant by these comments? Relate you answers to a specific Japanese firm.

10 Define:

(a) Export credits.

(b) SITPRO.

(c) Ethnocentric.

(d) Sogu Shosa.

(e) Globalization.

(f) Geocentrism.

(g) The multinational business.

(h) The stages of economic development.

(i) Forward buying of currencies.

(j) Trade mission.

EXTENDED CASE STUDY 12:
MARKETING IN THE SINGLE EUROPEAN MARKET

Introduction

The adoption of the Single European Act by the members of the European Community (now the European Union, EU) marked the start of a crucial phase in the economic progress of Western Europe. It is a development which has provoked widespread discussion, comment and concern inside and outside the EU. In the UK, the debate has caused turmoil, with some people saying the scale of the Conservative government defeat in 1997 was caused by this issue. This debate is inevitable. The Act has created a single internal market from some of the richest and most powerful economies in the world. The countries of the EU have a Gross National Product of $6 trillion and 360 million citizens. It is, perhaps, the single largest trading block in the world, with a significantly larger population and only slightly smaller GNP than the US. The EU's share of world trade, excluding the EU itself, is virtually the same as the combined share of the US and Japan. The likely addition of the former members of EFTA boosts both the population and GNP of the EU.

Although the debate is inevitable, it needs to be placed in perspective. It is a stage in a process that has been taking place for much of the last half-century. The European

Iron and Steel Community, the Treaty of Rome, the expansion of the Community, the Single European Act and the Maastricht Treaty are steps on a road to integration and expansion that seems set to continue for many more years with the creation of a single monetary system. It is a process driven as much by fear as by ambition. Some of the fears are self-evident. In this century, at least 100 million people in Europe and many more outside have died in conflicts driven largely by internal economic rivalries.

Other concerns are less striking but equally important. The economic standing of Europe was in decline compared with the US and Japan for most of the early 1980s. From 1979 to 1985, the European Community's share of world trade (excluding intra-EC trade) declined by almost 1.5 per cent. The US share of world trade increased by roughly 0.75 per cent and that of Japan by over 5 per cent. This pattern of decline and the underlying acceptance of failure, summarized in the term 'Euro-pessimism', was so well entrenched that only a major and dramatic initiative could reverse this process. A series of reports[38, 39] led eventually to the adoption of the Cockfield Report.[40] This proposed a seven-year timetable for the abolition of barriers to movement and trade within the Community. This report, its timetable for action and list of the 300 detailed decisions for the Council was the cornerstone of the Single European Act.

The Single European Act and the Maastricht Treaty extend far beyond the creation of an internal market. A series of decisions were made on majority voting, the powers of the European Parliament etc. which change significantly the balance of authority and power within the EU. In part these were enacted specifically to ensure that the timetable for dismantling internal barriers did not slip. Already, the impact of these decision is changing the nature of the EU. The vision of Jacques Delors:

> We would like to see the people of Europe . . . enjoying the daily experience of a tangible Europe, a real community where travel, communication and trade are possible without any hindrance.[41]

has by-passed the specific removal of barriers to internal trade. Even the collapse of Britain's membership of the ERM has not changed the basics of this agenda, with the EMU moving the agenda even further.

The emerging agenda for marketing change

The ultimate goal of creating a favourable atmosphere for European firms to expand and develop their marketing policies is accepted and endorsed by governments, industries and commerce across Europe, even the most reluctant to give up any degree of national sovereignty. The potential gains include:

1   Lower costs from the elimination of frontier controls and simplification of administrative proceeds.
2   Improved efficiency from increased competition.
3   Greater exploitation of economies of scale.
4   Reallocation of resources and greater comparative advantage.
5   Increased innovation.

These are closely linked to the kinds of changes in marketing practice identified by Lawrence.[42]

These changes in marketing practice include:

- the growing importance of market segmentation;
- bipolarization of companies in given industries;
- increased industrial concentration;
- closer links with Eastern Europe;
- more trans-European marketing such as cross-border branding, advertising and pricing;
- faster growth in southern Europe;
- increased emphasis on management quality as a source of competitive advantage.

The changes affect economic relations within the EU and with other countries and regions of the world. Agriculture and the Common Agricultural Policy have long been at the centre of EU policy. Economic and social policies have emerged to tackle problems of: job creation; working conditions, opportunities for the economic and socially disadvantaged; and training. Over the last decade concern grew about the needs of future generations. Programmes to provide access to new technologies were introduced. A determined effort was launched to create a stronger sense of the unity of Europe among young people, especially students. Mobility of citizens and better understanding of common interests and challenges are priorities.

The sense of declining capacity in advanced technologies and eroding competitiveness was a major motive for greater integration. The revolution in information technologies and computing in the late 1970s and early 1980s brought European leaders face to face with the absolute and relative decline in capacity and competitiveness. The Community moved from being a net exporter of information technology to being a net importer in less than ten years. The Community's share of high-technology exports stagnated over the 30 years from 1960, while the share of the US, Japan and other Pacific Rim countries increased. This aggregate pattern was vividly illustrated in specific products and sectors. In the early 1990s eight out of every ten microcomputers sold in Europe originated in North America or Japan while nine out of every ten video recorders originated in Japan. European firms have steadily lost ground in information technology industry and biotechnology.

Injecting resources into research and development and supporting innovation is a priority for marketing-orientated firms seeking to exploit new opportunities. Investment is concentrated in strategic areas. Here, the emphasis is on providing funds for leverage and to support collaboration across Europe. Programmes for specific industries, e.g. information technology,[43, 44] stand alongside more wide-ranging schemes.[45, 46]

The nature of the EU, especially the challenge of opening markets and equalizing factor endowments, leads to a special emphasis on transport and energy policies. Barriers to the free movement of goods increase industrial costs. The White Paper on completing the internal market included provision for a single administrative document for all cross-border movements of goods. More recently, the Transport Infrastructure Programme provided a policy framework and system of support to improve and expand transport links across the EU.[47] Problems still exist, notably in air transport where fares within the EU remain high in international terms. Energy policies pose similar problems of harmonization while raising additional issues of research and development. Attention has been focused on policies for specific sectors such as coal and nuclear power or R & D schemes. These are linked increasingly to the EU's programmes on the environment.[48] Policies on the environment highlight the extent to which EU policies cannot stand in isolation from wider, international concerns.

The Central European countries have a combined population of almost 100 million. Several, despite their current difficulties, are significant industrial nations. Key industries like steel, shipbuilding, mining, automotive and chemicals are well established. The addition of the Baltic republics, Russia and other West Asian countries expands both the population base, industrial potential and reservoir of natural resources. Their problems are immense. They include vast foreign debts, poor productivity, inefficient distribution, low morale and bad management. But there are clear benefits for the members of the EU if some form of economic integration and development can be achieved. Some of these gains are specific to individual countries.

These changes are having profound effects on the world vision of marketing strategists in Europe. Some are switching virtually all their attention eastwards. Others have drawn a wholly different lesson. These developments have increased the awareness of some leaders of the potential elsewhere.

Competitive challenges

The opportunities cannot mask all the hurdles. Some challenges are already visible within the EU. There is a major political debate on the overall political and economic direction of the EU. The central challenges facing the EU remain economic. Growth in Gross National Product is slow. Table 14.2 shows the gap between the EC and its main industrial rivals, the US and Japan.

Economic growth in most member states remains sluggish. This is especially noticeable when the rate of growth in GNP over the last 25 years is compared, as in Table 14.3.

The combination of diversity and fragmentation poses problems in a host of aspects of economic and social policy. Even Germany, the economic powerhouse of Europe, is described by Porter as having 'problems competing successfully in new industries ... [with] ... market positions gradually slipping in many sectors'.[49]

The variety of tax regimes, competition and public procurement policies in member states tie up scarce resources and add to the costs of companies. Value added taxes amount to just over 8 per cent of total tax receipts in Britain but 21 per cent in France.

Excise duty accounts for over 20 per cent of tax revenues in Ireland but less than 5 per cent in the Netherlands. Corporation taxes vary equally widely. They range from 15 per cent of revenues in Luxembourg to 3 per cent in Italy. Some of this variation is accounted for by patterns of consumption but much reflects the diversity of tax regimes. Establishing uniformity in VAT, excise duties, capital transfer taxes and reducing the costs of compliance are key aspects of the later phase of integration. The efforts to achieve greater European monetary integration centre on the wish to minimize these costs and establish a stable framework for financial planning and management.

Concern about lost competitiveness can be seen in worries about the policies being adopted by US and Japanese companies in Europe. Jacques Clavert of Peugeot expressed this when he commented:

> The Japanese, as we've discovered, are the best in the world at moving forward without being noticed. They move with apparent immobility. The day after the French government announced that Nissan cars built in the UK, were European, Nissan representatives announced, 'We don't know

Table 14.2 The Gross National Product of the EC, US and Japan

Nation	Gross National Product 1995 ($billion)
Belgium	269
France	1,549
Germany	2,420
Italy	1,091
Luxembourg	17
Netherlands	397
Greece	112
Ireland	60
Spain	557
Portugal	103
UK	1,100
Denmark	175
Total	7,850
US	6,981
Japan	4,961

Source: OECD[50]

Table 14.3 Comparative growth rates

	Average percentage rise in GNP			
	1966–1973	1973–1979	1979–1989	1989–1992
US	3.4	2.4	2.5	2.6
Japan	4.5	3.2	3.4	3.2
EC	4.4	2.4	2.0	.5

Source: OECD

why people are talking about producing only 200,000 cars in Europe. We've always been talking along the lines of 400,000.' Some of my American colleagues consider it almost certain that 40 per cent of the cars to be sold in America at the start of the next decade will have something to do with the Japanese – either Japanese cars imported from South East Asia, or Japanese cars made in America, or cars made through joint ventures with the Japanese.

The same concerns are seen in a host of industries. The exclusion of ICL from discussions about the ESPRIT project follows its take-over by Fujitsu. Information technology and telecommunications are especially sensitive given the rapid decline in international competitiveness by European industry. The EU has moved from being a net exporter of IT into a major import market especially for US and Japanese industry. In the last decade between 1978 and 1988 every major European country saw its share of world exports decline in computing, semiconductors, office equipment and telecommunications.

Figure 14.2 R & D as a percent of GNP. (From: Webster, A. and Etzkowitz, H., *Academic–Industry Relations: The Second Academic Revolution.* London: Science Policy Support Group, 1990 for 1975-1988, CSC for 1989.)

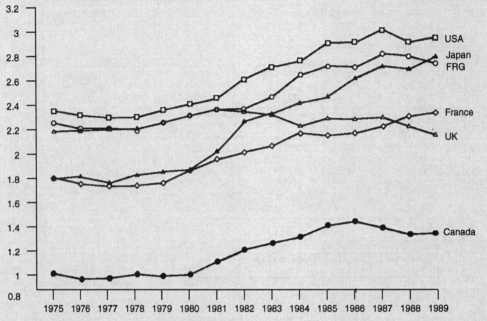

Figure 14.3 Patents registered at US Patents Office (1987)

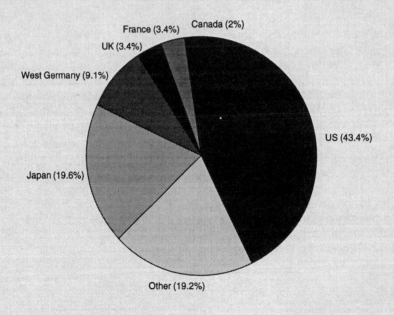

A single market?

The economic and industrial appeal of greater integration is based largely on the increased competitiveness of European industries. The effective working of a single market will determine the extent to which this goal is reached. An overarching structure exists to determine and deliver polices across Europe. The decision system is based on three components: the Council of Ministers (from each member state), the Commission and the European Parliament. These act through four mechanisms:

1   Regulations which are directly applicable in every state.
2   Directives which are binding within a fixed period.
3   Decisions which are binding on those at whom they are directed.
4   Recommendations and opinions; these are merely the views of those issuing them.

This policy framework is backed to an increasing degree by enforcement decisions of the European Court and policy in member states.

Western Europe

In Western Europe integration is well advanced. Large companies seek to establish a European perspective in their financing, production, logistics and markets. Corporations are financing their European operations through banks and financial institutions which are increasingly 'European' in their outlook, not national. This is made easier by electronic funds transfer and other technological developments in banking.

The realignment of the banking sector is well under way. Acquisition and merger is likely to be more attractive than organic development in crowded North European markets. Retail banking provides the most obvious opportunities for rapid development. 'Four major retail products appear ripe for growth [across Western Europe]: consumer credit, mortgages, credit cards and mutual funds'.[51] The extent of the opportunity is well illustrated by the wide divergences in use of different banking services. In Britain, for example, there are roughly 500 credit cards per thousand people. In contrast, France has 250, Italy 180 and western Germany only 150. An equally varied pattern is seen in smart-card operations.

The competition to develop European banking operations will be fierce over the next decade. This will increase rapidly as the ecu becomes the single currency for most of Europe. The pace of this development is well illustrated by Poldermans's comment[52] in July 1990: 'A common European currency seems as far off as Keynes's vision of a Bancor was 40 years ago. A European central bank is not regarded by many senior bankers as a serious proposition in their lifetimes.' In just over a year, most European governments were committed to both propositions. Recent setbacks have not eliminated the commercial case for a single currency.

Production and plant location decisions within the EU are shaped largely by access to markets, skills and raw materials. Inward investors tend to set access to the community as their primary requirement. The popularity of Britain and Spain with US and Japanese firms is largely a function of common standards, cost of labour and skill levels in the workforce. The firms originating within the EU show a tendency to concentrate production to achieve economies of scale. These concentrations are often close to their origins or the key markets. Satellite or branch production in peripheral regions was cut back drastically during the 1980s.

The free movement of goods and services is central to the successful development of the single market. Many of the formal and procedural barriers are already eliminated. Despite that, delays and waste persist. The Henley Centre estimates that 22 per cent of operating costs for road vehicles can be caused by cross-border customs delays.[53] Simplified customs procedures, increased competition and strategic changes in logistics policies are changing this. Hauliers in low-cost markets are winning business from those in high-cost areas. This enables firms to rationalize their warehouses and inventories. Tully illustrates the scope for savings based on this by pointing out that Philips maintains inventories of 20 per cent of annual sales in Europe but only 12 per cent in the US.

The highly fragmented nature of European distribution and retailing is changing. Some of the shift will occur through competitive and organic growth. Acquisition and merger will be even more important. The first signs of this can be seen in retailing. Major groups are seeking to establish themselves in other parts of the EU. Cultural and social diversity within the EU is a major barrier to change in local markets. Perhaps the greatest of these hurdles remains language. The countries of the EU speak eighteen languages and numerous dialects. These act as a brake on the rapid integration of consumer markets. The gradual emergence of English as the trade language might affect this but not in the short term.

Central Europe

The countries of Central Europe pose challenges, threats and opportunities to the European Union and those seeking to increase their economic links with Europe. Each nation has distinctive characteristics which will largely determine the likelihood of successful economic growth and improved links with the EU. The integration of East Germany into a reunified Germany was only achieved at a massive cost to Germany and its Community partners.

Some common building blocks are needed. Virtually every recent study has highlighted poor management as a common problem in Eastern Europe.[54] The EU, through its TEMPUS initiative, provides a framework for training, development and support for management education initiatives. Individual governments are working along parallel lines. The UK government has established 'know-how' funds to support training, development and technology transfer. Most Central European countries are keen to liberalize their markets. This can only occur if their banking and financial services are reformed. The privatization programmes advocated in these countries will be hard to deliver without a functioning stock market. These common problems are stimulating fairly consistent responses from Western institutions.

Elsewhere, the diversity of situation and the need to balance local, national and international interests makes consistency of approach harder to achieve. Two aspects of this will provoke increasing discord. The first is the nature of industrial and business developments in Central Europe. The second is the diversity of interest among separate European countries.

The industrial and business developments in Central Europe cannot be separated from those within the EU. In many fields there is competition for resources, even over-capacity. One of Europe's largest foodstuffs groups faces this dilemma today. It has substantial over-capacity in production of vegetable oils in Western Europe. Plans for rationalization are well under way. Now, it is under pressure to acquire several plants in the former East Germany and other parts of Central Europe. These factories are materially worse than the poorest of those plants in the West whose future is under review. Substituting Western output will reduce costs and improve product quality but increase unemployment in Central Europe. The alternative will lead to job losses in the West while improvements in quality and productivity will occur in the long term.

The right balance between the political and commercial interests of those involved is not easy to achieve. So far, the EU has proceeded cautiously. There is pressure from some member states to accelerate this progress. Germany is at the forefront, especially in terms of industrial investment in the former East Germany. The future scenario for the Community sees Hungary, Czechoslovakia and Poland taking the first steps toward membership. The members of EFTA and some of the peripheral countries of Europe are joining them. The total population of this enlarged Community exceeds 400 million. Table 14.4 indicates that the Gross Domestic Product would be close to that of the US.

Table 14.4 Population and GDP of Europe and the US in 1996

($billion)	GDP (millions)	Population
European Community	8441	373
Hungary	41	10
Czechoslovakia	36	10
Poland	97	38
Total enlarged EC	8615	431
US	9051	263

Sources: OECD[55]

Eastern Europe

Eastern Europe, i.e. the Baltic states and other former Soviet republics, pose a distinct set of challenges. The natural resource assets across Russia and the rest of the CIS are vast. They include most sources of primary energy, raw materials and precious metals. Reserves of oil and natural gas are hard to estimate but are likely to exceed those of any other country. Output remains high.

Table 14.5 Petroleum and natural gas outputs for 1996

Country	Crude oil (million barrels)	Natural gas (m^3)
Saudi Arabia	2,976	37,718
US	2,505	559,261
Russia	2,254	582,988
Mexico	994	38,454
UK	914	71,144

The agricultural sector is large but inefficient. These difficulties are made worse by major problems of logistics and distribution. This means that food may rot before it reaches the market. Similar difficulties face the manufacturing sector. Poor quality standards, low productivity and inefficiencies in the market and distribution systems recur throughout Russia. There is strength in some sectors. Educational standards are high. The education and medical services are sound. Certain types of R & D, notably aerospace, are well resourced. They can make a valuable contribution to economic growth if resources are redeployed and effective systems of technology transfer created.

President Yeltsin publicly espouses the 'free market' future of Russia. This has encouraged Russian and EU policy-makers and industrialists to seek ways to increase links between the two regions. These have highlighted some of the opportunities and many of the challenges. There is a large market in Western Europe for Russian natural resources. This is more important now that the Gulf crisis of 1991 has flagged the problems of continuity of supply from that region. The market in Eastern Europe for industrial and consumer goods is massive. There is, however, serious concern about the impact of large-scale exports on its growing shortages of foreign exchange. The Paris Summit established a framework for closer political links and greater economic collaboration.

The internal market

The broad pattern of the unified internal market can now be discerned. The goal of 'an area without internal borders, in which the free traffic goods, persons, services and capital are guaranteed' is gradually being achieved. The proportion of the 'external' trade of each member country which is with other member states is converging. Figure 14.4 gives an indication of these shifts in the proportion of total external trade which is within the EU for some of the larger EC countries. This process of convergence is likely to accelerate as firms become more comfortable with intra-European trade and communication becomes easier.

Opportunities

The development of 'European' business is spurred by a mixture of acquisition and organic growth. The last few years saw a sharp increase in the number and value of acquisitions of firms in one European country by businesses based in another. The UK has been at the centre of much of this activity. Despite this spurt, acquisitions by non-EC countries, notably the US, continue to exceed internal cross-border deals.

Organic growth is being driven by increased convergence in tastes and technical standards. Firms are exploiting this through:

1   Better integration of their business operations.
2   Diversification into related business.
3   Strategic alliances.
4   Specialization.

The increased scale of European operations places a premium on marketing and operational effectiveness. The costs of failure are increased with distance. These are heightened by the shorter product life-cycles of new products and higher costs of R & D.

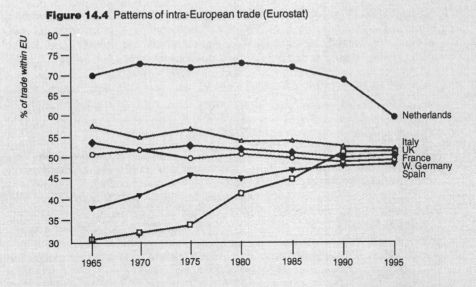

Figure 14.4 Patterns of intra-European trade (Eurostat)

Diversification into related industries has increased in most European markets. In part, this is a reaction to the high risks associated with non-related diversification. The notion of 'sticking to their knitting' has widespread currency among European industrialists. Companies relieve their need to expand into new areas through 'strategic alliances' to exploit particular opportunities, e.g. Central or Eastern Europe, or manage resource-intensive projects, e.g. the European Airbus project. Initially these links were largely 'horizontal', i.e. firms in complementary sectors. The buyback agreement between Siemens and Philips illustrates this. More recently, vertical alliances involving companies at different stages in the marketing systems are growing in importance in Europe. The link between the National Freight Company and Christian Salvesen gives some indication of the potential for this type of collaboration.

Challenges

The strategic planning of companies and within countries is directly affected by the creation of the single currency and the opening of Central and Eastern Europe. Corporations will need to redefine their corporate missions in terms of the integration of markets, not their separation. Small- and medium-sized firms will find that traditional sources of local protection will disappear.[56]

From inside

Within the EU, success turns on the ability to define, develop and exploit their competitive and comparative advantages. At the core of this is the effective audit of the resources at their disposal. All firms within the EU are faced with this challenge. The old hurdles of home and overseas trade will erode. It means that the local high street or industrial estate is an international market. The audit turns on appreciating the firm's strengths, weaknesses, opportunities and threats and the key to its competitive advantage locally, nationally and across Europe. The objectives of the firm cannot be separated from the audit. These goals will need to be actionable, communicable, consistent and quantifiable.

The strategies of the enterprise provide the means to achieve these goals. Marketing strategies have dominated much thinking about developments in the single European market. More recently, new strategic concerns have emerged. These centre on human resource policies and resourcing or purchasing strategies. The shift away from centralized procedures in these fields is slowing as firms find that headquarters control over standards can be mixed with local control over implementation. These processes accelerate with the increased mobility of labour, especially highly qualified or managerial staff.

From outside

The earlier discussion highlighted the extent to which the move towards greater European integration reflected fears about threats from US, Japanese and other international competition. The fear of an emerging 'Fortress Europe' shaped aspects of US policy during the GATT negotiations. In some sectors, notably cars, there was a clear sense that some European governments wished to increase barriers to entry. This aspect declined in importance only to be replaced by protectionist demands by agricultural groups. The greater emphasis on overcoming threats from outside the EU through improved competitiveness, not higher barriers to entry is largely accepted by industry. Effective defence policies are built around:

1   Exploitation of competitive advantages through stronger customer orientation and 'local knowledge'.
2   Strategic alliances with suppliers and customers.
3   Collaboration on a project basis with complementary or competitor companies.
4   Innovate and develop while fully exploiting EU and local support.
5   External, international growth.

These mirror in many ways the policies that non-European firms will need to apply to enter the European market successfully.

Entry strategies

There is no single strategy for the non-European company seeking to develop in the single European market or the evolving wider market. The diversity of cultures, environments, tastes and practices will persist for many years. This places a special premium on good-quality prior investigation. Almost inevitably, this highlights the need to adapt the firm's approach to circumstances and special conditions. In some cases, it is possible to concentrate operations in a single location. There are the exceptions. Most entry strategies require more than one point of access and route to development. The portfolio of policies is built from several alternatives:

1   Locally owned subsidiaries.
2   Joint ventures.
3   Acquisitions.
4   Partnerships.
5   Alliances.
6   Competitive development.

Each offers opportunities for the entrant to build up its position in Europe. Companies like Nissan established major manufacturing operations within the EU. These provide a basis for long-term business development. These are, however, expensive and involve long lead times. The Toyota production plant cost $1.2. billion and took four years to get to full production. Joint ventures reduce costs through sharing them with

Figure 14.5 Acquisition by non-EC companies of EC companies (1988)[57]

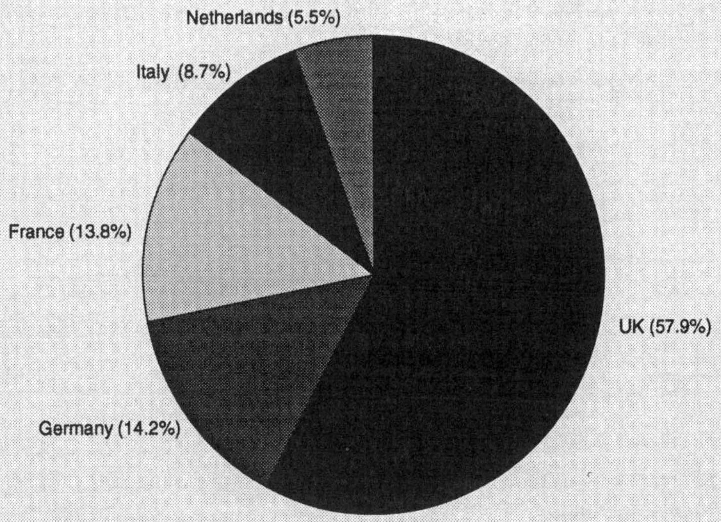

Netherlands (5.5%)

Italy (8.7%)

France (13.8%)

UK (57.9%)

Germany (14.2%)

the venture partner. Mitsubishi is joint venturing with Daimler-Benz in van production in Spain.

Acquisition of European companies by firms from outside the Community is an important feature of competitive positioning for Europe. In 1988 almost 300 European companies were acquired by non-EU companies. Their combined value was $19,718 millions. This greatly exceeds the value of acquisitions by EU companies of companies in other EU countries. These purchases were largely concentrated in the UK (see Figure 14.5).

The decision by the Italian telecommunications equipment company, Italitel, to establish a partnership agreement with AT & T calmed many fears about the strategic intent of European industry. This was followed by more extensive collaborations such as that involving GEC, GE (US) and Siemens.

The majority of entrants depend on their ability to compete in open competition with local companies. Their success turns on their prior research, effective product and market development and strong distributor and customer relationships. The opportunities persist but the competitiveness of local, European firms seems set to increase. The ultimate beneficiaries are customers.

Conclusion

The single European market, the single European currency, and the integration of Central and Eastern Europe create new challenges and opportunities for industry within and outside the EU. Some of the opportunities will grow from the greater cohesion and development of European markets. Others will emerge from the new attitudes and policies adopted by European and international industry. The real dividends from this development will only be earned if the opportunities and wealth created are distributed to create new opportunities and potential elsewhere.

Task

For a specific UK firm or organization of your choice develop and describe a European marketing strategy. This strategy should:

1 Identify the specific features of the European markets which justify this kind of approach.

2 Draw out the key features of the EU that the firm will seek to exploit.

3 Explain the changes in European marketing practice that will have the most immediate impact on your proposals.

4 Complete a SWOT analysis of the firm's market in Europe with clear reference to other European rivals.

5 Indicate any programmes initiated or managed by the European Commission that can be used to further the firm's ambition.

6 Spell out your marketing strategies and proposals.

7 Relate these proposals to opportunities elsewhere.

8 Highlight any operational changes or challenges that will face the firm as it expands its European operations.

9 Suggest the best mix of exports from the UK, joint ventures, acquisitions etc.

10 Include a brief executive summary of your proposals.

15

Managing the marketing mix

Introduction

For many years one of the most successful firms in the instant coffee market was a company which few, if any, consumers could name. Sol Café built up a significant share of a market where branding and heavyweight advertising were the norm by adopting a diametrically opposite route. In establishing their position as a producer of own-label coffee, personal selling, prompt delivery and meeting customer product and price requirements dominated their marketing mix.

The marketing mix is best defined as the distinct mix of marketing tools that the enterprise uses to meet the needs of particular customers or groups of customers in a market.

Avon cosmetics and Yardley present contrasting approaches to developing business in the cosmetics market. Avon concentrates on personal selling in the home, while Yardley backs its extensive dealer network with substantial advertising expenditure. However, they have one thing in common: success.

A mini-case study

In setting up his video business Dave Green faced the same basic problem as these giant firms had faced and, with varying degrees of success, had solved. He had decided on his market(s) and his offering: individuals and firms with video equipment and their need for blank video cassette tapes.

In a market such as this his options were wide open: should he concentrate on the commercial market, or perhaps on specific groups of the consumer market? Once he had made that decision he then had to decide what precisely his offering was. In raising that issue he was examining his marketing mix. The commercial and consumer markets differ significantly in composition and needs (Table 15.1).[1]

1 *Consumer:* affluent (A, B, C1 socio-economic groups), using purchased equipment; generally tapes erased after a short time; (important subgroup building up in libraries), use equipment to control viewing times, own small number of tapes but replace frequently.
2 *Commercial:* often media-related (ad agencies, marketing consultants) but growth in other sectors: mixture of bought and rented equipment; (in media) experienced with equipment and wide range held; tapes are often stored, large stock.

Dave Green's task is to decide which target market(s) he will concentrate his efforts around.

Table 15.1 The marketing mix for different markets

	Consumer	Commercial
Product	Good quality; preferably links with equipment manufacturer; robust technically for frequent erasures.	Very high quality; compatible with existing systems; professional use reduces technical risks.
Place	Links with rental or equipment sales firms very important; limited willingness to search; fears of direct mail or discount outlets.	Willing to search; technical knowledge reduces direct mail worries; outlets providing other needs make buying easier.
Price	Low enough to attract but not to undermine quality image; percentage discount for dealer may need to be high to persuade him to stock these instead of higher priced units.	Low prices, especially if sold through direct mail; supplies shops may accept lower margin than television shops as it is new line.
Promotion	Main media plus point of sale for quality reassurance, perhaps allied to promoting different uses or storage to increase usage.	Direct mail or personal selling to direct accounts.

He can, for example, decide that he wants to concentrate on producing cut-price high quality cassettes to the consumer market. He can operate using direct mail. He might even set up an electronic shop using the Internet. He will need to keep his costs down and concentrate all his advertising on classified advertisements in national newspapers.

Table 15.1 illustrates how managing the mix for different customers can produce very different offerings. The selection of mixes and the allocation of resources between the mix elements go far in determining the success of the firm and its customer proposition. The marketing person is:

> a mixer of ingredients, one who is constantly engaged in fashioning creatively a mix of marketing procedures and policies to produce a profitable enterprise.[2]

The essence of managing the marketing mix lies in providing each group of customers or segment of the market with the mix of product, price, place and promotion which most suits their needs. The design of specific mixes has variously been described as an art in which a unifying vision is the key and a science in which data, analysis and experimentation are the routes to success.[3] The product manager is in many ways turning the product or brand into a market in its own right.

Mass customization has the capacity to transform this situation by producing individually customized goods or services at the cost of standardized mass produced goods. Already in Japan, firms like National Panasonic Bicycles and Toyota have introduced this process to 20 or 30 per cent of their line. Mass customization means tailoring the product or service around the needs of a specific customer. [4]

National Panasonic developed its customized order system to allow purchasers to order mountain bikes designed around their preferences and physiognomy. Buyers indicate their preferences, then sit on a special frame which adjusts to their size and weight, etc. These facts are downloaded by computer where a customized bike is produced within days to their individual needs, at a price which is closer to that of a mass produced bike, than that of a traditional, custom-made bike.

Figure 15.1 *Mainichi Daily News*

Mainichi Daily News
Dedicated To International Understanding

Saturday, May 25, 1991

Nissan's Entire Line Going 'Made-To-Order' In August

Mainichi Shimbun

Nissan Motor Co., the second largest automotive manufacturer in the country, revealed Friday that it will drastically change its production system by introducing a made-to-order production setup in August for its entire line of automobiles.

Nissan's innovative system may mark an important step away from an age of mass production of a limited range of models into an age of individualized production suited to the diversified tastes of consumers, according to industry analysts.

Nissan's new production scheme, which will be known as the "ANSWER" system, will replace the traditional method of basing monthly output on forecasts of automobile consumption.

While Mercedes Benz, Jaguar, and some Japanese manufacturers have introduced made-to-order production for luxury cars, it usually takes such firms from two weeks to two months to fill a customer's order.

By introducing a computerized system which connects sales branches to its production center by a computer link, Nissan will be able to offer made-to-order production for all of its models, including cars for the mass market.

has ordered if the dealer does not have the model in stock.

As producers have had to increase their range of models to please the consumer, it has become increasingly difficult for dealers to stock all available models.

And when there is a surge of interest in specific models, customers may have to wait several months to receive their cars. Nissan's new system will enable customers to select the model type, color, upholstery material, and other features such as air conditioning when they submit their order. Nissan promises to fill these orders within two weeks.

Nissan plans to shorten the waiting time after the system is fully implemented.

Nissan will connect 221 of its domestic sales branches to its headquarters by computer, which will relay customer orders to its seven production plants.

Eventually, Nissan plans to expand the

The "ANSWER" system will enable Nissan to eliminate the disparity between monthly sales forecasts and actual demand, and to rationalize its production while increasing customer satisfaction.

The "ANSWER" system is the culmination of a project which was started in October 1988. It is based on a computer analysis of customer orders and inventory levels, and allows required adjustments to production lines to be made immediately.

The "ANSWER" system will enable dealers to inform a customer of an exact delivery right after an order is entered into the computer. It will also help Nissan reduce inventory costs, and its interest expenses.

Most car makers currently determine their monthly production after compiling statistics on orders placed at sales outlets the previous month. These figures are collected every 10 days, but do not allow the

The mix elements

The marketing mix is the set of controllable variables that the firm can use to influence the buyer's response.[5]

Although there are a number of different descriptions of the mix elements, probably the most popular is McCarthy's four P's: product, price, promotion and place.

Product

The product can be subdivided into quality levels, special features, styling, branding, product range or mix, service back-up, warranty, durability and packaging.

The product mix of these features can vary enormously. A firm might invest heavily in quality control and first-rate material to ensure a top quality, durable product, which would keep its service and quality costs down. Another company might provide an array of products each with a different combination of these elements, e.g. a low-quality product backed by a high service element in combination with a masthead, high-quality product.[6]

Price

Price is the mechanism of exchange between firm and customer. It incorporates level(s), credit (terms and sources), discounts, margins, resources, financial services (e.g. advice), allowances or trade-ins and strategy and tactics. As in the case of products, considerable scope exists for establishing a different sub-mix of price elements. One firm might have a high premium price but offer generous credit terms, while another might have a far lower price but give virtually no credit. The mix can vary between levels of the market. The retailer might be encouraged through high discounts to buy low and sell high to end-users.

Promotion

Promotion encompasses the two broad areas of *advertising* (including below-the-line) and *personal selling:* advertising (main media/display, main media/classified, below-the-line); merchandizing (promotional support for the retailer); personal selling (salesman's (special) discounts); and publicity (press and public relations).

There is a growing understanding of how these forces interact. The dangers of cold canvassing[7] are encouraging more and more firms to combine personal selling and media advertising.

Place

'Place' makes the product physically available. It falls into two broad areas – channels and physical distribution – and covers channel strategy, intermediary systems, outlet, warehouse and factory location, service levels, documentation, coverage, stocks, freight and insurance.

Some writers have suggested that the sheer size of this area, allied to a number of other factors, takes it out of marketing altogether. However, the importance of intermediary polices and physical distribution in making the product or offering available demands a powerful marketing involvement.

Although there is a tendency to think in terms of a mix of four factors, in reality the offering is made up of a series of sub-mixes of the variables listed above. Decisions taken in one area have effects which go far beyond their immediate context. For example, a decision to adopt a penetration pricing stance[8] calls for extensive distribution, probably high stocks, high customer awareness (perhaps from media advertising) and high-volume production capacity. With a new product the large amount of trial sought by this strategy may call for a high degree of confidence in the organization's ability to maintain quality levels.

Limitations to the four P's

The extent to which the notion of the four P's encapsulates the key areas of marketing action has disguised many of the problems of mix management that have emerged in practice. It is easy to become preoccupied with the challenges of making decisions on individual parts of the mix or creating blends which fit the internal requirements of the enterprise. Successful mix management is not built on this. It depends on the fit between manageable resources (mix elements) and the needs of specific customer groups. A mix created without targeting or focusing on a market segment has no value.

This is closely related with the common failure to appreciate the importance of placing mix decisions in their competitive and environmental context. The elements are designed to:

1 Create a combination meeting customer needs.
2 Achieve competitive advantage.
3 Satisfy legal requirements.

Driver[9] examined the importance of these and noted that:

> The prevailing conception of marketing in terms of the four P's, which largely excludes competitive and legal considerations, has tended to isolate marketing from a context which is a matter of practical and public importance.

Designing the optimum mix

Most mix-design blends intuition and research. As managers become more aware of the extent to which each variable is interdependent there is increasing interest in methods of designing the optimum mix.

The marketing mix depends on a clear vision of the *customer group* and target market and the *resources of the firm*. Marketing research, entrepreneurial insight and many other sources build the picture of the market or segment the firm wishes to satisfy, and the firm's resources include its personnel, history, current offering, and even the image currently held in the market of its offerings. Attempts by newspapers such as the *Daily Express* to reach new markets, e.g. to move from an older customer profile to a younger market, have often foundered on the clear vision the new target market has of the offering and their rejection of it. In many customer markets the phrase 'You can spin down but not up' holds true. It means that expensive products (or firms with high-quality images) can be a platform for cheaper derivatives but that cheap products cannot be a platform for expensive derivatives.

Borden suggests that designing the mix is a combination of arts and sciences, calling for a multi-step approach (Figure 15.2).

Some writers suggest that more quantitative approaches can be adopted to set the optimum marketing mix for a particular firm at a given point in time. The aim of such analysis is to use estimates of pay-offs from specific combinations to arrive at optimum mix.

In the discussion of this topic Kotler indicated how modern economic techniques along with improved data-handling systems in firms can help cope with the problems involved in this type of study. His analysis does not set out to handle the very important subjective or corporate dimensions of these decisions.

Even within specific areas, e.g. setting the advertising appropriation, short-term economic circumstances may directly affect resource allocation. David Corkindale[10] points out that one of the findings of a long-term research project at Cranfield is that subjectivity, interpersonal negotiations and external financial forces all have an impact on setting advertising budgets. In establishing both the overall mix of investment and expenditure in specific areas a much more extensive network of interacting forces comes into play.

Mixes for levels

Although a specific marketing mix is targeted on a group of end users, its impact on other parts of the environment is vital to its success. For example, in industrial markets, distributors frequently resist lower-priced substitute products. This derives from their

Figure 15.2 Building the marketing mix. [b]Borden, N.H., 'The Concept of the Marketing Mix'. In *Readings in Basic Marketing* (ed. McCarthy, E. J., Grastief, J. R. and Brogowicz, A. A.). Illinois: R. D. Irwin, 1975.

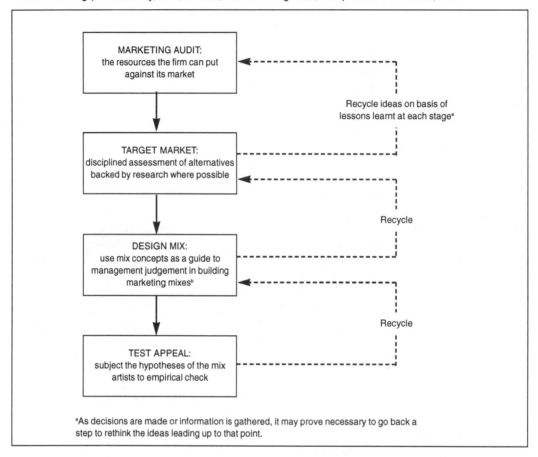

recognition that they have no direct interest in supporting a product selling for £4 against another selling for £5 if the margin remains the same and the volume is constant. For a manufacturer with only one line this may be solved by adjusting the margin. A producer with a large number of other lines going through the same dealers might find the cost of this enormous.

Just as mixes for the subgroups of end users are designed to meet their needs, the mixes for those involved in reaching these groups must similarly be considered. The interaction between these is important in determining the overall success of the policies.

Change over time

The optimum combination of elements changes as the product passes through its life-cycle, as environmental forces change, as the consuming and intermediary groups adapt, and as competition responds. The design of the initial mix will therefore need to be able to respond to these circumstances. The ability to adapt can be seen in brands (Oxo, Guinness), manufacturers (Philips, Wedgwood), intermediaries (Sainsbury, W. H. Smith) and service organizations (Sotheby's, Barclays Bank).

Record companies are very successful at building adaptations into the marketing mix. As the buying public for records grew and key retail groups increased in influence, they moved from the specialized record store, retailing at full price and using limited main media display advertising, to larger general stores and with substantial promotion (Figure 15.3).

The future

There is increasing pressure on marketing management to demonstrate the optimal nature of their mix decisions. Quantitative approaches are likely to play an increasing part in providing the guidelines for these decisions. Rapid change means that intuition and creativity have a continuing role to play in ultimate decision-making.

Figure 15.3 This advertisement demonstrated the effective combination of price, promotion and distribution. Reproduced by permission of Virgin.

SPECIMEN QUESTIONS

1   What are the options open to a firm in setting the price for a new product? How are these options influenced by knowledge of the different ways other marketing mix variables affect customers' expectations about price?

2   The four 'Ps' gives a false impression of the way the marketing mix operates. Discuss.

3   It is sometimes argued that the lack of real product differentiation, i.e. significant technical or performance differences between products, is the sole real justification for emphasis on other marketing mix elements. Do you agree with this proposition? Justify your answer in terms of both theory and practice in named firms or industries.

4   How true is the notion that 'mass customization' spells the end of both market segmentation and marketing mix management? Include detailed analysis of the true meaning of 'mass customization', 'marketing mix management' and 'market segmentation' in your answer.

5   Outline at least two different approaches to the design of optimal marketing mixes that have been developed over the last twenty years. Explain their strengths and weaknesses from both a practical and a theoretical perspective.

6   Explain the contribution that a marketing audit can make to the long-term effective management of one of:

   (a)   A university.

   (b)   A hospital trust.

   (c)   A political party.

7   Competitive bidding is commonly used in industrial and government markets; explain the way this approach is used and indicate the contribution that factors other than price can play in helping firms succeed in a competitive bidding situation.

8   Define:

   (a)   Place.

   (b)   The marketing mix.

   (c)   Marketing audit.

   (d)   Target market.

   (e)   Merchandizing.

   (f)   Market penetration.

   (g)   Market share.

   (h)   Push-pull.

   (i)   Bill of lading.

   (j)   Trade mark.

16

Product policy and innovation

Introduction

Japanese manufacturers in particular are changing the terms of the competition. They have moved from competing through low costs and high quality to competing by providing product differentiation and sophisticated multitechnology products.[1]

The above comment highlights the widespread awareness of the importance of the product, its features and quality to competitive success. The product is the cornerstone of the marketing mix, since it holds together promotion, distribution and pricing policies. Products are not necessarily tangible: the bank, travel agent, insurance company, consultant, architect, and designer all have product offerings, but these offerings are largely intangible; and although the foundry, plastics moulder or aluminium processor deals in physical products, these are frequently made to the buyer's specification, and the firm's real offering is technical skills or production capacity. Even the finished products in the shops are made up of the components or semi-finished products of a large number of manufacturers. Raw material, chemical, commodity, food and other primary product markets have their own special characteristics which the marketing managers in these areas have to understand. Planning, decisions and policies in all areas of marketing are directly affected by the product field in which the marketing manager operates.

This immense variety is reflected in the American Marketing Association's definition of a product:

Anything that can be offered to a market for attention, acquisition or consumption, including physical objects, services, personalities, organizations and desires.

Many firms owe their existence to an entrepreneur's determination to make a product. Often a market opportunity is recognized or there is a commitment to make something better or cheaper, but occasionally the simple desire to invent or to introduce a new service provides the spur to starting the firm.[2] The commitment of Dr Land of Polaroid to his product breakthrough led him to build up his business in defiance of the prevailing wisdom and market power of the photographic industry. Henry Ford's genius at manufacture led to the creation of the Model T and laid the foundations of the Ford Corporation. In Europe, François Michelin of Michelin and David Brown of DJB Engineering show the immense potential of inventiveness allied to a determination to succeed. In all these cases the product and its manufacturing process are the rocks upon which the firm's future stands. In the service sector,

Lord Sieff of Marks and Spencer and Richard Branson of Virgin demonstrate the continuing power of a commitment to a product offering in building up their firms in the service sector. Akio Morita of Sony even called his autobiography *Made in Japan*.[3]

The importance of the product to the firm and its profits means it lies at the centre of most managers' thinking about the company. In many cases the firm is identified in the minds of the general public with the product or process. To them, Parker makes pens, and to prove it most of the workforce are directly involved in manufacturing pens. British Gas supplies gas, and the majority of its management, staff and workers are involved in its storage or transmission, or associated services. This proximity and the resulting identification with the product go a long way towards explaining the product orientation, seen by Levitt as a source of potential danger to all firms:

> It is all too easy in this day and age for a company or industry to let its sense of purpose become dominated by the economies of full production and to develop a dangerously lopsided product orientation. In short, if management lets itself drift, it invariably drifts into the direction of thinking of itself as producing goods and services, not consumer satisfaction.[4]

Recognition of this does not detract from the importance of the product, but does call upon management to see it in a number of different ways: the route to satisfying complex customer needs; a part of a selection of opportunities buyers have to satisfy these needs; an aspect of the changing environment in which buyers' needs and their methods of meeting them are constantly evolving. Porter[5] notes that competitive advantage is sustained by constant improvement and upgrading.

The complexity of customer needs

Increased understanding of buyers and their needs has highlighted the large number of factors involved in product choice.[6] This goes far beyond the identifiable and relatively undifferentiated features of the *core product*. Commodity markets illustrate the characteristics of a core product market. It is almost impossible to separate the wheat produced by independent growers in Britain from that produced by their competitors. The market may be akin to the 'perfect competition' described in Chapter 1 with each producer having virtually no power to control the market or his own business future. Many new products go through a phase when a large number of 'me too' brands almost create a commodity-market situation. Alfred P. Sloan, former president of General Motors, pointed out[7] that during the period when the Model T Ford dominated the US motor industry the only real difference between it and the Chevrolet was the low price Ford could charge because of his massive economies of scale.

The homogeneity of need, implied by products showing virtually no difference, occurs very infrequently in the market-place. This was recognized in the era of the tea clippers, when ships like the *Cutty Sark* would race from India or Ceylon to be the first to market, hence getting the best price. The modern concept of the *augmented product*, with its emphasis on quality, features, style, name, packaging, service warranty, installation and instruction, and more recently environmental impact, plays a major part in effective product planning geared to winning real advantages in the market.[8]

Effective control in these areas is as important as the core product's basic characteristics in winning sales and establishing customer loyalty. Overseas customers have often criticized the poor quality control of British goods, and the Advisory Council on Applied Research and Development notes that:

> we believe that a major effort is due, indeed overdue, to place greater emphasis in Britain on the sciences related to manufacture with special attention to the relation between production processes and the design, quality and reliability of products.

Special features meeting the buyer's particular needs can often sway the buyer more effectively than lower prices. The inclusion by Japanese car manufacturers in the 1970s of features such as number plates and radios in the basic car was a real product advantage in the eyes of many customers, even if the final price was actually higher. This is important in service industries as in manufacturing. The core product of a bank may be its financial service, but special features such as easy access to cashpoint machines are important to many customers. Special services to manufacturers, ranging from advice and counselling to booklets on special topics, are also part of their augmented product.

In the tourist industry many areas of historic or leisure interest fail to realize fully their potential because of lack of facilities, the wrong type of services, or simply lack of thought about the total product requirements of the visitor. A research study compared the historic cities of York and Durham. Both share many core features of history, interest and reputation, but York had developed a wide range of catering and shopping facilities geared to the tourist and Durham had not. The effect was that the average visitor to York spent two-and-a-half times as long in York as his or her equivalent spent in Durham, with the resulting pay-offs for the local tourist industry.

It is seldom fully realized how important aspects of the augmented product can be to the intermediary. He or she can be reassured by those features which are passed on to the customer, but some features can be designed specifically for the wholesalers and retailers, e.g. protective packaging, multipacks and specific pack sizes. In certain instances palletization has made a dramatic difference to ease of handling, a feature equally important for industrial customers.

Recent research has highlighted the role of the user in initiating and advancing new product development ideas and projects: 'Innovatory success is associated with active user involvement in product specification, design and development.'[9]

This move to greater consumer involvement is made easier by new technologies which make customer involvement more practical. The power that buyers have always exercised in industrial and government markets is extending to consumer markets. Sometimes the results are surprising. In early 1997, the *Wall Street Journal*[10] reported that Procter & Gamble found that the volume and diversity of its promotions and brands was confusing and alienating customers. Consumers have less time for shopping today, but far more choice. A firm like Proctor & Gamble that offers over one hundred brands, backed by an average of four promotions and a variety of price offerings, risks alienating customers. Some end up preferring the simple product offering of the retailer's own brand. Research from Manchester Business School suggests that suppliers of branded goods face major problems as shoppers become more sophisticated, and more willing to trust the retailer to provide products of adequate quality irrespective of the name they carry.[11]

Selection of opportunities

Until now the discussion has tended to be centred on the single product, although this may encompass many features. However, there are very few single-product firms. Most firms, like Proctor & Gamble[12] or Unilever[13] offer a range of products or a *product line,* which is a broad group of products intended for basically similar uses and possessing similar physical characteristics. This tendency derives from a number of pressures. The internal economic logistics of products create the opportunity to introduce related products, or the same capital plant may be able to produce a very wide range of goods. External distribution or sales economies can create similar opportunities. A representative visiting a contact can probably introduce additional product ideas or offerings to the buyer at relatively little extra cost.

In some cases agents or intermediaries may expect or demand complementary products. It makes their purchasing more efficient and easier if valued suppliers provide additional related items. Analysis of the market-place may identify related items with market potential. Sometimes these are totally new sectors of the market, and at other times there may already be firms established there, but the sector shows signs of growth or appeals for other reasons.

The primary purposes are to achieve internal efficiencies and external *synergy,* which is achieved when the combined effect of a group of elements is greater that the sum of their individual impacts. The combinations of separate products and product lines make up the firm's *product mix,* 'the composite of products offered for sale by a firm or business unit'.

There is no need for a direct relationship between the items in a firm's product mix. In large firms a very wide spread of lines carried can be part of a deliberate policy of new venture development or may derive from a series of acquisitions. ICI, illustrates this. Its spread of activities ranges from tobacco, through plastics and packaging, to chemicals. Even after the firm split into two, ICI and Zeneca, the variety is immense. Within a giant firm there may be specific units with a very wide product mix. A food division's mix might include motorway service stations, frozen chickens, potato crisps and pet foods. Successful management calls for control of the mix in terms of three variables: product width (the number of different lines), product depth (the number of items in each line) and product consistency (the closeness of the relationships between the products).

In smaller firms the mix tends to be much narrower. The major exceptions to this are firms in process industries, producing goods using a particular technology or material, and component manufacturers. These groups generally produce items to a customer's specification to be incorporated in the end product. In the case of process industries such as plastics, steel, rubber and aluminium, many firms have no product of their own, but have the skill to produce a massive array of items using their specific technology, e.g. plastics injection moulding or aluminium extrusion. Their offerings are their skills and capacity. The component manufacturer usually provides a wide range of goods but will often adapt, amend or even redesign particular items for a customer. Smallness is a real advantage in this type of industry, as the commitment, flexibility, speed of response and low overheads of small firms offer major benefits to customers.

Brands and branding

Product and brand management policies were introduced by some larger firms to build the qualities of the small firm into the advantages of the larger firm. A *brand* is a name, term, symbol, design or combination of these which identifies the goods or services of one seller or group of sellers and differentiates them from those of other sellers.[14] Some brand names are so powerful that they are now in everyday use, e.g. to Hoover a room rather than to vacuum clean it, and to Xerox rather than photocopy.

Helena Rubenstein highlights the intangible features of the brand in quoting a definition of a brand as:

> the promise of the bundle of attributes that someone buys and that provides emotional satisfaction. These attributes may be tangible or invisible, rational or emotional.[15]

The development of brand- or product-management-based marketing organizations provide firms with the opportunity to establish internal profit centres. The brand manager is almost the 'managing director' for this specific product, with control over advertising, sales, distribution, price and even product development (usually within the range). In multi-brand firms, competition can emerge within the company, spurring each brand or product manager on to greater achievements.

The brand can provide the customer with a reassurance of quality and consistency. In some cases strong brand loyalty emerges, with the buyer actively searching out his preferred brand. The identification of brand and symbol or trademark can give protection from price cutting and individuality, and is a powerful cue for potential purchasers, occasionally worldwide. In Britain and in some other countries with strong retailing groups the phenomenon of 'own-label' brands has emerged. Firms such as Tesco, Sainsbury and Marks and Spencer introduced products under their own labels. These are either the same name as the store, e.g. Tesco coffee, or the company brand, e.g. Marks and Spencer's St Michael label. In the past the tendency for these to cost less contributed to a lower-quality image, but today the quality demands of the stores and the reputation of the retailers have led to their being viewed as equal to or better than manufacturer's brands.

All companies offering an array of products or brands can choose from a number of marketing strategies:

1   The entire output can be individually branded, with no obvious generic link, e.g. Procter & Gamble's Bold, Ariel, Daz, Tide and Fairy Snow.
2   There can be a series of family brands within firms, e.g. the Sunsilk range of shampoos, hairspray, conditioners and setting lotions within Elida Gibbs division of Unilever.
3   A powerful brand symbol can link all the firm's offerings; e.g. the Kodak name and symbol are used to link the firm's films, cameras, photographic chemicals and other activities.

There are many permutations of these within the overall need to earn the maximum advantage from the corporate reputation while protecting the individual identity of specific items, and the choice is a problem which firms face every time a new brand or new product is introduced on to the market.

The value of strong brands has been vividly illustrated over the last few years. Firms like Cadbury have built international brands to reinforce their market position. This prompted firms like Nestlé to place the acquisition of 'brand' rights at the core of the strategy to acquire firms like Rowntree.

The Coca-Cola brand name is the world's strongest image, with a power that extends across the USA, UK, Europe, Asia and Australia. *Financial World* magazine valued the Marlboro brand at $40 billion, followed by Coca Cola at $30 billion (see Table 16.1).

Table 16.1 The world's most powerful brand names

World	USA	UK	EU
Coca Cola	Coca Cola	Coca Cola	Coca Cola
Sony	Marlboro	Marks and Spencer	BMW
Mercedes-Benz	Pepsi-Cola	Kellogg	Adidas
Kodak	McDonald's	Gillette	Mercedes-Benz
Disney	Miller	=Guinness	Philips
Nestlé	Budweiser	=Mars	Kodak
Toyota	Ford	Heinz	Sony
McDonald's	Wendy's	Sainsbury	Volkswagen
IBM	Chevrolet	Nescafé	Gillette
Pepsi-Cola	Burger King	Cadbury	Pepsi-Cola

Source: Cannon, T. (ed.) *The Guinness Book of Business Records*, London, Guinness Publishing, 1996.

For the overwhelming majority of firms, prosperity is based on a balance between skilful management of existing products and the search for and successful introduction of new products and developments. Competitive pressures, changes in customer attitudes and behaviour, or political and economic forces mean that no firm can assume that the product which successfully met an important need yesterday will continue to provide customer satisfaction and corporate profits. In government markets, defence requirements and medical-product needs change and adapt. In industrial markets, plastic mouldings may replace timber or metal. Pressure on the consumer-goods manufacturer to innovate will be felt through the chain of supply. Even markets such as agriculture, often seen as stable, face the demands of a changing environment.

Barbie's Tale: The success of Barbie (and her partner Ken) highlights the value of a powerful brand identifier. Since Barbie was introduced in 1959, almost 600 million Barbie dolls have been sold, and the owners of Barbie, Mattel, have become the largest toymaker in the USA.[16]

Change for change's sake is either necessary or advisable, particularly when related to specific brands, products or lines. Stephen King points out that the constant search for new brands can lead to the premature withdrawal of support for brands with continuing potential for projects and sales:

> One result can be a self-fulfilling prophecy. The company's major brand has a bad year . . . funds are withdrawn from it . . . the next year it does even worse, this confirms the original diagnosis and panic increases; new brands are hustled along faster and faster, and most fail: the company has talked itself into a decline.

When creating a balance between supporting established products and brands and searching out innovations, one must recognize that the firm must survive today to prosper and grow tomorrow.

Failure to capitalize on branding opportunities can cost firms dear. IBM's failure to realize the potential inherent in brands cost it dear in the personal computer market. They were the first to label a personal computer as a PC but did nothing to protect the name 'PC' as a brand identifier. The term PC soon became generic. They followed up the PC with the name AT for 'advanced technology' – once again, making no effort to protect the brand. This term again became a generic for this category. Only with the OS/2 did IBM seek real brand strength.

Success with branding[17] allows firms to:

- build stable long-term demand;
- add values that attract customers;
- build and hold good margins;
- provide a platform for expansion;
- protect the firm against powerful intermediaries;
- enhance the appeal of the firm.

King[18] has argued that the advantages are so considerable that the creation of company brands, in which the reputation of the firm is equally high brings these benefits to recruitment, employee relations and finance, as well as customer relations.

A series of developments has reinforced the emphasis given to brands in contemporary marketing. Perhaps the most important is the value that firms can derive through increasing royalty and premium prices; even where there are major external problems, for example the Guinness Trial, where consumers stayed loyal to the brand. This prompted an analyst to say that: 'Branding is the DNA of competitive strategy for world class businesses.'[19]

The value of brands prompted some firms to put value on the brands when drawing up their balance sheets.[20] This type of development highlights the importance of brands across the firm. Rubenstein[14] argues that an understanding of the brand's essence, i.e. the 'main and distinctive characteristics that make the brand unique' are the main source of the brand's power in the market-place (Figure 16.1).

The changing environment and evolving needs

In a modern industrial society such as Britain, changes continually occur in the market. They can be caused by technological developments, fashions, political pressures, economic circumstances and many other factors. Technology 'push' and market 'pull' drive economies forward. The search for growth by companies, both in the home market and overseas, can itself be a major force in this process. This pattern of change and growth is probably the most important single factor distinguishing industrial from non-industrial societies, and as such it is something no firm can ignore, either in terms of pressure on the viability of its current offering or in terms of the opportunities it creates for projects and growth. No company can neglect it; nor can a country looking for national prosperity fail to recognize its importance or the vital role of marketing in this process. The first recommendation of the ACARD report was that:

> The Government should recognize the encouragement of industrial innovation as a major component of the industrial strategy.

Figure 16.1 Deconstructing the brand essence

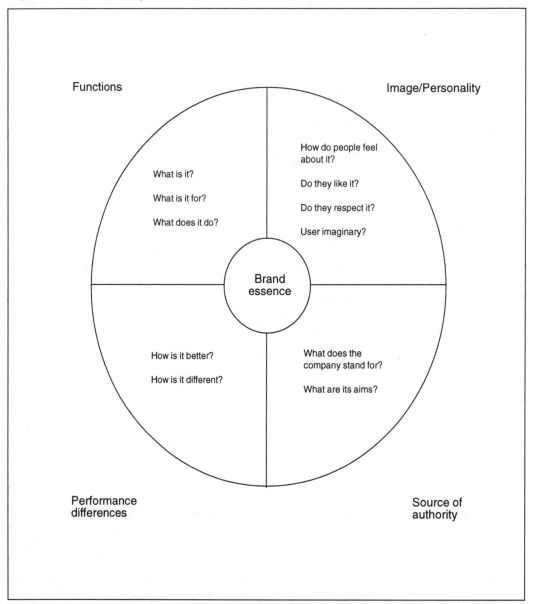

There are four basic elements in the pattern of change and growth: technical change, invention, innovation and product development:

1 *Technical change:* the environment of adaptation, development and modification in technology surrounding the firm, its customers and the market.
2 *Invention:* the process of creativity and discovery, generally involving a specific addition to the sum of human knowledge, but although new, not necessarily useful or desired by any potential market.

3 *Innovation:* the technical, industrial and commercial steps which lead to the marketing of new manufactured products or commercial services and to the use of new technical processes, products or services.

4 *Product development:* the introduction of adaptations, changes or modifications into existing products, brands or services designed to extend their viable life, adapt to new markets or introduce new uses.

Each can emerge out of the different perspectives of producers, intermediaries and customers.

What business am I in?

Even before 1960, when Theodore Levitt published *Marketing Myopia,* some businessmen realized the dangers inherent in too close an identification of the firm, with a specific product and the importance of meeting customer needs and specific products or offerings. Products might have very limited lives but needs might persist. Today, this issue is at the centre of marketing thought. The firm which narrowly defines itself in terms of a particular form of product runs the risk of being overtaken by changes in the ways in which customers seek to satisfy their needs. 'They have always bought it' and 'Everyone needs it' are phrases which have sounded the death-knell of or led to massive contraction in industries and companies ranging from cooperages to railways. Coopers saw themselves as being in the barrel-making rather than in the storage-container business, and railways identified themselves with trains rather than with transport. Even if outside factors lead to revival, for example oil shortages leading to a railway revival, many firms will have failed to survive and many of the remaining will have paid a high price for this marketing myopia.

Recognizing the dangers inherent of this identification with specific offerings has led to a more critical examination of how products and brands develop over time. The notion of a life-cycle has emerged as a useful mechanism for analyzing the process by which specific forms of meeting needs emerge, grow, stabilize and decline over time. Closely associated with this is the proposition that the marketing-orientated firm should closely study the needs which give rise to specific products as well as studying the progress of its own products or services.

The product life-cycle

The model suggests that all products go through a series of stages in their lives, as illustrated in Figure 16.2. At each stage the sales-profit relationship varies. Similarly, the relative importance of, appropriate form of, and interrelations between the marketing mix variables change. Product quality is vital during the introductory stage as failures during trial of a product can lead to long-term buyer rejection. Advertising may be more informative or educational during this period. In later periods, widening distribution or cutting prices may become more important. Besides giving cues to the appropriate strategies for the existing product, the model can help the firm to better exploit the market position of the product by providing leads to the timing of new launches, the move to new markets and diversification. More general analysis may indicate general patterns of behaviour, e.g. whether product life-cycles are shortening. The model provides a fertile source of ideas and developments within firms and among marketing people.

A number of writers have highlighted limitations to the use of the product life-cycle model, and have even questioned the value of the approach. Stephen King points out that it can be applied

Figure 16.2 The product life-cycle

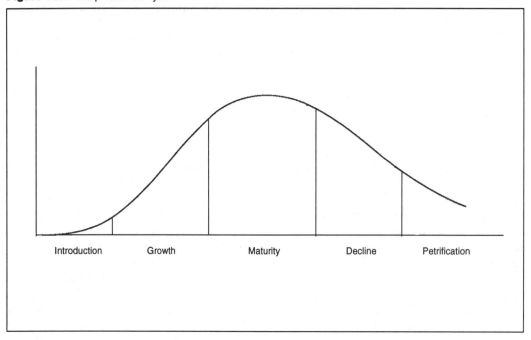

Figure 16.3 Exploiting the product life-cycle

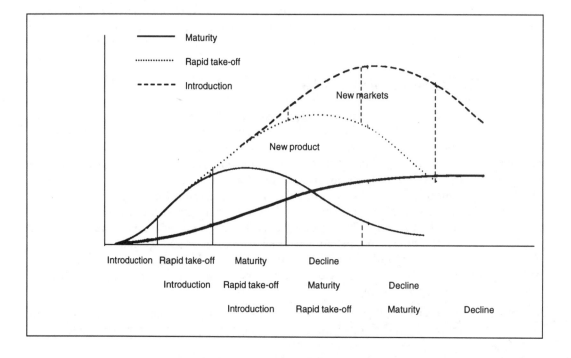

effectively only to a specific form of product or service. Brands can incorporate dramatic changes in composition, sustaining long-term growth, and any attempt to apply the life-cycle model is likely to do more harm than good. Brand names like Oxo, Bovril, Hovis and Persil in consumer markets, and Dexion, Xerox and Formica in industrial markets have incorporated substantial changes apparently without following a life-cycle model. The failure to identify a clear life-cycle for such important products as steel, aluminium, glass and bread leaves the model with limited descriptive validity.

Despite these criticisms the model retains an important role as a guide to analysis and planning, giving direct cues to decision-making without being a scientific tool. The firm can try to exploit the life-cycle by looking for new product developments, innovations or new markets to extend the life-cycle (Figure 16.3).

The life-cycle concept places particular emphasis on risks, for management in any firm, of failing to cultivate invention and innovation.

The product life-cycle illustrates the importance of adopting a process view of innovation. This means recognizing that 'the development of new products is not an instantaneous act but a series of activities that occur over time'.[22]

Invention, research and creativity

Successful products derive from a stock of ideas, concepts and prototypes which firms can originate themselves or obtain from external sources. The fertility of firms in this area is largely dependent on the creative climate in the firm. The potential sources of new products or services are enormous. They range from the 'Eureka'-type invention to the marginal improvement of existing products. All have a role in sustaining the firm's competitive position if they are conducted with a view to meeting buyer needs more effectively. Among the sources of new ideas are:

1 The firm's research and development department: this department may be working to a specific brief, e.g. to develop a drug capable of combating hay fever, but minimizing side-effects and avoiding the use of antihistamines; or it may have a much broader role, e.g. to explore new sources of energy or to spot new product opportunities. Generally there will be some relationship between the two, with ancillary roles such as reviewing related developments, e.g. by competitors.

2 Outside organizations: these can provide a continuing source of inventions and developments. They range from major government projects, e.g. the NASA space programme which incorporated a dissemination project for new products, to private concerns or individuals offering opportunities to license or buy.

3 The marketing department and other company units: these can produce leads through such activities as brainstorming, think-tanks, foreign search, market gap analysis, market research, activity analysis, long-range projections and segmentation analysis.

The establishment of an open, creative company environment stimulates a high degree of corporate inventiveness.[23] It is important to overcome the resistance to change which can emerge in companies, where fear, vested interest and risk avoidance can produce internal barriers to needed change.[24]

The stock of high-potential new product, process or service ideas is the vital base in the search for success. However, it is only the starting point in the development of offerings capable of making a real contribution to corporate performance. Successful innovation is the next crucial step.

Innovation

Innovation takes four basic forms:

1 Improvement and development of existing forms: the manufacturer of a piece of earth-moving equipment can introduce features geared to make it operate more quickly or efficiently. An advertising agency may offer new client services.
2 Improvement and development of existing processes: a printer may identify ways of printing a specific item to improve finish or reduce price, but calling for only minor modifications, if any, in a client's layout or presentation.
3 Introduction of novel production process: this has been the basis of the growth of industrial society. Suppliers introduce new technologies to the production of basically similar products, often generating dramatic price cuts and improvements in product quality and consistency. From the spinning jenny to the silicon chip (Figure 16.5), it certainly offers new horizons for the adapting firm.
4 The introduction of new products and services: in modern society, markets are in a constant state of flux, with modified, changed or revolutionary products or services being offered to potential customers. The craze for skateboards created massive but fleeting opportunities for those fast enough to adapt, and the digital watch threw the Swiss watch industry into confusion, while revitalizing the US industry. The emergence of media buying agencies is forcing many traditional advertising agencies to evaluate their operations carefully, while McDonald's hamburger franchises have affected the entire fast-food catering market.

The time taken to move from invention to innovation varies enormously. Some famous products have taken decades to reach the market (Table 16.2).

The opportunities for innovation are matched by the risks. It is estimated that between 50 and 90 per cent of new introductions on to the market fail. Disasters such as Ford's Edsel, Du Pont's Corfam and RCA's computers are the tip of an iceberg which also includes the Sinclair C5 and innumerable less well publicized failures. The mass evidence that has been accumulated indicates that the root cause of failure is commitment to a specific product, service or brand offering relatively little to the prospective buyer, but perhaps meeting some corporate need for representation in a sector of the market, meeting a specific launch date, or exploiting some internally developed technology.

Screening and testing

Effective market-orientated screening and testing procedures are essential to reduce these high rates of failure. The firm can also use these processes to turn ideas, inventions or possibilities into a producible, marketable reality.

The first stage involves evaluating all developments against the firm's current or foreseeable production capabilities. Although many new product proposals can be eliminated here, an open mind must be kept about those which do not fit into the firm's current technology. The

Figure 16.4 Missing opportunities

Figure 16.5 Early microchip. Reproduced with the permission of IBM United Kingdom Ltd

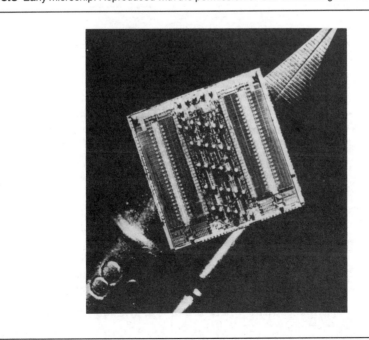

Table 16.2 The time taken from invention to innovation

Product and Process	Invention	Innovation	Years between invention and innovation
DDT	1874	1942	68
Ballpoint pen	1888	1946	58
Float glass	1902	1957	55
Synthetic detergent	1886	1930	44
Fluorescent lamp	1901	1938	37
Silicones	1910	1946	36
Automatic drive	1904	1939	35
Zipper	1891	1923	32
Helicopter	1904	1936	32
Tungsten carbide	1900	1926	26
Continuous steelcasting	1927	1952	25
Anti-knock petrol	1912	1935	23
Cotton picker	1920	1942	22
Hydraulic clutch	1925	1946	21
Catalytic cracking of petrol	1915	1935	20
Diesel locomotive	1895	1913	18
Radio	1900	1918	18
Phototypesetting	1936	1954	18
Cinerama	1937	1953	16
Penicillin	1928	1943	15
Rocket	1929	1944	15

Source: Cannon, T. *The Guinness Book of Business Records*, London, Guinness Publishing, 1996.

Table 16.3 Sources of stimulation for innovation in eight empirical studies

Study	Proportion of innovations from market, mission or production needs (%)	Proportions of innovations from technical opportunities (%)
Baker	77	23
Carter and Williams	73	27
Goldham	69	31
Sherwin	66	34
Langrish	66	34
Myers and Marquis	78	22
Tannenbaum	90	10
Utterback	75	25

Source: Voss, C. A., 'Technology Push and Need Pull: A New Perspective', *R & D Management,* 14, No. 3, 1984.

market potential of some products or processes may induce the firm to adapt their current capabilities to realize the opportunities in the market.

The remaining proposals then require careful business analysis. This involves exploring the market potential of the project, and 'concept research' makes a valuable contribution to this process. The underlying proposition is put before prospective purchasers, usually in visual form, although mock-ups are sometimes used. These can be explored generally through in-depth interviews or group discussions. Occasionally there are sufficient data for more quantitative approaches, giving clearer insights into prospective pay-offs.

These approaches are particularly useful where the prospective buyers are already familiar with the underlying ideas, language or terminology involved in the product. Radical new ideas, so new that the bases for communication do not exist, cannot effectively use these systems. More complex, projective approaches such as delphic or futures analysis are used increasingly. Traditionally there has been reluctance to use these approaches in industrial markets, and over the last few years there has been an increased use of empirical studies to analyze opportunities in these markets. A major goal of these initial screening stages is to minimize the costs involved in developing the idea, project or proposal to a finished stage.

Effective development is designed to ensure that the customer benefits underlying the initial proposal and providing the basis for business analysis are delivered by the final product. Some compromises may be necessary to arrive at an item capable of being produced efficiently or returning a reasonable level of returns for the firm, but these considerations should not be allowed to negate the primary buyer requirements. The smoker may want an absolutely safe cigarette, but does a merely safer cigarette have the same appeal? An aircraft capable of carrying passengers from London to New York in less than four hours has real appeal, but is that sustained when the payload is only 115 passengers? Plastic-coated steel may have real advantages for the auto industry, but are these sustained if storage and handling problems dramatically increase wastage? The development programme must encompass manufacturing capabilities, and efficient production problems in this area were major factors in the demise of Du Pont's Corfam.

The market-place is the final arbitrator of whether the final physical offering will deliver enough benefits to buyers to provide a long-term, profitable contribution to the firm. Test marketing has developed to provide a situation in which the maximum information can be gleaned from the market-place at the lowest cost prior to final commercialization. The aim is to replicate in miniature the complete market. There are two distinct approaches: test markets for forecasting and problem identification, using only one experimental area; and matched-area tests to obtain forecasts and identify potential problems but, equally important, to select the optimum marketing mix from a number of alternatives.

Test marketing

The value of test marketing largely depends on selection of the test area or areas and the process by which the experiment is conducted. Properly conducted, it invariably costs both time and money, but insights into the product's potential can be obtained. Discipline must, however, be exercised, particularly in the complex area of building up the forecasts. Simple extrapolation is dangerous; the complexity of the context must be built into the analysis. Equally important are experimental biases deriving from: concentration of effort behind the test, such as disproportionate support or over-involvement by management or sales staff; poor choice of test areas, perhaps because areas are chosen for convenience rather than from a desire to model the market; and competitive response designed to maximize their information and sometimes muddying the water for the test. A Lever Bros executive described a test conducted by that company when the competition 'came in so hard and heavy that as our sampling crews were going up one side of the block, the Procter [competition] men were coming down the other side'.

In Britain these problems have led to some reluctance to embark on large-scale test markets, particularly when the technological gap is so small that the competition can respond by introducing their own brands based at least in part on information obtained at the innovator's expense. In the US the complexity of the market, its size and the costs involved have created an environment in which the savings outweigh the risks, and it appears that companies here which are introducing products, particularly in industrial markets, for a wide European market are adopting a mode of behaviour akin to the US model.

Although these disciplines help to reduce risk, it will never be totally eliminated. For this reason it has been argued that, as companies become larger, more centralized and more bureaucratic, there is a reduced willingness to take risks for radical new developments. In some instances this has led to the development of new product management teams. At the centre of all these developments is the attempt to back small entrepreneurs with large-firm resources.[25]

Design is an increasingly important feature in product development and innovation for performance and sustainable quality. Total design strategies[26] and 'the idea of design as an active element in a company's approach to the market'[27] have grown in importance as firms recognize the crucial importance of delivered performance and assured quality.[28]

Success and failure

There is widespread evidence that high rates of failure are common in new products, brands, or service developments. The attrition starts long before an idea or concept reaches the market. In many firms, it takes tens of proposals to produce one product launch. As the ideas are reduced through each stage in the developmental process, the costs increase (Figure 16.6)

Figure 16.6 Stages in the developmental process and associated costs

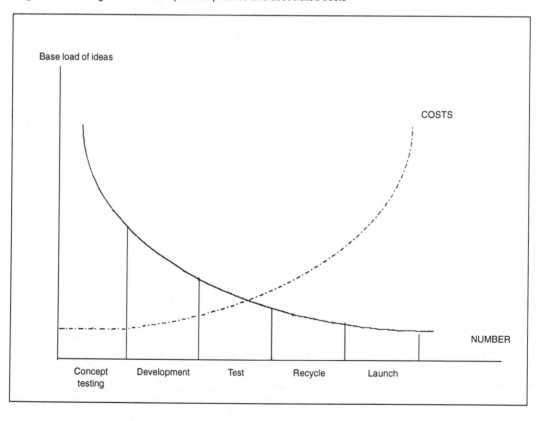

Despite the selection process, evidence continues to mount that firms pay more attention to their business priorities than customer needs in selecting the projects to introduce – with resultant high failure rates. Davidson's research[29] (Table 16.4) shows that successes, not surprisingly, occur when consumers are offered a better product at a better price, while failures are concentrated where the product and/or price is worse than existing offerings.

Table 16.4 Price and performance advantages in new product launches[30]

	50 new product successes	50 new product failures
Significantly better performance, higher price	44	8
Marginally better performance, higher price	6	12
Better performance, same price	24	0
Same performance, lower price	8	0
Same performance, same price	16	30
Same performance, higher price	2	30
Worse performance, same or higher price	0	20
	100	100

Note: Performance was, as far as possible, evaluated by blind product tests among target consumer groups.

The entrepreneur and the small firm

The ability of the risk-taking entrepreneur to break out of the narrow bounds of the established situation and fan the flames of enterprise has been the basis of the growth of many of today's great industries. Ford, Durant, Kellogg, Singer, Krupp, Eastman, Courtauld, Daimler, Biro, Siemens and Dassault all created giant enterprises which are almost synonymous with the industries they built. The entrepreneur still plays a major part in the process of product management and development.

There is some evidence to suggest that in both new technology-based firms (NTBFs) and in the majority of smaller firms the scope for and interest in effective product management and innovation are at their highest. At the same time their involvement in the product creates the dangers associated with a product orientation with a real need for a more powerful, structured and systematic marketing orientation. These policies must go beyond the product.

Effective product management calls for an approach incorporating current products, innovation and, where necessary, product abandonment strategies.

SPECIMEN QUESTIONS

1 Outline the research problems facing a company that has developed a wholly new consumer product or service. Indicate ways in which the firm can build up sufficient understanding of the market potential to determine production levels and launch advertising budgets.

2 Morita argues that 'Japanese manufacturers in particular are changing the terms of the competition'. In what ways are these companies using innovation to change the nature of competition in international markets?

3 How can an ancient city like York use innovation to strengthen its position in the tourism market? Illustrate your answer with specific examples from tourism marketing in a city such as York.

4 Why do you think McCrae described branding as the DNA of competitive shopping? Do you agree with this view? Illustrate your answer with at least one brand role.

5 It is estimated that between 60 and 80 per cent of innovations fail in the market. Why do you believe this high rate of failure occurs and what role can marketing play – if any – in reducing this rate of failure?

6 Many of the most successful and important innovations, new products and services, emerge from small and medium sized firms despite the much higher investments by larger companies in R & D.

   (a)   Why do you think this occurs?

   (b)   What can large firms do to change this balance of success?

   (c)   What can marketers learn from this?

7 What specific problems does a company face in launching a new product in several markets (home and overseas) at the same time? Why, despite these problems, might a firm decide on this course of action?

8 For a market of your choice, analyze the reason for the success or failure of three recent products or brands. Highlight in particular any more widely applicable lessons for these successes or failures.

9 Why have process based innovations proved to be so much more profitable to innovating companies? In the light of this, why do you think British firms seem to invest far more resources in new product development?

10 Define:

   (a)   Invention.

   (b)   Innovation.

   (c)   Technology push.

   (d)   The augmented product.

   (e)   The product mix.

   (f)   Brands.

   (g)   NTBF.

   (h)   Total design.

   (i)   Market gap analysis.

   (j)   Brainstorming.

CASE STUDY 13:
DEVELOPMENT AND LAUNCH OF THE NEXO PLASTICS COMPOUND HOPPER-FEEDER

For most of its history NEXO Plastics (Nottingham) Ltd has been firmly established as a good quality injection moulder. In 1995 the firm had a turnover in the region of £10 million. Strong links exist with major firms in the locality (John Player and Sons, Raleigh Industries, Boots and Pedigree Petfoods) as well as with a large number of medium and small firms.

This array of blue chip accounts has led the firm to place considerable emphasis on increasing the efficiency of its production process. Jack Wills, the production director, has shown himself to be extremely talented at this, and his efforts are complemented by the small and enthusiastic technical staff he has built up.

One of the firm's recurrent problems lay in filling the hoppers on its injection-moulding machinery with plastic compounds at an efficient and consistent rate. After a number of abortive attempts to solve the problem, sometimes with bought-in equipment and sometimes with units built by the firm itself, the staff eventually developed a very effective piece of hopper-feeder equipment.

This home-made item seemed to do the job more efficiently and at a lower cost than any other equipment with which they were familiar, and the hopper-feeder was soon making a significant contribution to the smooth running of their production process and reducing costs through waste.

About a year after the equipment became fully operational a 'productivity mission' from France, organized in association with the British Plastics Federation, visited the factory. Apart from making a number of more general comments, a number of the members of the mission expressed considerable interest in the hopper-feeder. A medium-sized moulder from Lyons was so keen that he offered to place an order for one immediately. A technical expert from RAPRA (the Rubber and Plastics Research Association) was also very complimentary about it.

This outside interest stimulated considerable discussion in the firm. The hopper-feeder had not been developed for sale, but was merely an aid to its current production. The low cost of producing it, along with its contribution to production efficiencies and the interest which had been shown in it, indicated that the firm had a highly-marketable item. The only serious reservation they had about selling it lay in their reluctance to supply the fruits of their ingenuity to their competitors.

In spite of these reservations it was decided to place the hopper-feeder on the market. There was some discussion about licensing manufacture to an existing equipment supplier, but Jack Wills was keen to keep it in-house, as this would provide them with ready access to any related developments. Alan Leith, the newly appointed sales director (he had been with the firm for many years), was confident that the company could handle the sales and marketing.

Funds were put aside for further development to make the hopper-feeder a more saleable item. The foreman in the technical department was given responsibility for setting up production facilities capable of earning £400,000 from sales in the first year, £750,000 in the second year and £2m by the fifth year.

It was decided to launch the product at the international plastics exhibition (INTERPLAS) at the National Exhibition Centre, Birmingham, in ten months' time. The company was committed to having the equipment in a fully commercialized form by then. However, far more problems emerged than had been anticipated, and Jack Wills was very unhappy about the amount of time he ended up spending on the project. Eight weeks before the exhibition a fully operational production unit was installed in their factory, and although there were minor teething troubles it was felt that it was now saleable.

To coincide with the exhibition, advertising space was taken in the exhibition catalogue, *Rubber and Plastics Weekly* and *Plastics and Rubber International*. Alan Leith invited journalists from these journals to the factory to see the hopper-feeder in action. In Rubber and Plastics Weekly a very favourable report was published ten days before the exhibition. (*Plastics and Rubber International* is a monthly so their feature did not appear until later.)

It was decided that Jack Wills and his foreman would work with Alan Leith and his staff manning the stand. Peter Needham, the managing director, spent the first four days on the stand and was available in Nottingham at fairly short notice should any problems occur.

The exhibition was a tremendous success. Large numbers of firms visited the stand, a number of orders were taken, and there were far more enquiries than they had anticipated. When the results of the exhibition were reviewed it was found that the first year's output was almost taken up by orders received at the exhibition and those inquiries which Alan Leith felt confident would mature.

Because of this early breakthrough Alan Leith was keen to expand production more rapidly than originally intended, perhaps looking for £1m in the second year. The overseas interest was particularly exciting, as the firm had never exported before. Within two months Alan had followed up a number of enquiries in Europe and these, combined with the firm orders taken at the exhibition, meant that orders worth £275,000 had been taken. Over 60 per cent of these were export orders.

The care taken in designing and testing the product now paid off handsomely, since there were very few problems or complaints. Despite this, the sheer size of the demand placed the very limited resources devoted to this exercise under considerable pressure, and there was some tendency to drain resources from other areas of the firm's activities. It was well into the second half of the first operating year before equilibrium was established.

More worrying for the firm's sales management was the rapidly lengthening delivery times for the equipment, which had stretched from two months to eight months. They felt that the technical staff and engineering were not giving it sufficient priority. At the same time grumbles were starting to come from their major customers for plastics processed goods. They complained that deliveries to them were stretching out, key staff were not available and rival companies were giving better prices. In June 1996, Raleigh placed a major order, which NEXO expected to win, for components on a new range of mountain bikes with another plastics processor.

Task

In the light of these factors review the firm's operations to date, bringing out any lessons for future introductions and making practical proposals for the future marketing of the hopper-feeder.

17

Test marketing

Introduction

No aspect of marketing poses more challenges than the effective management of change. This is true whether change is prompted by external forces or derives from internal initiatives. Both create uncertainty. This uncertainty involves risk for the individual and the firm. In marketing, this can be seen in a wide range of areas. Demands for new products and services, pressure for increased product use, improved packaging, improved productivity and the constant drive for competitive success combine to create the need to adapt through innovation and change, with all the associated risks. Managing these risks is an integral part of effective marketing management. A major tool in this effort to reduce work is *test marketing*.

> Test marketing is a controlled experiment conducted in one or more limited, but carefully selected, parts of a market. These are chosen to be representative microcosms of the total market. The aim is to use the test to predict and explore the consequences of one or more proposed marketing actions, notably new product introductions.

The above definition of test marketing differs from some of those more commonly used, by broadening the term to include experiments on other aspects of marketing besides new product launches. Many firms use the same techniques to explore the implications of change in other aspects of the marketing effort. The physical aspects of the product may remain the same but the total product proposition in the eyes of the consumer may be transformed. This is akin to introducing a new offering.

Changes in the test market environment influence this. New technologies have emerged which enable firms to adopt novel approaches. At the same time the techniques are employed in a wide range of circumstances. The decision by Tesco to join Lunn Poly in a test market to examine the scope for selling holidays through supermarkets took the techniques into two unusual areas: retailing and services. The same pressures which led manufacturers to employ this approach to gauging the market potential of their goods – expense and high risk – encourage other firms to follow this route. Despite the growing use of the technique, many questions persist about its role and value.

The controversy

Test marketing is a subject on which many different and strongly held views exist. Philip Kotler in his classic marketing textbook[1] stated that:

Test Marketing is rapidly approaching the state of a science.

This contrasts with Stephen King's comment[2] that:

The delays of Test Marketing have often spoilt what might have been successful businesses.

These views are not necessarily contradictory but they do focus attention on the two issues around which much of the test marketing debate revolves:

1   Is test marketing an important contribution to the scientific process of gathering useful information to aid marketing decisions?
2   Even if this is true, is the real price, in terms of money spent, delays, warnings to the competition, worth the effort?

In this chapter these topics, plus the issues which emerge from them, are studied.

The scientific dimension

The process of marketing research – gathering empirical evidence to assist in marketing decision-making – owes a great deal to the scientific tradition. Anyone reading marketing research textbooks continually comes across the notion that market research aims to, or actually does, introduce science into marketing.

Marketing research . . . the application of scientific method to Marketing.[3]

Although this is less confidently asserted today than it was once, the link between the process of systematically gathering, recording and analyzing marketing information and the empirical tradition of the natural sciences cannot be denied.

Experimentation is an almost essential part of that tradition.

It is experimentation that expresses the basic empiricism of science.[4]

Test marketing is the attempt to apply the framework of the scientific experiment: constructing a situation in which certain developments and interrelationships of interest to the researcher can be observed and measured, with conclusions about relationships being drawn.

The laboratory experiment focuses attention on the questions under consideration, *excluding as far as possible all other influences.* The test market by its very nature is as closed, as self-contained, as the laboratory experiment. Although this is a limiting factor, it is a mistake to assume that researchers in the natural sciences successfully exclude all possible sources of bias and every non-experimental influence. We are usually talking about matters of degree and the commitment to a research discipline. These qualifications accepted, test marketing provides access to a rich and powerful source of marketing intelligence.

Mini-case study: Campbell's food

The problems which faced Campbell's range of frozen food in 1980 highlight the variety of lessons that can be learned. Their objectives were clear and fitted neatly into an overall corporate commitment to growth and diversification. The range was targeted on the customer seeking new tastes and willing to pay a premium for quality and uniqueness. In the test, problems emerged which brought major features of the proposition into question.

Retail buyers challenged both the underlying proposition – 'There is a limit to what customers would pay in this sector' – and the practicality of opening up this sector under the Campbell's label at this time – 'The Campbell's name doesn't guarantee success. There are too many frozen food lines on the market'. The Campbell's test enabled the firm to assess these reactions in a limited experimental area. This was done at a far lower cost than a national introduction. It is estimated that the 'test' cost the firm around £750,000, including research costs but excluding product development. A national introduction into that market at the time would cost about £5 million excluding stock. Clearly, the data above beg the question whether the same insights could be obtained from more conventional, lower-cost research. Normally the test is conducted after a programme of market research is completed. This is especially true in new product development.

The challenge of innovation

Most discussion of test marketing centres upon its role in innovation. Until fairly recently, this was seen largely in terms of new consumer products. There is now a rapidly growing awareness of the scope for using it effectively in a number of novel situations:

1 Improved performance in traditional areas: getting the best out of current brands, products and lines through optimizing advertising, price, service display and other features of the marketing mix.
2 Use in areas such as services, retailing and industrial goods.

In all these areas, the act of innovation is acknowledged as probably posing more risks to management than any other area of marketing. It is estimated that the failed 'Mr Burt' development by the Burton Group cost over £5 million during the mid-1970s. Test marketing is part of the battle to:

1 Limit these risks.
2 Help with the 'Go/No Go' decision.
3 Provide volume, profit and share predictions.
4 Eliminate bugs from the system.
5 Examine alternative approaches.
6 Bring out aspects of the product or service that can be improved for the firm's competitive advantage.
7 Supply data on as many aspects of the innovation and its performance in the market as possible.

Ansoff's framework[5] for exploring alternative growth paths demonstrates the strategic options open to firms. Evidence to date indicates that the likelihood of failure increases as the firm moves away from familiar markets and known products.

In each of the strategies in Table 17.1, a need exists to break free from the conventional notion that innovation can only be thought of in terms of the physical product. It is the total offering which matters, including image, cost, expectation, etc.

The risks associated with new products and services and the associated costs are enormous. Most marketers are familiar with new product failures, ranging from the almost legendary stories of the Ford Edsel and Du Pont's Corfam to the more routine failures of brands like Wills Ambassador. In very many cases, major contributory factors to their difficulties would have been spotted in test marketing.

The 1950s – Ford Edsel: serious difficulties made worse by the glare of publicity.

> Within a few weeks after the Edsel was introduced, its problems were the talk of the land. Edsels were delivered with oil leaks, sticking hoods, trunks that wouldn't open, and push buttons that couldn't be budged with a hammer.[7]

The 1960s – Du Pont's Corfam: major problems with customer acceptance.

> Corfam shoes had to fit properly in order to be comfortable: they did not stretch and mould to one's feet even after prolonged wearing.[8]

The 1970s – New Smoking Material: proposition did not match up to customer expectations. Customers wanted and expected a safe, cheap product, not a safer, similar-priced product.

The 1980s – IBM's PCjr: this did not have the specification, support or price to justify software houses in developing games, or customers in switching from existing equipment. The IBM name was not strong enough to carry a disappointing product.

The 1990s – Euro Disney: Faced problems of climate, cost and market acceptance.

A cautionary note should be made here. Test market success does not guarantee the same pattern nationally. There are a number of examples of products performing well in a test market, but failing to make the grade nationally. Both Heinz Toast Toppers and 'Dine' Instant Mashed Potato performed sufficiently well in tests for large-scale, national launches to take place. Their failure highlights the importance of the market as arbiter of success and failure.

Table 17.1 Alternative growth strategies

		Products Existing	New
Markets	Existing	Market penetration	Product development
	New	Market development	Diversification

Source: Ansoff.[6]

Success, survival and failure

Most contemporary studies put the rate of new product failure between 30 per cent and 60 per cent. Perhaps even more important, studies of truly successful brands put the chances of achieving this success at less than one in ten. Although there is relatively little research in the area, there is scant evidence that rates of failure are any lower in services, retailing or industrial goods. In a comprehensive study, John Madell[9] found that only 4 per cent of new product launches in the British food market were truly successful.

Test marketing can help firms to:

1. Avoid expensive failure.
2. Identify the factors in the firm's offering which need to be changed in order to maximize the firm's chances of success.
3. Improve performance of existing products, services and brands.

Once the decision to test is made, performing these tasks efficiently calls for the imposition of a rigorous discipline on the testing process. This discipline should be applied to all aspects of the test itself – opportunity, methodology, location, scheduling and duration – and the measurement and analysis of the research results.

Table 17.2 The chances of success

Year	1969	70	71	72	73	74	75	76	77	78	Total
Total food products launched	53	76	94	92	64	81	55	70	73	72	730
£4m+ Turnover	1	1	2	5	2	5	1	4	7	3	31
per cent	2	2	2	5	3	6	2	6	10	4	4

Source: Madell.[10]

Are test markets worth doing?

It is foolish to deny that there are problems, risks and costs involved in test marketing. Some of these are, broadly speaking, controllable and linked to the research discipline and design itself: what to test, when to test, the controls to be imposed, choice of area, timing, measuring and assessing results, besides the techniques of projection, prediction and forecasting. These are examined in depth later. Other difficulties are associated with the non-laboratory, competitive nature of this marketing action.

Placing the new product, service, other offering, or changed policy on the market exposes it to the public eye. Part of that public is the competition, and many of the advantages of surprise are forfeited. The benefits which come from surprise are lost, and only lead times remain to offer the bonus of being first.

There are important areas in which this competitive dimension gives cause for serious concern. This is notably when the tester is entering a totally new market against well-established rivals. Faced with this dilemma when launching their Snack Soup, Cadbury, a firm usually convinced of the value of test marketing, decided to:

> pre-empt the competition by introducing, distributing and promoting
> our brand nationally and being the first on the market. (N. D. Cadbury)

Tests: exceptions and opportunities

Cadbury pointed out the risks for the newcomer conducting a test market in a field dominated by established producers. Although lead times can protect, the combination of established power and inherent risk is a strong argument against this experiment. Incidentally, the evidence on innovation to date suggests that simultaneously introducing new products into new markets is the most dangerous launch policy. This is illustrated by the difficulties encountered by Wiggins Teape when moving into toys, Woolworth into durables and clothing, and even Marks and Spencer with its knitting wool.

At the other end of the spectrum, testing may be unnecessary where the costs and risks of national launch are low. Typically, this is the situation in which spare capacity on existing machinery can be employed for a minor product adaptation with low promotional costs. The firm's familiarity with the market can provide clear indications of the potential.

Other situations in which testing is probably impractical are:

1 *Fashion lines,* footwear or clothing, seasonal lines.
2 *Fads,* such as cyberpets.
3 *Other short-life-cycle items,* such as CDs and fiction books.

In each of these situations, their very nature is incompatible with the time needed for the process of constructing, performing and evaluating the experiment. It ought to be stressed that these criteria hold true for *risk avoidance* strategies.

It is possible that *opportunity maximizing* can be at least as important. Therefore, test marketing alternative strategies may bring to the fore combinations offering significantly better prospects for sales and/or profits.

Until now, discussion concentrated on the marketing costs and implications of testing. Often production, sourcing and delivery factors weigh more heavily with management. It has been suggested that consumer durables and other items calling for high pre-launch investment are not worth market testing, as there is so much 'up front' money spent that the launch has to proceed.

This reflects much of what is known about the psychology of innovation. It is very difficult for company management to accept that the item upon which so much time, money and effort has been spent can fail. Unfortunately failure is endemic. When marketing costs are likely to be high, it is usually worth testing either to cut losses, even if marketing costs are a small percentage of total investment, or *improve the total offering* through product testing, service levels, promotion or prices.

In the mid-1970s, BP introduced a low-viscosity oil. The product had major technical merits which produced significant savings in petrol consumption. However, after two years, it had gained only 2 per cent of the market versus a target of 5 per cent. It became clear that many factors contributed to this: significant differences in results between new and older cars, doubts among customers about the product, and the low overall share of BP outlets in the total oil market.

The initial failure of BPVF7 in distribution and communication would probably have been identified in a test market. High development costs in this case were an argument for, not against, test marketing. In consumer durables, launches are regularly criticized for their poor quality, inadequate instructions etc. If the firm is lucky, the product survives long enough to be debugged, albeit with national attention focused upon it and possibly a widespread body of resentment. The technical and distribution problems that plagued the Waddington's Video-master vividly illustrated the costs and risks that can occur with new consumer durables. These cost Waddington's an estimated £2 million in 1979–1980.

To the question, 'Under what circumstances should I test?', the basic answer is *always*, unless certain specific and definable circumstances exist.

In general, the costs and risks of new product development are now so great that, assuming the product or services can be supplied in sufficient quantities, at an acceptable price, testing should take place.

More formal approaches for deciding when to test markets include Bayesian and other decision analytic techniques where values can be put against the pay-offs from reduced risk because of improved information.[11] Cost-benefit analysis of test marketing has been used to further explore this key issue.[12]

What can be tested in test markets? (Variables)

Although most British test marketing is concentrated on new products or services, in other countries, notably the US, a far wider array of factors are subjected to tests. Overall increases in marketing costs, allied to recognition of the critical role played by these non-product features, has put the spotlight on their testability. At the same time, there is increasing research and media sophistication to make such research more practical and profitable. These developments enable test markets to explore most aspects of the marketing mix, notably:

1 *Product:* overall appeal and performance, quality, ranging, mix, presentation, packaging.
2 *Price:* appropriateness, levels, range, mix and their impact on sales.
3 *Distribution:* optimal combination of outlet choice, stock level, display, movements, trade terms, besides overall acceptance.
4 *Promotion:* advertising budgets, schedules and mix, creative approach, below-the-line merchandizing and sales force effort.

The importance of this was illustrated with the success of Dettol Deep Fresh, a new bath foam which combined the Dettol image with the characteristics of a luxury soap foam. David Beauchamp of Reckitt and Colman acknowledged that, once the concept emerged, 'developing advertising was difficult because we knew that if we missed the pinhead of acceptance it might not work'. Dettol Deep Fresh was tested in two areas.

Test markets enable the firm to monitor performance of these factors acting either in concert or (to some degree) separately. This can take two forms, as follows:

1 *Single test of the marketing package in the market.* Here overall performance is closely monitored to answer:
   (a)   the Go/No Go question;
   (b)   the performance question;
   (c)   specific questions about aspects of the package.
2 *Multiple test of different combinations in the market.* Some features may be held constant, e.g. advertising copy, but others changed in various locations, e.g. Peterborough, Ipswich and Luton.

The Go/No Go decision focuses attention on avoiding failure. Overall acceptance can be measured and, equally important, the nature of the good or service appeal can be measured: who is buying it? where from? under what conditions? in what volume? how often? The latter two questions are particularly important in gauging long-term market penetration and performance. Most brand share prediction techniques call for purchasing patterns over a period of time. Some success has been achieved using repeat purchased rates to predict ultimate market shares.

Defining information needs, decisions and controls

Even if the company does not take its analysis as far as detailed forecasts, test marketing is a decision tool and the criteria for decisions should be established before introduction. These will include:

Targets

1 *Sales:* total and by target market. The target market should go right down the distribution chain, including distributors and retailers as well as consumers.
2 *Shares:* including not only introductions' performance, but impact on own and competitors' brands.
3 *Advertising and promotion response:* the whole gamut of goals from awareness and attitude to reaction.
4 *Product performance:* this goes beyond technical evaluation to include match of consumer expectations and product delivery.
5 *Distribution:* the pattern of acceptance, in terms of individual stores, types and any regionalism which emerges. These might incorporate desired stock levels, even the amount of discounting.

All have to be linked to decisions which must be made and the criteria on which they will be based. The quality of the research facilities which the tester can use is vital to implementation.

In building the bases upon which this type of analysis if performed, the inherently dynamic nature of the market should be borne in mind constantly. This is clearly shown in one of the more successful food market innovations in the late 1970s: instant pot snacks. This market grew from a relatively small base to over £30 million in a few years. Soon the novelty began to pall with Pot Noodle, Snack Pots, Quick Lunch and Knorr Knoodles competing vigorously for a stable market. Under these conditions, the chances of success for new offerings reduced rapidly.

The corollary to establishing targets is defining the conditions under which they will be achieved. These will include:

1 Advertising and promotional budgets.
2 Sales force activity.
3 Product availability.
4 Distribution.
5 Support services: technical etc.
6 Competition: nature and activity.

Setting up the test

Careful preparation is vital to experimental success. The more complex the situation being studied, the more critical the controls. This is clear in test marketing, as few areas are more prone to the accusation 'garbage-in, garbage-out'. Setting up the test calls for a clear definition of the research brief.

The research brief

This defines as clearly and as operationally as possible the problem under investigation and the material required from the study. The three simple rules for a brief are that it should be *actionable, communicable* and *internally consistent.*

Definition of the three types of variables

1 *Dependent variables:* those to be measured, on which performance will be judged.
2 *Independent variables:* those that are being examined or are the subject of the experiment.
3 *Exogenous variables:* those that are outside the test and, although they may have an impact, are not manipulated.

The *dependent variables* are sales, the *independent variables* include different advertising levels and creative treatment, whilst the weather is an *exogenous variable*. It is within this framework that the controls mentioned earlier are established to:

1 Minimize personal or company involvement.
2 Establish performance norms.
3 Facilitate management.

Effectively combined, the brief, management and definition of variables and implementation of controls should ensure an effective marketing test or experiment, provided the appropriate practical disciplines are imposed.[13]

Are there alternatives?

The costs and risks of test marketing, particularly the full-blown pre-launch test of a new product (sometimes called the experimental launch), prompt a continuing search for more limited, lower-cost alternatives. Two roles are ascribed to these alternatives:

1 A substitute for the full test, i.e. if their ability to predict is as good, why incur the additional expenditure?
2 A final pre-test research stage to screen out potential loss makers.

There is no general agreement that any of the methods so far tried provides a complete substitute for the full test. There are, however, a number of alternatives which can give some approximation of likely results in test and be valuable pre-test research steps. Among the most successful of these are:

1 *Limited area testing,* using small test towns or limited catchment areas.
2 *Outlet tests,* where one type of store (e.g. chemist shops) or main trade customer (say Asda) is used.

Mini area tests

Two factors combine to heighten interest in the use of cities or more limited areas as test areas. These are:

1 Increasing costs of testing.
2 Desire to use tests to explore more detailed aspects of the marketing effort while certain factors, e.g. advertising, are held constant. These can include display material, differences in product or packaging for manufacturers, types of services offered, hours of opening, etc., for retailers and service firms.

Areas with the advantage of having a number of major cities (population over 100,000), physically very separate, but no dominant conurbation, e.g. London, Birmingham, Southampton/Portsmouth, Liverpool/Manchester, Newcastle/Sunderland are invaluable.

When conducting these more limited area tests, it ought to be recognized that the smaller the area, the greater the likelihood of significant variation from the national average. This demands greater stringency in applying the controls previously mentioned.

Micro-market testing (the mini-test) shows particular promise. The basic technique involves using panels of people from a 'Shoppers Club'. Periodically each panel member receives a catalogue listing typical supermarket lines. At more frequent intervals, a 'promotions' bulletin is distributed, listing special offers and price changes.

Each week a van calls to collect the club's orders, meeting them from its stocks. This combination of catalogue, promotions bulletin and van provides a controllable, market-based environment in which new products can be tested, aspects of their marketing mix varied, while the entire process is closely monitored. Alternative formulations of the mini-test have mobile supermarkets or automarts as substitutes for the catalogue and van.

Evidence to date suggests that, for reformulations of existing products, the mini-test is a reasonably good predictor of likely response. The forecasts for new brands have been reasonably accurate. It is, however, no substitute for the full test in highlighting the multitude of market-place, logistical, physical or competitive variables which can:

1 Determine the likely success or failure of the product.
2 Determine the best available information for either a new or modified offering.

Where should I test? (The external variables)

All experiments – and test markets are no exception – turn upon the appropriateness of the laboratory situation set up for them. In the natural sciences, setting up the experiment is as important as the conduct of the test. In test marketing the costs, risks and demands are at least as great. A test conducted in an inappropriate location, perhaps unrepresentative of the total market, can result in, at best, valueless and, at worst, dangerously misleading information.

The first step in choosing the locale is to carefully review the total market in which the firm is interested. When the company seeks to extrapolate the results, the criteria upon which this is done must be defined early in the planning process. The test market area ought to be typical or representative of the total market.

Choice of location was central to the thinking when Heinz Coleslaw (tinned) was tested in Anglia, ATV and other areas in 1980. The product broke new ground, as the major competition was chilled cabinet coleslaw, and was compatible with brands in the Heinz salad range. The test provided an opportunity to evaluate overall acceptance and likely penetration. The promotional mix of TV, radio and 5p-off coupons in *TV Times* was evaluated in terms of both consumer and retail appeal. The area chosen provided a bench mark for judging the brand's likely achievement throughout the marketing system.

Often the target market is Britain itself. In this case, the company needs to explore carefully how Britain is really divided in terms relevant to its markets. The dynamic nature of today's environment adds a new dimension to this, as the composition of different areas, lines of communication and distribution, besides media mix, can vary rapidly over time.

Carlson Lite (a low carbohydrate beer) was tested in the Southern Region test area. It was very successful during its test and the firm moved into a roll out. Unfortunately for the firm, the test area successes were not repeated, and the product enjoyed only limited success.

> Terrestial television areas do not remain static. The introduction of a new booster signal – or the removal of an existing one – greatly affects the number of homes which can receive a particular channel. Cable, satellite and digital TV provide massive increases in flexibility and adaptability.

For many consumer markets, the key variables in establishing the target markets and hence the sought-after features of the test area are:

1 Demographic characteristics.
2 Industrial and occupational structure.
3 Distribution patterns and retail structure.
4 Media pattern.
5 Company and brand strength.

Demographics: the age, sex and social class structure of the population.

Industrial and occupational structure: the balance of industrial, agricultural and other types of work and related work patterns, besides the general level of economic activity.

Distribution patterns and retail structure: these are the channels through which the goods must move to reach the ultimate buyers.

Media pattern: includes factors such as the range of media available and the ITV media weighting.

Any special features of product usage or consumption should be included in this analysis.

Seagram recognized this in the test market for its sparkling wine, Crocodillo. The target was overwhelmingly young women 'who are experimenting with drinks'. This was reflected in both the choice of test area and the factors both producer and retailers were keen to measure: attitudes in target market and repeat buying among a group happy to experiment.

In reviewing these variables, extreme care is needed so that no major bias is inbuilt. A test area may appear attractive, but an occupation structure dominated by, say, the service sector, could distort results and give a misleading impression of the market potential. The test market-place variables typically ought to be distinguished from experimental control factors and roll-out features.

The *control* features include:

1 *Discreteness* of the experimental situation. This includes both the extent to which the area as a whole can be handled separately from the total market, and the scope for treating specific parts as separate.
   It is a harsh fact of life that no major test area can have a wall built around it. Some degree of overlap is inevitable in Britain, whether it is in TV transmission or large numbers of people moving in and out of the test area. When the extent of overlap is fully understood, greater control can be built into the situation.
2 *Area structure.* This is an important factor if matched area experiments or other attempts to compare and contrast aspects of the test are sought. An area containing broadly comparable, but physically quite separate, areas is invaluable in tests geared to produce the best possible offering. Cambridge, Norwich and Ipswich for example, are broadly comparable in size, but an average of 50 miles apart. Separate formulations of product, promotion etc. could be tried with the vital element of the control in the third.

3 *Location.* This is critical if the offering is to be introduced initially into the next-door areas. It is desirable to ensure that a balanced move across to national launch, e.g. introduction to adjacent Southern, Midland and Northern areas simultaneously, is achieved. This helps to protect against regional competition or regional distortion in performance.

In the real world the *size/cost* factor plays a powerful role.

Assuming the points made earlier are applied, the area chosen should be large enough to increase the probability of its being representative, but small enough to make costs acceptable and effective management and control viable.

How long should the test last?

Many pressures combine to encourage firms to cut test markets short: the relatively high cost, the desire to exploit any competitive lead, etc. It is a temptation which affects each stage in the process: pre-, during and post-test.

The pre-test. This is the base period in which the product, service or other change is judged. It has to be long enough to allow the natural fluctuations which occur in every market to work their way through the experimental and control areas.

The test proper. This starts the moment the first sell-in starts. It has to be long enough to allow the experimental or test factors to pass right through the system as, at each stage, distortions can occur. The trade may be over-enthusiastic – for example, Cadbury's Chillo failed despite high trade ratings. Consumers may buy at high initial levels, but reject it subsequently. Key weaknesses in delivery and performance sometimes emerge late in the day. However, the reverse can occur quite easily – trade reservations can be overcome by consumer demand or new and potentially profitable uses may emerge later.

The key variables in this are the repeat purchaser rate and the pattern of consumption. These are also important in allowing the tester to forecast long-term performance.

Post-test. This calls for a thorough review of the test and all the internal and external factors which influence performance and judgements. A production problem, a strike, even things like the weather can distort results. The buyer for Laws stores in the North East highlighted the importance of weather on the test launch of Bovril Chicken – it simply was not 'chicken cube weather'. This point was endorsed by the buyer from Amos Hinton: 'Summer is not the best time anyway, so we'll hope for some improvement in the next few weeks'.

All data should be thoroughly reviewed and related to targets. This is particularly important, as there is a common tendency to fudge results by ignoring targets set initially in the hope that something will turn up.

The test

The value of the test market depends upon the quality and range of information collected. Many aspects of this are devolved to the associated advertising and research agency, within the controls mentioned earlier. The main data sources are the following.

Factory sales. All goods dispatched from factory or warehouse, preferably broken down by type of account or location. Extra controls are needed to assist both production and dispatch, while ensuring no slippage in area definition occurs. When the firm is dealing with large direct accounts, care is needed so that their timing and distribution of orders does not distort results.

Store audits. These give a picture of the movement of goods through outlets, stock-holding and purchase pattern. The importance of the major multiples in most fast-moving consumer-goods markets puts special emphasis on this step.

Trade research. The support and involvement of the trade is vital for successful test marketing. Lack of information and the casual assumption that they will play a part causes considerable resentment in some quarters.

Consumer research. Panels, omnibus surveys, tracking studies and specially commissioned surveys play a vital part in the ongoing evaluation of the test. This research provides the framework for both revision as the experiment progresses and final evaluation in the key Go/No Go, Recycle and Abandon decisions. John Davis[14] points out:

> Too often research in this area is merely confined to a single *ad hoc* survey
> some weeks or months after the launch which will show some single
> measure of awareness.

The performance of a brand, product or service emerges over time. A single snapshot can easily give a distorted picture. The recurrence of retail buyer comments like 'The tourist trade this summer hasn't provided a steady demand' (Cussons 'Only You' hand care) and 'The TV advertising definitely gave the product the boost it needed, but don't think Polyripple would be selling as well without this support' (Polycell Products Polyripple) demonstrate how important continuing systematic study is in order to get a true picture of performance.

Test area overlap

One of the most striking differences between the regions defined by research organizations like A. C. Nielsen and those of the TV region is 'area overlap'. The nature of television transmission and the continual efforts by contractors to improve their range and quality has led to considerable and changing areas of overlap. There is an average of 10 per cent across the various regions. This means that it is virtually impossible to neatly define a test area and cut it off from all external media influences.

John Davis[15] highlights the advantages which can be taken of this by running two experiments side-by-side in the two adjacent areas. Different campaigns or approaches can be employed. Research in the overlap areas can be used to bring out key aspects of the different approaches, highlighting their relative effectiveness.

To be wholly effective, the overlap areas should be scrupulously examined. The firm must ensure that quality of transmission, patterns of usage and previous advertising are, broadly speaking, constant. The test in both areas can be very useful in advertising research and to explore competitive approaches to a key innovation.

How is performance judged?

Evaluation can be based on two separate, but inter-related criteria:

1 Did the tested product or service meet its targets?
2 Do our forecasts for national performance indicate a successful product or change in policy?

As indicated earlier, arriving at clearly worked-out objectives is an integral part of effective testing. These should incorporate such variables as penetration, repeat-purchase rates, impact on competitor and own brands, distribution pattern, and returns on budgets. Performance should be carefully checked against these and other goals for the product or change in presentation. Alternative formulations being examined can be compared. It is largely in terms of relative performance that the innovation or change will be judged. At the same time, lessons learned in logistics, physical characteristics, promotion and competitiveness have to be explored in terms of the twin criteria of pay-offs and practicality.

The targets set for the test are the bench mark, but increasingly there is a desire to convert test market sales into longer-term forecasts. This area has been full of controversy. Gold[16] indicated the fallibility of test market results. A great deal of work has been conducted in the intervening period to produce major improvements in projection, production and forecasting from test markets. Davis[17] developed a *projective technique* based on the proposition that differences between areas are reflected in existing (pre-test) brand shares. The extent to which existing brands lose share to the test brand in the test market indicates their overall vulnerability. The likely national brand share is likely to emerge from the combination of the test market's losses. Algebraically, estimated brand share nationally, T, will be:

$$T_1 = 100 - \left\{ X_0 \frac{x_1}{x_0} + Y_0 \frac{y_1}{y_0} \ldots \right\}$$

Hence if the pre-test market has four major brands, x, y, z and n:

Test Area Shares (%)		National Shares (%)	
x_0	40	X_0	45
y_0	30	Y_0	25
z_0	20	Z_0	15
n_0	10	N_0	15

x, y, z and n are the shares post-test. Test brand 'T' takes 10% from X_0, 5% from Y_0 and 3% from N_0.

Therefore:

$$T = 100 - \left\{ 45 \frac{30}{40} + 25 \frac{25}{30} + 15 \frac{15+7}{20 \quad 10} \right\}$$

Only equilibrium-state market shares ought to be employed. Time lags, peaks and troughs in performance must be taken into account. This means that measurement of the entire market and the test is an ongoing process.

It is possible to arrive at an early forecast of ultimate performance using a forecasting technique. The amount of work in this field means that it can only be dealt with in a cursory way here.

Three basic approaches can be used:

1 *Judgemental forecasts.* Test market performance can be a key part of the data on which the judgements can be made. Particularly interesting is the use of the Delphi Method. In this technique, a panel of 'experts' respond individually to questionnaires demanding a forecast and the assumptions behind them. Responses are anonymous and exchanged between the experts until a consensus is reached.

2 *Time series analysis.* A variety of methods have been used here. The availability of consumer panel data and recognition of the critical importance of repeat buying has heightened interest in this area. Rawlins and Sparks[18] highlighted the relative robustness of commonly used models such as the Parfitt–Collins[19] and Fourt–Woodlock[20] approaches. At the same time, they put forward a model to predict the steady rate volume of the brand.
Thus,

$$\text{Volume} = \text{Units per buyer} \times \text{number of buyers}$$

$$= \frac{\text{weight of purchase by repeat buyers}}{\text{relative purchasing by repeat buyers}}$$

multiplied by

$$\frac{\text{no. of repeat buyers}}{\text{proportion of repeat buyers}}$$

The later paper by Parfitt and Collins[21] develops this further.

3 *Causal methods.* These involve the development and use of a forecasting model in which sales changes derive from changes in specified variables. Surveys of buyer intentions are perhaps the most commonly used form. Chambers *et al.*[22] provide a very useful framework for choosing the most appropriate technique.

In most of these approaches, there is an assumption that effective management and control of the test has taken place and that sufficient time has been given to enable the test to properly develop and for equilibrium to have been reached.

From test to launch

One of the most remarkable features of current research and writing on test marketing and innovations is the lack of attention paid to the process of moving from test to commercialization. Even Philip Kotler, the US authority on marketing – quoted earlier as describing test marketing as rapidly approaching the state of a science – covers the problem in a few brief comments. A number of practical problems face the firm after the test has been completed. Hard decisions have to be made as to whether the offering has been a failure or a success.

An unsuccessful test product can be very de-motivating for all those involved, from field force through to retailers stocking the product. Debriefing them and revitalizing their interest in the range of corporate activities is an investment in the firm's competitive future.

Often, a generally unsuccessful product is rejected totally. Recycling aspects of the proposition calls for the maximum benefits to be gained from the test. This might lead to the modified offering or a new product incorporating certain features being due for test again. Faced with this issue, management must add broader, more subjective criteria to the objective criteria for area choice mentioned earlier. It is unwise to test frequently in the same area, particularly if a specific pattern of response (failure or success) has occurred.

Following a successful test, a number of important questions face the firm, notably:

1 Do I roll out gradually?
2 Do I go national immediately?
3 How do I deal with the test area(s) in the post-test, but national launch, period?

Three factors determine the optimum course of action between progressive roll-out and national launch. These are:

1 The scale of the success.
2 The likely pattern of competitive response.
3 The practical considerations of producing, stocking, distributing etc.

The greater the success, the shorter the competitive lead time, the more important an immediate shift to national production. Gearing up for this may take longer than the 'end of test/go national' schedule permits. This increases the importance of pre-launch research, notably of the mini-test type. Equally, forecasting techniques capable of giving early predictions of likely brand shares are essential to the continuing process of research.

Despite the urgency which can emerge in these circumstances, caution is essential. Often the deteriorating product quality or reduced service which emerges during this early launch period provides competitors with their greatest chance to erode the brand's position or introduce alternatives. The opportunity for rivals is greatest during periods of stock-out or rationing. Among the most commonly reported reasons for failure following a successful test are poor product quality, irregular supplies and non-competitive pricing. Marketing managers responsible for this stage in the commercialization process are generally better advised to roll-out, rather than attempt a full national extension, if there is a real danger of these difficulties emerging.

In coping with the post-test but national launch period, two interrelated strands exist. Often it is to the firm's advantage to maintain a lag between activity here and national activity. For a period of time, this enables the firm to contrast two different stages in the product's life-span. It is tempting to persist with this. It can seldom, however, be maintained for long without undue investment of resources and distortions in behaviour patterns. These typically occur after a few trading periods. It is then in the firm's interest to restore the broad balance of area activity.

Conclusion

Test Marketing provides an experimental environment in which firms can explore the extent to which they truly understand needs. Recent developments, notably mini-tests and simulations, may be able to further reduce costs by providing many of the benefits associated with large-scale experiments. They will not, however, eliminate the need for rigour and control.

SPECIMEN QUESTION

One of the major clearing banks has developed a new package of financial services for younger, working women. Among its key features is an early career and returner assurance policy that guarantees women who take a career break to have children an income for five years after the birth of their first child if they are not in paid employment, plus a guaranteed low interest loan for an MBA or similar for qualifying students. Design a test market for this new 'product', taking into account:

1　The arguments for and against such a test market.

2　The choice of variables to test.

3　The best location.

4　The optimum timing.

5　The kinds of decisions which the bank needs to make and the value of test markets in these cases.

6　Any staff support or training required to support the test.

7　The ways performance can be measured during and after the test.

8　Any alternatives.

9　Form of 'roll-out' that might be appropriate.

10　Other issues you recommend should be noted.

18

Price

Introduction

Few company decisions create as much interest or stimulate as much external involvement as those concerning price. Customers, intermediaries and the firm's personnel, especially those in marketing and selling, are all directly involved. The prices themselves, particularly in aggregate, affect political and economic processes, and politicians, economists, civil servants, commentators and pundits study, comment and try to take action over prices (Figure 18.1). This interest derives from the pivotal role which price plays in the exchange process between buyers and sellers.

Figure 18.1 The newsworthiness of price: lead story, *Guardian*, December 1994

Index points to 4 per cent inflation –
mortgage rise likely

Oil firms put
petrol up 3p a litre

The reality of pricing

Price is the amount for which product, service or idea is exchanged, or offered for sale, regardless of its worth or value to potential purchasers.[1] Although a monetary equivalent or value can be imputed, prices can incorporate goods exchanged, e.g. cars traded in or similar deals.

Within the framework of classical economic theory, prices are arrived at in a relatively deterministic manner, emerging from the interplay of supply and demand:

The quantity of a good that people will buy at any one time depends on price.[2]

In a perfectly competitive market manufacturers have virtually no influence on their prices. These are determined by market forces created by competitive pressures and consumer buying patterns. The 'invisible hand' of the market establishes rates. The salient features of this perfectly competitive market – a homogeneous product, complete information among buyers, economically rational buying behaviour and large numbers of small competitive producers – are almost impossible to achieve in a complex modern industrial society. Even in an apparently homogeneous product field, such as wheat, differences exist, e.g. North American wheats tend to be harder, and thus more easily milled.

Economic theory has incorporated these realities within the notion of pricing under imperfect competition:

> All sellers in the oligopolistic industry[3] [where a few producers dominate the market] recognize a mutual inter-dependence of the price-output decisions, and therefore act interdependently rather than independently in adjusting their prices or outputs.[4]

Although terms such as oligopoly, imperfect markets and interdependence have accumulated certain pejorative associations, their true meaning is important. Simply, all that is being said is that in modern markets, industrial, consumer and service, a firm setting its prices must have one eye on its customers and another on its competition. Nowadays more eyes have to be grown to study government, pressure groups, the media, financial institutions and owners and shareholders.

Although price formation can be described within a framework of economic theory, for the practising manager it means hard work, carefully tested assumptions, expectations, research and judgement in what is probably the most difficult area of marketing decision-making.[5]

The just price

Underlying much discussion about price is the notion of the 'fair' or 'just' price, the price that could be called correct on the basis of social considerations. A great deal of government, pressure group and media action and discussion is geared towards achieving just prices, but it is seldom fully appreciated how sensitive this concept is to the point of view of those discussing it.

For the seller a fair price is probably the amount he or she needs for their offering in order to make a reasonable profit. The notion of a reasonable profit itself has to be discussed, as there are different approaches to this. To the customer a fair price probably refers to some general idea of affordability allied to some sense of intrinsic value, with previous experience a contributory factor.

In entering into the exchange both are seeking some degree of profit from it. Sellers want some excess of income over costs, while buyers want an excess of satisfaction from the goods or services over the satisfaction from holding on to their money or purchasing something else. In determining pricing policies the company needs to understand both the costs involved and alternatives open, and the responses of the different groups and the values they place on the goods or services (Figure 18.2).

The political dimension

At a seminar at Durham University in 1979, a senior marketing executive from a nationalized industry asserted that price flexibility was a thing of the past. Prices were now so important to the political and economic management of the country that government was gradually eliminating any managerial discretion (Figure 18.3). (This comment was made before the election of the first Thatcher government, which took as one of its main goals the reduction of government interference in the market. 'Let the market decide' became the catch-phrase of the 1980s.) The recently elected (1997) Labour government in Britain places the same priority on price stability and low inflation.

Figure 18.2 The exchange and interplay between costs and values. Adapted from Hesketh, J. L., *Marketing*. London: Collier-Macmillan, 1976

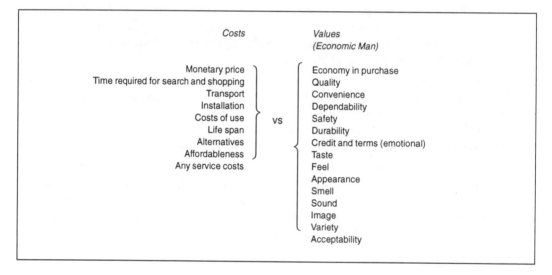

Costs		Values (Economic Man)
Monetary price		Economy in purchase
Time required for search and shopping		Quality
Transport		Convenience
Installation		Dependability
Costs of use	vs	Safety
Life span		Durability
Alternatives		Credit and terms (emotional)
Affordableness		Taste
Any service costs		Feel
		Appearance
		Smell
		Sound
		Image
		Variety
		Acceptability

Figure 18.3 Price: the political dimension

How Labour plans to keep prices down.

Prices and inflation dominated political discussion and each general election during the 1970s, 1980s and 1990s. Even the non-interventionist policies of the Conservative Thatcher and Major governments did not preclude some action on prices within specific areas or under the auspices of the Monopolies and Mergers Commission or the Office of Fair Trading. The latter's role has been expanded in collaboration with the regulatory bodies set up to monitor the newly privatized utilities, e.g. OFTEL.

Even within this framework it is a mistake to take the marketing executive's comment at its face value. Price is an area of considerable freedom of action, albeit within limits. The company's flexibility will depend to a considerable extent on specific circumstances. Price is an especially sensitive marketing instrument which can be changed to suit circumstances. In a recent study over half of the respondents indicated that the importance of different pricing objectives varied over time.[6]

The price decision

The need to make decisions about prices occurs under a number of specific circumstances for different types of products and services. For an existing brand or product the decision can incorporate increases, reductions and holding price. In the late 1960s Rothman's King Size cigarettes made significant inroads into the market share of the Benson and Hedges King Size brand leader, simply by holding prices when cigarette duty was increased.

The major circumstances in which pricing decisions need to be made are: new product introductions; changes in external circumstances, e.g. raw material, tax or duty changes; competitive action in raising or lowering prices; internal changes, from new products to new processes; promotions; and changes in market structure or size. In each of these situations, the objectives, short or long term, of the firm must be clearly set before action is taken.

Table 18.1 Pricing objectives

	Included among the set of objectives (%)	Principal objectives (%)	Rank
Target profit or return on capital employed	88	67	1
Prices fair to firm and customers	49	13	2
Prices similar to those of competitors	48	8	3
Target sales volume	47	7	4
Stable sales volume	25	5	5
Target market share	18	2	6
Stable prices	17	2	7
Other	5	1	8

Source: Shipley.[7]

Although specific goals are set in initiating an action, increasingly managers are recognizing the need to adopt policies with medium- to long-term consequences in view. A market skimming price[8] might be seen as a mechanism for opening up a market with a view to penetrating new segments, with progressive lowerings of price.

New product pricing

The pricing of a new product is the purest pricing situation the firm is likely to face, particularly if there are no existing, direct competitors. The firm is in a position to set its goals in terms of itself, its intermediaries and the end customer.[9] Dean[10] suggests that three factors determine the new product price: getting the product accepted; maintaining the market in the face of growing competition; and producing profits.

To achieve the goals related to these, Dean suggests two strategies lying at the extremes of a spectrum: skimming prices and penetration prices. Skimming prices are high prices, probably backed up by heavy promotion which are used to open up the market. The manufacturer usually tries to position the product as the leading, highest-quality, most prestigious offering. The firm steadily lowers its prices to meet competition or open up new markets but generally holds on to a slight price advantage. A number of firms in the calculator market adopted this strategy when this market emerged. A similar process exists in personal computers. The most likely markets – education and business – were opened up first, and later other markets were penetrated by progressive price reductions. The success of this strategy has now created a significant defence reaction among customers: they are reluctant to buy new products 'because the price is bound to come down'. Computer software companies face massive problems with this expectation among users.

Penetration prices are the opposite end of the spectrum. Everything is done – promotion, discounts, publicity, high stocks etc. – to open up the market as quickly as possible.

At one time it was very difficult to escape from a pricing policy adopted at launch. An overpriced product could not easily be brought into a different price bracket without questions about quality and reliability being raised, and an underpriced product could not easily have its price raised because of the buyer's pricing assumption. Inflation during the 1980s has done much to alter this. Change is now expected and customers accept frequent modifications: up and down.

A major exception to the concept of penetration prices being difficult to increase is introductory offers. In consumer markets at least,[11] this type of promotional action appears to have virtually no effect on perceptions of quality unless it is held over indefinitely without any explanation (price legislation permitting).

Briscoe and Lewis,[12] in a substantial study of the interaction between price and the product life-cycle, highlight the importance of linking pricing policies with the stage in the life-cycle. They suggest that even when it is undesirable to vary monetary price overtly, 'by using these disguised price variables (credit, discounts, rebates) which can be more readily varied over the product life-cycle, price can be made a more effective marketing tool'.

Changing external factors

During an inflationary period such as the late 1980s, perhaps the most significant factors influencing firms to modify their prices were the external changes affecting them, especially price increases by suppliers, wage increases by workers and dividend pressure. These increases must be met through internal economies, the use of alternative materials or price increases. The overwhelming majority of firms review the first two alternatives thoroughly before embarking on the third, potentially dangerous, step. A number of industries were rocked by price increases in materials during the late 1970s. Plastics and other petroleum-based industries were particularly severely hit. After a long history of growth, the plastics industry's competitiveness was weakened by increases which were running at 50 to 60 per cent at times. The ramifications spread to boatbuilding, caravans, toys, construction, automobiles, electronics and many other high-plastics-consumption industries. Twenty years later, raw materials prices are still monitored as the earliest indicator of inflation.

Most firms are reluctant to modify their prices frequently, and this poses a major forecasting problem during an inflationary period (Figure 18.4). The scale of the price increases and their timings are based on estimates of inflation. Failure to get either right can mean the firm trading at a loss for long periods of time. The problem is made more difficult by two recent developments: materials shortages, perhaps requiring the purchase of more expensive stocks, and the tendency for inflation to be non-linear, accelerating over time.

Figure 18.4 The impact of inflation

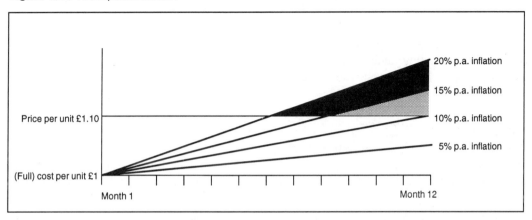

In retail markets the scheduling of buying can influence the firm's profitability dramatically. Warnings of imminent price increases are a common ploy by salesmen to increase volume sales and establish stronger rapport with customers. The real impact of this on their own firm may be extra sales of money-losing lines, but most companies recognize this and build it into their costings.

Competitive action

The concentrated nature of most consumer and industrial, and some service, industries means that few firms can ignore the pricing policies of their rivals. This 'competitive' aspect of pricing creates both problems and opportunities.[13]

None of the manufacturers mentioned in Table 18.2 can ignore the pricing policies adopted by their major competitors. Increases, reductions and stability create new opportunities and problems. For example, Unilever (Birds Eye) might announce a price increase. Faced with probably the same basic cost position, rivals can respond either by increasing in time, knowing volume losses will be slight, or by holding or reducing prices to search out extra volume.

There is a common assumption among economists that the only real means of appraising these options is through holding or reducing prices.[14] Hence markets in which this does occur indicate some degree of collusion or excess market power. In fact, most firms and managers have experimented at some time with both these policies and when faced with an increase they apply the knowledge acquired in these situations. However, there is a sense in which the

Table 18.2 Concentration: a perspective

Product field	Major manufacturers	Share of three largest firms (%)
Ready-to-eat breakfast cereals	Kelloggs Nabisco Quaker	95
Frozen foods	Unilever Imperial Group Findus	86
Soups (canned)	Heinz Crosse and Blackwell Campbells	95

Source: Cannon, T., Advertising: The Economic Implications. London: Intertext, 1975.

circumstances have changed and past experience may be a poor guide. Against this is the risk and cost involved in holding or cutting price. Most firms manage this balance by occasionally holding prices to gauge the opportunity for competitive advantage but generally keeping in line with their rivals.

Internal change

It is sometimes convenient to think of pricing in terms of single-product, single-market situations, but the dominant pattern for companies is multiple products and multiple markets. The responsibility of corporate marketing management is to balance the different pricing policies and structures to gain the best returns for the firm.

Product line pricing occurs in a number of different situations. Sometimes the price of one product or brand affects the price of another. This can be a deliberate part of company policy General Motors pioneeered brand range pricing in the 1920s. Alfred P. Sloan describes how.

> The special committee . . . recommended that the policy of the corporation should be to produce and market only six models, and that as soon as practicable the following grades should constitute the entire line of cars:
>
> (a) $450–600   (c) $900–1,200 (e) $1,700–2,500[15]
>
> (b) $600–900   (d) $1,200–1,700

Here, in a relatively simple situation, the network of prices has been established and, perhaps more importantly, the relationships are set. These relationships provide a guide for product, promotion and distribution policies.

These interrelationships exist in many situations. For example, petrol sales, car repairs, and new and used vehicle sales are all part of the motor trader's interrelated product range. Petrol sales might dominate the business at a major service station, with repairs merely as a service, or new car sales may be the main business, with used car sales being merely a method of disposing of trade-ins. Over time, however, these priorities will change, e.g. shortages of supply might lead to a re-examination of the returns from the used-car operations and a realignment of priorities.

In many situations of this type of interaction the notion of the loss leader plays a part. A *loss leader* is a product or service sold at lower-than-normal margins for the purpose of attracting customers who might then purchase other items at normal margins. Traditionally it has been associated with supermarkets, where staple products such as sugar and butter are often sold cheaply to attract trade. It occurs in many other situations, however. Industrial suppliers might price the initial project for a major customer below cost merely to become an accredited supplier, and management consultants will often perform a small limited project at a low price with a view to longer-term, more substantial contracts. The special offers made by many banks to students might even be described as loss leaders.

Interrelated prices take a very different form in those industries where costs of raw materials, production and labour are tied together. A tannery might specialize in high-quality suede but use all its waste to make garden or industrial gloves, or a manufacturer of sheep-skin gloves might use his offcuts to make belts. At any point in time one line may appear dominant, but the contribution of the other lines may be significant in real profit terms if the marginal cost is borne in mind.

Promotional prices

A glance at any newspaper or a walk through any shopping area will show the importance of the price cut or special offer (Figure 18.5).

There are dangers in promotional pricing: it builds short-term volume but no loyalty, and the customer's image of the product can deteriorate.

In some consumer-goods markets, trade discounts and volume bonus (dealer loading) can be an important part of key-account management. The supermarket group will share the cost of the price reduction in order to increase turnover.

Non-core-price policies

So far much of the discussion has centred on the cash or monetary price of the product, but in industrial markets credit terms play a major part. A supplier may give 7, 30, 90, even 120 days to pay as a major part of the offering. Some firms adopting this policy balance long terms to some clients with shorter terms to others, while other companies offer prompt-payment discounts to minimize the costs of credit.

Moving into international trade or exporting to a new country is very similar in pricing terms to launching a new product. The firm may be facing a new demand situation, perhaps with very little or no competition, and tariff barriers and government attempts to restrain imports may limit the firm's freedom of action. However, although a new and perhaps very different demand situation may exist, it is clear from the research into the area that careful study of the market plays only a minor part in price setting for most firms.

Setting prices

The majority of firms follow policies which can be broadly described as 'cost plus' pricing. In a large-scale study in the US, Lanzillotti[16] recorded the responses of a sample of major corporations (Table 18.3). Broadly, the same questions asked in Britain today produced a similar type of response from both large and small firms (Table 18.4). In the retail business it would probably be defined as a combination of gross margin and stock-turn.

Table 18.3 Pricing goals of major companies

Company	Major pricing goal
General Foods	33.5 – 3% gross margin
US Steel	8% on investment (after taxes)
International Harvester	10% on investment (after taxes)

Table 18.4 Pricing techniques

	All products (%)	Some products (%)	Some or all products (%)
Cost-plus method	59	33	
Marginal analysis	3	13	–
Other (e.g. competitor analysis, 'blind guess')	–	–	27

Source: Shipley.[17]

These answers reflect the desire of most managers to achieve what they would define as reasonable profits, perhaps a combination of funds for reinvestment, income for wages, salaries and other overheads, material and processing costs, resources for promotion, distribution and product development, returns to shareholders, enough to keep the financial institutions supportive, and taxes. For the company to survive, the money for all or most of these must come from what it earns from its product array. Individual products may follow routes which do not directly contribute to this, but overall the price mix has to be viewed in this light.

Competitors cannot be ignored, so the firm might adopt a competitive pricing stance. Here the company will try to find itself a niche in the market. Using the prices of other companies as cues it can try to charge the going rate, seek to undercut or keep a good 'price advantage'.

Gabor,[18] in an important series of studies on prices, highlighted the importance of customer-orientated pricing:

> There is no uniform formula by which a price could be judged. It will be
> a good price or a bad price according to how well it serves the aims of the
> firm.

The response of the customer is the key to effective pricing within this frame. Systematic research should be conducted by a firm to establish the price which most closely meets the customer's needs. This involves building up estimates of both the returns on specific prices and the shape of the demand curve under different circumstances. One company might find that its demand increases with price (to a point), while another might find that the way to satisfy its customers is by combining high-priced prestige with low-priced bread and butter brands. The optimum policies will depend on the estimated response.

Breakeven analysis

Breakeven analysis is a straightforward device for enabling a manager to estimate the minimum sales required in a given period or in the launch of a product to ensure that the product does not make a loss. It consists of three basic elements: fixed overheads (or fixed costs), marginal costs, i.e. those that change with sales, and income. In Figure 18.5, at each given price the sales volume required to break even (B) can be established from the point where total costs (F(i) and F(ii)) intersect with income (total revenue).

Although it has some value, breakeven analysis is based on three major assumptions:

1 A fixed relation between sales volume and returns.
2 The firm can accurately forecast the demand curve.
3 A true picture of the cost situation can be established.

Figure 18.5 Breakeven chart

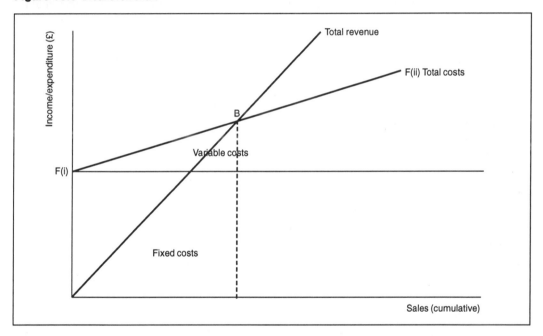

Marginal pricing

Marginal pricing is based on the proposition that many of the firm's costs are fixed, and whether the company sells 100 or 1,000 items will not affect rent, rates, interest on loans or depreciation on machinery, and once these fixed costs have been met the returns are on each extra unit sold under the average pricing method assumed in the breakeven chart.[19]

The firm bases its prices on the cost of each extra unit of output sold after the fixed overheads have been met. It has been suggested that the ability of the Japanese to undercut European firms is derived from their widespread adoption of marginal pricing policies.

Conclusion

In developing pricing policies in the firm there is seldom complete freedom for any one area or manager. Corporate management may provide an overall framework such as that described earlier by Sloan, or perhaps even a more general one, e.g: 'Seek growth in high-technology fields'.

Invariably there is a sales and marketing dimension. The sales force may report back about fierce overseas competition. Ignoring this can cause production disruptions and erosion of the competitive position. Marketing may advise the 'milking' of existing brands to finance new developments.

The finance department has the responsibility for ensuring effective cash flows and maintaining the financial stability of the firm, so it will set targets for returns and impose constraints on action. Effectively balancing these corporate, financial, competitive and marketing forces is the essence of successful pricing. It should not be assumed that these are incompatible. Gabor mentions the importance of the relationship between price and quality, pointing out that many buyers use price as an indicator of quality. The strategic dimension to pricing policies is increasingly important in shaping and developing marketing programmes.[20]

SPECIMEN QUESTIONS

1 Many pricing decisions by UK firms are based on the addition of a percentage to cost and cost is usually established by full/absorption costing methods.

    (a)   What difficulties exist in establishing a reliable measure of the full cost of a product or service?

    (b)   What non-cost factors should be taken into account in pricing decisions?

2 Economic theories of price often include the notion of 'search time' as a factor. What aspects of marketing can be included in this notion and why?

3 Is there any value in the notion of the 'just' price?

4 Firms have many objectives when setting their prices. Indicate the types of objectives that are likely to be especially important to:

    (a)   The dominant manufacturer in a fast-moving consumer goods market.

    (b)   A bank setting charges for the time of bank managers.

    (c)   A specialist design agency with a strong track record for brochures and advertising but now trying to enter the magazine market (as a designer for the publisher).

    (d)   A capital good manufacturer selling equipment to a government agency in a developing country.

5 Explain the ways in which the pricing of new products differs from that of established products.

6 Construct a break-even chart for a community co-operative serving an island community. It is considering the purchase of a tractor-trailer but faces the following costs and likely revenues:

Expenditure (est.)

    (a)   Purchase price of tractor-trailer £14000—likely grant 35%.

    (b)   Current interest rates 8%.

    (c)   Annual insurance, tax etc. £850.

    (d)   Estimated maintenance and repair costs £350 p.a.

    (e)   Salary for driver (pt) £8,000.

    (f)   Other variable costs £500 p.a.

Income (est.)

    (a)   Casual rentals to local crofters 60 days at £40.

    (b)   Harvest time rentals 50 days at £50.

    (c)   Contract from Western Islands Council for refuse collection service; two days per week for 50 weeks at £45.

    (d)   Other income £1,000.

Advise the co-operative the likely break-even date and the wisdom of a decision to acquire the tractor trailer.

CASE STUDY 14: A MINI PRICING POLICY

Few cars have achieved either the volume sales or the eclectic appeal of the Leyland Mini. In the twenty years from its introduction in 1959 to 1979 over 4.5 million Minis were sold. It was consistently among the top five best-selling cars in the UK. However, serious reservations were expressed about its financial contribution to the British Motor Company (BMC), British Leyland (BL), Leyland Motors or even Rover today.

When introduced, the car was targeted on first-time car buyers primarily in the C1 and C2 socio-economic groups. Employing tremendous technical and design skills, Sir Alec Issigonis produced a car with a low petrol consumption and capable of carrying four adults, for less than £500. A policy broadly akin to penetration pricing was adopted to achieve maximum penetration in this sector.

John Barber, then with Ford, recalls that:

> Ford was amazed that BMC priced the Mini down to compete with the very old and very basic Ford Popular.

The low price was very much a double-edged sword. It made the car more accessible to the target market but drastically reduced the dealers' freedom of action, as well as causing the customer to have some doubts about the car's quality.

Despite this pricing policy the car was slow to move into high-volume sales (Table 18.5). A number of other factors eventually combined to stimulate substantial sales volume, notably fashion changes in the 1960s and rally successes.

Table 18.5 Price and market shares of the Mini

Date	Total Mini price (£)	Market Share	Indexed Mini price Oct. 59 = 100	Oct. Retail Price Index	Total Mini price in 1959 prices
Oct. 1959	496.95	NA	100.0	100.0	496.96
Oct. 1960	496.95	NA	100.0	102.0	487.21
Oct. 1961	496.95	NA	100.0	106.0	482.35
Oct. 1962	526.25	NA	105.9	109.1	482.35
Oct. 1963	447.65	14.0%	90.1	111.5	401.48
Oct. 1964	469.90	10.8%	94.5	116.0	405.00
Oct. 1965	469.80	9.5%	94.5	121.6	386.35
Oct. 1966	478.00	8.7%	96.2	126.2	378.76
Oct. 1967	508.75	7.4%	102.4	128.7	395.30
Oct. 1968	561.10	7.8%	112.9	135.9	412.88
Oct. 1969	595.50	7.0%	119.8	143.2	415.85
Oct. 1970	738.50	7.5%	128.5	153.8	415.15
Oct. 1971	640.63	7.9%	128.9	168.1	381.10
Oct. 1972	695.15	5.9%	139.9	181.4	383.21
Oct. 1973	738.84	5.8%	148.7	199.3	370.71
Oct. 1974	1003.26	7.1%	201.9	233.4	429.85
Oct. 1975	1299.00	7.1%	261.4	293.8	442.14
Oct. 1976	1496.00	6.4% (to end Oct.)	301.0	324.6	460.87

Reproduced with permission. Sharman, H. and Rines, M., 'The Maxi Task of Marketing the Mini', *Marketing*, January, 1977.

By the mid-1970s the market for the Mini bore only limited resemblance to its initial target. It was far more classless, its major customer groups being AB women and first-time buyers among ABC1 C2 men.

During the period of its success the fortunes of Leyland Motors (formerly BMC and BL) waned considerably. It has been suggested that a factor in this decline was the poor returns earned from the Mini, its best seller. This coincided with a long period (for most of the 1960s) of underinvestment by BMC.

Task

Explore the issues affecting the pricing policies adopted for the Mini and consider the wisdom of the choices made.

19

Channel management

Introduction

In Chapter 11, intermediaries and intermediary systems were examined from the point of view of the middle men themselves. The problems they face in developing their markets were explored. Manufacturers are dependent to a considerable degree on the effectiveness of their intermediaries in this area if their channels of distribution are to meet their marketing goals. The creation of the single European market has increased the importance given to effective channel management.

Channels are the networks of intermediaries linking or capable of linking the producer to the market (Figure 19.1). The term 'channel' is used to symbolize the flow of goods and services around the network. This movement is not merely physical, i.e. of the goods, but includes title (ownership), payment, information and promotion.

In building up an effective channel system or managing a current one, the firm is faced with a number of decisions:

Figure 19.1 Channel flows

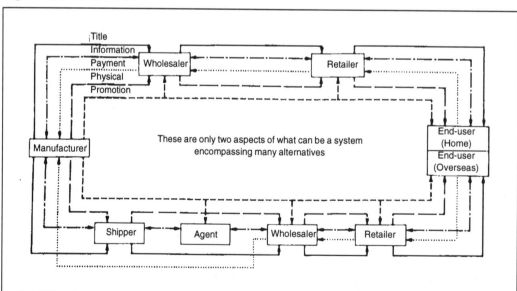

1 The levels (different stages in the system between producer and user) and numbers (the width of distribution at each level) of intermediaries.
2 The roles the different channel members will play in the flows.
3 The support that will be offered (level and type).
4 The extent of channel leadership that will be sought.
5 The level of integration between the middle men in the marketing of the firm's offerings.

This may imply a degree of manufacturer dominance that may not exist, since these decisions are also faced by other channel members. For example, giant retailers buying a wide selection of own-label goods might decide either to buy-in supplies or to use only wholly-owned suppliers. They can decide on the availability of these goods to other traders (perhaps overseas). Their promotions might feature the store or particular private-label goods.

The role of intermediaries

Channel intermediaries have many roles. One is to perform the distribution at a lower cost per unit than the manufacturer could, and to balance the production efficiencies of the supplier with the purchasing needs of the customer. For example, a cigarette machine might produce ten million cigarettes of a fixed size per day, but if sizes and specifications were changed to match the needs of small-volume buyers this could drop to one or perhaps two million. The wholesaler or retailer, through volume buying, gives the producer the opportunity to maximize production efficiencies while keeping prices down for customers.

Another intermediary role is to break down the large volumes produced into the small quantities bought. For example, a retail furniture company might place an order for 100 suites of furniture but the individual customer buys only one suite.

Intermediaries can minimize the number of transactions involved in the selling process, as Figure 19.2 shows. They may also assist in cash management by producers, e.g. small craft and clothing firms may provide the small producer with the income needed to increase production.

Figure 19.2 The economies of intermediary systems. Reproduced with permission. Gattona, J., 'Channels of Distribution', *European Journal of Marketing*, 12, No. 7, 1978

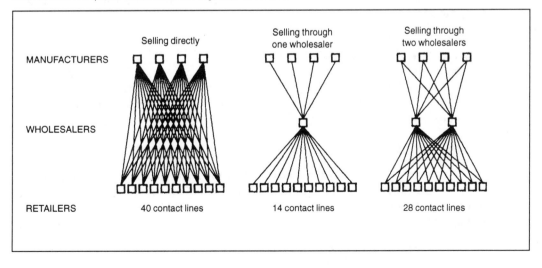

Providing information and insight into markets is another role of the intermediary. Small firms entering into exports often benefit enormously from the practical insight and guidance provided by buyers from such stores as Macy's or Gimbel and Saks.

Some intermediaries provide limited processing services, e.g. timber merchants or steel stockholders may cut to length or do some finishing work.

In some markets channel members may lead the marketing and promotional effort.

Intermediaries bring together a range of similar or related items into a large stock, thus facilitating the buying process. For example, the supermarket buys in 6,000 to 10,000 lines to provide the shopper with choice, and the builders' merchant will provide everything (from sand to light fittings) that the builder can use, on occasion even assembling some parts.

After-sales service and some filtering and management of warranty are also provided by intermediaries.

These are some, though not all, of the tasks performed by intermediary channel members. Manufacturers are faced with a range of different types of intermediary and an array of possible services when determining channel policies. Their decisions gain added significance when the relatively long-term character of these decisions is considered.

Channel choices are long term

The company adopting a specific channel strategy usually cannot extract itself easily if difficulties arise. It is the practice in many markets to invest significant sums in supporting middle men, providing them with anything from relatively small point-of-sale items to substantial kiosks or gantry units, and promotional investment may be used to support this effort. Customer loyalty is frequently shared between the outlet and the product. For example, a retailer may regularly purchase a specific branded product from the local cash and carry, and unless customers' demand for that line is substantial, will not visit another cash and carry if that line is dropped. The individual consumer can often be persuaded by the retailer to switch to a substitute if the original is not available.

The agent or intermediary in many countries is afforded legal protection if the producer wishes to transfer his or her trade, and contractual agreements are sometimes used in Britain to achieve the same effect.

Channel networks

The construction or modification of the channel requires careful and thorough review from a marketing perspective, in which the number of intermediaries sought is a fundamental consideration. Four basic options exist.

Intensive distribution

This involves seeking every possible outlet for the firm's product. It is characteristic of fast-moving consumer goods, e.g. cigarettes, soft drinks and sweets, where every exposure to the customer is an opportunity to buy. The outlet has relatively little impact on the customer's impression of the product.

Selective distribution

The manufacturer limits the search for outlets to a limited number of fairly broad categories. These can be related to type (e.g. only pharmacists for the firm's toothpastes) or style (e.g. only large, clean outlets with adequate display area for the firm's products). Selective distribution is employed when there is some limited interaction between product and outlet.

Exclusive distribution

The producer selects the intermediary very carefully and then provides him or her with exclusive rights to a particular area. Certain cosmetics firms demand some customer advisory service, and car manufacturers insist on repair, service and warranty handling facilities. This characterizes markets where the interplay between product and outlet is considerable. Part of the basic customer proposition may involve close links with the retailer.

Vertical integration

Under certain circumstances the producer might need to become directly involved with its intermediaries. It may buy itself into them or start its own wholly-owned outlets; e.g. Virgin started as a music retailer, moved into record production, then sold its music business to EMI. The firm is then faced with a major problem of integration; whether or not the intermediary should buy on the open market, i.e. be an independent profit centre. Closely related to this problem is the horizontal competition (i.e. wholesaler v. wholesaler, retailer v. retailer) that can emerge. Vertical integration can quickly alienate the firm's existing customers, since the firm will then be in direct competition with them.

Channel design

Channel design calls for the firm to conduct a thorough review of the objectives of the system and the constraints under which it will operate. The channel must match the capabilities of the firm, a point shown to be very important in the case of a small Scottish golf club manufacturer seeking a US distributor. A major group was interested in the product, but expected back-up promotion expenditure of about $200,000, more than the firm had spent in its entire existence.

The marketing-orientated firm focuses its attention on the needs of the different customer groups it is trying to interest. This may mean other intermediaries as well as end-users.

The amount of search time the customer is willing to invest can directly affect the extent of distribution sought.[1] Perishable goods require intermediaries willing to invest in special storage equipment. Bulky or heavy goods need investment in handling equipment.

Once the goods are out of the manufacturers' hands they have relatively little control over their display and merchandizing, although some firms have their own merchandizing or display teams. For complex or technical products adequate customer service can be vital. Interest in the retail-selling process itself may be critical, since there is belief among some middle men that they are merely stockists, and therefore have little need to try to build in any customer service or systematic selling effort. In most builders' merchants and hardware stores, and even in some appliance or department stores, this is clearly demonstrated. Sales staff use incomprehensible technical jargon and provide limited advice and assistance, if they are found at all. Anthony Jay once commented, 'The problem in Britain isn't selling, but buying.'

Hunt *et al.*[2] emphasized the different behavioural aspects of relations between channel members. Words like bargaining, conflict, co-operation, power, performance, role, satisfaction and politics recur in their analysis. They illustrate the ways in which channel members work together and the issues which affect these relationships.

Push and pull

Effectively moving a product through the channels and managing the various flows of information, title etc. is a combination of push and pull. The push is the manufacturer's or first-level intermediaries' efforts to persuade other channel members to stock or promote the product. The pull is the pressure exercised by customers on the trader to stock the item. Balance here is essential, as Figure 19.3 illustrates. Excess push may lead to the middle man overstocking the line.[3] In the short term this disrupts demand, as the trader holds back orders to achieve a more balanced position. Excess demand may lead the dealers to seek new sources of supply.

Figure 19.3 The balance between supplier push and customer pull

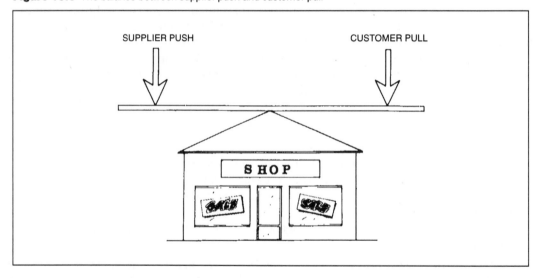

Achieving effective distribution is a mixture of pull and push. Pull is placed first simply because the trader's basic interest is in lines which effectively meet buyer needs, and which move through their outlet:

> There is no point in their offering me a 50 pence per case bonus if the goods never move out of my shop. (Supermarket owner's comment)

Insights into future promotional activities play a part in this.

Trade prices and discount structure are the basis of the relationship between producer and intermediary. The increased concentrated buying power and purchasing skills of dealers have created severe strains on traditional regional sales structures. Key-account management has emerged to play a major part in handling the special needs of and to cope with the massive power of major retail groups.

Originally this was concerned with price negotiations, including special discounts, volume bonuses and even agreements to develop own labels. At a conference in 1979, Andrew McDonald of Robinson, McDonald Marketing suggested that the major retailers were now so significant that products and brands could be designed to meet the special needs of their target customers, e.g. the Tesco customer or M&S customer. Firms now produce speciality products for these firms which do not sell elsewhere.

Intermediary responsibilities

Producers seeking to realize fully the potential of their dealers start with a clear idea of the degree of responsibility being transferred to them. This can encompass freedom over pricing. In some situations, e.g. where the agent or distributor is the principal (has title to the goods), the producer's power is limited once the sale is completed. Giving the intermediary responsibility for price is a major step which the producer should never take without careful consideration.

The pricing policies adopted by the dealer can have a major effect on the image and viability of the product. For example, Hathaway Shirts was forced to invest heavily to rectify problems created by the pricing policies adopted by its US distributors. In a number of instances, notably industrial markets overseas, the degree of ignorance about the prices being charged for the firm's products is alarming.

The amount of service back-up provided by the dealer must be established at a very early date. This can encompass both repair and warranty as well as information and advisory services.

Responsibility for business development and meeting targets is particularly important in opening up new middlemen accounts. The firm should always spell these out even to the point of defining the manufacturer's rights of access to clients. Many small firms face particular problems here, as intermediaries can control all the flows in the system.

Conflict and co-operation

The idea of a channel may leave readers with the impression that movement downwards is smooth and even. Although this may be the case, there are areas in which conflicts can and do emerge. The root of this lies in the attempts of the independent channel members to maximize their profits. The intermediary is both a customer involved in an exchange and a partner in distribution.

Some forms of conflict are beneficial to the system. They can create better balances of resources, skills and abilities can be improved, and inefficient, even dangerous or dishonest traders or manufacturers can be eliminated from the system.

Particular problems can emerge when specific channel members have too much power or act negatively. The desire of some retailers or wholesalers to restrict their lines, limit the numbers of new products, or demand promotional bonuses can stifle competition and innovation. At the same time, the policies of some manufacturers to restrict supplies or even refuse to supply certain traders may seriously reduce the end-customer's freedom to buy. Moore points out that 'conflict is a fact of life in the Marketing Channel, as it is in any social system, and one with which managers inevitably struggle on a regular basis'.[4]

Conclusion

The growing complexity of modern industrial societies has pushed the producer further and further away from the prospective or actual buyer. However, channels of distribution have emerged to provide links, and many manufacturers are increasingly dependent on intermediaries to manage the flows that link them with their customers. Effective channel management calls for a determination to fully realize the opportunities available. Change has long characterized channel systems, so marketing-orientated managers must build up their systems with the expectation that changes will create new opportunities for or real threats to their firms. The single European market, the opening up of Central and Eastern Europe and powerful new technologies will transform channels of distribution during the years to come. Keeping pace with these, winning advantage and avoiding problems, may prove to be one of the single greatest marketing challenges of the dawning millennium.

SPECIMEN QUESTIONS

1 For a firm of your choice draw up a picture of their channels of distribution. Indicate clearly the different flows and the marketing opportunities and threats that this structure and pattern of flows creates for the firm.

2 What is meant by the 'sort and allocation' role of intermediaries? How does this change as their market power over manufacturers increases?

3 What are the factors that will determine the choice between intensive, selective, exclusive and vertically integrated distribution? Illustrate each of your answers with examples of firms that are likely to use these approaches and the determinants of their decisions.

4 What contribution can marketing play in improving the supply and distribution of agricultural produce in developing countries?

5 Outline the ways in which the advertising of a range of garden products can help persuade a major group of garden centres to carry and display effectively this range. How would you advise the firm to respond to the suggestion by the head buyer that the firm drops media advertising and increases trade discounts by the same amount?

6 Moore has pointed out that 'conflict is a fact of life in the Marketing Channel'. How would you use this information to advise a wholesaler and cash and carry stores to cope with the pressure on the manufacturer from large retailers to cut out middle men and sell direct?

CASE STUDY 15: ASKO

ASKO is a publicly quoted $15 billion German retailer. ASKO is one of Germany's five largest food retailers and is the premier out-of-town retailer in Germany. ASKO is the German market leader in four retail lines: out of town hypermarkets, do-it-yourself building marts, furniture, and discount clothing in out-of-town locations.

Sales in the consolidated ASKO Group are around DM 26 billion; another DM 10 billion sales are made in a hypermarket joint venture with Metro, called MHB, so that a total sales volume of some DM 36 billion will be achieved in 1997. About half ASKO sales are in food – classical discount supermarkets and out of town hypermarkets as well as wholesale. The other group sales are in discount speciality retailing lines: do-it-yourself building marts, furniture, discount clothing.

Since going public in 1984, ASKO has been one of the fastest-growing retail companies, and, in 1990, had the highest net profit of any publicly listed German retailer.

ASKO is Germany's:

mart chain;

counter;

mission is to be a leading, global-orientated
ore concepts, for its profitability, and for the

nding, in which the suppliers may get stronger,
e its mission?

20

Physical distribution management and logistics

Introduction

Few management concepts have excited more interest over the last decade than physical distribution management and logistics:

> Physical distribution is the broad range of activities within a company (or other type of organization) concerned with the efficient movement of goods and raw materials – both inwards to the point of manufacture and outwards from the production line to the customer.

> Logistics and physical distribution management (PDM) is that part of management which is responsible for the design, administration and operation of systems to control the movement of raw materials and processed goods. (Both quotes from the Institute of Logistics)

Crucial to the logistics concept is the belief that management in this area calls for the integration of all parts of the organization involved in the movement and storage of goods, the need to view in terms of the efficiency of the total organization, and recognition that this efficiency is defined in terms of effectively and profitably meeting customers' needs, and that the goals of management in this area are the creation of time, place and form utility.

'Time, place and form utility' means getting the goods and any associated documentation and services to the right place, at the right time, and in the form required by the recipient. For example, a production manager may need 15 tonnes of zinc-coated steel (zintec) on a certain date. If he gets it too soon the firm pays interest on the capital involved, storage space is taken up unnecessarily, handling costs are involved and pilferage and wastage can occur. If he gets it too late, production lines are disrupted, delivery schedules can be affected and customer dissatisfaction can be caused.

A historical perspective

Given these dimensions of physical distribution management, it is perhaps surprising that the concept did not emerge earlier. It is estimated that about 15 per cent of the US Gross National Product, i.e. about $1,400 billion, is involved in this area of business. It is little wonder that Peter Drucker[1] described it as 'the economy's dark continent'.

The last two decades saw many moves towards redressing the balance. These were spurred partly by a combination of inflation and technical change. Inflation has hit particularly hard those companies whose stocking and warehousing policies were inefficiently managed. The technical changes affecting physical distribution management (PDM) have been extensive, and include containerization, roll-on/roll-off ships, wide body jets, palletization, and computerization of warehousing and stocking.

The EU, with its interest in direct transport methods (equipment, operating methods, axle weights, drivers' hours etc.) and increasing involvement in other areas, has accelerated the process, and the changing documentation and legal requirements and the work of bodies such as SITPRO (Simplification of International Trade Procedures Board) have also played an important role.

Although these environmental pressures have helped to stimulate interest, a number of organizations and bodies have played a major part. The National Council of Physical Distribution Management (US) has played a major part in refining and developing the area, and the Institute of Logistics, although a very young organization, has already become a focal point for discussion, research and the dissemination of ideas.

The combination of these factors makes physical distribution management one of the most dynamic areas of opportunity for the student or young business person. Companies like Boots, GKN, ICI, Johnson and Johnson, RHM Foods, and United Biscuits have developed or are in the process of developing fully integrated PDM systems.

The increased integration of European markets is creating new opportunities and posing novel challenges to effective PDM. These are highlighted by related developments in transport and technology. A clear illustration of this can be seen in the 'new railway revolution' in Europe. New track and rolling stock mean that rail transport will be as quick as air between many major mainland European cities.

The physical distribution and logistics system

As indicated earlier, logistics encompass all functions directly involved in the movement of goods. The primary areas are transportation, materials handling, packaging, warehousing, inventory, location and processing (orders and associated communications and documentation).

A research project conducted by the CPDM Research Liaison Committee broke this down even further when examining the main areas of work by management in these areas:

1 *Transportation:* vehicle utilization, selection of model, vehicle schedules and routes, vehicle design specifications, vehicle selection, use of third-party contractors, direct v. indirect deliveries, load planning, vehicle rent, purchase and lease and carriage of specialized products, e.g. glass and dangerous materials.
2 *Materials handling:* in-plant movement, order picking techniques, sorting systems, pallet movement, unit loads and handling systems.
3 *Packaging:* packaging warranty.
4 *Warehousing:* warehouse space, facilities utilization and warehouse layout.
5 *Inventory:* stock-holding policy, stock-level requirement forecasts and control procedures.
6 *Location:* best methods of achieving national distribution coverage and location of field warehouses and depots.
7 *Processing:* order processing, administrative systems and drop size/cost analysis.

8 *Costs:* audit procedures, refusals, transport and handling, customer account profitability, cost allocation, backhaul waste capacity and labour incentives.

9 *Strategic and general issues:* service level offerings, service levels and their cost/revenue sensitivity, policy formulation, legislation, policy towards shared transport and other facilities, incentives, motivation of distribution staff and balance of own fleet versus use of third-party contractors.

It is clear from this not only that the range of activities is enormous,[2] but also that there are significant areas of overlap, particularly in marketing. Much of the pressure for the introduction of legislation to introduce the Single European Act came from those concerned with the high cost of PDM in Europe. It is estimated that 20 per cent of total product costs were tied up in the 'extra' costs of tariff and customs barriers in Europe.[3]

Marketing, PDM and logistics

Bowersox *et al.*,[4] in their authoritative book on the subject, place PDM and logistics firmly as part of the marketing mix, not as a separate function. Physical distribution can be 'a positive force in obtaining a competitive advantage in the market-place' through: achieving a balance of customer service and efficiency capable of meeting real customer time, place and space needs profitability; building up optimization policies which can identify internal and external efficiencies, helping to protect the firm from the worst effects of inflation; providing an approach which views the channel and physical distribution system as a whole, thinking it through and maximizing benefits for the entirety rather than for the parts. The overall purpose is synergy through integration and efficiency.

The scale of physical distribution has led some commentators to view PDM and logistics as related to but separate from marketing, and a number of firms have established independent (of marketing) units to reinforce this autonomy. Regardless of the perspective taken in this debate, the interdependencies are extensive, and effective company management calls for these areas to work together, whether formally independent or not.

The goals of PDM and logistics

Although the overall objective of an efficient distribution system was described earlier in terms of creating time, place and form utility, this can be usefully divided into two sub-goals. PDM is concerned with both internal efficiencies and external services.

The success of PDM and logistics is dependent on its contribution to the more efficient operation of the elements listed earlier within some identifiable objective of a certain level or type of customer service. Traditionally the various parts of the distribution system (transport, materials handling, packaging etc.) have operated independently of each other, and their interactions with other parts of the firm have tended to be individual. This has created massive system inefficiencies.

The freight manager may cut back on his or her fleet to reduce costs, and this in turn may place extra pressure on the warehousing or parts department to hold extra stocks. If both decide to cut back or not adapt, the end customer will suffer, and perhaps extra marketing costs will be required to recruit new buyers. A number of gas regions faced this problem recently. Under pressure to reduce overhead costs, parts departments were running down their stocks. The immediate result was that service engineers were forced to reduce the amount they carried with them, and thus were often unable to effect a repair on their first visit, so there were sometimes long delays before appliances were repaired. Eventually consumer complaints departments had to expand to cope with the greater numbers of dissatisfied customers.

Customer service is difficult to define. To the customer it probably means the effort made by the manufacturer to ensure that the product is made available at the time, in the place, and in the condition requested. Companies, however, tend to use specific measures when considering customer service.

Order lead time is the period from the moment the customer first places the order or request (including repairs) until it is received. This may be measured in terms of days (same-day delivery, repairs within 48 hours) or by some other objective criteria.

Percentage of orders satisfied provides an objective measure of the stock levels required to supply a fixed proportion of requests from stock. The cost of trying to satisfy all customers will be prohibitively high, so most firms target on an 'achievable' proportion.

The efficient operation of the physical distribution system calls for the various parts to work efficiently internally, but, more important, also to work effectively as a whole. System inefficiencies are caused by the desire of each part to achieve its own goals (Figure 20.1).

Figure 20.1 Ordering a book (an extreme example)

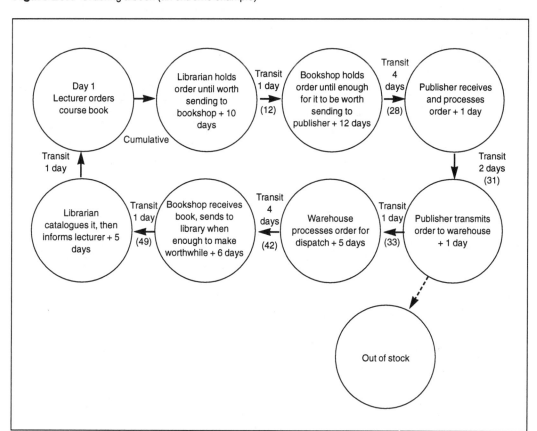

The total-cost approach to distribution

This focuses on the interrelationships that exist within the parts of the system. Trade-offs are sought between the different elements, and there is scope for both direct savings and improved customer service.

Savings may be achieved in areas outside the scope of specific managers. For example, the cost of holding production stocks may not lie with either purchasing or production, and as a result these stocks may creep up until they are a drain on corporate resources. The total-cost approach highlights these areas.

More importantly, the total-cost approach focuses on the effect on the total system. This approach demands that the effects of changes in each item are reviewed in terms of their overall impact. This can be seen in terms of the effect of increasing or reducing the expenditure on quicker delivery through transport and communication. As a result, the total-cost graph differs dramatically from the graph of the individual area (Figure 20.2).

Conclusion

The creation of the single European market poses some of the most immediate challenges to marketers involved in physical distribution. Major distribution firms, e.g. P&O, are responding by creating integrated, Europe-wide logistics support systems. The extent of the opportunity will prompt firms to seek greater effectiveness, e.g. through better integration of telecommunications, computing, storage and transport studies. In a very real sense, physical distribution will be the main competitive battleground of the late 1990s.

Recent research on innovation has reinforced the emphasis given to physical distribution management and logistics. The cost of inventory can destroy margins and eradicate the gains from a new product launch. Yamashina[5] (Figure 20.3) shows how quickly an out of stock position can be transformed into an excessive inventory policy. Information technologies are transforming both the costs and capabilities of distribution and logistics systems.

Figure 20.2 The full cost of transport alternatives

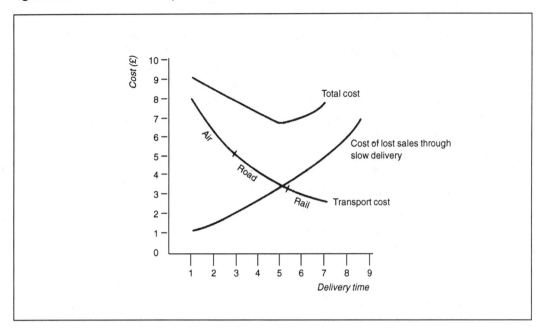

Figure 20.3 Product life-cycle and transition of inventory level (*Source:* Yamashina)

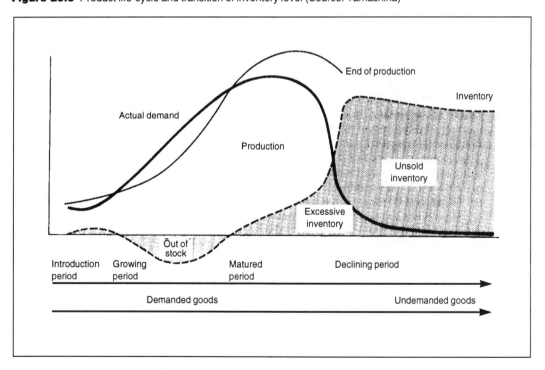

SPECIMEN QUESTIONS

1 Why did Peter Drucker describe physical distribution as 'the economy's dark continent'? What opportunities does this relative neglect create for firms that are awake to the opportunities created by effective physical distribution management?

2 Indicate ways in which the increased integration of European markets is creating major opportunities for the better use of physical distribution and logistics.

3 Outline the main goals of physical distribution management and show how improved PDM has produced significant marketing gains for a firm of your choice.

4 What is the total-cost approach to distribution and how can it produce significant improvements in the working of the marketing mix?

5 It has been argued that distribution is often the key to success in international markets.

   (a)   Why might this be the case?

   (b)   What example can you give of this kind of success?

   (c)   How can lessons of overseas success be used to improve the management of PDM in home markets?

6 Yamashina's research draws out the fine line that lies between stock shortages and excess stock during the launch period of a new product. What are the operational implications of this finding for the successful management of innovation?

7 Explain why the 'cost of possession' is such an important issue for companies like steel stockholders and other intermediaries in industrial markets.

8 'Environmental fears and the pressure for greener marketing will transform the packaging industry over the next decade.'

   (a)   How true is this comment?

   (b)   What risks do these twin pressures pose to manufacturers of packaged goods?

   (c)   How can marketing help threatened firms respond?

9 Advise a manufacturer of fast-moving consumer goods seeking to strengthen its market position in domestic markets on the relative merits of road, rail, air and seaborne transport.

10 Define:

   (a)   Time utility.

   (b)   Form utility.

   (c)   Inventory.

   (d)   Material handling.

   (e)   Logistics.

   (f)   Zero inventory.

   (g)   Containerization.

   (h)   AGVs.

   (i)   Pallet racking.

   (j)   Load matching.

CASE STUDY 16:
THE NO HANDS FOOD MIXERS DIVISION OF
HOPEFUL DURABLES LTD

The year is 1996. No Hands Food Mixers division of Hopeful Durables Ltd has been in existence for eight years and was originally set up as an organizational entity to exploit the growing demand for kitchen gadgetry in the UK. Hopeful Durables is currently turning over £6 million a year, of which No Hands contributes about a third.

Recently a number of problems have emerged which have resulted in a decline in net margin of the No Hands business even though turnover has steadily risen. It is felt within Hopeful Durables that a number of major decisions have to be taken.

The market

The market for food mixers is small and is dependent upon imported products. As can be seen from Table 20.1, no real growth has been evident in recent years but Hopeful Durables is optimistic about long-term growth and has formed No Hands to develop sales and distribution, within the UK, of its existing lines. The Managing Director, Mr Ian Moody, has been given this task.

The relatively low sales in 1995 are due to lower imports from the Netherlands and France. Preliminary estimates for 1996 showed an increase and it was hoped that they would be back to the 1994 level. The value of the market (1995) at retail was estimated at about £10 million.

Table 20.1 UK sales (including imports)

	Units (000)
1992	979
1993	667
1994	980
1995	736

In the past ten years imported mixers have become the most important source of supply. In 1995 imports accounted for about 60 per cent of supplies compared with 40 per cent from home sources, a reversal of the situation prevailing six years previously.

Products and prices

There are many different kinds of food mixers and a wide range of attachments. The largest are table mixers, retailing at between £100 and £115. The smallest, hand mixers, sell at between £50 and £60. No Hands have products throughout the entire price range. (These are typical 'realized' retail prices, i.e. after all manner of discounting activities. Hopeful, on average, gets 75 per cent as its NSV.)

Companies in the market

Whiskers Limited has the dominant market share, with three others, No Hands, Kordless and No Fuss, as main competitors. Market shares are estimated in Table 20.2.

Table 20.2 Market shares

	%
Whiskers	35
No Hands	25
Kordless	25
No Fuss	5
Others	10
Total	100

Whiskers' position has been eroded by increased competitive activity from No Hands and Kordless.

Mixer ownership is extremely low when compared with other European countries. Hopeful considers that there is a lot of room for expansion in the British market. It is felt that it is unlikely that the low UK ownership is caused by price, as the cheaper mixers are well within the housewife's reach, but rather is due to cooking habits. Many British housewives only occasionally prepare elaborate meals and even when they have a mixer it is used infrequently.

Distribution

Most purchases are made at independent electrical dealers. Multiples have been growing increasingly important and now account for over 10 per cent of mixer sales. Electricity Board showrooms are believed to have 12 per cent of sales. A further 12 per cent of sales are made through department stores and a similar percentage through mail order. Some 7 per cent of consumer sales are directly accounted for by wholesalers. This is summarized in Table 20.3.

The normal channel flow is for manufacturers to deal through electrical wholesalers and, because of the high proportion of imports, the importance of such wholesalers is likely to continue.

Although many retailers are prepared to stock more than one brand, it is nevertheless very difficult for the smaller companies to obtain distribution.

Table 20.3 The pattern of sales by outlet types

	%
Independent electrical dealers	47
Multiples	10
Electricity Board showrooms	12
Department stores	12
Mail order	12
Wholesalers – direct sales	7

Within No Hands, the managing director, Mr Moody, thought that the future development of his company's logistics function should be the responsibility of an expert. He appointed a director to be responsible, Mr R. Suppards.

Mr Suppards immediately commenced an appraisal of No Hands' existing capabilities and the specific physical distribution service requirements of retailers. A review of the situation is presented below.

Sales force

Until recently No Hands food mixers were sold by all Hopeful salesmen. However, this policy has just been changed and a specialist sales force recruited. At present it numbers 20, based on regional sales offices as shown in Table 20.4.

Table 20.4 Regional sales

	Per cent sales		
	All Hopeful Products	No Hands	No. of No Hands salesmen
South East, London	30	50	8
West and South West, Bristol	15	15	3
Midlands, Birmingham	25	20	3
North West, Manchester	10	5	2
North East, Newcastle	10	5	2
Scotland, Glasgow	10	5	2
	100	100	20

Salesmen perform varied functions, i.e. taking orders, checking inventory, arranging displays, dealing with customer complaints and other general selling activities as directed from time to time. A breakdown of the time used by salesmen shows that on average each salesman makes eight calls per day and each call takes some 40 minutes. Of this time the various functions accounted for are as shown in Table 20.5.

Table 20.5 Breakdown of time used by salesmen

	%
Checking inventory	50
Arranging displays	10
Customer complaints	10
Selling	10
General chat	20
	100

No Hands sales had increased slowly but steadily over the past five years and it was this slow and steady growth that had prompted the company's reorganizations.

Facilities locations

Hopeful has warehousing facilities close to each of the regional sales offices. These have each been fed from production sources in Birmingham and from the Netherlands. Each is at capacity loading and a decision is required on whether to extend the warehouses or to review the service policy.

Inventory

Inventory levels are currently based on sales forecasts. For each location and item maximum sales levels are forecast. In recent years inventory holding has increased, due basically to two factors, an ever-widening product range with increases in model types, colours etc. and the need to carry higher safety stocks of those items imported from the Netherlands. A further source of concern is that, in order to achieve possible production economies, senior management in Hopeful are considering concentrating production in the Netherlands and in France. Such a change is becoming even more likely in the face of UK industrial relations problems.

Management has always considered that the cost of holding inventory (valued on an NSV basis) should be most carefully and stringently examined. Recent estimates have been of the order of 24 per cent p.a., a significant increase from the mid-1980s, when it was just less than 20 per cent p.a. Much of the difference can perhaps be accounted for by the higher cost of capital, but obsolescence is playing a significant role.

Transportation

Hopeful's distribution manager, N. N. Kelley, was for many years the company's transport manager. In 1995 he was awarded the Gold Medal of the Institute of Transport. He was considered by many as the best freight rate negotiator in the business and was proud of the low rates obtained from carriers. These low rates invariably necessitated maximum cube use on all carriers and vehicles, both for trunking and for deliveries to retail and trade outlets. Kelley's policy had always excluded any own-transport fleet.

Order processing

Orders are received in a number of ways, i.e. phone, mail, fax and from representatives by mail or phone at the regional offices. Dispatch notes are prepared and forwarded to the warehouse staff. Invoices are all raised by head office in Birmingham.

Order cycle times vary because Kelley's policy is to accumulate orders until such time as full vehicle loads can be dispatched, and thus lowest unit transport cost obtained.

Trade relations

In the past Hopeful has enjoyed good relations with the trade. However, in the past year some murmurs of discontent have been apparent. The trade appears to be satisfied with discounts but feels that inventory investment is growing too high. Paradoxically, lost sales due to stock-outs are beginning to occur on some lines which to Hopeful seems illogical when total investment in inventory is increasing.

Task

Describe how an integrated approach to physical distribution can give Hopeful an edge in building their markets.

This case study is reproduced with the permission of Dr David Walters of Cranfield School of Management.

21

Advertising and sales promotion

Introduction

Advertising and sales promotion are the most obvious aspects of marketing effort. To many people, they are synonymous with marketing itself. Media advertising stares down from posters, enters the home through television, radio and newspapers and is in the workplace through the industrial, trade and technical press. Promotional activity is frequently related to the act of purchase, meeting the shopper in the outlet or geared to influence the middle man's buying behaviour. When asked to describe marketing, most consumers would start off with specific advertisements they have seen and offers they have taken up or rejected. This awareness reflects the success of advertising and sales promotion in establishing their presence. It is this access to the buyer or prospective buyer that the firm seeks when considering an investment in advertising or sales promotion.

The nature and scale of advertising

Advertising is purposive communication. The firm spends its money to communicate with groups in the market-place and achieve certain results. The objectives can vary enormously and the means of reaching customer groups have evolved over time to service these needs. The simplest form is the individual trying to sell her car through classified ads; the most complex form is corporate advertising for a giant multinational, trying to create a favourable climate for the firm's operations, improve the image of its product offerings, boost company morale and establish specific links with the market. Although advertising has established a high level of awareness, the proportion of the UK Gross National Product invested in media advertising is small – 1.37 per cent in 1988 (see Table 21.1). This is high in European terms but lower than in the US. Even if the most generous estimates of the scale of sales promotional activity are incorporated, it is still below 2 per cent.

Media advertising

The American Marketing Association defined advertising as:

Any paid form of non-personal presentation and promotion of ideas, goods or services by an identifiable sponsor.

The overwhelming majority of the expenditure is directed through press and television (Table 21.2).

Table 21.1 Advertising as a percentage of Gross National Product

Country	1984	1985	1986	1987	1988	1992	1996
Belgium	0.53	0.54	0.56	0.56	0.58	0.70	0.76
Denmark	1.02	1.06	1.11	1.11	1.10	1.10	1.09
France	0.56	0.59	0.63	0.70	0.73	0.90	1.00
Germany	0.90	0.88	0.89	0.90	0.79	1.00	1.12
Greece	0.44	0.44	0.55	0.60	0.57	0.60	0.70
Ireland	0.65	0.70	0.80	0.77	0.76	0.80	0.95
Italy	0.69	0.74	0.78	0.74	0.62	0.90	1.05
Netherlands	0.90	0.90	0.99	0.98	1.00	1.10	1.21
Portugal	0.27	0.24	0.35	0.37	0.37	0.60	0.70
Spain	0.92	1.00	1.16	1.30	1.32	1.30	1.30
UK	1.27	1.26	1.37	1.47	1.50	1.50	1.56
US	1.55	1.48	1.59	1.62	1.61	1.70	1.72
Japan	0.74	0.71	0.70	0.71	0.70	0.90	1.00

Table 21.2 Total advertising expenditure, including direct mail, for the UK, £m

	1990	1991	1992	1993	1994	1995
National newspapers	1,187	1,121	1,155	1,220	1,336	1,433
Regional newspapers	1,715	1,628	1,640	1,715	1,871	1,963
Consumer magazines	541	506	466	448	499	533
Business and professional	790	708	746	714	828	898
Directories	492	504	523	551	589	639
Press production costs	412	417	427	438	478	514
Total press	5,317	4,884	4,957	5,085	5,600	5,980
Television	2,325	2,295	2,472	2,605	2,873	3,103
Direct mail	979	895	945	90	1,050	1,135
Outdoor and transport	282	267	284	300	350	378
Radio	163	149	157	194	243	296
Cinema	39	42	45	49	53	69
Total	8,925	8,532	8,859	9,140	10,169	10,961

Source: Advertising Association.

Advertising as an industry has emerged partly in response to the needs of firms to communicate with their customers during a period in which markets have become larger, more diffuse and more competitive, and partly as a reflection of the media owners' ability to provide the means of effective, purposive communication.

The revolution in thinking about newspaper financing initiated by Lord Northcliffe with the *Daily Mail* in 1896 brought together the need of manufacturers to reach their customers and that of newspaper proprietors to keep their cover prices down through the sale of advertising space, and this is still an important part of the current advertising industry. New media have emerged, with the balance of relationships, the skills and the techniques changing over time, but the mutually supportive relationship persists.

There are now three parties involved in the advertising process: the advertiser, who supplies products or services; the advertising agency, who translates the advertiser's message into a form appropriate to the medium and relevant to the prospective customer, places the advertisements and are legally responsible for the space bought;[1] and the media owner, who provides the vehicle for reaching the specific target groups or audiences. Originally the agencies were literally the agents of the media, paid a commission on their sales of space.

Although the character of the relationship has changed over the years, with agencies focusing their talents and developing skills to meet the needs of advertisers, the form of payment, by commission from the media, has remained basically constant.[2] In a sense this meets the needs of all parties: the agent has increased independence, the media owner has a secure relationship with a body of experts in communication, and the advertiser has access to a wide and varied group of autonomous specialists. The complexity of the media, their interplay, the varied goals of firms and the different responses of consuming groups all call for highly developed talents in communication.

Table 21.3 Total advertising expenditure, including direct mail, as a percentage of total (UK)

	1990	1991	1992	1993	1994	1995
National newspapers	13.3	13.1	13.0	13.3	13.1	13.1
Regional newspapers	19.2	19.1	18.5	18.8	18.4	17.9
Consumer magazines	6.1	5.9	5.3	4.9	4.9	4.9
Business and professional	8.9	8.3	8.4	7.8	8.1	8.2
Directories	5.5	5.9	5.9	6.0	5.8	5.8
Press production costs	4.6	4.9	4.8	4.8	4.7	4.7
Total press	57.6	57.2	55.9	55.6	55.1	54.6
Television	26.0	26.9	27.9	28.5	28.3	28.3
Direct mail	11.0	10.5	10.7	9.9	10.3	10.4
Outdoor and transport	3.2	3.1	3.2	3.3	3.4	3.4
Radio	1.8	1.7	1.8	2.1	2.4	2.7
Cinema	0.4	0.5	0.5	0.5	0.5	0.6
Total	100.0	100.0	100.0	100.0	100.0	100.0

Source: Advertising Association.

The agency may be called upon to devise a campaign to put across varied and subtle ideas to an audience which may not be particularly interested in them and may be unaware of the transmission of the message, in the space of a 15-second commercial or in a newspaper advertisement. At the same time, the scope for a particular form of expression is limited by the regulations of the British Code of Advertising Practice.

Table 21.4 All-Europe advertising media split

Year	Print (%)	TV (%)	Radio (%)	Cinema (%)	Outdoor (%)
1985	68.0	21.2	4.1	0.8	5.9
1986	67.5	21.8	4.2	0.7	5.9
1987	66.4	22.7	4.2	0.7	6.0

Source: Andrew Green, 'International Advertising Trends', *International Journal of Advertising*, 8 , No. 1, 1989, p. 92

Advertising media

The media have played a major part in the evolution of advertising through the provision of access to consuming and decision-making groups, by supplying an environment for specific forms and styles of advertisement, by developing a cost structure and research into audience characteristics, and through a recognition of the interplay of specific media, advertisements and campaigns.

Access

The media provide advertisers with access to prospective purchasers both in general and in specialist groups.[3] Before the advent of television, the national newspapers were the sole means (in the UK) of reaching the mass market quickly and effectively. The huge circulations of the 'popular' daily and Sunday papers were the major incentive for firms to use them. However, the growth of television has led to a revision of thinking about newspaper audiences, and it has been recognized that the selective character of readership is as important as the sheer size of the market. This has coincided with a progressive change in the relative market share of the 'quality' compared to the 'popular' press. The regional newspapers have for many years been the largest single area of advertising expenditure. Their firm basis in the local community has given them real strength in specific areas, particularly classified advertisements. These dominate the advertising expenditure in the regional press, accounting for 60 per cent of all expenditure compared to 12.5 per cent in the nationals in 1989.

This reveals how important the local press can be to advertisers. Messages directly relevant to the community served, perhaps geared to action in the near future, can have great impact. Retail advertising, local event promotions and producers attempting to build a strong regional base for their output provide the majority of non-classified regional advertising, and the low absolute cost of space allows these small advertisers to use the medium. Under certain circumstances the local press has been used in national campaigns, e.g. to boost coverage in areas of special interest or to bring out regional aspects of the message.

Achieving access to the many specialist-interest groups is made relatively easy for the advertiser through magazines catering for specific market segments and the trade press. These range from the huge-circulation women's magazines to relatively small-volume technical and trade publications. The advertiser can define the target group with a high degree of accuracy and can focus all media expenditure on them. The detailed interest which readers have in the subject matter of specialist magazines usually means that they carefully read all the content, including advertisements. Many non-regular readers purchase such magazines when considering purchases, partly to search the advertisements. A clear definition of the target market should be compared with the readership profiles of the magazines, and much background information about their readers is available from publishers themselves.

Industrial and commercial advertising has grown dramatically during the1970s and 1980s partly because of the five-fold increase in retail advertising. During the same period industrial advertising has increased two and a half times. A great deal of expenditure has been directed towards the trade and technical press and magazines, which provides advertisers with the opportunity to direct their messages towards the experts in the field of interest. The purchasing and influencing power of relatively few people can determine the success of these efforts, and the interest in the product offerings often leads to follow-up of advertisements. British industrial advertisers have the advantage of being able to advertise in leading UK and US journals, which often reach overseas markets and provide valuable export leads.

Magazines such as *The Engineer, Design* and *Nuclear News* have a worldwide readership and reputation which advertisers can turn to their own advantage. In the context of industrial media it is worth noting the growth of trade directories, buyers' guides, annuals and, a more recent development, controlled circulation papers. Trade directories have long been invaluable to the professional buyer, who knows that a careful search of the ABC directory will identify a number of prospective suppliers. More recently, specialist-interest groups have published guides to their industry, e.g. *The European Plastics Guide*, or even to their region, e.g. *North East Buyers' Guide*. There is some evidence that purchasing officers are increasingly using these as the starting point in their search for supplies.

So far our attention has been focused on the variety of the press media, but interest in the selectivity of these media has been stimulated by the growth of television as the dominant mass medium. Only the Sunday papers can effectively compete with the top television programmes.

The overwhelming majority of homes in the UK have television receivers capable of receiving ITV programmes from the regional contractors (Figure 21.1). Using this network it is possible to reach an enormous national audience simultaneously with a single message. However, only the largest advertisers would beam their transmission out in this way. Most advertisers use the regions selectively, attempting to combine number of 'impressions' with a degree of targeting. Major regional advertisers will direct their efforts solely towards their particular areas. Some organizations combine national campaigns devised centrally with regional messages; for example, British Gas will run campaigns nationally while locally it promotes on Granada Television the range of cookers in gas showrooms. Some smaller television regions obtain a significant proportion of their income from test marketing in their region, with local advertising often earning significant media discounts.

> New products or services, or products or services not advertised on
> television before and which are advertised either exclusively in Scotland,
> or in Scotland and one television area within the UK, will qualify for a 25
> per cent reduction. (*British Rate and Data*)

Major changes have been taking place over the past few years, notably Channel 5, Satellite TV and cable television. The next few years will see new developments as hundreds of digital channels come on air.

In 1973 the first commercial radio stations based on the mainland of Britain started broadcasting, the way having been paved by Radio Luxembourg and the off-shore 'pirate' radio stations. Although many of the pioneer stations suffered teething troubles, commercial radio has now long been established as an important part of the media profile. Now, the range of specialist national radio channels is expanding through stations like Classic FM, Jazz FM and Virgin. Many British stations are confined to specific urban areas (Piccadilly in Manchester, Radio Clyde in Glasgow, Radio City in Liverpool). Their specific audience profiles vary considerably, with overall strengths among housewives, young people and commuting motorists. Leading national advertisers are finding that radio provides an access to specific groups that are difficult to reach by other media, e.g. the young, or provides access in particularly favourable circumstances, e.g. housewives planning their shopping. More recently specialized stations such as Manchester's Sun Radio and a network of community radio have added further diversity to the system.

Poster and transport advertising has traditionally been faced with severe access problems. The most important of these for the poster industry have been the lack of detailed audience data

Figure 21.1 The IBA companies and their potential audiences

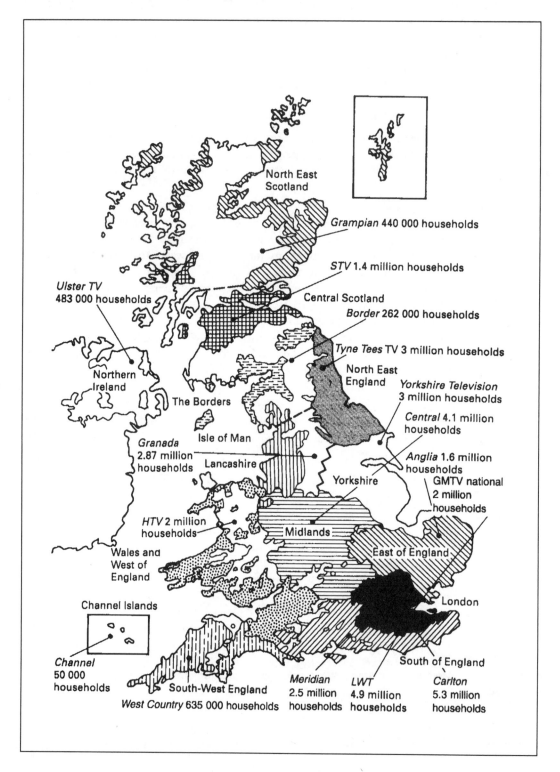

and the overwhelming dominance of the best sites by relatively few industries, which hold them on long-term contracts. The majority of the population has the opportunity to see (OTS) posters every day, and certain specific sites have very high OTS scores for their area. The cigarette and liquor industries have built up massive portfolios of such sites in order to keep their products visible to customers,[4] and until recently this prevented the generally fragmented poster industry from offering meaningful coverage to prospective clients.[5]

The 1980s saw progressive rationalization and a greater willingness to co-operate in the poster industry, which in turn encouraged more advertisers to use posters. However, further broadening of the industry's base is dependent on the policies adopted towards and by the cigarette and liquor advertisers. Transport advertising, with its similar dependence on these advertisers plus a few specific groups, e.g. cinemas and 'own' advertising (BR, London Regional Transport), has long been the Cinderella of the outdoor media. It offers a large number of access points to the travelling public on road and rail in airports and ports. Transport authorities, particularly London Regional Transport, are now adopting a much more aggressive approach to marketing their product, but there is still the major problem that the lack of data leads the advertiser to view the poster or transport media audience as relatively undifferentiated other than by area. The emphasis on selectivity of audience by advertisers has created problems for the industry.

This interest in selectivity has helped the cinema advertising industry to maintain its share of media advertising despite the rapidly escalating costs of producing films suitable for cinema broadcast. The boom in cinema audiences in the late 1980s and 1990s shifted the audience profile from its traditional dominance by the young (under 24) and unmarried. This powerful consumer group, with its high discretionary income and little reluctance to spend it on acquiring material possessions, is of tremendous importance to producers of leisure goods, clothing, cosmetics and specific consumer durables (cars, motorbikes, watches etc.). Although these factors are important to the national advertiser, local advertisers use cinema to reach specific local-interest groups. The cinema audience has shown itself to be extremely changeable; new styles, notably the multiplexes, have changed the profile and range of audiences. Popular films such as *Trainspotting* and *Titanic* reached new and diverse audiences. These are important considerations for any prospective cinema advertiser, whose returns on a major investment in a commercial are partly dependent on the success of specific films.

Environment

Although the access to an audience provided by a medium is a critical factor, very few advertising media are thought of by their audience as merely a source of advertising information, or by the advertiser as a blank sheet of paper to be managed to the advertiser's specific advantage. All the media and the specific advertising vehicles impart their own characteristics to the advertisements appearing in them. These may be structural (newspapers are static and generally black and white, while television commercials are mobile and usually in colour) or they may be determined by specific contexts (the *Mirror* and the *Sun* have a specific style and method of presentation which can make an advertisement designed for the *Financial Times* totally ineffective). These environmental factors provide the canvas for the creativity of the advertiser and determine the effectiveness of the copy placed in front of specific customer groups.

The complexity of the press media almost defies any global categorization. Even the conventional notion of the static nature of media can be confounded by the near genius of some creative teams. Creativity in the face of the variety of the media is capable of refuting almost any of the general points made below. Traditionally, there has been some tension between researchers and creative groups. This is slowly eroding as both learn to appreciate the contribution each makes to effectiveness.[6]

The static character of newspapers is a constraint on advertising. However, the impact of effective copy can be tremendous. The reader makes a conscious effort to purchase a newspaper, searching for news, interest and stimulation. This provides the opportunity to relate the advertisements to this search. However, those who really satisfy these needs are the paper's own journalists and editorial staff. Advertisements are competing for impact against immediacy of the news itself. Two positive[7] approaches to this problem have been adopted. The advertisements can compete for impact (Figure 21.2):

Figure 21.2 Stanley's advertisement competes for impact with the headlines. Reproduced with the permission of the *Daily Record*.

> Out of 4,850 (newspaper ads) I managed to find nine. (John Webster, Creative Director of BMP)[8]

or they can recognize their difference (Figure 21.3):

> An advertisement either has to set out to do what the editorial does or it has to do the opposite . . . Most of the eight (ads) I have picked are opposites. (E. McCabe, Senior Vice President, Scali, McCabe Sloves Inc.)[9]

Figure 21.3 The Mitsubishi ad communicates movement in a static medium

Magazines add another dimension to the environment of the advertisements that appear. Many offer colour, which brings a vitality and impact achievable in only the very best black and white copy. The interest and involvement of the readers provide the ideal focus on leisure; the traditional women's magazines (*Woman's Own*), with their emphasis on the home; the modern women's magazines (*Vogue, Cosmopolitan, Company, Minx, Frank*), catering for very diffuse groups, and the special-interest magazines (*Custom Car, Popular Photography, Byte*) are only a few of the vehicles offering opportunities to weld a specific offering to the acknowledged interest of the reader. The success of men's magazines like *Loaded* has created new promotional opportunities.

These often have the great advantage of gaining longer and repeated exposure: a newspaper is normally finished within a day, while the *TV Times* boasts that it is 'the nine-day magazine'. The potential impact of the TV magazines has increased with the freedom to include full listings, i.e. all channels. Regular contributors to specialist magazines may keep them indefinitely. The use of magazines as reference sources is an important characteristic of much of the trade and technical press. Company libraries and individuals will keep specific periodicals for many years, referring back again and again to specific issues and occasionally even individual advertisements. This information element has led David Ogilvy to recommend advertisers to use case histories and testimonials, demonstrate and use long copy. The readers are specialists and will be selective. When they refer to an advertisement it will be for a purpose, and information will help them to recognize the value of your offering in solving their problems.

> Print is the purest form of advertising. It puts the creative mind one-on-one against a blank sheet of paper. With no outside influences. No tricks. No gimmicks. No hiding behind actors or music jokes or props. When it comes to print, it's just you, that blank sheet of paper – and the moment of truth for the creative person. (Hank Seidon, Executive Vice President, Hacks and Greist) [10]

Marshall McLuhan, the media expert, contrasts the 'hot' medium of paper with the 'cool' medium of television. The emergence of television, entering the audience's homes with vision, sound, movement and colour, added a new dimension to the media environment. The home environment is both a blessing and a curse. The well-designed advertisement is like a welcome visitor, achieving an impact and audience unrivalled by other media. The structural characteristics of the medium are creatively combined with the specific context of the transmission to achieve a rapport with the target audience.

The poor advertisement, however, is an unwelcome intrusion into the evening's enjoyment and can alienate prospective purchasers. It must be recognized that these advertisements are directed towards specific audiences and objectives, and it is their contribution in those directions which determines their value, not winning awards or praise from non-target groups. The medium does have operational constraints. In 15 to 30 seconds a message which may have taken months to develop must be delivered in such a way as to elicit the required response from the audience without unnecessarily alienating other groups and at the same time comply with the regulatory requirements of the government and other agencies. The following simple rules appear to contribute to more effective commercials: [11]

1 The picture must tell a story.
2 Provide a 'key visual'.
3 Grab the viewer's attention.
4 Be single-minded.
5 Register the name of your product.
6 Show people, not objects.
7 Have a pay-off.
8 Reflect your product personality.
9 Avoid 'talky' commercials.
10 Build campaigns, not individual commercials.

This recognition of the environment in which the message is received is particularly important for the minor media, i.e. posters and transport, radio and cinema. Much of their value is derived from the specific circumstances in which messages are received and the attitude of the audience towards them.

Posters are seldom studied carefully. They are geared towards the passer-by, who may even be isolated from the media in a car or on a bus, so the copy or visual must break into the audience's consciousness to deliver its message. A great deal of poster advertising is effective in providing supportive, reminder impacts behind a campaign being carried on through other media. Smaller sites are used in shopping centres to trigger off purchase-linked behaviour. Different effects can be achieved by different poster sizes and locations. Sizes are usually in multiples of 30 by 20 inches (Figure 21.4).

Figure 21.4 Poster sizes

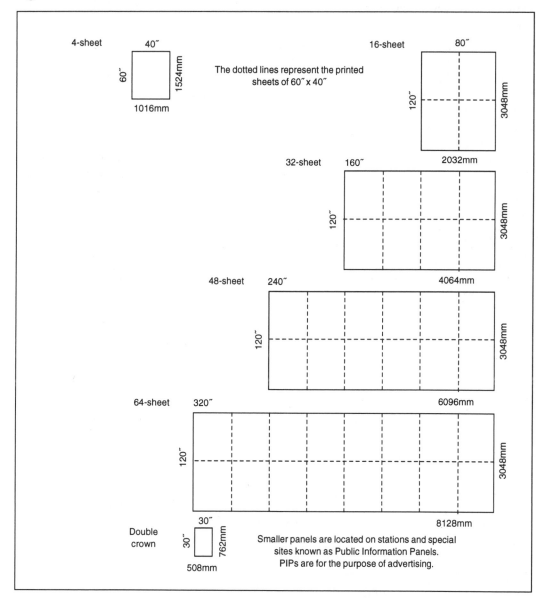

The last decade has seen the emergence of radio as an important medium, with its own distinctive style and environment. Most of the stations are based in urban centres, drawing their audiences from the locality and rapidly establishing powerful links with the immediate community. The music of local radio has rapidly become the continuous background in houses while the housework is being done and in the car while travelling. The nature of the content has led to local radio being particularly popular among the young, who are both difficult to reach by other media and often fiercely loyal to the local station and specific DJs. During the day local radio creates an environment in which shopping-linked, local messages can be transmitted, e.g. 'Visit Savacentre now for bargains in the food department'. Directed at both the housewife and the motorist, these messages can establish a strong purchase link.

However, messages which fail to recognize the impact on their advertisements of the context of 'music background' can easily be lost in that background. The message must instantly establish a memorable impression on the target audience. It appears that listeners are willing to stretch their imaginations in interpreting messages, and this has allowed some advertisers to be extremely imaginative and evocative. Other advertisers have effectively translated campaigns from other media to radio. Problems do exist, however, particularly in adapting for radio advertisements which normally have powerful visual images. As indicated above, involvement is an important aspect of any medium. It is difficult to achieve this in the home, where many distractions surround the commercials. It has been estimated that over half the audience are engaged in some other activity during commercial breaks – leaving the room, doing domestic chores, switching channels etc.

However, this is not a problem for cinema advertisers. The cinema is blacked out and attention is focused on the screen, so the opportunity exists to establish a powerful link with the audience. However, the audience is generally young and expects to be entertained, so the entertainment value of any cinema advertisement must be extremely high, competing as it does with the multi-million dollar movie offering which follows. Effectively produced commercials can thrive on the atmosphere, but poor advertisements quickly die.

Costs

Advertising costs are made up of two distinct but interrelated elements: exposure costs for space and time, and production costs. A rough rule of thumb puts production costs at 10 per cent of exposure costs, although specific circumstances can distort that balance. *British Rate and Data* is the bible of the UK media planner. It appears every month and provides details of the costs of all media for specific spaces and timings. These costs must be viewed in terms of both absolute cost, e.g. £32,500 for an unspecified[12] page in *The Mirror*, and cost to reach a specific audience. The concept of cost per thousand is used to highlight the real costs per thousand of the audience using specific media. For example, the absolute cost of a full page in the *News of the World* is far higher than a full page in the *Daily Post*, but the readerships are so different in size that the cost per thousand is far higher in the *Daily Post* than in the *News of the World*. It is therefore better for an advertiser who can afford the absolute cost to invest funds in the medium offering the lowest cost per thousand for the target audience. This proviso about the target audience is very important. There is generally little point in investing funds in getting the lowest absolute cost if the cost of reaching the target audience is higher.

Research into audiences and their characteristics is a continuing process. The basic source of newspaper-audience data is the National Readership Survey, which annually samples 30,000 individuals aged 15 and over. The survey measures readership of over 100 publications, including all major newspapers and magazines. A similar function is performed for television by JICTAR, which is a national panel of 2,700 homes containing 7,000 individuals aged four and over. Minute-by-minute home ratings for all channels are produced by a meter on the TV set. Similar information on poster audiences is collected by JICPAS, and on radio audiences by JICRAR. The Screen Advertisers' Association performs a roughly similar service for cinema. These surveys are only the tip of a massive iceberg of continuing study: advertising agencies, large advertisers and the media owners themselves perform regular studies of their audiences and their characteristics.

Interplay

It is dangerous to think of advertising in terms of single advertisements in individual media. Even the smallest advertisers should plan their activities in terms of bringing all their sales promotion together in a promotional campaign. The classified advertisement provides the information to stimulate contacts, and the selling process relates to the classified advertisement to ensure that the best sales prospects are seen, with neither seller nor prospective purchaser wasting time. In planning substantial advertising efforts a campaign approach is central. The overall plan is identified, and each advertisement and all the media are reviewed in terms of their contribution to the plan. The target audience can be as specific as 'all readers of the *Manchester Evening News*', but a significant proportion of *News* readers will not buy the paper on a specific night, and a large number will not notice the advertisement. Thus even defining the market in terms of a specific newspaper will involve repeats, which pose their own creative problems, e.g. what is the advertisement's effect on those seeing it for the third or fourth time?

Very seldom is the specific audience of an individual medium anything better than an approximation of the firm's target audience. A million buyers of *The Mirror* are only a small part of the C2DE population of the UK, although it is true that repeats in *The Mirror* will gradually increase the coverage of the newspaper[13] (Figure 21.5). Using other newspapers and additional media may mean better returns (in terms of market penetration) for additional expenditure (Figure 21.6). This pattern occurs in both one-medium and multi-media advertising: repeated exposures in a single medium lead to diminishing returns for money spent in terms of audience reached, and adding further media, even with smaller audiences, may improve penetration of the target audience. It is worth remembering that people employ a number of media in their lives (an estimated 40 per cent of *Mirror* readers also read the *Sun*, and the majority of TV viewers will also see posters), so a scheduling decision must take this into account. This interplay can also be effectively used to add further dimensions to the campaign, e.g. to build up images using TV and colour magazines, to remind and heighten brand-name consciousness through posters, to suggest action in the press and on radio, and to trigger purchase at point of sale. The concepts of campaigning and interplay are central to any decision on budgets and schedules.

Figure 21.5 Diminishing returns from concentrating on a single newspaper

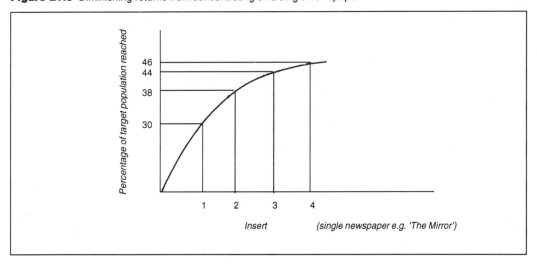

Figure 21.6 Increasing returns from spreading coverage

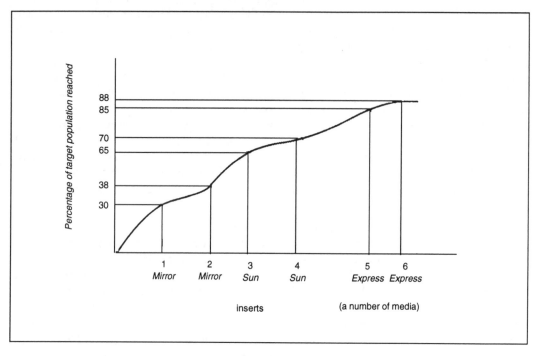

Setting the advertising budget

The firm's advertising budget sets the limits within which the media planner must operate and is thus a major factor in determining the extent to which the firm's advertising objectives can be achieved. A certain minimum level of exposure is necessary before even the best advertising can have any effect. There are a number of basic approaches to setting the total budget.

Affordability

Setting the budget on the basis of affordability is probably the most fundamental approach. The company decides (probably subjectively) how much it can afford, and these funds are then allocated to the different media. Although this approach is very common, particularly among small and industrial firms, it derives from a total misconception of advertising by which advertising is treated as a luxury to be indulged in when times are good and dropped when times are bad. In fact, advertising is vital for building links with customers, the basis of every strong firm. Research has indicated that

> (increased) advertising during depression generally resulted in an increase in sales relative to the sales of competitors who did not make such increases.[14]

Percentage of sales method

The percentage of sales method sets the advertising budget as a simple percentage of either sales during last full year or forecast sales of the budget year. This avoids the severe fluctuations in expenditure which often occur with the 'affordable' approach. At the same time, it is a simple method of solving the problem of different opinions about what the firm can afford; for example, the sales manager may say £100,000 and the finance director £1,000. However, this approach treats advertising almost as a tax on sales, implying that advertising results from sales, not vice versa.

The competitive parity approach

Taking the competitive parity approach looks beyond the firm to the competitive environment. The company locates itself in terms of its perceived competitors and invests the amount appropriate to its position in the market. This method almost totally ignores the firm's customers and its own needs, assuming that its goals and objectives are the same as its competitors'. Equally important, it presupposes that the competition know what they are doing and are adopting a planned approach to setting their budgets.

The objective and task method

The objective and task method involves the firm establishing its advertising goals and making available funds sufficient to achieve them. It is usually seen as the optimum method of exploiting the purposive character of advertising. The resources are made available to perform the task set.

Combining the approaches

In fact the majority of firms adopt some combination of these methods. Setting the budget is not a once-and-for-all task. Appropriations are proposed (by line managers), discussed and reviewed (by managers, agencies and directors) and determined (by the board). When circumstances change, the sensible firm modifies its position. In this process all four approaches described above play a part:

1 Advertising objectives are set by top management for all brands. The brand managers (probably after discussions with the agencies) indicate the budgets required.
2 Top management relate these to hard criteria such as current sales of brands, perhaps indicating a percentage of sales which might be available. Some firms will even distinguish between types of sale, e.g. 5 per cent of historic sales, 15 per cent on new sales.
3 Considerable discussion usually ensues, particularly in firms with a number of products and brands attempting to achieve their objectives with limited resources. Competitive advertising levels play a major part in establishing the realistic nature of budgets and objectives.
4 Assuming that the budgets finally agreed can be 'afforded', given the many other demands on company resources, the firm determines its advertising budget. The agency is then officially notified of the sums it can spend to achieve agreed objectives.

Throughout this process the lessons that the firm has learned in previous years provide the backcloth to discussions and decisions. Information about responses in the market-place to company expenditure is a vital element in budgeting, and in the US larger firms conduct market experiments to help determine advertising expenditure.

Scheduling

Once a budget is set, the media scheduling task is to achieve the most efficient allocation of the funds among alternative media and over time. These two decisions, where and when, constitute the basic task of the media planner. A good brief is vital to the planners as their proposed schedules in terms of number of media and alternatives within media, number of insertions and balance of types of insertion, and timing are functions of the type of audience wanted, target number of exposures and desired response. Scheduling is an area which involves both sophisticated computer-based models, based on linear programming, simulation and other techniques, and individual media-buying skills where the buyer's negotiating ability is critical.

The role of an advertising agency

Throughout this discussion advertising agencies and specific tasks identified with them – media buying and scheduling, creative development, communications development – have been mentioned. This reflects the development of the agency from the days when its brokerage task dominated, to today, when an awareness of the total communication is vital. Through this process two key features have been important:

1 *Agencies are outside the advertiser's firm.* The independent perspective they can provide is necessary for the firm wanting a realistic judgement of its work. This independence allows a degree of honest appraisal not always within the producer's firm.
2 *Agencies work for many clients.* This enables them to feed into the companies' policies an extremely wide range of ideas and experiences. It is particularly important for creative workers to avoid the staleness which can occur when handling only one product or a narrow range of products.

Although this implies that all advertising agencies are very similar, in fact they operate as very individual entities. Powerful and creative personalities dominate the agency world to a degree unusual in industry. The character of the industry provides the talented with almost unrivalled opportunities to stamp their own personalities both on their firms and on advertising in general. The industry's role today is very much the creation of people like Charles Saatchi and David Ogilvy.

The structure of an agency

Agencies differ enormously in size, structure and range of services. There are creative 'hot shops' whose sole activity is creative development, with very few ancillary activities. Media-buying agencies have emerged over the last few years to provide centralized space-buying services. Their expertise is in media, in which they offer special discounts, but they offer little support in other areas. However, the majority of agencies retain a full service capability, attempting to match the complete range of client needs with the services they offer, i.e. creative services, media services, marketing services, account planning and handling and occasionally PR and below-the-line promotions. An example of the structure of an advertising agency is shown in Figure 21.7 (see page 388).

The recruitment, selection, management motivation and control of agencies is a continuing concern of most firms. An outsider looking at the advertising press would get the impression that accounts are constantly on the move from agency to agency, but in fact many of the most successful agency–client relationships endure for decades. Some degree of mobility is probably an advantage, as it introduces new ideas and keeps agencies alert, but although it may be a good thing in general, it is not necessarily so for specific accounts. This is one reason why the largest advertisers employ a number of agencies.

They are often involved in new product launches, and a successful launch may mean long-term good billings for the agency. The Creative Business was founded by David Bernstein, one of the leading company image specialists in Britain, to provide a hot shop environment for company image development. He comments:

> Image is reality.
>
> It is the result of our actions.
>
> If the image is false and our performance is good, it's our fault for being bad communicators.
>
> If the image is true and it reflects our bad performance, it's our fault for being bad managers.
>
> Unless we know about our image we can neither communicate nor manage.[15]

Objectives in advertising

The clear communication of objectives is essential to a strong client–agency relationship. In this discussion two distinct areas are examined: how advertising works – the overall ways in which advertising can contribute to company objectives; and the definitions of specific tasks for individual campaigns or advertisements.

How advertising works

A number of models which attempt to describe the way in which advertising affects the customer have been suggested. The majority assume that the task of advertising is to help the customer move through a series of states of mind, usually starting with 'unawareness' and ending with 'action' (Table 21.5).

These models provide a useful way of thinking about the way consumers respond to advertising and the consequent tasks of advertisements or campaigns. They are used in both industrial[16] and consumer advertising[17] There is, however, no evidence that consumers move through the stages in the manner described or that any specific advertisements propel the prospective buyers along in the way suggested. However, advertising does appear to be important in:

1 *Information communication:* in terms of absolute expenditure this is probably the single most important task set.
2 *Highlighting specific features:* the concept of the unique selling proposition (USP) suggested that by bringing out a single unique element in the product offering, directly related to a buyer need, advertising could establish a link between prospect and product that would lead to purchase-directed action.
3 *Building up an overall 'brand image':* image-building advertising contrasts with USP advertising by emphasizing the total product offering. The different characteristics of the brand are brought together in a creative whole which relates to the overall needs of groups of buyers of the product category.

4   *Reinforcing behaviour:* research has indicated that attitudes are very dependent on previous behaviour. The positive attitudes of existing buyers can be effectively reinforced, enhancing brand or product loyalty.

5   *Influencing intermediaries:* much advertising is geared to winning shelf space in retail outlets for the company's offerings. Even when this is not a primary task of advertisements, it is still an important function.

In achieving all these goals it must be stressed that it is the product or service offered which is important and the consumer's positive responses must be in that direction, not towards the advertisement or slogan.

Table 21.5 Advertising task and consumer's state of mind

| | Models | | |
| | | | |
DAGMAR	The Lavidge and Steiner Model	AIDA	Advertising task
1. Unaware	1. Awareness	1. Awareness	Moving the customer through the early
2. Aware	2. Knowledge	2. Interest	stages is usually seen as the information task
3. Comprehension	3. Liking	3. Desire	of advertising. Ultimately the consumer
4. Conviction	4. Preference	4. Action	must be persuaded to take action to
5. Action	5. Conviction		purchase the product. Starch argues that an
	6. Purchase		advertisement must be seen, read, believed and then acted upon.

Defining specific tasks for individual campaigns or advertisements

Clear and actionable objectives and goals are very important in advertising, with the advertisers' need to operate through intermediaries, their distance from the point of purchase and long response time scales. Objectives must be set, openly discussed with the agency and clearly communicated to all those involved in achieving them. The primary objectives set by a firm may be:

1   *To inform:* on its own 'to inform' is meaningless. The target group and the time scale within which it will be informed must be identified, e.g. 'to inform all C2DE housewives currently using electric cookers over ten years old that the South-Eastern Electricity Board is offering £25 on their cookers with new cooker purchases'. The information can be directed to many groups and focuses on many marketing areas, e.g. price offers available in new outlets, new forms, at new terms or in new markets.

2   *To build up an image of the brand or highlight certain features:* this must be stated much more clearly. The statement or objective should be clearly reviewed so that the firm can measure its effectiveness, e.g. 'To establish X as the most prestigious brand in the market-place, it should be clearly preferred by all buyers to whom price is relatively unimportant. It should be aspired to by all other buyers.' Images can be defined in many ways and in many circumstances: a common image-building objective in fast-moving consumer-goods markets is to distinguish clearly the brand from own-label products.

3   *To reinforce behaviour:* this can be restated to highlight the specific behaviour patterns that are to be reinforced, e.g. 'To increase usage of the drink among AB customers who currently only purchase it at Christmas. The overall special image is

to be maintained by focusing on other family festivals: birthdays, weddings, Easter etc.' This reinforcement can even involve persuading buyers to act now; e.g. reducing the period between furniture changes will dramatically improve the furniture industry's profits.

Although the definition of advertising goals lies at the core of effective advertising, rigour is often neglected in favour of detailed discussion of specific creative presentations, artwork quality or even appropriateness of particular models.

Evaluating advertising

It is perhaps characteristic of the advertising industry that one of the most popular quotes about the effectiveness of advertising is 'We know that 50 per cent of our advertising is effective but we don't know which 50 per cent'. This reflects the difficulty of making any universal comments about attempts to measure the effectiveness of advertising, particularly in increasing sales. A number of large-scale studies have been sponsored by research institutes, government departments and firms themselves. Some have shown considerable promise in specific product fields and under particular circumstances, but none has been universally applicable.

This is not surprising in the light of the relatively small amount of marketing expenditure accounted for by advertising, the diffuse objectives set by advertising, the heterogeneous nature of markets and the very complex nature of consumer behaviour. For the individual firm at a specific point in time these studies are not important. The key is still the firm's objectives and the contribution of advertising to achieving these objectives.

A carefully planned, implemented and sustained process of monitoring the performances of advertising in the market-place is essential. This can be directed towards the broad advertising tasks identified earlier.

1   *Task: to inform.* Evaluation: recall – the extent to which the advertising message is read, noted and remembered (spontaneously and prompted). 'Reading and noting scores' are regularly collected for the main press media and spontaneous and prompted recollection of the advertisements and specific features is measured by a number of market research agencies.
2   *Task: image-building.* Evaluation: awareness – overall awareness of the firm, its specific product offering and the message of specific advertisements can be studied through structured questionnaires.
3   *Task: behaviour reinforcement.* Evaluation: attitude research – this is a critical area of modern research. However, there are problems of effective measurement and interpretation of results. In-depth interviews and group discussions are often used to study this area.
4   *Task: action.* Evaluation: sales research – a regular appraisal of sent-out sales, retail ordering, stocks and consumer purchases geared to both the immediate and lagged effects of advertising.

Hastings and Leather[18] propose a model (Figure 21.8) of the advertising research process which highlights the continuous nature of research and the value of feedback loops.

Most of this discussion has been directed towards mainstream media advertising. Direct-mail advertisers to both industrial and consumer groups have coupon returns, product purchases and the number of sales visits stimulated as a basis for measurement.

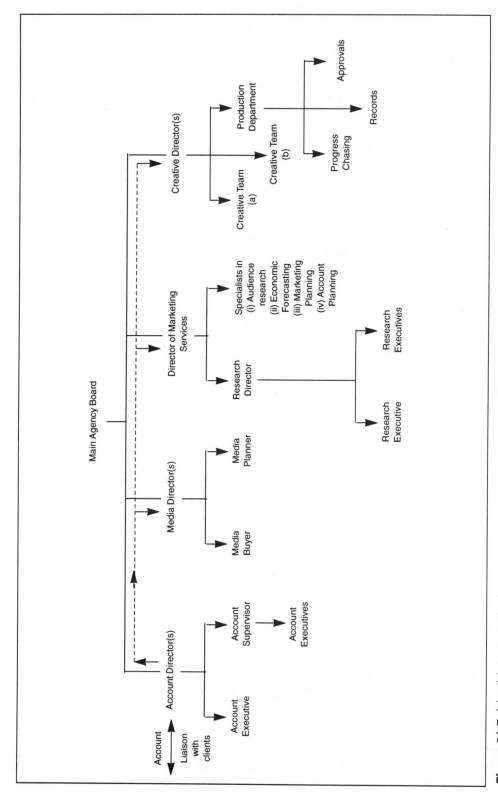

Figure 21.7 Advertising agency structure

Non-media advertising

Non-media or below-the-line[19] advertising is one of the fastest-growing areas of activity in modern marketing. Much of this growth has been stimulated by the direct purchase link which often occurs with a sales promotion: the promotion can be taken up only if the product is bought (sometimes repeatedly). This is important in building up short-term sales volume and provides an effective means of directly tracing the pay-offs from any promotional activity. Growth in this area over the last decade has been considerable, in both the absolute amount of activity and the areas in which non-media advertising is used.

Figure 21.8 The advertising research process. (*Source:* Hastings and Leather[18])

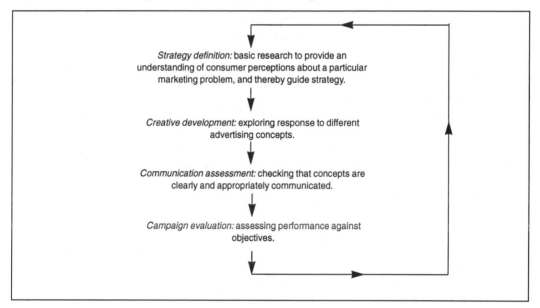

Typology of non-media advertising

Consumer

1 *On-pack offers:* free flowers with detergents are the classic example; they are often used by magazines, e.g. motoring magazines giving away simple tools.
2 *Free samples:* small packing pushed through letter-box or invitations to be sent in to manufacturer for samples.
3 *Free gifts:* these are frequently linked with loyalty-building activity requiring a number of packet tops, coupons or trading stamps.
4 *Coupon offers:* distributed through retailers and door to door, they often involve money off the purchase of specific products or in particular outlets.
5 *Competitions:* this activity, although still popular, faces problems of the ingenuity of professional entrants and the complexity of the law.
6 *Exhibitions and demonstrations:* these range from giants such as the Ideal Homes Exhibition and the Motor Show to small in-store demonstrations.
7 *Mail-in offers:* these include reduced prices and premium gifts, e.g. sets of glasses,

requiring the customer to send off to the manufacturer or agent some evidence of purchase and, often, money.

8 *Catalogues, leaflets and brochures:* usually distributed at the point of purchase but include the giant mail-order catalogues.

9 *Personality offers:* these experienced a boom in the 1960s, with White Tide Men, Egg Chicks and many others visiting customers and outlets. Activity in this area is now relatively limited.

10 *Price cuts:* these involve short-term price cutting in-store. The normal pattern is for both a retailer and manufacturer to finance the offer in order to increase store throughput in a specific line.

Trade

1 *Point-of-sale material:* usually distributed by salesmen to establish maximum in-store impact. It ranges from the substantial in-store sales units of the cigarette firms to shelf strips, wobblers and many other items.

2 *Merchandizing support:* manufacturers introduce their own merchandizing staff into outlets, including wholesalers. They will exhibit, demonstrate and sell the product in support of the retailer.

3 *Exhibitions:* these provide the backbone of the attempt of many firms, particularly in consumer-durable markets, to place their products in front of the middle men.

4 *Catalogues:* these are widely distributed throughout the retail trade.

5 *Special discounts:* usually short-lived and often allied to other promotions.

Industrial

1 *Exhibitions and trade fairs:* the diffuse locations of large buyers make exhibitions a critical part of industrial sales promotion. They range from domestic exhibitions (Inter-build, the British Medical Equipment Exhibition) to major international exhibitions (International Leatherweek (Semaine de Cuire), Paris, Nudex (International Nuclear Exhibition, Basle)).

2 *Catalogues:* showing the range of products and production capability of firms. Mail-in offers: usually associated with advertisements in the trade and technical press.

3 *Price-off deals and trade-in allowances:* these are given to dealers, distributors and end users. Premiums and inducements: usually of the desk-top or executive-gift type, including diaries, calendars etc.

4 *Systems and installation support:* the concept of systems selling has already been discussed; systems or installation support is a facet of this. It is the free provision of services necessary for the effective use of a product or service.

Dangers of non-media advertising

The enormous range and scope of non-media advertising have led many firms to employ it in many situations, and in volume-sensitive markets its appeal is enormous. However, dangers do exist. A product or brand's long-term future depends on the attitudes and behaviour of the purchasers. Cutting back on media advertising to build up short-term sales may mean that the customer's overall impression of the product deteriorates. A strong individual product may end up being seen as the product that is always on offer. Very seldom can short-term increases in volume fully compensate for the promotion costs. An effective balance of media and non-media advertising will sustain the overall consumer image of the brand while building long-term volume.

Economics and ethics in advertising

The growth of advertising as a substantial industry has been marked by the emergence of two interrelated debates on the role of advertising in society. The first centres around the role of advertising in the competitive process, and the second focuses its attention on the impact of advertising on the moral fabric of our society. Both are legitimate areas of concern, assuming that a responsible and rigorous approach is adopted by all parties. Unfortunately, much of the debate has consisted of argument between two parties holding specific polarized views:

1 *Advertising is anti-competitive,* building barriers to entry into markets and preventing smaller firms from making any headway against the power of major manufacturers. At the same time, it encourages consumption for its own sake, allied to a hedonism which undermines our moral codes.
2 *Advertising is competitive.* The media are open to all, with the success of the larger firms merely reflecting the efficiency with which they meet consumer needs. Any impact on the values of society is primarily reflective. Advertising is such a small part of our total communication that it cannot determine values. In fact, it is most effective when operating within existing norms and values.

The past 25 years have seen a large number of studies of the economics of advertising, and certain key themes have been identified.

The competitive process

Much of the debate centres around different views of the competitive process. To the traditional economist the notion of 'perfect competition' is an ideal at which to aim. However, the underlying assumptions of product homogeneity and perfect information are difficult to achieve in the majority of markets in modern industrial economies, since product differences are introduced to satisfy the varying needs of different consumers. A great deal of evidence has now been accumulated to indicate that advertising is particularly effective when real product differences exist. A more recent feature of the argument focuses on the idea of spurious product differentiation. It is suggested that advertising acts to create differences between products which have no basis in the product's physical characteristics, e.g. 'Daz whiteness' and the 'little perforations' in tea-bags. However, these points may merely reflect the different values of specific commentators. The majority of these concepts emerge from pre-testing of advertisements and are sustained because they have some meaning to buying groups. The real danger is if the power of certain manufacturers is so great that consumer rejection of these implied qualities could be ignored by firms whose market position enables them to prop up

> inferior products . . . enabling them to survive longer than would otherwise be the case. (Rt Hon. Roy Hattersley)

Empirical investigation indicates that the capital costs of entry and other non-marketing costs are normally more important in building barriers to entry than is advertising. In many consumer markets, as well as among manufacturers, there is also competition among stores, which often offer the same brand at different prices and have own-label brands. Intermediaries are thus a major force in preventing any abuse of market power by manufacturers. In some markets abuses may exist, but the problems probably have more to do with the infrastructure of the market than the promotional superstructure.

The claim that there are too few manufacturers is complemented by an alleged information problem, and this is at the core of the marketing process. The notion of perfect competition solves the problem by proposing that all product offerings in a market are the same, e.g. Canadian wheat is more or less the same as US, Soviet or British wheat. In highly differentiated markets the buyer faces problems of gathering, understanding and organizing information. Brand images can play a major role in identifying a totality with which the purchaser can identify, particularly when backed by previous purchasing experience. At the same time the manufacturer investing £3 million in advertising should maintain product quality to ensure repeat purchase. It is possible for major manufacturers to use the information power of large budgets to direct product-selection criteria along the lines most favourable to them, e.g. appearance more important than safety in cars, and to swamp the advertising of the competitive products of smaller firms or counter-advertising, e.g. the £12 million spent by cigarette companies against the £2 million spent on anti-smoking advertising.[21]

There is some evidence to suggest that even regular purchasers of products are ignorant of many key product features, including price, competitive offerings, and size. However, it is important to recognize that most consumers are unable to handle the amount of information which even relatively limited weekly shopping would need if full price/quality buying were carried out. The purchase of 40 items under these conditions might involve awareness of perhaps six brands with different prices in four shops and encompassing four meaningful product differentiations for each brand: a total of 4,240 pieces of information. Access to media and communication skills presents a much more serious problem. Reductions in the number of newspapers, increasing advertising rates and discount structures constitute real problems for the small manufacturer trying to place a product before a potential audience. The tendency of some advertising agencies to cut back on their smaller accounts may prevent small firms from gaining access to the best talents. However, the highly competitive nature of the advertising industry does operate as a constraint to this.

The ethics of advertising

Comment in the area of ethics has been directed at false and misleading advertising and immoral and amoral advertising. False advertising is all advertising which is demonstrably untrue. It is the side of advertising which all responsible persons involved in the industry work hard to stamp out. Misleading copy is a grey area open to a considerable amount of debate, as what is misleading to some is clear to others. Puffs, blandishments and emphasis often fall into this area. For example, the Royal National Institute for the Deaf criticised advertisements for hearing aids which included phrases such as 'like having new ears' on the grounds that hearing aids do not restore hearing, but merely amplify sound. The RNID felt that false hopes were being raised by misleading copy.

Any view of immorality or amorality in advertising depends very much on the standpoint of the commentator. Some writers argue that the harm done by certain advertised products, e.g. cigarettes and alcohol, is so great that a total advertising ban is necessary to discourage consumption and progressively erode demand. Ultimately the responsibility for decisions in this area lies with the country's political leaders, who must gauge the evidence and be willing to pay at least part of the price in lost tax revenues and any industry support necessary to ensure employment for workers and compensation for others involved in the industry. The most common moral criticism of advertising is that it encourages materialistic values. In a society such as ours, with complex and constantly changing values, any attempt by advertising to promote specific values would most certainly be resisted by many, and it does appear that advertising is most effective when it reflects values rather then teaching them. It is possible that this may lead to the amplification of certain trends in society, and in this area socially responsible executives must act to impose controls. The British Code of Advertising Practice, as revised in 1974, is important in this:

> The Advertising Standards Authority . . . discharges its duty to keep advertising legal, decent, honest and truthful with speed and success. (Rt Hon. Roy Hattersley)

It is inevitable that society will take a keen interest in the impact of advertising on the economic and moral structure of society, and the British Code of Advertising Practice is an important source of information and guidance to advertising and marketing executives whose commitment to specific messages and themes may lead to some neglect of broader issues. In the past the response of the industry has been positive: there has been a willingness to listen which would be welcomed in other industrial, political and academic communities.

Public relations

Awareness of the need to draw together the range of corporate activities and present them to the public has led many firms to identify clear public relations (PR) policies. Industry and commerce are central features in modern society and the specific communities in which they are based, and PR policies are designed to bring out that role. At the same time the responsible PR executive feeds back to the firm the likely overall impact of its broader range of industrial and commercial policies. Many firms, particularly smaller firms, fail to realize the contribution an intelligently designed PR policy can make to supporting general promotional policies. Trade press, local press and even the national media will respond positively to approaches featuring company achievements. The Central Office of Information will assist firms wishing to place their major accomplishments before a large audience.

Conclusion

Advertising and sales promotion provide a diffuse and exciting range of opportunities for the marketing person. Effectively used and integrated with other aspects of the marketing mix, the scope for the effective presentation of the firm's offering to the market is almost unlimited. Costs, with their associated need for control, are involved, but these costs are directed towards building business in both the short and the long term. Successful advertising and promotion emphasizes pay-offs rather than payments, within a socially responsible perspective. Few aspects of marketing are likely to see more changes than advertising, with the Internet, cable and digital TV all opening up new opportunities in the very near future.

SPECIMEN QUESTIONS

1   What impact has satellite, cable television and Internet advertising had in (one of) the USA, the UK or Europe?

2   You are the advertising manager of a medium-sized departmental store in Bolton.

   (a)   What advertising media are available to you?

   (b)   What are their relative merits?

   (c)   Which media would you select either to increase use of the store by locals or widen your catchment area?

3   A report by the Department of Trade and Industry has concluded that 'eventually the cost of advertising is paid by the customer through increased prices'. As the best qualified recent graduate working for TTA Advertising, you have been asked by your MD to brief her on a response for an interview with Jeremy Paxman on tonight's Newsnight. Outline your response.

4   You are the advertising director of a medium-sized importer of fashion clothing (£30 million turnover p.a.) largely sold through C&A, BHS and J. D. Williams. Last night your chairman – and the owner of the company – had dinner with Richard Branson. He has come in convinced that a radio advertising campaign using stations like Virgin can be used to establish a range of branded knitwear on the market. Spell out your response to this proposal, indicating any research you might commission to explore this issue.

5   Outline the contribution that poster advertising can make to an effective advertising campaign. Illustrate your answers with examples of the effective and, if possible, ineffective use of posters.

6   What is the 'law of diminishing returns' in advertising budgeting? Outline ways in which a media scheduler would overcome this problem in maximizing the 'reach' of a newspaper campaign.

7   What is the role of an advertising agency? How does the work of a 'full service' agency differ from that of a specialist creative consultant?

8   Use a model of how advertising works to advertise a small, specialist snacks manufacturer on the development of an effective main media campaign. Indicate the tasks to be undertaken and the role of advertising at each stage.

9   Assess the view that the convergence of national markets and improved international communication will lead to globally standardized advertising.

10   Define:

   (a)   GDP.

   (b)   Advertising.

   (c)   Strap line.

   (d)   OTS.

   (e)   CPT.

   (f)   'Below-the-line' advertising.

   (g)   The 'competitive parity' approach to setting ad budgets.

   (h)   Image.

   (i)   USP.

   (j)   On-pack offers.

EXTENDED CASE STUDY 17: VW GOLF

Marketing conditions

For twenty years Volkswagen's production programme centred on the Beetle, which accounted for the major share of its turnover. By the beginning of the 1970s the Beetle no longer fulfilled the consumer's expectations as to what a modern automobile should be, and VW was therefore forced to switch as quickly as possible to a new, modern, progressive and comprehensive model programme.

In 1973 and 1974 VW incurred losses of DM950 million as a result of the problems caused by a difficult international economic situation and the oil crisis, which led to a world-wide recession and a shift in consumer attitudes towards economy and energy-awareness. Not only in Germany, but to a comparable extent all over the world, there were the first concrete signs of a downward trend in the automobile market since the Second World War.

After various market studies had been analyzed, several new aspects of domestic automotive demand in particular were revealed: the development of motorization by no means always runs parallel to overall economic conditions but according to its own laws of growth towards a total market saturation which is estimated to be approximately 800 cars per 1,000 adults and is expected to be reached at the end of the century; demand depends on the amount of disposable income in private households, on levels of private consumption and the accumulation of wealth by these households. Within these development parameters, the market for cars in the 1-litre to 1.5-litre class grew during the crisis by 40 per cent, to be superseded two years later by a renewed increase in demand for larger automobiles.

In Germany the automobile market plays a fundamental role; consumer behaviour regarding the automobile is determined by lifestyle, standard of living and by a sense of status. The automobile provides a feeling of personal freedom and of belonging to a certain stratum of society; at the same time factors which influence purchasing change as time goes by, so that in periods of economic difficulty initial and replacement buying are often postponed. This insight was partly responsible for VW modifying its rather production-orientated attitudes, which it had adhered to in the past, to a more market-orientated mode of operating, which was based on the customers and their wishes. The most important marketing instrument in this revised company philosophy was the new range of Volkswagen models, which was introduced successively in the period 1974–75 and consisted of the Golf, as focal point, accompanied by the Passat and the Scirocco. (These models are sold in the United States under the names Rabbit, Dasher and Scirocco respectively.)

Particularly the Golf met the purchasers' demands for functional styling, high utility value, high chassis, engine and engineering standards and outstanding economic performance. It formed the focal point for a range of VW models, upon which the recovery of the company ultimately depended. These models encompassed a broad range from the smaller to the larger class of automobile but with the main emphasis on the middle-class vehicle. Within each class VW offered a basic version with a wide selection of decor, styling, performance and comfort extras.

An after-sales service policy, which was particularly important for VW and was based on the maximum quality service for customers as well as automobiles, was successfully established through a comprehensive series of measures.

The network of service outlets and dealers was more tightly organized, and VW assured itself of marketing control by acquiring direct holdings in wholesaling companies. At the retail level, VW operated with independent firms by means of franchising arrangements. As a whole, the service network was more tightly organized and the mechanics trained so as to secure optimal market coverage.

The pricing policy placed VW's various new models just above the competitors' comparable models without, however, crossing the threshold of the consumers' price-sensitivity; VW wanted to be presented in all of the most popular categories.

The Golf was positioned in terms of its major rivals as shown in Figure 21.9.

In view of the hoped-for market position as well as VW's other marketing objectives (consolidation and expansion through a modern range of automobiles in a variety of classes, all tailored to consumer demand and incorporating the very latest technology), it was quite evident that considerable importance would have to be placed on communication as a marketing instrument if success was to be achieved.

Figure 21.9 A graphical representation of the results of a Volkswagen image analysis regarding the product characteristics, performance and economy. *(Source:* Volkswagen)

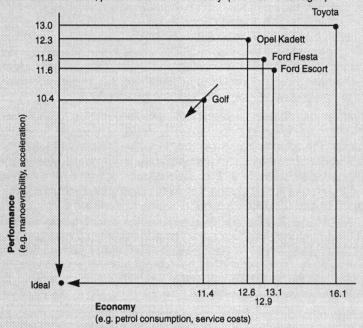

Communication strategy

Communication policy was VW's most important tool for realizing its marketing-strategy decisions. Volkswagen here made the distinction between dealer- and consumer-orientated communications.

Dealer-orientated communications strategy

In the context of a dealer-orientated communication policy, three instruments were especially important:

1. The company's information and training activities.
2. The company's advertising activities aimed at the dealers.
3. The dealer's advertising activities aimed at the consumers.

When the Golf was launched, these three instruments formed the core of all of the company's communication activities vis-à-vis the VW dealers.

Before, and also during, the launch period the VW company above all had to generate enthusiasm for its new product and keep it constantly alive. In order to achieve this, VW used information and training events, as well as dealer meetings, both at a regional and at a national level, in order to stay in constant communications contact with retailers and wholesalers.

In 1974, for example, a dealers' congress was held just shortly before the launch of the Golf. This congress was attended by more than 10,000 people from the VW and Audi sales organizations from all over Europe.

They were divided into various groups, e.g. directors and executives, salespeople, service department employees, supervisors, parts managers, as well as other employees with primarily technically orientated jobs. The main purpose of these activities (including training courses) was to provide these various groups of employees with information on the new car, to familiarize them with it and to motivate them.

Furthermore, these activities were intended to provide the dealers with a standard set of sales arguments for their customers and to prepare the ground for effective post-sales service. In addition, communications with the dealers were to ensure uniform and effective conduct of the dealers towards their customers.

In co-ordination with the dealers, VW had developed an advertising concept, which had the crucial task during the launch period of familiarizing the public with the new model and making it popular. The main idea was to talk about the new car as often as possible and make it sound as interesting as possible, to show pictures of it and also have it appear 'in person'.

The dealers' advertising activities, which were mainly aimed at establishing a connection between dealer and product performance, were characterized by a common colour. As a result, all advertising media used by the dealers had a high recognition value, which was particularly important in view of the large number of various activities carried out.

The dealers' launch strategy consisted of three elements:

1 *Preparations:* a number of particularly impressive media were employed before production of the new car was started in order to draw the public's attention to the coming event. The media used for this purpose were: large 18/1 sheet posters; joint ads commissioned by several dealers; ads by individual dealers; and the 'Golf Post', consisting of a letter with the Golf journal (mass circulation pamphlet) and a bumper sticker for potential Golf buyers taken from the dealers' customer files, as well as for people who sent in ad coupons.

2 *Product description:* a description of the new car and its main technical data was provided by means of outdoor advertising (18/1 large size and Fries posters), ads commissioned jointly by several dealers and ads by individual dealers. These primary advertising media were supplemented by display materials such as large-size transparent PVC stickers for showroom windows, rear window car stickers, advertising racks for holding pamphlets and showroom design.

3   *Merchandizing activities:* the public's interest in the new model was aroused through a large number of activities that simultaneously helped the Golf to become a popular, well-known and prominent car.

Consumer-orientated communications strategy

Objectives. The communication objectives were partly derived from the problem of substituting the Golf for the Beetle and were partly determined by the general marketing idea.

The short-term objective during the launch period of the Golf was to convince the buyers that the Golf was not the successor to the Beetle, but rather a partner model, in order to avoid an abrupt loss of all the old, loyal Beetle drivers.

In addition, the public, and especially the fans of the traditional VW concept, had to be convinced of the Golf concept. The attention of potential buyers had to be drawn to the fact that VW, too, was now offering a modern, pace-setting product concept in the lower middle-class range, a product which furthermore could be 'smoothly' integrated into VW's product family.

VW wanted to make potential buyers familiar with their new top-of-line product, the Golf, in a very short period of time. In fact, they wanted to make the Golf known to 80 per cent of the population within only two months!

A major long-term objective was to achieve a high-level image. In this context, two aspects had to be taken into consideration simultaneously. First, the traditional VW image with its characteristics 'quality, reliability, and good service' had to be transferred to the Golf, which additionally was described as being 'practical, trouble-free, fun to drive'.

And secondly, the modern concept of the Golf, in combination with the existing company image, was intended to add the aspects of progressiveness and modernness to VW's image.

Secondly, VW's advertising style consisted of several material guidelines to be followed:

1   As a general rule, the advertising message must be consumer-orientated, realistic and credible, with the major emphasis on product-related information.
2   The presentation of the product should be perceived as something quite natural.
3   There should be a smooth transition from the advertising style for the Beetle to the advertising campaign for the Golf, with a strong emphasis on the particular product characteristics.
4   Adjustments to short-lived fashion trends should be avoided when this affects the basic concept.

These guidelines were applied both to the Golf's launch campaign and to the period following the launch. But in this later stage, more emphasis was placed on an adaptation to the buyers' objectives and their experiences with the Golf. The typical character of VW's advertising style, which can be accurately described as 'product-orientated advertising', was, however, maintained.

This indicates that the Golf campaign was to be built on a clear presentation of the most essential facts (note following the motto: 'Something for everybody'). The arguments presented were to have a very strong reference to the product's practical uses, i.e. they had to be mainly rational. The key idea around which the advertising concept was built was the following promise:

VW is offering a practical, trouble-free car that the whole family can enjoy because it suits all their various needs as a result of its product concept.

Furthermore, the Golf's compact design had to be popularized. The consumers had to be made aware of the fact that despite its small outer appearance, the Golf was a fully-fledged, middle-class car that was in line with current automotive trends.

VW wanted to prevent the consumers from confusing a compact with a sub-compact car. At any rate, VW had to prevent the Golf from being regarded as a small car or as a sober, functional 'mini station-wagon', when compared with Opel's Kadett and Ford's Escort.

Another long-term objective of VW was that Golf buyers should be characterized as having 'neutral status' in order to prevent the Golf from being associated with a very specific, closely defined market segment.

The advertising concept for the Golf was in principle a continuation of VW's advertising strategy, which is characterized by consistent advertising style. The most important elements of this style are partly of a purely formal nature. The standard VW advertising layout, which had been built up in the course of the years, was to be maintained in order to obtain a high recognition value for VW's advertising activities.

Basically, every Volkswagen ad had to be composed of three elements: picture, headline and text, with possible variations of these three fixed elements to allow for interesting advertising layout and message suggestions.

The presentation's central theme was therefore the product's versatile uses, such as a family car, a shopping car, a city car, a travel car, and the family using it in these various situations.

One of VW's strategy principles has always been a uniform European communications policy. The communications concept was therefore regarded as a concept for the whole of Europe.

Target groups. The Golf's main function as VW's major source of revenue in the future made it necessary to take into consideration specific buyer wishes when planning the new automobile, but also to make sure that the Golf would appeal to a quantitatively large segment of automobile buyers. Socio-demographic and psychological analyses of the potential buyers of the Golf led to the following results.

Demographic profile:

1 Sex: 70 per cent men, 30 per cent women.
2 Professional status: self-employed, 5 per cent; white-collar workers, 43 per cent; blue-collar workers, 32 per cent; civil servants, 10 per cent; others, 10 per cent.
3 Age: 20 to 49 years (average 34).
4 Income: net household income: minimum, DM 1,000; average, DM 1,700.

Psychological profile:

1 They are individuals who have a pronounced tendency to follow society's norms and conventions, and who tend to have a rather timid personality and therefore try to avoid being conspicuous in any way.
2 When buying cars, they prefer trouble-free and practical models to streamlined body-work, rapid acceleration and high speed.
3 The importance of the car and emotional attachment result from the high investment value that the car represents for this type of person. They do not regard their cars primarily as status symbols, but they expect their cars to meet certain standards and look after them and treat them with care.

As far as the owner structure was concerned, the two groups that VW's campaign was supposed to appeal to were first of all people currently owning Beetles, and secondly people who had driven Beetles in the past, but had switched over to competitors' models (both German and foreign) in the meantime. VW hoped to be quite successful with the Golf in attracting owners of competitor models. Studies had shown that people who had been driving cars like Opel Kadett, the Fiat 127/128, Ford Escort, Simca 1100 and Peugeot 102/104 for the last two to four years would be particularly susceptible to the Golf.

Strategy. The advertising objectives and the size of the target group led to the following strategy considerations.

The Golf must be optically presented in such a way that the consumers rate it one class above most of the smaller models with a similar concept. The Golf must acquire an unmistakable character of its own.

The Golf with its product characteristics must be shown in an explanatory environment because VW must convince the consumers of its ability to offer and manufacture genuinely compact cars.

The Golf must become a popular and attractive car that everybody likes. VW has to be credible in describing the car's benefits to the consumer. Therefore, Volkswagen expressed the entire concept of the Golf in a simple, straightforward motto:

> Golf, der Kompakt-VW:
> Auto, Motor und Spass.
> (Golf, the compact from VW:
> Auto, Motor and Fun)

All expectations that are nowadays associated with a car in this class are communicated by this slogan.

The 'compact from VW' stands for a full-fledged middle-class car that is small in size and as reliable as all VW products. 'Auto' represents the company's claim of having developed an adequate and superior overall concept. 'Motor' stands for sophisticated engineering, value and dynamic performance, a car promising manoeuvrability and liveliness. 'Fun' to drive, fun in everyday life, but also enjoying more serious things such as economy, roominess and reliability.

With these statements, the Golf's image profile was given the widest scope possible. As a result, the market segment was not artificially limited and the product's expected benefits were communicated in a way that was credible to everybody.

The advertising media to be selected had to measure up to the following requirements which were based primarily on the advertising strategy considerations mentioned above:

1   The Golf's overall concept must be communicated to a large group of the population.
2   Advertising messages that deal with the Golf must become predominant in this market segment, i.e. the media strategy has to be aimed at quantitative predominance.
3   The Golf must be present in the potential buyers' awareness; the potential buyer has to be constantly confronted with various types of advertising messages that are related to the Golf.

Other major factors that influenced the selection of advertising media were the main advertising messages, the division of the campaign into a launch period and follow-up period, the specific advertising objectives and the cost factor (finding the most cost-efficient way of reaching the desired target group).

Print media, i.e. newspapers and magazines, and television were chosen as basic media. In the print media group, consumer magazines were of primary importance because they fulfilled the necessary prerequisites for realizing an optimum advertising effect. The relevant target group could be reached accurately and extensively, and the creative possibilities that magazines offered facilitated an optimal translation of the advertising message into a visual image and a written text as required by the basic concept.

The launch campaign was primarily aimed at achieving the greatest possible coverage and the highest possible contact frequency. In order to reach this objective, identical ads were placed in several magazines at the same time, and in individual publications different ads were not inserted one after the other, but several at a time. In these advertising activities, VW concentrated mainly on the publications with the highest circulations in the German magazine market, i.e. general-interest and programme magazines.

The follow-up campaign was dominated by consumer magazines to an even greater extent. After reaching the objectives of the launch campaign, i.e. familiarizing a large percentage of the population with the Golf, this medium was particularly suitable for emphasizing or playing down specific product characteristics perceived by customers as positive or negative. But at the same time it was the most suitable medium for realizing product- or experience-orientated advertising concepts during the follow-up period.

Television was used mainly to familiarize as many people as possible with the new product as quickly as possible. In the follow-up campaign, the relevance of this medium diminished. However, VW continued to make use of it in accordance with its position in the German media scene.

Daily newspapers also played a certain role in the campaign, but they were a medium which was used primarily by the dealers (see section on dealer-orientated communications policy). Especially during the launch campaign, the information character of this medium corresponded to the topical and innovative nature of the advertising message about the Golf. After the launch, dealers advertised in dailies only sporadically.

Radio and special-interest publications, such as automobile and sports magazines, did not initially play a very important role. Radio was used only during the launch campaign, and this only in a few isolated cases, and there were also relatively few ads in special-interest publications. However, this must be seen against the background that the primary function of these journals in the automobile industry is not that of an advertising medium, but rather that of a medium for forming opinions or for objective reporting and evaluating.

As the Golf's primary task was to avoid losing VW's customers – especially Beetle drivers – in the future, a direct mail campaign aimed at 425,000 VW owners was carried out during the launch period.

A supplementary medium that VW used during the launch period was outdoor. Impressive poster designs updated and emphasized the information that the observer had already been given on the Golf by other media and added to the impression that the Golf's presence on the road was quite natural. During the launch period, outdoor advertising reached a level of 6 per cent of the total advertising budget, but played no role in the follow-up period.

Advertising message. The central theme of the launch campaign was the car's suitability for the family, as manifested by the product concept, as well as the versatility and the roominess of the Golf. The key features of the advertising message were: practical, trouble-free, fun to drive (lively).

These key features were rounded off by the following supplementary features, which could in turn be associated with the key features: economical (trouble-free), versatile use (practical), suitable for shopping, suitable for city driving and easy to park, suitable for long-distance travelling, safe handling characteristics (fun to drive).

In those export markets that closely resemble the German market's demographic and psychological buyer structure (Austria, Switzerland, the Netherlands, Denmark, UK), the advertising message basically consisted of the same elements as in Germany.

Apart from this, the VW Company shifted the emphasis between the various key elements of the advertising message in different domestic markets. Depending on the particular target group that VW primarily wanted to reach within the Golf market segment (e.g. sporty drivers, drivers with an interest in the car's engineering, women), different elements of the advertising message were stressed.

The major theme that was chosen for the Golf's ad campaign was the Golf's positive characteristics that its drivers experienced, e.g. the car's excellent cornering ability, the comfortable and hard-wearing seats, the good mileage, its 'suitability' for women. At the same time, the continuous checks in the Golf's ranking as compared to its competitors, based on a large number of criteria, provided some useful clues for the advertising message, e.g. the themes 'reasonable price' and 'comfort'.

The Golf's styling, which was unconventional for its price category and was also rather sober, had to be made attractive to conservative tastes of the above-mentioned psychological segment to be reached. Thus the aim was to interpret the car's sober, clear design in combination with its distinct overall concept as being technically aesthetic.

Seen from this perspective, it would have been conceivable to present the vehicle 'as such' in its 'pure' form. But on the other hand, such a confrontation with the new product appeared inappropriate in view of the psychological characteristics of the main target group.

Instead, the process of getting to know the new car has to be emotionally supported by a familiar, general setting, i.e. a context in which the new product would look quite natural: the versatile car and various situations in which it can be used by the entire family.

The technical product characteristics were explained in the context of a given use; the novel product concept was much more convincing when shown directly in a practical situation. Despite its technical soberness, the Golf had to be, and could be, presented in a personified, emotional environment.

In this way, undesirable defence reactions which might have been provoked by the association with the unexpected and the new were diverted to produce positive associations about the car's versatile use for the whole family so the new product concept could gradually become the accepted standard, as planned.

Communication budget. The Volkswagen Company fixes its communications budget annually. Plans for concrete measures are drawn up on the basis of the marketing and advertising objectives. This then automatically leads to the required budgets for the various communication instruments. If the required budget exceeds the funds available, a feedback process sets in to modify the measures planned. As regards the absolute size of the budget, only figures on expenditures in the major advertising mass media are available. Table 21.6 shows that over a period of three years, VW's advertising budget for the Golf stayed at a rather high level then receded to a lower level from 1977 onwards.

Table 21.6 Total advertising expenditures for the Golf in West Germany in DM000s

1974	1975	1976	1977
9890	7912	8036	3236

Source: Schmidt and Pohlmann.

The development of the budget distribution for the Golf was a direct consequence of advertising strategy considerations on one hand, and VW's experience with media on the other. The budget distribution in Figure 21.10 shows that the statements made above about media selection or reasons for choosing particular media have consistently been put into practice.

Figure 21.10 Development of the advertising budget distribution for VW's Golf shown as percentages. (*Source:* Schmidt and Pohlmann.)

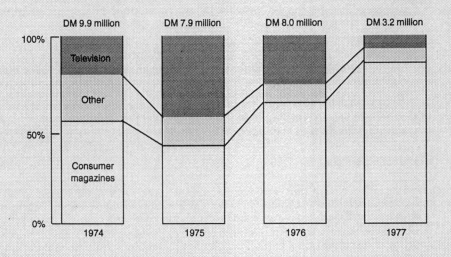

During the launch campaigns (1974), VW's main emphasis in media advertising was clearly placed on ads in consumer magazines (approximately 60 per cent of the budget). In 1975, the two major advertising media used were television (about 45 per cent) and consumer magazines (about 40 per cent). In the following years, consumer magazines played the predominant role (at times exceeding 90 per cent of the advertising budget).

These figures again show that media such as special-interest publications, radio and cinema advertising were of little or no importance in the realization of the Golf advertising objectives. Outdoor advertising and direct mail played a minor role during the launch campaign when their shares in the Golf's total budget amounted to 6 per cent and 9 per cent respectively.

A comparison of this budget distribution with that of the Golf's main competitors (Opel Kadett, Ford Escort) shows that VW's activities lay within the industry's usual range. VW's most important competitors also concentrate their advertising activities on consumer magazines.

The realization of the communication strategy and the desired advertising objectives required exact timing of all activities aimed at the 'outside world'.

In August, 1974, the first Golf came off the line. Catalogue sales started as early as June 1974, in order not to surrender the time between the popularization of the new car and the first deliveries without a defection to competitors. Local and national advertising activities for the Golf started in July 1974. The actual launch campaign lasted till the end of 1974 and was then succeeded by slightly modified follow-up advertising.

An analysis of the seasonal distribution of VW's communication activities shows that VW concentrated its consumer-orientated media advertising on the periods from February to May and from mid-September to mid-December. The resulting advertising gaps were filled with special campaigns (e.g. discontinued models, new models) and with stronger regional orientation. Regional particularities (e.g. school holiday dates) were given special consideration in the dealers' advertising activities, which as a result were less uniform in their timing, especially since special campaigns played the main role in the dealers' advertising.

Examples of advertisements. The balanced and consistently pursued advertising strategy can be easily illustrated by means of a few examples. During the launch campaign, ads with the following slogans were used: 'Golf, the compact from VW: Auto, motor and fun'; 'The new popular sport: Golf'; 'A new car, hot off the press'; 'Here you can stretch out on long stretches'; 'Easy open, easy close'; '3.75 metres short, 1 family large'.

Examples taken from the follow-up advertising period used the following slogans: 'Golf. It helps you around the corner'; 'Ace acceleration'; 'A star with curves'; 'The key to success'; 'It's a sure thing – the Golf'.

Marketing success

Overall objectives reached

The precarious development of the entire VW group, which started at the beginning of the 1970s and reached its peak in 1974–75, was warded off by means of the Golf's striking success in the market, and the company's development subsequently took an extremely positive turn.

Car sales rose to 2.14 million vehicles in 1976 and reached another record peak in 1977 when 2.28 million cars were sold.

The sales volume reached DM 21.4 billion in 1976 and about DM24 billion in 1977.

Profits (annual balance sheet surplus) amounted to roughly DM1 billion in 1976 and ranged in the same order of magnitude in 1977.

The Golf's market success is documented by the following sales data. From the Golf's launch in July 1974 till June 1978, about 1,950,000 cars were delivered worldwide to the VW organization. This figure can be broken down as follows: West Germany, 775,000 units; US, 460,000 units; European volume markets, 550,000 units.

When data were broken down to individual markets, the Golf turned out to be a 'best seller' in several countries (see also Table 21.7).

Table 21.7 Development of Golf sales (worldwide and in selected markets) in units

	1974	1975	1976	1977	Jan.–May 1978
Worldwide	110,000	426,400	496,000	602,000	260,000
West Germany	71,000	168,000	206,000	216,000	93,000
Europe	37,000	140,000	132,000	156,500	67,000
US	58	98,000	112,000	165,000	59,000
Canada	–	10,600	17,900	23,000	10,000
Mexico	–	–	–	10,200	11,000

Source: Volkswagen.

In Switzerland and in West Germany, the Golf has been, since its launch, the most frequently sold automobile ever. In the twelve most important European volume markets the Golf was number two in 1976 and in 1977 behind the Ford Taurus and followed by the Fiat 127 (Ford Taurus: 397,000; VW Golf: 364,000; Fiat 127: 335,000).

If all European automobile markets are considered as a whole, the Golf ranks fourth.

In 1977, the Golf was number four worldwide.

Golf's market success is also clearly reflected in the development of its share in the market. Looking at the class relevant to the Golf (comprising a segment of roughly 35 per cent of the total market), the data listed in Table 21.8 give clear evidence of VW's very positive development. Not only was the company successful at an early point in stopping and neutralizing any fading of its share in the market which might have been caused by the Beetle's collapse, but it even succeeded in increasing its market share in this class with the help of the Golf.

Table 21.8 Market shares of new car registrations in West Germany (in the Golf's class) as %

	1970	1971	1972	1973	1975	1976
VW Group	44	42	38	38	40	45
Ford	5	6	6	6	12	11
Opel	24	19	20	20	17	17
Foreign manufacturers[a]	27	33	36	36	31	27
	100	100	100	100	100	100

[a] Mainly Simca, Renault, Fiat.
Source: Volkswagen.

Communication success

The criteria applied by VW to determine the communication success of the campaign were media efficiency, level of familiarity, image and brand preference.

The media efficiency, particularly during the launch campaign, is impressively demonstrated by the following data: the chosen media combination resulted in a coverage of 96 per cent of the total adult population (14 years and over); and the average number of contacts per person reached amounted to 17 for the total population.

The Golf's level of familiarity among the population was determined by means of an initial market research survey carried out six weeks after the beginning of the launch campaign. Even after this brief period, it had already reached 90 per cent (normally 60 per cent after six weeks).

The first check on the Golf's image was also made six weeks after the launch, and the result was compared with the desired image. This then provided an important basis for adjusting the image by modifying the contents of the advertising messages.

After the launch period, annual image analyses were carried out, mainly concentrating on the image that the Golf had for non-buyers when compared to the Golf's competitors. These brand preference analyses were a useful source of information for determining the various product-orientated components of the advertising message.

All in all, the image objectives envisaged for the Golf were reached to a large extent. The Golf was primarily considered a modern, progressive and sporty car which the buyers regarded as being extremely manoeuvrable and fuel-saving.

In general, the Golf was rated as a car for younger people, while some important competitors had images associated more with older members of the population.

Undesirable impressions existed mainly with regard to the statements 'reasonable price' and 'easy to get in and out of'. Non-owners of the Golf rated the car as being relatively expensive – despite its other economic benefits, which were widely recognized (e.g. fuel consumption, insurance cost, maintenance) – and, because of the car's compact outer appearance, they were also rather sceptical with regard to the ease of getting in and out.

As far as Golf owners were concerned, a survey by the 'mot'-magazine (*Testen Sie Ihr Auto Selbst* (*Test Your Car Yourself*), Motor-Presse, Stuttgart, 1977) by and large confirmed the impression held by the Volkswagen Company. Nine hundred and forty Golf drivers rated their cars as 'very good' or 'good', particularly for the criteria 'top speed', 'acceleration', 'oil consumption', 'cornering ability', 'cross-wind sensitivity', 'room in front'. Poorer ratings were given for the Golf with regard to the bumpers, room in the back, standard equipment and shelf space.

An important indicator of the economic and communicative success of a car is its 'capture rate', i.e. the number of buyers who had previously driven competitors' models. The Golf confirmed – as expected – that it is very capable of attracting drivers of competitor's models. In 1976, 29 per cent of the Golf buyers had driven other brands before, and in 1977, 40 per cent of the buyers had switched to the Golf from competitors' models.

An analysis of the structure of models formerly owned by Golf buyers shows that in 1976 and 1977, for instance, it was mainly former Beetle drivers (48 and 30 per cent respectively), Opel Kadett drivers (4 and 3 per cent respectively), Ford drivers (5 and

3 per cent respectively), Fiat drivers (3 and 5 per cent respectively) and Renault drivers (4 and 5 per cent respectively) who were attracted to the Golf.

The Golf's success in terms of sales and communication, as described above, shows that the strategy pursued by the VW company (i.e. drawing the buyers' attention to the Golf by means of product-orientated advertising which emphasized the Golf's specific product advantages and using magazines as the main medium for communication, as well as creating a clear product image distinguishing the Golf from its direct competitors) was right and still is.

The case study is reproduced with the permission of Gruner and Jahr Advertising.

22

Sales and sales force management

Introduction

In his book *The Rise and Fall of the British Manager,* Alistair Mant places a special emphasis on the role and responsibility of the sales professional:

> The salesman's job is shot through with technical skill, leadership and trusteeship – he goes into the environment and, so to speak, takes the skin of the organization with him when he goes – he *is* the organization so far as his prospects and clients experience it.[1]

This is something which any well-run organization recognizes, and something which is given special emphasis by some of our trading rivals. In Germany, for example, salespeople, particularly the engineering or technical representatives, are part of the corporate elite, and their skills in establishing links with customers, building up relationships and closing and following up orders are an essential part of the success of many German companies.[2] It is a pattern reflected in France, Italy, the US, Scandinavia, Japan and the better UK firms. In Eastern and Central Europe the export salesman holds a special place.

In North America there has been a surge in the attention given to sales and selling recently. In part this rejects the transformation produced by the use of information technology in sales management and operations. This 'revolution'[3] has re-emphasized the traditional role of sales staff, improved their productivity[4] and extended their portfolio of activities.[5] These developments have helped management to address Lidstone's 'three stark facts of economic life'[6] facing sales management. These are: (1) a sales force is expensive; (2) profits not sales justify investments in selling; and (3) a sales force can play a key role in the 'fight' for markets.

For many companies the emphasis on sales and selling is natural. The salesperson is the key intermediary, the presenter of company offerings and the interpreter of customer needs. Closing a sale is the tangible sign that all the efforts of development, promotion and pricing have been worthwhile, and the salesperson is in the fortunate position of being 'in at the end'. Sale closing and order taking are distinct tasks that the salesperson is uniquely able to undertake.

Despite these factors there has been a tendency to play down the role of the salesperson in modern British society. To a considerable degree this derives from a failure to appreciate the nature of the selling task, the many different types of salesperson, the skills required and their central role in corporate effectiveness. This is especially worrying in an economy which is highly dependent on successful industrial marketing. In this environment the skilled, graduate engineering salesperson can be crucial to success.[7]

Selling is a rapidly evolving discipline. Changes are being forced by new understanding of the nature of the relationship between customer and client, awareness of the factors which influence the individual spending so much time (up to 90 per cent) out of the firm, with no direct contact with other company staff, technological developments, recruitment problems and the changing structure of the market. Although these are changing the form of selling, they have not changed the basic tasks that the people involved in sales and merchandizing perform.

Selling

No other function which involves so many skilled individuals operating in so many different environments can be as neatly compartmentalized into one simple task as can selling. Seven selling tasks can be identified:

1 *Product delivery:* sales are secondary to milk or bread salesmen. They may be able to produce some increases in sales, but orders generally have been placed earlier. There may be some scope for selling in extra volume, notably new products[8] or those on offer.

2 *Inside order-taking:* perhaps the largest group of sales staff is those in stores, car showrooms, parts departments and at the end of telephones waiting for the potential buyer to arrive. Although their role is sometimes played down, any Boots or Marks and Spencer's executive will explain the important role that shop staff have played in their success. The car manufacturers invest considerable time and effort in attempting to stimulate positive selling attitudes in auto salesmen.

3 *Outside order-taking:* the field forces of many large consumer-goods fields are actively involved in this area. It ranges from regular calls to small outlets, where the salesperson almost does the ordering for the owners, to visits to the branches of large outlets, where lists of suppliers are carefully defined but the value of giving the local manager some discretion is recognized.

4 *Goodwill building:* often staff whose job is goodwill building are given no freedom to solicit orders. They educate customers, assist with display and have many other roles. They are often tied in with the firm's merchandizing force, and some operate in specialized areas such as pharmaceuticals.

5 *Technical or engineering representation:* here the emphasis is placed firmly on the technical and product knowledge of salesmen. They will give advice and guidance, even to the point of helping to draft specifications.

6 *Creative selling of tangibles:* this encompasses every sphere from the door-to-door encyclopaedia salesman to the defence salesman negotiating billion-pound contracts for aircraft or tanks.

7 *Creative selling of intangibles:* this is the selling of services, including insurance, banking credit, advertising and consultancy.

Although it is useful to present these as different types of selling, in fact many salespeople will perform all or most of these tasks. For example, the car salesman will usually have responsibility for: delivery, or at least handing over the key; inside order-taking, when the client is in the showroom; outside order-taking, generally with fleet or company buyers; goodwill building, including in-store display; advice to former buyers; reassurance about faults; technical representation; providing insight into the vehicle's specification and performance; creative selling of intangibles, i.e. the vehicle and accessories; creative selling of intangibles, perhaps a hire-purchase agreement, insurance or even membership of a motoring organization. In many cases the freedom to negotiate trade-ins and discounts also adds a pricing dimension to the salesman's role.[9]

There is, however, a powerful trend towards increased specialization, especially in high ticket item sales and those in which specialist or technical expertise is required.[10] At the same time, new technologies are eliminating or inducing the salesperson's role in some aspects of order-taking and administration.

The salesman's task

To perform in these very different situations, salespeople perform a number of distinct tasks:

1 *Develop product and market knowledge:* salespeople should be knowledgeable about both the offering and the firm's objectives for each segment of the market.
2 *Prospect for potential clients:* within the framework or territory given to salespeople, it is their task to identify prospective clients, e.g. through *Yellow Pages,* buyers' guides etc.
3 *Prepare the sale:* each potential buyer or group of buyers should be studied as closely as possible, e.g. by examining company reports, and a sales plan prepared.
4 *Sales pitch:* the potential buyer should be approached in the way and with the offer most likely to succeed. This may take place in one visit or over many, e.g. in a capital project two, four, six or more visits may be necessary.
5 *Close:* the ultimate purpose of most sales contracts is to close the sale effectively. This should be carefully considered and the optimum time and form determined.
6 *Follow-up:* there are two elements in this: to avoid loss of the contract and to be in a good position to win future contracts.

To successfully follow this system the salesperson must perform a number of related tasks as well as calling on more general corporate resources.

Negotiating

Few activities are more closely linked with sales and selling than negotiating. Despite its importance, negotiating has received little substantive attention in the sales or marketing literature. The most authoritative ideas tend to be those associated with 'famed' negotiators like Mark McCormack[11] and Robert Townsend[12] or populist books like *Getting to Yes*[13] or *The Haggler's Handbook.*[14] They tend to be strong on 'assertions' like McCormack's 'As a general rule, you are far better having meetings at your own office. This has very little to do with "power offices" and everything to do with territorial imperative.'

Elsewhere lists of rules proliferate such as:[15]

- Don't bargain over positions – concentrate on real issues.
- Don't mix personalities with issues – separate the substance from the person.
- Don't lose track of each party's real interests – always ask why people are involved and what they want.
- Don't close lines of negotiation too early – always give each party some options.
- Don't lose track of real issues – use objective criteria to resolve issues wherever possible.

These heuristics have their value but this is limited by the lack of research into the specific merit of particular rules or the general value of this type of approach.

Related tasks

These will include careful monitoring of the environment in the salesperson's territory, e.g. a local newspaper might feature a local firm winning a major contract, and this can provide opportunity. Communication is a major part of the salesperson's job. This goes far beyond merely setting up meetings: an important aspect may be effectively transmitting the customer's comments and complaints to head office. Planning is often neglected by salespeople who prefer 'to be getting on with the job', but properly conducted it can make a major contribution to effective resource and time allocation. Administration plays a major part in any sales operation. Many firms are now giving salespeople a major customer-information gathering role.[16]

Linking with other corporate resources

Theodore Levitt,[17] in an excellent paper on the subject, highlighted the important part that advertising can play in preparing the ground for effective selling. The salesperson must be fully integrated in the firm's marketing effort.

Integration is an important part of the management of any sales force. Most salespeople spend the majority of their time 'out in the field', and this can lead to a situation in which they start to identify with those they spend most of their time with – customers – rather than with the firm.

Some firms who have attempted to maximize eye-contact time, i.e. the time the salesperson spends in front of the customer, have actually found that performance deteriorates. This does not mean that there is no value in 'eye-contact time': it merely highlights the importance of planning it carefully and recognizing that it is merely one of many variables influencing performance.

Training has emerged as an area of vital importance in sales development.[18] New technologies[19] make the delivery of these training programmes to a widely distributed sales-force easier and more effective. The well-trained salesperson has greater credibility with potential clients. This increases the chances of a sale while reinforcing post-purchase confidence.[20]

Sales management

Few areas of management contain more simplifications and myths than sales management. Films such as *Glengarry Glen Ross* with Al Pacino, *The Cadillac Man* with Robin Williams, and *Tin Men* with Danny De Vito and Richard Dreyfuss, supply grim and unyielding stereotypes of sales and sales management. In each, a crude and unyielding mixture of stick and carrot is used to 'motivate' and direct the efforts of sales staff. These images bear little resemblance to the techniques and skills employed in well-organized, modern sales organizations.

In practice a clearly thought-out and professional approach to sales force management is necessary. Effectiveness here is built up through recruitment of the right staff, allocation in the optimum manner, management of the staff and other resources for maximum returns, motivation to ensure consistently high performance, and control to maintain the sales force's continuing contribution to effective company performance.

Recruiting

Recruiting the right kind of sales staff is a recurrent problem for most firms. The company will have its own individuality, the customers will be of a particular type, technologies and the kinds of technical skills needed will vary, and the current staff will do much to create the environment in which the salesperson must operate. The problem is finding the right person for the job. Some writers have suggested that the firm should seek out 'good sales types', and there are a number of suggestions about what are the traits to be sought in the good salesperson.

1 *McMurry and Arnold's traits:*[21] high level of energy; abundance of self-confidence; chronic hunger for money, status and other rewards; well-established industriousness; perseverance; competitiveness.
2 *Mayer and Greenberg's traits:*[22] empathy (ability to identify with prospects, customers and their needs); ego drive (the determination to succeed).

Murray[23] has highlighted the different challenges faced by companies recruiting a sales force from scratch – in a new market, territory or industry – versus recruiting individual salespeople. The former gives the firm a 'blank sheet of paper' on which a distinct design can be imposed, while the latter places the emphasis on effective integration into current operations and team members.[24]

Whether one of the basic models of salesperson behaviour traits is adopted or a specific company approach is used, a number of good-quality recruits will be a major first step. A well-thought-out and clear job description allied to a carefully designed recruitment campaign is necessary. It is now estimated that the cost of keeping one salesman on the road is over £50,000 per annum. Investment in this valuable resource needs careful planning.

The challenging nature of the modern sales environment is prompting many British and European firms to widen their search for quality recruits. Graduates, especially those in engineering, are a key target group. This is closely linked with the changing role of the buying or purchasing function.[25] Modern supplier development strategies place a considerable emphasis on the integration of the supplier's sales team with innovation, design and engineering.[26] This, in turn, requires sales staff capable of making a genuine strategic contribution to this function.[27]

Allocation

Allocation of the sales force plays a major part in ensuring that the optimum returns are earned. Three basic approaches have been adopted to the allocation of field forces:

1 *Geographical:* here the salesperson represents the entire offering of the firm in a specific geographical area or patch. These areas can range in size from a part of Central London to 'Africa and the Middle East'. The essential feature of this system is that it combines local knowledge with organizational simplicity.
2 *Product:* each representative is given responsibility for a part of the company's offering. It might be a particular product line in which he or she has special knowledge, e.g. cooker clocks and timers, or a particular service, e.g. marketing consultancy. In-depth knowledge of the offering and an ability to respond authoritatively to specific queries are the strengths of this approach.

3 *Customer:* in situations in which the firm is dealing with a heterogeneous group of clients, e.g. footwear manufacturers, car makers, or furniture producers, knowledge of their special needs and awareness of any particular strength of the company's offerings in this area can provide a real asset to sales development.

Key-account handling, i.e. when major customers are dealt with by special sales teams, has emerged over the last few decades as a major aspect of sales force organization. Although it can be linked with the customer approach (differentiation by customer size is still customer-based), its significance goes beyond this.

Key accounts can be so substantial that individual approaches, treating each account almost as a market segment, can be devised. A major grocery account could be worth 10 to 15 per cent of turnover for specific lines. Handling these customers calls for special skills, and the high investment of the retailers in their buyers is a good measure of the investment the producer should make in the key-account team.

Before embarking on a key-account development programme, six questions should be asked:[28]

1 What is the maximum share of our business that these top customers should account for?
2 How can we organize ourselves to best deal with them?
3 What information do we need?
4 How should our relationships with them develop?
5 What sales and marketing policies should we adopt?
6 What sales and marketing staff and what skills are needed to work most effectively in this area?

A number of developments are directly affecting the role of the salesperson in this area. Key-account staff need highly developed negotiating skills and considerable awareness of business development, and it is normal to give staff considerable negotiating discretion and even some responsibility for product development, advertising, promotion and price. This has led to increasing involvement by corporate marketing management – marketing directors and product and brand management – in key-account work, and this type of interaction is improving their understanding of each other's roles.

Management

Management of the sales force goes far beyond recruitment and allocation. It calls for clear insight into the different selling situations faced by sales staff. Newton[29] suggests that four basic situations face the salesperson: trade selling (volume building through intermediaries); missionary selling (assisting intermediaries to sell); technical selling (providing the array of support needed in industrial markets); and new business selling (opening up new accounts, making new contacts). The sales manager must instil:

1 A sense of identification between the salesperson and company goals, i.e. overcoming some of the barriers that can be built up from factors such as spending so much time outside.
2 An effective operational balance. This often means that a constant search for new accounts is weighed against ensuring good service for existing clients.
3 A commitment to enable the company to capitalize fully on the store of knowledge and awareness of customers held by the salesperson. More and more companies are recognizing the value of sales force and marketing think-tanks in establishing a good cross-fertilization of knowledge and ideas.

Lidstone[30] links many of the problems faced by sales managers with the four operational 'realities' of sales force organization. The four 'ds' – diffusion, dissent, distance and deskilling – challenge the management capabilities of sales management.

Table 22.1 The four difficulties facing sales management

Issue	Difficulty	Implications
Diffusion	Sales forces are often geographically spread across a wide area.	Communicating Motivating Controlling
Dissent	Sales staff regularly face rejection and disagreement from customers.	Loss of morale Erasing of technique
Distance	The distance between sales operations and management means staff are unsupervised for most of the time.	Leadership Support Training Control
Deskilling	Selling is a social skill.	Maintaining skill level

Adapted from Lidstone, J., *Training Salesmen on the Job*. Gower, 1986.

Motivating

Motivating the sales force calls for a clear understanding of the forces that influence performance. The very high turnover in many sales forces and sales departments suggests that a combination of the personalities of the staff involved and the policies adopted are not preventing de-motivation and the desire to leave. Replacing top-quality staff is expensive and the costs incurred during transfer can sometimes be enormous. The recurrent problem in advertising, for example, is that those closest to being sales staff – account executives – leave, taking their major accounts with them. Despite this, management often seem to be unwilling to invest time or effort in trying to understand the forces that affect sales force motivation. Communication and involvement in decision-making appear to be very important, and close contact with a clearly communicated sense of belonging are often needed by sales staff to sustain their commitment.

A recurrent complaint of sales staff in both small and large firms is the apparent lack of response to their comments and suggestions:

> We are told we are the main point of contact with the customer but no-one appears to listen when we report what the customer is saying. (Comment by experienced salesman with large firm.)

The normal approach to motivation is defined in terms of sales force incentive payments and bonuses, but there is some evidence[31] to suggest that remuneration is best seen as a control mechanism rather than a motivator:

> Payment systems are best thought of in terms of their ability to demotivate rather than motivate.

The increasing importance of 'team selling'[32] has forced many firms to review radically their systems of reward or incentive. These often shift attention toward business development, loyalty and profits and away from volume, especially in industrial markets.[33]

Control

Control is generally exercised through three vehicles: payment and supervision, promotion and targets. Remuneration can be seen in terms of both level and form. Payment is usually in terms of a fixed salary, salary plus commission, or straight commission. The individuality of salespeople and the varied nature of marketing conditions suggest that any general analysis of strengths and weaknesses should be handled with care in any specific situation, but it does appear that overall these appear to be as shown in Table 22.2.

Table 22.2 Alternative payment systems for sales staff

	Strengths	Weaknesses
Salary only	Provides security for opening up new territories. Minimizes internal tensions. Achieves effective balances when lengthy negotiations can be followed by long-term repeat orders. Easy to administer.	No incentives for extra efforts. Does not fit in with achievement and reward needs of many salesmen.
Salary plus commission	Achieves balance between incentive and security. Stimulates marginal opportunity spotting. Makes salespeople more likely to be creative in pushing for new development	Incentives for efforts still limited. Difficult to administer, particularly if target-related.
Straight commission	Maximizes effort. Provides powerful reward-stimulus learning pattern. Leads to attempts to fully exploit major accounts. All costs are tied to returns.	May cause jealousy and antagonism among staff. Danger of short-term pay-offs with accounts rather than long-term relationship being emphasized. Little incentive for missionary work. May deter some applicants. Can create some financial distress when performance is poor.

Sales force targets are infrequently associated with these payment systems. Targeting has been the cause of fierce debate among marketing and sales staff, the arguments of each being: 'If the person is doing the job properly, targets are expensive and cumbersome methods of restating the inevitable' and 'Targets provide salesmen and managers with clear ideas about expected performance and added incentives for achievement'. The move towards tailoring sales force compensation to specific management objectives has done much to sustain interest in targeting.

It appears that many of the criticisms are related to systems of arbitrary targeting. Management may decide on the basis of some evidence or analysis that specific targets should be set, and these are then set to the sales force. Although the response may be short-term uplifts in sales, in the medium to long term it appears that sales force turnover increases, sales in some accounts decline in the medium term as orders, brought forward to meet targets, lead to increased stocks, and sales costs increase dramatically.

Mutual targeting appears to overcome many of these problems. The salesperson, his or her immediate superior and perhaps the relevant manager work together to establish agreed targets and the best means of achieving them. It is essential that the firm has a clear idea of its priorities in this area. Multi-brand or multi-product firms sometimes adopt the dangerous stance of changing or modifying targets, e.g. for each journey cycle.[34]

Evaluating performance may be related to these targets or defined in terms of some other criteria. Although there is much discussion about evaluating individual salespeople, relatively little research has been carried out into measuring the overall effectiveness of the sales force.

Some analyses have implied that evaluation of the sales force is perhaps best seen in terms of measuring the impact of increasing (or reducing) the sales force size. The sales force can thus be increased or reduced until the maximum returns, as defined by the firm, have been earned.[35]

Evaluation of the individual salesperson is usually conducted in terms of two parallel sets of criteria:

1   *Quantitative:* meeting targets; sales volume and profitability; visits, usually split between established and new accounts; promotional or display work, i.e. placing display material; customer comments.
2   *Qualitative:* assessed contribution to company achievements; satisfying superiors' expectations; attitude and contribution to development of sales force and his colleagues; organizational skills; longer-term potential; customer relationships; appearance.

The heart of the matter

At the heart of modern sales and sales management lies an understanding of the sales process, sometimes called the sales interview. Typically, this can be broken down into six phases:[36]

1   The opening.
2   Need and problem identification.
3   Presentation and demonstration.
4   Dealing with objectives.
5   Negotiation.
6   Closing the sale.

Successful sales staff identify and employ strategies and tactics to take them through each of these phases. Sometimes these policies are designed around common features such as the famous IBM emphasis on 'needs, features, benefits'. Elsewhere priority is given to individual actions to tackle particular challenges.

Effectiveness often depends on thinking the process through in advance, assessing likely barriers to progress and devising ways to overcome these. Sometimes the challenge lies outside the direct control of the individual. In international markets these often emerge because of cultural difficulties[37] or barriers.[38] There is, however, growing recognition of the strategic value of a skilled and motivated salesforces. In *Thriving on Chaos,*[39] Tom Peters advises top managers to recognize this value by spending time with sales staff, giving them the resources to do their job and placing them at the heart of the sales and marketing effort.

Conclusion

The last two decades have seen dramatic shifts in trading conditions. Resource shortages in the mid-1970s gave way to buoyant markets in the mid-1980s. The late 1980s and early 1990s saw a dramatic shift from the high optimism of the period just after the destruction of the Berlin Wall, to grave concerns during the Gulf War and the boom then collapse of the 'Tiger' economies of Asia. Exchange rate fluctuations, technological restrictions and new priorities have appeared and will continue to happen. This situation poses particular problems for sales staff. Even when their own firms are not directly affected, their supplies may be limited, so they may have to modify their operations to incorporate the skills to effectively allocate, perhaps even ration, supplies. At other times, production schedules demand that product is shifted as quickly as possible. In some industries this has even led to sales personnel taking a positive role in the reallocation of stocks from one outlet to another one day and allocating orders between production units later.

The pressure of costs and liquidity today means that sales staff in many companies also have to become actively involved in debt collection. This has created severe problems of behaviour modification for some staff, who may be forced to restrict supplies to well-established clients whose payment record is poor, thus affecting the overall profitability of the account.

This broader role, with sales staff acting almost as account managers in some instances, is leading to an increasing information and communication need among sales staff. In the short term this has led to a pattern of feeding increasing amounts of market intelligence to the field sales force, and on-line link-ups through computer or video systems.

As communication systems between the firm and its sales force improve, many of the traditional problems of sales force management – geographical dispersion and lack of immediate control, notably of the consistency of messages – are likely to be reduced. It is quite likely that this, along with environmental changes, will lead to a revitalization of the role of the salesperson. This is already occurring in industrial markets,[40] and may soon happen in consumer markets. The importance of sales staff, already great, may steadily increase, as will the demand for high-quality recruits. Often these will come from non-traditional groups with skills, access and backgrounds to open new markets. Traditional prejudices against women, ethnic minorities, the disabled are being replaced by decisions to choose the right person for the right job.[41]

At the same time, there is constant pressure on the sales force to move key staff into other areas[42] and use their expertise elsewhere.

SPECIMEN QUESTIONS

1 'The sales representative is the most effective but least appreciated member of the marketing team.' Assess this comment – indicating as far as possible why you think this type of view is held.

2 Outline the impact of new information technology on the sales function – illustrate your answer in terms of at least three of McMurry's seven selling tasks.

3 You are the owner of a small, high technology, bio-tech company. Draw up the job description for a new salesperson.

4 'Bank managers are merely money salesmen.' Discuss this comment and suggest ways in which banks might refine the role of bank managers in the light of this view.

5 Why is personal selling generally viewed as the most important element in the industrial marketing mix? How might the effectiveness of this kind of selling be improved by the greater use of other, non-price, marketing mix elements.

6 The newly appointed sales director of a local firm has asked you to advise on the organization of her national sales force. The firm sells a range of products into the construction and DIY industry. These range from packaged, decorative tiles for use by householders to plain tiles typically bought by local authority direct works departments. Recent acquisitions have widened the range of products to include bathroom and toilet fixtures and fittings. At present 27 sales staff are organized regionally and are paid on a basic salary and small commission (maximum 15 per cent of total remuneration). Prepare and defend your recommendations.

7 What are the relative merits of a home-based sales representative and an overseas agent in opening up a market for plastic components for the 'white goods' and 'automotive' markets?

8 Apart from personal attributes and selling skill, what factors can affect the ability of sales staff to reach their targets?

9 Discuss the relative merits of:

(a)   very high, hard-to-achieve sales targets;

(b)   forecast-based targets;

(c)   no targets

in sales force management.

10 'I watched *Glengarry Glen Ross* and felt that the tough stance adopted by the sales manager from head office was exactly what this group needed – if anything, he was too soft.' Comment.

CASE STUDY 18: ROYALE MOTORS LTD

Jean Brown had recently been appointed Sales Director of Royale Motors of King's Lynn. In her first two months in her new job she had conducted a thorough review of the firm's operations, and this filled her with foreboding about the future.

The company consisted of four garages and showrooms, all holding Rover franchises in the King's Lynn area. For the last three years the firm had suffered badly from increased competition, especially from new products by foreign producers and vigorous price competition by UK producers; the entire range, from the Metro to the top-of-the-range Rover 600 and 800 series had been affected. Now, although new stock was available in all the showrooms, sales were very sluggish.

Little of this could be blamed on Rover's overall performance, as Rover nationally was winning the market share. Her sense of disquiet was made worse by a number of unhealthy behaviour patterns, which she observed among her sales staff. While sales force turnover was steadily increasing, notably among younger men, a passive attitude to winning business existed. On one day alone she noted seventeen visitors to one showroom; of these, only three were spontaneously approached by a salesman; six called into the sales office for attention, and the rest left. Also, trade-in values and price discounts were increasing as a proportion of the purchase value of new and used vehicles sold, and increasing numbers of old and difficult-to-sell foreign cars were being accepted. In contrast to this, fewer cars from the 'majors' (Ford, Fiat, VW and the leading Japanese manufacturers) were being traded in for new Rovers. 'The only major manufacturer whose cars are traded in is Rover, and often the impression is that Rover dealers were the only ones offering acceptable trade-in.' The major bright spot was the relative strength of second-hand sales. She knew that the new link with BMW would place these problems under an even greater spotlight.

Jean put these points to the board at the first board meeting after completing her review. There was some discussion of the scope for seeking out the franchise to link with Rover. Jean, along with her fellow board members, rejected this on the grounds that they had for over forty years 'invested in Rover', and besides they had to get their problems sorted before BMW would consider extending their franchise at the expense of their local BMW dealer. It was generally agreed that revitalized sales and marketing would go a long way to resolving their problems, at least in the short to medium term.

Jean decided upon a number of immediate steps:

1   She reorganized the sales force, giving each outlet far more freedom and responsibility for turnover and profitability. She then looked for a method to generate a spirit of constructive competition between outlets.

2   She restructured the payment system. In the past the commission element had been very small ('Rover cars sell themselves' was almost the message). Now commissions allied to agreed sales targets would constitute a significant part of the sales rep's income.

3   Layout of the showrooms was drastically changed. The sales offices were eliminated and a more open-plan format adopted: 'They must not hide behind glass walls'.

4   Stricter controls over trade-ins and discounts were introduced. These were linked to the commission system.

5 The sales manager in each outlet was given special responsibility for 'fleet' business. The type of 'fleet' sought was closely defined, i.e. small firms with seven to ten company cars. The managers and their staff were required to go out and actively seek this business.

6 Advertising and sales expenditure were boosted, primarily through local radio.

7 Links were established with the East Anglia Regional Management Centre for a continuing counselling relationship.

8 Rover inspectors were actively involved in future developments.

These were put before the board at the next board meeting. Some of the board members were already aware of complaints among the sales force about the scale of these changes.

Task

1 Review the proposals.

2 Relate these to the type of promotions to be seen on offer from rival car dealers.

3 Decide which to support and make specific recommendations to Jean on implementation, especially in terms of winning active support from the sales force.

CASE STUDY 19: AVON COSMETICS LTD

Avon Cosmetics is the world's largest direct shopping company. Today's sales-force numbers in the millions worldwide. This results from Avon's commitment to recruit and train more people, and target their efforts towards the modern, professional woman.

In the US, Avon representatives who recruit or 'sponsor' new sales staff are paid a bonus, besides receiving a commission on the recruit's sales, as long as both remain in the company.

Staff loyalty is an important part of Avon customer care. Customers prefer sales staff who are highly experienced and familiar to them.

Over the years, Avon has experimented with a number of additions to their core of cosmetics, toiletries and fragrances. These include home health-care, medical supplies and chemicals, few of which had any significant impact on their customers. The decline in overall sales figures during the 1980s forced a rethinking of Avon's marketing strategy. Avon widened its appeal, for example to target women of differing ethnic origins. Avon product catalogues are available in different languages, to cater for multi-lingual societies.

23

Marketing communications

Introduction

A communications revolution is occurring that is changing the nature of marketing. It affects every feature of the process of exchange – from the identification of opportunities, through the design and delivery of goods and services to the feedback process on customer satisfaction.[1] New technologies allow retailers to download designs to clothing producers in Hong Kong as quickly as they can be sent to Leeds. Related technologies allow a small further education college to produce an 'in-house' newspaper to high standards using desk-top publishing. New graphics software permits the lecturer to include visuals, images and a host of audio-visual aids to present ideas, concepts and issues. Kenichi Ohmae[2] suggests that these communication system developments will create a 'borderless world' in which ideas spread quickly[3] and control systems change. The very nature of the firm will be transformed. Buttle[4] argues that this transformation has advanced so far that 'communication' is now 'the process by which we construct our social reality'.

Much of marketing activity centres around the communication process. Despite this, there has until recently been relatively little attention paid to the total communication process. Writers have preferred to concentrate on the more specific areas of communication such as advertising, press relations, selling and personal contact. Failure to understand the underlying process can undermine the dialogue the firm is seeking to establish with its client groups.

Communication has been defined by Delozier[5] as:

> The process of establishing a commonness or oneness of thought between a sender and a receiver.

This places emphasis on two vital but often neglected features of communication:

1 It involves a number of partners.
2 The reception of the message is as important as its transmission.

The 'classic' communications error assumes virtually the opposite: that the needs of the receiver and the sender are the same, and that all receivers of information are the same.

The communication process

All communication processes have certain features in common, whether they involve a salesperson speaking to a client or an advertising campaign using a number of media. In Figure 23.1 a model of this process is presented.

Transmission

It is useful to describe the communication process as starting with the 'transmitter's' rather than the 'receiver's' data. Most of the time, however, it is difficult to draw the line between the two, as the interactions in healthy communication are ongoing, with dialogue being the most important feature. In their study of industry marketing negotiations, Alexander, Schul and Babakus[6] highlight the multidimensional nature of interpersonal communications. People interact and communicate on a number of levels. Understanding these levels is an important aspect of the attempt to appreciate how and why people respond the way they do.

Figure 23.1   The communication process

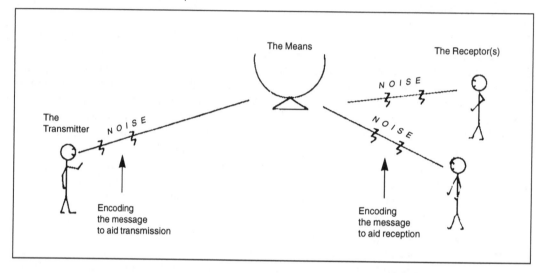

At the same time it is necessary to recognize that communication is not necessarily a conscious process. We are continually taking in or giving out impressions through our appearance, manner and attitudes, as well as the words we say and the images we project. Informal communication – internally through the business grapevine or externally through rumour or endorsement – can have a direct impact on such issues as product support, endorsement or appeal.[7] Anyone seeking a career in marketing needs to be as conscious of the unintended impressions as of the thought-out and designed campaigns. This can include the appearance of the salesperson, the frontage of the shop and the appearance of the factory or workplace. The company is constantly transmitting messages even if it does not know it. Marketing's function in this area is to ensure that the message transmitted is the one the firm seeks to send. Figure 23.3 illustrates how the sender and receiver are in constant interaction with roles continually changing.

Different participants play varying roles. Opinion leaders,[8] for example, can shape views far beyond their immediate networks.

Figure 23.2 Different ways of sending the same message. From *Build a Better life by Stealing Office Supplies*, by Scott Adams, published by Nicholas Brealey Publishing Ltd, tel: 0171 430 0224, fax: 0171 404 8311.

Figure 23.3 The simple two-way communication model

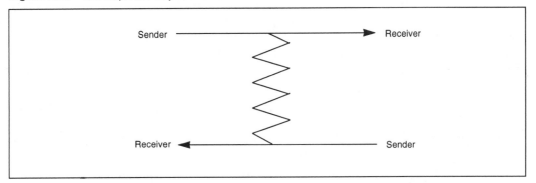

Encoding

Sending any message involves choices about the best way to send it and then the way to convert the message into the form required by that means. In the personal sales situation it involves choosing the right terms to use, the language best suited to get across the message and providing supportive cues. This is most obvious in international trade where the sales staff is dealing in a foreign language. It is equally true in the home market where the sales staff need to phrase their message in ways which relate to the understanding and information needs of the client.

In certain international markets there is increasing reluctance to deal always in English with British salespeople. The story is told of the Managing Director of the German firm who arrived in his office to find the salesman from a US company waiting to see him. He took him into his office, sat him down and asked:

'Are you selling to me or am I selling to you?'

When the salesman replied he was selling to the Managing Director, the German replied:

'Well, now we speak in German.'

This was a perfectly proper and suitable response.

Often the process of encoding calls for more obvious marketing skills and disciplines, such as:

1　Phrasing market research questions so that the respondent understands and can respond to them.
2　Designing a TV commercial in a way which gets across a complex message, reflecting a challenging marketing strategy to a largely indifferent audience in 15 seconds.
3　Building an exhibition stand which attracts customers, allows the firm to display its products and meets safety standards . . . comfortably.

The process of encoding involves converting the message the firm wishes to send into terms which meet the needs of the medium in which it is being transmitted.[9]

Noise

The sender has another all-pervasive factor to deal with in any encoding process – noise. This is the general term used to describe the variety of external and potentially distracting influences or stimuli, which affect the transmission. Noise can be very basic, such as background noise from the factory making it hard for the salesperson to be heard. It can be totally negative, such as the loud complaining previous customer distracting current buyers. It can be intangible and positive, such as the delicious smells from the kitchen of a restaurant, or tangible and negative, such as black smoke from the next-door café.

Certain forms of noise can be unavoidable. Many messages are converted into forms that cannot communicate the full nature and character of the product and service. Often the firm can avoid the negative effects with care and attention to detail. The then Marketing Director of the Scottish Development Agency described how she was frequently addressed in letters from overseas as 'Mrs Scottish Development Agency' in letters that then proceeded to say 'Dear Sir'. There is no doubt that British firms are as guilty as anyone in this process of failing to appreciate the impact that noise can have on any process of turning an idea into a tangibly expressed concept. Recently, there has been a growing awareness of the impact of such issues as gender on the way messages are treated.[10]

Terpstra[11] identifies many of these 'noise' communication barriers. He indicates how they can both distort messages and produce very different results from those sought (Figure 23.4).

Figure 23.4 Communication barriers in international marketing. Adapted from Terpstra[12]

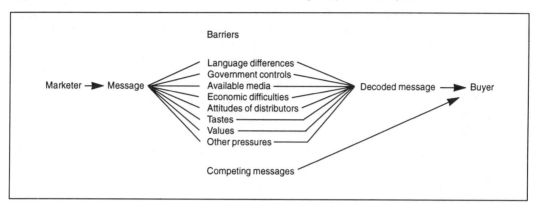

The means

The range of opportunities for transmitting messages is virtually endless, from the direct mail letter via the satellite to the beer mat. The options are enormous, especially when the scope for combined means is included. Despite that, until some form of telepathy is available, all have limitations. Each has its strengths and weaknesses under different conditions and in getting various messages across. The options open are discussed at length in Chapter 2. However, it must be recognized that all have their impact on:

1 The nature of the message.
2 The process of transmission.
3 Reception.

Preparing a message for transmission, sending it and organizing for its reception involves a series of transformations. Each of these creates an opportunity for noise and distortion. These problems are made worse when the firm fails to keep clearly in mind the objectives of the exercise and the needs of the receiver.

Symbolism

Symbols are very important in marketing communication. The Kodak K, the Coke bottle, the leading Jaguar, are intrinsic features in the offering made to current or potential buyers. The McDonald 'golden arch' has a meaning that extends far beyond a logo and way of identifying an outlet.[13] Some symbols can become so familiar that there is almost no need for the full name to be used. M and S, IBM and BBC are good illustrations of this process. The corporate logo can reach the same status. The Shell 'shell' and the Mercedes-Benz 'badge' have reached this point of awareness and recognition.

This type of symbol can become part of a global system of communication. They make it easier for clients to recognize the product or its message. A symbol like the Esso 'tiger' takes this even further by making an overt link between the product offering and certain characteristics of the tiger. This can have positive features but contains some risks. Symbolism varies between countries and over time. An image can be powerful and positive in one country but negative in another. Animal symbolism, notably parrots, elephants and tigers, is a common feature of advertisements and logos in India. In Europe animals are seldom used.

Sometimes, this symbolism extends beyond the firm or the country. Bradley[14] shows how German companies are expected to be strong on product features in the marketing mix. Consumers believe that Italian companies will be good at communications. US firms are assumed to emphasize R & D. Sometimes these 'images' are negative. Saghafi[15] highlights the problems faced by Latin American firms entering the US market.

Against these generalized views and the proposal that 'The world's needs and desires have been irrevocably homogenized by technology'[16] there is evidence that even within Europe there are deep-rooted cultural differences.[17] These need to be recognized if marketing policies are to work. Whitelock and Chung[18] concluded that standardization of advertising occurs in only a small minority of cases and that 'universal standardization of advertising is not possible for all products'.

Symbols are increasing in importance, as markets become more international and competitive:

> The symbol becomes shorthand for the personality of the company. If the personality (reputation) represents values, then the symbol itself comes to represent values. It thus has a worth.[19]

The value of symbols extends through the enterprise to the entire communication process.

The receiver

Both the transmission and reception of information and communication are personal processes. The individuals who are expected to 'take in', 'understand' and 'act on' the message are diverse and subject to many other influences and pressures.

As receivers of information, human beings are relatively imperfect. They are not standardized or specialized like television sets or computers. It is surprising that so many firms act as if this were the case. Companies seldom take into account the physical limitations of individuals.

> Friends of the Earth in Durham was one of the earliest organizations to recognize the importance of good household insulation to protect the elderly from the worst aspects of cold northern winters. With the help of the Manpower Services Commission, Friends of the Earth embarked on a campaign to persuade pensioners to let them insulate their homes at no cost.

> They undertook an extensive poster campaign to reach the elderly. However, in the first month they had virtually no takers. They stood back and looked at their advertising with the help of a marketing lecturer from the university. It soon became apparent that the size of the writing on the posters was so small that it was virtually invisible to most old people, especially when stuck on the inside of a post office window.

Problems of hearing and sight are seldom taken into account by marketing staff, although it is estimated that over 70 per cent of the population over the age of 30 have problems in these areas.

A number of models have been developed to describe the process by which information is taken in, organized and acted upon. In applying these or other approaches, firms seldom take into account the double loop, which is involved in converting learning to action. The loops in Figure 23.5 describe how developing the means to ensure the reception of a message is intimately associated with the mechanism for ensuring that routes to action are included.

Figure 23.5   Learning and action loops

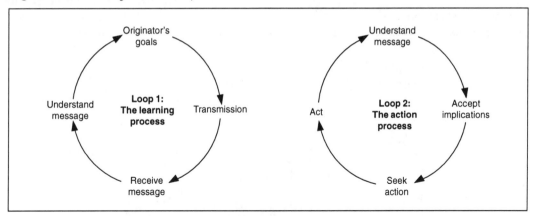

Problems of communication

These can be summarized as:

1 Biases by the receiver – we only hear or see what we want to.
2 Omission or distortion by the sender – the dangers of gaps and misleading messages.
3 Lack of trust.
4 Non-verbal forces always obliterate verbal.
5 Overload.
6 Hidden sources and data.
7 Distance.
8 Fear.
9 Immediacy – the present always obscures the future.
10 Conflict – pulling people in many ways usually means they go somewhere else.
11 Obscurity.

Overcoming these problems is partly a function of the means being used to transmit the message. However, certain basic rules should be applied:

1 Recognize the problem.
2 Use a variety of means to get messages across.
3 Build campaigns, not individual actions.
4 Encourage two-way communication.
5 Keep the links in the chain of communication as few as possible.

These steps, allied to a programme of research to understand the needs of the receptor group, provide the best promise of getting the desired message across.

Conclusion

Communication has always been at the centre of marketing theory and practice. Technological changes have the potential to transform marketing communications by giving producers far more scope to offer highly selective and carefully directed messages to their markets. Consumers and intermediaries will have far more power than in the past to inform and influence suppliers. Morgan[20] explores the ways in which firms are using electronic commerce to extend their horizons.[21] The Internet is only part of this picture. Intranet developments[22] allows firms to integrate their information and communication systems.

Figure 23.6 This Liverpool Victoria Insurance advertisement plays on the 'image' of insurance salesmen

SPECIMEN QUESTIONS

1 Indicate three ways in which an understanding of the multidimensional nature of communication is reflected in an advertisement or promotion of your choice.

2 Your advertising agency has spent the last six weeks working on a radical reappraisal of your advertising. The creative director of the agency is full of enthusiasm for the new treatment because, as he says, 'like all good advertising it is built around a genuine dialogue with people – inviting and encouraging them to bring something to the communication process'.

   At a seminar at the local university sponsored by your firm, the Professor of Marketing spontaneously expresses a similar view to the marketing director (who is yet to see the campaign). Your director calls it airy-fairy nonsense.

   The agency is due to present in three days; what do you do?

3 'Culture is the ultimate determinant of the effectiveness of all communication.' How far can this notion be used to explain the success of two of:

   (a) The McDonald 'Golden Arch'?

   (b) The Kodak 'K'?

   (c) The Shell 'shell'?

   (d) The Coke 'shape'?

4 If 'culture is the ultimate determinant of the effectiveness of all communication', how far can this notion be used to explain the failure of two of:

   (a) *The BIZ* business magazine?

   (b) The Sinclair C5 electric car?

   (c) Kevin Costner's films *Waterworld* and *The Postman*?

   (d) American football in Britain?

5 Define:

   (a) Communication.

   (b) The borderless world.

   (c) Encoding.

   (d) Noise.

   (e) Video vultures.

   (f) Symbolism.

   (g) Overload.

   (h) Cognitive dissonance.

   (i) Perceptual bias.

   (j) Feedback.

PROJECT

1   Prepare a report on the way a selected international firm promotes its identity and portfolio of products locally and in two other markets.

2   Give a presentation on the message(s) being transmitted and the points of similarity and difference.

24

Strategic marketing

Introduction

The economic turbulence of the early 1990s prompted many firms to review their approach to marketing and its role in the firm. Fluctuating rates of growth in North America, parts of Asia and Europe were associated with increasing budget deficits in the US, an increasing gap between the rich and the poor and concern about the ability of local and world economics to sustain current levels of expansion. Policy-makers found themselves faced with visions of expanded opportunities and growing risk. The strategic challenge facing marketing becomes more important under these circumstances. This challenge is to help firms position themselves to win competitive advantage. This is achieved by meeting customer needs more effectively in the short term while establishing an enhanced competitive capability in the long term.[1]

Strategic positioning which places the enterprise in the best place to capitalize on opportunities lies at the core of effective marketing today. This approach acknowledges the limitations on immediate action. An enterprise cannot change overnight simply because old markets contract and new opportunities emerge. Senior management's task starts long before the specific opportunity or threat occurs. Marketing policy-makers are responsible for ensuring that the venture is in the best position to spot, employ or respond to customer needs.

Changing conditions

The nature of the opportunities open to a firm and its freedom to manoeuvre are determined by its core competences and capabilities. Prahalad[2] views the core competences of the firm as the cumulative results of the lessons learned over time. These competences draw together skills in managing technologies, the ability to mobilize resources and an understanding of particular marketing. The integration of these competences permits the firm to succeed in some markets and under specific conditions. Central to the strategic marketing position of a firm is its understanding of these competences and the ability to direct them to achieve results.

Kay's[3] notion of distinctive capabilities takes this type of analysis further by suggesting that long-term competitive advantage derives from capabilities 'which other firms lack', that are 'underpinned' by 'supporting strategies' in a specific 'industry' to gain market advantage against specific rivals. Kay suggests that specific distinctive capabilities recur in successful firms. These are the ability to innovate within a distinctive corporate architecture, i.e. system of relationships, so successfully that the company's reputation reinforces its long-term success.

Initially, changes in markets and conditions provoked a range of responses from marketing managers and academics. Some emphasized diversification and high levels of activity as means of 'covering the risks' of getting it wrong. The notion that product life-cycles were contracting encouraged some firms to increase the rate of new product introduction and abandon some well-established products. Elsewhere, the emphasis was on specialization. Niche marketing seemed to be the ultimate marketing solution in static markets until Tie Rack, Knickerbox, Sock Shop and Next 'hit the wall' and were forced to rethink themselves in the late 1980s. Exciting ideas became transformed into panaceas. Total Quality Management (TQM) at its best reaffirms the importance of customer satisfaction.[4] It challenges the compromises and complacency that grew up in the buoyant and less competitive markets of the 1950s, 1960s and 1970s.

Tom Peters talks of the Japanese providing the first cars that did not need a built-in mechanic. Others note that the great Japanese achievement lies in making available technology work. Sadly, the substance behind the idea was not as widely recognized as the value of the basic idea. There was a failure to develop the back-up systems to make the intensive quality programmes work. This has prompted Oakland to talk of TQD: Total Quality Disillusionment.[5] A similar fate seems to be affecting the idea of Total Customer Responsiveness (TCR) put forward by Tom Peters.[6] The excitement of the idea can blind managers to the hard work and strategic commitment needed to make it succeed. The current re-examination of these ideas is leading to a reappraisal of the central task and role of marketing. This highlights the importance of marketing in giving the firm a sense of direction. From this comes recognition that the formulation of strategies to manage and take advantage of all the challenges posed by the market is a vital task for marketing management.

Strategic management is a critical element in helping firms to:

1 Cope with the increasing complexity of business operations today, especially in large organizations.
2 Provide a sense of direction and basis for co-ordinating corporate activities.
3 Identify and capitalize on developments in the market-place.
4 Achieve competitive advantage.

This approach to marketing strategy provides the framework within which a definition of strategy can be developed. A number of approaches to identifying the features that distinguish strategy and strategic decisions from operational and tactical issues have been developed. Luck and O'Ferrel[7] suggest a relatively simple definition of strategy:

> The fundamental schemes or means for reaching objectives.

Weitz and Wensley[8] place their emphasis on:

> (the progress by which) a company determines where to 'place its efforts, which markets and market segments it chooses to participate in, and what product it attempts to sell in those markets'.

Andrews[9] emphasizes the importance of defining the nature of organization and integrating its operations. This role is especially important in larger and more diverse ventures:

> Corporate strategy is the pattern of decisions in a company that determines and reveals its objectives, purposes, or goals, produces the principal policies and plans for achieving those goals and defines the range of businesses the company is to pursue, the kind of economic and non-economic contribution it intends to make to its stakeholders, employees, customers and communities . . . [it] defines the businesses in

which a company will compete, preferably in a way that focuses resources to convey distinctive competences into competitive advantages.

In sum, it encompasses those activities which:

1 Define the nature and distinctive competences of the enterprise.
2 Give the firm its sense of purpose.
3 Provide a measure against which proposed actions can be assessed.
4 Provide a framework for integrating diverse operations.
5 Highlight the firm's differential advantage in the market.

The nature of strategic decisions

A number of writers[10, 11, 12] have suggested that the distinctive nature of strategy lies in the types of decisions involved. These choices enable executives to distinguish between the tactical and strategic in their work. Two approaches to this are presented, shown in Table 24.1.

The varying emphasis of the sets of authors reflects the rather different nature of their preoccupations. Johnson and Scholes[13] focus on the strategic decision as it affects the organization, while Steiner and Miller[14] give their attention to the challenges this type of decision poses to the manager. However, the consistency of their emphasis on the relative importance of the strategic decision, its long time horizon and its complexity gives some flavour of the nature of the task faced by the marketing strategist. In this context, his or her skills in strategic analysis are the major determinants of success.

Table 24.1 The characteristics of strategic decisions

Johnson and Scholes[15]	Steiner and Miller[16]
1. Importance	1. Importance
2. Long time horizons	2. Long time horizons
3. Matching the firm to its environment	3. Top-level decision makers
4. Matching activities to resources	4. Level of detail
5. Allocation of major resources	5. Regular formulation
6. The values of policy makers	6. Unstructured and unique problems
7. The scope of the firm's operations	7. Largely subjective information
8. Complexity	8. Difficulty of evaluation

Sources: Johnson and Scholes;[17]

Strategic analysis

In Chapter 8, many of the major issues in this area were introduced. Effective analysis calls for the knowledge to wed the skills introduced in that chapter to an ability to place the strategy into a wider context. Successful analysis requires as much insight into the capabilities of the enterprise as the environment in which the firm operates. Figure 24.1 highlights the multifaceted nature of strategic decision-making.

A host of environmental forces can influence the firm. Some are general, affecting all types of companies. The tax system in a country will influence the behaviour of most companies. The Single European Act and the Maastricht Treaty touch virtually all European companies. Other

Figure 24.1   The context for formulation of marketing strategy: a summary model of the elements of strategic management. (*Source:* Johnson and Scholes.[18])

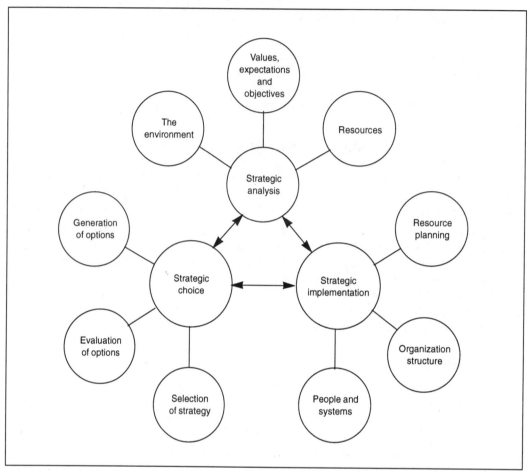

environmental influences are more specific in their effects. Construction firms are among the first to feel the results of changes in mortgage rates. Companies like British Aerospace were steeling themselves for large reductions in defence expenditure until the 1990–91 Gulf crisis. The growing awareness of threats to the natural environment makes 'green' marketing one of the driving forces in contemporary marketing thought.[19, 20, 21]

Skilled marketers understand the environmental forces that shape performances and the ways they determine performance. The choices, selections and appraisals made as part of strategic analysis are shaped by the values, expectations and objectives of those involved in the analysis. People are influenced in this analysis by their training and the reward systems which operate in the company. Their freedom of action and the options open to them are determined by the resources at their control. A small firm might want to open new accounts across Europe but they lack the resources to tackle more than one fairly small market in mainland Europe.

Porter[22] draws attention to the importance of value chain analysis. This type of analysis breaks down the activities performed by companies and the resources available to the firm into a small number of strategically important categories (see Figure 24.2).

Figure 24.2 The generic value chain. Source: Porter.[23]

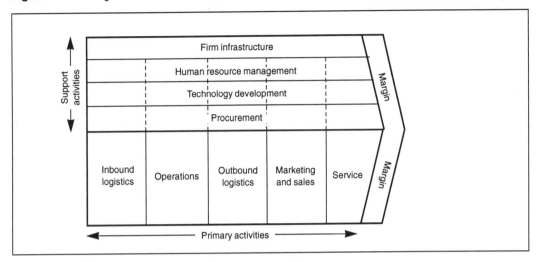

These are defined in terms of either their effects on costs or the scope within them for achieving competitive advantage through differentiation. They are:

1 Inbound logistics (all activities associated with goods and services bought in).
2 Operations (production and manufacturing systems).
3 Outbound logistics (all activities linked with dispatch, delivery and stocking of goods and services produced).
4 Marketing and sales.
5 Service.

The choice of strategy depends on a proper understanding of the options open to the firm. The ability to identify and develop the choices open to the firm is especially important. Scenario analysis is part of this. It involves the construction of models of the 'scenarios' facing the firm and the strategies that will provide a maximum opportunity and/or minimum risk. Choice of strategy is determined in part by the resources available to the firm and partly by the extent to which the possible strategies fully exploit the firm's strengths and opportunities while overcoming weaknesses and countering threats.

There is a tendency to underestimate the problems faced in ensuring the effective implementation of selected strategies. The history of warfare is full of grand strategies which failed because the logistics failed to keep pace with the troops, events did not combine as planned, or the things that could not go wrong did go wrong. The same patterns can be seen in marketing. This means that the resources required for implementation have to be sufficient. 'Sufficiency' is seldom the bare minimum but enough to cope with failures and setbacks. The organization will need to respond and adapt to the needs of the strategy. The people involved ought to have the skills and knowledge to play their part in effective implementation. This is especially true where change or adaptation to new circumstances is required.

Marketing strategies turn on the three basic elements: analysis, choice and implementation. The analysis calls for a clear understanding of the environment in which the firm operates. The extent of change, plus the complex and sometimes conflicting signals from the environment, calls for a detailed analysis of the key market conditions. This form of analysis was introduced earlier. It is possible for the firm to review the market in which it operates in terms of a

Figure 24.3   The environment turbulence mix

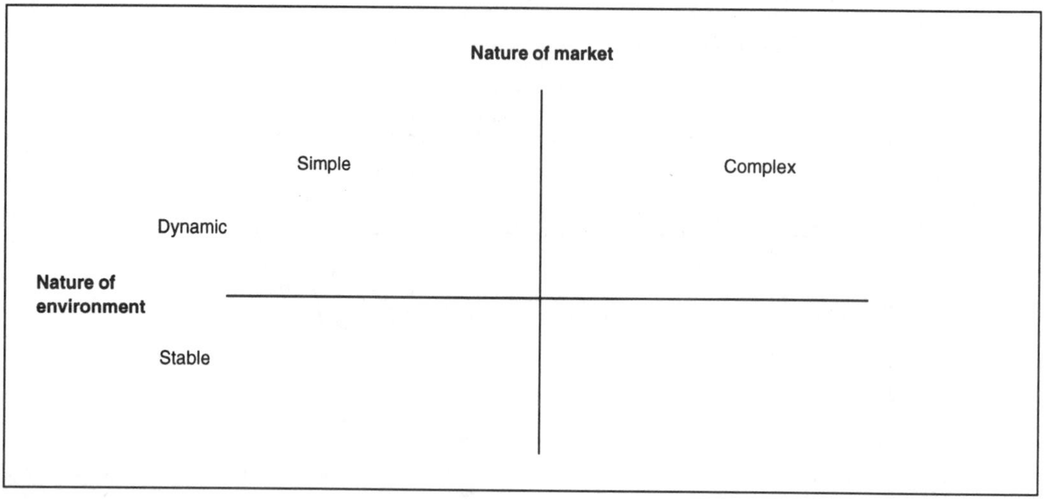

'turbulence matrix' (see Figure 24.3). The firm can locate its various offerings within this framework to explore the nature of the strategic planning tasks it will face.

An understanding of the process involved is only one aspect of the process of successful strategic management. *Choice* of appropriate strategies must be based on an understanding of the enterprise and its capabilities. The internal organization and resources of the organization need to be in tune with the strategies being pursued if they are to be achieved. This is a two-stage process:

1   Understanding the needs and capabilities of the firm (the internal, marketing audit).
2   Communicating strategies and overcoming internal resistance.

SWOT analysis and other related techniques are regularly used by firms seeking the maximum fit between strategies and capabilities. SWOT calls for a detailed and critical appraisal of the Strengths, Weaknesses, Opportunities and Threats facing the enterprise in the market.

There has, however, been far less attention paid to the tasks of communicating and *implementing* strategies. This is especially true of the issues involved in building support within the firm and overcoming resistance inside and outside the organization. This area has received increased attention following evidence that in many situations, internal resistance posed the biggest threats to effectiveness:

> Real live businessmen have learned that the big challenge is not in concocting strategy but making it work. (*Fortune,* 27 December 1982)

Ansoff[24] identifies a number of forms and explanations for the resistance to the introduction of marketing strategies, notably:

1   Delays and procrastination as those involved express their fears and lack of confidence in both the policies and the management's commitment to the changes.
2   'Sabotage' or 'absorption' by those who see their current activities placed at risk in the proposed changes.
3   'Deflection', as those with alternative approaches attempt to bend strategies to their ends.

These barriers are situations which senior management must tackle if their policies are to be effective. The first stage of this lies in the process of developing strategies. The greater the degree of pre-involvement, the greater the later commitment. At the same time, once the programme has been established and communicated it is the responsibility of top management to ensure compliance.

Tight-loose strategy

Peters and Waterman[25] highlight the effectiveness of a particular form of strategy in the most successful firms: the tight-loose approach. It has two distinct characteristics:

1 Strategies are 'tightly defined' but kept to critical and fundamental areas.
2 Management are 'loosely directed', i.e. given considerable discretion in the ways they work to achieve the strategy.

The underlying philosophy of the approach is that, provided the marketing manager is committed to the direction the firm is going in and understands his or her role in this, he or she is the person best able to choose the directions and make the operational decisions.

Strategies and portfolios

The appeal of the strategies and portfolios approach lies in its ability to wed the underlying strength of strategic planning to the real-world limitations on management control in marketing today. The problems should not let us lose sight of the importance of strategy in allowing the firm to locate itself and its product in the market-place. In this work, 'portfolio analysis' has emerged to play a central and important role. This approach has developed in a number of forms, but these have certain characteristics in common. The most critical of these is the notion that the products of the firm should be reviewed as if they represented a 'portfolio' of investment opportunities. A number of criteria can then be used to explore the nature of the investment opportunity, and the likely benefits and risks of expending additional funds and efforts to support the product to penetrate the market. The best-known of the approaches to portfolio analysis is that employed by the Boston Consulting Group.[26]

Examination of the firm's position, allied to knowledge of the general characteristics of these markets, prompts consideration of a number of approaches to these situations. The two determining variables are growth rates and market share. It is suggested by Headly[27] that these are the two single most important criteria on which investment decisions should be based. There is a close relationship between the returns a firm earns from a brand or product in a market, and its strength in and experience of a market. Both these factors are associated with larger market shares. At the same time:

> The growth of a business [market] is a major factor influencing the likely ease . . . and hence cost . . . of gaining market share.

Each of the following categories (see also Figure 24.4) will place particular demands on marketing resources, have differential potential and call for different strategic responses:

1 *Stars*. These absorb considerable resources but have considerable potential for growth and profitability.
2 *Cash cows*. These were probably 'stars' once, but there is now little growth in the market. They offer good returns now, but may have reached their peak.

Figure 24.4   The business portfolio or growth share matrix

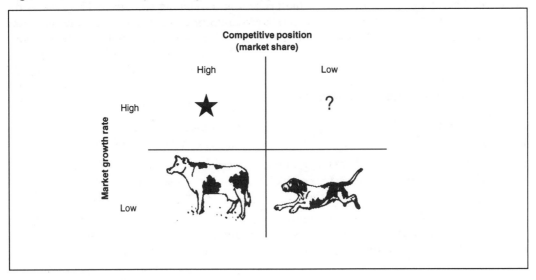

3   *Question marks.* 'High growth, low share – have the worst characteristics of all.' They consume major resources but offer little prospect of good returns.

4   *Dogs.* These consume relatively little in the way of resources but offer little prospect of returns to the firm.

A number of other approaches, such as the Shell Directional Mix, provide a similar framework but within the same overall method.

Recent research has added new light to these concepts. Perhaps the most important is that despite the strength of the underlying relationship between cash flow, market growth and competitive position, the appeal of the concept can be deceptive:

> The simplicity of this alleged principle makes it appealing as a foundation for planning. The problem is that it is often wrong. (Buzzell and Gale,[28] p. 11)

The PIMS researchers[29] highlighted the interrelationship between a number of important variables and performance. Ultimately, however, it is the relationship between quality of products and service to customers relative to competitors that determines the performance of business. This in turn depends on investment in marketing, R & D and capacity. As Morrison and Wensley[30] point out, 'No planning technique alone will guarantee good strategies'. The approach helps to structure thinking about analysis but contains inevitable dangers if viewed as a panacea.[31]

Ansoff's product/market opportunity matrix, described in Chapter 17, places its emphasis on the relationship between these product offerings and market conditions. Ansoff emphasizes the options open to the enterprise under different market conditions. In established markets, where the firm is managing existing offerings, the strategic option open to the firm is market penetration. It is obliged to seek ways to improve sales to existing or new customers through more intensive distribution, increased promotion, and price competition. The primary goals are to increase consumption among current buyers or win sales from rivals.

In established markets where there are new products, i.e. product development, the strategic options change. The emphasis is on new variants, range extensions, new models and other innovations. These are designed to increase awareness and opportunity to buy. In contrast, market development opportunities occur where established products can be introduced into new markets. Success will often depend on identification of these new markets, adapting promotional policies to new client groups and winning over distributors. In many ways, the greatest challenges are faced when the firm introduces a new product into a new market. This process of diversification places major demands on the marketing intelligence systems of the firm as it tries to cope with novel marketing conditions and an unfamiliar offering. It seems that the probability of success is lowest where uncertainty is greatest.

Figure 24.5 The product/market growth matrix: illustrations.

Market penetration
Airlines Frequent Flier Programme promotions to persuade business users to use the airline repeatedly.
Volume discounts by steel stock-holders to construction companies.
10p off next-purchase promotions by drinks companies.

Product development
Mars Ice Cream Bars.
Speciality stores within Safeway supermarkets.
ICI introducing fire-resistant polymers for furniture products.

Market development
Manchester Business School offering three-week Senior Executive Programme in Hong Kong.
Disney Corporation opening EuroDisney in Paris.
Launch of Guinness into German market.

Diversification
Acquisition of Rover by British Aerospace.
Estate agents owned by banks and building societies.
Philips' introduction of personal computers.

A further dimension is added to the analysis of strategies by Porter.[32] He emphasizes the relationship between environmental conditions and competitive pressures. His analysis concentrates on the scope firms have to compete and means available to gain competitive advantage. The competitive scope open to firms is either to attempt to reach a broadly defined target group or to target on a narrowly defined group. These can be reached through offering lower prices or by differentiating the offering (see Figure 24.6).

This approach highlights the scope for firms to succeed with strategies which fit their circumstances. It does, however, emphasize the distinction between price competitiveness and differentiation. It suggests that firms must choose between quality-based differentiation and lower prices. In the majority of cases this is true. There are notable exceptions to this. Sainsbury supermarkets have succeeded with a best-for-less type policy. Amstrad works hard to deliver relatively high technology and good quality at lower prices than its rivals.

Figure 24.6 Porter's generic stragey model

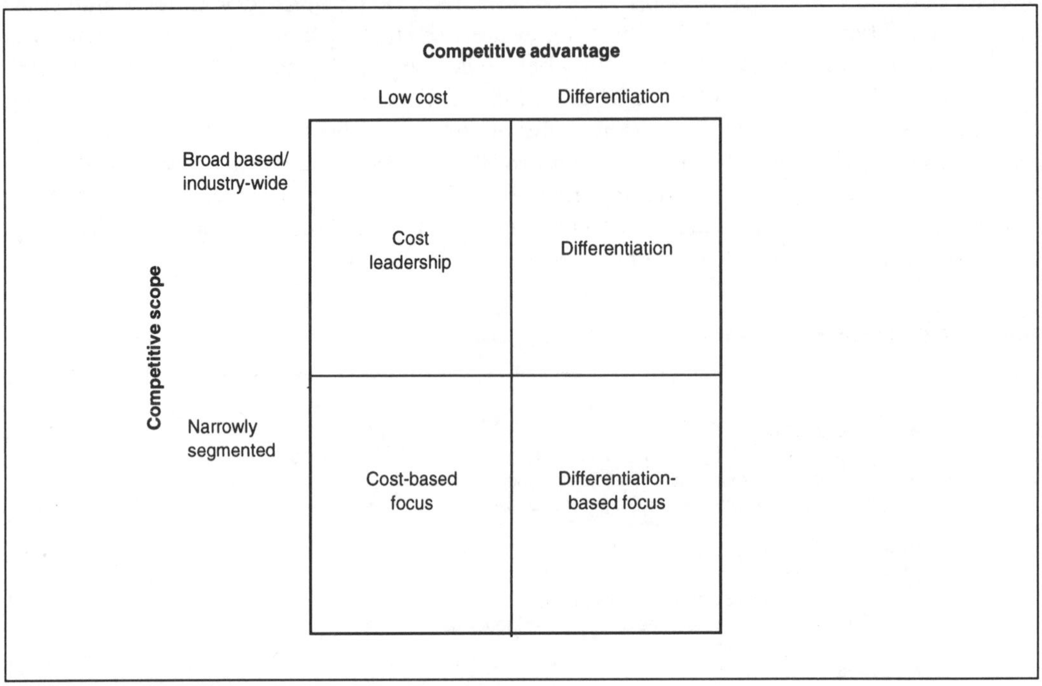

Competitive advantage

Low cost | Differentiation

Broad based/
industry-wide

Cost
leadership

Differentiation

Competitive scope

Narrowly
segmented

Cost-based
focus

Differentiation-
based focus

Strategic business units

The analysis of markets in this type of strategic framework has led to the identification of these areas of activity as 'Strategic Business Areas' (SBAs).

> This is a distinctive area of business in which the firm does (or may want to do) business.[33]

Recognition of these SBAs has led firms to seek ways of matching these with 'Strategic Business Units'. These may be defined as:

> a unit of a firm which has the responsibility for developing the firm's strategic position in one or more SBAs.[34]

The SBUs focus managers' attention on the areas for development without imposing the types of operational constraints typically associated with brand and product management. The market could be developed as an integrated totality rather than in a piecemeal way through specific offerings. At the same time, management are forced to look at markets in terms of benefits and costs. Attention is redirected towards the returns being earned. Simultaneously, senior corporate management has the freedom rigorously to appraise the different areas of activity within an internally consistent framework. Despite these claims, it is clear that SBUs have not lived up to their early promise. It would appear that simply devising alternative organizational structures cannot compensate for a lack of strategic insight.

There is increasing criticism of the approach of modern writers on marketing strategy. This criticism centres on the emphasis on analysis, and the priority given to positioning over action and implementation. Bleeke[35] says that the failures of current approaches are:

1 Too much emphasis on *where* to compete and not enough on *how* to compete.
2 Too little focus on uniqueness and adaptability.
3 Inadequate emphasis on *when* to compete.
4 Too much attention to firms as competitors rather than individuals as competitors.
5 Too much use of the wrong measures of success.

These observations fit into the more general comment that the development and implementation of marketing strategies are inseparable. Success turns on the ability of marketing managers to identify areas of strategic advantage which meet customer needs in ways which build on the organization's strengths and overcome weaknesses. This is done in a competitive environment in which skilled rivals are seeking to achieve the same results.

Mathur[36] takes this argument further by suggesting that the focus for competitive strategy must be the business or business unit 'in a single competitive market'. This does not necessarily match the traditional notion of the SBU as it excludes multiproduct, multimarket administrative units and re-emphasizes the fit between the offering and the market.[37]

The mind of the strategist

In his examination of business policy in Japan, Ohmae[38] places considerable emphasis on the thought processes and mental disciplines associated with success in this field.

What marks the mind of the strategist is an intellectual elasticity, or flexibility of response, that enables him to come up with realistic responses to changing situations, not simply to discriminate with great precision among different shapes.[39]

It is the ability to integrate this creative insight with the effective use of disciplines of marketing strategy that will mark the effective marketing person of the future.

SPECIMEN QUESTIONS

1 What are the key characteristics of strategic marketing decisions? Illustrate your answer in terms of specific firms or markets.

2 What is meant by either the macro or the micro environment of the firm? Why is it important in marketing to draw this distinction?

3 Use Porter's notion of the value chain to provide guidance on strategy for one of:

(a) A university.

(b) A local firm.

(c) A government agency

4 Explain the notion of 'core competences' as employed by Prahalad. Why are these ideas so important in determining the approach to business and market development employed by strategy-led businesses?

5 Why do firms tend to underestimate the difficulties of implementing strategies?

6 Use the environmental turbulence matrix to analyse the situation facing companies in:

(a) The oil industry.

(b) PC business software producers.

(c) Local radio stations.

(d) Manufacturers of branded detergents.

7 Use the Boston Consulting Group product portfolio analysis to assess the current status of the different products and services of two organizations of your choice. One should be drawn from the public sector, e.g. a university, and the other from the private sector, e.g. a confectionery firm.

8 Under what circumstances should the global strategy of a multinational firm take precedence in determining the policies employed by local subsidiaries?

9 What are the differences between the management, policy and co-ordination problems faced by:

(a) A multinational with a globally integrated and co-ordinated strategy?

(b) A multinational with a country-centred organization and structure?

What factors in the firm or its business would prompt the choice of approach?

10 Define:

(a) Ratio analysis.

(b) Strategy.

(c) Differentiation.

(d) Networking.

(e) Inbound logistics.

(f) The built environment.

(g) Deflection.

(h) PIMs.

(i) Cash cow.

(j) Portfolio analysis.

CASE STUDY 20: THE MACPHERSON CARR GROUP

Macpherson Carr is a medium-sized corporation trading across a number of areas with a significant income from exports and overseas earnings. It is based on two old-established companies: Macpherson Engineering and H. A. Carr Engineering. Most of the manufacturing is done in the Midlands or the South of England. Macphersons was originally a Midlands company founded in the early 1920s which steadily expanded through the 1930s, 1940s and 1950s. It took over Anderson and Thompson in 1952. H. A. Carr Office Furniture was founded somewhat later (the mid-1930s). Its fabrication company was the original point of contact between the two firms. Their joint wish to move into plastics and other materials provided much of the spur to merge the cash-rich Carr's with the capital-intensive Macpherson company.

1993 Sales (£000s)	Net assets (£000s)	Pre-tax profit (£000s)	Net current assets (£000s)	UK employees
386,275	126,528	14,787	75,452	6,150

Group activities include engineering, plastics, packaging and office equipment. In 1989 approximately 18 per cent of sales were exported, primarily by three firms, Anderson and Thompson (manufacturers of special-purpose vehicles), H. A. Carr (office equipment) and BIG Precision Ltd (manufacturers of mechanical power transmission equipment). These firms account for 50 per cent of total sales and 80 per cent of exports. However, only BIG Precision exports a large proportion of its turnover. These are largely to the US and Germany. The group has some holdings overseas:

H. A. Carr has manufacturing and sales subsidiaries in Germany, South Africa and Australia; Anderson and Thompson has an assembly plant in India and joint ventures in Nigeria and Iran. Both joint ventures are largely assembly plants.

Effective control of the overseas operations rests with the UK manufacturing units rather than the group. The group has traditionally been highly devolved, with the trading companies (manufacturing units) exercising considerable discretion. The main group Board has consisted of the Chairmen of the five divisions – engineering, vehicles, plastics, office equipment and chemicals – with some limited service support. These vary enormously in size and structure (Table 24.2). The group has grown largely through a series of mergers, primarily during the 1960s. Throughout the early 1970s the high degree of decentralization produced a number of new formations – Arnold Hydraulics, Macpherson Systems, Synthetic Rubber Inc. – but most notably the growth of the chemicals division.

Table 24.2

Division	Sales (at 1993 prices)		
	£000 1979	£000 1989	£000 1993
Vehicles	65,210	81,125	10,1125
Engineering	24,700	37,150	57,150
Plastics	10,850	30,910	50,910
Office equipment	49,140	79,030	89,030
Chemicals	10,710	50,060	70,060
	160,610	278,275	368,275

During the two years after 1989, growth (by value) took place in virtually all units, notably those tied to the automotive industry: more recently Arnold Hydraulics and Bilson Mouldings were hit badly by cut-backs in the UK with sales in 1993 actually lower than 1991 for both divisions. It is strongly felt that the devolved nature of the group, allied to the relatively poor exports of most firms and weak overseas representation, has played a major part in making the company vulnerable to the decline in the market. These sentiments are supported by the continuing success of the chemicals sector, which has been closely involved in setting up partly-owned manufacturing units in Venezuela, Peru, Mexico, and is in negotiations for projects in Indonesia and Malaysia. The relative prosperity of BIG Precision adds extra weight. The enormously successful introduction of the BIG Torque Limiter into the US is held up as showing just what can be done, even in difficult times.

The Big Torque Limiter

BIG Precision had traditionally conducted a great deal of its business with the steel industry in North America. One particular customer, Crucible Steel, was having recurrent problems with one of the strands of its 80-inch hot-strip mill. The rolls were jamming frequently. This resulted in broken couplings and extensive down-time. It was necessary either to improve the process and do away with jams, or find a means of eliminating the resulting damage and lost time, or both.

Crucible's close links with BIG led it to approach the BIG sales engineer in Pittsburgh. Together the firms identified the possibility of employing a torque-limiting coupling to overcome the problem. The unit operates as a 'weakest link', or circuit breaker, in the drive. It disengages, in the event of a jam, before damage can be done. The unit could then be reset to resume operations with a minimum loss of time. Identifying and solving this problem opened up a major new market for the firm. Although it took three years to get it right, within a year 150 units were sold (50 UK, 100 US). By the end of the 1989–1990 financial year, sales of this one line and spin-offs were over £16 million, with 80 per cent exported. Five years ago the first enquiries were received from German steel companies. Unfortunately none of the sales or marketing staff spoke German so there was a slow response. A new German agent has since been appointed. In the first six months of 1991, enquiries worth £2 million were obtained. £250,000 worth of orders were dispatched by the end of 1991. During 1992, orders from Germany grew to £5 million with £3 million dispatched but there was a 40 per cent drop in demand in 1993.

Corporate perspective

At the annual Chairman's Conference, the Chairman used the comparison of this success and failure elsewhere to focus attention on the poor transfer of internal skills, expertise and contacts. The Chairman felt that the moment had come for the group to be reorganized with a high degree of decentralization. He identified four key steps in this:

1   Reorganization of main board with functional responsibility.
2   Production of standardized marketing plans by the company, the divisions and each operating unit.
3   The determined effort to improve skill in certain key areas, notably marketing, innovation and international trade.
4   The formulation of a 'priority Europe' top management team to produce a strategy for growth in Europe.

Implementing the proposals

As indicated above, the Chairman's first proposal was for a major expansion in group functions and responsibilities. Main board directors would hold responsibilities for Marketing, Finance, Personnel, Engineering, R & D and International. This last director was to be responsible for the newly-formed International Division. In future it would be responsible for all overseas manufacturing or sales subsidiaries, besides servicing and co-ordinating export development for group companies. The International Directorate was given special responsibility for building up sales in mainland Europe. Currently these accounted for less than 5 per cent of total group sales.

In the future the functional specialists, plus the chief executive based at Carr House, would have a working majority on the Board. Using a famous firm of management consultants, the firm had arrived at a standardized business plan format. The purpose was to simplify the submission of stragetic planning, business and marketing data, while additionally providing a standardized format for presentation. A 'plan' was to be produced for each country being developed by the firm. It was split into four sections:

1 *Country summary.* Standard 'guidelines for growth' were produced for completion by the Managing Director.
2 *Business development by product or service.* This was to explore the different aspects of performance and special problems or opportunities.
3 *Business plan schedules.* This was to include detailed financial budget forms for the different areas of business development.
4 *An action plan for Europe.* This was to identify the opportunities open to the firm within the single European market.

Co-ordination of planning was to be the responsibility of the Group Marketing Director. The first stage in implementing this programme and improving key skills to be a series of corporate planning and business policy workshops organized through a major university business school.

Reaction

The proposals on first presentation to the Board generated fierce resistance from many quarters. This turned on three key issues:

1 *The cost:* particularly in terms of extra group overheads for the operating units.
2 *The home market implications:* this degree of standardization would stifle initiative.
3 *The overseas market implications:* the economic, cultural, technical and general trading conditions of the overseas units were so different that centralization would be totally dysfunctional.

The challenge was led by Jack Hodson, Chairman of the Vehicle Division and Managing Director of Anderson and Thompson. He argued that the group was reasonably efficient with a range of products it could be generally proud of. The central problem to him was that his firm in particular was badly hit by market conditions over which it had no control. Most of its vehicles went to municipal (airports, port authorities) or government (defence, health) customers. The cut-backs there had knocked a massive hole in its market. It had not been able to build up exports because its product was 'better than most countries wanted': 'They just aren't willing to pay'. In his eyes, adding further overheads would make him even less competitive. He was especially suspicious of this emphasis on Europe: 'It's only relevant if we want to export and I'm not sure we do – look at the cost . . .'

His views were endorsed by Ian Carr of the Office Furniture division. He suggested that the reasonable performance of his subsidiaries overseas owed a great deal to their historic association with H. A. Carr. 'They depend on us for design and development – without us they'd be lost.'

Task

Assess the position faced by Macpherson Carr.

Put forward your appraisal of the competitive situation faced by the firm.

Taking the role of the new International Director or Marketing Director, prepare a brief strategic plan.

Highlight the ways the firm might develop into Europe.

Comment on any opportunities in Central or Eastern Europe.

25

Market planning

Introduction

Marketing is essentially an operational and purposive pursuit. The firm adopting a marketing perspective is building its business around the specific proposition that 'success is based on effectively meeting customer needs'. In implementing this concept the forces outside the firm and the resources at the company's disposal must be wedded to an idea of how these are going to be made operational. This is linked to an understanding of the direction the organization is taking. This is closely associated with the strategic direction of the enterprise and the strategic alternatives open to the firm.

The plan

The marketing plan provides both the vision and the direction. Winkler,[1] in what remains as probably the best practical book in the UK[2] on this subject, states:

> The planning process does two supremely important things. First, it identifies corporate problems and searches for alternative solutions. Then it provides the corporate body with a focus and a direction.

In his excellent book *Marketing-Led Strategic Change,* Piercy takes the issue further by integrating information systems marketing programmes and policies with plans, strategies and operations.[3] Piercy links an understanding of the capabilities of the firm within the market to an analysis of the market-place or environment.

In coping with the environmental pressures on the company and managing the resources at its disposal and their complex interplay, a clear sense of direction is invaluable. In discussing the planning process, two terms drawn from military usage are frequently used: strategy and tactic. Here they will mean:[4]

1 *Marketing strategy:* the art or science of projecting and directing the larger movements and operations of the firm,[5] in the market-place, to the company's advantage.
2 *Marketing tactic:* the art or science of managing or manoeuvring the specific resources of the firm, usually within a framework defined in the overall strategy.

Kotler[6] encompasses both these notions within his concept of strategic marketing. He sees it as

> the process of analysing opportunities, choosing objectives, defining strategies, formulating plans and carrying out implementation and control.

Brownlie[7] develops this further by relating it to the wider plans and strategies in the firm. He describes strategic marketing planning as

> the formulation of marketing strategy within the framework of the strategic planning process.

McDonald [8] gives as his planning model the methods by which 'stratgic decisions are reached by use of a sequential, planned search for optimum solutions to defined problems. This process is highly rational and is fuelled by concrete data'.

Turning plans to reality

The process of analysing opportunities to define the direction in which the firm wishes to move is central to strategic marketing. It is made up of three distinct but interrelated elements. These have been explored in earlier chapters but can be summarized as:

1 Examine and analyse the environment and marketing system(s) in which the enterprise operates.
2 Identify the options open to the firm, i.e. what business the firm is in and what are the customer needs which underpin this business.
3 Assess and mobilize resources at the firm's disposal that can help identify these options, bringing out those most capable of being met by the firm, and the differential advantages that the company may have in this process.

In these terms, planning is best seen as a continuous feedback loop with the options and resources interacting (Figure 25.1). This interplay is managed by the marketing or corporate staff, whose understanding, determination and ability can influence both options and resources. Strategic marketing and the plans which emerge are dynamic.

Figure 25.1 The continuous feedback loop

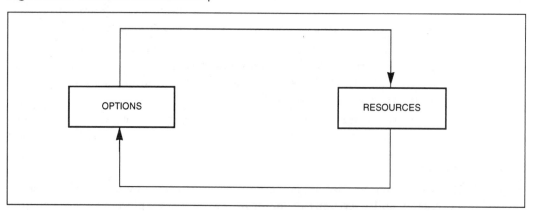

This approach to marketing planning is illustrated by the core marketing plan structure shown in Figure 25.2.

The process of developing the marketing plan provides an opportunity to review, debate and develop ideas and think about the ways the venture is adapting to its environment and the challenges it faces in winning competitive advantage. The plan is not written on tablets of stone: it is an operational document in the real world.

Figure 25.2 The basic marketing plan

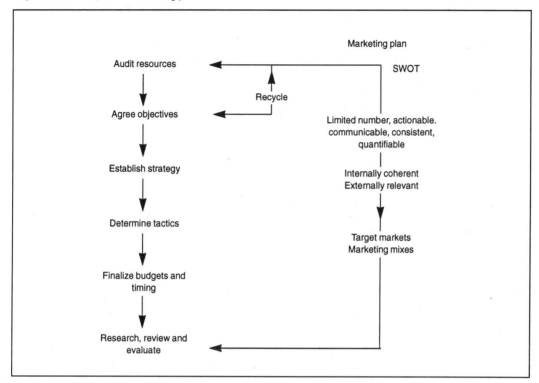

Greenley[9] points out that planning is a continuing process with adjustments and adaptations occurring constantly. In part this reflects changes to adapt to new conditions. At the same time, it reflects the interpretations made by managers when they try to match the simplifications inevitable in plans to a complex and changing world. This issue is explored at length by Piercy and Giles.[10] They argue that the

> current understanding of the environment . . . (is) a fundamental shaping force on managers' perceptions of the market and what actions are possible and potentially effective.

This 'grounded theory' will be shaped by a variety of experiences and attitudes. The planning process should reflect this managerial reality, not an externally imposed and artificial structure. They present a planning model based on adjustment and correction of an existing programme (Figure 25.3). This approach serves as a useful counterpoint to more traditional approaches. Its value lies in providing a new perspective on a process that can easily become routinized and lacking in creativity. It highlights the value of basing the approach adopted in the reality faced. It is, however, subject to the danger implicit in all grounded theory, i.e. it can confuse description with analysis and understanding.

Barriers to effective planning

The idea that plans contribute to greater effectiveness has widespread support. Despite this, large numbers of firms either fail to plan or miss the chance to use planning to gain real competitive advantages. The barriers to planning range from the entrepreneurs'

Figure 25.3 The environment- and tactics-driven plan. Source: Piercy, N. and Morgan, N.A., 'Organisational Context and Behavioural Problems as Determinants of the Effectiveness of the Strategic Planning Process', *Journal of Marketing Management,* 6, No. 2, 1990, p. 24

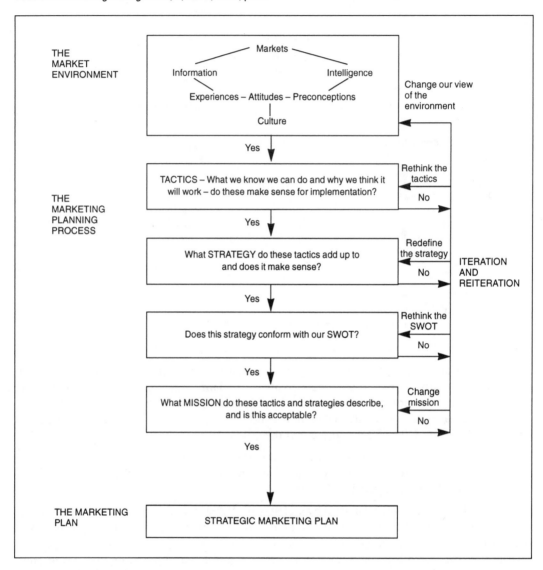

distrust of the process to the criticisms of writers like Mintzberg[11] who question the value of the effort. McDonald[12] identifies in Table 25.1 institutional barriers which range from corporate cultures in which the leadership team abdicate their responsibilities, to environmental problems which make planning hard to perform effectively.

Marketing audit

Successful planning is based on an understanding of reality. Objectives which can neither be achieved nor evaluated play no part in practical marketing, and tactics or strategies

Table 25.1 Marketing planning barriers

Roles people play
        Lack of chief executive/senior management involvement
        Lack of cross-functional involvement
        Lack of top management support

Cognitive
        Knowledge and skills
        Lack of innovation/non-recognition of alternatives

Systems and procedures
        Lack of care in marketing planning introduction
        Forecasts without documentation of intervention
        Inflexible application of textbook process
        Lack of follow-through to tactics
        Too much detail

Resources
        Lack of time (elapsed and/or effort)
        Lack of money (for market research etc.)

Organisational environment/culture
        Organisational structure inappropriate
        Stage of organisational developemt
        Corporate politics
        Short-term orientated reward systems
        Culture stifling idea generation/openness

Data
        Lack of information

Environmental
        Difficulty of forecasting in times of turbulence and inflation

which are beyond the firm's resources can be an impediment to action. The marketing planner must start the planning process with a thorough review of the firm's current position. Access to good-quality and relevant information is crucial to this.[13] Information has a dual value:

1 It provides insights and understanding of the environment and likely response to marketing action.
2 It integrates the different parts of the plan – resources, strategies and tactics – while enabling those responsible for different areas to interact and understand their roles and responsibilities.[14]

This link between information, plans and learning is developed further by de Geus[15] in a discussion of the ways in which managers learn from planning. Planning forces managers to expand their understanding of the enterprise, its capabilities and competences. The extent to which managers, especially those in senior management, build up their understanding of the enterprise and the challenges it faces through planning is often underestimated by writers on the topic.

Gaining this understanding takes time. It means that the marketing staff must start with an awareness that few plans of any real value can be prepared quickly. In some firms the planning process is a year-long activity. This may be necessary when one is

drawing on the past, to decide in the present what to do in the future.[16]

The marketing audit calls for an investigation of the demand variables in the immediate market network, including suppliers, intermediaries, competitors and more general economic forces.

This picture of the current and historical situation facing the firm provides the background for all other action. The company is not locked in to its current environment but it is very difficult to separate completely the situation in the firm and how the firm is seen in the market-place from its history. The shortage of firms and industries which have repositioned themselves in time for a major shift in demand is not simply a matter of 'marketing myopia', but is because this is very difficult. It calls for a very rare vision of the future.

> It may not be generally known that at the turn of the century Mr Durant
> . . . was the leading wagon and carriage producer in the United States . . .
> [long before] Mr Durant incorporated General Motors Company on
> 16 September, 1908.[17]

The marketing audit should be conducted on a regular basis. Some firms prefer to use outside consultants, while others employ their own staff. Out of the audit should emerge a diagnosis of the current situation facing the firm and an evaluation of the situation, across its different areas. A rigourous assessment of the enterprise's own strengths, weaknesses, opportunities and threats can be linked to a similar appraisal of its rivals. This provides an insight into the options open to it and the ways its competitors can respond. Out of this should emerge an understanding of the keys to the firm's competitive success. The audit should provide a picture of the likely futures for the firm, perhaps through a mixture of analysis, prognosis (extrapolating trends) and scenario development, the latter through a series of hypotheses about development under certain clearly definable circumstances.[18]

Forecasting

In defining the future of either the firm or its specific products or offerings, forecasting plays a major part. Managers have always built up pictures of the future of their firms and the likely response to their actions, and recently there has been a more systematic search for methods of prediction or forecasting.

> World economic growth will be lower over the next ten years than the
> rates seen in the 1960s.[19]

> Junior executives with good career prospects are increasingly reluctant to
> invest time and money in an MBA programme, particularly in today's
> difficult job situation.[20]

All efforts at forecasting share the problems encountered by these commentators. Economic growth continued throughout the 1970s and the 1980s while MBA programme admissions boomed and continue to do so.

Estimates from informed opinion

Informed opinion still plays a major part in forecasting. This may come from within the firm. For example, the agreed sales targets discussed in Chapter 22 can provide guidance, or the sales staff can be asked for estimates, or other staff and management can give estimates of future demand based on their expectations. Forecasts may also be built on estimates from outside opinion. Expert comment can play a part here. This usually derives from general economic or market projections such as those published in the media, or industry-specific estimates, often produced by trade associations or the industry research association. Some firms also approach specialist experts for their opinions. The Delphi method is also being used by a number of companies. This provides estimates from experts in a systematic and structured way.

Considerable success has been reported with this approach in novel situations; for example, it was used very effectively to forecast visitors to the Tall Ships Race visit to Liverpool in the early 1990s. Consumer marketing research can be used to provide a picture of customer intentions, but care must be taken in projecting from this. There has been a dramatic growth in the use of quantitative methods of forecasting in marketing.[21] These have encompassed most areas of marketing activity: estimating effects of changes in advertising, promotion, distribution and price; predicting the future of a new product; determining the potential of possible retail or catering outlets etc.

Time series projections

A time series projection depends on the analysis of past behaviour to determine the future. It may be a trend projection, where the pattern is expected to be repeated in the future (Figure 25.4). The basic assumption is that past patterns reflect an underlying causality which will recur in the future.

The simple projection shown in Figure 25.4 seldom occurs in reality. Erratic events, business cycles, seasons and marketing action by the firm, its competitors and its intermediaries combine to produce a more obscure situation (Figure 25.5). It is in these circumstances that the firm must answer questions about the future viability of the product, the effect of promotional activity and the returns from further investments. Statistical demand analysis can be used, providing there are sufficient observations to make projections, the variables examined are fully independent, a normal distribution exists, causality is one-way, and no more factors emerge on the market to distort the results. In the situation described above the firm can attempt to smooth out the variation in a number of ways. One of these ways is by simple moving averages. As each new observation becomes available, the average is updated and used to modify the forecast (Table 25.2). The more observations that are included, the greater the

Figure 25.4 The simple linear projection

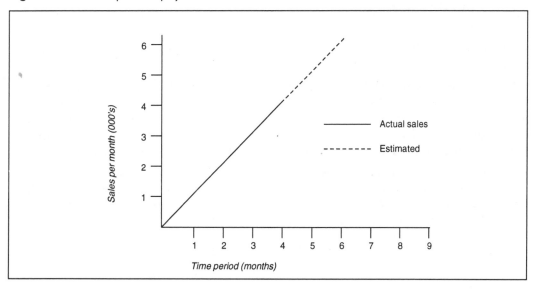

Figure 25.5 An erratic market situation

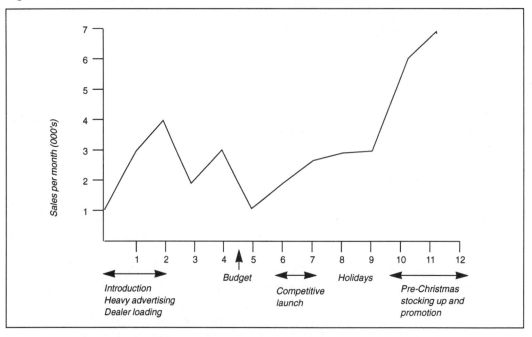

Table 25.2 Simple moving averages

Month	1	2	3	4	5	6	7	8	9	10	11	12
Sales (000)	3	4	2	3	1.5	2	2.5	3	3	5	6	
Three months' moving average				3	3	2	2	2	2.5	3	3.5	4.5
Five months' moving average						2.5	2.5	2	2	2.5	3	4

All numbers are rounded to the nearest 0.5.

smoothing effect is. In a stable situation this improves accuracy but, as can be seen here, the more erratic figures, the greater the discrepancy.

Although this approach has proved useful, interest in forecasting has led to a number of other developments. Exponential smoothing (Table 25.3) overcomes some of the data-handling problems of the moving average, as well as giving extra weight to the most recent period; thus, $St + 1 = St + a (Xt - 5)$, where $St + 1$ is the forecast sales for the next month, St is the forecast for this month, Xt is the actual sales for this month and α is a smoothing constant.

Among many other approaches that have been used (with varying degrees of success) to forecast aggregate sales and the response to specific actions are simple and multiple regression, correlation, and simultaneous equations. The use of quantitative techniques is likely to grow still further in importance in modern marketing.

Table 25.3 Exponential smoothing

Month	1	2	3	4	5	6	7	8	9	10	11	12
Sales (000)	3	4	2	3	1.5	2	2.5	3	3	5	6	
Smoothing values ($\alpha = 0.3$)		3	3	3	3	2.5	2.5	2.5	2.5	2.5	3.5	4.5

All numbers are rounded to the nearest 0.5.

Objectives

The marketing audit and the picture of the type of futures facing the firm provide the framework in which the firm's objectives can be set. Setting objectives is a critical part of planning, since objectives can originate from any part of the organization and can be short, medium or long term. The objectives that the firm or marketing group is seeking to achieve shape the policies and tactics adopted. Marketing objectives describe the purposes or goals that the firm is seeking to achieve through its strategies and tactics. Properly constituted objectives should normally meet five specific criteria. They should be:

1 *Actionable*, otherwise they are merely wishes or dreams.
2 *Achievable*, otherwise they produce frustration, not a sense of purpose.
3 *Consistent*, otherwise different objectives can cancel each other out.
4 *Communicable*, otherwise those with responsibility for implementation do not know the ways in which they are contributing.
5 *Quantifiable*, otherwise progress towards their achievement cannot be measured.

Often firms seek to achieve too many objectives simultaneously. This can breed confusion and conflict. The most productive objectives are those accepted and understood by those responsible for implementation.[22]

The objectives of a firm or marketing group can evolve over time. This can be a response to changing external circumstances, new attitudes or ideas. Smith[23] shows how the type of objectives espoused by one firm were very specific and commercial in the mid-1960s:

> Increase our share of home and export markets. Launch the product coding system during the first quarter of 1967.

These became more general and wide-ranging in the mid-1970s.

> It is essential that we develop long-term strategic planning techniques to establish the future of the company.

By the 1980s issues of consensus and ownership emerged to dominate the process of setting and defining objectives. Objectives were included in an 'Annual Strategic Statement'. They became 'intentions to take innovative steps forward'. In the 1990s, vision statements which directly or indirectly refer to the firm's underlying values have had a key role to play in shaping strategies.

Marketing decision variables

Marketing decision variables are those factors capable of affecting demand under the firm's direct control:

I can decide on the number of vans, their communication tie-ups, the advertising, their location and hours of work, but I can do nothing about the numbers of windscreens shattered. (Managing Director of windscreen repair service company)

Glueck and Jauch[24] describe many of these controllable variables as 'strategic advantage factors' (SAF). In a firm's marketing they include the following variables:

Competitive position	Market share
Quality of marketing research	Product/service mix
Product line	New products
Patents	Customer loyalty
Packaging	Price position
Sales force size/quality	Advertising quality/expenditure
After-sales service	Distribution and service system
Coverage	Merchandizing and promotion
Protection in market	Total resources.

The firm has the opportunity to exploit these SAFs by enhancing those which work to its benefit, integrating them for greater effectiveness, or diminishing the effectiveness of the SAFs of its rivals. These provide opportunities to enhance the effectiveness of marketing[25] and improve the efficiency of internal marketing systems.[26]

Marketing mix and sub-mixes

The marketing mix defines the key, controllable features of marketing over which the firm has some control. Its role, value and effectiveness is shaped by the ways in which the market responds to the effort invested and the allocation of resources.

1 The marketing effort includes both the level of investment or effort in a specific mix element and any awareness of their effectiveness.

2 The marketing allocation is the deployment of the firm's resources between products and markets, even internal investment against external:

In the first year we found that the bulk of our investments were in staff mortgages. (Director of major foreign bank in Britain)

3 The marketing response is how the market will react or how it is believed the market will react to particular actions.

4 Marketing procedures are the methods by which decisions are made and implemented.

In some firms advertising and market research agencies are actively involved in the entire decision-making process, including planning; in others they are outsiders, brought in for their specialist skills.

The marketing organization is the structure, responsibilities and procedures adopted by the firm in order to manage its marketing.

All marketing policies are implemented on the basis of some form of forecast, estimate projection or prediction about the response in the future to these efforts.

The relationship between the character of objectives and their perceived difficulty is illustrated in Figure 25.6.

Figure 25.6 The relationship between performance and difficulty

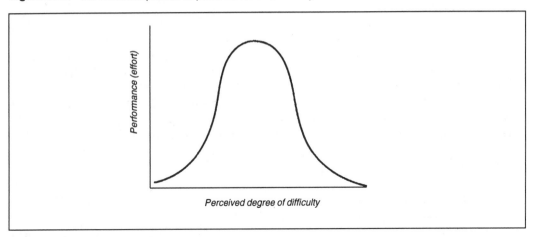

Research

At this stage, or even earlier, the firm might find it necessary to gather further market intelligence. These information needs should be defined early in the plan. The research may be needed to establish the relative priorities of goals.

Strategy

As indicated earlier, the strategy shows the overall direction that the firm will adopt to achieve its purpose or objectives. A clear and communicable strategy statement can play a major part in facilitating the evaluation of tactics. The strategy statement should be capable of being measured against the objectives and the tactics defined later. For example, a medium-sized engineering firm might set itself the strategy of developing overseas business through networks of strong relationships with customers designed to establish the firm in their eyes as a producer of high-quality, precision-engineered goods. This type of strategy can be measured against the firm's objectives: 20 per cent of business from overseas; improved profile of work, i.e. x per cent of work to technically advanced fields; and access to innovative technologies. At the same time specific tactics can be judged in terms of the strategy, for example the sales manager's suggestion that they appoint a commission agent in the Netherlands, with responsibility for Benelux and Germany.

Tactics

The tactics define precisely the actions to be taken, e.g. investment in different mix elements, planned interplay, besides giving specific responsibilities for their implementation. They should be carefully drawn up to provide a consistent presentation of the organization to the market. They must fit in with the strategy. Their contribution to achieving the stated objectives should at least be able to be described if not quantified.

Controls

The measures described above for ensuring that the elements in the plan hang together are only a part of the control system. This requires clear patterns of responsibility and authority. Control procedures need to be built in to monitor the overall performance of the actions laid out in the plan. Over time a series of reference points in the marketing system can be established to provide an early warning of potential problems, e.g. sales force resistance to new display material may lead to poor distribution, with serious consequences for business developments. An important part of the planning process is that over time the firm monitors its performance in certain key areas. The lessons learnt may be capable of incorporation into the system of controls.

Contingencies

In the real world, few plans, no matter how carefully detailed and researched, can be expected to run smoothly, with no competition, environmental or organizational problems. Sets of contingencies should be drafted to cope with specific situations. Scenario analysis has emerged as an increasingly important feature of contingency planning. This kind of analysis poses 'What if' questions to proposals about policies and direction.

Costs and timings

Costs and timings should be described in considerable detail. The effect of time in certain areas can be critical. It may be especially important when corporate management are reviewing the interplay between certain discrete areas; for example, should two independent units introduce major new brands simultaneously?

Evaluation

There are elements of both art and science in the drafting of plans, and learning is important in building up the knowledge of those involved in drafting and implementing plans. A systematic approach to evaluation is needed to ensure that all the lessons learned during one period are built into succeeding periods.

Different approaches to plans

Although the framework provided above generalizes about the experiences of many firms, there is a wide scatter of practice in industry. In some multinational corporations, headquarters management are so distant from local management that the plan is their only mechanism of management and control. In such organizations the plan has taken on a major corporate role. Some firms have developed a consistent planning format which is employed through the organization from the corporation itself to the smallest national firm, product or brand. In many small firms planning as a formal or written-down activity scarcely exists. This is due partly to the entrepreneurial nature of managers themselves and partly to a certain mystique about planning itself. Instead of a plan being a simple, practical and disciplined guide to action, far more complex notions have been built in. In specific circumstances these can play a part, but only when they add to rather than detract from understanding and action.

Implementing plans

One of the truisms of marketing is that anyone can plan; the test of quality is implementation. Brilliant, creative, even visionary plans come to naught in the market-place because the firm underestimates the challenge of implementation. Much traditional thinking assumed that implementation followed automatically or easily, from the conceptualization of the plan. This ignores the gaps that exist between the plan as formulated and the plan as delivered. Cespedes[27] describes this as the 'formulation–implementation dichotomy'. This means that these represent different activities placing different strains on the enterprise and calling for different skills. A variety of approaches can be used to ensure the implementation of plans (Figure 25.7)

Figure 25.7 Getting action on plans[28]

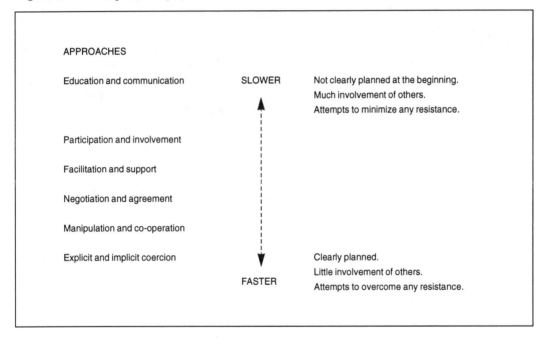

Barriers to effective implementation

Successful implementation of plans means overcoming the many stumbling blocks that may exist in the firm. These can range from senior management inertia to the determined resistance by vested interests. McDonald[29] summarizes these as:

1 Confusion between tactics and planning.
2 Isolating the marketing function from operations.
3 Confusion between the marketing function and marketing concept.
4 Organizational barriers.
5 Lack of in-depth analysis.
6 Confusion between prices and output.

7   Lack of knowledge and skills.
8   Lack of systematic approach to marketing planning.
9   Failure to prioritize objectives.
10 Hostile corporate culture.

Successful implementation of marketing plans calls for these barriers to be overcome by committed senior management backed by effective and well-integrated marketing systems. Driver[30] suggests that this can only be done if the 'people' dimension to plans and their implementation is explicitly recognized and the nature of the organization, its 'values' and the 'styles' adopted by managers are explicitly recognized.

Conclusion

Planning is playing an increasing part in corporate activity, and plans and controls in specific areas of marketing – innovation, pricing, communication, sales and many others – are being subjected to rigorous scrutiny. There is a danger that poorly introduced (perhaps in an over-rigid or negative manner) plans can stifle the creativity that is crucial to these areas, but this is not a weakness of planning itself. Plans can provide a solid base for creative development. At the same time the effective implementation of plans integrates the marketing effort into the total corporate effort. The growing evidence that marketing improves profits and overall company performance makes this a priority for business today. Narver and Slater[31] found that

> after allowing for important market level and business level influences,
> market orientation and performance are strongly related.

This link, allied to the business survival and growth relationships already established, makes effective marketing planning a company priority.

SPECIMEN QUESTIONS

1 List the three main aspects of marketing planning that a small firm should take into account in preparing its first, formal marketing plan. Justify your choice of these factors and give reasons why formal planning gives benefits that cannot be gained through informal or no planning.

2 In 1933 Charles P. Darrow of Philadelphia, USA, invented the game of Monopoly. The following year Packet Bros of Massachusetts rejected the product partly because it contained 52 errors. This lost Packet Bros the rights to a game that has now been translated into over 90 different languages.

   Would modern methods of product development, analysis and marketing planning prevent this type of failure? If your answer is yes, indicate how; if your answer is no, indicate why not.

3 Outline the main steps in preparing a marketing plan; indicate why it is often argued that successful planning depends on the maximum amount of transparency, debate and discussion.

4 Explain the distinctive contribution that mission statements can make in marketing planning. Give some illustration of productive and, if possible, non-productive mission statements.

5 Ashleigh Brilliant comments that 'the difference between science and magic is that magicians usually know what they are doing'. What does the unpredictability of science and technological forecasting suggest about the value of technological forecasting in business planning?

6 Describe the Delphi approach to forecasting and outline its specific strengths and weaknesses.

7 What are the internal barriers to effective marketing planning in a small, privately-owned firm? Outline ways in which these barriers can be successfully overcome.

8 Compare 'added value' and 'price cutting' as marketing weapons in two of the following markets.

   (a)   Retail car sales.

   (b)   Endowment-based mortgage policies.

   (c)   Fast food catering.

   (d)   Management training.

9 Your father is the managing director of a medium-sized British footwear company. An opportunity has arisen for the firm to acquire a US footwear producer. What advice would you give him on how to proceed?

10 'The development of strategic alliances lies at the heart of international business development over the next decade.' What are the implications of this statement for international marketing planning?

CASE STUDY 21: FALKIRK UNIVERSITY

Falkirk University is one of the newest universities in Scotland. It has 6,850 students (1,850 full time and the rest part time). It has an immediate catchment of 120,000 centred on Falkirk itself, population 35,000, the town of Larbert and communities across the Central Region of Scotland. The university operates through five divisions, each containing several areas of study. The broad structure is described below.

The divisions

1 Business and Management.
2 Hotel and Catering.
3 Electronics and Computing.
4 Mechanical, Construction and Production Engineering.
5 Social Sciences.

The subjects taught include accountancy, business, law, secretarial studies, catering, hotel management, tourism, electrical and electronic engineering, computer science, IT, recreation, building, manufacturing sciences, mechanical engineering, sociology, psychology, and economics.

The employment patterns and industrial structure of the region around Falkirk are broadly similar to those of the central belt of Scotland as a whole. Recently, however, trends in the overall pattern of employment and industry in Scotland seem to be having a more marked effect in Falkirk. There has been a shift away from traditional manufacturing industries and a reduction in the levels of activity in construction as well as a move towards tourism. This has been stimulated by a lively local authority. A number of novel initiatives have been introduced, including the Falkirk Technology project. Growth is expected in other services besides some 'revival' in primary industries.

Table 25.4 The local economy versus Scotland

	Employment structure	
	Scotland (%)	Falkirk (%)
Primary	6	7
Secondary	29	27
Construction	8	6
Services	57	60

During the period 1979–1992 the numbers in employment declined in the area around Falkirk. Manufacturing jobs dropped by 33 per cent, construction by 19 per cent and primary industries by 9 per cent. These losses were partially compensated by a gain of over 18 per cent in the service sector. The adverse effects of these changes in the overall economic structure had been mitigated by some slight increase in the overall population of the area, new firms moving into the area, such as Compaq Computers, and the university's ability to recruit in subjects in which it had a high reputation, notably the pop music courses it pioneered, and computing and business.

Some subjects have gained. This has been especially noticeable in the Division of Business and Management. In other fields, the impact has been inconsistent. Innovations such as the Information Technology programme, especially the ITEC, and a speciality in pop music have been successful. The progress made with these initiatives encouraged a large number of similar 'launches' during 1990–91. Relatively few of these were successful.

The problems of structural and economic change have hit the Divisions of Construction and Environmental Studies, Mechanical and Production Engineering and Social Sciences especially hard.

Until the present review, the university's central promotional expenditure was small (Table 25.5). Divisions have been able to use their own budgets to supplement this. It is hard to be precise about the amount spent, but it appears to range between the £2,500 spent by Business and Management and the £450 invested by Social Sciences. The college became a University during 1992.

Table 25.5 College expenditure on promotion

	1995 £	1996 £	1997 £
Media expenditure	5,000	5,350	6,320
Prospectus	10,000	11,000	12,500
Brochures etc.	2,500	3,000	3,750
Events	1,000	1,500	2,000

The new Vice Chancellor is determined to use this new status to grow and develop despite her fears that the local economy will continue to languish. Some of her fears were confirmed by a downturn in local applications (–5 per cent) after the imposition of student fees and evidence that local firms are cutting back on training. She was, however, pleased to see other UK applications up 60 per cent and overseas applications double. A study of the local environment provided a useful picture of the local markets. Tables 25.6 and 25.7 give some indication of the findings.

Table 25.6 Knowledge of locally provided courses

Course	Yes	No
Appropriate for new staff	18	43
Appropriate for existing staff	16	45

Table 25.7 Form of contact with college

Form	Average number of contacts (monthly) over the last year
One-off (by chance)	3
One-off (problem driven)	2
Occasional (chance)	2
Occasional (planned)	7
Frequent (planned)	8

Her concerns were increased by the evidence that links were weakest with the newer, growing companies (Table 25.8).

Table 25.8 Form of contact with college

| | Established firms | | New firms | |
	Yes	No	Yes	No
Organization has approached	15	46	7	66
Organization would approach	21	40	11	76

There is some evidence that local student groups are seeking new opportunities elsewhere, either at the local college of further education or in Glasgow or Edinburgh. Data on sources of information about courses and activities highlight some problems and opportunities (Table 25.9).

Table 25.9 Form of contact with college

Source	Percentage
Advertising	20
Word of mouth	20
Enquiry	10
Job Centre	10
Advisory	10
Don't know	30

The issue

The Vice Chancellor has been approached by the leader of the local council. The Region and District councils want the University to play a much larger role in the community. They have already given some help in promoting its work. They now want the university to become an important vehicle for establishing Falkirk as an international centre for learning and research. They have indicated a willingness to invest significant new resources in marketing the university if an acceptable 'Marketing and Development Plan' can be produced. The Vice Chancellor has called upon the heads of the five divisions to advise her on the marketing policies that should be adopted. She is especially keen to hear their comments on:

1 The best ways to operate in the current environment.
2 How the marketing effort should be organized, especially the split between central and divisional activities.
3 The university's strengths, weaknesses, opportunities and threats.
4 The ways in which the university and the divisions should direct their efforts.
5 Levels of expenditure and forms of activity.
6 Key target markets.

Task

The groups should produce a comprehensive marketing plan covering these issues.

Marketing: the social, ethical and environmental dimensions

Introduction

Perhaps the clearest illustrations of the dynamic nature of marketing have emerged from the discussions on, and research into, the various social, ethical and environmental dimensions of marketing. No area of business activity is as strongly defined in terms of its interaction with the corporate social responsibility, ethical and environmental concerns, as marketing. This means that it cannot afford to stand back from the fierce discussion taking place in the countries of the West about the future direction of modern industrial society.

> Consumerism, environmentalism, re-ordering of national priorities, urban renewal, price controls, education, welfare, shortages of natural resources, economic development, social costs of products and services and a host of additional quality of life factors are among the challenges now facing marketing. (William Lazer[1])

The wider agenda

To these concerns can be added: food and production standards; responsibilities to other communities; fairness in the workplace; cultural sensitivity; large-scale environmental concerns.[2] Each of these issues poses a challenge to aspects of modern business and the environment in which the marketer operates. The advertisement from Women in Marketing and Design goes to the heart of many of these issues of fairness and responsibility (Figure 26.1). In response to them, a number of different policies are emerging. These include:

1 *Ethical standards:* the values which firms use to make choices about responsible and proper behaviour.[3]
2 *Environmentalism:* the impact human beings have on the natural and built environment through the products produced, their development, composition, use and disposal.[4]
3 *Consumer action:* the way customers are organizing themselves to achieve their goals, from the green consumer to positive purchasing.[5]
4 *Consumerism:* this has posed in the most forthright way a challenge to certain aspects of the marketing concept. The most fundamental question that can be asked is how, when marketing is at least tacitly accepted as the basic business approach by many firms, consumerism can emerge and gain such growth. Marketing is about meeting customer needs, so why do some customers demand protection from marketers?

5 *Social responsibility:* this takes the debate about consumerism on to a much broader level. It raises questions about whether marketing management should adopt particular stances in the firm about a wider range of 'social issues'.

6 *Marketing and non-profit making organizations:* although not strictly linked with these earlier concepts, this issue is often raised in this context. At its most basic the question here is the degree to which marketing is context linked or implies a more general approach to organization, free of industrial links.

Some authors argue that marketing is essentially a business discipline[6] and these wider issues are not relevant or appropriate concerns. Others suggest that it is about the broader 'exchange' process and has merely developed in a business context.[7, 8] Linked to these notions of the transferability of the marketing concept to different social and economic circumstances is a wider discussion on the contribution that marketing, its underlying ideas and applications, can make to the most dramatic economic challenge of today: economic development.[9]

Although many of the ideas which underlie these discussions emanate from the US, the issues themselves are worldwide. The subject is not new: there has been discussion and action in both Europe and Britain for many years. In the middle of the last century Charles Dickens was writing about 'advertising traps', and at the turn of the century Sweden was passing consumer-protection legislation. The formulation of the Co-operative movement was part political and part consumerist. There is a burgeoning literature on the role of marketing in environments as diverse as Co-operatives[10] and local authorities.[11]

This work gains a new relevance with the transformation of Central and Eastern Europe from 'command' economies into 'market' economies. Although this has reduced the external threat to the market economies, it has coincided with the emergence of a new set of questions about the standards, behaviour and contribution of those with market power in the Western economies.

An essential feature of the responses of different societies to the questions posed has been the individual or culturally related nature of these responses. A major tenet of marketing is that the marketing system is affected by and in turn affects the broader environment. This interrelation will determine the nature of responses in Britain and Europe to the issues raised in this worldwide debate. These issues range from the specific activities of marketers, e.g. their approach to packaging, to their wider contribution to business behaviour.

Digital Equipment, for example, showed how it was possible to reduce drastically the volume (and negative environmental impact) of packaging equipment through a sustained campaign.

Table 26.1 The characteristics of strategic decisions

Computer product	Product vol. (cm^3)	Packaging vol./Product vol. Before	After	Reduction (%)
Mouse	216.96	8.62	0.94	89.1
Module	791.98	2.79	0.72	74.3
Software	181.90	15.17	1.79	88.2
Cabinet	900 472	0.36	0.25	31.0

Source: Larry J. Nielsen, *Measurement Techniques in Packaging Waste Management* (Proceedings of Corporate Quality/Environmental Management, 9–10 January, 1991, Washington DC).

Figure 26.1

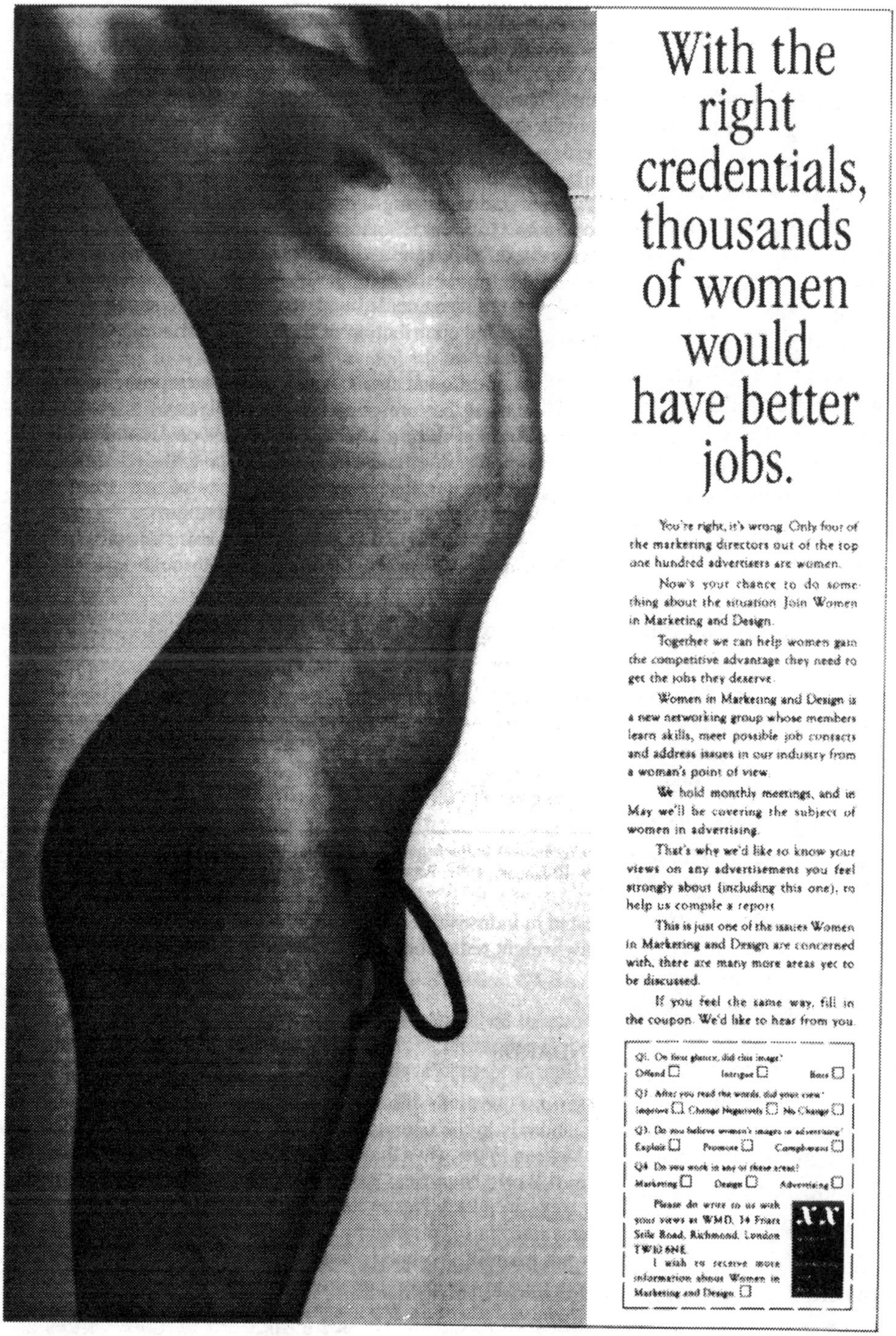
With the right credentials, thousands of women would have better jobs.
You're right, it's wrong. Only four of the marketing directors out of the top one hundred advertisers are women.
Now's your chance to do something about the situation. Join Women in Marketing and Design.
Together we can help women gain the competitive advantage they need to get the jobs they deserve.
Women in Marketing and Design is a new networking group whose members learn skills, meet possible job contacts and address issues in our industry from a woman's point of view.
We hold monthly meetings, and in May we'll be covering the subject of women in advertising.
That's why we'd like to know your views on any advertisement you feel strongly about (including this one), to help us compile a report.
This is just one of the issues Women in Marketing and Design are concerned with, there are many more areas yet to be discussed.
If you feel the same way, fill in the coupon. We'd like to hear from you.
Q1. On first glance, did this image?
Offend Intrigue Bore
Q2. After you read the words, did your view?
Improve Change Negatively No Change
Q3. Do you believe women's images in advertising?
Exploit Promote Complement
Q4. Do you work in any of these areas?
Marketing Design Advertising
Please do write to us with your views at WMD, 34 Friars Stile Road, Richmond, London TW10 6NE.
I wish to receive more information about Women in Marketing and Design.
XX

Their approach has been replicated in industries as diverse as aluminium can production and milk bottles. Both industries saw weight reductions (grams per unit) between 40 and 60 per cent.[12]

Ethics, values and standards

A series of events have raised serious questions about the willingness of firms to accept and implement acceptable ethical standards in the operations of their firms in markets. Perhaps the most dramatic of these can be seen in the ways that international firms sell their products in poor and underdeveloped Third World countries. Worldwide attention was drawn to this issue following reports of the ways in which Nestlé and others promoted their powdered baby milk products in developing countries. This vividly illustrated the type of ethical issue faced by firms. The product is not harmful if properly used and in the right circumstances. Neither of these conditions was met in the poor countries of sub-Saharan Africa, Latin America and Asia, in which powdered baby milk was promoted. Advertising associated the product with strong, healthy infants. Merchandizing and promotion encouraged hospitals to recommend the product. Parents were not made fully aware of the dangers from improper use. These included: dehydration from the wrong mix of powder and water; dysentery from impure water; and malnutrition from weak mixtures. Tragically, very few mothers needed this product. The natural alternative, breast milk, suffered from none of these problems. This case raises two distinct issues. First, there is the decision to introduce the product into markets where these risks might exist. Second, there is the way in which a firm responds when the matter is raised.

Much of the recent debate has concentrated on the first issue. Donaldson[13] has highlighted the importance of 'awareness of ethical issues in business and management'. In particular he emphasizes the need 'to counter over-deterministic or fatalistic views that management does not have any options, and to reflect on the possibility of moral development: the "only doing my job" response is not the only option'. In essence this means that management is not value-free. Membership of a firm or executive responsibility is not a substitute for membership of a society and personal responsibility.

The ways in which Nestlé responded to criticism provide many lessons to firms facing similar challenges today. 'At first, Nestlé largely ignored the problem.'[14] As the volume of criticism grew and political support for the concerns increased, the firm became more hostile and defensive. It took almost a decade for the firm to establish a constructive working relationship with those raising concerns. Eventually, Nestlé established an effective and open system for monitoring and managing the way its products were sold. Its difficulties were observed by companies across the world. Some recognized the risks of political and consumer pressure building against them. They acted quickly to set up their own internal systems. Faced with potential problems they act quickly and openly. The Perrier product withdrawal in 1989 re-emphasized the problems associated with company resistance to admitting problems. Refusal to acknowledge the problem allied to an apparent desire to blame 'the messenger' cost the firm $100 million in lost sales and market share in the two years after the US Food and Drug Administration's identification of the problem.

Other firms have acted to win marketing advantage from prompt action even before the concerns are politically significant. Heinz was among the first major food companies to insist on changes in tuna fishing techniques. The Co-op Bank highlighted its core values as a key feature in its advertising. Success seems to go to firms that: recognize issues early; are open and responsive; involve staff and intermediaries in producing a prompt response and establish self-sustaining systems for the long term.[15]

Environmentalism

Fortune magazine has predicted that:

Saving the environment will climb to the top of the East–West as well as the West–West agenda.[16]

This view vividly illustrates the importance attached to environmental concerns in modern markets.[17] Virtually every aspect of marketing, from its role in the firm to the workings of the marketing mix, is affected. Sustainable development is replacing short-term advantage as a corporate and marketing priority. It means that:

1 *Product development is being shaped by a desire to avoid potentially harmful side-effects from products.* Carl Sagan calls for 'a commercially feasible fuel that delivers 60–100 miles per gallon' while Frank Popoff of Dow Chemicals acknowledges that the 'costs [of] . . . helping our customers dispose of products, for protecting the ozone layer and groundwater . . . [will be borne] . . . partly by the market'.

2 *Distribution systems will affect and be affected by changes in the environment.* Almost 60 per cent of the food grown in Russia is lost because of poor storage and distribution. The winter food crisis in Russia in 1991 would not have occurred if effective distribution systems existed. At the same time road haulage is an environmentally poor alternative to rail in small, crowded countries like Britain.

3 *Packaging is under close scrutiny.* Firms like McDonald's became increasingly aware of the negative customer reaction to packaging that littered the streets and was thought to harm the ozone layer. The firm now uses 'ozone-friendly' packaging.

4 *There is increased awareness that the total, real price of goods and services extends beyond the money paid at a specific moment.* The success of the differential pricing of 'lead-free' petrol has increased interest in 'green' taxes as a way of shaping market behaviour and introducing differential costs into commercial relationships. The Economist in a comment on carbon dioxide emissions pointed out that 'a tax in the order of $5–10 per ton would be a reasonable insurance premium to pay given the risks to mankind'.

5 *Advertisers are increasingly aware of the benefits from positive action and equivalent costs of failure.* Bottle banks outside supermarkets are an important symbol of their awareness of this issue. The ozone-friendly sticker on aerosol cans means the difference between consumer acceptability and rejection.

So far, responses by marketers to environmental concerns have been *ad hoc* and piecemeal. Increasingly, these concerns are moving to the centre of strategic marketing planning. Firms will develop integrated, company-wide responses.[18]

Green marketing

The notion of 'green marketing' has emerged as a response to the challenges that environmental decline poses to firms and communities. Initially, however, the notion of 'green marketing' carried clear perjorative connotations as firms tried to exploit consumer concerns by image changes without substantive shifts in behaviour. At the heart of green marketing is the notion that significant behaviour changes by marketers will create a virtuous circle of addressing environmental needs while winning competitive advantage. There is some evidence that, for example, consumers will pay a premium for greener products. Specific campaigns like the 'dolphin-friendly' tuna campaign, to force fishermen to use different fishing techniques, clearly had effects in Western markets.

Until recently, however, there was little structure to the analysis of ways firms could adapt strategically to these shifts. Peattie and Charter[19] have shown how Porter's Value Chain approach can be adapted to provide a strategic view of green marketing.

Figure 26.2 Components of environmental performance[20]

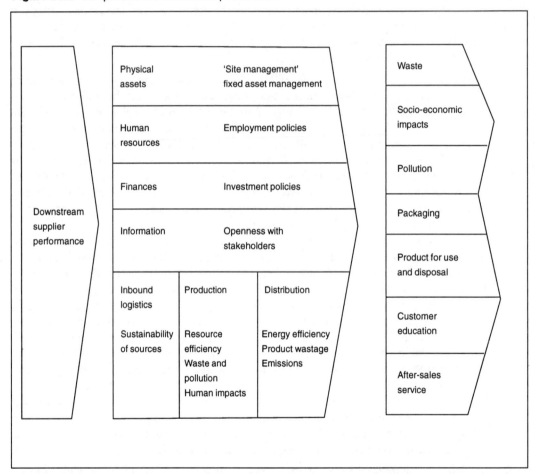

Using this approach, inbound resources are managed to maximize sustainability while production and distribution minimize waste and seek high levels of resource efficiency. The combination produces a value chain which produces both competitive advantage and the minimum negative effect on the environment.

Consumer action

Direct customer action to achieve wider goals has grown in importance during the 1980s and 1990s. It is not a new phenomenon. In the US 'affirmative action' purchasing has been a continuing feature of government buying. Those wishing to sell to the federal government know that there are quotas for small firms, women-owned businesses, veterans and minorities. Sub-contractors are expected to follow the same principles. Some large companies have responded to new social and environmental concerns in the same way. McDonald's informed its packaging suppliers that it was stopping buying containers using CFCs by a given date. The Body Shop will not use products which have been tested on animals. Supermarkets like Safeway will not sell tuna caught using drag netting.

Often these corporate responses are a reaction to action by end consumers. Any parent whose twelve-year-old daughter objects to buying a can of tuna without the 'little dolphin' symbol knows the power of this type of pressure. The extent of this action has grown over the last decade. Smith[21] details a number of the more famous illustrations of organized consumer action producing changes in marketing. California grapes, Barclays Bank, Angolan coffee, Tarmac and Nestlé are among the more famous cases. The list now extends to hardwoods, aerosols, E-numbers, cigarettes, DDT, ivory, sausages and many others. The increased skills of pressure groups and the growing responsiveness of consumers are making firms more aware of the need to respond early and constructively to consumer concerns and action.

The special case of food

The late 1980s saw a dramatic increase in the number of specific concerns about food production and processing standards. These 'scares' included:

> endemic salmonella in chicken flocks and the consequent contamination
> of eggs, the presence of listeria in pâté, cook chill foods and soft cheeses,
> glass in baby foods . . . bovine spongiform encephalopathy (BSE).[22]

These problems reflect increases in the number of reported incidents of problems of contamination. An illustration of this was reported by Goldie:

> The Central Public Health Laboratory serotyped less than 50 strains of
> monocytogenes in 1967, compared to 214 cases in the year ended
> 30 November, 1987.

These developments reflect a mixture of changes in food processing technology, increased concern among consumers and growing criticism of the food industry. Technology provides producers and processors with an increasing number of technological alternatives. This allows them to process food more quickly, store it within narrower bounds, extract more from the raw material and present products in different ways. These opportunities pose new demands for care and attention to maintain standards. New, long-shelf-life, cold food products illustrate these opportunities and risks. Many have a long shelf life at 4°C. After proper storage they can be eaten without cooking. Unfortunately 'listeria monocytogenes can grow at 4°C, and is resistant to nitrates and sodium chloride which normally inhibit growth of other bacteria'.[23] The response to these challenges is criticized by writers like Geoffrey Cannon. He comments[24] that:

> The British food manufacturing industry may diversify into new business,
> but resists making higher quality food from healthier ingredients.

The mixture of increased awareness about risk and greater consciousness about healthy eating makes consumers very responsive to food scares[25] and increasingly discriminating in products bought. Difficulties with the former have encouraged firms to establish systems to deal with specific problems. These policies include:[26]

1   Stop production and inform health authorities.
2   Stop deliveries of raw materials.
3   Recall products already distributed.
4   Provide quick advice to consumers, wholesalers and retailers.
5   Arrange alternative supplies.
6   Plan rehabilitation of brand image in the market.
7   Monitor financial implications constantly.
8   Reassure all stake-holders – media, shareholders, employees, customers etc. – with regular and honest updates on position.

This combination of rapid response, concern for the total effect on the product, the firm and the market and planning for rehabilitation is increasingly important in responses to the effective management of the wider responsibilities of the firm.

Consumerism

Consumerism has been defined as:

> a social movement seeking to augment the rights and powers of buyers in relation to sellers up to the point where the consumer is able to defend his interests.[27]

As such, it has a history which stretches back at least to the nineteenth century, when there were protests against company shops.[28] The consumer movement today differs from most earlier similar movements in two ways:

1   *Adoption of an apolitical stance.* In the past similar movements linked themselves with formal political groups, generally populist, liberal or socialist. Most modern groups, however, adopt a firm policy of avoiding such links. This does not preclude links with government, local authorities or quasi-government bodies.
2   *Interaction with marketing.* Although it is an exaggeration to suggest that businessmen in the last century and the first half of this century were ruthless in their approach to customers, there was far more general acceptance of ideas such as 'Never give a sucker an even break', 'Buyer beware' and 'Any profit we can make is a fair profit'. The advent of marketing has changed this. Customers and their needs have supposedly become the firm's primary interest.

In the development of consumerism from the 1960s to the present day a number of overall trends can be distinguished. The first of these is that its forays into the international environment generally follow a path of affluence. The US and Sweden were at the forefront of this penetration, followed more recently by Western Europe and Japan. Although there are consumer groups in many parts of the Third World, consumerism is relatively unimportant when set against the crushing economic problems that many of these countries face. This path of affluence appears to recur in the franchise of the consumer groups in individual countries:

> At the beginning members [of the Consumers' Association] were recruited almost entirely from the AB and C1 social classes . . . Nor has

the CA succeeded in widening its membership to embrace a more representative cross-section of the population.[29]

In their study of the economic determinants of complaints, Morris and Reeson[30] found that:

> Complaint rates (complaints recorded per 1,000 population) are closely related to the level of expenditure on consumer advisory services.

This suggests that access to a mechanism for complaint, allied to awareness of the freedom to complain, is a significant factor in generating action. This has now gone so far that Crozier[32] suggests:

> Some commercial firms are at last treating 'consumerism' as an unsolicited market research feed-back from a highly significant segment of the total consumer population.

TMI[32] argue that good service recovery can be built on converting the dissatisfaction of the complaining customer into satisfaction. In these groups and probably also in the broader population the growth of consumerism is a function of:

1 *The dangers associated with the product:* actual or apparent physical danger related to certain products gave rise to many consumer groups, e.g. Nader's 'Unsafe at Any Speed'.
2 *The perceived honesty or otherwise of the producer or seller:* examples of dishonesty provide a constant spur to the growth of consumerism.
3 *The abuse of power:* a great deal of discussion now centres on the actual or alleged ability of some firms to control the market by manipulating supplies, make excess profits and generally act with little external restraint.
4 *Inequality:* in the majority of areas there persists a sense of inequality which needs to be resolved through various means, from trust breaking to product information.

The consumer movement[33] has taken a number of different stances in its relationships with producers. These can be broadly divided into responsible and liable stances.

Responsible stance

A 'responsible' stance is based on the proposition that the overwhelming majority of manu-facturers generally accept that there is a mutual interest between them and their customers or clients. Decisions may have been made in the past which do not agree with this notion but these are neither irrevocable nor malicious. Within this framework a continuing dialogue (with inevitable highs and lows) will provide the optimum mechanism for change. Kotler[34] brings this view out clearly when he asserts that:

> consumerism was inevitable; consumerism will be enduring; consumerism will be beneficial; consumerism is pro-marketing; and consumerism can be profitable.

Liable stance

A 'liable' stance is based on a much more conflict-based view of the relationship between producer and consumer. Within this framework the producer is held liable in law for the product's shortcomings. In the US the special character of the legal system has led to a certain punitive element in this area.

Thus when corporations rape the environment or abuse us as guinea pigs, we awaken to our individual powerlessness and our dependence on their smooth and presumably benign functioning. Then our frustrations and resentments surface, and we demand that corporate power be brought to heel and that corporate officials be made accountable.[35]

> There are some fears that a similar punitive aspect could emerge in the UK. It is, however, probable that even if 'product-liability' legislation was enacted, the very different legal customs would not lead to the same situation.

Seller's response

Management's response to the challenges posed by consumerism has varied enormously in terms of specific management groups, the approach to the consumer groups and the consumerist issue. In general, there is broad recognition by American[36] and European[37] executives that consumer pressure has been generally beneficial to the buyer. There are some, however, who suggest that the price paid in some circumstances was not fully appreciated.

> I merely ask whether the people of Europe – or indeed, the people of America – have asked whether they really want this state of affairs.[38]

In general there is little dispute about the need for and value of restraint on dangerous goods and dishonesty. Far more open to dispute, however, is the question of whether outside pressure groups, often drawn from specific subgroups in the population, play any significant part in improving overall standards or educating suppliers to their wider responsibilities. This is especially true, given the existing competitive pressure of the market, in dealing with alleged abuse of power and inequalities. Overall, it appears likely that consumerism will remain part of the marketing environment for the foreseeable future.

Marketing management and consumerists generally have a common interest in improving standards and offerings. Where disputes are likely to arise is over the recognition by marketing management that requirements differ significantly between groups. At the same time, these standards are related to cost, and communicating this to certain consumer-interest groups can play a part in the true dialogue from which both are likely to benefit.

Marketing and non-profit-making organizations

Interest in marketing among non-profit-making organizations has grown rapidly over the last twenty years. Politicians are aware of the scope for using marketing research to build up a picture of the attitudes and expectations of the electorate. Political leaders in the US[39] and Britain[40] employ marketing to shape the presentation, development and implementation of policies. Government departments are among the heaviest advertisers. They employ media advertising to create awareness of schemes like the New Deal. Universities, colleges and other parts of the public sector are learning the same lessons. A university will manage its portfolio of courses to maximize the effective use of its resources. University for Industry teaches users in novel ways. Universities seek to make their staff more aware of the value of the marketing concept to improve client awareness and better service. An ambulance service will inform casual users of the costs of each 'call' to encourage those able to use taxis or other transport. A hospital will collaborate with a retail developer to improve retail and catering services and generate new forms of income.

Developing this view of the market-place in terms of the complex networks of needs which face an organization is central to the marketing concept. It highlights the impact of the environment on the enterprise. Recognition of the different kinds of needs and the variety of relationships sought by clients is perhaps the greatest single contribution that marketing can make to non-profit-making organizations. It is a view that is being increasingly recognized by a host of non-profit organizations.

Simmons[41] brings out the rapid rate of growth in the use of market research by these organizations (Table 26.2). This probably under-represents the non-profit-making sector as some voluntary bodies conduct the research themselves and others, e.g. charities, may have access to expert but free assistance. This use has grown throughout the last two decades.

Table 26.2 Users of market research

	1966	1974	1976
Total user members	1,100	1,400	1,400
	(%)	(%)	(%)
Food, drink and tobacco	19	19	22
Other manufacturing	32	28	28
Service	3	7	6
Advertising	30	19	15
Media	8	9	8
Academic institutions	4	9	10
Public sector	4	9	11

The argument for the introduction or acceptance of marketing in non-profit-making organizations is based on the proposition that:

1 They face a host of problems that would be analyzed as straightforward marketing problems if found in the profit sector.
2 Just like any business trying to manage its relationships or its exchanges with a franchise, they seek to manage their demand, need to understand their markets and franchises, operate within a system and are influenced by their environment, and have at their disposal a marketing mix.

The understanding that is called for can operate at many levels, as an example used already shows. It will be remembered that Durham's Friends of the Earth group were actively involved in insulating the homes of the elderly. They decided to produce a poster. A number of activitists drew it up, had it printed and placed copies in friendly shops. There was no reaction. They then examined the problem in greater detail with some residents of a nearby old people's home. Problems emerged immediately: type-faces that were legible to students were difficult for old people to see and 'friendly' record shops, clothes shops and craft shops were seldom visited by old people.

In a situation like the one in the Friends of the Earth example the parallel between profit-making and non-profit-making organizations is fairly close. The problems become far more serious when the body has multiple goals. A sense of direction is essential to effective marketing. In any commercial concerns this derives from the stated goals, probably co-ordinated or established by a clearly defined executive structure. In some non-profit-making organizations, however, the scope for this does not exist.

This is particularly true when inner-directed goals clash with outer-directed goals, as can often be seen in the case of historical sites, academic institutions, and government departments. Using the historical site illustration, the inner-directed goal might be the historical studies of the research staff, the excavations etc. The income from visitors may contribute towards the funding of this but interfere with the real work. Resolving the clashes between these internal goals and an external 'Bring more visitors' goal puts serious strains on the setting of objectives. Ideology or strongly held attitudes can play a significant part in this.

The director of the historical site might be a committed historian who is unwilling to invest time and effort worrying about the marketing infrastructure. In some instances the product may be the sole reason for involvement in the institution, and an activist for a pressure group or political party may totally reject the notion of 'modifying the product' to suit the needs of specific target groups. In the case of the historical site it may be argued that a high-level marketing officer should be employed or that the organization ought to buy marketing services. Unfortunately, the narrowness of vision of some organizations will lead them to recruit another subject specialist, e.g. an archaeologist, rather than a marketing person. The overwhelming majority of non-profit-making organizations lack the resources to adopt either policy, and in these organizations the production of a simple marketing plan is probably the most important first step. Agreeing to invest resources in this is a necessary prerequisite.

Government

The state is by far the largest, single non-profit-making organization. In managing its exchanges with the environment an increasingly positive attitude to marketing is being adopted at senior levels. Investment in research into such critical areas as energy conservation, family planning and allocation of social services is making a significant contribution to policy formulations.[42] However, as was noted in the section on service marketing, the impact of this will be restricted until methods of communicating this notion throughout the organization are established.

Conclusion

Throughout this text the need to develop a broader perspective on marketing and the different contexts in which managers operate has been emphasized. This broader social dimension to marketing both poses a challenge and gives an opportunity. The challenge lies in the failure to recognize that many of the criticisms contain an element of truth. The challenge to the concept itself is whether the emergence of consumerism is derived from a weakness in marketing or from flaws in its application. The opportunity is provided for marketing people to contribute to some of the areas of social, environmental and economic difficulty facing the world. At the same time the horizons of marketing people can be widened by their attempt to understand and adapt to the needs of non-profit-making organizations. There is a new recognition that values are central to decision-making in marketing. Recognition of these values calls for a review of the ways in which resources are allocated:

> There is a bewildered embarrassment that the system that serves 80% of us so well should leave the other 20% so obviously deprived.[43]

The need to respond extends beyond the local market to the global market.[44] It is part of the excitement of marketing that it provides:

1 Insights into the nature of response – by striving to understand and appreciate the nature and diversity of needs.

2 Policies for appropriate responses – adapting and developing the total relationship between the customer and supplier to ensure that they want the relationship to persist and develop.

3 Appreciation of the unity of interest between the individual, the group, the organization and the wider environment.

The interdependence of people, systems and the wider environment has long been recognized by successful marketing executives, academics and students. It is impossible to be an effective marketer without appreciating that decisions, policies and acts have consequences far beyond their immediate and obvious environment. A simple mistake in naming a product can ruin its prospects. Poor packaging can undo years of product development. This same understanding must now extend even further. Failure to appreciate the values and concerns of others produces racial, sexual and cultural stereotypes. Product development which ignores environmental impacts ruins the prospects of our children.

The challenge to marketing in the late 1990s is to play its part in shaping sustainable, prosperous, equitable development for all participants in the marketing system. In the global market-place, it is as important to make this contribution in the post-Gulf War Arab world, the newly emerging economies of Central and Eastern Europe and the developing economies of Africa, Asia and Latin America as in the richer nations of the West.

CASE STUDY 22:
KNOXBRIDGE – A SUITABLE CASE FOR TREATMENT?

Introduction

The closure by British Rail of the Knoxbridge Engineering works brought the problems of this once-prosperous town in the central belt of Scotland to national attention. The loss of 500 jobs was a severe blow to a community which had seen its major industries and leading firms steadily decline for a number of years, and with increasing speed during the recession in the early 1990s and has not recovered.

Knoxbridge has an industrial history dating back as far as that of Scotland itself. Although links with the railways have always been strong, the industrial base was much wider. Coal and fireclay were mined for much of the last century. The last pit closed in 1962. Although there was a steady rundown in the mining industry, jobs emerged in new industries such as papermaking, refractory brickmaking, iron castings, general engineering and more recently plastics processing and some chemicals manufacture. As recently as the late 1960s, Knoxbridge was sufficiently prosperous to offer most of the youngsters leaving its schools a good chance of an apprenticeship or a job.

Aside from being a manufacturing base, Knoxbridge has been an important commercial centre for the nearby rural community. The shopping centre is large and contains a number of major retail outlets, such as Marks and Spencer and House of Fraser. However, trade has been lost to nearby Silvertown. The new indoor shopping centre in that town has drawn some trade from Knoxbridge.

Although Knoxbridge is within 30 miles of both Edinburgh and Glasgow, access to the motorway network could be improved. Rail links are good, but the closure of the engineering works has raised some questions about this.

Recent decline

There are now about 46,000 people living in the Knoxbridge area. The conurbation is bounded by the motorway to the west. With the exception of some more recent housing developments, the town is skirted by good A-roads to the east and south. The newer developments mentioned above were primarily developed to accommodate overspill from Glasgow – almost 90 per cent of the houses there are council houses. An industrial and commercial estate was developed nearby; unfortunately, this has been especially hard hit by the recession. Unemployment in this area is very high.

The rest of the township is less well defined and concentrated. Home ownership is low, with 77 per cent of all houses council-owned. There are a number of relatively isolated communities in outlying areas, such as the old mining community of Kintry. Here there are major social problems, especially with the ageing population.

These particular problems have to be seen in the context of the area's progressive decline. Unemployment has grown rapidly. At the same time there is low demand for existing skills. The College of Technology has recently opened an Information Technology Centre. The College of Commerce has a well-established programme of work, but there has been a dramatic increase in youth unemployment. These have to be seen in the national context of long-term decline in industrial output, rising unemployment of surviving firms, and a number of major closures such as that experienced in Knoxbridge recently.

Figures from the Knoxbridge Employment Office show that it is proportionately one of the worst-affected areas in Scotland. Although relatively small and with significant numbers of employed people in the community in relation to other areas, it is now estimated that the workforce has contracted to just over 7,500 in 1996 from just under 14,000 in 1982.

The general picture is dismal, with:

1   A number of recent closures.
2   Negligible growth in existing firms.
3   Low rate of new company formation.
4   Poor prospects of inward investment.

Between 1979 and 1996 there was a 35 per cent decline in total employment in the area. At least 34 companies have closed and job losses of at least 1,400 people have occurred between the beginning of 1990 and March 1996. Twenty-five of these closures were in manufacturing and construction, accounting for over 1,000 of the jobs lost.

Although the last few years have seen some new developments, notably a new hypermarket and a major DIY superstore, these have done little to arrest the overall decline.

Table 26.3 Overall employment changes (Knoxbridge Employment Office)

Sector	1988	(%)	1993	(%)	Change
Primary	386	(2.7)	222	(2.0)	−164
Manufacturing	7,226	(51.5)	5,424	(54.0)	−1,802
Construction	1,484	(10.6)	1,404	(14.0)	−80
Services	4,946	(35.2)	3,084	(30.0)	−1,862
Total	14,042	(100.0)	10,134	(100.0)	−3,908

Community action

The announcement of the closure of the railway engineering works prompted a number of people from different parts of the community to come together to explore ways of tackling their problems. The Regional and District Councils, along with the Chamber of Commerce and a number of other employers, met with Scottish Enterprise. The latter strongly advised them to set up an Enterprise Trust. This has now been done with the Regional Council, the District Council providing 'pump-priming' financial support and ABL distilleries providing a secondee as director.

Task

'What part can marketing play in reviving this community?'

Appendix: Managing a marketing project

THE RESEARCH-BASED THESIS, project report or dissertation on marketing provides a most complex, information-hungry environment. Those involved in enterprise will find the underlying disciplines invaluable in virtually all investigative project work. The entrepreneur starting a new commercial enterprise requires a business plan based on a coherent structure. A research paper without a clear framework will ramble and confuse readers. The initiators of a charitable venture need a clear understanding of the role and purpose of their work. A project report needs to be clear and relevant to the brief. A theatre group blends a sense of direction with personal insights. A dissertation gets its direction from knowledge of the literature and insights from the evidence gathered. Underlying each of these aspects of enterprise is a use of networks and information. Students undertaking a marketing project face all these difficulties.

Defining the task

At the core of any marketing project is a definition of the task or work to be done. The researcher faces several common problems. He or she may have a body of knowledge to draw on but it is inadequate. Established wisdom provides the hypothesis, the questions, an insight into the opportunity, even a view of the most promising way forward. Enterprising investigators will generally make the initial mistake of trying to do too much in the time available. Fascination with the issue blinds enthusiasts to the limitations of resources. The final-year student seeking to understand the implications for technology of high-temperature superconductivity has much in common with the entrepreneur striving to launch a new business based on teleshopping. Unless they are uniquely skilled or backed by the equivalent of Huber Corporation's superconductivity experts or Tesco retail specialists they will fail. Successful project management depends on an appreciation of the challenge faced and the resources needed. In research, this means a summary statement of the issue and the hypothesis to be tested. In a commercial enterprise, the equivalent is a description of the business and an answer to the question: Why will I succeed? If you are looking for ideas, go through the projects or dissertations in the university. Many often concluded by indicating promising areas for future research. The abstracts section in the *Journal of Marketing* is an invaluable source of ideas and references.

Project search and initial development

In the research situation, the investigator often faces a need to seek out ideas and projects. The primary, initial assignment lies in defining an achievable project and programme of work that can be undertaken. It is useful to ask:

- Is the project interesting?
- What is known about the issue? or, more important, What do I know about the issue?
- Do I have access to relevant information?
- Can I complete the project in the time available?
- Is success dependent on forces outside my control?
- Is help easily and readily available?

Only move forward if most of the answers are 'Yes'.

The preparation of a time-based plan of action, with contingencies built in, often provides useful insights. The time plan (below) from the fictitious University of Inverness Marketing Project indicates just some of the constraints based on a 'final-term' project:

4 June	Hand in project.
24 May	Proof-read the project.
18 May	Type up the project.
7 May	Revise and edit final draft (1).
23 April	Start final write-up.
17 April	Collate information (1).
6 April	Send out reminders to respondents.
23 March	Mail survey.
19 March	Type up final questionnaires.
12 March	Review pilot survey.
7 March	Start pilot survey.
1 March	Draft questionnaires (r2).
26 February	Complete initial literature review.

Some of the basic planning ground rules are outlined above. The most basic is 'Plan from the end-date'. It is easy to look forward and believe time stretches out indefinitely. This is dangerous in itself and can be fatal when absolute and practical restrictions exist. Make sure the computer you're using can format the document properly, and that the printer will print it to a suitable standard. The last-minute rush can destroy the value of earlier painstaking work. The examiners' irritation at poor English, recurrent spelling mistakes and bad presentation will soon blind them to intrinsic merit.

At most stages of a project some scope for recycling work is necessary. The (r) identifies the more common areas. The draft is unlikely to be 'right first time'. The initial sort through responses will not bring out all the main issues. Questionnaires take several efforts to get things right. In this illustration a project based on a mail survey is proposed. The scope for delays and difficulties is as great in personal questionnaires and experiments. Some problems are shared.

Equipment failure with an experiment is akin to the respondent refusing to answer. Sitting in front of a person who clearly has no knowledge of the issue is as wasteful as finding that the computer is 'down' or the equipment is broken.

In research projects Murphy's Third, Fourth and Fifth laws are a sure guide to planning:

- *Murphy's Third Law*
  In any field of scientific endeavour, anything that can go wrong, will go wrong.

- *Murphy's Fourth Law*
  If there is a possibility of several things going wrong, the one that will cause the most damage will be the one to go wrong.

- *Murphy's Fifth Law*
  If anything just cannot go wrong, it will anyway.

It is, however, unlikely that the researcher will be able to use Maier's Laws to win past the astute supervisor. These are:

- If facts do not confirm to the theory, they must be disposed of.
- Knowledge advances more by what it has learned to ignore than what it takes into account.

Notes, references and further reading

Chapter 1: Notes and References

1. Hammer, M. and Champy, J., *Reengineering the Corporation*. New York: HarperCollins, 1993.
2. Peters, T. J. and Waterman, R. J., *In Search of Excellence*. New York: Harper and Row, 1982.
3. Whiteley, R. C., *The Customer Driven Company*. London: Business Books, 1991.
4. Pine II, J. B., Victor, B and Boynton, A. C., 'Making Mass Customisation Work' *Harvard Business Review*, September–October 1993.
5. Hamel, G. and Prahalad, D. K., *Computing for the Future*. Boston: Harvard Business Publications, 1994.
6. Kay, John, *Foundations of Corporate Success*. Oxford: Oxford University Press, 1995.
7. Saunders, J. and Wong, V., 'In Search of Excellence in the UK', *Journal of Marketing Management*, 1, No. 2, Winter, 1985, pp. 119–138.
8. Cannon, T., 'Internationalisation of the Growing Company', *Interchange*, 1990.
9. Porter, M., *The Comparative Advantage of Nations*. London: Macmillan, 1990.
10. Kay, J., *Foundations of Corporate Success*. Oxford: Oxford University Press, 1995.
11. Department of Employment, *Keys to Business Growth*. London: Department of Employment, 1990.
12. Cannon, T., *The Guinness Book of Business Records*. Bath: Guinness Publishing, 1996.
13. Beal, T., 'Domestic Consumer Demand and Global Marketing Strategy', *Second World Marketing Congress*, Stirling, 1985.
14. Packard, V., *The Waste Makers*. Harmondsworth: Penguin, 1960.
15. Mant, A., *The Rise and Fall of the British Manager*. London: Macmillan, 1977.
16. Webster, F. E., 'Top Management's Concerns about Marketing', *Journal of Marketing*, Summer, 1981, pp. 9–16.
17. Bennett, R. C. and Cooper, R. G., 'Beyond the Marketing Concept', *Business Horizons*, June, 1979, pp. 76–83.
18. Wong, V., Saunders, J. and Doyle, P., 'The Quality of British Marketing: A Comparison with US and Japanese Multinationals in the UK', *British Journal of Marketing*, 4, No. 2, Winter, 1988, pp. 107–130.
19. Marcus, B. W., *Competing for Clients in the 90's*. New York: McGraw-Hill, 1992.
20. Drucker, P., *Management: Tasks, Responsibilities, Practices*. London: Harper and Row, 1973.
21. Dixon, D., F. and Blois, K. J., 'Some Limitations on the Four 'P's' as a Paradigm for Marketing', Marketing Education Group Annual Conference, Cranfield, 1983.
22. Hamel and Prahalad, *op. cit.*
23. Runyon, K. E, *The Practice of Marketing*. Columbus, Ohio: C. E. Merrill, 1982.
24. Kotler, P., *Marketing Management: Analysis, Planning and Control*. Englewood Cliffs: Prentice-Hall, 1987.
25. Crosier, K., 'What exactly is marketing?' in Thomas, M., and Waite, N. (eds) *The Marketing Digest*. Oxford: Heinemann, Professional Publishing Ltd, 1989.
26. Baker, M., 'One More Time: What is Marketing?'. In Baker, M. (ed.) *The Marketing Book*. Oxford: Butterfield Heinemann, 1994.

27. Grouroos, C., 'The Rebirth of Modern Marketing', Swedish School of Economics and Business Administration Working Paper 307, Helsinki, 1995.

28. Report of the Central Committee of the 9th Congress of the Socialist Unity Party of the German Democratic Republic.

29. Brown, A. C., 'Eastern Europe: A Dilemma for the Strategic Planner', *Quarterly Review of Marketing,* Autumn, 1990, pp. 14–18.

30. Hammarkvist, K. O., 'Markets as Networks', Marketing Education Group Annual Conference, Cranfield, 1983.

31. Crosby, P., *Quality is Free.* London: McGraw-Hill, 1979.

32. Norburn, D., Birley, S. and Dunn, M., 'Marketing Effectiveness and its Relationship to Customer Closeness, Corporate Values and Market Orientation', Proceedings 20th Annual Conference Marketing Education Group, Warwick, 1987.

33. Uttal, B., 'The Corporate Culture Vultures', *Fortune,* 17, October, 1983.

34. Business Week, 'Marketing: The New Priority', November 21, 1983.

35. Helbroner, R. L., *The Making of Economic Society.* Englewood Cliffs: Prentice-Hall, 1968.

36. Braudel, F., *Civilisation and Capitalism 15th to 18th Century, Volume 3: The Perspective of the World.* London: Collins, 1985.

37. Belshaw, C. S. *Traditional Exchange and Modern Markets.* Englewood Cliffs: Prentice-Hall, 1965.

38. Deane, P., *The First Industrial Revolution.* Oxford: Oxford University Press, 1969.

39. Lorenz, C., 'How Japan Is Dumping a Dated Global Dogma', *Financial Times,* 27 October, 1986.

40. Clark, R., *Aspects of Japanese Technical Innovation.* London: Technical Change Centre, 1987.

41. Dace, R., 'Japanese New Product Development', Proceedings 21st Annual Conference Marketing Education Group, Huddersfield, 1988.

42. Discussion in this section is based primarily on the description provided by Alfred P. Sloan in his detailed and insightful review of the events of the period in *My Years with General Motors.* Harmondsworth: Penguin, 1986.

43. Thomas, M., 'The Alpha and Omega of the 4 Ps – Planning and Productivity', Marketing Education Group Annual Conference, Cranfield, 1983.

44. The dispute at the end of 1990 between Nissan and its main UK dealer vividly illustrated this.

45. Reid, D., 'Strategic Marketing Planning: Shortfalls and Implications', Second World Marketing Congress, Stirling, 1985.

46. Gray, D., 'Uses and Misuses of Strategic Planning', *Harvard Business Review,* January–February, 1985.

47. Baker, M. and Black, C., 'The Competitiveness of British Industry: What Really Makes the Difference', Proceedings Marketing Education Group Annual Conference, 1987.

48. Wilson, R. M. S., *Management Controls and Marketing Planning.* London: Heinemann, 1979.

49. Parkinson, S., 'World Class Marketing: Lost Empires of the Image Men', *Journal of Marketing Management,* 7, No. 3, July 1991.

50. Peters and Waterman, *op. cit.*

51. Thulliez, G. J., 'French CEOs Look Ahead,' *The McKinsey Quarterly,* Autumn, 1989, pp. 33–40.

52. Morita, A., *Made in Japan.* London: Fontana, 1990.

53. Peters and Waterman, *op. cit.*

54. Piercy, N. and Evans. M., *Managing Marketing Information.* London: Croom Helm, 1985.

55. Cannon, T., *Corporate Responsibility.* London: Pitman, 1994.

56. Smith, N. C., 'Teaching Ethics in Marketing: One Approach and Some Caveats', *Quarterly Review of Marketing,* Autumn, 1988, pp. 10–16.

57. Pirenne, J., *Tides of History.* London: George Allen and Unwin, 1963.

58. Cannon, *op. cit.*

59. 'American Competitiveness', *Business Round Table.* New York, 1992.

60. Kaynak, E., *Marketing in the Third World.* New York: Praeger, 1982.

61. Chok, M. K., 'Export Pricing of China's Industrial Goods', World Marketing Congress, Halifax, Nova Scotia, 1983.

62. Rostow, W. W., *The Stages of Economic Growth.* London: Cambridge University Press, 1960.

Chapter 1: Further Reading

Baker, M., *The Marketing Book*. Oxford: Butterfield Heinemann, 1994.

Brown, S. *Postmodern Marketing*. London: Routledge, 1995.

Ellsworth, J. H. and Ellsworth, M. V. 'Marketing of the Internet'. London: Wiley, 1995.

Hart, C., 'The Power of Unconditional Service Guarantees', *Harvard Business Review*, July–August, 1988.

Kay, John *Foundations of Corporate Success*. Oxford: Oxford University Press, 1995.

Kotler, P., *Marketing for Non-Profit Organisations*. London: Prentice-Hall, 1982.

Levitt, T., 'Marketing Myopia'. In *Fundamentals of Marketing* (ed. Taylor, J. L. et al.). London: McGraw-Hill, 1978. Brings out the importance of a marketing vision or perspective in looking beyond the current offering into new areas.

Peters, T. J. and Waterman, R. H., *In Search of Excellence*. London: Harper and Row, 1982. Explores the key lessons for corporate success from the experiences of 60 of the most successful US corporations in the 1970s.

Pine II, J. B. *Mass Customisation: The New Frontier in Business Competition*. Cambridge, Mass: Harvard Business School Press.

Sampson, A., *Company Man*. London: HarperCollins, 1995.

Weitz, B. A. and Wensley, R., *Strategic Marketing*. Boston, Mass.: Kent Publishing, 1983. The introduction provides an excellent summation of the vital and central role of strategy in modern marketing thinking.

Zemke, R., *The Service Edge*. New York: New American Library, 1989.

Chapter 2: Notes and References

1. Griffin, T., 'Marketing Management – The Top and Bottom, Short and Long of It All', Proceedings Marketing Education Group Annual Conference, Cranfield, 1983.

2. Piercy, N., *Marketing Organization*. London: George Allen and Unwin, 1985.

3. Middleton, B. and Long, G., 'Marketing Skills: Critical Issues in Marketing Education and Training', *Journal of Marketing Management*, 5, No. 3, 1990, pp. 325–342.

4. Doyle, P., 'Management Structures and Marketing Strategies in UK Industry', *European Journal of Marketing*, 1990.

5. Payne, A. F., 'Developing a Marketing Oriented Organization', *Business Horizon*, May–June, 1988.

6. Piercy, N., 'The Role and Function of the Chief Marketing Executive and the Marketing Department', *Journal of Marketing Management*, 1, No. 6, Spring 1986, pp. 265–290.

7. McDonald, M., 'Planning the Marketing Function', in *The Marketing Book* (ed. M. Baker). Oxford: Heinemann, 1991.

8. Ballantyne, D., 'Internal Networks for Internal Marketing', *Journal of Marketing Management*, 13, No. 3, July 1997.

9. Coulson-Thomas, C., 'Customers, Marketing and the Network Organization', *Journal of Marketing Management*, 7, No. 3, July 1991.

10. Kotler, P., 'The Major Tasks of Marketing Management', *Journal of Marketing*, October 1973.

11. Hilgard, E. R., Atkinson, R. C. and Atkinson, R. L., *Introduction to Psychology*. New York: Harcourt Brace, 1965.

12. Festinger, L., *A Theory of Cognitive Dissonance*. Stanford, CA: Stanford University Press, 1957.

13. 'High Speed Travel in Europe', The Economist, 3 February 1990, pp. 23–26.

14. Thomas, R. E., *Business Policy*. London: Phillip Allen, 1983.

15. Johnson, G. and Scholes, K., *Exploring Corporate Strategy*. London: Prentice-Hall, 1984.

16. Piercy, N., *Export Strategy: Markets and Competition*. London: George Allen and Unwin, 1982.

17. Channon, D., *The Strategy and Structure of British Enterprise*. London: Macmillan, 1973.

18. Collins, J. C. and Porras, J. I., *Built to Last*. New York: HarperCollins, 1997.

19. Mintzberg, H., *The Structure of Organizations*. Englewood Cliffs: Prentice-Hall, 1979.

20. Johnson and Scholes, *op. cit.*

21. Kay, J., *Foundations of Corporate Sucess*. Oxford: Oxford University Press, 1994.

Chapter 2: Further Reading

Collins, J. C. and Porras, J. I., *Built to Last.* New York: HarperCollins, 1997.

Gillinham, D. W., 'The Marketing Management System', in Thomas, M. and Waite, N. (eds.) *The Marketing Digest.* Oxford: Heinemann, 1989.

Hart, C., 'The Power of Unconditional Service Guarantees', *Harvard Business Review*, July–August 1988.

Simon, H., *Hidden Champions.* Cambridge, MA: Harvard University Press, 1996.

Stalk, G. jnr. and Hout, T. M. *Competing Against Time.* London: Collier Macmillan, 1990.

Treacy, M. and Weirsema, F., *The Disciples of Market Leaders.* New York: Addison-Wesley, 1995.

Chapter 3: Notes and References

1. Kotler, P., *Marketing Management: Analysis Planning and Control.* Englewood Cliffs: Prentice-Hall, 1997.
2. Pettigrew, A. and Whipp, R., *Managing Change for Competitive Success.* Oxford: Blackwell, 1991.
3. Mitchell, V-W, 'Assessing the Perceived Risk Associated with Appointing Planning Consultants', *Journal of Marketing Management,* Vol 11, 1995.
4. Wilson, A., *Practice Development for Professional Firms.* London: McGraw-Hill, 1984.
5. Kotler, *op. cit.*
6. Cannon, T., 'Marketing Problems in the Food Chain', *Food Marketing*, 1, No. 1, 1985.
7. King, S., 'Has Marketing Failed or Was It Never Tried?', *Journal of Marketing Management,* Summer 1985.
8. King, *op. cit.*
9. Doyle, P., 'Marketing and the Competitive Performance of British Industry', *Journal of Marketing Management,* Summer 1985.
10. Parkinson, S., 'Successful New Product Development', *British Graduate,* Spring 1982.
11. Amine, L., 'Marketing and the Performance of the British Textile Industry', PhD dissertation, University of Bradford, 1976.
12. NEDO, *Industrial Performance: Trade Performance and Marketing.* London: HMSO, 1981.
13. NEDO, *International Competitiveness: R & D and Action by EDC's.* London: NEDO, 1988.
14. Brownlie, D., 'Environmental Scanning', in M. Baker, *The Marketing Handbook.* Oxford: Butterfield Heinemann, 1994.
15. Diffenbach, J., 'Corporate Environmental Change in Large US Corporations', *Long Range Planning,* 16, No. 3, 1983.
16. McDaniel, G., 'The Meaning of the Systems Movement to the Acceleration and Direction of the American Economy', in *Analysis for Military Decisions* (ed. E. S. Quaile). California: Rand Corporation, 1975.
17. Wind, Y. and Robinson, P. J., 'Product Positioning: An Application of Multidimensional Scaling', in *Attitude Research in Transition.* Chicago: American Marketing Association, 1972.
18. Abell, D. F., 'Strategic Windows', *Journal of Marketing,* July 1978.

Chapter 3: Further Reading

Ballance, R. H. and Sinclair, S. W., *Collapse and Survival: Industrial Strategies in a Changing World.* London: George Allen and Unwin, 1983.

Cannon, T. *Welcome to the Revolution.* London, Pitman, 1996.

Gershung, J., *After Industrial Society.* London: Macmillan, 1978.

Hamel, G. and Hammarkvist, K. O., 'Markets as Networks', Cranfield, Marketing Educators Group Annual Conference, 1983.

NEDO, *Industrial Performance: Trade Performance and Marketing.* London: HMSO, 1981.

Pickering, J. F. and Cockerill, T. A. J. (eds), *The Economic Management of the Firm.* London: Philip Allan, 1984.

Chapter 4: Notes and References

1. Dawson, J., 'Retailer Differentiation through Services', Third Bi-Annual Conference on Food Marketing, Cranfield, 1989.
2. Shaw, S. and Muir, J., *Salmon: Economics and Marketing*. London: Croom Helm, 1987.
3. Rawlings, C. M., 'Developments in Packaging and Food Marketing,' *Food Marketing*, 2, No. 3, 1986, pp. 116–122.
4. Houghton, T., 'Political Policy, Legislation and Business Strategy', *British Food Journal*, 54, No. 5, pp.16–20.
5. Frank, J. and Wheelock, V., 'International Trends in Food Consumption', *British Food Journal*, 90, No. 1, pp. 22–29.
6. Mintel, *Retail Intelligence*, January–February 1988, Vol. 1, p. 2.1.
7. Davis, G., 'Healthier Eating and the Effects on Health Food Retailing', *British Food Journal*, 94, No. 2, 1992, pp. 30–36.
8. Thompson, K. E., 'International Competitiveness: British Food Industry Post-1992', *British Food Journal*, 94, No. 6, 1992, pp. 5–9.
9. Swaminathan, M. S., 'The Emerging Global Agricultural Scenario', *Royal Society of Arts Journal*, No. 5376, November, 1987, pp. 891–909.
10. Mackenzie, D., 'Greener Than Thou', *Marketing Business*, April1992, pp. 10–13.
11. Slattery, J., 'Current Diet and Health Recommendations –The Response of the Food Industry', *Food Marketing*, 2, No. 3, 1986, pp. 180–186.
12. Black, Sir D. Chm., *Diet, Nutrition and Health*. London: British Medical Association, 1986.
13. Bernstein, D., *The Company of Green*. Sheffield: Green Leaf Publishing, 1992.
14. Charter, M. and King, R., 'Issues Emerging in Environmental Marketing', *Greener Management International*, April, 1993, pp. 72–80.
15. Food and Agriculture Organization, *World Food Report 1986*. Rome: FAO, 1986.
16. Brown, S., 'Retailing Change: Cycles and Strategy', *Quarterly Review of Marketing*, 13. No. 3, Spring, 1988, pp. 8–11.
17. Sawyers, L., 'The Effect of the Introduction of New Technology upon Female Labour in Retailing', PhD thesis, University of Stirling, 1985.
18. Dawson, J., Findlay, A. and Sparks, L., 'The Impact of Scanning on Employment in UK Food Stores; A Preliminary Analysis', *Journal of Marketing Management*, 2, No. 3, Spring 1987, pp. 285–300.
19. Burrough, B., and Helyar, J., *Barbarians at the Gate*. London: Jonathan Cape, 1990.
20. *Fortune*, 'Managing Now for the 1990's', 26 September 1989, p. 34.
21. Blair, L. and Shaw, S., 'Product Sourcing in the Food Chain', Third Bi-Annual Conference on Food Marketing, Cranfield, 1989.
22. Nicholls, J. R., 'The EC: Dancing with a Gorilla', *British Food Journal*, 90, No. 6, November–December 1988, pp. 263–267.
23. Wheelock, J. V., 'Coping with Change in the Food Business', *Food Marketing*, 2, No. 3, 1986, pp. 20–45.
24. Cannon, G., *The Politics of Food*. London: Century, 1987.
25. Elkington, J. and Hayes, J., *The Green Consumer Guide*. London: Gollancz, 1988.
26. Goldie, F. J., 'Thinking about the Unthinkable: Disaster Management in the Food Industry', *British Food Journal*, July–August 1988, pp. 155–158.
27. Duke, R., 'Post Saturation Competition in UK Grocery Retailing', *Journal of Marketing Management*, 7, No. 1, 1991.

Chapter 4: Further Reading

Daly, L. and Beharrel, B., 'Health, Diet and the Marketing of Food and Drink – Some Theoretical Problems', *British Food Journal*, 90, No. 1, 1988.
Jukes, D. J., 'The Structure of Food Law Enforcement in the United Kingdom', *British Food Journal*, 90, No. 6, 1988, pp. 239–249.
Local Authorities Co-ordinating Body On Trading Standards, Report of the Factory Enforcement Working Party. London: LACOTS, 1984.

Chapter 5: Notes and References

1. Barney, J., 'Firm Resources and Sustained Competitive Advantage', *Journal of Marketing*, 17, No. 1, 1991.
2. Now almost impossible under EU competition policy.
3. Hooley, G., Cox, A. and Adams, A., 'Five Year Mission: To Go Where No Man Has Been Before', *Journal of Marketing Management*, 8, No. 1, 1992.
4. Sheaff, R., *Marketing for the N.H.S.* Milton Keynes: The Open University Press, 1991.
5. Cunningham, M., 'International Marketing and Purchasing of Industrial Goods', Edinburgh, Marketing Education Group Annual Conference, 1980.
6. Beal, T., 'Domestic Consumer Demand and Japanese Global Marketing Strategy', Second World Marketing Congress, Stirling, 1985.
7. Porter, M., *The Competitive Advantages of Nations.* London: Macmillan, 1990.
8. Nerlove, M. and Waugh, F. V., 'Advertising without Supply Control', *Journal of Farm Economics*, November 1961.
9. Barker, J. W., *Agricultural Marketing.* Oxford: Oxford University Press, 1981.
10. Cannon, T., *Marketing Problems in the Food Chain*, Sheffield: Agricultural Economics Society, 1984.
11. Much of this discussion is based on Barker.
12. *Ibid.*
13. Jukes, D. J. 'European Developments in the Foodstuffs Sector', *British Food Journal*, 92, No. 2, Winter 1990, pp. 3–10.
14. Fletcher, K., Wheeler, C. and Wright. J., 'The Role and Status of UK Database Marketing', *Quarterly Review of Marketing*, October 1990, pp.1–14.
15. Cannon, *op. cit.*
16. Nerlove and Waugh, *op. cit.*
17. Cannon. T., 'Marketing Problems in the Food Chain', *Food Marketing*, 1, No. 1, 1985.
18. Hill, R. W. and Hillier, T. J., *Organisational Buying Behaviour.* London: Macmillan, 1977.
19. Barnes, J. and Glynn, W., 'The Customer Wants Service, Why Technology Is No Longer Enough', *Journal of Marketing Management*, 9, No. 1, 1993.
20. Grouros, C., 'A Service-orientated Approach to Marketing of Services', *European Journal of Marketing*, 9, No. 1, 1975.
21. McKechnie, S., 'Consumer Buying Behaviour in Financial Services: An Overview', *International Journal of Bank Marketing*, 10, No. 5, 1992.
22. Robinson, R. D., *International Business Management.* Illinois: Dryden Press, 1978.

Chapter 5: Further Reading

Baker, M., *Marketing Strategy and Management*, 2nd edn. London: Macmillan, 1992.
Browlie, D., 'Organising for Environmental Scanning: Orthodoxies and Reformations', *Journal of Marketing Management*, Vol. 10, 1994.
Goldsmith, W. and Clutterbuck, D., *The Winning Streak.* London: Weidenfeld and Nicholson, 1985.
Pettigrew, A. and Whipp, R., *Managing Change for Competitive Success.* Oxford: Blackwell, 1991.
Suttoa, J., *Sunk Costs and Market Structure.* Boston: MIT Press, 1991.

Chapter 6: Notes and References

1. Simmons, M., *The British Market Research Industry*, Annual Conference of the Market Research Society, 1977.
2. Crimp, M. and Lea Lui Wright, *The Market Research Process*, 4th Edition. Hemel Hempstead: Prentice-Hall, 1997.
3. AMSO, *Annual Report.* London: Association of Market Survey Organisations, 1997.
4. HYPERLINK http://www.marketresearch.org.uk.
5. HYPERLINK http://www.iccwbo.org.

6.   HYPERLINK http://www.esomar.nl.
7.   Green, P. E. and Tull, D. S., *Research for Marketing Decisions.* Hemel Hempstead: Prentice-Hall International, 1995.
8.   Hund, S. D., *Marketing Theory.* Columbus, Ohio: Columbus Grid Inc., 1976.
9.   Harper, M. Jr, 'A New Profession to Aid Management', *Journal of Marketing*, January 1961.
10. Perreault, W. D. jnr., Green P. E., and Malhotra, N., 'The Shifting Paradigm in Marketing Research', *Journal of the Academy of Marketing Science*, 2, No. 4, Fall 1992.
11. Durkheim, E., *Rules of Sociological Method.* 1895.
12. Watson, J. B., *Psychology from the Point of View of the Behaviouralist.* 1919.
13. Marx, K., *Capital.* 1, 2nd Edition, 1873.
14. Kaplan, A., *The Conduct of Inquiry.* New York: Chandler Publishing, 1964.
15. Ryan, A., *The Philosophy of the Social Sciences.* London: Macmillan, 1971.
16. Ehrenberg, A. S. C., 'Laws in Marketing: A Tail-piece', in *Consumer Behaviour* (ed. Ehrenberg, A. S. C. and Pyatt, F. G.). Harmondsworth: Penguin, 1971. (Title in these readings, 'Regularities of Behaviour'.)
17. Zaltman, G., Christian, R. A., Angelman, P. and Angelman, R., *Metatheory and Consumer Research.* New York: Holt, Rinehart and Winston, 1973.
18. Hesketh, J. L., *Marketing.* New York: Macmillan, 1976.
19. Ehrenberg, A. S. C. 'The Research Brief', in *Marketing Research* (ed. Seibert, J. and Wills, G.). Harmondsworth: Penguin, 1970.
20. Crisp, R. D., 'Marketing Research Organization and Operation', Research Study No. 35. pp.39–47. New York: American Management Association, 1958. Reproduced with the permission of the American Marketing Association.
21. Definition Committee for the American Marketing Association.
22. A good guide to a practical approach to coping with large amounts of raw data is Ehrenberg, A. S. C., *Data Reduction.* Chichester: Wiley, 1975.
23. HYPERLINK http://www.dnbcorp.com.
24. HYPERLINK http://195.92.16.244/cso http://195.92.16.244/cso.
25. HYPERLINK http://www.doc.gov/bureaus.
26. HYPERLINK http://www.un.org.
27. HYPERLINK http://europa.eu.int/index.htm.
28. HYPERLINK http://www.oecd.org.
29. HYPERLINK http://www.un.org.
30. HYPERLINK http://www.imf.org.
31. HYPERLINK http://europa.eu.int/eurostat.html.
32. HYPERLINK http://www.oecd.org.
33. HYPERLINK http://www.warwick.ac.uk/services/library/library.html
34. HYPERLINK http://www.dnbcorp.com.
35. HYPERLINK http://www.dnbcorp.com.
36. HYPERLINK http://www.companies-house.gov.uk.
37. HYPERLINK http://www.glen.co.uk/cbd.
38. HYPERLINK http://www.adassoc.org.uk/aa/gial.html.
39. HYPERLINK http://www.adassoc.org.uk/aa/members/isba.html.
40. HYPERLINK http://www.ipa.co.uk/contents.html.
41. HYPERLINK http://www.cbi.org.uk/cbi/htdocs/unregindex.html .
42. HYPERLINK http://www.marketresearch.org.uk.
43. HYPERLINK http://www.casba.co.uk/cim.
44. HYPERLINK http://www.mintel.co.uk.
45. HYPERLINK http://www.eiu.com.
46. HYPERLINK http://www.frost.com.
47. HYPERLINK http://www.adassoc.org.uk/aa/gial.html.
48. HYPERLINK http://www.inst-mgt.org.uk.

49.   HYPERLINK http://www.casba.co.uk/cim.

50.   HYPERLINK http://www.city.ac.uk/library.

51.   HYPERLINK http://www.csv.warwick.ac.uk/services/library/library.html .

52.   HYPERLINK http://www.cs.aston.ac.uk/oldbrum/Library.html .

53.   HYPERLINK http://www.lse.ac.uk/m25/LSECON.1.HTML.

54.   HYPERLINK http://www.lbs.ac.uk/facres.htm.

55.   HYPERLINK http://www.mbs.ac.uk/lis/bis.

56.   HYPERLINK http://www.bbc.co.uk.

57.   HYPERLINK http://www.2000.osgm.vanderbilt.edu/baseline/internet.demos.july9.1996.html.

58.   HYPERLINK http://www.mit.edu:8001/people/mkgray/growth.

59.   HYPERLINK http://www.spectraweb.ch/~werbal/english/10commandments.html.

60.   See Moser, K. and Kalton, G. G. W., *Survey Methods in Social Investigation.* London: Heinemann, 1971.

61.   Moore, P. G., *Statistics and the Manager.* London: Macdonald, 1966.

62.   HYPERLINK http://www.marketresearch.org.uk.

63.   HYPERLINK http://www.marketresearch.org.uk.

64.   Kempner, T., *A–Z of Management.* Harmondsworth: Penguin, 1973.

65.   Gouldner, A. W., *Patterns of Industrial Bureaucracy.* New York: Free Press, 1975. Whyte, W. F., *Street Corner Society.* Chicago: University of Chicago Press, 1954. Both these studies employed the specialized form of observational study known as participant observation. Very little use has been made of this approach in marketing, except for some limited use in industrial studies.

66.   Market Research Development Fund Seminar, 'What Matters in Qualitative Research', *Journal of the Market Research Society,* 33, No. 1, January 1991.

67.   HYPERLINK http://www.milkround.co.uk/industry/advert/company/acniel.html.

68.   Brown, G. H., 'Brand Loyalty', in *Consumer Behaviour* (ed. Ehrenberg, A. S. C. and Pyatt, F. G.). Harmondsworth: Penguin, 1971.

69.   HYPERLINK http://www.gallup.com http://www.gallup.com.

70.   Smith, S. V., Brien, R. H. and Stafford, J. E., 'Marketing Information Systems: An Introductory Overview', in *Readings in Marketing Information Systems* (ed. Smith, S. V., Brien, R. H. & Stafford, J. E.). Boston: Houghton Mifflin Co., 1977.

71.   Briscoe, G., *The Sources and Uses of Marketing Information in the British Steel Corporation.* London: British Steel Corporation Fellowship Scheme, 1972.

72.   Jobber, D. and Rainbow, C., 'A Study of the Development and the Implementation of Marketing Information Systems in British Industry', *Journal of the Market Research Society,* 19, No. 3, July 1977.

Chapter 6: Further Reading

Bagozzi, R. P. (ed.) *Advanced Methods in Marketing Research.* Cambridge, Blackwell, 1994.

Birks, D. F., 'Market Research', in Baker, M., (ed.) *The Marketing Book.* Oxford, Heinemann, 1991.

Bradley, U., *Applied Marketing and Social Research.* Chichester: Wiley, 1987.

Crimp, M. and Lea Lui Wright, *The Market Research Process,* 4th Edition. Hemel Hempstead: Prentice-Hall, 1997.

Chisnall, P., *Marketing Research,* 4th edn. Maidenhead: McGraw-Hill, 1992.

Chapman, M. and Mahon, B., *Plain Figures.* London: Cabinet Office, HMSO, 1985.

Green, P. E. and Tull, D. S., *Research for Marketing Decisions.* Englewood Cliffs: Prentice-Hall International, 1996. This seventh edition, with its confirmed quantitative and decision-making approach, sustains the commitment to quality of the earlier works.

Chapter 7: Notes and References

1.   Kotler, P., *Marketing Management: Analysis, Planning, Implementation and Control. 9th Edition.* Englewood Cliffs: Prentice-Hall, 1997.

2. Adapted from Kotler, P., *Marketing Management: Analysis, Planning and Control*. Englewood Cliffs: Prentice-Hall, 1997.

3. Yankelovich, D., 'Market Segmentation', in *Consumer Behaviour* (ed. Ehrenberg, A. S. C. and Pyatt, F. G.). Harmondsworth: Penguin 1971.

4. Engel, J. F., Blackwell, R. D. and Minard, P. W., *Consumer Behaviour*, 8th edition. Hinsdale, Illinois: Dryden Press, 1995.

5. Packard, U., *Hidden Persuaders*. Hammondworth: Penguin, 1962.

6. Howard, J. A., *Marketing Management*. Illinois: R. D. Irwin, 1963.

7. Maslow, A. H., *Motivation and Personality*. New York: Harper and Row, 1954.

8. Chisnall, P. M., *Marketing A Behavioural Analysis*. London: McGraw-Hill, 1992.

9. Allport, G. W., *Handbook for Social Psychology*. Worcester, Mass.: Clark University Press, 1975.

10. Bird, M., Channon, C. and Ehrenberg, A. S. C., 'Brand Image and Brand Usage', *Journal of the Market Research Society*, 7, 1970.

11. Fishbein, M., 'The Relationship between Beliefs, Attitudes and Behaviour', in *Cognitive Consistency* (ed. Feldman, S.). New York: Academic Press, 1966.

12. Chisnall, *op. cit.*

13. Engel, J. F., Blackwell, R. D. and Minard, P. W., *Consumer Behaviour*, 3rd edition. Hinsdale, Illinois: Dryden Press, 1995.

14. Fletcher, W., *Adweek*, 22 March, 1974.

15. This section draws heavily on Howard, J. A., *Marketing Management*. Illinois: R. D. Irwin, 1963.

16. Kotler, P., *Marketing Management: Analysis, Planning, Implementation and Control. 9th Edition*. Englewood Cliffs: Prentice-Hall, 1997.

17. Foxall, G., 'The Consumer Situation – An Ingegrative Model for Research in Marketing', *Journal of Marketing Management*, 8, No. 4, 1992.

18. Rogers, E. M., *The Diffusion of Innovations*. New York: Macmillan, 1962.

19. Lancaster, G. and Taylor, C. T., 'The Diffusion of Innovations and the Attributes', *Quarterly Review of Marketing*, Summer 1986, pp. 13–19.

20. Cunningham, R. M., 'Brand Loyalty: What, Where, How Much?', *Harvard Business Review*, January-February 1956.

21. Cannon, T., Ehrenberg, A. S. C. and Goodhardt, G. J., 'Regularities in Sole Buying', *British Journal of Marketing*, 1970.

Chapter 7: Further Reading

Chisnall, P. M., *Marketing: A Behavioural Analysis*. 4th Edition. London: McGraw-Hill, 1992. A lucid drawing-together of the various strands which make up our current knowledge, providing an insight into a consumer-behaviour perspective on marketing.

Engel, J. F., Blackwell, R. D. and Minard, P. W., *Consumer Behaviour*, 8th edition. Hinsdale, Illinois: Dryden Press, 1995. Note particularly Chapters 2 and 19.

Foxall, G. R. and Goldsmith, R. E., *Consumer Psychology for Marketing Managers*. London: Routledge, 1994.

Howard, J. A., *Consumer Behaviour in Marketing Strategy*. London: Prentice-Hall, 1988. This represents an important contribution to the integration of theories of consumer behaviour with strategic marketing issues.

Chapter 8: Notes and References

1. Makridakis, S. *Forecasting Planning and Strategy for the 21st Century*. New York, Free Press, 1990.

2. Weitz, S. and Wensley, R., *Strategic Marketing*. Boston, Mass.: Kent Publishing, 1984.

3. Piercy, N., *Marketing-Led Strategic Change*. Oxford: Butterworth-Heinemann, 1992.

4. Abell, D., *Defining the Business: The Starting Point of Strategic Reviewing*. Englewood Cliffs: Prentice-Hall, 1980.

5. Moore, R. A., 'Conceptual and Empirical Developments in Marketing Channel Conflict', *Journal of Marketing Management*, 4, No. 3, Spring, 1989.

6. Daft, R., Sormunen, J. and Parks, D., 'Chief Executive Scanning Environmental Characteristics and Company Performance', *Strategic Management Journal*, 9, 1988.

7. Browlie, D. 'Environmental Scanning', in Baker, M. (ed.), *The Marketing Book*. Oxford, Heinemann, 1994.

8. Parkinson, S., 'The Role of the Buyer in Successful New Product Development', *R and D Management*, 12, No. 3, July, 1982.

9. Paliwoda, S. and Thompson, P., 'Industrial Product Classification and Market Behaviour', *Proceedings Research Developments in International Marketing*, Manchester, 1984.

10. Piercy, N., 'Information Processing: The Newest Mix Element', Marketing Education Group Annual Conference, Cranfield, 1985.

11. Piercy, N. and Evan, M., *Managing Marketing Information*. Beckenham: Croome Helm, 1983.

12. Rubin, S., 'Save Your Information System from the Experts', *Harvard Business Review*, July-August, 1986.

13. Lyons, H. and Thakur, S., 'New Information Technologies. The Educational Implications for Marketing Management', 2nd World Marketing Congress, Stirling, 1985.

14. Cunningham, M. and Culligan, K., 'Competition and Competitive Groupings: An Exploratory Study in Information Technology Markets', *Journal of Marketing Management*, 4, No. 2, 1988, pp. 148–174.

15. Turnbull, P. and Lewis, B., 'Bank Marketing', *European Journal of Marketing*, 16, No. 3, 1982.

16. Mitchell, J. W. and Sparks, L., 'Technology and Bank Marketing Information', *Journal of Marketing Management*, 4, No. 1, 1988, pp. 50–61.

17. Turnbull and Lewis, *op. cit.*

18. McKay, J. and Fletcher, K., 'Consumers' Attitudes towards Teleshopping', *Quarterly Review of Marketing*, 13, No. 3, Spring 1988, pp. 1–7.

19. Arnold, M. E. and Penn, J. M., 'The Information Technology Revolution in Marketing: A Review of Current Applications', *Quarterly Review of Marketing*, 1, No. 2, Winter, 1987, pp. 1–6.

20. Cairncross, F., *The Death of Distance*. London: Orion, 1997.

21. *Ibid.*

22. Buzzell, R. D., Gale, B. T. and Sultan, R. G. M., 'Market Share – The Key to Profitability', *Harvard Business Review*, January–February 1975.

23. Buzzell, R. D. and Gale, B. T., *The PIMS Principles*. New York: The Free Press, 1987.

24. *Ibid.*

25. Runyon, K. E., *The Practice of Marketing*. Columbus, Ohio: C. E. Merrill, 1982.

26. Hammermesh, R. G. Anderson, M. J. and Harris, J. E., 'Strategies for Low Market Share Business', *Harvard Business Review*, May–June 1978.

27. Walsh, V., Roy, R and Bruce, M., 'Competitive by Design', *Journal of Marketing Management*, 4, No. 2, 1988, pp. 201–16.

28. Porter, M., *Competitive Strategy*. New York: The Free Press, 1980.

29. Peters, T. and Waterman, R., *In Search of Excellence*. London: Harper and Row, 1985.

30. McBurnie, T. and Clutterbuck, D., *The Marketing Edge*. Harmondsworth: Penguin, 1987.

31. Dawson, J., Shaw, S. and Harris, D., *Impact of Changes in Retailing and Wholesaling*. Stirling University, 1987.

32. *Ibid.*

Chapter 8: Further Reading

Aaker, D. A., *Strategic Marketing Management*. New York: John Wiley, 1992.

Ackoff, R. L., *Creating the Corporate Future*. New York: Wiley, 1981.

Drucker, P. F., *Managing in Turbulent Times*. London: Heinemann, 1980.

Strategic Planning Institute, *The PIMS Programme: The Strategic Planning Brochure*. Cambridge, Mass.: 1980.

Wilson, R.M.S., and Gilligan, C., *Strategic Marketing Management*. Oxford: Butterworth-Heinemann 1997.

Chapter 9: Notes and References
1. Cairncross, F., *The Death of Distance*. London: Orion, 1997.
2. Eaton, J. and Smithers, J., *This Is IT*. London: Philip Allen, 1982.
3. Fletcher, K., 'The Evolution and Use of Information Technology in Marketing', in Baker, M. (ed.) *The Marketing Book*. Oxford: Heinemann, 1994.
4. Buzzell, R., 'Marketing in an Electronic Age', in *Marketing 1995; A Scenario for the Future* (ed. Buzzell, R.). Cambridge, Mass.: Harvard University Press, 1985.
5. HYPERLINK http://www.chemie.fu-berlin.de.
6. HYPERLINK http://europa.eu.int/index.htm.
7. Budd, S. A., *The EEC: A Guide to the Maze*. London: Kogan Page, 1987.
8. HYPERLINK http://www.inslantweb.com.
9. Arnold, M. E. and Penn, J. M., 'The Information Technology Revolution in Marketing (1) and (2)', *Quarterly Review of Marketing*, 12, Nos. 2 and 3, 1987.
10. Zuboff, S., *In the Age of the Smart Machine*. London: Butterworth-Heineman, 1988.
11. Cannon, T., *Accelerated Information Systems and New Technologies*. London: Aslib, 1986.
12. Hammer, M. and Champy J., *Re-Engineering the Corporation*. New York: Harper Business, 1993.
13. HYPERLINK http://www.cnn.com.
14. Sawyers, L., *The Impact of New Technology on Female Employment in Retailing*. Unpublished PhD thesis, University of Stirling, 1986.
15. HYPERLINK http://www.amazon.com.
16. HYPERLINK http://www.wal-mart.com.
17. HYPERLINK http://pathfinder.com/fortune.
18. Vyssotsky, V. A., 'Computer Systems: More Evolution Than Revolution', *Journal of Systems Management*, 13, No. 2, 1980.
19. Watkins, T., 'Marketing Information Systems in Insurance', 2nd World Marketing Congress, Stirling, 1985.
20. Fletcher, K., 'Information Systems in British Industry', *Management Decision*, 21, No. 2, 1983, pp. 25–36.
21. HYPERLINK http://www.philips.com.
22. Piercy, N., 'Information Processing – The Newest Mix Element', Marketing Education Group Conference, 1983.
23. Worthington, S., 'Credit Cards in the United Kingdom', *Journal of Marketing Management*, 4, No. 1, 1988, pp. 61–70.
24. Zuboff, S., *The Age of the New Machine*. Oxford: Heinemann, 1990.
25. Watkins, I., The Use of Microcomputers in Teaching Marketing in UK Universities and Polytechnics', *Quarterly Review of Marketing*, Spring, 1986, pp. 14–16.
26. This glossary is reproduced with permission from Technology: The Issues for the Distributive Trades. Distributive Trades Economic Development Committee, London: NEDO.

Chapter 9: Further Reading
Curry, D., *The New Marketing Research Systems*. New York: John Wiley, 1993.
Fletcher, K., 'The Evolution and Use of Information Technology in Marketing' in Baker, M. (ed.) *The Marketing Book*. Oxford: Heinemann, 1994.
McIver, G. and Naylor, G., *Marketing Financial Systems*. London: IOB, 1986.
McKenna, R. *Real Time*. Cambridge, Mass.: Harvard Business School Press, 1997.
Negraponte, N. *Being Digital*. New York: A. A. Knopf, 1995.
Parkinson, S., 'Computers in Marketing', in Baker, M. (ed.), *The Marketing Book*. Oxford: Heinemann, 1994.
Piercy, N and Evans, M., *Managing Marketing Information*. London: Croom Helm, 1983.
Shaw, R. and Stone, M., *Database Marketing*. London: Gower, 1989.

Chapter 10: Notes and References

1.   Piercy, N., *Market-Led Strategic Change*. Oxford: Heinemann, 1992.
2.   HYPERLINK http://www.pathfinder.com/fortune.
3.   HYPERLINK http://www.amazon.com.
4.   Economist Intelligence Unit, 'Own Brand Marketing', *Retail Business,* October, 1968.
5.   Darby, G., 'A Manufacturer's Views on Below the Line Activity', *Admap,* 4th World Advertising Workshop, 1971.
6.   Reilly, W. J., 'Methods of Studying Retail Relationships'. In *Research Monograph* 4, Bulletin 2994. Austen: University of Texas Bureau of Business Research, 1929.
7.   The reader is referred to Stuart Price's excellent book on franchising, *The Franchise Paradox.* London: Cassell, 1997.
8.   Christopher, M., *The Customer Service Planner.* Oxford: Heinemann, 1992.
9.   Albrecht, K. and Bradford, L. *The Service Advantage.* Homewood, Illinois: R. D. Irwin, 1990.
10. Walters, D. and Laffy, D., *Managing Retail Productivity and Profitability.* London: Macmillan, 1996.

Chapter 10: Further Reading

Bowers, D. and Cooper, M., *Strategic Marketing Channel Management.* New York: McGraw Hill, 1992.
Christopher, M., *Logistics and Supply Chain Management.* London: Pitman, 1992.
Ennew, C. T., Watkins, T., and Wright, M. *Marketing Financial Services.* Oxford: Heinemann, 1990.
Hardy, K. G. and Magrath, A. 'Ten Ways for Manufacturers to Improve Distribution Management' *Business Horizons,* November–December 1988.
McDonald, M. and Tideman, C. *Retail Marketing Plans.* Oxford: Heinemann, 1992.
McNair, M. P. and May, E. G., 'The Next Revolution of the Retailing Wheel', *Harvard Business Review,* September–October, 1978. A stimulating review of the problems and opportunities in retailing today.

Chapter 11: Notes and References

1.   Wilson, A. (ed.), *The Marketing of Industrial Products.* London: Hutchinson, 1966.
2.   Marrian, J., 'Marketing Characteristics of Industrial Goods and Buyers'. In *The Marketing of Industrial Products* (ed. Wilson, A.). London: Hutchinson, 1966.
3.   Levitt, T., *Industrial Purchasing Behaviour.* Harvard University Graduate School of Business Administration, 1965.
4.   Done, K., 'Shockwaves Still Coming' *Financial Times* Survey: World Automotive Suppliers 28 June, 1993.
5.   Briscoe, G., Cannon, T. & Lewis, A. L., 'The Market Development of New Industrial Products', *European Journal of Marketing,* 6, No. 1, 1969.
6.   Gross, A. C., Banting, P. M., Meredith, L. N. and Ford I. D., *Business Marketing.* Boston: Houghton Mifflin, 1993.
7.   Foxall, G., Johnson, B. and Murphey, F. S., 'The Development of Control Software for Flexible Manufacturing Systems by British Aerospace', *Journal of Marketing Management,* 2, No. 3, 1987, pp. 259–274.
8.   The notion of 'satisfying' means setting certain minimum job performance criteria, enough to perform tasks with no risk to position. Cyert, R. M. and March, J. G., *A Behavioural Theory of the Firm.* Englewood Cliffs: Prentice-Hall, 1963.
9.   Wootz, B., *Communications Patterns in Industrial Purchasing,* Workshop on Industrial Marketing, Brussels, 1975.
10. Levitt, T., 'Communications and Industrial Setting', *Journal of Marketing,* April, 1967.
11. Ford, I. D. (ed) *Understanding Business Markets.* London: Academic Press, 1990.
12. Hakansson, H. (ed.), *International Marketing and Purchasing of Industrial Goods.* Chichester: Wiley, 1982.
13. Little, D., Bunce, M., Leverick, F. and Wilson, D., *Collaboration in Product Development,* mimeo. Manchester School of Management, UMIST, 1993.

14. McDonald, M. and Leppard, J., *Effective Industrial Selling*. London: Heinemann, 1988.
15. Voss, C., *Just In Time Manufacture*. London: IFS International, 1992.
16. Sheth, J. N., 'A Model of Industrial Buying Behaviour', *Journal of Marketing*, October, 1973.

Chapter 11: Further Reading

Axelson, B. and Easton, G. (eds.) *Industrial Networks: A New View of Reality*. London: Routledge, 1992.
Blois, K. 'Are Business to Business Relationships Inherently Unstable?' *Journal of Marketing Management* Vol. 13, July 1997.
Ford, I. D. (ed) *Understanding Business Markets*. London: Academic Press, 1990.
Gross, A. C., Banting, P. M., Meredith, L. N. and Ford, I. D., *Business Marketing*. Boston, Mass.: Houghton Mifflin, 1993.
Hakansson, H. (ed.), *International Marketing and Purchasing of Industrial Goods*. Chichester: Wiley, 1982. Describes some of the most valuable recent work in the field. A powerful, strongly empirical study of a critical issue.
Hart, N. (ed.), *The Marketing of Industrial Products*. London: McGraw-Hill, 1984.
Hill, R. W. and Hillier, T. J., *Organisational Buyer Behaviour*. London: Macmillan, 1977. Provides a valuable insight into a critical area of interest.
Wilson, A., *The Assessment of Industrial Markets*. London: Associated Business Programmes, 1974. Based on a wealth of experience.

Chapter 12: Notes and References

1. Fuchs, V. R., *The Service Economy*. New York: National Bureau of Economic Research, 1968.
2. Zemke, R., *The Service Edge*. New York: The American Library, 1989.
3. Hart, C., 'The Power of Unconditional Service Guarantees', *Harvard Business Review*, July–August, 1988.
4. Lewis, B. 'Editorial', *Journal of Marketing Management*, April 1995.
5. Stanton, W. J., *Fundamentals of Marketing*. New York: McGraw-Hill, 1978.
6. Grönroos, C., 'A Service-orientated Approach to Marketing of Services', *European Journal of Marketing*, 12, No. 8, 1979.
7. Lowell, D. 'Marketing of Services' in Baker, M. (ed.) *The Marketing Book*. Oxford: Heinemann, 1994.
8. Worthington, S., 'Affinity Credit Cards: Card Issues and Strategies and Affinity Group Aspirations', *International Journal of Bank Marketing*, 10, No. 7, 1992.
9. Mastersbrook, W. F. *Managing for Quality in the Service Sector*. Oxford: Basil Blackwell, 1991.
10. Walsh, K. 'Marketing and Public Sector Management' *European Journal of Marketing*, vol. 3, 1994..
11. Grönroos, *op. cit.*
12. *Ibid.*
13. Berry, L. and Parasuraman, A. *Marketing Services: Competing Through Quality* New York: The Free Press, 1991.
14. Ballyntyne, D. F. 'Coming to Grips with Service Intangibles using Quality Management Techniques' *Marketing Intelligence and Planning* vol. 6, 1990.
15. Gummesson, E. 'In Search of Marketing Equilibrium: Relationship Marketing versus Hypercompetition' *Journal of Marketing Management* vol. 13, July 1997.
16. Scarbrough, H. and Lannon, R., 'The Management of Innovation in the Financial Marketing Sector', *Journal of Marketing Management*, 5, No. 1, Summer, 1989, pp. 51–62.
17. Zemke, R. & Schaaj, D., *The Service Edge*. New York: New American Library, 1989.

Chapter 12: Further Reading

Berry, L. and Parasuraman, A. *Marketing Services: Competing Through Quality*. New York: The Free Press, 1991.

Christopher M., Payne, A. and Ballyntyne, D. *Relationship Marketing: Bringing Quality, Customer Service and Marketing Together.* Oxford: Heinemann, 1991.

Cowell, D. W., *The Marketing of Services*, 2nd edn. Oxford: Butterworth Heinemann, 1994.

Ogilvy, D., *Confessions of an Advertising Man.* New York: Atheneum, 1963. Amusing and well written insight into the ideas and actions which led to the development of one of the most successful advertising agencies in North America by a Briton.

Journal of Marketing Management Special Issue on The Marketing of Services, April 1995.

Chapter 13: Notes and References

1. OECD (HYPERLINK http://www.oecd.org http://www.oecd.org)
2. Directives of the German Democratic Republic's Five-year Plan, 1976–80.
3. Terpstra, V. and David, K., *The Cultural Environment of International Business.* Cincinnati, Ohio: Southwestern, 1985.
4. Posses, F., *Selling to the Americans.*
5. Mortmore, T. and Siddal, J., *The Importance of Cultural Trends in Marketing Planning.*
6. Barclays Bank Report, *Factors for International Success.* London: Barclays Bank International, 1979.
7. 'Silentnight Wakes up to Exporting', *Marketing*, June, 1978.
8. British Overseas Trade Board *15 Export Case Studies.*
9. BETRO Trust Committee, *Concentration on Key Markets.* London: Royal Society of Arts, 1977.
10. Both quotes from Hill, R., 'How Durco Europe Went Direct', *Marketing*, March, 1977.
11. Business International Corporation, *Managing Global Marketing: A Headquarters Perspective.* New York: Business International, 1976.
12. *Planned Innovation,* April, 1979.
13. Kempner, T., *A Handbook of Management.* Harmondsworth: Penguin, 1976.
14. Barclays Bank Report on Uruguay, 1976.
15. Burkart, A. J. and Medlik, S., *Tourism: Past, Present and Future.* London: Heinemann, 1974.
16. Keegan, W. J., 'Five Strategies for Multinational Marketing', in *International Marketing Strategy* (ed. Thorelli, H. B.). Harmondsworth: Penguin, 1973.
17. Buckley, P., 'Developments in International Business Theory in the 1990s', *Journal of Marketing Management,* 7, No.1, January, 1991.

Chapter 13: Further Reading

Aaby, N. E. and Slater, S. F. 'Management Influences on Export Performance: A Review of Empirical Literature 1978-88' *International Marketing Review* vol. 6 1989.

Bradley, F. *International Marketing Strategy.* Hemel Hempstead: Prentice Hall, 1991.

Casson, M., *The Growth of International Business.* London: George Allen & Unwin, 1983.

Day, A. J., *Exporting for Profit.* London: Graham and Trotman, 1976. Authoritative and comprehensive review of the area.

Lessem, R., *The Global Business.* London: Prentice-Hall International, 1987.

Paliwoda, S. J., *New Perspectives on International Marketing.* London: Routledge, 1992.

Tookey, D., *Export Marketing Decisions.* Harmondsworth: Penguin, 1975. Succinctly and clearly reviews the subject from a practical perspective.

Chapter 14: Notes and References

1. Baker, M., *Marketing: An Introductory Text.* London: Macmillan, 1985.
2. Majaro, S., 'International Marketing', in *The Marketing Book* (ed. Baker, M.). London: Heinemann, 1987.
3. Buckley, P. J., and Ghauri, P. *The Internationalisation of the Firm.* London: Dryden Press, 1993..
4. Ricardo, D., *Principles of Political Economy and Taxation,* 1817.
5. Heckscher, E and Olin, B., in *Interregional and International Trade.* Cambridge, Mass.: Harvard University Press.

6. Porter, M., *The Competitive Advantage of Nations*. London: Macmillan, 1990.

7. Buckley, P. J., Pass, C. L. and Prescott, K., 'Measures of International Competitiveness: Empirical Findings from British Manufacturing Companies', *Journal of Marketing Management*, 6, No. 1, 1990, pp 1–16.

8. Enderwick, P., 'Multinational Corporate Restructuring and International Competitiveness', *Californian Management Review*, 32, No.1, Fall, 1989.

9. Cannon, T. & Willis, M., *How to buy and sell overseas*. London: Century Hutchinson, 1982.

10. Anderson, O. 'On the Internationalisation Process of Firms' *Journal of International Business Studies* Vol. 2 1993.

11. Fitzpatric, P. D. and Zimmerman, A. S., *Essentials of Expert Marketing*. New York: AMA, 1985.

12. Ohmae, K., 'Effective Strategies for Competitive Success', *McKinsey Quarterly*, Winter, 1978, pp. 50–59.

13. Collins, R. S. and Owens, J. K., 'Swiss Francs and Rising Exports: A Paradox', *The Business Quarterly*, 43. No. 2, 1978, pp. 59–64.

14. Piercy, N., *Marketing Led Strategic Change*. London: Harper Collins, 1991.

15. Cannon, T., 'Managing International and Export Marketing', *European Journal of Marketing*, 14, No. 1, Summer, 1981, pp. 34–48

16. NEDO, *International Price Competitiveness, Non-Price Factors and Export Performance*. London: National Economic Development Office, 1977.

17. Kono, T., 'Corporate Culture and Long Range Planning', *Long Range Planning*, 23, August, 1990.

18. Wells. L T. Jr, 'A Product Life Cycle for International Trade', *Journal of Marketing*, July, 1968, pp. 1–6.

19. Driscoll, A. M., and Paliwoda, S., 'Dimensionalising International Market Entry Mode Choice' *Journal of Marketing Management*, April 1997.

20. Keegan. W., 'Future Strategies for Multi-National Marketing'., in *International Marketing Strategy* (ed. Thorelli, H. B.). Harmondsworth: Penguin, 1973.

21. Levitt, T., 'Globalisation of Markets', *Harvard Business Review*, May-June 1983, pp. 92–102.

22. Hill, J. S. and Kwon, U., 'US Multinational Product Strategies for Europe', *Journal of Marketing Management*, 6, No. 3, Winter, 1990, pp. 195–208.

23. *Ibid.*

24. Letovsky, R., 'The Export Finance Wars', *Columbia Journal of World Business*, 25, Spring/Summer, 1990.

25. Douglas, S. and Craig, S., 'Global Marketing Myopia', *Journal of Marketing Management*, 2. No. 2, Winter, 1986, pp. 155–169.

26. Hite, R. E. and Fraser, C., 'Configuration and Co-Ordination of Global Advertising', *Journal of Business Research*, 21, December, 1990.

27. Curry, D., *The New Marketing Research Systems*. New York: John Wiley, 1993.

28. Renzetti, C. M. and Lee, R. M. (Eds.), *Researching Sensitive Topics*. Berkeley, CA: Sage Focus Editions, Sage Publications, 1993.

29. Wells, *op. cit.*

30. Haigh, R. W., 'Selecting a US Plant Location: The Management Decision Process in Foreign Companies', *Columbia Journal of World Business*, 25, Fall, 1990.

31. Perlemutter, H. V., 'The Tortuous Evolution of the Multinational Corporation', *Columbia Journal of World Business*, January-February, 1969, pp. 9–18.

32. Treasure, J., *British Exports – Three Myths*. London: Institution of Practitioners in Advertising, 1966.

33. Heenan, D. A. and Perlemutter, H. V., *Multinational Organisational Development: A Social Architecture Perspective*. Reading, Mass: Addison-Wesley, 1979.

34. Cerruti, J. L. and Holtman, J., 'Business Strategy in the New Industrial Landscape', *Harvard Business Review*, 11, November–December, 1990.

35. Nicoliades, P., 'The Growth of Japanese Direct Investment in the EC', *Economic Trends*, No. 3. 1990, pp. 66–73.

36. Wong, V., Saunders, J. and Doyle, P., 'The Quality of British Marketing: A comparison with US and Japanese Multinationals in the UK Market', *Journal of Marketing Management*, 4, No. 2, Winter, 1988, pp. 131–148.

37. Brouthers, L. E. and Werner, S., 'Are the Japanese Good Global Competitors', *Columbia Journal of World Business*, 25, Fall, 1990.

38. Albert, M. and Ball, R. J., *Towards European Economic Recovery*. European Parliament Working Document.

39. Dooge Committee, *Ad Hoc Committee for Institutional Affairs*. Council Document SN/1187/85.

40. Cockfield Report, *The White Paper on Completing the Internal Market*. Commission Document.

41. Ceccini, P., *The European Challenge 1992: The Benefits of a Single Market*. European Commission, 1988.

42. Lawrence, P., 'The Single European Market in Context', *Journal of Marketing Management*, 9, No.1, January 1993.

43. ESPRIT is the European Strategic Programme for Research and development in Information Technology.

44. A major initiative in biotechnology is developing between the Community and Europe's leading agrochemicals companies.

45. BRITE (Basic Research in Industrial Technologies for Europe) was launched to provide help for research into advanced technology for traditional industries: aeronautics, cars, textiles, etc.

46. RACE (Research into Advanced Communications in Europe) is designed to help shape pan-European communications systems.

47. *The Transport Infrastructure Programme*, Commission Document, COMDOC 86/340 and COMDOC 86/674.

48. Community Programmes are extensively detailed in Haigh, N., *EEC Environment Policy and Britain*. London: EDS, 1989.

49. Porter, M., *The Competitive Advantage of Nations*. London: Macmillan, 1990.

50. OECD (HYPERLINK http://www.oecd.org http://www.oecd.org)

51. Poldermans, R., 'European Banking in 1993: All Change?' *Prism*, Spring, 1989, pp. 63–73.

52. *Ibid.*

53. The Henley Centre, *The United Markets of Europe: Transport*. London: Henley Centre, 1988.

54. *The Economist*, 'Eastern Europe's Economics: What Is to Be Done?', 13 January, 1990, pp. 21–26.

55. OECD, *op. cit.*

56. The Small Firms Task Force was created specifically with the aim of increasing competitiveness; see *Action Programme for SMEs*, ComDoc (86) 45.

57. KPMG, *Deal Watch*, London, March, 1989.

Chapter 14: Further Reading

Bartlett, C. A., Doz, Y. L. and Hedland, G. (eds.) *Managing the Global Firm*. London: Routledge, 1990.

Buckley, P. J. and Casson, M., 'The Economic Theory of the Multinational Enterprise'. London: Macmillan, 1985.

Budd, S., *The EEC: A Guide to the Maze*. London: Kogan Page, 1985.

Cavusgil, S. T., and Li, M.T. *International Marketing: An Annotated Bibliography*. American Marketing Association, 1992.

Cundiff, E. W., *Marketing in the International Environment*. London: Prentice-Hall, 1984.

Doyle, P. & Hart, N. (eds.), *Case Studies in International Marketing*. London: Heinemann, 1982.

Dudley, J. W., 1992: *Strategies for the Single European Market*. London: Kogan Page, 1989.

Egan, C., and McKiernan, P. *Inside Fortress Europe: Strategies for the Single Market*. Wokingham: Addison-Wesley, 1994.

Majaro, S., *International Marketing*. London: Routledge, 1993.

Quelch, J. A., Buzzell, R. D. and Salama, E. R., *The Marketing Challenge of Europe 1992*. New York: Addison-Wesley, 1991.

Rothery, Brian *What Maastricht Means for Business* Aldershot: Gower, 1993.

Terpstra, V., *International Marketing*. New York: The Dryden Press, 1987.

Chapter 15: Notes and References

1. This was Dave's model of the market in the early days – subsequently modified as experience and information grew.
2. Borden, N. H., 'The Concept of the Marketing Mix', in *Readings in Basic Marketing* (ed. McCarthy, E. J., Grastief, J. R. and Brogowicz, A. A.). Illinois: R. D. Irwin, 1975.
3. Brown, S. 'Art or Science?: Fifty Years of Marketing Debate', *Journal of Marketing Management* vol. 12 1996.
4. Pine, B. J., Peppers, D., and Rogers, M. 'Do You Want to Keep Your Customers Forever?' *Harvard Business Review,* March–April 1995
5. Kotler, P., *Marketing Management*. Englewood Cliffs: Prentice-Hall, 1996.
6. A masthead product carries the firm's flag i.e. establishes the highest standards for the range, e.g. Cadillac for General Motors.
7. Selling without any preparations of the ground with the particular prospect or group of potential buyers.
8. Pricing low for high volume (see Chapter 20).
9. Driver, C., 'Marketing Planning in Style', *Quarterly Review of Marketing,* June, 1990.
10. Corkindale, D. A., 'A Practical Way to Set Advertising Budgets', *Marketing,* August, 1978.

Chapter 15: Further Reading

Borden, N. H., 'The Concept of the Marketing Mix', in *Readings in Basic Marketing* (eds. McCarthy, E. J., Grastief, J. R. and Brogowicz, A. A.). Illinois: R. D. Irwin, 1975. Effectively sets out the essential character of marketing mix management.

Christopher, M., McDonald, M. and Rushton, A. (eds.), 'Back to Basics: the Four P's Revisited', Marketing Education Group Annual Conference Proceedings, 1983.

De Chernatony, L. and McDonald, M. H. B., *Creating Powerful Brands*. Oxford: Butterworth Heinemann, 1992.

Chapter 16: Notes and references

1. Department of Trade and Industry, November, 1989.
2. Kodama, F., 'Technology Fusion and The New R&D', *Harvard Business Review*, July–August, 1992.
3. Morita, A., *Made in Japan*. London: Fontana, 1990.
4. Levitt, T. 'Marketing Myopia', *Harvard Business Review*, July–Aug 1960.
5. Porter, M., *The Competitive Advantage of Nations*. London: Macmillan, 1990.
6. Venkatraman, M. P., 'The Impact of Innovativeness and Innovation Type on Adoption', *Journal of Retailing*, 67, Spring, 1991.
7. Sloan, A. P., *My Years with General Motors*. Harmondsworth: Penguin, 1989.
8. Hamel, G. and Prahalad, C. K., 'Corporate Imagination and Expeditionary Marketing', *Harvard Business Review,* July–August, 1991.
9. Rothwell, R., 'Innovation and Reinnovation: The Role for the User', *Journal of Marketing Management,* 2, 1986, pp. 109–123.
10. Naisecti, R. 'Too Many Choices; P & G, Seeing Shoppers Were Being Confused, Overhauls Marketing', *Wall Street Journal,* January 15th, 1997.
11. Mitchell, P. 'Brand Imaging Costs Pilloried', *Financial Times,* January 6th, 1997.
12. (HYPERLINK http://www.pg.com http://www.pg.com)
13. (HYPERLINK http://www.tasteyoulove.com http://www.tasteyoulove.com)
14. Bennett, P. D. (Ed.), *Dictionary of Marketing Terms*, Chicago, Illinois: Marketing Association, 1988.
15. Rubenstein, H., 'Brand First Management', *Journal of Marketing Management*, vol. 12, 1996.
16. Cannon, T., *The Guinness Book of Business Records*. London: Guinness Publishing, 1996.
17. Doyle, P., 'Building Successful Brands: The Strategic Options', *Journal of Marketing Management,* 6, No. 1, January 1989.

18. King, S., 'Brand Building in the 1990's', *Journal of Marketing Management*, 7, No. 1, January, 1991.
19. McCrae, C, *World Class Brands*. London: Addison Wesley, 1991.
20. Wood, L. M., 'Brands: The Asset Test', *Journal of Marketing Management*, vol. 11, 1995.
21. Rubenstein, H., 'Brand First Management', *Journal of Marketing Management*, vol. 12, 1996
22. Johne, A., 'Substance versus Trappings in New Product Development', *Journal of Marketing Management*, vol. 1 no. 3, 1986 pp 291-301.
23. Kautor, R. M., *The Change Masters*. New York: Simon and Schuster, 1983.
24. Peters, T., *Managing Chaos*. New York: A. A. Knopf, 1987.
25. Peters, T., *Liberation Management*. New York:, A. A. Knopf 1992.
26. The Design Council, *Design and the Economy*. London: The Design Council, 1990.
27. Grafton-Small, R., 'Marketing by Design', *Quarterly Review of Marketing*, 12, No. 3, Summer, 1987, pp. 1-4.
28. Crosby, P., *Quality Is Free*. New York: McGraw-Hill, 1979.
29. Davidson, J. H., *Offensive Marketing*, 2nd edition. Harmondsworth: Penguin Books, 1987.
30. The Design Council, *op. cit.*

Chapter 16: Further Reading

Advisory Council on Applied Research and Development, Industrial Innovation, HMSO, 1978. Report bringing out the importance of effective innovation to Britain's industrial future and the critical role of marketing in this process.
Brooks, J., 'Xerox, Xerox, Xerox, Xerox'. In Brooks, J., *Business Adventures*, Harmondsworth: Penguin, 1971. A perceptive and lucid account of the development of this major corporation.
Cannon, T., 'New Product Development', *European Journal of Marketing*, 12, No. 3, 1978.
Cannon, T., 'Test Marketing', *Anglia Television*, 1982.
Crawford, M., *New Products Management*, Homewood, Illinois: R D Irwin, 1991.
HMSO, 'The Competitiveness White Paper'. London: HMSO, 1995.
Leavitt, T., 'The Marketing Imagination'. New York: Free Press, 1986.
McCrae, C., *World Class Brands*. London: Addison Wesley, 1991.

Chapter 17: Notes and References

1. Kotler, P., *Marketing Management: Analysis, Planning and Control*. Englewood Cliffs: Prentice-Hall, 1980.
2. King, S., *Developing New Brands*. London: Pitman, 1973.
3. Green, P. E. & Tull, D. S., *Research for Marketing Decision*. Englewood Cliffs: Prentice-Hall International, 1st ed., 1966.
4. Kaplan, A., *The Conduct of Enquiry*. New York: Chandler Publishing, 1964.
5. Ansoff, I., *Corporate Strategy*. Harmondsworth: Penguin, 1968.
6. *Ibid.*
7. Brooks, J., *Business Adventures*. Harmondsworth: Penguin, 1971.
8. *Ibid.*
9. Madell, J., 'Where Do Successful New Brands Come From?', *New Product Development Seminar*, Univas, Paris, 1979.
10. *Ibid.*
11. Rice, F. 'Secrets of Product Testing', *Fortune,* November, 1994.
12. Rawlins, T. C. and Sparks, D. N., 'The Use of Repeat Buying Measures in Evaluating New Product Launches', MRS Eighteenth Annual Conference, 1975.
13. Saunders, J. A., Sharp, J. A., and Witts, S. F., *Practical Business Forecasting*, Aldershot: Gower, 1987.
14. Davis, E. J., *Experimental Marketing*. London: Nelson, 1970.
15. *Ibid.*

16. Gold, J. A., 'Testing Test Market Predictions', *Journal of Marketing Research*, August, 1964.
17. Davis, *op. cit.*
18. Rawlins, *op. cit.*
19. Parfitt, J. H. and Collins, B. J. K., 'The Use of Consumer Panels for Brand Share Prediction', *Journal of Marketing Research*, May, 1968.
20. Fourt, L. A. and Woodlock, J. W., 'Early Prediction of Market Success for New Grocery Products', *Journal of Marketing*, October, 1960.
21. Parfitt, J. H. and Collins, B. J. K., 'The Use of Consumer Panels for Brand Share Prediction', *Journal of Marketing Research*, May, 1967.
22. Chambers, J. C., Mullick, S. K. and Smith, D. D., 'How to Choose the Right Forecasting Technique', *Harvard Business Review*, July–August, 1971.

Chapter 17: Further Reading

Cannon, T., 'New Product Development', *European Journal of Marketing*, 21, No. 3, 1978.
Clancy, K. J., Schulman, R. S. and Wolf, M., *Simulated Test Marketing: Technology for Launching Successful New Products*. New York: Lexington, 1994.
Cooper, R. G. and Kleinschmidt, E. J., *New Products: The Key Factors in Success*. Chicago: American Marketing Association, 1990.
Hirsrick, R. D. and Peters, M. P., *Marketing a New Product*. Menlo Park, Calif.: Benjamin Cummins, 1978.
Wills, G., 'Cost Benefit Analysis of a Test Market', Management Decision, 1, No. 1, 1967.

Chapter 18: Notes and References

1. Adapted from the definition of the Definitions Committee of the American Marketing Association.
2. Samuelson, P. A., *Economics*. New York: McGraw-Hill, 1996.
3. Oligopoly is where a small number of manufacturers control a large part of the market.
4. Bain, J. S., *Industrial Organization*. New York: Wiley, 1968.
5. There is not scope here for a full discussion of pricing under imperfect competition from the economist's perspective. The reader is directed to Bain, J. S., *Industrial Organization*. New York: Wiley, 1968.
6. Shipley, D., 'Dimensions of Flexible Price Management', *Quarterly Review of Marketing*, 11, No. 3, Spring, 1986, pp. 1–7.
7. *Ibid.*
8. These are high prices probably backed by extensive promotion.
9. This slightly exaggerates the situation as few innovations are totally new and the probability of competitive introductions in response influences thinking.
10. Dean. J., 'Pricing a New Product', in *Fundamentals of Marketing* (ed. Taylor, J. L. and Robb, J. F.). New York: McGraw-Hill, 1979.
11. There is some limited evidence that a similar pattern exists for supplies, components and end products in industrial markets.
12. Briscoe, G. and Lewis, A. L., *The Marketing of Steel Products and the Role of Innovation*. London: British Steel Corporation Fellowship.
13. Munro, K. B. *Pricing: Making Profitable Decisions* New York: McGraw-Hill, 1990.
14. Nagel, T. T. and Reed, K. H. *The Strategy and Tactics of Pricing* New Jersey: Prentice Hall, 1995.
15. Sloan, A. P. Jr, *My Years with General Motors*. Harmondsworth: Penguin, 1989.
16. Lanzillotti, R. F., 'Pricing Objectives in Large Companies', *American Economic Review*, December, 1958.
17. Shipley, *op. cit.*
18. Winkler, J. *Pricing for Results* Oxford: Heinemann, 1983.
19. Simply stated, the average pricing would be: total costs, £10,000; mark-up, 20 per cent; volume sold, 5,000; price, 12,000 – 5000 = £2.40 per unit.

20. Robicheaux, A., 'How Important Is Pricing in Competitive Strategy?', in *Proceedings of the Southern Marketing Association* (ed. Nash, H. W. and Robin, D. P.). Southern Marketing Association, 1976.

Chapter 18: Further Reading

Mann, M. V. and Rosiello, R. L. 'Managing Price: Gaining Profit', *Harvard Business Review*, Sept–Oct 1992.
Munroe, K. B., *Pricing*. London: McGraw-Hill, 1990.
Nagel, T. T. and Reed, K. H. *The Strategy and Tactics of Pricing*. Englewood Cliffs: Prentice Hall, 1995.
Winkler, J. *Pricing for Results*. Oxford: Heinemann, 1983.

Chapter 19: Notes and References

1. Economists have suggested that to the customer real price (P) is actually a function of search time cost (c) and monetary price (p). Thus $P = c + p$.
2. Hunt, S., Ray, N. M. and Wood, V. R., 'Behavioural Dimensions of Channels of Distribution', *Journal of the Academy of Marketing science*, 13, No. 3, Summer, 1985, pp. 1–24.
3. The concept of 'stock push' has been developed to describe the practice of supplying excess stock to force the retailer to work hard setting the product out, sometimes called 'dealer loading'.
4. Moore, R. A., 'Conceptual and Empirical Developments of Marketing and Channel Conflict', *Journal of Marketing Management*, 4, No. 3, 1989, pp. 350–369.

Chapter 19: Further Reading

Christopher, M., Payne, A. and Ballantyne, D., *Relationship Marketing*. Oxford: Butterworth-Heinemann, 1991.
Moore, R. A., 'Conceptual and Empirical Developments of Marketing Channel Conflicts', *Journal of Marketing Management*, 4, No. 3, 1989, pp. 350–369.
Schonberger, R., *Building a Chain of Customers*. New York: The Free Press, 1990.
Stalk, G. and Hout, T. *Competing Against Time* New York: Free Press, 1990.
Stern, L. W. and El-Ansany, A. I., *Marketing Channels*, 3rd ed. Englewood Cliffs: Prentice-Hall, 1988.

Chapter 20: Notes and References

1. Drucker, P., *The Economy's Dark Continent*. Edinburgh: Fortune Press, 1962.
2. One could identify a number of areas of activity that could reasonably be included, such as documentation, forecasting and purchasing.
3. Cecchini Report, *The Cost of Non-Europe*. European Commission, 1988.
4. Bowersox, D. J., Smykey, E. W. and Lalonde, B. J., *Physical Distribution Management*. New York: Macmillan, 1965.
5. Yamashina, H., 'Integrated Logistics and Distribution', *Mimeo*, Group Ambrosetti, April, 1992.

Chapter 20: Further Reading

Bowersox, D. J., Smykey, E. W. and Lalonde, B. J., *Physical Distribution Management*. New York: Macmillan, 1965. A powerful and comprehensive review of the topic.
Wentworth, F., *Handbook of Physical Distribution Management*. London: Gower Press, 1976. A practical approach including a number of excellent specific articles. Note especially Chapters 1 and 3.

Chapter 21: Notes and References

1. Not all agencies perform all functions: media agencies and creative hot shops have emerged as major forces over the last twenty years.
2. Commissions provide approximately 60 per cent of total agency income, although importance of fees has gradually increased. Recently the NPA (Newspaper Publishers Association) has indicated its interest in revising the system.

3. Large-scale audience research is conducted under the auspices of the Joint Industry Research Committee: JICTAR (Joint Industry Committee for Television Audience Research), JICNAR (Joint Industry Committee for Newspaper Audience Research), JICPAS (Joint Industry Committee for Poster and Audience Surveys) and JICRAR (Joint Industry Committee for Radio Audience Research).

4. Another factor has no doubt been the threats to advertising by these industries in other media and the ban on TV advertising of cigarettes.

5. The number and location of sites is regulated by the Town and Country Planning Acts.

6. Vaughn, R. L., 'Creatives and Researchers: Must They Be Adversaries?', *Journal of Advertising Research*, 22, No. 6, 1982, pp. 45–48.

7. There is little doubt that some advertisers give up the struggle and look merely to gain access to the customer.

8. Webster, J., *Advent*, June, 1978.

9. McCabe, E., *Advent*, August, 1976.

10. Seiden, H., *Advertising Pure and Simple*. New York: American Management Association, 1976.

11. Roman, K. and Mass, J., *How to Advertise*. New York: St Martin's Press, 1976.

12. Particular pages and spots are 'specified' and carry a premium charge.

13. Only part of the readership buys it every day. The audience is constantly changing, with new readers joining and old readers leaving each day.

14. Vaile, R. S., 'The use of advertising during depressions'. *Harvard Business Review*, April, 1927.

15. Bernstein, D., *Company Image and Reality.* London: Cassell, 1984.

16. Abratt, R., 'Advertising Objectives of Industrial Marketers', *International Journal of Advertising*, 6, No. 2, 1987, pp. 121–31.

17. Runyon, K. E., *Advertising.* Columbus, Ohio: Charles E. Merrill, 1984.

18. Hasting, G. and Leather, D., 'The Creative Potential of Research', *International Journal of Advertising*, 6, No. 2, 1987, pp. 159–168.

19. Called 'below-the-line' as no media commission can be charged on it by agencies.

20. Hasting, *op. cit.*

21. These sums are purely illustrative.

Chapter 21: Further Reading

Broadbent, S. R., (ed.), *20 Advertising Case Histories.* London: Cassell, 1984.

Cannon, T., *Advertising Research.* London: Intertext Marketing Research Series, 1973.

Cannon, T., *Advertising: The Economic Implications.* London: Intertext, 1975.

Chiplin, B. and Sturgess, B., *Economics of Advertising*, 2nd ed. London: Holt, Reinhart and Winston, 1981.

Driver, J. C. and Foxall, G. R., *Advertising: Policy and Practice.* London: Holt, Rinehart and Winston, 1984.

Martin, D. N. *Romanticising the Brand: The Power of Advertising and How to Use it.* New York: Amacom, 1989.

Ogilvy, D., *Confessions of an Advertising Man.* New York: Athenium, 1963.

Toop, A., *European Sales Promotion: Great Campaigns in Action.* London: Kogan Page, 1992.

Chapter 22: Notes and references

1. Mant, A., *The Rise and Fall of the British Manager.* London: Macmillan, 1977.

2. Barclays Bank Report, *Factors for International Success.* London: Barclays Bank International, 1979.

3. Donaldson, B., *Sales Management: Theory and Practice.* London: Macmillan, 1990.

4. McKay, S., Fair, J., Johnson, M., Sherrell, D., 'An Exploratory Investigation of Reward and Corrective Responses to Salesperson Performance', *Journal of Personal Selling and Sales Management*, 11, Spring, 1991.

5. Comer, J. M., *Sales Management.* Boston: Allyn and Bacon, 1991.

6. Lidstone, J., 'Selling' in Baker, M. (Ed.), *Marketing*. Oxford: Heinemann, 1993.

7. Alexander, J., Schal, P. and Babakus, E., 'Analysing Interpersonal Communications in Industrial Marketing Negotiations', *Journal of the Academy of Marketing Sciences*, 19, Spring, 1991.

8. New products here would include new to the firm, e.g. milkmen selling fruit juice or eggs.

9. Given the range of skills required, it is perhaps surprising that research has shown that car salesmen hold their job in very low esteem.

10. Frazier, G. L. and Rody, R. C., 'The Use of Influence Strategies in Interfirm Relationships in Industrial Product Channels', *Journal of Marketing*, 55, January 1991.

11. McCormack, M., *What They Don't Teach You at Harvard Business School*. London: Collins, 1984.

12. Townsend, R., *Further Up the Organisation*. London: Michael Joseph, 1984.

13. Fisher, R., Ury, W. and Patton, B., *Getting to Yes*. London: Century, 1992.

14. Koren, L. and Goodman, P., *The Haggler's Handbook*. London: Century, 1992.

15. Based on Fisher, R., Ury, W. and Patton, B., *Getting to Yes*. London: Century, 1992.

16. Although this can prove useful it can also be dangerous. The firm must be clear about the primary task of its sales force, since all too often salesmen are given so many ancillary tasks – information-gathering, display, stock checks, allocation – that they have almost no time left for selling.

17. Levitt, T., 'Communications and Industrial Selling'. In *Readings in Marketing Management* (Ed. Kotler, P. and Cox, K. K.). Englewood Cliffs: Prentice-Hall, 1972.

18. Sager, J., 'Recruiting and Retaining Committed Salespeople', *Industrial Marketing Management*, 20, May, 1991.

19. Rottenberger, K. J., 'Sales Training Enters The Space Age', *Sales and Marketing Management*, 142, October, 1990.

20. Sharma, A., 'The Persuasive Effect of Salesperson Credibility', *Journal of Personal Selling and Sales Management*, 10, Fall, 1990.

21. McMurray, R. N. and Arnold, J. S., *How to Build a Dynamic Sales Organisation*. New York: McGraw-Hill, 1968.

22. Mayer, D. and Greenberg, H. M., 'What Makes a Good Salesman', *Harvard Business Review*, July–August, 1964.

23. Murray, T., 'Starting a Salesforce from Scratch', *Sales and Marketing Management*, 143, April, 1991.

24. Vaccaro, J., 'Organisational Issues in Sales Force Decisions', *Journal of Professional Services Marketing*, 6, 1991.

25. Stalk, G. Jr. and Hout, T., *Competing Against Time*. London: Collier Macmillan, 1990.

26. Tzokas, N. and Saren, M., 'Innovations Diffusion: The Emerging Role of Suppliers versus the Traditional Dominance of Buyers', *Journal of Marketing Management*, 8, No. 1, 1992.

27. Greatorex, M., Michell, V-W. and Cunliffe, R., 'A Risk Analysis of Industrial Buyers', *Journal of Marketing Management*, 8, No. 4.

28. From an article on the subject by Lidstone, J. and Melkman, A. 'Make Marketing Plans for Major Customers', *Marketing*, October, 1977.

29. Newton, D., 'Get the Most Out of your Salesforce', *Harvard Business Review*, September–October, 1969.

30. Lidstone, J., *Training Salesmen on the Job*. London: Gower, 1986.

31. Zachariades, C. Z., *The Management Motivation and Control of Salesmen*. Durham: Unpublished MSc dissertation, 1976.

32. Murray, T., 'Team Selling: What's The Incentive', *Sales and Marketing Management*, 143, June, 1991.

33. Wilson, K., 'Managing the Industrial Sales Force of the 1990s', *Journal of Marketing Management*, 9, No. 2, 1993.

34. The time taken by the firm's sales force to complete a regular tour of its accounts.

35. Salmon, W. J., 'How Many Salesmen Do You Need?' In *Analytical Marketing Management* (Ed. Doyle, P., Law, P., Weinberg, C. and Simmons, K.). London: Harper and Row, 1974.

36. Lancaster, G. and Jobber, D., *Sales Technique and Management*. London: MacDonald and Evans, 1985.
37. Francis, J. N. P., 'When in Rome? The Effects of Cultural Adaptation in International Business Negotiations', *Journal of International Business Studies*, 22, 1991.
38. Katsikeas, C. S. and Piercy, N. F., 'The Relationship Between Exporters from a Developing Country and Importers Based in a Developed Country', *European Journal of Marketing*, 25, No. 1, 1991.
39. Peters, T., *Thriving on Chaos*. London: Pan, 1989.
40. This has probably been more fully realised in Britain's trading rivals than in Britain itself.
41. Cannon, T., *Corporate Responsibility: A Textbook on Business Ethics, Governance and the Environment*. London: Pitman, 1994.
42. Strafford, J., 'Fred's our Best Salesman – Let's Promote Him', *Industrial Marketing Digest*, 5, No. 3, 1980.

Chapter 22: Further Reading

Anderson, R. *Essentials of Personal Selling*. Englewood Cliffs, N.J.: Prentice Hall, 1995.
Fierman, J. 'The Death and Rebirth of the Salesman' *Fortune*, July, 1994.
Lidstone, J., *Beyond the Pay Packet*. New York: McGraw Hill, 1992.
Smallbone, D., *An Introduction to Sales Management*. London: Staples Press, 1971. A thorough and comprehensive study of the entire process.
Wilson, M., *Managing a Sales Force*. London: Gower, 1983.

Chapter 23: Notes and References

1. Mueller-Heuman, G., 'Market and Technology Shifts in the 1990s', *Journal of Marketing Management*, 8, No. 4, 1992.
2. Ohmae, K., 'The Borderless World', *McKinsey Quarterly*, No. 3, 1990, pp. 3–19.
3. In Moscow during the winter of 1990 there were over 300 'free' newspapers available.
4. Buttle, F., 'Marketing Communication: A Primary Process View', *Proceedings*, Marketing Education Group Annual Conference, Huddersfield, 1988.
5. Delozier, M. W., *The Marketing Communication Process*. New York: McGraw-Hill, 1976.
6. Alexander, J. F., Schul, P. L. and Babakus, E., 'Analysing Interpersonal Communications in Industrial Marketing Negotiations', *Journal of the Academy of Marketing Science*, 19, Spring, 1991.
7. Jejkins, F., *Marketing Communications*. London: Blackie, 1990.
8. Chan, K. K. and Misra, S., 'Characteristics of the Opinion Leader', *Journal of Advertising*, 19, No. 3, 1990.
9. Smith, R. E. and Buchholz, L. M., 'Multiple Resource Theory and Consumer Processing of Broadcast Advertisements: An Involvement Approach', *Journal of Advertising*, 20, September, 1991.
10. Meyers-Levy, J. and Sternthal, B., 'Gender Differences in the Use of Message Cues and Judgements', *Journal of Marketing Research*, 28, February, 1991.
11. Terpstra, V., *The Cultural Environment of International Business*. Southwestern Publishing Co., 1978.
12. Terpstra, V., *International Dimensions of Marketing*. Boston, Mass.: Kent Publishing, 1981.
13. Levy, J., 'Symbols for Sale', *Harvard Business Review*, July–August, 1959, pp. 117–124.
14. Bradley, F. M., 'Developing Communication Strategies for Foreign Market Entry'. In *Research Developments in International Marketing* (Ed. Turnbull, P. and Paliwoda, S.). Manchester: UMIST, 1984.
15. Saghafi, M. M., Varroglis, F. and Vega, T., 'Why US Firms Won't Buy from Latin American Companies', *Industrial Marketing Management*, 20, August, 1991.
16. Leavitt, T., 'The Globalisation of Markets', *Harvard Business Review*, May–June, 1983, pp. 92–102.

17. Dunn, S. W. and Yorke, D. A., 'European Executives Look at Advertising', *Columbia Journal of World Business*, Winter, 1974, pp. 54–60.
18. Whitelock, J. and Chung, D., 'Global Advertising', *Proceedings*, Marketing Education Group Annual Conference, Huddersfield, 1988.
19. Bernstein, D., *Company Image and Reality*. London: Cassell, 1984.
20. Morgan, R. F. 'An Internet Marketing Framework for the World Wide Web' *Journal of Marketing Management* vol. 12, 1996.
21. (HYPERLINK http://www.netrez.com/business.commerce.html)
22. (HYPERLINKhttp://www.intranet.co.uk/intranet/intranet.html

Chapter 24: Notes and References

1. Ohmae, K., *The Mind of the Strategist*. London: McGraw-Hill, 1982.
2. Prahalad, C. K. and Hamel, G., 'The Core Competences of the Corporation', *Harvard Business Review*, May–June, 1990.
3. Kay, J., *Foundations of Corporate Success*. Oxford: Oxford University Press, 1993.
4. Garvin, D. A., *Managing Quality – The Strategic and Competitive Edge*. London: Collier Macmillan, 1988.
5. Oakland, J. S., *Total Quality Management*. Oxford: Heinemann, 1989.
6. Peters, T. J., *Thriving on Chaos*. London: Pan, 1989.
7. Luck, D. J. and O'Ferrel, C., *Marketing Strategy and Plans*. Englewood Cliffs: Prentice-Hall, 1979.
8. Weitz, S. and Wensley, R., *Strategic Marketing*. Boston, Mass.: Kent Publishing, 1984.
9. Andrews, K. R., *The Concept of Corporate Strategy*. Homewood, Ill.: R. D. Irwin, 1980
10. Hax, A. C., *Strategic Management*. Englewood Cliffs: Prentice-Hall, 1984.
11. Johnson, G. and Scholes, K., *Exploring Corporate Strategy*. London: Prentice-Hall, 1988.
12. Steiner, K. and Miller, R., *Making Management Decisions*. London: Prentice-Hall International, 1984.
13. Johnson and Scholes, *op. cit.*
14. Steiner and Miller, *op. cit.*
15. Johnson and Scholes, *op. cit.*
16. *Ibid.*
17. Johnson and Scholes, *op. cit.*
18. Johnson and Scholes, *op. cit.*
19. Cannon, T., *Corporate Responsibility: A Textbook on Business Ethics, Governance and the Environment*. London: Pitman, 1994.
20. Peattie, K., *Green Marketing*. London: Pitman, 1992.
21. Kleiner, A., 'What Does it Mean to be Green', *Harvard Business Review*, July–August, 1991.
22. Porter, M. E., *Competitive Advantage: Creating and Sustaining Superior Performance*. New York: The Free Press, 1985.
23. *Ibid.*
24. Ansoff, L., *Corporate Strategy*. New York: McGraw-Hill, 1967.
25. Peters, T. J. and Waterman, R.H., *In Search of Excellence*. London: Harper and Row, 1982.
26. Boston Consulting Group, *Perspectives on Experience*. Boston: Boston Consulting Group, 1968.
27. Headley, S., 'Strategy and the Business Portfolio', *Long Range Planning*, February, 1977.
28. Buzzell, R. D. and Gale, B. T., *The PIMS Principles*. New York: The Free Press, 1987.
29. *Ibid.*
30. Morrison, A. and Wensley, R., 'Boxing-up or Boxed in?: A Short History of the Boston Consulting Group Share/Growth Matrix', *Journal of Marketing*, 7, No. 2, 1991.
31. Kotabe, M. and Duhan, D., 'The Perceived Veracity of PIMS Strategy Principles in Japan', *Journal of Marketing*, 55, January, 1991.
32. Porter, M. E., *Competitive Strategy: Techniques for Analysing Industries and Competitors*. New York: The Free Press, 1980.

33. Ansoff, *op. cit.*
34. *Ibid.*
35. Bleeke, J. A., 'Peak Strategies', *McKinsey Review*, Spring, 1989, pp. 19–27.
36. Mathur, S., 'Talking Straight about Competitive Strategy', *Journal of Marketing Management*, 8, No. 3, July, 1992.
37. Bonoma, T.V., *The Marketing Edge: Making Strategies Work*. New York: The Free Press, 1985.
38. Ohmae, L., *The Mind of the Strategist*. London: Pan Books, 1984.
39. *Ibid.*

Chapter 24: Further Reading

Easton, G., Burell, G., Rothschild, R. and Shearman, C., *Managers and Competition*. Oxford: Blackwell, 1993.
Wensley, R., 'Strategic Marketing: A Review'. In Baker, M. *The Marketing Book*. Oxford: Heinemann, 1994.

Chapter 25: Notes and References

1. Winkler, J., *Winkler on Marketing Planning*. London: Associated Business Programmes, 1972.
2. This area is reasonably well served for good books. Another particularly useful one is: Stapleton, J., *How to Prepare a Marketing Plan*. London: Gower Press, 1971.
3. Piercy, N., *Marketing-Led Strategic Change*. Oxford: Heinemann, 1992.
4. Adapted from the definitions given in the *Shorter Oxford English Dictionary*, 1973.
5. Although the term 'firm' is used, it can incorporate all types of organization.
6. Kotler, P., *Marketing Management*. Englewood Cliffs: Prentice-Hall, 1973.
7. Brownlie, D., 'The Anatomy of Strategic Marketing Planning', *Journal of Marketing Management*, 1, No. 1, 1985, pp. 35–63.
8. McDonald, M. 'Strategic Marketing Planning: Theory, Practical and Research Agendas' *Journal of Marketing Management* vol. 12, 1996.
9. Greenley, G. E., *Strategic Management*. London: Prentice-Hall, 1989.
10. Piercy, N. and Giles, W., 'The Logic of Being Illogical in Strategic Marketing Planning', *Journal of Marketing Planning*, 5, No. 1, Summer, 1989, pp. 19–31.
11. Mintzberg, H. *The Rise and Fall of Strategic Planning* Englewood, Cliffs, N.J. Prentice-Hall, 1994.
12. McDonald, *op. cit.*
13. Wind, Y., 'Marketing and Other Business Functions'. In *Research in Marketing* (Ed. Sheth, J. N.). Greenwich, Conn.: Jai Press, 1981.
14. Peattie, J. K. and Notley, D. S., 'The Marketing and Strategic Planning Interface', *Journal of Marketing Planning*, 4, No. 3, Spring, 1989, pp. 330–349.
15. de Geus, A. P., 'Planning as Learning', *Harvard Business Review*, March–April, 1988, pp. 70–74.
16. Stanton, W. J. *Fundamentals of Marketing*. New York: McGraw-Hill, 1978.
17. Sloan, A. P., Jr, *My Years with General Motors*. London: Pan Books, 1969.
18. Wilson, A. *Aubrey Wilson's Marketing Audit Checklists* London, McGraw Hill, 1992.
19. Morrell, J., *The 7th Transfleet Lecture*. London: Centre for Physical Distribution Management, 1979.
20. Anonymous director of Masters Programme.
21. For a thorough review of the subject see Briscoe, G. and Hirst, M., *An Appreciation of Alternative Sales Forecasting Models: Recent Techniques Based on Historical Data*. Warwick: Centre for Industrial, Economic and Business Studies, 1972.
22. Humble, J. W., *Management by Objectives in Action*. London: McGraw-Hill, 1970.
23. Smith, R. A., 'Formulating Objectives – What Really Can Happen', *Journal of Marketing Management*, 1, No. 6, 1986, pp. 227–257.
24. Glueck, W. F. and Jauch, L. R., *Business Policy and Strategic Management*. London: McGraw-Hill, 1984.

25.   Biggadike, R., 'The Contributions of Marketing to Corporate Strategy', *Academy of Management Review*, 6, No. 4, 1981, pp. 621–632.
26.   Brownlie, D. T., 'Scanning the Internal Environment', *Journal of Marketing Management*, 4, No. 3, Spring, 1989, pp. 300–329.
27.   Cespedes, F. V. and Piercy, N. F. 'Implementing Marketing Strategy' *Jounal of Marketing Management* vol. 12 April 1996.
28.   *Ibid.*
29.   McDonald, M., 'Ten Barriers to Marketing Planning', *Journal of Marketing Management*, 5, No. 1, Summer, 1989, pp. 1–18.
30.   Driver, J. C., 'Marketing Planning in style', *Quarterly Review of Marketing*, 15, No. 4, Summer, 1990, pp. 16–21
31.   Narver, J. C. and Slater, S. F., 'The Effect of Market Orientation on Business Profitability', *Journal of Marketing*, 54, No. 4, October, 1990, pp. 20–34.

Chapter 25: Further Reading

Ball, R., *Management Techniques and Quantitative Methods*. London: Heinemann, 1986.
Greenley, G., *The Strategic Operational Planning of Marketing*. London: McGraw-Hill, 1986
Mintzberg, H. *The Rise and Fall of Strategic Planning* Englewood Cliffs, N.J.: Prentice-Hall, 1994.
McDonald, M., *Marketing Plans*. Oxford: Butterworth Heinemann, 1989.
Stapleton, J., *How to Prepare a Marketing Plan*. 4th edn. London: Gower Press, 1989. Gives a detailed picture of the fundamental processes involved in effective planning.
Winkler, J., *Winkler on Marketing Planning*. London: Associated Business Programmes, 1972. An invaluable guide to the manager or student who is serious about building practical plans.

Chapter 26: Notes and References

1.   Foreword to *Marketing and Social Priorities* (Ed. Fisk, G.). New York: American Marketing Association, 1974.
2.   Cannon, T., *Corporate Responsibility: A Textbook on Business Ethics, Governance and the Environment*. London: Pitman, 1994.
3.   Beauchamp, T. and Bowie, N., *Ethical Theory and Business*. New Jersey: Prentice-Hall, 1988.
4.   Hooper, T. L. and Rocca, B. T., 'Environmental Affairs; Now on the Strategic Agenda, *Journal of Business Ethics*, 12, May–June, 1991.
5.   Smith, N. Craig., *Morality and the Market*. London: Routledge, 1990.
6.   Luck, D. J., 'Broadening the Concept of Marketing – Too Far', *Journal of Marketing*, July, 1960.
7.   Kotler, P. and Levy, S. J., 'Broadening the Concept of Marketing', *Journal of Marketing*, January, 1969.
8.   Drucker, P. F., 'Marketing and Economic Development', *Journal of Marketing*, January, 1958.
9.   *Ibid.*
10.   Finnegan, C., *Marketing for Co-ops: A Practical Guide*. London: ICOM C-Publications, 1985.
11.   Walsh, K., *Marketing in Local Government*. London: Longman, 1989.
12.   Waller, D. L., 'Technology Challenges for Industry', *Greener Management International*, Issue 2, April, 1993.
13.   Donaldson, J., *Key Issues in Business Ethics*. London: Academic Press, 1989.
14.   Smith, N., *Morality and the Market*. London: Routledge, 1990.
15.   Cook, L. M., and Welch, J. F., 'What CSR Means to Me', *Business and Society Review*, No. 18, 1992.
16.   Nulty, P., 'How the World Will Change', *Fortune*, January 15, 1990, pp. 22–26.
17.   Davis, J. J. 'A Blueprint for Green Marketing', *Journal of Business Strategy*, 12, July–August, 1991.
18.   Srodes, J., 'Corporations Discover It's Good To Be Good', *Business and Society Review*, Summer, 1990.
19.   Peattie and Charter.
20.   *Ibid.*

21.	Smith, *op. cit.*

22.	Beardsworth, A. D., 'Trans-science and Moral Panics: Understanding Food Scares', *British Food Journal*, 92, No. 5, 1990. pp. 11–18.

23.	Goldie, F. J., 'Thinking about the Unthinkable: Disaster Management in the Food Industry', *British Food Journal*, 90, No. 4, 1988, pp. 155–158.

24.	Cannon, G., 'Diet and the Food Industry', *Journal of the Royal Society of Arts*, May, 1988, pp. 398–411.

25.	Mitchell, V.–W. and Greatorex, M., 'Consumer Perceived Risk in the UK Food Market, *British Food Journal*, 92, No. 2. pp. 16–22.

26.	Goldie, *op. cit.*

27.	Mann, J. and Thompson, P., 'Consumerism in Perspective'. *European Journal of Marketing*, 12, No. 4, 1974.

28.	These protests were about the activities of some employers, who paid workers in tokens which could be traded only for goods, usually of poor quality, from company shops.

29.	Fulop, C., 'Twenty Years of Which?', *European Journal of Marketing*, 12, No. 4, 1978.

30.	Morris, D. and Reeson, D. I., 'The Economic Determinants of Consumer Complaints', *European Journal of Marketing*, 12, No. 4, 1978.

31.	Crozier, K., 'The Contribution of Market Research to Social Marketing', *Journal of the Market Research Society*, 21, No. 1, January, 1979.

32.	TMI, 'A Complaint Is A Gift', Solihull: TMI, 1993.

33.	The notion of a consumer movement should not hide the true heterogeneous nature of consumerism.

34.	Kotler, P., 'What Consumerism Means for Marketers', *Harvard Business Review*, May–June, 1972.

35.	Heilbroner, R. L., *Controlling the Corporation. In In the Name of Profit* (Ed. Heilbroner, R. L. et al.). New York: Doubleday, 1972.

36.	Greysa, S. A. and Diamond, S. L., 'Business is Adapting to Consumerism', *Harvard Business Review*, September–October, 1974.

37.	Straver, W., 'The International Consumerist Movement', *European Journal of Marketing*, 11, No. 2, 1977.

38.	Methven, Sir J., 'Market Research in Business and Industry', *Journal of the Market Research Society*, July, 1968.

39.	Mauser, G. A., *Political Marketing: An Approach to Campaign Strategy*. New York: Praeger, 1983.

40.	Smith, G. and Saunders, J., 'The Application of Marketing to British Politics', *Journal of Marketing Management*, 5, No. 3, Spring, 1990, pp. 307–323.

41.	Simmons, M., 'The British Market Research Industry', *Journal of the Market Research Society*, July, 1978.

42.	Philips, N. and Nelson, E., 'Energy Savings in Private Households', *Journal of the Market Research Society*, October, 1976.

43.	The Economist, *The World in 1989 and on to the 1990's*. London: Economist Publications, 1989.

44.	Hall, J., 'Values – The Key to Business in 1990 and Beyond', *Journal of Marketing Management*, 5, No. 2, Winter, 1989, pp. 123–132.

Chapter 26: Further Reading

Donaldson, J., *Key Issues in Business Ethics*. London: Academic Press, 1989.

Goyder, G., *The Just Enterprise*. London: Deutsch, 1987.

Kotler, P., *Marketing for Non-Profit Organizations*. Englewood Cliffs: Prentice-Hall, 1975.

Mann, J. (Ed.), 'Consumerism', *European Journal of Marketing*, 4, 1978.

Smith, N., *Morality and the Market*. London: Routledge, 1990.

Walsh, K., *Marketing and Local Government*. London: Longman, 1989.

Appendix: Further Reading

Turbian, K. L., *A Manual for Writers of Research Papers, Theses and Dissertations*. London: Heinemann, 1982.

Name index

Adams, Scott 423
Alexander, J. F. 422
Andrews, K. R. 432
Ansoff, I. 321, 322, 436, 438
Arnold, J. S. 412
Arnold, M. E. 155

Babakus, E. 422
Barber, John 348
Beal, T. 93
Beauchamp, David 325
Bernstein, David 385
Bird, M. 138
Birley, S. 10
Blackwell, R. D. 141, 144
Blair, Tony 61
Bleeke, J. A. 440
Boase, Martin 237
Borden, N. H. 295, 296
Bowersox, D. J. 360
Bradley, F. M. 426
Branson, Richard 67, 236, 300, 394
Brilliant, Ashleigh 461
Briscoe, G. 126, 340
Broadbent, Simon 174
Brown, A. C. 6
Brown, David 299
Brown, G. H. 124
Brown, M. 95
Brown, S. 84
Brownlie, D. 448
Buckley, P. 261, 267, 276
Budd, S. A. 182
Buzzell, R. D. 156, 438

Cadbury, N. D. 323
Cannon, Geoffrey 89, 471
Chambers, J. C. 333
Chisnall, P. M. 137
Chung, D. 426

Churchill, Sir Winston 2
Clark, R. 13
Clavert, Jacques 280
Clinton, Bill 182
Clutterbuck, D. 176
Collins, B. J. K. 333
Conran, Terence 204
Corkindale, D. A. 295
Craig, S. 271
Craze, Mark 237
Crimp, M. 108
Crisp, R. D. 112
Crozier, K. 473
Culligan, K. 154
Cunningham, 220
Cunningham, M. 154
Cunningham, R. M. 145

Dace, R. 13
Darby, Geoff 200
Darrow, Charles, P. 461
Davis, John 331, 332
Dawson, J. 85, 177
de Geus, A. P. 451
De Vito, Danny 411
Dean, J. 340
Dekker, D. 183
Delozier, M. W. 421
Demming, Bill 100
Deng Xiaoping 6
Dickens, Charles 466
Donaldson, J. 468
Douglas, S. 271
Doyle, P. 3
Dreyfuss, Richard 411
Driver, J. C. 460
Drucker, P. 3, 358, 364
Durant, Mr 408
Durkheim, É. 109

Egan, Sir John 9
Ehrenberg, A. S. C. 110, 112, 145
Engel, J. F. 141, 144
Etzkowitz, H. 282

Fishbein, Martin 139
Fletcher, K. 155, 194
Ford 220
Ford, Henry 299
Forte, Charles 18
Freud, Sigmund 137

Gabor, A. 344, 346
Gale, B. T. 156, 438
Gattona, J. 351
Giles, W. 449
Glueck, W. F. 456
Gold, J. A. 332
Goldie, F. J. 89, 471
Goldman, M. I. 20
Goodyear, J. R. 115
Gorbachev, Mikhail 6
Gray, D. 18
Green, Andrew 371
Greenberg, H. M. 412
Greenley, G. E. 449
Griffin, T. 32
Grönroos, C. 5, 237

Halpern, Sir Ralph 205
Hammarkvist, K. O. 7
Hammermesh, R. G. 156
Harriman, Sir George 12, 27
Hastings, G. 387, 389
Hattersley, Roy 391, 393
Headley, S. 437
Heckscher, E. 266
Heenan, D. A. 275
Hesketh, J. L. 110, 338
Hill, J. S. 270
Hill, R. W. 222, 223
Hillier, T. J. 222, 223
Howard, J. A. 137, 139, 140, 142, 143
Hunt, S. 354

Issigonis, Sir Alec 348

Jauch, L. R. 456
Jay, Anthony 353
Jobber, D. 126
Johnson, G. 52, 433, 434

Kay, J. 431
King, Stephen 304–5, 307, 320
Kotler, P. 4, 39, 60, 132, 141, 144, 295, 319,
    333, 473
Kwon, U. 270

Lancaster, G. 145
Land, Dr Edwin 299
Lanzillotti, R. F. 343
Lawrence, P. 278
Lazer, William 465
Leather, D. 387, 389
Levitt, Theodore 220, 300, 307, 411
Lee Kuan Yew 21
Lidstone, J. 408, 414
Lipton, Thomas 204
Long, G. 35
Lorenz, C. 13
Luck, D. J. 432
Lyons, H. 154

Madell, John 322, 323
Major, John 64, 339
Mant, A. 3, 408
Marco Polo 10
Marx, Karl 109
Maslow, A. H. 137
Mathur, S. 441
Mayer, D. 412
McBurnie, T. 176
McCabe, E. 376
McCarthy, E. J. 296
McCormack, Mark 410
McDonald, Andrew 355
McDonald, M. 459
McKay, J. 155
McLuhan, Marshall 378
McMurray, R. N. 412, 418
Michelin, François 299
Middleton, B. 35
Miller, R. 433
Mintzberg, H. 52
Mitchell, J. W. 155
Moore, P. G. 118
Morgan, N. A. 450
Morita, Akio 19, 316 (300)
Morrel, David 200
Morris, D. 473
Morrison, A. 438
Murray, T. 412

Nicholls, J. R. 88
Nicoliades, P. 275
Nielsen, Larry J. 466
Northcliffe, Lord 370

O'Ferrel, C. 432
Ogilvy, David 377, 384
Ohmae, Kenichi 421, 441
Olin, B. 266
Oppenheim, Sally 67
Owen-Jones, Lindsay 19

Pacino, Al 411
Packard, Vance 3
Palin, Michael 72
Paliwoda, S. 152
Parfitt, J. H. 333
Parkinson, S. 151
Penn, J.M. 155
Perlemutter, H. V. 275
Peters, Tom 1, 2, 18, 19, 175, 416, 432, 437
Piercy, N. 19, 34, 35, 154, 158, 194, 195, 201,
     447, 449, 450
Polderman, R. 283
Popoff, Frank 469
Porter, M. 2, 276, 280, 300, 434, 435, 439–441,
     470
Posses, F. 223
Prahalad, C. K. 2, 431, 441

Rainbow, C. 126
Rawlins, T. C. 333
Reeson, D. I. 473
Reid, D. 18
Reilly, W. J. 206
Ricardo, David 266
Rines, M. 348
Rodgers, Francis G. 1
Rogers, E. M. 145, 186
Rostow, W. W 22, 247
Runyon, K. E. 4

Saatchi, Charles 384
Sagan, Carl 469
Saghafi, M. M. 426
Sainsbury, Lord 204
Sawyers, L. 85, 188
Scholes, K. 52, 433, 434
Schul, P. L. 422

Seidon, Hank 378
Seiff, Lord 204, 300
Shersby, Michael 61
Shipley, D. 344
Simmons, M. 108, 475
Slattery, J. 83
Sloan, Alfred P. 14, 300, 342, 346
Smith, Adam 245
Smith, N. C. 20
Smith, R. A. 455
Sparks, D. N. 333
Sparks, L. 155
Spedding, C. 81
Steiner, K. 433

Taylor, C. T. 145
Terpstra, V. 424
Thakur, S. 154
Thatcher, Margaret 6, 64, 339
Thomas, M. 15
Thomas, R. E. 50
Tookey, D. 253
Townsend, Robert 410

Utterback, J. 19

Von Hipple, E. 19
Voss, C. A. 312

Waterman, R. H. 437
Waterman, R. J. 1, 18, 19
Watkins, T. 193
Watson, John B. 109
Webster, A. 282
Webster, John 376
Weitz, S. 432
Wells, Louis T. Jnr 248
Wensley, R. 432, 438
Wheelock, J. V. 88
Whitelock, J. 426
Williams, Robin 411
Wilson, A. 214
Winkler, J. 447
Wolfson, Isaac 204
Wyles, Ian 9

Yamashina, H. 362–4
Yeltsin, Boris 286

Subject index

account 54
acquisitions 290, 300
advertising
  affordability of 382
  agencies
    role of 383
    structure of 383–4, 386
  budget for 382–3
  case study 395–407
  economics and ethics in 391–3
  evaluation of 388
  for exports 250–1
  in international marketing 271–2
  media 370–88
    access to 371–4
    costs 380
    environment of 375–80
    interplay of 380–1
    scheduling 383
    totals 370, 371
  models of 386
  non-media 388–91
    dangers of 391
    typology of 390–1
  objectives 385, 386, 388
  as percent of GNP 369
  and public relations 393
  research process 390
  and sales promotion 369–407
  in services 237
agents
  in advertising see agencies under advertising
  in intermediate markets 203
  in overseas trade 252
agricultural markets
  food chain in 98
  institutions in market place 97–8
  organizations for 96–8
Albania 284

alphanumeric key pad 195
Association of South East Asia Nations 245, 266
auction markets 98
audits 54
  marketing planning 449–50
  in test marketing 331
Austria 85
Avon cosmetics 294

Baltic states 286
banks, information technology in 154
bar coding systems 191, 196
barter 22, 26–7
Belgium
  advertising expenditure 369
  consumer protection bodies 68
  GNP of 281
  hypermarkets and superstores 85
  market research revenues 113
benefit 158
Benetton 175, 176
Benson & Hedges 332
Blackthorne Publishers Ltd (case study) 28–30
Body Shop 471
brands, and product policy 300, 301
breakeven analysis 345–6
British Aerospace 245, 438
British American Tobacco 149
British Gas 297, 372
British Telecom 234
budget 54
Bulgaria 284
business and financial community 73
buy-back 26
buyers 133–46
  attitudes of 138–9
  behaviour of
    clothes marketing 178
    models of 140–5

brand loyalty of 145–6
in industrial markets 219–20
   expectations of 220
   risks 221–2
influences on 134
market segmentation 135–7
   by lifestyle 137
   by location 135–6
   by socio-economic factors 136
motivations on 137–8
   behavioural approach 138
   psychoanalytic views on 137
new products, diffusion and adoption of 145
problem solving by 142–3
and reality, images of 139
social and economic variables of 135
buying
   black box system of 134
   coalitions in industrial markets 222–3
   stages in process 144

Cadburys 301, 323
CAD/CAM 185
calculators, diffusion curves 187–8
Caledonia Plain Chocolate (case study) 56–7
Campbell's foods 320
Canada
   petroleum and gas output 286
   R&D in 282
capital, organizations for 102
car market, Europe 79
Caribbean Community and Common Market
      246
Caribbean Free Trade Area 246
case studies
   advertising 395–407
   exports and overseas trade 263–5
   industrial markets 228–9
   intermediary markets 212–13
   market effort, managing 56–7
   marketing 28–30
   marketing analysis 158–74
   offerings and organization 96–7
   physical distribution management 365–8
   planning 462–4
   price awareness 129–31
   sales management 419–20
   services 242
   social responsibilities 477–9
   strategic marketing 442–6
   test marketing 317–18
catalogues, as non-media advertising 389

Ceefax 117
Central African Customs and Economic Union
      246
Central American Free Trade Area 246
Central Europe 279, 284–5
channels 349–56
   conflict and co-operation 355
   design of 352
   flows 349
   intermediaries 350–1
      responsibilities of 354–5
   long term 361
   networks 361–2
   push and pull 362–4
China: petroleum and gas output 286
cinema advertising
   access to 374
   environment of 379
   totals 370, 371
clothes marketing 176–81
   buyer behaviour 181
   context of 176–7
   future of 180
      market changes 176–8
      domestic 177–8
      international 178
   market structure 178–83
   and technology 179–90
Cockfield Report 278
commercial research 116–17
communications 54, 421–30
   barriers 425
   and learning process 427
   means of 428
   problems of 427–8
   process of 421–2
      encoding 423
      noise 423–5
      transmission 422–3
   receiver of 426–8
   symbolism in 425–6
Community Inter-Institutional Information
      System 182
comparative advantage, theory of 245–6, 266–7
Competition Act (1979) 67
components, organizations for 100–1
computers 196, 466
   diffusion curves 186–7
   hardware 196
   major companies 188
   in marketing information systems 188–90
   program 197

software 197
user friendly language 197
visual display unit 197
consortia in overseas trade 255
consumer action/consumerism 471–4
and food marketing 471–2
liable stance 473–4
responsible stance 473
seller's response 474
consumer goods 26
consumer panels, for research 123–4
Consumer Protection Acts (1961,1971) 68
Consumer Safety Act (1978) 74
consumers 133–48
advertising, effect on 385–6
attitudes of 138–9
brand loyalty of 145–6
market segmentation 135–7
by lifestyle 137
by location 135–6
by socio-economic factors 136
motivations on 137–8
behavioural approach 138
psychoanalytic views on 137
new products, diffusion and adoption of 145
non-media advertising on 389–90
problem solving by 142–3
and reality, images of 139
social and economic variables of 135
Consumer's Associations 62, 75, 80, 470
consumption 27
Co-op Bank 467
Co-operation in Automation of Data and
Documentation for Exports, Imports and
Agriculture 183
Copyright Act (1956) 68
Council for Mutual Economic Assistance 246
coupons, as non-media advertising 389
Cranfield School of Management 358, 367
creativity, and product policy 302–5
culture
and international marketing systems 248
and market effort 46
and marketing system 71–3
customer pull 352–4
customer satisfaction 28
customers
allocation of sales force by 413
and commitment to excellence 18
complexity of needs 298–9
identification of 17
customs unions in overseas trade 245

data processing 196
databases 196
dedicated lines 196
demand
law of 28
in marketing environment 40–7
supply and 15–16
demographics 80
and market effort 41–2
and test marketing 328
Denmark
advertising expenditure 367
GNP of 282
hypermarkets and superstores 86
market research revenues 117
deregulation 64, 80
derived demand, in industrial markets 218–19
Dettol (case study) 158–74
developing countries 28
differentiation 157
Digital Equipment Corporation 466
digital exchanges 196
Direct Information Access Network for Europe
183
distribution
channels for 351
as environmental issue 467
in international marketing 272
physical see physical distribution management
and test marketing 330
distributors
in intermediate markets 203
in overseas trade 252
diversification
in international marketing 275
and Single European Market 287
Du Pont 320, 327
Dysan Corporation 149

East African Community 246
Eastern Europe 281, 285–6
economic factors in international marketing
systems 247–8
economic growth, stages of 22–3
economic policies, and marketing 68–70
economics of advertising 390–1
electronic funds transfer systems 189, 195
electronic point of sale systems 189–90, 195
electronic pricing 195
encodation 195
encoding, in communication process 424
environment 19–20, 80

environment of marketing 39–49
    demand in 40–7
    food, pressures on 83
    institutional demand in 46–7
    supply in 47–9
environmentalism 467–8
Esso 425
ethics
    in advertising 392
    case study 477–8
    in marketing 18–19, 465–78
Europe
    car market 79
    services, employment in 232
European Society for Opinion and Market
        Research 250
European Strategic Programme for Research and
        Development in Information Technology
        (ESPRIT) 182–3, 283
European Union 68, 250, 279–93
    and food marketing 87
    market research revenues 114
excellence, commitment to 17–18
exhibitions, as non-media advertising 389
expert systems 186
exports and overseas trade 243–65
    advertising and sales promotion 250
    case study 263–5
    comparative advantage, theory of 244–5
    costs over time 256
    customs unions in 245
    developments in 245–6
    and export-led growth 248–9
    historical perspective on 243–4
    intermediaries in 251–3
    and international marketing 255–7
        distribution 255
        pricing 255
        products 257
    international marketing systems 246–7
        culture 247
        economic factors 246–7
        political factors 247
        technology 247
    invisibles, trade in 257–9
        consultancies 259
        finance 258
        shipping and freight 258
        tourism 259
    market selection and development 249
    marketing perspective on 244
    and multinational enterprises 259–61

new issues in 260
selling overseas 251

Fair Trading Act (1973) 67
Falkirk University (case study) 462–4
Fiat Automobiles 22
fibre optics 195
films, diffusion curves 187–8
finance, overseas trade in 258
finished goods 100–1
Finland 86
firms
    concept of 8
    marketing, role in 37–9
    marketing throughout 10–11
    organizational forms 39, 52
    research in 111–12
    small, and entrepreneurship 310
Food and Agriculture Organization (FAO) 83
food marketing 81–90
    environmental pressures 83
    future of 88–9
    grocery sales, shares 84
    investment and technology 85–6
    operations 88
    and policy changes 82–3
    regulation and control 75
    structural and behavioural changes 85–6
    tradestructure 87–8
    work patterns 86–7
Ford Motor Company 13, 259, 300, 309
forecasting 451–3
    estimates 451
    time series projections 451–3
Fortune Products of the Year 21
France
    acquisitions of companies 289
    advertising expenditure 367
    consumer protection bodies 68
    exports as share of GNP 243
    GDP activity shares 93
    GNP of 281
    hypermarkets and superstores 85
    intra-European trade 287
    market research revenues 114
    R&D in 282
franchising 213
    in food 88
    international 269
    in services 238
free gifts, as non-media advertising 389
Friends of the Earth 63

Furniture Industry Research Association 114–15

General Agreement on Tariffs and Trade (GATT) 95, 245, 280, 288
General Electric 244
General Motors 13, 298
generic value chain, in strategic marketing 434
Germany
  acquisitions of companies 290
  advertising expenditure 367
  consumer protection bodies 68
  exports as share of GNP 243
  GDP activity shares 93
  GNP of 281
  hypermarkets and superstores 85
  intra-European trade 287
  market research revenues 114
  population crisis in 280–1
  R&D in 282
government
  attitudes to marketing 474
  research agencies 116
  services by 237–8
Greece
  advertising expenditure 369
  GNP of 281
  market research revenues 114
grocery multiples 98
grocery sales, shares 83
Gross Domestic Product 71, 87
  industrial activity shares 93
Gross National Product
  advertising as percent of 369
  in European Union 280
  exports as share of 243

Halfords Drop Forgings (case study) 228–9
Heinz Corporation 480
Henley Centre for Forecasting 363
heterogeneity of service industries 231
Hewlett-Packard 149
Holiday Inn 231
Hong Kong 176–7
Hungary 284, 285
hypermarkets, in Europe 85

IBM 1, 6, 13, 322, 329, 415
ICI 244, 301
Independent Broadcasting Authority 374
Independent Television 373
industrial markets 214–29

buyers' risk 218–19
buying coalitions 219–20
capital goods 225–7
case study 228–9
and derived demand 215–16
differences 214–15
engineering firms 227
non-media advertising in 390
process producers 226
segments 225–6
sellers and buyers 216–17
tackling 222–4
Industrial Revolution 28, 68
industrialization, impact of 11–15
inflation 87
and prices 339, 342
information, in test marketing 331
information technology 181–99
  computing and telecommunications 188–9
  diffusion curves in 186–7
  and distribution 189–91
  EU initiatives 182
  impact of 182–7
  in marketing analysis 154–5
  marketing information systems 125–6, 191–5
    features and uses 194
    management control 191
    user friendliness 192
innovation 28
  adoption of, time 145
  and product policy 298–300
  and test marketing 308–9
inseparability, in service industries 232
intangibility, in service industries 231–2
intermediaries
  channels for 350–1
  in overseas trade 251–4
  responsibilities of 354–5
intermediate markets 200–13
  agents 202
  case study 212–13
  changes in 200–1
  distributors 202
  franchising 209
  future of 209–10
  retail marketing 203–7
    location of 204–5
    outlet, types of 203
    and price 205–6
    product mix 203–4
  wholesalers 202–3
international agencies for research 116

international marketing 246–7, 251–3, 266–90
  building markets 269–72
    adaptation 270
    advertising 271–2
    distribution 271
    price 270–1
    standardization 269–70
  culture 247
  distribution 252
  diversification in 274
  economic factors 246–7
  and export marketing 267
  moving overseas 267–9
  operational structure 273–5
  overseas trade, development stages 268
  political factors 247
  pricing 252
  products 254
  research base 272–3
    integration 273
    sources 272
    value 273
  technology 247
International Monetary Fund 245
invention, and product policy 299–300
inventory 358
  levels, costs 360, 361
investment, in food marketing 92–3
invisibles, overseas trade in 254–6
  consultancies 256
  finance 255
  shipping and freight 255
  tourism 256
Ireland
  advertising expenditure 369
  GNP of 281
  market research revenues 114
Italy
  acquisitions of companies 289
  advertising expenditure 369
  GNP of 281
  hypermarkets and superstores 84
  intra-European trade 287
  market research revenues 114

Japan
  advertising expenditure 369
  consumer protection bodies 68
  exports as share of GNP 243
  GDP activity shares 93
  GNP of 281
  R&D in 282

JICPAS 381
JICTAR 381
just price 330
just-in-time manufacturing 185, 219

Kirkby Carpets (case study) 263–5
knowledge revolution 18
Knoxbridge Engineering (case study) 477–9
Kraft Jacob Suchard 92

laser scanner 196
Latin American Free Trade Area 245
learning process, in communication 427
legislation in the marketing system 67–9
libraries, for research 117
lifestyle 157
  market segmentation by 137
location
  allocation of sales force by 413
  market segmentation by 135–6
  and physical distribution management 360
  population, and marketing 43–4
  in retailing 205–6
  and test marketing 328
Lomé Treaty 279
loss leaders 342
Luxembourg
  GNP of 281
  market research revenues 114

M1 (money supply) 79
M2 (money supply) 79
Maastricht Treaty 68, 277–8
MacPherson Carr Group (case study) 442–6
magazine advertising
  access to 374
  environment of 378, 379
  totals 372–3
manufacturers
  channels for 350
  in marketing system 74–6
marginal prices 345
market 79
market effort, managing 31–58
  case study 56–8
  environment of marketing 37–47
    demand 36–45
    institutional demand 44–5
    marketing mix 47
    needs 36–44
    supply 45–7
  marketing, role in firm 35–7

marketing controls 54
and marketing management 31–3, 37
marketing manager in 33–5, 55
and marketing policy 47–52
organizational chart 37
market segmentation 135–7, 157
analysis of 151–3
and industrial markets 225
by lifestyle 137
by location 135–6
by socio–economic factors 136
market share 155–6
market structure in clothes marketing 178–9
marketing
case study 28–30
controls 54, 55
definitions 4–6, 27
emergence of 9–15
ethics in 19–20
throughout firm 8–9
global concept of 20–2
hierarchy 8
management and market effort 31–3, 37
organizational chart 37
role in firm 35–7
marketing analysis 148–80
case study 158–80
competitive positions, analysing 152–3
market, defining 149–50
market shares and competition 154–5
new information technologies 153–4
purchasing process, diagnosing 150
target groups and segments 150–2
Marketing Development and Export Services
(case study) 241
marketing manager 33–5, 55
marketing mix 27, 291–7
building 295
changes over time 295–6
for different markets 296
elements of 293–4
limitations of 294
future of 296
for levels of markets 295
and marketing environment 48
optimum, designing 294–5
planning for 465
marketing policy 48–52
strategy and structure 51–3
marketing project, managing 478–9
marketing system 23–5, 58–80
and business and financial community 74

and culture 73–4
and direct intervention 65–6
and economic policies 69–70
environment for 64–74
interacting forces in 24, 73
legislation in 67–9
manufacturers in 75–7
mapping the market 77
and media 73–4
opportunities in 80
participants and partners 79–80
and pressure groups 63, 74
primary producers in 75
regulation, inducement and direction 66–7
systems approach to 77
and technology 70–2
and trade associations 75
Marks and Spencer 133, 176, 204, 300, 323
in food product development 86
Marlboro cigarettes 21
McDonald's 269, 469
media
in advertising 369–87
costs 378
environment of 374–8
interplay of 378–80
scheduling 382
totals 369–70
and marketing 73
and test marketing 328
Mexico: petroleum and gas output 292
Mini, pricing of (case study) 348–9
MITI 64
Monopolies and Mergers Commission 67, 207,
331
motivation of sales force 415–16
motivations of buyers and consumers 137–8
behavioural approach 138
psychoanalytic views on 137
motives 55
Multi-Fibre Agreement 279
multinational enterprises
international marketing strategies 273
in overseas trade 260–2
multiple markets, conversion processes 77

National Council of Physical Distribution
Management 359
National Economic Development Office 64,
269, 272
National Enterprise Board 64
National Readership Survey 378

needs, and marketing environment 38–43, 54
Nestlé 87, 302
  and consumer action 467–8
Netherlands
  acquisitions of companies 289
  advertising expenditure 369
  GNP of 281
  hypermarkets and superstores 84
  intra-European trade 287
  market research revenues 114
  networks, of channels 352–3
newspapers
  advertising
    access to 372–3
    costs 380
    environment of 376–7
    interplay of media 380–1
    returns for 381
    totals 371–2
  diffusion curves 187–8
Nexo Plastics hopper-feeder (case study)
    317–18
niche retail marketing
  in clothes 180
  in food 88, 90
Nissan Motors 6
No Hands Food Mixers (case study) 365–8
noise, in communication process 424–5
non-media advertising 387–9
  dangers of 389
  typology of 388–9
non-profit-making organizations 472, 474
North American Free Trade Area 246, 265
Norway 87

objectives 54
offerings 91–107
  in agricultural markets 91–107
  capital 103
  components 100–1
  finished goods 101–2
  industrial 91–107
  plant 103–4
  processed products 100
  raw materials 93–6
  services 102–3, 238–9
Office of Fair Trading 67–9, 338
Organization for Economic Co-operation and
    Development (OECD) 250, 272
Organization of Petroleum Exporting Countries
    (OPEC) 246
organizational chart in marketing 37

organizations 91–107
  for agricultural markets 97–99
  for capital 103
  case study 96–7
  for components 100–1
  for finished goods 101–2
  for plant 103–4
  for processed products 100
  for raw materials 94–7
  for services 102–3
overseas trade see exports and overseas trade
ownership, lack of in service industries 237

Pacific Basin 27
packaging
  as environmental issue 467, 469
  in physical distribution management 359
packet switching 195
Pandora (Arts and Crafts) (case study) 212–13
Parker Pens 52, 299
patents 282
Patents Act (1977) 68
penetration prices 333
perishableness, in service industries 236–7
Perrier 468
Philip Morris Organization 92, 201
Philips of Eindhoven 150
physical distribution management 358–68
  alternatives, cost of 362
  case study 365–8
  future of 362
  goals of 360–1
  historical perspective 358–62
  and marketing 360
  system of 359–60
  total-cost approach 361
Pilkington Glass 51
pilot studies, in field research 118–20
PIMS, in strategic marketing 437
place
  in marketing mix 14, 50, 296
  in test marketing 326
planning 447–64
  barriers to 460
  basic plan 449
  case study 462–4
  contingencies 459
  controls 459
  costs and timing 459
  differing approaches to 459
  environment-driven 451
  evaluation 459

feedback loop for 449
forecasting 453–5
    estimates 453
    time series projections 453–55
market audit 450–1
marketing decision variables 456
marketing mix 456
objectives 455–6
research 458
strategy 458
tactics 451, 458
plant, organizations for 102
P&O 362
point of sale material, as non-media advertising 389
Poland 283–4
political factors in international marketing systems 248
population, location and marketing 43–4
portable data capture unit 198
portfolio approach to strategic marketing 436–8
Portugal
advertising expenditure 367
GNP of 281
hypermarkets and superstores 85
market research revenues 114
poster advertising
access to 375
environment of 378–9
sizes 379
pressure groups 63, 74
price 336–49
breakeven analysis 345–6
case study 348–9
cuts, as non-media advertising 388
decisions on 340–3
    changing external factors 341–2
    and competition 342–3
    and internal change 343
    new products 341
    promotions 343
as goal 345
in international marketing 256, 270–1
and just price 337
marginal 346
and market concentration 342
in marketing mix 14, 50, 296
non-core-price policies 344
objectives 344
politics of 337–8
in real world 346
and retailing 206–8

setting 344–5
in test marketing 324
price awareness (case study) 129–31
Price Commission 67
primary producers in marketing system 75
privatization 65–6
product
allocation of sales force by 412
launch of, and test marketing 327
in marketing mix 14, 50, 296
policies on 299–318
    brands 303–4
    changing environment and evolving needs 305
    customer needs, complexity of 300–1
    entrepreneurs and small firms 314
    innovation 310–12
    invention, research and creativity 307–8
    opportunities, selection of 301–2
    product identification 307
    and product life cycles 307
    screening and testing 313–14
in test marketing 324
product life-cycle 216
international 248–9, 268, 270
and inventory levels 364
and product policy 307
product management 38
product/market growth matrix, in strategic marketing 439
programme 54
promotion
in exports and overseas trade 250–1
in marketing mix 14, 50, 296
and price 343–4
in test marketing 324
protocols 197
public sector 65
purchasing process, analysis of 151

radio
advertising
    access to 374
    environment of 378–9
    totals 370–1
diffusion curves 187–8
Rank Xerox 22
raw materials 27
organizations for 93–6
Reckitt and Colman 326
recruitment of salesmen 411–12
regulation
in food marketing 75

in marketing systems 65–6
Resale Prices Act (1977) 66–7
research 108–31
 briefing for 111
 case study 129–31
 decision analysis 126
 field research 118–24
  consumer panels 123–4
  experimentation 121–2
  observation 122
  omnibus surveys 124
  piloting 118–20
  qualitative research 122
  questionnaires 120–1
  sampling 118
  syndicated research 123–4
  trade audits 123
  TV ratings 124
 and firm 110–11
 and GNP 282
 industrial marketing research 124
 in international marketing 272–3
  integration 273
  sources 272
  value 273
 marketing information systems 125–6
 by non-profit organizations 126
 planning for 458
 and product policy 299–300
 as 'science' 109–10
 scope of 112–13
 secondary sources in 113–16
  commercial 115–16
  government agencies 115
  international agencies 115
  libraries 116
  videotex 116
 in service industries 125
 in test marketing 331
 users of 475
Research in Advanced Communications for
  Europe 182
Restrictive Practices Acts (1956, 1976) 67
Restrictive Practices Court Act (1976) 67
retailing
 channels for 351
 clothes 178–9
 and intermediate markets 204–8
  location of 205–6
  outlet, types of 204
  and price 206–8
  product mix 204–5

return on investment 158
Romania 284
Rothmans 339
Rover Cars 49, 149, 198, 256
Rowntrees 86
Royale Motors Ltd (case study) 419–20
Russia 285–6, 470

Sainsbury's 205
Sale of Goods Act (1983) 68
sales management 408–20
 allocation 412
 case study 418–20
 control 414–15
 current climate of 416
 difficulties facing 413
 motivation 413–14
 payment systems 414
 recruiting 411–12
 of sales force 413
 sales process 415
 training 411
sales promotion see advertising
salesmen
 in intermediate markets 201
 tasks of 409–12
  linking to corporate resources 410–11
  negotiation 410
Saudi Arabia: petroleum and gas output 286
scenario analysis 54
selling 409
 and consumerism 473
 in industrial markets 220–1
 and marketing 3
 overseas 251
services 80, 230–42
 advertising for 237
 case study 242
 definition of 230–1
 employment in 230
 future of 238
 by government 234–5
 growth, source of 231
 innovation and productivity 238
 offerings, managing 235–6
 organizations for 102
 and product industries, differences 231–4
  heterogeneity 231
  inseparability 232
  intangibility 231–2
  ownership, lack of 234
  perishableness 232–3

range of 234–5
research in 125
shampoo market, mapping 78
shipping and freight, overseas trade in 259
Single European Act 88, 278, 433
Single European Market 45, 278, 433
  and Central Europe 284–5
  challenges in 287–8
  competitive advantages 280–3
  and Eastern Europe 285–6
  entry strategies 288–9
  and food marketing 82
  GNP in 281
  internal market of 286
  intra-European trade 287
  marketing change, agenda for 278–80
  opportunities in 286–7
  as single market 283
  and Social Charter 278
  timetable for 277–8
  and West European integration 283–4
skimming prices 341
snack pots 327
social responsibilities, in marketing 465–79
  case study 477–9
socio-economic factors
  of buyers and consumers 134
  market segmentation by 135–6
socio-economic structure 45–6
Sock Shop 149, 179
Spain
  advertising expenditure 369
  GNP of 281
  hypermarkets and superstores 87
  intra-European trade 288
  market research revenues 114
Standard International Industrial Classification
  48
strategic business units 440–1
strategic marketing 431–46
  case study 442–6
  changing conditions 431–2
  decisions in 432–3
  environment turbulence matrix in 435
  formulation of strategy 434
  generic strategy model 439
  generic value chain 434
  planning in 458
  and portfolio approach 436–8
  product/market growth matrix 438
  and strategic analysis 433–6
  strategic business units 439–40

strategist, mind of 440
  tight-loose strategy 436
superstores in Europe 87
supplier push, and channels 353–5
supply
  and demand 16–17
  in marketing environment 47–9
  offerings
    consumer 48
    industrial 48
Supply of Goods (Implied Terms) Act (1972)
  68
Sweden
  consumer protection bodies 68
  hypermarkets and superstores 86
switch trading 27
Switzerland 86
SWOT analysis
  in marketing system 78
  in strategic marketing 435–6
symbolism in communication 424–5
syndicated research 122–4
systems 80

tactics 54
target groups, analysis of 151–3
technology
  in clothes marketing 179–80
  in food marketing 86–7
  and international marketing systems 248
  and marketing system 70–1
telecommunications in marketing information
  systems 189–90
television
  advertising
    access to 371–3
    environment of 373, 375
    potential audiences 372
    totals 369–70
  diffusion curves 187–8
  ratings, in research 124
Tesco Stores 149, 201, 202, 319
test marketing 319–35
  alternatives to 327–8
  case study 317–18
  controversy over 319–20
  evaluation 331–2
  exceptions and opportunities 324–5
  external variables 328–9
  information needs, decisions, and controls 326
  innovation, challenge of 320
  length of 330

mini area tests 327–8
and product launch 334
scientific dimensions 320
setting up 326–7
success of
   chances of 323
   survival and failure 323
the test 331–2
test area overlap 332
value of 323–4
variables in 325–6
Third World 472
multinational enterprises in 261
toilet soap market (case study) 129–31
Total Quality Management 99, 187
in strategic marketing 432
tourism, overseas trade in 256
trade
evolution of 10–11
non-media advertising in 390–1
overlapping patterns 202
trade associations 72
trade audits, in research 123
Trade Descriptions Act (1968–1972) 68
Trade Marks Act (1938) 68
transmission, in communication process 422–3
transport, and physical distribution management
      359

Unfair Contract Terms Act (1977) 72
Unilever 245, 260
United Kingdom
acquisitions of companies 290
advertising expenditure 367
age profiles 43
exports as share of GNP 243
GDP activity shares 93
GNP of 281
hypermarkets and superstores 85
intra-European trade 287
market research revenues 114
petroleum and gas output 286

R&D in 282
regional profiles 44
services, employment in 230
socio-economic divisions 45–6
textiles, suppliers 95
visible exports 70
United Nations 271
United States
advertising expenditure 367
consumer protection bodies 68
exports as share of GNP 243
GDP activity shares 93
GNP of 281
petroleum and gas output 286
R&D in 282
Uruguay Round of GATT 95

venture management 54
vertical integration, channels for 352
videotex, for research 116
Viewdata systems 190
Virgin 302
vision statements 456
Volkswagen Golf (case study) 395–407

Waddington's 325
warehousing, in physical distribution
      management 358
Water Share Offer 60
West African States Customs Union 246
West Indies Associated States 246
Westward Plastics (case study) 96–7
wholesaling
channels for 350
clothes 181
in intermediate markets 203–4
Wiggins Teape 323
W. D. and H. O. Wills 313
World Bank 249, 270

Yardley cosmetics 291
York, tourism in 303